THEORIES OF ENTREPRENEURSHIP

THEORIES OF ENTREPRENEURSHIP

Nurturing Growth. Harnessing Excellence.

Dr. VASANT DESAI
Director,
Visvesvaraya Institute of
Socio-Economic Research (VISER),
Mumbai.

Himalaya Publishing House

MUMBAI • DELHI • NAGPUR • BENGALURU • HYDERABAD •
BHUBANESWAR • CHENNAI • PUNE • INDORE • AHMEDABAD
LUCKNOW • ERNAKULAM • KOLKATA

FIRST EDITION : 2011

Reprint : 2025

PUBLISHED BY : Mrs. Meena Pandey
for **HIMALAYA PUBLISHING HOUSE PVT. LTD.**
"Ramdoot", Dr. Bhalerao Marg, Girgaon, **Mumbai-400004**
☎ 23860170 • 23863863 • Fax: 022-23877178
Email: himpub@vsnl.com
Website: www.himpub.com

BRANCH OFFICES

Delhi : "Pooja Apartments", 4-B, Murari Lal Street, Ansari Road, Darya Ganj, **New Delhi-110 002.** ☎ 23270392 • 23278631 • Fax: 011-23256286

Nagpur : Kundanlal Chandak Industrial Estate, Ghat Road, **Nagpur-440018** ☎ 2738731 • 3296733 • Telefax: 0712-2721215

Bengaluru : No. 16/1 (Old 12/1), 1st Floor, Next to Hotel Highlands, Madhava Nagar, Race Course Road, **Bangalore-560001.** ☎ 22281541 • 22385461 • Fax: 080-22286611

Hyderabad : No. 3-4-184, Lingampally, Beside Raghavendra Swamy Matham, Kachiguda, **Hyderabad-500027,** ☎ 040-65501745 • 09848130433

Chennai : No. 85/50, Bazullah Road, T-Nagar, **Chennai-600017.** ☎ 044-28144004 • 28144005

Pune : No. 527, "Laksha Apartment", 1st Floor, Mehunpura, Shaniwarpeth, Near Prabhat Theatre, **Pune-411030** ☎ 020-24496323 • 24496333

Lucknow : Jai Baba Bhavan, Near Dr. Sanjiv Awasthi, Church Road, Kurshi Road, Aliganj, **Lucknow-226024** ☎ 9305302158, 9415349385, 9389593752

Ahmedabad : 114, Shail, 1st Floor, Opp. Madhusudan House, C.G. Road, Navrangpura, **Ahmedabad-380009.** ☎ 079-26560126 • 09327324149, 09314679413

Ernakulam : No. 39/104A, Laxmi Apt., Karickamuri Cross Road, Ernakulam, **Cochin-622011.** ☎ 0484-2378012 • 2378016. 09344199799

Bhubaneswar: 5, Station Square, Bhubaneshwar, Orissa-751001. 9861046007.

Indore : Kesardeep Avenue Extension, 73, Narayan Bagh, Flat No. 302, IIIrd Floor, Near Humpty Dumpty School, Narayan Bagh, **Indore (M.P.)** 99301386468

Kolkata : 108/4, Beliaghata Main Road, Near ID Hospital, Opp. SBI Bank, **Kolkata-700010,** 09910440956

DTP by : Sudhakar Shetty (HPH Pvt. Ltd., Mumbai)

Printed by : **Delhi.**

DEDICATION

JOHN KENNETH GALBRAITH

(1908-2006)

A mirror to affluent society

Born on October 15, 1908 in a Iona Station, Ontario, Canada.

Died on April 29, 2006 at a hospital in Cambridge, Massachusetts, USA.

Renowned liberal economist focused on core issues like the distribution of wealth.

Author of The Affluent Society, one of the rare works that forces a nation to re-examine its values. A friend of India. This study is dedicated in his remembrance.

Economist John Kenneth Galbraith, who focused on core issues like the distribution of wealth, died on Saturday at a hospital in Cambridge, Massachusetts, at the age of 97, *The New York Times* reported.

Galbraith was one of the most widely read authors in the history of economics. Among his 33 books was *The Affluent Society,* one of the rare works that forces a nation to re-examine its values, the obituary said. He wrote fluidly, even on complex topics, and many of his compelling phrases. Among them, 'The Affluent Society,' 'Conventional Wisdom' and 'Countervailing Power' — became part of the language.

THE INDIA CONNECTION

- Galbraith's involvement with India began in 1958-59. He was in Switzerland at that time, working on his famous treatise — initially titled *Why The Poor Are Poor* but later, on his wife's suggestion, changed to *The Affluent Society*.
- In Switzerland he had a chance meeting with Professor P.C. Mahalanobis, India's Chief Economic Planner. Mahalanobis told him about Jawaharlal Nehru's request to the then US President Dwight D. Eisenhower for the services of an economic expert to help with India's planning process.
- Galbraith interrupted his work and came to India for three months and worked with the Planning Commission on problems related to agriculture.
- Galbraith had predicted during his tenure in the 1960s that one day India would be Asia's breadbasket. "Agriculture is one economic activity that does not obey the laws of demand and supply," he said.
- Professor Galbraith is also credited to have seeded India's entry into information technology. He began the first computer science department, at IIT Kanpur.
- Jawaharlal Nehru and Galbraith shared a good rapport which could be traced back to their *alma mater.* Both studied in Cambridge.

— Agencies

ENTREPRENEURIAL MISSION STATEMENT

- The entrepreneur lives and works in an environment that is fiercely competitive. It is therefore crucial that the entrepreneur sharpens his/her cutting edge to stay ahead.
- The entrepreneur as the engine of economic growth, job creation and prosperity, always served the society. Customer priority and quality are his mission and passion.
- The entrepreneur shall adopt organisation structures to speed up communication, decision-making, job creation, income generation and wealth creation.
- The entrepreneur displays courage to take risk of putting his own money into an idea; courage to take on the competition and courage to take a leap into an unknown future and create new enterprises/businesses. This creative process is the lifeblood of the strong enterprise that derive growth and propel nations forward.
- The entrepreneurial activities blossom and thrive under conditions where citizens participate and compete in the market place under conditions of equality and are not unduly burdened by regulation.
- The entrepreneur will always strive for a neutral and sustainable enhancement of entrepreneurial society.
- Entrepreneurism is the lifeblood of any economy; but in India, where first-generation innovators are still battling the odds to make a mark on the global economy, enterprise is an idea whose true potential is yet to be realised. Ironically, Indian entrepreneurism is more about overcoming barriers — be it finance, bureaucracy, and infrastructure — than about achieving the fruits of liberalisation. That is not an inspiring image for a country that dreams of being a critical component of tomorrow's knowledge economy; of creating vibrant digital valleys; and of having its own Bill Gates and Michael Dells. Yet the changing Indian economic arena is always a buzz with the news of mavericks that have discovered bold new ways of competing. And they have done so in areas that have been extremely tough to compete in, dominated as they are by mighty multinationals.
- Entrepreneurism triggered by liberalisation and the advent of the brain power industry, demands the systematic development of business clusters in India, or geographical concentrations of competitiveness where technology diffusion is rapid and supply chains are short and efficient. Clusters, where the levels of competitiveness are always high, are the breeding grounds of entrepreneurism. They need adequate supportive infrastructure, like educational institutes and research centres, and a good quality of life, to thrive. A hassle-free environment can leverage the diverse capabilities of Indian entrepreneurism.

CREDO OF ENTREPRENEURS

THE WORLD NEEDS

The World Today is looking for

Entrepreneurs who are honest

Entrepreneurs who are innovative

Entrepreneurs who are optimistic

Entrepreneurs who will stand for the right

Entrepreneurs who care for the society

Entrepreneurs who stand for values

Entrepreneurs with conscience

Entrepreneurs who neither brag nor run

Entrepreneurs who neither flag nor flinch

Entrepreneurs who know their place and fill in

Entrepreneurs who know their business and attend to it

Entrepreneurs who are not too crazy

Entrepreneurs who are not too lazy to work

Entrepreneurs who will prosper with society

Entrepreneurs who will lead and motivate

Entrepreneurs who always dream for change

Entrepreneurs who live for their principles

The ultimate measure of a man

Is not where he stands

In moments of comfort and convenience,

But where he stands

At times of challenge and controversy

— Martin Luther King

PREFACE

In creating and growing a new venture, the entrepreneur assumes the responsibility and risks for its development and survival and enjoy the corresponding rewards. In fact, economic development depends on the allocation of entrepreneurial resources to efforts to discover new profit opportunities.

In the 21st century, entrepreneurship has assumed great importance. Globalisation on coupled with information technology has given a fillip to entrepreneurship in a big way. Entrepreneurial activities are getting broad-based. All along, there is big leap in employment opportunities and rise in income.

Literature on entrepreneur has been growing in recent years. Though there have been numerous articles in various journals on entrepreneurial development, especially in India and quite a few edited books containing articles on different aspects of the subject by different authors, there remains an imbalance in the coverage of topics. It is, therefore, no exaggeration to say that there has not been a single comprehensive book on the subject, explaining, analysing and assessing the various aspects of the subject. This book is intended to help evolve a perspective of development of the vital sectors of the national economy and furnish the much needed information on this subject.

The factors contributing to economic development are labour, technology, natural resources, capital and entrepreneurship. New business formation is the result of harassing human skills with the developed technology, added by available capital as well as other infrastructure to set in a development process. The key factor in this development process is the entrepreneur. This is the forte of the entrepreneur whose policies and strategies cover such broad areas as production, marketing, financing, pricing and personnel relations. The growth of entrepreneurship largely depends upon effective policies and their efficient implementation.

Whose contributions as an innovator and co-ordinator will go towards the economic development of the country. Thus, entrepreneurship is the co-ordination of the production elements.

The role of the entrepreneur in the history of economic thought is reviewed. An interdisciplinary approach to the understanding and development of entrepreneurship theory is the need of the hour. The study should be on the basis of contributions from economic decision theory, sociological system theories, psychological research and behavioural studies.

Over the years, social scientists, economic thinkers, psychologists and anthropologists have contributed to the entrepreneurial literature with their theories and models.

The present study *Theories of Entrepreneurship* consists of Ten chapters.

In all, FORTY Theories relating to entrepreneurship are presented for the FIRST-TIME in this study.

Theories of entrepreneurship are broadly grouped into:

1. Economic Theories of Entrepreneurship
2. Socio-cultural Theories of Entrepreneurship
3. Motivation of Theories of Entrepreneurship
4. Entrepreneurial Leadership

The theories of entrepreneurship helps students and teachers in understanding the varied facets and evolution of entrepreneurship environment fostering and accelerating the growth of entrepreneurs and entrepreneurship activities.

The study of nature is the main objective of all sciences. There is no greater weapon than science to do away with human ignorance. The combination of modern culture and knowledge of science play an important role in the Life of man. It also influence and foster entrepreneurship in the country.

In order to facilitate the students to understand the above concepts, the fundamental theories are introduced.

We sincerely hope that the text book will meet the expected needs of students and teachers. We solicit constructive suggestions from students and teachers for improving the text and content.

ACKNOWLEDGEMENTS

My debt to those who have helped me in one way or the other is heavy indeed. While I take this opportunity to thank all of them — they are too numerous to mention individually in a brief preface — I would like to acknowledge my deep sense of gratitude to Ms. Pratibha Chaudhari, Mr. K.N. Pandey, Mr. Anuj Pandey, Mr. Neeraj Pandey, Ms. Phalguni Ravi and Mr. M.V. Desai for their ungrudging help at all stages.

I wish to place on record my sincere thanks to, Mr. Sudhakar Shetty, who has done a commendable job in designing creatively and presenting the study in new dimensions. And, Mrs. Y.S. Shetty who has added depth to the study by her meticulous presentation and deligient reading.

No words can adequately express my debt of gratitude to my late father, Shri Ranganath Balawant Mutalik Desai (1909-2006) and my late mother Smt. Laxmidevi (1914-2000), for generating in me a perennial interest in higher studies.

I am particularly indebted to my wife, Mandaramala, whose patience, support, encouragement, understanding, and love helped this effort to fruition.

The Himalaya Publishing House, which is in the forefront of publications, enthusiastically came forward to undertake the publication of this book. I wholeheartedly thank them.

Finally, I thank all those who directly or indirectly helped me in bringing out this unique study on time.

Mumbai
October 25, 2010

VASANT DESAI

Expert advice to the budding entrepreneur

"Think big. Never compromise on fundamental values. Look ahead, be self confident and have the best around you. Be committed to quality and play to win."

Azim Premji *Chairman, Wipro*

"Vision and ebullience. Perseverance, commitment, tenacity and a bias for action. You also need attitude and above all, passion."

Kumaramangalam Birla,
Chairman, Aditya Birla Group

"Speed and imagination. Global business skills. Also aspiration, patriotism, excellence in execution and communication skills."

Narayana Murthy,
Chairman and Chief Mentor, Infosys

CONTENTS

IN SEARCH OF VISION

Indian enterprises have realised that a well-defined purpose or goal is necessary, whether they call it mission or vision or both. This is the fallout of the liberalisation ushered in the early 1990s. The reforms and the consequent competition forced on industry — made imperative to have a road map and a target. It is a tool that is necessary to navigate the minefields of competition.

Jamsetji Nusserwanji Tata
The Tata Group founder is hailed as a visionary

Actually, Indian industry wasn't so far behind. In the West too, articulated vision statements arose only as a consequence of the Total Quality Movement (TQM) of the 1980s.

Today, scores of companies are codifying their ethics, values, corporate culture, and goals. "This is the value proposition and market discriminator," says Arjun Malhotra, CEO of Techspan and one of the founders of HCL. With so many companies competing for the same space, particularly in fast-paced new generation industries, it is necessary to be different to stand out from the herd.

Though all the best companies have mission or vision statements, there are still some people who dismiss them as just so much management jargon, rarely disseminated to the grassroots and with limited impact on the bottomline. There's also a certain amount of confusion about what the terms actually mean.

It is not helped by the fact that vision is a slightly nebulous concept. It can often be something unachievable — for instance, attaining unachievable — for instance, attaining a "zero defect" level. It can be vague — for instance, selling hope (remember the famous quote of the cosmetics manufacturer: "In the factories, we make lipstick; in the marketplace, we sell hope").

Management consultant John Walker has attempted to define the different terms. According to him the mission or purpose defines an organisation's generalised niche — its business and arena of operation, as well as some generalised goals ("to be the best", for instance). Values are derived from a closer look at the individuals currently defining the organisation; they are the strong, common veins of belief and drive that run through this group. Values are a primary source of strong motivation for the group. A vision is a specific medium-range goal measurable and deliverable. It is timed too quick and it becomes a mere plan; too long and it is rendered a fantasy. The vision symbolises achievement of the values and the mission.

Understandably, there is much dispute about these definitions. There's also argument about which needs to come first —vision or mission. At one level that should be a no-brainer; men like Jamsetji Tata or Dhirubhai Ambani are hailed as visionaries, not missionaries. But the truth of the matter is that these concepts are new to India and each CEO or company has been deciding on its own interpretation of mission, vision, and values.

But almost all agree on their need. "We find it very useful to have a vision statement," says a Wipro spokesperson. "For one thing, it sets an internal target. It acts as a turbocharger that ignites the combined enthusiasm of the team. Hence, the employees can aim to perform higher."

Aptech chairman Atul Nishar says: "A vision statement refers to a vividly descriptive image of what a company wants to be or wants to be known for. It represents an organisation's dream and intended destination. A powerful organisational vision inspires and engages its employees into a highly motivated and empowered team."

Aptech's vision for the new millennium is to emerge as:

- the IT and education megacorp,
- the preferred choice of customers in all market, and
- the best place to work in.

Mirc electronics Chairman and Managing Director Gulu Mirchandani describes it evocatively: "A vision statement is like a beacon of light that beckons people in an organisation towards a common destination. It is a dream that inspires everyone to rise above his or her limits of competence, and surge ahead."

At Tata Steel, which in the late 1980s was a large, slothful steel producer with huge societal obligations, the vision statement to enter a new era took former Managing Director J.J. Irani six months to formulate. It runs like this: "Tata Steel enters the new millennium with the confidence of a learning organisation; a knowledge-based and happy organisation. We will establish ourselves as the supplier of choice by delighting our customers with our services and our products. In the coming decade, we will become the most cost-competitive steel plant and so serve the community and the nation." The exercise — which was christened Turning the Titanic — involved a great deal of attention to the nitty-gritty. It worked; today Tata Steel is a world-class steelmaker.

For the Tata group at large, it is obviously difficult to have such a specific mission or vision. That's why the stress there is more on a value system, a Tata code that supreme Ratan Tata is trying to instil in all the group companies. The group purpose, according to Tata, is "to improve the quality of life of the communities we serve."

Kumar Mangalam Birla, Chairman of the Aditya Birla Group, defines the group vision as "to be a premium conglomerate with a clear business focus in each sector. In essence, it means getting into a leadership position in the businesses that we are in and will get into."

Asian Paints has a carefully articulated Vision 2003. The broad objective is to become one of the top five decorative companies worldwide. The new vision was flagged off in 1998 and includes a detailed road-map of how to get there. There are other milestones as well — for example, a group turnover of Rs. 2,500 crore by 2003.

BEL India says it wants to be "the market leader in defence electronics and in other chosen fields and products". BSES has a 15-year corporate plan. Godrej Consumer Products says its corporate mission is, among other things, "to delight both in India and abroad."

At Reliance, they firmly believe in two things — betting on opportunity and betting on people. The corporate slogan is "where growth is a way of life". Reliance Industries, however, is one of the few top-drawer companies that does not have a formal, written mission statement.

Infosys has three principal corporate objectives:

- To be a world-class software house in the global market.
- To be one of the first "names" to come to mind for software solutions.
- To create wealth for the company, shareholders, and employees by legal and ethical means.

The Infosys vision is: "We will be a globally respected corporation that provides best-of-breed software solutions delivered by the best-in-class people." The company believes that in software, as in no other industry, mindshare precedes marketshare.

This is, of course, the encapsulated vision or mission. In most cases — given the ambiguity of the terms — the statement extends to several pages. But there are some points in common.

Most companies want to be the best in their category; in fact, several say that they will abandon a sector if they do not see a chance of figuring amongst the top three.

There is focus on quality; understandable, as it was TQM that inspired the entire exercise. As a corollary, there is a quest to "delight" the customer.

Finally, there is an accent on people, which far-sighted companies are realising is their biggest asset. "Companies that don't take care of their people can hardly expect them to adopt any worthwhile vision," says a management consultant.

How does one get the employees of a company to accept a vision statement and work towards its success? It's true that most companies start with the vision of one man, the original entrepreneur. But today companies need to reinvent themselves, as the environment has started changing rapidly. What's the best way to get an insight into the most appropriate vision?

As usual, there is no agreement on the issue. Some feel that for an ongoing concern which lacks a vision or needs a newer one, the process should not be top-down. People should be asked for suggestions, they should be made to buy into the idea at the formation stage itself. "Employees should be made to feel that the vision belongs to them," says a management expert. "There should be a sense of ownership."

"Vision is an emotional issue," says Nishar of Aptech. "Hence 'vision' is something which must be continuously communicated to the employees. Mere communication is not good enough but, for employees to get emotionally engaged to the organisation, it is equally important that they 'own up' the vision of the organisation." He adds that it is vital to "walk the talk".

At Aptech, the first vision statement was formulated 10 years ago by the senior management team after several brainstorming sessions and meetings. It has undergone minor revisions in line with the company's business focus. At Pune-based Thermax, a written vision/mission statement was adopted in January 1997. "It has remained fairly constant over the years as there was no need felt to change it," says chairperson Anu Aga. The Thermax vision focuses on best technologies, customer satisfaction, values, and its people.

One company that has had a vision statement for a long time is Wipro. It may be worthwhile to look a little closer at its experience. A spokesperson says: "We evolved the beliefs of the company in 1972, when not too many companies in India had articulated beliefs or values. The beliefs were debated, articulated, and practised by every member of Wipro. A periodic review of these beliefs has led to the current ones — human values, integrity, innovative solutions, and value for money."

Wipro says the vision should be ambitious and set a stretch for the team. "Challenge is inspiring because it taps all the inner strengths, abilities, and energies that bring out the best in a person or a team," says Chairman Azim Premji. "Nothing excites a team or pushes it to a greater height as common challenge with which the team identifies itself. At the same time, the vision cannot be completely safe. It should be beyond reach but not an impossible dream either."

At Wipro, the vision formulation process involved over 250 team members from different business units. The vision was communicated to every team member in the organisation. Every business unit head met his team members across the globe and communicated the vision to the team.

In addition, after the annual performance results are out, Chairman Premji and senior officers meet employees in different locations to speak on the performance and plans.

At this time, Premji keeps aside separate time to talk about vision and promise. During induction, there is always a separate session where new employees are introduced to the Wipro promise and vision.

Such emphasis on vision and mission is not true of every company. If the formation of vision statements is a bottom-up process, it becomes much easier to get the rank and file involved. If it is imposed from the top, as it very often is, it needs a concerted effort to spread the culture in the company. In some places, communicating vision means nothing more than framing the statement all over the office and the factory. But the more effective CEOS make it a structured exercise. Today, internal communication has become far more important than external communication.

How do the rank and file look upon mission statements? In a workplace environment where there is antagonism between the management and workers, such statements don't do much. But the process of involving the workforce can lead to reduction of the antagonism. Implementation of a mission statement can be the precursor to healthy industrial relations. "You are all working towards a common cause," says a management expert.

The other piece of advice experts give companies that are commencing their first vision exercise is to keep the essential message simple. Jargon doesn't work. Secondly, in the initial stages, it is very necessary to set up quantifiable milestones. It doesn't matter that they are not achieved; their effectiveness is in just being there. For a company that has matured on the vision trail, targets are not imperative; they get achieved along with the assimilation of the value system.

Vision is likely to become an integral part of corporate India because it is much a part of our cultural ethos. By contrast, it may not work so well in the US, which has a quick-fix mentality. CEOs in the US are quick to discard ideas if they take too much time working out.

They would be wrong. For vision is the corporate life-jacket of the future. Helen Keller, who turned blind and deaf at 19 months but still managed a successful career working for those similarly afflicted, was once asked: "What can be worse than losing your sight?" Her answer: "Losing your vision." Companies in India have begun realising that if they don't have begun realising that if they don't have vision, we won't be seeing much of them in the future.

This quiz is on entrepreneurs who have had the guts to strike out on their own and grasp success which would otherwise have eluded them.

1 He once said, "When I was 19, I caught sight of the future and based my career on what I saw. I turned out to have been right." He founded a company with his classmate from Lakeside School in 1975 and together they built it into a $500 million behemoth, steering it through a turbulent business history. Name him and his friend.

2 This retailing genius introduced a novel inventory control system of "Cross Docking" — in which goods move from one loaded dock to another in 48 hours or less. He opened his first store in 1962 and now his chain of stores has a storage capacity second only to the US government. Name him.

3 As a young graduate, he was a shop assistant at his father's saree shop in Nai Sarak, Delhi, and went on to start his own shop at Kamla Nagar. In 1979, he started a company that sold song lyric books (including "The Best of ABBA"), posters and leather patches, and is now India's largest chain of gift/greeting card stores. Name him.

4 In 1979 five friends set up a unit, to produce and export shirts, with a capital of $10,000. This single unit is now a huge conglomerate of firms, including the world's largest exporters of washing machines and other home appliances. It is one of Korea's largest Chaebols. Name the group.

5 This Australian comes from a family of newspaper magnates. He ran his first paper, the Adelaide Herald when he was 23 years old. He took over 20th Century Fox in 1985. His effort to enter the US direct satellite market by purchasing 49 per cent of the satellite "Echo Star" was a failure, and he has suffered several setbacks in publishing and electronic media as well. However, he is one of the largest media tycoons in the world. Name him.

6 His father was a turmeric farmer from a small village in Andhra Pradesh. He was the first graduate in his family. He quit Indian Drugs and Pharmaceuticals to set up his own company, which initially produced variants of Bayer's Ciprofloxacin and Astra Zeneca's Omeprazole.

His firm is now one of India's major pharma companies, and has invested millions in R&D. Name him.

7 In his hook "Surviving at the Top" he wrote, "A person's worst potential enemy is himself." He also said "Cash is King" and that he wanted to be the "King of Cash". A hereditary millionaire with family holdings in real estate, he became a billionaire at the age of 28, with substantial investments in hotels and casinos, among other things. Name him.

8 He started his publishing career with a quarterly magazine called "Business Today" (and no, he is not connected with the Living Media Group). He is the only person to win the prestigious "Crystal Owl" award four times for making the most accurate economic forecasts. He once contested for US President with the offbeat mandate "Elect me because I am not a politician". Name him.

9 He was the only person in the class to get an A from his professor Benjamin Graham at Columbia University. He bought a failing textile firm in 1965 and retained its name, turning it into a colossal investment firm. His assets include a huge quantity of silver, which he keeps acquiring on a regular basis. Name him, and his investment company.

10 In January 1975, he enrolled as an MBA student at Ohio State University. Now the billionaire CEO of one of India's largest IT giants, he attributes his success to "education" and his recipe for success is "Read, Read, Read". Name him.

ANSWERS

1. William Henry (Bill) Gates and Paul Allen, Microsoft
2. Sam Robson Walton, Wal-Mart
3. Anil Moolchandani, Archies Greetings and Gifts
4. Daewoo, founded by Kim Woo-Choong
5. Keith Rupert Murdoch, News Corp, which owns, among other things, Star TV
6. K. Anji Reddy, Dr. Reddy's Laboratories
7. Donald Trump
8. Steve Forbes, Editor in Chief, Forbes Magazine
9. Warren Edward Buffett, Berkshire Hathaway
10. B. Ramalinga Raju, Satyam — now listed on the NASDAQ as SIFY

This quiz has been provided by K Circle Quizzing Club, Secunderabad.

http://www.kcircle.com

The Tata Group

At the Tata Group our purpose is to improve the quality of life of the communities we serve. We do this through leadership in sectors of national economic significance to which the group brings a unique set of capabilities. This requires us to grow aggressively in focused areas of business.

"Our heritage of returning to society what we earn evokes trust among consumers, employees, shareholders, and the community. This heritage will be continuously enriched by formalising the high standards of behaviour expected from employees and companies.

"The Tata name is a unique asset representing leadership with trust. Leveraging this asset to enhance group synergy and becoming globally competitive is the route to sustained growth and long-term success.

Wipro

Vision for 2004

Business leadership

Among the top 10 information technology services companies globally and the No. 1 information technology company in India.

Customer leadership

The No. 1 choice of customers through innovative solutions and Six Sigma processes.

People leadership

Among the top 10 most preferred employers by creating an environment of empowerment, intellectual challenge, and wealth-sharing.

Brand leadership

Wipro brand to be among the five most admired brands in India.

The Aditya Birla Group

Our vision

To be a premium conglomerate with a focus at every business level.

Our mission

To pursue the creation of value.

Our aim

To deliver value for our customers, shareholders, investors, employees, and society at large.

Management ethos

Focus on value-added growth through:

- **Strategic thrust:** Fundamental value-creation and sharper business focus.
- **Structural initiatives:** Internalising the concept of value-creation.

Godrej Consumer Products

We shall operate in existing and new businesses which profitably capitalise on our corporate image of quality and integrity.

"Our objective is to delight both in India and abroad.

"We shall achieve this objective by re-engineering our business and through continuous improvement in quality, cost, and customer service.

"We shall strive for excellence by nurturing, developing, and empowering our employees and suppliers. We shall encourage an open atmosphere, conducive to learning and teamwork."

SUCCESS MANTRAS

Nothing succeeds like success, which is the only route to emerge a winner in life.

Life, as we know it today has become very fast-paced and has undergone myriad changes from what it was a decade ago. These changes make it increasingly difficult to find satisfaction and contentment. Success, which is not so easy to achieve, has become a part and parcel of today's fast changing world. Nonetheless, a few simple steps can help you outline and reach your goals.

Success

Everyone wants to be successful. However, in order to be successful, you have to first determine what success actually means to you, personally. Does success mean mere accumulation of material wealth and power or something else? One has to decide this factor while he or she treads on the path of achieving success in life. Moreover, do not try succeeding at something just because others want you to, or you see others doing the same. Attempting to succeed in areas that you are unsuited to only leads to depression and unhappiness.

Set your goals

Once you have determined what success actually means to you, you can set goals for yourself to achieve. Another Gene Donohue recommends that one should set goals in all areas, which include educational and mental, home and family, financial and career, social and cultural and health and spiritual. It has been suggested the goals should be specific, measurable, action-oriented, realistic and time-bound (SMART). Writing your goals down on paper motivates you towards achieving them, as the process of setting them down on paper leaves a firm imprint on your mind.

Working towards your goals

Knowing what you want in life is just the first step. The next and most important one is to turn your dreams into reality. For instance, if your goal is to do an MBA from a specific institute, say from IIM, collect information on entrance tests and admission requirements. Once you have your information, allot time-frames to achieve each step.

Apart from this, try and anticipate the possible difficulties that you may face while achieving your goal. So, it is better to develop a strategy to bypass your goal or keep more than one option open to fall back on as an alternative. Also, if the situation requires you to change your goals, do so. Do not consider it a failure, consider it a victory, as you had the insight to realise that something had changed.

While you are working towards your goals, take some time every now and then to monitor your progress. Acknowledge yourself when you complete each step. This will help motivate you to work harder and complete the remaining steps. Note your achievements as well as your mistakes. This will help you in working through the rest.

Motivation

Whenever you are putting in your best efforts at getting somewhere, it is extremely important to be constantly motivated. In life, one often goes through many ups and downs and you must always take full advantage of the 'Ups' and overcome the 'Downs' if you want to carry on consistently and with full force. Motivation does not come from external sources. Although one can be motivated by a parent or a teacher, external motivation can keep you going only up to a certain point. Ultimately, it is you yourself, who provides the best motivation to reach your goals successfully.

- **Stay current:** Be in tune with latest developments in technology, trends, business and market development and pay attention to the latest development and trends in IT outsourcing, application development, disaster recovery/co-location, wireless networks, VOIP, 64-bit computing. Internet security, etc.
- **Stay connected:** Many of us work long hours with little time left for anything else. However, to stay marketable it is critical to stay connected to the industry we work in. Attending networking events or seminars allows you to stay in touch with your peers and monitor industry trends. It also enhances your visibility with potential employers. Join associations and memberships in relevant societies.
- **Track record:** Most associates track record with the number of years one needs to stay in an organisation. It goes beyond that. Staying a long time in a job is no guarantee of a greater market value. Today's economy is more dynamic and ever changing. Organisations are constantly re-inventing themselves to stay ahead. Being an old timer does not ensure a job when you leave. In today's business environment, a credible record means having a combination of achievements, fulfilling commitments to your employer and staying abreast of current and emerging technologies and trends.
- **Be business savvy:** In today's competitive market environment, organisations cannot afford to isolate their IT personnel from day-to-day business operations and strategies. IT managers must develop their business acumen and be more savvy in their overall contribution to the organisation, be able to propose meaningful technology solutions or deploy technology as a strategic tool to bolster business potential and growth. The IT manager's role as a strategic business contributor cannot be underestimated.
- **Upgrading IT skills:** In a rapidly changing IT industry, one must constantly upgrade. If you are a programmer who'd like to move into a systems administrator role, a CCNA or a DBA certification would increase your market value and open doors to new opportunities. If you are a Java professional, you may want to go for additional Java certification. IT skills can also be acquired through hands-on experience. Exposing yourself to new technical skills within your current work environment can also enhance your potential market value.

- **Continuous learning:** IT managers need to get familiar with other key business areas such as accounting, budgeting, profit and loss, financial statement analysis, business strategy, marketing, etc. In their future capacity as a CIO, CTO or IT director, they would need to display competencies in these vital areas.
- **Be proactive:** Many of us think that being proactive would leave us with more work and less pay. Look at it this way: By being proactive, you are seen as a team player with initiative. We tend to overlook the fact that when one takes on more roles to ensure projects are completed, we are also increasing our value personally. Volunteering can also unleash a skill you may think you don't have.
- **Soft skills:** Most technical professionals neglect their soft skills. With sufficient time and effort, you can boost your interpersonal, presentation and communication skills, people management skills and in the handling of difficult tasks or issues. This goes a long way in enhancing your market value and career options.
- **Being happy:** Love the work you do and you never have to work at all. Many times, we think of our job as a chore. Lack of enthusiasm reflects in the way you contribute to the firm.

Remember, to remain constantly marketable, you need to be clear about what you want to achieve. Once you have clarity, everything you set out to do will lead you to your own professional and personal success.

In today's dynamic business environment, it is important to stay 'relevant' with the ever-changing economy. Information Technology is constantly undergoing changes, leading to jobs losses and new jobs being created with every passing moment. To adapt and accept new job roles and environments is crucial to one's career. Here are some tips that will help you ride and stay afloat on the choppy seas of Information Technology.

❒ ❒ ❒

Box - 1

ENTREPRENEURS WHO CHANGED THE FACE OF CORPORATE INDIA

Source: A Pictorial History of Indian Business (FICCI)

Late Cowasjee Nanabhai Davar
(1814 – 1873)

The Inspiration to Invest: Cowasjee Davar inaugurated India's industrial revolution. In 1854, he set up India's first steam-powered textile mill in Bombay. Capitalised at Rs. 5 lakh, the Bombay Spinning and Weaving Company paid a 10 per cent dividend for six years straight. Davar set the stage for the safety of industrial capital in India. Galvanised by his example, others too made industrial investments. Among them: were Wadias and the Tatas.

Late Sir Jamsetji Nusserwanji Tata
(March 3, 1839 – May 19, 1904)

The Father of India's Industrial Revolution: J.N. Tata was the first Indian to understand the significance of the industrial revolution. At his Swadeshi textile mill, he instituted pension funds and accident compensation. He believed India's progress hinged around steel, hydroelectric power, and technical education. The industrialist in Jamsetji Tata was a pioneer and a visionary, possessed of a spirit of entrepreneurial adventure and acumen never seen before or since in a native of colonial India. The nationalist in him believed unwaveringly that the fruits of his business success would enrich a country he cared deeply about. These attributes, by themselves, would have been enough to mark him as an extraordinary figure. But what made Jamsetji Tata truly unique, the quality that places him in the pantheon of modern India's greatest sons, was his humaneness. He inspired creation of the Indian Institute of Science, formerly Tata Institute, in Bangalore. In 1900, when he was 60, he set up Jamshedpur Steelworks after learning steel-making in Europe. He was the giant who touched tomorrow.

Late V.O. Chidambaram Pillai
(September 5, 1872 – November 18, 1936)

The Steamships That Cried Freedom: Pillai was a nationalist who entered business to prove a point as much as to make profits. His Swadeshi Steam navigation Company Ltd. broke the monopoly of British shipping in coastal trade with Ceylon. VOC, as he was popularly called, was a radical Congressman who was arrested in March 1908 on charges of sedition. He was finally released in 1912. Pillai inspired an entire generation of conservative southerners to plunge into business.

Late Rai Bahadur Mohan Singh Oberoi
(August 15, 1898 – May 3, 2002)

The Brown Sahib's Opportunity: In 1934 Oberoi mortgaged his wife's jewels while scratching together Rs. 20,000 to buy his British partner's stake in the Clarke's Hotel, Simla. He put in money while the Brits pulled their out, and a decade later, he was the first Indian to run a hotel chain. In 1965, he opened the first five-star international hotel in India in Delhi. Thirty-four hotels in seven countries later, Oberoi was the first real Indian multinational. It is difficult to believe that the man who had established 28 fabulous properties, 13 of them abroad, by the time he passed away at age 104 in 2002, grew up as charity student in the obscurity of a Punjabi small town, Bhaun. His entry into his ordained orbit was as unredeeming.

Late J.R.D. Tata
(July 29, 1904-November 29, 1993)

A Visionary of the New Generation: Late Jehangir Ruttonji Dadabhoy Tata (Popularly known as JRD) is a visionary industrialist of the 20th century. Titan of the Times. J.R.D. Tata left an indelible mark on industry. He built the industry on the cornerstones of integrity and honesty. He played a critical role in increasing India's scientific, medical and artistic quotient.

Born in Paris on July 29, 1904, Jehangir Ratanji Dadabhoy Tata was the second child of Ratanji Dadabhoy Tata and his French wife Sooni. JRD was barely 34 when he took over as the forth chairman of a 13-company group with sales of Rs. 280 crore. India's industrial revolution mirrored his entrepreneurship as he set up businesses ranging from trucks to locomotives, cement to pharmaceutical, hi-tech enterprises like TCS to agri businesses and services including airlines and hotels. When he stepped down in March 1991, the conglomerate earned Rs. 10,627 crore. Under JRD. The Tata name became a synonym for probity and integrity and was India's most respected business brand. His people-centric model kept Tata workers from going on strike at a time when trade unions ruled industry. JRD also recognised the importance of access to technology and having good managers on board. He founded the Tata Institute of Fundamental Research, funded Indian Institute of Sciences, and set up the Tata Administrative Service along the lines of the British Administration Service.

Late Henning Holck Larsen
(July 4, 1907-July 27, 2003)

The Dane Who Never Went Home: One of a small flock of Europeans who refused Quit India, Larsen and his partner Soren K. Toubro – both came here to set up a cement plant for a British employer — set up a company in 1938 that became India's pre-eminent engineering giant. Larsen knew independent India offered much scope for his company and his skills. Worth Rs. 5,400 crore today, Larsen's push to manufacture it all in India sparked off an engineering boom that hasn't quit. From nuclear plants to new expressways, Larsen's stamps on India's is indelible. His spirit continues to find expression in the products we make, in the projects we execute, and indeed in everything we do, as we make the things that make India proud.

Dr. Verghese Kurien
(November 26, 1921)

Father of the Unlikely Entrepreneur: Dr. Kurien created Operation Flood, the largest dairy development programmme in the world. He made India the World's largest milk producer. But most importantly, he put economic power in the hands of the producers, all 10 million families at last count. The Kaira District Cooperative Milk Producers' Union, or Amul, as India knows the giant, is modern and fleet enough to lord it over an array of multinational competitors. Humble farmers, and cowherds – they all have a stake in one of the world's best dairy operations. He created India's White Revolution. His Operation Flood, launched in 1970, followed a simple structure (called the Anand Pattern); at the core were farmers and the co-operatives; on top was a district-level milk producers' union, and finally there was a state federation that did the marketing. The National Dairy Development Board, which Kurien founded in 1963 (he won the Ramon Magsaysay Award for Community Leadership in the same year), today runs a co-operative network comprising 170 milk unions and 10.7 million farmer members. The 80-year old Kurien retired in 2000 as NDDB's chairman.

Karsanbhai Khodidas Patel
(March 10, 1944)

The Power of the Grassroots: Patel knew no marketing, had no management qualifications and no collaborator, Indian or foreign, when he created the first Indian brand to humble the best multinationals. The saga of this Gujarat government chemist began with a 12 yard shed in his backyard in 1969. Worth Rs. 2,440 crore today, Nirma's cut-price detergent shook the likes of Lever. Patel, who speak little English, inspired legions of Davids to do entrepreneurial battle with India's corporate Goliaths.

Late Aditya Vikram Birla
(November 14, 1943 – October 1, 1995)

The First Mogul of Globalisation: When MIT graduate Aditya Vikram Birla returned to India to be a part of his grandfather G.D. Birla's sprawling empire in the 1960s, he could have gone with the flow. But when it took Indian bureaucrats 11 years to clear a refinery project, Birla did not believe it worth his while to work the licence raj. Instead long before globalisation became a buzzword, he spread outward, setting up a textile mill in Thailand; late the world's largest palm oil refinery in Malaysia. When he died in 1995, his group had 17 companies in 14 countries.

"The late Aditya Vikram Birla inherently believed in the trusteeship concept of management. Simply put, he said that the wealth that one generates and holds is to be held in trust for its stakeholders.

This meant not only rewarding shareholders and employees, but reaching out to communities.

Late Dhirubhai Hirachand Ambani

December 28, 1932 – July 6, 2002

The Saga of New India: Truly an entrepreneur for the tumultuous, new India. Poor son of Gujarat village school teacher, he reached Aden at age 17 and worked as petrol station attendant. Mixing grand opportunism with extreme guile, he clambered his way up, manipulating the licence raj to his advantage. He created an equity cult by going to millions of small investors when the big bankers refused him money. He adapted as easily to liberalization. At Rs. 60,000 crore, there's quite simply nothing larger than Reliance in India today.

Dhirubhai always encouraged people to think big, think fast, and think ahead. He often said, "Our dreams have to be bigger. Our ambitions higher. Our commitment deeper. And our efforts greater. This is may dream for Reliance and for India.'

He was the first Indian to truly understand the term 'economies of scale.' At a time when government decided capacities for business, Dhirubhai thought otherwise. He outwitted the system and built capacities that were not based on reasonable projections of demand. When times were good, he had the bandwidth to meet demand. When times were bad, he had the economies of scale on his side or that extent, the global ambition Indian Inc now harbours and the beligerence it exhibits, is Dhirubhai Ambani's legacy. What makes Dhirubhai the most dynamic of all Indian entrepreneurs is not only the fact that he single-handedly built an empire in the shortest possible time but he also ushered in the cult of equity and wealth creation. Ambani not only clothed Indians; he also put money in their pockets.

N.R. Narayana Murthy

(August 23, 1946)

Messiah of the New Middle Class Nagavara Ramarao Narayana Murthy (N.R. Narayana Murthy) created a world class a new kind of IT company along with his seven colleagues with middle-class ethics and global ambitions from Rs. 80,000 as initial investment in 1981. The Infosys is an embodiment of middle class values, hardwork, humility, honesty and innovation — and inspired unaccountable thousands on the good way to make money.

Narayana Murthy is undoubtedly the great Indian middle-class hero, an achiever who proved that merit does matter, that you don't have to do bad things to make good, that even an engineer from a lower middle-class family who didn't inherit a business empire and refused to pay bribes can become a corporate czar. He had turned into a venture capitalist and mentor.

Kiran Mazumdar Shaw

Biotech Baroness: It's rare for a women to be the CEO of a company that leads it industry. Its rarer still for that woman to also have pioneered the industry. But then, Kiran Mazumdar Shaw is no ordinary woman. When she returned from the UK with a master's degree in brewing (her father R.I. Mazumdar was India's first brew master), she was all of 25 years old. Her original idea was to take up a job as a brewmistress. But fate willed otherwise. As it happened, she couldn't find a job. Far from being deterred, the young Mazumdar launched her own company with Biocon, an Irish firm, to manufacture enzymes for packaged fruit juices. Now Biocon is moving into even greener pastures.

It will use its technology to manufacture recombinant human insulin. It is a multi-billion dollar market that is expected to revolutionise diabetes treatment and the product will pit Biocon with MNCs like Eli Lilly. Her dream: To propel Biocon into the world's top 10 biotech firms.

It is Kiran's people-centric nature that makes her rise above mundane things like gender differentiation. Her style is hands on and she usually puts in 15 hours of work daily.

Today, Biocon (the Irish partner sold out to Mazumdar Shaw in 1999) is India's largest biotech company with revenues of about Rs. 200 crore, and focused on pharma products such as anti-infectives. It also has a subsidiary called Helix that carries out Biuocon's biopharm operations. Kiran Mazumdar Shaw, Chairman and Managing Director, Biocon has won the 'Nikkei Asia Prize' 2009 for her pioneering achievements in the field of Biotechnology. Shaw was nominated for her pioneering work in the field of Biotechnology in India by establishing a business model that believes in innovation and intellectual excellence, her achievements as a first generation entrepreneur and her status as an icon of entrepreneurship in the country.

Azim Premji

(July 24, 1945)

Creator of the New Wealth: Azim Hasham Premji who inherited an oil mill from his father Mohammed Hush Premji, diversified and entered the knowledge economy in 1979. From there on, he led his way to software superpower status. His vision, determination has created new wealth and newer opportunities.

So it's remarkable that Azim Premji unwittingly serves as inspiration for hundreds to technics — around the country and within his company — to strike out on their own Many CEOs of tech startups launched in the late 1990s were once long-serving employees of Wipro. Others who couldn't get into Wipro, made it on their own.

Faquir Chand Kohli

(February 28, 1924)

Father of Indian Software Industry: As an electrical engineer, F.C. Kohli was an unlikely candidate to be India's software revolutionary. But, as it turned out, J.R.D. Tata couldn't have picked a better man to lead the Tata group's foray into the then esoteric software business. When Kohli took over the reins at Tata Consultancy Services in 1969, the electrical engineer from the Massachusetts Institute of Technology only had experience in managing power plants. Worse, computer technology wasn't really a priority for the government. Kohli battled on, managing to get a modest share of the software boom that had begun in the US in the early 60s. The arrival of Rajiv Gandhi and his technology-friendly team opened up opportunities for TCS, and a horde of other software wannabes. Today, TCS is Asia's largest software and service company. A company with strong heritage, high level of ethics and integrity and a respected technology leader with proven track record. People are proud to work on cutting edge technology that transforms people's lives in every corner of the world. The company culture and values provide people a distinct environment where they can focus on making a difference, learning and growing while maintaining a healthy work/ life balance.

Late P.C. Mahalanobis
(June 29, 1893 – June 28, 1972)

India's Quality Guru: Prasanta Chandra Mahalanobis was India's answer to the American quality guru Edwards W. Deming. Just like his American peer, Mahalanobis was a statistician. And like Deming, Mahalanobis (called 'Professor' by his friends) sought to create prosperity through the use of statistics. When Mahalanobis was in his late 20s, he set up the Statistical Laboratory within the Physics Department of Calcutta's Presidency College. By 1931, it became the Indian Statistical Institute, and in 1959 it was a national institution. Mahalanobis also showed India the use of sample surveys, by employing them to study Bengal's jute production and yield in 1937. Statisticians today consider that Professor's greatest contribution. But in popular memory, the Cambridge graduate is best remembered for his seminal work on the Five-Year Plan. While the decay of Nehru's command capitalism may be at the root of India's economic problems, the Mahalanobis model did give a newly independent India a spring-board to prosperity. It's a pity that the expected leap did not take place.

John D. Rockefeller
Once controlled 90 per cent of the nation's **oil** business

Cornelius Vanderbilt
Undercut competitors' **steamboat** prices; bought **railroad** lines in his late 60s

John Jacob Astor
Sold his **fur** business to invest in New York City real estate

Stephen Girard
Used his shippiing fortune to enter **banking;** helped finance the War of 1812

Bill Gates
Co-founder of **Microsoft**

Andrew Carnegie
Built a **steel** empire, then gave most of his money away

A.T. Stewart
Founded the first **department store** in New York, on lower Broadway

> *"Industrialisation is an ongoing process which accelerates economic growth and induces social change."*

ONE

Introduction

INTRODUCTION

The Process of Change

The process of socio-economic change is an intrinsic part of human civilisation. Man has been striving ceaselessly to discover the secrets of nature and thereby benefit immensely in creating a peaceful, rich life for himself and his fellow-beings. Man has benefited by agricultural, industrial and information activities. According to J.K. Galbraith, there are three types of economic development that are currently in vogue. These are symbolic modernisation, maximised economic growth and selective growth. Economic growth is the *sine qua non* of change and better living standards. Over the years, a middle-of-the road social democratic thinking is becoming consolidated.

Sustained Growth

The primary objective of developing countries like India is to achieve rapid, balanced and sustained rate of economic growth. Hence, efforts are directed towards the creation of conditions in which a fast development of productive resources can take place. This inevitably necessitates the transformation of social and economic structures which will not restrain the potential productive forces and inhibit the development of resources. The state has, therefore, to devise efficient and effective strategies, at once political, economic, social, technological and cultural, so as to ensure a desirable co-ordination of all sectors of the economy and assure deliberate and requisite interest and involvement of the people. This is largely secured by adopting, politically, the technique of planning and, economically, the tool of management. Country after country in the underdeveloped world is progressively and intensively resorting to centralised state management of the economy and to a restructured and neo-cultured society.

Economic development, if conceived without appropriate social changes, becomes soon stultified and stagnated. Social change cannot be achieved, if political, technological and cultural aspects are combined and woven into the fabric of economic planning. Comprehensive national planning is increasingly becoming an instrument of socio-economic transformation in developing countries. Planning delineates strategies. It also determines policies consistent with the political philosophy of the party in power and largely of the country voting the party to power. There seems, however, nothing like universal precepts of planning, though concepts of planning are emerging with experience gained all over the world. One does not naturally observe a uniform approach to planning. There is bound to be as much diversity in national planning, as multiplicity of political philosophies and dissimilarity in the state of economies.

Objectives of Planning

There would, however, be no two opinions on the basic objective of planning. Planning must impart dynamism to the process of development. In different developing countries, diverse economic systems exist. Despite the apparent similarities between the different economies, they are at various stages of development. Furthermore, different regions and sub-regions in the same country are also not at the same levels, economically, socially, technologically and culturally. Dissimilarities are wide. The process of planning in one and the same country, therefore, tends to be very complex and, at times, beset with formidable problems obstructing the process of rapid, balanced and sustained economic development. It is, thus, becoming patently evident that planning to become a potent tool and an effective technique of economic development must descend from the Olympian altitudes of the national level to the low lands of the regions. Formulation of development plans can be all-inclusive and well-integrated only at the regional and the sub-regional level. Every region and sub-region, due to its distinctive character, demands a special treatment. It is relatively easy and simple to accelerate production, stimulate consumption and motivate transformation of the economic and social structure at the regional and sub-regional level, particularly in a vast and diverse country like India. Some of our states and regions are as big as nations. If the creation of conditions facilitating rapid growth of physical and human productive resources is the aim of planning, the peculiarities of the region and sub-regions have to be taken into account — perhaps more than the points of similarity. Rapid the balanced economic development pre-supposes co-ordinated and deliberate activity in all sectors of the country.

Public Response

In a country like India, economic development must be consistent with the principles of democracy, ensuring that the economic tasks will be in full accord with the interest of the vast mass of humanity, ground for ages in chronic and abysmal poverty. Poverty has killed interest, initiative and enterprise. The greatest social tragedy in a poor country is the loss of will. There is an urgent need to overcome their economic backwardness and cultural weakness and to promote their social and intellectual advance. The challenge to developmental planning in countries like India lies in laying down the firm material foundations for a more equitable, equal and egalitarian society. This is possible when backwardness of regions and sub-regions is clinically examined and correctly diagnosed. Prescriptions need to be written on the basis of social psychology and economic pathology of the regions and sub-regions and medication, nursing as well as nourishment provided to gain economic strength and infuse 'development will.' The success of planning is closely linked with the readiness with which the people respond to the demand of economic progress. Rapid economic development is largely dependent on the degree of popular response, and the intensity of this response indicates the extent of development will generated in the community or the region concerned. The first task, therefore, is to be stimulate and arouse the people to action aimed at improving their lot by undertaking productive, economic activity. Such an awakening will facilitate numerous changes in the social and economic fabric of the region concerned and will also catalyse structural transformation. The process of regional and sub-regional development is triggered off by combining all aspects of economic development into meaningful policies, quantified targets and viable programmes. It must be appreciated that planning goes beyond purely economic factors.

Man — A Crucial Factor in Development

The absence of universal precepts of planning should not worry any planner unduly, because it is still possible to enunciate the basic laws that motivate economic development, drawing on the experiences of planning under different political systems. These should hold good in all economies and for all countries at any time. There is something which can be described as the laws of dynamics of economic development. If they are respected while planning and complied with while implementing, the process of economic development may not prove to be unfruitful and wasteful. Like the laws of nature, these laws of dynamics of economic development are inexorable and the degree of alienation with them will render planning unsuccessful. "These laws embrace various aspects of the process of planning. As has been emphasised above, economic development is a multi-lateral and multi-directional movement. In fact, economic developmental potential remains a dormant asset due to the undeveloped or underdeveloped economic man. Man is much more crucial to development than other economic factors. As such, when man wills to change, economic development rolls on. Other factors are ancillary, though quite necessary. Sufficiency of other resources, without the necessary human "development will" does not lead us anywhere. Developable resources may exist in plenty. But, if development-wedded human minds are absent, hardly any economic development will take place. So, the creation of the development will is the key factor which engines the economic progress. Once such a will emerges, it is necessary to see that the laws are correlated and co-ordinated action is planned, and whatever is planned is well executed. A humble attempt has been made below to present the seven laws of dynamics of economic development, as they are quite relevant to the regional and sub-regional planning contemplated in India at present.

Entrepreneurship

The words *"entrepreneur", "intrapreneur"* and *"entrepreneurship"* have, acquired special significance in the context of economic growth in a rapidly changing socio-economic and socio-cultural climate, particularly in industry, both in developed and developing countries. The experience in the industrialised countries like the United States of America, Germany, Japan and the United Kingdom are authoritatively cited in support of this claim. An in-depth study of the subject thus becomes not only relevant but also necessary.

An entrepreneur is one of the important segments of economic growth. Basically, an entrepreneur is a person who is responsible for setting up a business or an enterprise. In fact, he is one who has the initiative, skill for innovation and who looks for high achievements. He is a catalytic agent of change and works for the good of people. He puts up new greenfield projects that actually creates wealth, opens up employment opportunities and fosters other sectors.

The techniques of planning may have to be based on these laws of dynamics of economic development. Their ignorance or non-compliance is likely to retard and restrict the process and pace of economic development, which all the developing communities and countries cherish. Development is essentially a matter of social and economic management. In India, perhaps, the emphasis was and still is largely on the economic aspect rather than on the social. If the social motivation is taken care of, economic development will begin to take care of itself. Perhaps, our planners need this advice. But will they heed?

Trends in Economic Development

There are seven major trends affecting the direction of economic development.

1. Technology as a resource
2. Competition in domestic and international markets
3. The role of invention
4. Government as stimulator
5. Entrepreneurial and Intrapreneurial development
6. Innovative capital formation
7. Collaborative relationships

Technology is more than a thing, a gadget, or even a process. It is a self-generating resource that is not consumed in the process of use. Consequently, it is an important form of economic wealth.

Competition is forcing a reassessment of our individual and collective responses to the marketplace. Fierce domestic and international competition for scientific, technological, and economic preeminence is forcing communities and regions to leverage all their resources — human, technological and financial — to compete effectively for vibrant and diversified economies.

The countries are experiencing an unprecedented burst of invention. Myriad technological advances are occurring with incredible speed and frequency. The ability to commercialise these inventions will have direct and immediate economic consequences.

The governments are trying to find positive non-interventionist approaches to encouraging entrepreneurship and technological diversification. They seek to create jobs, provide benefits to the small business sector, and push technology. The creation of an environment that promotes entrepreneurial activity has become a more important focal point in government's policy on development.

People with raw energy and a proclivity for risk-taking built and sustained the countries. They are continuing to build it today — in new ways, with new approaches. These entrepreneurs and intrapreneurs are breaking tradition and providing a dynamic source of creative and innovative enterprises.

Innovative capital formation is providing the catalyst for the entrepreneurial process. Mechanisms for providing seed capital and venture capital as well as expanding venture capital industry are helping to build new ventures. If the entrepreneurial process is to succeed, it is essential to continue to support and expand the formation of capital and its innovative utilisation in new business development.

Finally, creative collaborative relationships are being formed between business, government, and academia. These ties are forging new opportunities for commercialization and are accelerating the technology transfer process.

The World Bank's Report

The World Bank's Report, *"India — Poverty, Employment and Social Services"*, stresses that if India were to build on its improved economic performance, it would have to improve agricultural growth rate, continue her policy of industrial deregulation and rationalisation of trade policies, improve public sector finances and increase efficiency in the social sectors. Simultaneously, export growth will have to be stimulated and domestic fiscal imbalances reduced.

In India, agricultural growth is still governed by the seasonal rains. The phenomenal growth in agriculture is attributed to the entrepreneurial skills and hard work. Yet, industrialisation is widely recognised as one of the important means to usher in economic and social transformations. Industrialisation is a *sine qua non* of economic progress, an effective instrument of growth and welfare. Industrialisation is essential not only for the generation of employment and achieving industrial self-sufficiency but also for the accelerated development of agriculture and other sectors through the backward and forward linkages.

Objectives of Industrialisation

Industrialisation accelerated economic growth, increases national income, brings about structural changes in the economy, induces social changes and promotes entrepreneurship.

The motives or objective of industrialisation are:

(*i*) To promote economic development;

(*ii*) To increase employment;

(*iii*) To increase levels of income;

(*iv*) To strengthen foreign trade;

(*v*) To develop strategic industries;

(*vi*) To safeguard defence requirements;

(*vii*) To stimulate development of other sectors;

(*viii*) To promote entrepreneurship;

(*ix*) To strengthen the social fabric; and

(*x*) To effect structural changes in the economy.

Fig. 1: Objectives of Industrialisation

Industrial development depends on a number of important factors as follows:

1. Entrepreneurship.
2. Capital.
3. Human resources.
4. Infrastructure.
5. Market.
6. Technology.
7. Government Policies.
8. Natural resources: *(i)* Mineral resources, *(ii)* Energy resources, *(iii)* Forest resources, *(iv)* Marine resources; and *(v)* Water resources.

Other factors determining industrialisation are geographical and climatic factors, agricultural development and innovation.

Industrial development is fostered and sustained by innovation. Joseph Schumpeter has assigned a very important role to innovations and entrepreneurship in industrial development. Peter F. Drucker has also laid special stress on these two aspects.

Innovation is the specific tool of entrepreneurs, the means by which they exploit change as an opportunity for a different business or a different service. It is capable of being presented as a discipline, capable of being learned, capable of being practised. Entrepreneurs need to search purposefully for the sources of innovation, the changes and their symptoms that indicate opportunities for successful innovation. And they need to know and to apply the principles of successful innovation.

Innovation, however, does not have to be technical, does not indeed have to be a "thing" altogether.

Entrepreneurship/innovations are not an inspiration, a gift, a talent or a "flash of genius" but are purposeful tasks that can be organised as a systematic work. Peter Drucker's basic postulate is that systematic entrepreneurship and purposeful innovation create an entrepreneurial economy.

Human Resources

While the availability of industrial resources is an important advantage for development through industrialisation, responsive human resources are the major conduit for the development and upgrading of technology. After all, the human factor is the greatest factor in the process of its own development.

Among the inputs that go into industrial development, such as capital, industrial resources, scientific research and human resources, social scientists emphasise the last-named factor as perhaps the most significant for achieving rapid industrialisation. The human factor consists broadly of individuals with a reasonable level of general education and skills in specific areas. While human skills include manufacturing, technical, supervisory, managerial, administrative and entrepreneurial competence, it is the entrepreneurial quality which is a key ingredient. It often sets the limit to the degree of industrial development and the speed with which it can be achieved in a particular country or region.

Lack of entrepreneurship inhibits the process of industrialisation in the newly-developed countries. Although there is no such thing as a zero level of entrepreneurship, it is well recognised that entrepreneurs can be developed through appropriately-designed entrepreneurship development programmes (EDP). These programmes broadly consist of three distinct stages; firstly, that of developing achievement motivation, and sharpening entrepreneurial traits and behaviour; second, that of project planning and development; and at the third stage, guidance is provided on industrial opportunities, incentives and facilities, rules and regulations and the development of managerial and operational capabilities. With the growth of technical manpower, it is necessary to organise entrepreneurship development programmes in a widespread manner to attract potential entrepreneurs to small business. While doing so, the characteristics of an entrepreneur have to be kept in view.

Broadly, they are as follows:

- Development in any walk of life has always depended on individual qualities of entrepreneurship. A study of human history shows ample evidence of the role of individuals in the process of development.
- Industrial development in almost all countries has always started with individual enterprises.
- Even huge multinational and national corporations have mostly received their inspiration from one or a few individuals.
- In the case of small industries, the project is usually centered round a single individual.

— Small enterprises are mostly initiated, managed and developed by one or a few individuals.
— Qualities of entrepreneurship constitute one of the major resources in the promotion of any enterprise.
— An entrepreneur, by implication, is someone who ventures out; prefers change as a means of growth; and is prepared to take calculated risks.
— He analyses the pros and cons carefully before making decisions.
— He is involved in the planning activities, both before and after the decision to start the enterprise.
— He is motivated by an urge to make a success of the project.
— He proceeds to challenge the situation.
— He equips himself with all the necessary tools.
— HP is persistent and is full of perseverance for making a success of himself.
— Entrepreneurship is a product of interaction among a number of factors. Some of these factors are in the individual (psychological) and the rest are in the social, cultural and economic milieu.

In brief the ingredients for a successful entrepreneur are:
— He is confident in facing challenge and is eager to achieve.
— He identifies the product.
— He plans for a venture.
— He selects the technology commensurate with the means available and tuned to the social and economic environment.
— He is eager to improve quality.
— He is able to manage men and material.
— He finds markets.

In India, a large number of institutions and organisations are engaged in the development of entrepreneurship, resulting in the speedy growth of industrial ventures.

The example of India is fascinating. During its First Five Year Plan, the pride of place was given to technical education. Industrial training institutes for low-level semi-skilled workers, polytechnic and prototype development and training centres for skilled workers and supervisors, engineering colleges for managers and institutes of technology for the higher managerial group were established all over the country. This resulted in India becoming the third largest technical power in the world.

Industrialisation

Industrialisation is one of the important means to usher in an economic and social transformation in the developing countries. More so, when agriculture cannot sustain the burden of the population growth, it is the industry and service sectors which have to shoulder the responsibility to sustain as well as, at the same time, accelerate the pace of growth. It is indispensable for survival and growth.

Industrialisation results from the interaction of technological change, innovation, entrepreneurial growth, specialisation and trade. Good transportation and an efficient communication system and an educated labour force help promote the rapid development of industries. Well-defined rules reduce the costs of transactions as specialisation increases and economies become more complex.

Large industrial units and business houses have also an important role to play in developing and sustaining new entrepreneurship. For, it should be noted that while the growth of entrepreneurship in India in the last 25-30 years has been remarkable, entrepreneurship is still a comparatively scarce factor in India, as indeed in all developing countries. In spite of our fairly good economic progress, India is one of the poorest countries in the world. On the other hand, our natural and human resources are such that we can be a fairly prosperous country. So, what we require is more entrepreneurship on the part of the government and the private sector. Entrepreneurship is a plant which can be developed in a big way. What with so many technological and management institutes in India, it should not be difficult to develop thousands of entrepreneurs every year. In this connection, government economic policies have an important impact on the growth of entrepreneurship. Sometimes, the government gives the impression that the private sector will only be tolerated. This impression should be removed and there must be a formal recognition of the fact that in a country like India, we require entrepreneurship at various levels and of various sizes — Central Government, State Government, large, medium and small private sector units and also foreign entrepreneurship.

The entrepreneurship development movement in India has received significant attention; this is borne out by the fact that the small manufacturing enterprises have made phenomenal progress during the last three decades and today occupy an important position in the industrial economy of India.

Entrepreneurial Culture

The entrepreneurial culture is the rock bed of economic growth and development. It fosters the growth of enterprises/businesses with a vision and accountability for the betterment of a society. Entrepreneurial culture implies a set of values, norms and traits that are conducive to the growth of entrepreneurship. It is the corporate culture that focuses on the emergence of new opportunities, the means of capitalising on them, and the creation of the structure appropriate for pursuing them. Entrepreneurial culture should be differentiated from administrative culture. Administrative culture is the corporate culture which focuses on existing opportunities, organisational structures and control procedures. An ideal administrator would ask such questions as "What resources do I control? What structure determines our organisation's relationship to its market? How can I minimise the impact of others on my ability to perform? What opportunity is appropriate?" On the contrary, an ideal entrepreneur would ask very different questions such as 'Where is the opportunity? How do I gain control over them? What structure is best?"

An ideal entrepreneur is one who combines values in the market economy; that profits do not somehow preclude ethical behaviour; that growth is possible even if political patronage is not used to bend rules and cut corners, and quite simply that pursuit of wealth can be grateful and mannerly one. He takes with him the interest of his people, his country, his natural resources, the ecology and sees that his enterprise becomes a catalytic agent of development. There is thus a need of true entrepreneurs, who do not wait for incentives, infrastructure, government support; but build their enterprises, harness the resources and develop. They adopt a responsible value-driven corporate philosophy for their enterprises and/or business activities. As such, there is no dispute among economists and social thinkers about the urgent need for the emergence of an entrepreneurial society as a forerunner of accelerated development of the economy in an integrated manner.

In short, the entrepreneurial culture develops entrepreneurial focus while the administrative culture develops administrative focus.

The most important characteristics of entrepreneurial focus are:

(*a*) Strategic orientation, that is, the entrepreneurial kind of managers will be driven by perception of opportunity.

(*b*) Commitment to seize opportunities, they will be revolutionary with short duration.

(*c*) Commitment and control of resources, effective utilisation of resources.

TRENDS DRIVING ENTREPRENEURSHIP

How will the new entrepreneurs realise their ambitions? What are the fundamental changes urging them to strike out on their own in increasing numbers. An irreverent take on the times.

Smaller Government: As the size of the state as an employer shrinks it will spur private enterprise.

Easier Money: With banks getting more entrepreneur-friendly and venture capitalists spreading their wings, money will be more accessible.

Nuclear Families: With more women working, a double income in the family will allow more budding entrepreneurs to take the plunge.

Less Economic Controls: As bottlenecks and entry barriers come down further it will make the entrepreneurs' life easier.

Technology: With new technologies come new opportunities.

Growing Services: The low-capital option for the small-scale entrepreneur.

Instant Gratification: An instant-mix generation that will reach out for quick success.

Just-do-it Effect: Entrepreneurial success stories in the peer group will spur more to take the risk.

Growing Consumer Class: More types of consumers lead to more entrepreneurial opportunities.

Globalisation: As barriers come down opportunities will increase.

Knowledge Economy

The knowledge economy stands on three pillars. The first: Knowledge has become what we buy, sell, and do. It is the most important factor of production. The second pillar is a mate, a corollary to the first: Knowledge assets — that is, intellectual capital — have become more important to companies than financial and physical assets. The third pillar is this: To prosper in this new economy and exploit these newly vital assets, we need new vocabularies, new management techniques, new technologies, and new strategies. On these three pillars, rest all the new economy's laws and its profits.

In computerese, eight bits equal one byte. But eight, or zillion, bits of information do not equal a byte of knowledge. Knowledge is not a sum but a summation, a relation. Data and information plug into knowledge: They are tiles in a mosaic, but they are not its design.

Knowledge involves expertise. Achieving it involves time. It endures longer than information — sometimes forever. Alan Greenspan, chairman of the Federal Reserve Board, has estimated that the US GDP, if it could be gathered together and weighed, would tip the scales at about the same amount today as it did a hundred years ago. But its real value, adjusted for inflation, is more than 20 times what it was. The difference does not come from atoms and molecules, it comes from intangibles. But the difference, in health, in wealth, in living standards, is tangible indeed.

CHARACTERISTICS OF A KNOWLEDGE ECONOMY

	Industrial economy	*Knowledge economy*
Objective of society	Basic needs for all through development	Empowerment
Education	Text book and formal teaching	Creative, interactive, self-learning and informal with focus on values, merit and quality
Workers	Skilled, semi-skilled	Flexibly skilled, knowledgeable, self-empowered
Type of work	Structured & hardware driven	Less structured and software driven
Management style	Directing	Delegative
Quality of personnel	Performance based	Knowledge based
Impact on environment and ecology	Heavy	Strikingly less
Economy	Industrial	Knowledge driven

Source: Knowledge society: approach and action plan.

How many people actually become entrepreneurs?

The creation of the Global Entrepreneurship Monitor (GEM) in 1999 represented the first attempt to provide a regular annual review of the state of entrepreneurship around the world. The two principle measures of entrepreneurial activity cover start-up entrepreneurs (companies less than 42 months old), and individuals who are owners of established businesses. The 2006 report, covering 42 countries, found that the overall entrepreneurship rate including both measures expressed as a percentage of the total working population, varied widely. The extremes were the Philippines at around 40% and Belgium at just over 4.5 %. The figure for the US stood at 15.5%. That for India was slightly higher at just over 16%.

According to the figures quoted in the 2005 GEM report, on average male entrepreneurs outnumber their female counterparts by a factor of around two to one. This is a surprisingly high ratio in the light of other figures. For instance, in 2002 a Canadian study reported that as of 2000, women were majority owners in only 15% of Canadian SMEs. And four years earlier, a study of the 500 fastest growing entrepreneurial companies in Europe included just 7% of companies run by women owner/CEOs. A likely explanation for the apparent discrepancy is that the GEM figures include both people who are opportunity-driven and necessity-driven entrepreneurs, and the report found that there tend to be higher shares of female necessity-driven entrepreneurial activity in countries where women have reduced access to established labour markets, thus pushing up the overall figure of women entrepreneurs.

Conclusion

India is an untidy and disorganised country in many ways. It is difficult to work in India as L. N. Mittal found. He left the country and built the world's largest steel company abroad. He has made all Indians proud. Hundred years ago, another Indian had a dream: to build a steel industry in India. When Jamsetji Tata announced his intention, the British governor-general dismissed the idea and said he would personally eat every pound of steel that Tata would produce. When Jamsetji arrived in London to raise money for his venture, he was turned away. On his return many Indians gave him their jewellery and their life savings to invest in his dream, which was theirs too — a dream of an independent and self-reliant India. Now, a 100 years later, Tatas have bought the largest steel company in Britain. Returning from a visit to Jamshedpur recently. L.N. Mittal wrote how much he was impressed by tata Steel's continuing care of the environment and the people in and around it. He said what he was at jamshedpur made him proud to be an Indian.

We yearn for more integrity in our leaders. Integrity is a composite of two qualities. On one hand, integrity is the quality of being honest and uncompromising of values and principles. Many leaders of our times, in business and government in India and elsewhere, fail this test. On the other, integrity also means the quality of being integrated, of being in tune with and connected with wider society, which is something business leaders in India and elsewhere need to think about.

We also want more value-based leadership. 'value' and 'worthiness' have been hijacked by the world of business and economics into monetary concepts as in shareholder 'value' and personal 'worth'. Surely we need to live by more fundamental values and therefore need other measures of value and worth. We need leaders who are 'real value' creators who care for and create the common good that we all share. In recent years, Mr. Narayana Murthy, Mr. Nandan Nilekani have laid stress on value-based corporate growth. The country needs visionaries and value sustained economic development.

Unfortunately we tend to describe all those who have positions and titles, such as government ministers and CEOs, or those who have great wealth and fame, such as wealthy business tycoons and film stars, as leaders in our societies. The media perpetuates this notion. It prefers to tell the stories of such people. It magnifies their power: True leadership, however, lies in the being of the person, rather than in the having of something. The leaders we must honour are those who respect the rights of those with less power than themselves, who do not inconvenience others by their importance; and who are role models of integrity in its complete sense.

Three IT men, Business leaders, visionaries and trend setters — TCS CEO S. Ranadorai, turned 60 in October 2004: Wipro Chairman Azim Premji reached the milestone in July 2005; and Infosys Chairman N.R. Narayana Murthy turned 60 in August 2006.

THESE INDIANS HAVE BEEN THERE, DONE THAT.......

The list of Nobel laureates is embarrassingly short

Rabindranath Tagore, *Writer*
Won the Nobel Prize for Literature in 1913 for *Gitanjali*, an anthology of poems.
Chandrasekhara Venkata Raman, *Physicist*
Won the Nobel Prize for Physics in 1930 for work on radiation.
Hargovind Khurana, *Biologist* Won the Nobel Prize for Medicine in 1968 for interpreting the genetic code and analysing its function in protein synthesis.
Mother Teresa, *Christian missionary.* Who the Nobel Peace Prize in 1979 for work among Kolkata's poor.
Subramanyan Chandrasekhar, *Physicist.* Won the Nobel Prize for Physics in 1983 for work on theoretical studies of the physical processes of importance to the structure and evolution of stars.
Amartya Sen, *Economist.* Won the Nobel Prize for Economics in 1998 for work on developmental economics.
V.S. Naipaul, *Writer.* Won the Noble Prize for Literature in 2001 for his entire body of work which "unites perceptive narrative and incorruptible scrutiny in works that compel us to see the presence of suppressed histories" says a statement from the Nobel Committee.

Note: Hargovind Khurana, Subramanyan Chandrasekhar and V.S. Naipaul are of Indian origin but are not Indian citizens.

These Indians Missed Out

Mahatma Gandhi, *Father of the Nation,* apostle of peace and, in Albert Einstien's words, "the only true Christian since Christ."

Jagdish Chandra Bose, *Physicist.* Guglielmo Marconi beat him to the invention of the radio by a matter of a few days only.

Satyen Bose, *Physicist.* Immortalised in science for the Bose-Einstein Theory of matter and the Bose-Einstein condensate.

ECG Sudarshan, *Physicist.* His contribution to quantum theory of optical coherence was ignored.

G.N. Ramachandran, *Physicist.* His work on triple helix was considered Nobel-worthy.

But these may still make it

The following names crop up every year when Nobel prizes are discussed

C.N.R. Rao, *Structural Scientist.* Lauded for achievements in solid state chemistry and material sciences.

Ashoke Sen, *Physicist.* One of the high priests in the quest for sciences' Holy Grail – The String Theory.

Salman Rushdie, *Writer.* Burst on the literary scene in 1980 with Midnight's Children. Has penned several masterpieces since.

Vikram Seth, *Writer.* Another Indo-Anglian literary giant who might still make it.

Jagdish Bhagwati, *Economist.* His work on trade and globalisation is considered path breaking.

What do the laureates win?

- The Nobel Diploma
- The Nobel Medal
- The Prize Amount
  (over $ 1 million)

How are the Winners Selected

In each case, nominations are invited from scientists, heads of academies, researchers from various countries and in the case of the peace prize, nominations are invited and awarded by a committee of five, appointed by the Storting (the Norwegian Parliament). Easily over a 100 nominations are made in each category (more than the number of nominators since there are many duplications). The prizes for physics and chemistry are awarded by the Swedish Academy of Sciences; for physiology or medical works by the Karolinska Institute in Stockholm; for literature by the Academy in Stockholm; and for champions of peace by a committee of five persons elected by the Norwegian Storting. No consideration is given to the nationality of the candidates.

The will to win, the desire to succeed, the urge to reach your full potential... these are the keys that will unlock the door to personal excellence — Eddie Robinson

TWO

The Enterprise

Introduction

Industrialisation is widely recognised not only as one of the important means to usher in socio-economic transformations and achieving industrial self-sufficiency but also for the accelerated development of agriculture, transport, trade, services and other sectors through the forward and backward linkages. It is a process which accelerates economic growth; effects structural changes in the economy, particularly in respect of resource utilisation, production functions, income generation, occupational pattern, population distribution and foreign trade; and induces social

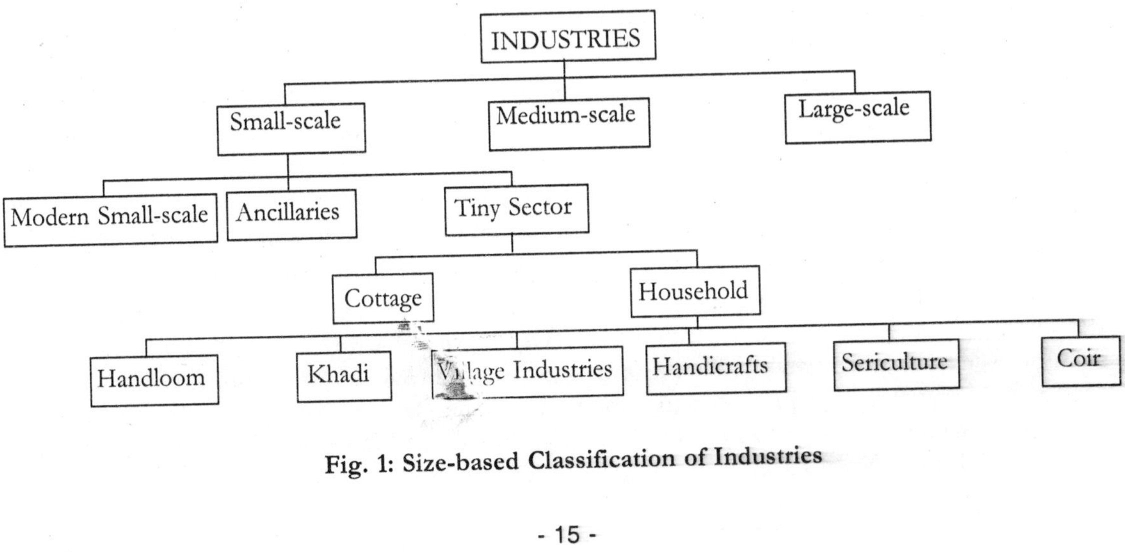

Fig. 1: Size-based Classification of Industries

change. Jawaharlal Nehru had emphasised that "Real progress must ultimately depend on industrialisation. Throughout the world, industrialisation has indeed become the magic word of the mid-twentieth century."

Industrialisation is brought about by the teaming entrepreneurs. Entrepreneurship is one of the most important factors of industrialisation. Entrepreneur is a kingpin in the process of economic growth.

Mixed Economy

India adopted a mixed economy, wherein the state and the private sectors play a vital role in accelerating the process of economic growth. Planned industrialisation has ushered in India after independence. Industrialisation has been conceived as one of the methods by which we can realise social and economic change which would lead to higher standards of living and greater equality of opportunity. Jawaharlal Nehru, the first Prime Minister of India, stated: "The growth of industry, big and small, is essential for any modern nation. Indeed without industrial development, there cannot be any higher standard of living of our people or even strength for it to preserve its freedom."

Industrial development gained more importance since the second Five Year Plan (1956-61). Indeed, industrialisation was given a new orientation with the Industrial Policy Resolution of 1956 which was formulated in the light of the socio-economic and political objectives and the Directive Principles of State Policy enshrined in the Constitution of India and the adoption by the Indian Parliament of the principle of socialistic pattern of society as the objective of social and economic policy. Industrial policy has been modified a number of times, albeit the basic tenets remain the same, and certain measures like the Industries (Development and Regulation) Act and the MRTP Act have been taken to reinforce the policy directives.

Indian Competitiveness

In a rapidly shrinking world, where national boundaries are becoming increasingly transparent, transnational trade is on the increase. This increase in world trade has led to greater competition — both internal and external.

It is in this context that the World Competitiveness Report 1990, prepared by (IMD) and the World Economic Forum, gains in significance. But can nations be competitive? Yes, because today, education, research support and fiscal and labour legislation are just a few of the policies recognised as major components of a country's competitiveness. In a world of increased capital technology and labour mobility, countries have to compete internationally for their prosperity.

Competitiveness, according to the report, "is the ability of entrepreneurs to design, produce and market goods and services, the price and non-price characteristics of which form a more attractive package than that of competitors." The report analyses the competitiveness of 34 countries. These countries are broken into two groups, industrial countries and newly industrialised countries (NIEs). The industrial countries are basically the member countries of the Organisation for Economic Co-operation and Development. The NIEs are Hong Kong, Brazil, India, Indonesia, Republic of Korea, Malaysia, Mexico, Singapore Taiwan and Thailand.

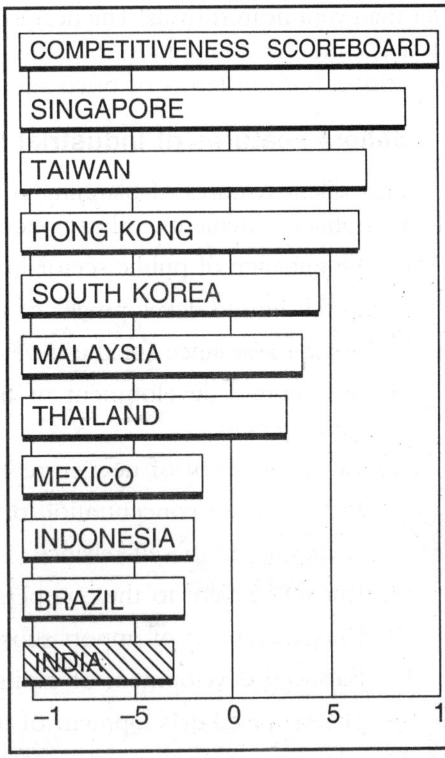

Fig. 2

In order to make the report objective and meaningful, some 326 criteria have been selected on the basis of their relevance to international competitiveness. While some of the criteria are very relevant to competitiveness (example, cost of labour), others have a longer term impact (percentage of GDP spent on research and development). Also, certain criteria have been given additional weightage. The criteria are divided into ten subject factors such as dynamism of the economy, industrial efficiency, market orientation, financial dynamism of the economy, industrial efficiency, market orientation and international orientation, among others.

But as the report rightly points out, competition can be both measured and perceived. The criteria mentioned above measure competitiveness. However, the perceptions of businessmen are taken into account by a Business Confidence Survey. This was done by circulating a questionnaire (126 questions) to 10,000 selected executives in all the 34 countries.

The world competitiveness scoreboard combines the quantitative and the qualitative analysis and ranks the countries in two groups. In group I, Japan is the most competitive nation followed by Switzerland, the US, West Germany and Canada. On the other hand, Spain, Portugal, Turkey, Greece and Hong Kong were the laggards in the descending order. In group II, Singapore is by far the most competitive nation followed by Taiwan and Hong Kong. The bottom three in the descending order are Indonesia, Brazil and India. It is indeed a tragedy that India ranks at the bottom of even the developing countries. Of course, this does not mean that India is the most uncompetitive nation in the world, because if certain countries in Africa, Latin America and Asia are included in the world rankings, then India would surely do much better.

Be that as it may, the Business Confidence Survey revealed some interesting facts. In growth optimism, the countries of South East Asia stand out as the best. This is because many of the countries like Thailand, Malaysia and Singapore have registered very high growth rates in the past decade. Here, India has also done fairly well and ranks sixth among the 34 countries surveyed.

As mentioned earlier, the 326 criteria are broken up into 10 factors that affect competitiveness and India stands out only in two factors. For instance, in 'dynamism of the economy' India is sixth among the 10 group II countries. The only other factor is 'future orientation' where India ranks fourth after Taiwan, Singapore and Korea.

The international communities' perception of the rising stars are Korea, Taiwan, Thailand, Spain and Singapore. On the question of entrepreneurs' expectations for future investment, India ranks fifth, behind Japan, Thailand, Ireland and Malaysia.

Indeed, in a world that is becoming more and more competitive, it is absolutely imperative that the planners, the government and industry realise that competition means moving at a pace faster than your nearest rivals. The nearest rivals to India today are countries like Thailand, Malaysia, Indonesia and the Philippines, to name just a few. All these countries are becoming increasingly competitive, both in terms of price and quality. Will India rise to the challenge?

Salient Features of Industrial Planning and Development

The salient features of planning and development of industries in India, as clear from the industrial policy statements, other policy announcements, plan documents, etc. are as follows:

1. Dominance of public sector in the key industries.
2. Synchronised development of small and large industries.
3. Special assistance for the development of small industries.
4. Accelerated development of backward areas and achievement of balanced regional development.
5. Encouragement of new entrepreneurs and diffusion of ownership.
6. Prevention of concentration of economic power.
7. Achievement of self-reliance.
8. Encouragement to the co-operative sector.
9. Encouragement of import-substituting and export-promoting industries.
10. Balanced development of capital goods and consumer goods industries.
11. Synchronised development of industrial, agricultural and other sectors.

The development of small-scale industries has been one of the most significant and characteristic features of industrial development in India. One of the distinctive characteristics of small-scale sector is that, the development of these industries would create broader employment opportunities, assist in entrepreneurship and skills development, and ensure a better use of scarce financial resources and appropriate technology. Furthermore, they can play a main role in the achievement of national economic and socio-political objectives. The gestation period is very short and they need smaller amount of capital to start. It also helps in the dissemination of productive capacity unlike the large-scale industries which tend to concentrate in a few hands. This part, establishment of such industries in rural areas and small towns helps to check the influx of population into bigger towns.

Basic Objectives

The basic objectives underlying the development of small and medium scale industries are the increase in the supply of manufactured goods, the promotion of capital formation, the development of indigenous entrepreneurial talents and skills and the creation of broader employment opportunities. In addition, they include socio-economic goals such as the decentralisation and dispersal of manufacturing activities from the metropolitan to the non-metropolitan and rural areas, the reduction of regional economic imbalances within a country and the diffusion of entrepreneurial and managerial abilities and skills and technology throughout the country.

In the Indian Economy, cottage and small-scale industries have a significant role to play. With increasing pace of industrialisation and sophistication of the large-scale industries, a new

Steps of the ladder the entrepreneur (Small) has to climb

It is a continuous process of industrialisation:

STEPS OF THE LADDER THE ENTREPRENEUR (SMALL) HAS TO CLIMB. IT IS A CONTINUOUS PROCESS OF INDUSTRIALISATION

34. ANCILLARY DEVELOPMENT
33. GROW BIGGER
32. COMPETE WITH OTHERS
31. MODERNISATION
30. DIVERSIFICATION
29. PLOUGH BACK PROFITS
28. KEEP UP-TO-DATE
27. SELL
26. PRODUCE
25. PLAN OUT RECORD-KEEPING
24. ORGANISE MARKETING
23. DECIDE ON PRICING POLICY
22. TRIAL RUN
21. RECRUIT PERSONNEL
20. PROCURE MATERIALS
19. INSTAL MACHINERY
18. PLAN BUYING
17. APPLY FOR MATERIALS (IF IMPORTED OR CONTROLLED)
16. PLACE ORDER FOR MACHINERY (PREFERABLY ON HIRE-PURCHASE)
15. PLAN SOURCES OF MACHINERY
14. PLAN FINANCE
13. OBTAIN CLEARANCE FROM CENTRAL, STATE & LOCAL AUTHORITIES AND SSI REGN. NO.
12. MAKE SURE WHAT LAWS WILL PARTICULARLY AFFECT YOU
11. ARRANGE THE WORKSHED WITH FACILITIES (PREFERABLY ON RENT)
10. DECIDE ON LOCATION AND SITE
9. OBTAIN THE PROJECT REPORT FROM SISI OR ELSEWHERE OR PREPARE IT YOURSELF
8. DECIDE WHETHER TO PURCHASE A GOING CONCERN OR TO START A NEW ONE
7. DECIDE ON FORM OF OWNESHIP [SOLE-PROPRIETORY] PARTNERSHIP/CO-OEPRATIVE/COMPANY (PRIVATE/PUBLIC)].
6. CHOOSE A LINE
5. DATE WITH YOURSELF FOR A DECISION
4. DISCUSS WITH ALL AROUND YOU AND WITH SISI & D.I. OFFICE
3. CONSULT PUBLICATIONS AND AGENCIES
2. DATE YOURSELF FOR NEWER IDEAS
1. ANALYSE YOURSELF AND YOUR OBJECTIVES

Fig. 3

Note: This is a bare outline. The next chapter contains some details and suggestion for step-by-step planning.

Box - 1

A rare entrepreneur who spurns collaboration ventures, his cement plants work effortlessly on the flawless technology he has developed —

In 1981, Durga Prasad Saboo, a would-be entrepreneur, applied to the Rajasthan government for 200 bags of cement. He was allotted only ten. Taking this as an affront, Saboo refused to accept the government quota. Instead, he decided to make his own cement. He began to design several tiny and mini cement plants — a profession he has stuck to across all these years and made a big success of.

Saboo began by experimenting with different grades and quantities of limestone, clay and coke. The first tiny plant he designed had a capacity of 10 tonnes per day. And he has never looked back since then. Without any publicity whatsoever, he sold the first 20 tiny plants he designed and for which he made his own machinery.

His company is equipped to supply six plants in a month. Saboo is one of those rare small scale entrepreneurs who spurn collaboration overtures from corporate giants. He refuses to sell his VSK technology or even allow them to market the plants he designs.

Winner of the Outstanding Entrepreneur award for the small scale sector, Saboo likes to do things on his own. Already Saboo Engineers has supplied no fewer than 101 tiny cement plants of different capacities (maximum capacity 200 tonnes per day) while another 14 will be put up shortly. Nine plants are in the process of being set up.

The basic advantages of the tiny cement plants are that they help dispersal of industry to rural areas. Compared to the large plants, the employment potential of these plants is much more whereas, power consumption is almost half that consumed by the big plants (70 units per metric tonne as against 125 to 135 units in the case of large plants). Moreover, the installation cost is hardly Rs. 800 per metric tonne compared to Rs. 2,000 pmt in the large plants.

Another significant advantage of the tiny cement plants is that they can be set up anywhere even if they are based on imported limestone. On the contrary, the large plants can be set up only where huge limestone deposits are locally available.

Sabbo began his career in 1940 as a store keeper at Patna in a roller flour mill. But, soon, family requirements took him back to his home town. In the sleepy little town of Kuchaman in Rajasthan, Saboo set up a unit in 1950 which manufactured components for flour mills.

But the real break for Saboo came in 1979 when he shifted to Jodhpur and set up four units for grinding of oilseeds and oil extraction. These units were started in less than two months. Today, he is assisted in the expansion of his business by his three sons.

The VSK technology developed by Saboo is significant. This technology, with slight modifications can be used to set up plants that can produce different varieties of cement like high strength cement, rapid hardening portland cement, rapid hardening non-shrinkage grout, sulphate resistance cement, oil well cement, etc. The varieties of cement fetch better returns than ordinary portland cement.

Personally, Saboo prefers to set up only tiny cement plants to meet the growing demand. There are reasons for this — the large savings in installation and fuel consumption and creation of more employment in rural areas are some.

No less than 99 per cent of the plants based on these technologies did not work. But the plants supplied by Saboo have never failed. These plants have been working without any trouble at 20 per cent to 30 per cent above their rated capacity. Even the National Productivity Council has paid rich tributes to Saboo for the flawless technology he has been able to develop for his tiny plants.

Apart from tiny plants, Saboo has also supplied a large-size bauxite calcination plant to Gujarat Mineral Development Corporation. Costing Rs. 7.11 crore, the entire plant has been supplied on a turnkey basis.

orientation is inevitable in the relationship of the SSIs with the large and medium industries. This relationship calls for integration of the production methods, upgradation of the qualities of production, ability to meet stringent delivery schedules and very many other problems that arise in a dynamic and changing environment not only in the country but also in the international field.

India is One of the Worst Cases

A recipient of the Magsaysay Award *Dr. Zafrullah Chowdhury* is one of the founders of a people-oriented health care system in Bangladesh and is known as the architect of the rational drug policy developed there in 1982. Chowdhury speaks to Jeanne Prasad of *Business India* on an appropriate health care policy for the developing countries.

What are the Essentials of a 'Rational' Drug Policy?: A rational drug policy is nothing new. Since the seventies, there has been a movement to develop a limited list of drugs which doctors and hospitals all over the world should follow. A drug policy which imposes rational drug use and behaviour already exists in Western countries. In Britain, under the National Health Scheme, the government will not pay for irrational use of drugs. In the US, the insurance companies will not pay for over-medication. Germany, France and Holland have a negative list of drugs. India is one of the worst cases of irrational drug use. Despite the presence of educated people and highly qualified medical personnel, anarchy reigns in the fields of both medicine and drugs.

Any medical textbook would tell the doctors to use drugs as a single ingredient product as far as possible. There are only a few exceptions such as iron and folic acid, which must be taken together in cases of anaemia. In 95 per cent of illnesses, a single ingredient product is sufficient: only about 5 per cent cases need treatment with two or three drugs acting together. In India, the opposite is the case. Here, drugs are mixed into a cocktail that can be found nowhere else in the world. Drugs that create addiction, like cough syrups — all of which contain opium are freely available cough syrups sold in Bangladesh.

How does such a Policy Protect Consumers and Control Prices?: A drug is one commodity for which the consumer cannot make a purchase decision himself but must depend on the doctor or chemist. Drug prices must be regulated by establishing norms for pricing of all drugs. Unlike India, which has a list of special drugs, in Bangladesh price of all drugs are regulated through a simple procedure that takes into account the actual cost of ingredients and packaging material. Only essential packaging material is included but extra packaging for protection is allowed, for unnecessary packaging used for promotion or exploitation is not included. However, this is essential because, in a poor country, people may believe that fancy packaging means a better drug.

Special conditions of manufacturing, such as separate enclosure, air-conditioning, no-touch methodology involving higher investment in manpower, machinery and buildings are also considered when setting the price. However, the same drug must have these same price, regardless of the location of production. The drug cannot be priced higher, if labour costs are higher in different regions, for instance. This may not be a foolproof or the most effective system, but it is good enough for a Third World country.

How was Bangladesh's rational drug policy developed and how has it fared?: The World Health Organisation has developed a list of 250 essential drugs, which can treat 90 per cent of all diseases. Top physicians and pharmacologists of the world worked for two years to develop this list, which was adopted by WHO in 1974.

Bangladesh decided to follow the WHO list in 1982. As a result, 40 harmful and 1,500 useless drugs were banned. Useless vitamin and enzyme preparations were withdrawn from the

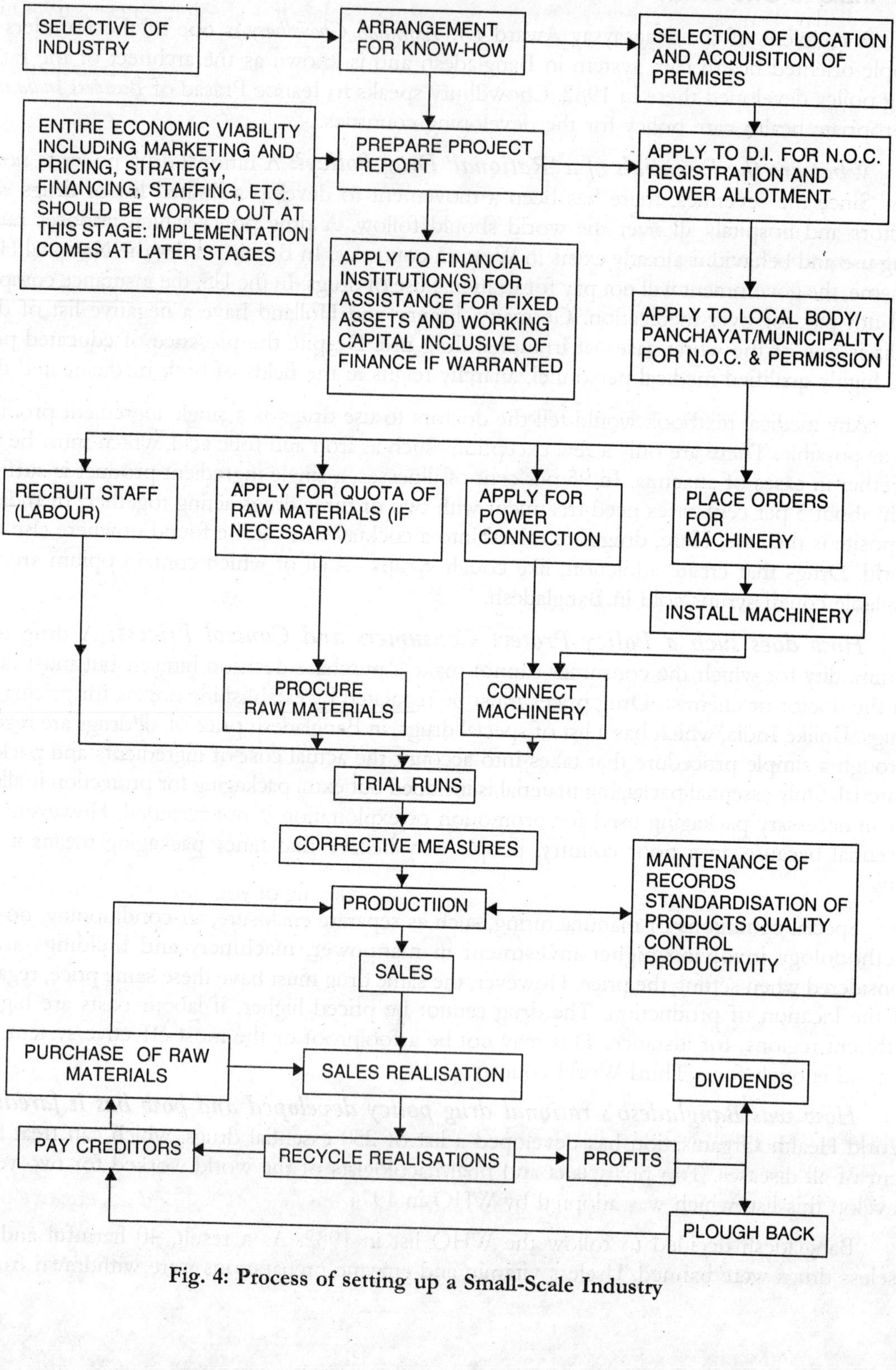

Fig. 4: Process of setting up a Small-Scale Industry

market. Today, Bangladesh allows no combination drugs, unless it is absolutely necessary. Out of the 250 essential drugs, only eight or ten combinations are allowed. Another policy — marketing of drugs under generic rather than brand names — has resulted in cheaper drugs and strengthening of the drug control system. It has also reduced the number of drugs prescribed.

Selection of a Small-scale Industry

The process of setting up a small-scale industry has been indicated in Fig. 4 which has been drawn on the basis of practical experience gained in its promotion. It indicates all the important stages in the setting up of a small-scale industry.

The objectives of the promotional regulations are to provide an impetus to the growth of a small-scale industry and regulate the supply of machinery, electricity, water, premises, finance, raw materials and markets. The process of production and marketing is governed by a series of rules and regulations. In a way, these regulations are a boon to the small entrepreneur.

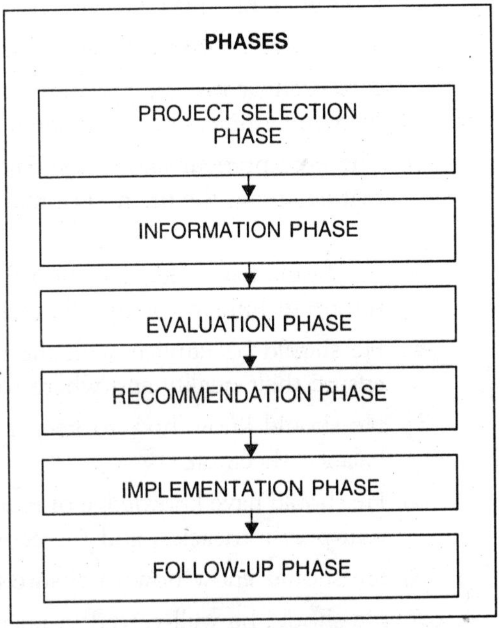

Fig. 5

Starting a Small-scale Industry

A small entrepreneur is the chief executive of his unit, its floor supervisor, accounts clerk, purchase manager, salesman, legal and economic advisor, planner and visionary — all rolled into one.

Every now and then, you will come across advertisement and announcement enticing you to set up small industries under the aegis of the State Small Industries Corporations, which promise a fully developed industrial shed with power and water, assistance in getting you raw materials, machinery on hire purchase basis, common services facilities, training facilities and facilities in the marketing of your product. Assurance term loans on attractive terms and working capital in time and at concessional rates. In backward areas, a number of additional subsidies are available.

To select those products, processes or systems in an organisation where the value and cost ratio is low and where analysis will lead to increased benefits:

(*a*) To gather, organise and analyse data.

(*b*) To define functions.

(*c*) To establish a functional monetary value.

To generate alternative methods for providing necessary functions:

(*a*) To develop, refine and evaluate alternative methods generated during the creative phase.

(*b*) To determine the cost.

(*c*) To select a feasible method offering best value.

To prepare and present a report containing recommendation along with benefits:

(*a*) To establish a plan of action for implementation of the selected method.

(*b*) To obtain approval.

(*c*) To perform all other actions necessary to put the proposal into effect.

(*d*) To follow-up and audit actual results.

(*e*) To resolve problems, if any, during proposal implementation..

An entrepreneur may be a qualified engineer. Even so, he should not dream of becoming a small entrepreneur unless he is confident of meeting the following twelve essential requirements:

(*i*) The entrepreneur should be fully conversant with the product line. It is not enough that he knows the method of manufacture; he has to know how to operate the machines, etc.

(*ii*) He should have adequate shop-floor experience to guide the machine operators in fool-setting techniques or the die-maker on the specific needs of his press tools.

(*iii*) He should be familiar with the raw materials he requires, their specifications, how to ensure their quality and where to get them at reasonable prices.

(*iv*) He should know how to keep accounts, how to maintain stores, how to prepare the balance sheet, etc.

(*v*) He should have knowledge of marketing channels, distribution network, agency practices, transport intricacies, and the economic of packaging.

(*vi*) He should know how to ensure the stipulated quality of his product.

(*vii*) He should be well-versed in taxation and other laws governing SSIs.

(*viii*) He should be willing to put up with bureaucratic regulations and insults, and be fractional under any circumstances.

(*ix*) He should know how to avail himself of the various benefits available to the SSIs.

(*x*) He should possess expertise, shrewdness, resourcefulness and, most important, perseverance in his business dealings. There is no substitute for hard work.

(*xi*) He should have the guts to withstand the high pleasure climate in which he has to build his unit.

(*xii*) He should pursue his dream project with a passion to succeed and perseverance. Hard work is a key ingredient.

Objectives to succeed

Any entrepreneur desirous of starting a small-scale industry should have a clear picture of the objectives of his project. It is advisable to prepare a comprehensive check list. Such a list, embracing all the important matters, has been given below for the guidance of prospective entrepreneurs. Students will get an insight into the various processes of a small-scale industry.

Box - 2

DO YOU HAVE THE PASSION TO SUCCEED?

A success story may start with a dream. But to reach its zenith, there are many other factors involved.

Many years ago, SRK declared that he'll rule Mumbai one day. And today, he's the King Khan of Bollywood. Fellow actor Manoj Bajpai, while growing up in a small town in Bihar, dreamt of tinseltown too. And he has managed to impress many with his talent. Car designer Dilip Chhabria, who confesses to "eating, living and sleeping cars" too worked tirelessly for a decade making car accessories in order to raise the money for his design studio.

We all dream. And we all hope that some day, our dreams will turn into reality. But, have you ever wondered why some people, like Khan, Bajpai and Chhabria succeeded where others didn't? The answer lies in the passion with which they pursued their dreams. As Chhabria, promoter of Dilip Chhabria Design, says, "One needs to be' obsessively passionate' as passion can vary, but obsession can't. It's the distinguishing factor. One must be restless all the time to do what one wants to do." He should know as he gave up a lucrative opportunity of working with General Motors, USA, all in his quest to designing cars.

Manoj Bajpai, who used to watch almost 120 movies a year at one time, says, "To make the dream a reality, you need loads of patience, self-belief, and most importantly the ability to take criticism on your face."

While some dream of reaching personal goals, others harbour dreams for the larger good. Like Bangalorean, Ramesh Ramanathan, who, while working with Citibank in New York and later in London, as MD and European head of corporate derivatives of a $100 million business, realised that his professional achievements were not solely his, he had a system to thank. "I began to appreciate what it takes to succeed — It's the conditions provided to people." says Ramanathan. Guided by this thought, he decided to create a similar base back home. So Janaagraha, an NGO, came into being in 2001, with the purpose of providing opportunities to people to be the best that they can be. Today, the NGO is working for people's participation not just in Karnataka, but also in Rajasthan, Maharashtra and West Bengal!

Listening to success stories seldom gives us an idea of the fears, doubts and uncertainties faced by an individual. "It's a lonely journey, till you get lucky." remarks Bajpai, adding, "When I first came to Mumbai and didn't have any work, the thought of going back did occur, but that was a short phase that lasted only for a couple of days, "Bajpai is not alone as director Nagesh Kukunoor in a recent interview revealed that five years ago when he wasn't able to rope in financiers for his projects did consider going back to his regular job of environment consultant. "With every film, I had to prove myself to the producers, and to be honest, the thought of leaving films did cross my mind," he says.

In Manoj Bajpai's words, these "battles with the self" once triumphed, make one strong enough to take on the world outside. As in Ramanathan's case, the biggest external hurdle was dealing with a traditional and rigid Indian mindset. "We might be an economically liberated society, but when it comes to social values, we are cynical. Initially, our motive of doing something for society was met with suspicion," he says. When it comes to overcoming difficulties on the way to success. Chhabria believes in the *mantra* — don't allow yourself choices. "If you have choices, then you won't put in 100 per cent effort. Then, it doesn't remain a life and death situation for you," he says.

It's interesting that these dreamers too look forward to acceptance at various levels. Bajpai revels in self-adulation. He says "Whenever I see my performance and feel it's someone else on screen, it gives me a high." On the other hand, Chhabria confesses that he's like a child who looks forward to appreciation. "When people give me a thumbsup sign on the road or say 'wow' after seeing my designs, I find it exhilarating," he remarks. For Ramesh Ramanathan, doing his bit for society encourages him to strive harder.

For these achievers, reaching their goal was merely a milestone crossed in the journey of life. As Bajpai puts it succinctly, "My dream was never materalistic. It's an evolving journey; I grow as I live every moment of my dream."

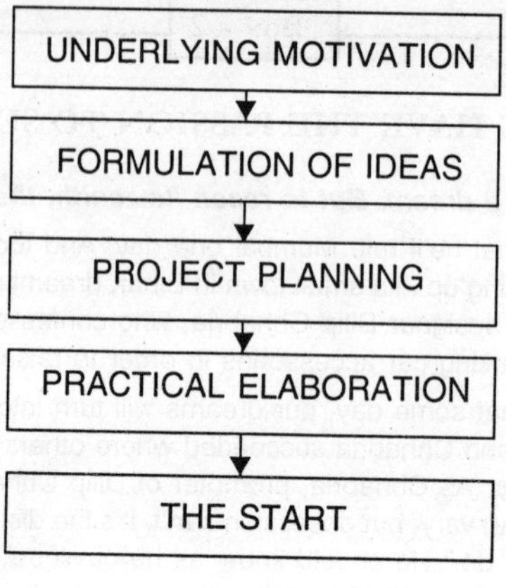

Fig. 6: Process of Starting a Small Enterprise

The Winning Edge

The opening up of the Indian small industry sector to competition as well as the increase in the need to the global market, demands fresh perceptions to respond to the radical changes in the 90s. Consequently, this sector must change first to survive as well as restructure itself to meet the new challenges through a critical evaluation of the forces of free global trade and increased competition. These events demand quantum strategic changes in terms of industry culture, flattening of the organisation structure, employee empowerment as well as team building. Only those organisations which can respond to these changes will be able to survive and retain a winning edge.

Some of the important characteristics that differentiate the successful organisations from the unsuccessful ones are:

1. The most important aspect of successful business is leadership. It calls for clear vision, goals and objectives, well defined mission, passion, perseverance, integrity, intuitiveness and employees' participation.
2. Adequate but well-orchestrated control. Constant feedback of results as well as setting and adherence of high standards give an organisation a cutting edge over others. Planning, foresight and analysis are other important qualities.
3. To be able to extract the best from its employees through total involvement, the organisations put a lot of emphasis on proper internal communication and on training employees.
4. The successful organisation is one which is very close to the market place. The process of systematic market is used to develop products or process of systematic market research is used to develop products or process and to provide value for money to the customers. This helps to gain the market share.
5. The next most important characteristic of a winning business organisation is "Zero Basing" or sticking to the best knowing what business the company is in, swiftly recognising and preventing when it has diverted into an unsuitable path and preventing risks.

DOING BUSINESS IN INDIA

The World Bank's recent publication, *Doing Business* bravely tries to develop a methodology to yield comparability across countries for medium-sized businesses.

The methodology starts with a hypothetical medium business, and posits scenarios. Then experts and businessmen are surveyed to assess the issues such a typical firm will face in these scenarios. This is an inherently in exact way of assessing problems faced by businesses. Yet it provides approximate comparisons across countries.

The data suggest that India's biggest problem is slow contract enforcement and liquidation, aggravated by poor credit to medium business (which can be eased by creating credit bureaus). Labour inflexibility turns out to be a lesser problem.

The study looks at five issues.

1. How easy is it to start a business?

This remains difficult in India. Start-ups require 10 procedures and take 88 days, costing 49.8% of per capita income. This is better than in Angola (146 days costing 838% of per capita income). Yet India lags well behind Asian neighbours. China has more procedures (12) than India (10), but these take just 46 days, costing 14.3% of per capita income. The champion here is Australia; just two procedures taking two days, India should aim for this too.

Many countries have no minimum capital requirement for a limited liability company. India does have a minimum but China's minimum is far higher, and it booms nevertheless.

2. How easy is it to hire and fire workers?

The hypothetical firm has 201 workers. The methodology develops indices to measure flexibility of hiring, conditions of employment (hours of work, paid leave, etc.), flexibility in firing, and an overall employment laws index. Each index varies from 100 for total rigidity to 0 for total freedom.

Major surprise: India is reasonably competitive. Its overall index is 51, against China's 47 and Thailand's 61. India is far more rigid than Singapore (20) or the US (22). Yet labour flexibility alone is no guarantee of success, as shown by Zimbabwe (27), Papua New Guinea (26) and, Kenya (34).

On the other hand, some rigid countries have fared very well, such as Taiwan (57), Germany (51) and France (50). Clearly some inflexibility can aid welfare without unduly hampering efficiency.

3. How good is enforcement of contract?

The time taken to judicially enforce a hypothetical supplier's contract (without allowing for appeals to higher courts) is estimated at 365 days in India, much better than in Guatemala (1,460 days). But India is way behind Tunisia (7 days), Netherlands (39 days), Singapore (50 days) or Botswana (56 days). I suspect the World Bank has underestimated the time for enforcement in India, but perhaps the problem is less severe for medium companies considered in this study.

India has 22 procedures for contract enforcement, comparable with China (20), Singapore (23) and Thailand (19). Nor are Indian laws especially complex. The real problem is time.

4. New difficult is it to close a business?

India is the world champion here. It takes 11.3 years to close a hypothetical medium-sized business in India. Closure is far quicker in neighbours like Singapore (0.7 years), China (2.6 years) and Thailand (2.6 years).

The Indian cost of winding up is only 8% of the cost of the estate in question, much lower than in China (18%) or Thailand (38%). But time is money.

In China and Singapore, the priority of lenders over other claimants is preserved 100%. But in India, the government and workers get seniority over creditors. The goals-of-insolvency index in this study measures the extent to which a satisfactory resolution is made for all stakeholders. India (21) scores badly compared with China (57), Thailand (62) and Singapore (99).

5. How easy is it get credit?

The study recommends creating public credit registries and private credit bureaus that collect and share data on the credit record of borrowers from all sources. This reduces the information asymmetry that makes lenders reluctant to lend, and has facilitated the explosive growth of credit cards in the west. India, alas, has neither public credit registries or private credit bureaus, and urgently needs this relatively painless reform.

STARTING-A-BUSINESS INDICATORS

	India	*China*	*Singapore*	*Thailand*	*Australia*
No. of procedures	10	12	7	9	2
Time (days)	88	46	8	42	2
Cost/per capita income	49.8	14.3	1.2	7.3	2.0
Min. capital to register (% of per capital income)	430.4	3,856	0	0	0
Hiring-firing Indicators (100 = total rigidity)					
Flexibility of hiring index	33	17	33	78	
Conditions of employment index	75	67	26	73	
Flexibility of firing index	45	57	1	30	
Employment laws index	51	47	20	61	
Contract-enforcement Indicators					
No. of procedures	122	20	23	19	
Time (days)	365	180	50	210	
Cost (% of per capita income)	95	32	14.4	29.6	
Procedural complexity index	50	52	49	53	
Closing-a-business Indicators					
Time (years)	11.3	2.6	0.7	2.6	
Cost (% of estate)	8	18	1	38	
Absolute priority preserved	33	100	100	67	
Goals-of-insolvency index	21	57	99	62	

Source: Doing Business in 2004, World Bank.

Only when the legal rights of creditors and secure will they lend with confidence. India makes it sc difficult for creditors to legally recover their dues that they are reluctant to lend to small and medium industry. Credit is the lifeblood of business, yet this is choked by defective laws and legal delays.

The bottom line: labour reform, while desirable, is by no means the biggest hurdle to doing business in India. Creating an environment that promotes credit flows, and providing for rapid enforcement of contract and closure will do far more for business. These are the microeconomic reforms needing most attention.

Key success factors for tomorrow's business managers and leaders

- Impart experiential knowledge
- Rope in cultural issues — because business is not only about economics anymore. Success depends on who we are as people.
- Built credibility to gain visibility
- Be simple; be honest; be frugal.
- Don't underplay yourself — be confident with functional expertise
- Respond to change immediately
- Create a global mindset by benchmarking to global standards
- Develop people skills
- There's likely to be less competition and more co-optation in the future.

CHECK LIST

Does your industry have scope for development? Consult Director of Industries)	Yes - No
Is there enough demand for the item you propose to manufacture?	Yes - No
Do you have some experience of	
(*a*) Manufacturing?	Yes - No
(*b*) Marketing	Yes - No
Have you studied the viability of your scheme? (Consult the Small Industries Service Institute)	Yes - No
Is factory space available	
(*a*) In the Industrial Estate?	Yes - No
(*b*) In an Industrial Area?	Yes - No
(*c*) In some other approved place?	Yes - No
Have you obtained the necessary licence from the Municipality or the Local Body?	Yes - No
Are the necessary raw materials available	
(*a*) Indigenously or are they to be	Yes - No
(*b*) Imported?	Yes - No
Are facilities available for	
(*a*) Tooling,	Yes - No
(*b*) Quality Control	Yes - No
Is necessary labour available	
(*a*) Of skilled workers	Yes - No
(*b*) Of semi-skilled workers?	Yes - No

Have you the necessary technical background for

(a) The erection of the machinery, Yes - No
(b) Operations? Yes - No

Have you studied your product in respect of

(a) The manufacture of the various parts, Yes - No
(b) Production Planning, Yes - No
(c) Inspection and Quality Control Yes - No
(d) Assembly Yes - No
(e) Packaging, Yes - No
(f) Diversification Yes - No

Have you the necessary finance?

(a) Are you a client of any bank?
(b) Has any bank offered to lend you —
(i) Short-term loans? Yes - No
(ii) Long-term loans? Yes - No
(c) Have you any assets? Yes - No
(d) Are your assets adequate for obtaining the necessary funds? Yes - No
(e) Have you other source/ways of raising money? Yes - No
(f) Have you approached the Director of Industries/State Financial Corporation for financial help? Yes - No
(g) Do you propose to approach the NSIC/SSIC for machinery on hire-purchase basis? Yes - No
(h) Have you adequate cash/bank arrangement to furnish the earnest money required by the NSIC?

What are your markets?

(a) Local, Yes - No
(b) Countryside, Yes - No
(c) Export? Yes - No

How would you market your product(s)? Through

(a) Retailers,
(b) Wholesalers, Yes - No
(c) Agents? Ye - No

Are the necessary transportation facilities available by

(a) Road,
(b) Rail?

Have you attended a course on

(a) Production, Planning and Control, Yes - No
(b) Purchasing and Marketing Yes - No
(c) Finance and Cost Control, Yes - No
(d) Personnel Management, Yes - No
(e) General Industrial Management. Yes - No

Have you entered into a foreign collaboration agreement for

(a) Technical Know-how,
(b) Royalty/Commission on sales? Yes - No
(c) Has your agreement been approved by the Government? Yes - No

Once the industry is identified, the SISI prepares a feasibility report and project report, giving one a comprehensive idea of an industry's prospects and profitability.

The Future of Business

There are many forces that are shaping the future. Until the 1980s and the early 1990s, it was enough for entrepreneurs to employ a battery of forecasters to correctly anticipate future trends and respond to them on a strategic plan. No longer it holds. Today, it isn't enough to merely know the future as difficult as the task is. Successful entrepreneurs must invent the future for themselves — impossible though it may seem.

The Ten fundamental principals are:

- They must set their own agendas, not allow them to be set by others.
- They must invent products that revolutionise people's lives, not copy them.
- They must create brand new technologies, not adopt them from others.
- They must redraw industry/business borders, not respond to their being redrawn.
- They must define new markets, not respond to their emergence.
- They must organise to be competitive, not depend on others.
- They must draw their own strategies, not allow them to be drawn by others.
- They must lead with a sense of vision and sense of purpose, not to be led by others.
- They must redefine entrepreneurial cultures that acts as anchors to help them adapt to the rapidly changing business environment, not allow it to happen.
- They must utilise the available resources productively to maximise benefits, not allow to be utilised by others.

In fact, the process of business transformation has become a race in itself. Those that take too long at this process may become laggards or, at worst, may never get back in the race. Instead, we will have to achieve the radical metamorphosis of our organisations while the race is in progress. Today, a simple choice faces every individual, every corporation, every government and every society on earth. That choice is: rethink the future, or be forced to rethink the future. Those who choose the first option will have the best chance of surviving and thriving the turbulent terrain ahead.. Those who procrastinate will quickly find themselves overtaken by change.

Visionary Perspectives on Tomorrow

Twenty five tenets of visionaries on the future of business, of corporations, of work, of strategy, of culture, of leadership:

1. Comparative advantage is now man-made, anybody having brainpower can compete.
2. Companies must reconnect to strategy.
3. Success is a function of making choices.
4. The energies of the whole enterprise must be mobilised around its strategic intent.
5. Competing for the future requires a commitment to creating new businesses and new products.

6. The goal is to try to imagine a future that is plausible — the future that you can create.
7. Harness the things that drive change.
8. If people are good at work, then they are too valuable to be put into management.
9. Small is beautiful, but what is really beautiful is the appropriate scale.
10. Knowledge is defined as the capacity for effective action.
11. High income consumers will demand high-quality products and personalised service.
12. Low-income consumers who will just want basic, no-frills products and services at the lowest possible price.
13. Having high quality won't be enough. It must be offered at a lower price.
14. Every product should be designed with a specific group of customers — and a price they are willing to pay — in mind.
15. Services will grow increasingly important as a competitive tool, especially as products become more similar.
16. In niches there are riches. Usually, only one or two firms serve a niche and serve it well and consequently earn a high margin.
17. The best way to win a war today is to mass your forces against a narrow target.
18. Marketers are essentially honing in on improving everything they do, whether it's distribution or improving their relationship with customers.
19. In marketing, you win by massing or concentrating your forces. This is essentially the concept of focus.
20. The other component of a good marketing strategy is predicting the future (convergence).
21. Leaders must learn to develop a social architecture that encourages bright people.
22. A sense of vision and purpose is the essential difference between leading and managing.
23. The capacity to clearly articulate a vision, communicate it simply, but also compellingly is the second important attribute of a leader.
24. Corporate cultures must act as anchors to help us to adapt to the rapidly changing business environment.
25. The core elements of corporate culture are, honesty, values, initiative, innovation and leadership.

Mark Johnson

Establishing a successful business no longer means that you will still be successful a few years down the line. As the rate of change rapidly accelerates, so does the possibility of your company becoming obsolete. According to Mark Johnson, co-founder and chairman, Insight, a strategic innovation consulting and investing company, a major reason companies often fall by the wayside is because they are unable to deal with disruptive innovations. One often hears of companies that didn't last out because a competitor came in with a disruptive technology that rendered them useless. Johnson offers a slightly different perspective. The issue isn't that the company affected could not develop the disruptive technology. For instance, Digital Equipment Corporation had the technology for the personal computer but failed to capitalise on it as it didn't get prioritised internally, and this is because it required a different business model.

Companies are no longer built to last, but must be built to transform. In other words, companies must pick up on when they need to switch from their existing processes to a new way of functioning. In cases where companies were affected by a disruptive competitor, they either didn't recognise the need to do so, or didn't do it successfully.

Most companies tend to avail at business model innovation because they are unsure about how to make the transition from the existing model to a new one. And to do this, the first step is to clearly understand the existing model. "Business model innovation is something that is more core than the core."

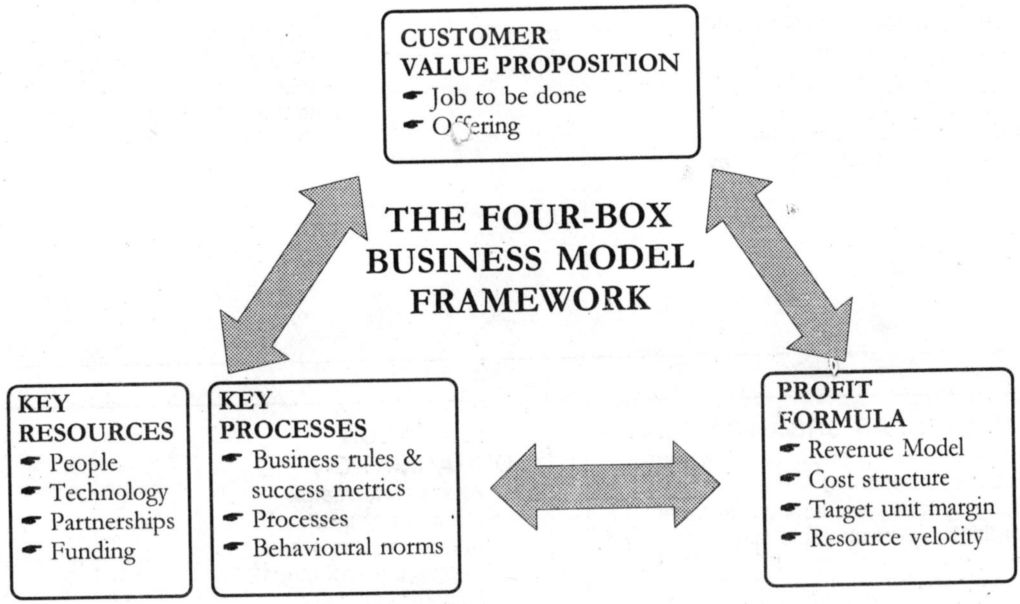

The entrepreneurs should focus their energies on pursuing untapped needs. Whether or not these opportunities quality as white spaces would then determine if it needs a new business model. Outlining the process, Johnson says that it has to start with wanting to satisfy a customer need. Once you know what the customer wants, design a business system which both delivers a value proposition and allows you to make money out of it. One needs to document what the original business system looks like and whether you need a new system to deliver the new value proposition after comparing the key critical processes and resources. The final step is to then connect with the real customer in a foothold market and test the assumptions before scaling it up — it works.

Ultimately, it is about finding a sustainable business model. Simply put, it's a model that repeatedly delivers value to the customer and also provides a sustainable way of making money while doing it.

Transformed Organisations

Organisations as we know to-day will disintegrate in the future. The new structures will be more fluid. Departments, units and divisions are expected to disappear and give way to multi-disciplinary and multi-skilled teams. In fact, management experts have visualised that the future organisations will be small, lean and integrated.

Organisation Structure

Six futuristic organisation models at work elsewhere in the world.

THE AMOEBA ORGANISATION

- Self-learning horizontal teams are fluid, based on emerging products
- Employees 'move around' until they find the products where they can add the most value

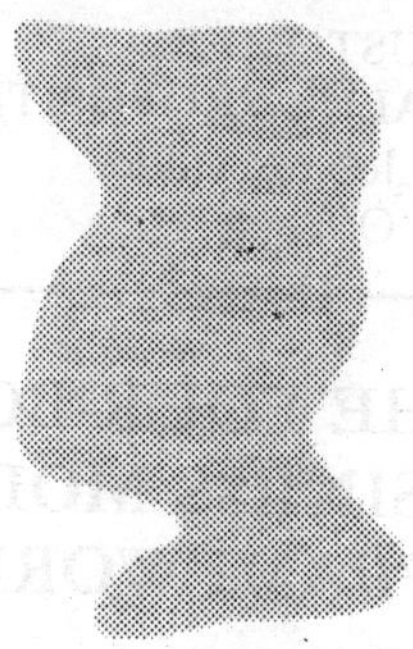

- Guided by "waterline principles (if risky area, check with key people)
- Ranks an titles avoided — leadership is defined by followers

Source: Anderson

THE MOLECULAR ORGANISATION

- Customer-focused business units with all functions represented
- Entire enterprise represented at tactical, coordinative and strategic level

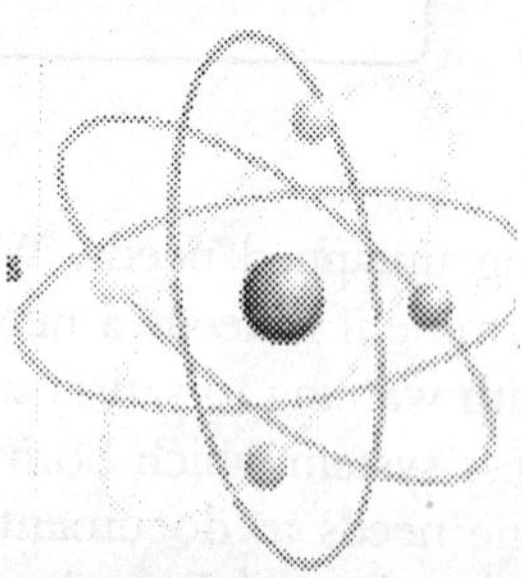

THE ABACUS ORGANISATION

- Abacus-like matrix structure of product areas (products) and geography (countries)
- Networks transfer knowledge, provide support, and open communications
- Able to escalate globally through sharing information

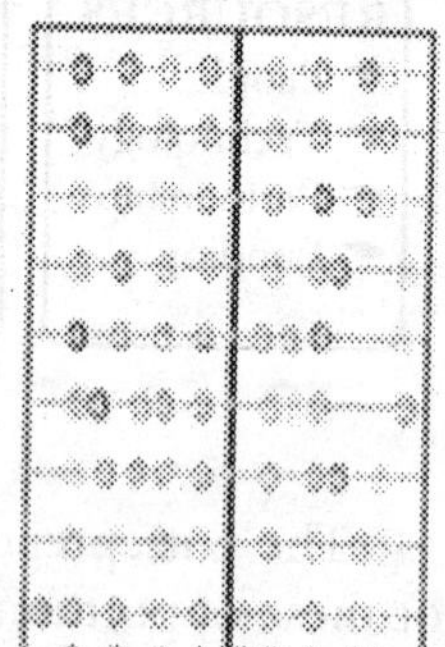

THE PIZZA ORGANISATION

- Competency based, people are resources
- Resources are the pizza base, competencies and responsibilities are toppings
- Reinvesting self into a flatter organisation, and outward focus through project teams
- Support services like HR, are matrixed to foster team-development
- Culture of teaming spreads from the top of the organisation

THE ECONETS ORGANISATION

- The EcoNet structure looks like this (small circles represent businesses)
- Markets are more efficient portfolio managers at a time when the world is moving fast
- Small is beautiful; emphasis on speed and boldness in decision-making, culture, and remuneration, therefore, access to talent.

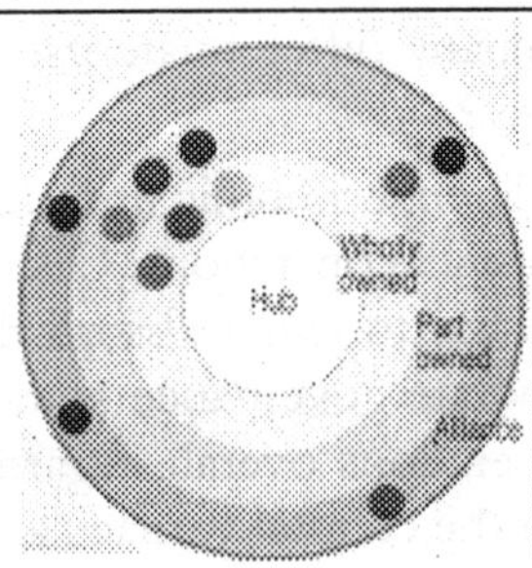

THE SPAGHETTI ORGANISATION

- No titles, no departments, no personal office space
- Small management teams sponsor and lead projects
- Key is the information system and knowledge base
- Physically and organisationally informal
- Initiatives interwine in this open environment

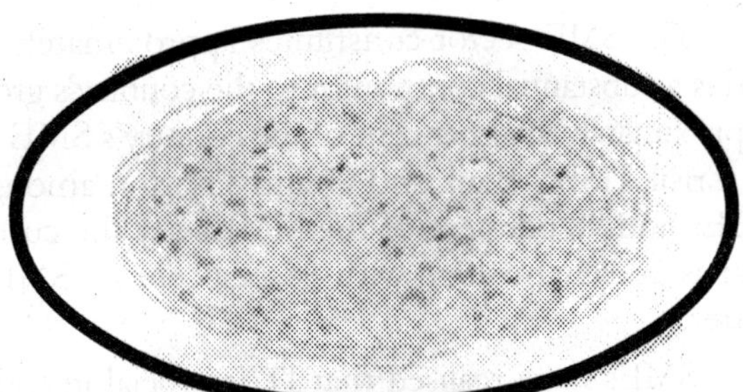

Conclusion

Starting an enterprise is not easy. It is ninety per cent perspiration and hardly ten per cent profit. It calls for vision, perseverance, co-operation and hardwork. The entrepreneur has a uphill task in co-ordinating multifarious activities and turn into a viable enterprise. It calls for a thorough business plan and prompt implementation. The entrepreneur needs a number of skills to set up a small industry, which will grow into a giant in coming years. Many of the giants of today *viz.,* Kirloskar, Honda, Escort, Camlin, Reliance were started small, it calls for a missionary work with a purpose. Then the joys of fulfillment is like a beautiful rainbow.

Annexure - 1

SME GROWTH: CLICKING ON THE RIGHT TECHNOLOGY

With an integrated, affordable, business management solution, SAP is ready to take SMEs to the next level

SMEs today must contend with considerable challenges that have the potential to directly affect their bottom line. Businesses today must be prepared to deal with an educated, savvy, global client base that has access to extensive information *via.,* the Internet and global markets. The proliferation of information available to prospective customers poses a formidable challenge. How does a company differentiate itself from competitors who offer similar products or services at reduced rates?

In addition, economic uncertainty adds to the mix, with fluctuations in world markets directly affecting business operations. Cost increases felt by suppliers are quickly passed on to the business owner who has to either absorb the cost directly or pass it on to their customer base. Further, recent corporate governance scandals in larger organisations have shed a more critical light on business operations overall, regardless of company size. The term "accounting irregularities" is now part of the cultural vernacular, further underscoring the need for business to manage a tight-run ship, with operational transparency being the standard, not the exception.

SMEs: The Right Technology

The SME sector constitutes approximately 95 per cent of the total industrial units in India and is a substantial contributor to the country's gross domestic product. Small enterprises constitute approximately 99.4 per cent of the country's SME universe. According to a global survey conducted by Crisil, HSBC Bank and Grand Thorton among SMEs and MMEs, in India, 88 per cent of the SMEs and 98 per cent of the MMEs say the current economy is very good. The outlook for the year is equally positive with 88 per cent of SMEs saying the economic situation will turn even better.

SMEs have realised that IT is crucial in today's economic environment and that they need to focus more and more on IT to stay ahead of the competition, especially as the "big players" of a globalised industry now enter traditional SME business sectors. A recent study by EIU reveals that majority of SMEs considers IT as a key aspect of their strategy to competitiveness and to economic growth. More than two-thirds of all SME CEOs think that IT is a determining factor to generate growth and to stay flexible. IT also supports companies in understanding their customers' behaviour and ability to meet their clients' needs. The majority of SME managers are also convinced that the integration of IT and business strategy is essential.

How does a small to mid-sized enterprise (SME) grow profitably in spite of growing competition? By employing the right technology that will provide a unified, up-to-the-minute view of operations, allowing for improved business-process efficiency and a more efficient business.

SMEs: The Scalable Solution

The task of aligning IT investments with business goals can be challenging. Most small businesses begin with a simple system, one that works to maintain the basic business operations indicative of a start-up company. As business expands, however, many companies do not keep up technologically, resulting in either inadequate or poorly integrated collections of outmoded applications. The implications of having an out-of-date system are numerous and far-reaching; most importantly, information gaps ensuing from disparate systems often result in business process break-downs and lost revenue. In addition, data stored in multiple locations is often not connected, often abandoning valuable customer and production knowledge and slowing business processes. Time is money; accordingly, using an outdated solution can adversely affect a company's bottom line.

In order to be successful, an SME should utilise a system that at once optimises business processes, decreases operational costs, and improves customer acquisition and retention. By employing the right technology that will provide a unified, up-to-the-minute view of operations, allowing for improved business-process efficiency; an SME can cut down its total cost of ownership with increased profitability. Also, to avoid hefty costs often associated with integrating vendors' products, an SME can opt for a fully integrated, affordable and scalable business management solution.

SMEs should look for a business solution that offers the following:

The Calculus to Keep Growing Businesses Growing

For small and mid-sized businesses that have been hardened in the old days of slow growth and limited demand, the past 3-4 years have come up as booster shots. With a wider spectrum of opportunities that exists today, growth has become # 1 imperative for the CEOs of small and mid-sized businesses. As these businesses participate in the growing demand curve, there is a simultaneous realisation that the rule book of business strategies that worked so well for them in the past may not remain appropriate for them as they harness the future.

Small and medium-sized businesses are increasingly asking themselves: how can they keep the growth momentum? While there is a wider consensus that the Indian economy will keep growing at a healthy 8-10 per cent year-on-year, the key distinction between the winners and the have been will be the capabilities that they posses to take an increasing pie of the growth market opportunities.

A comparative analysis between the large enterprises and SMB firms reveals one of the areas of structural weaknesses for SMBs is that of Information Technology. While SMBs have invested in basic accounting applications, the premise of the simplified world with which these accounting applications were built now lies in tatters. SMBs are becoming too complex and growing too fast to the extent that these accounting applications are the bottlenecks that SMBs must overcome. Simultaneously, unlike large enterprises that have invested in custom-built applications, SMBs are unlikely to take this route because of limited IT budgets, limited IT sophistication and limited in-house talent. The new category of business solutions for SMB markets are making strong inroads for the past 3-4 years. The new generation of these solutions for SMBs are refreshingly unique, eliminating complexity where it is not desired. Also, unlike accounting applications that portray a myopic view point of businesses, SMB ERP applications can provide views across business functions and across value chain. While many of SMB business application vendors exist, some of the key differentiators that CEOs need to look out for while choosing their ERP partners are as following:

- **Best Practices:** While businesses impete globally, embedding global best practices in the ERP solution can mark to market cost efficiencies and productivity for implementing organisations. Look out to the extent to which solutions have been designed with micro verticalisation framework that best suits your industry.
- **Lowering Implementation Costs:** Choose a vendor who has made special efforts to lowering implementing costs:
  - (*i*) Compare solutions: More gap between desired features means more costly customisation, choose that fits need best.
  - (*ii*) Compare solutions that are offered on a fixed cost contract instead of open time and material contracts that can lead to implementing budgets going haywire.
  - (*iii*) Build flexibility into the contract to accommodate changing technology.
- **Customer References:** While customer references is a fairly obvious means, many a times references are conducted superficially. See if your ERP partner can help you achieve deeper interactivity.
- **Address key functional issues:** There exists significant difference between ERP vendors on the functional issues. Look out for the best methodologies for:
  - (*i*) Need and gap analysis
  - (*ii*) Process engineering
  - (*iii*) Process documentation
  - (*iv*) Audit of data and system
  - (*v*) Conference room pilot
  - (*vi*) Validation of data and systems
  - (*vii*) Staffing and training
- **Industry Specificity:** Bring to bear the Business Best Practices and domain Knowledge of the vertical/sub vertical that the SME operates in.
- **Flexibility/Scalability:** The ability to integrate current systems with existing disparate or outmoded applications is essential. Small to mid-size enterprises are wise to utilise a system that is quickly and seamlessly integrated with their current applications.
- **Operational Transparency:** Stricter global accounting and corporate governance requirements have put pressure on businesses to have greater transparency, timeliness, and accuracy in both financial reporting and managerial control. Smart business owners will utilise solutions that will facilitate minimal error in the form of a singular, integrated system.
- **End-to-End and Real-Time Visibility:** The current fast-paced global business environment demands that business utilise a system that can at once deliver up-to-the-minute critical information across manufacturing, customer relationship management, and finance. Adopting a system that provides a full view of operations will allow for greater insight and costs savings.
- **Integration:** The ideal business software for SMEs is one that is intuitive, accurate and easy to use. Robust capabilities delivered in a familiar environment will result in a shorter learning

curve and more timely results. Business owners should look for software that can be easily integrated into the company's existing system, in an easy-to-use interface.

- **Ease-of-Use and User Empowerment:** When determining the technology or software of choice, a company should consider usability to be a key component. Information gathering should be quick and easy, allowing the user to gain knowledge regarding specific processes. Customised preferences for specialised users and managers will also allow for greater efficiency and user control.

- **Analytics:** A facts-based understanding of a company's customers and prospects in addition to suppliers, partners and employees, combined with broader economic indicators, are fundamental to experiencing both strategic and operational successes. Credible, clear, and comprehensive insights into every aspect of the business will give a company the competitive advantage.

Traditionally, the business software choices for SMEs have been limited. A typical SME would run an off-the-shelf accounting and financial reporting package and deploy separate software to handle areas such as payroll or sales management. The benefits offered by the sort of sophisticated, integrated company-wide ERP systems used by big businesses were, quite simply, out of reach. The level of investment required was unaffordable. Also, SMEs felt that they did not need the functionality that these systems offer. Today, this situation is changing.

From the top end of the business software market, Business Solution vendors like SAP have introduced business management systems designed specifically for SMEs. For the first time, SMEs now have the opportunity to deploy the most sophisticated business software solutions that offer more than vanilla accounting and financial reporting, and provide capabilities for managing the entire business from sales to fulfillment. By selecting solutions that are designed specifically for growth, companies can positively impact the bottom line and look to provide a greater return on their investment.

Financing to The Rescue

While SMEs are focusing more and more on IT in order to stay competitive, they sometimes face difficulties in their ability to invest. Their equity capital is traditionally rather low and the requirements to receive a bank's credit are higher than ever before — due to many compliance regulations. As a result, SMEs are pushed into a dilemma: Without investments, they cannot come up with innovations that are urgently needed. On the other hand, making investments with equity capital can increase entrepreneurial risk. New financing concepts like SAP Financing can help solve this problem.

The Global Challenge

- The software needs of SMEs are changing. With the complexity and global reach of today's business environment, SMEs are under great pressure to monitor their processes and financial performance even more closely. Since 2002, the introduction of stricter accounting and corporate governance requirements is intensifying the challenge.
- The need to comply with the U.S. Sarbanes-Oxley Act and adhere to International Financial Reporting Standards is forcing companies to reconsider their approach to business software. Organisations of all sizes are under pressure to provide greater transparency, timeliness and accuracy in reporting and managerial control.

- The new solutions that are becoming available to SMEs make this possible. But such companies can be forgiven for treating vendor claims with caution. Surveys suggest that SMEs are frequently disappointed by limitations with existing financial and accounting software. A study released in 2005 by PMP Research found that only one quarter (25 per cent) of companies feel their software had completely met their full objectives.

Dream Come True

A home textile manufacturer from Karur goes global, using his own business model of providing total retail solutions

He is an entrepreneur by accident. Son of a judge and a Chartered Accountant by profession, S. Susindran, CEO and founder promoter of the Karur-based Sabare International, has only two years' experience in the field — as General Manager, Pasupathi Textiles — and is an absolute novice to home textile manufacturing. Yet, when he claims that his vision is to create an Infosys of home textiles', it doesn't sound pompous. "I dreamed of something big in life. But when I started this small home textile enterprise, I initially invested only Rs. 15 lakh and reaped an average income common to home textiles, of Rs. 1-2 crore, for seven years. I was content with this. But then, I had a few European buyers and that made me think — why can't I go global?"

Susindran not only went global in the intervening years before quota abolition in 2005, but also developed his own yet-to-be patented business model TRSP (total retail solutions provider), integrating production and supply chain management (SCM), at the same time. He has now established a US subsidiary, Sabare US, in Atlanta, with an office in Phoenix, and plans to have three subsidiaries in China, the biggest being in Shanghai. The revenue has now gone up to Rs. 200 crore and he now projects Rs. 500 crore worth of sales by 2007-08.

Largely responsible for Sabare's success is Susindran's post-quota strategy for growth, which attracted capital from financier Kotak, who put in Rs. 30 crore equity. The promoter of Sabare has the right ideas as to why India has been a late starter in the home textile race (when compared to China and even Pakistan) and about how India can catch up because it has "fewer disadvantages and more potential in home textiles than garments."

Home textiles may well be the next big gold mine for India, but it is not going to be a cakewalk. The US garment industry is practically dead — unable to face competition from the likes of China. But both in the US and EU, home textiles is still alive and kicking and is today one of the most promising domains, as home beautification and decor have seen a healthy revival, thriving as never before. Susindran talks about why Indian players need to latch on to more creative thinking and innovative solutions, to take on the US competition on their own turf and become another China in home textiles."

It is not yet adieu to the US companies. The world's biggest home textiles company is Springs Industries. Yet, all the quota protection could not inure big names like Pillowtex and West Point (now under Chapter II). It is against the backdrop of such new circumstances that his claims about taking on the US players on their own turf are to be evaluated.

All Operations under One Roof

To begin with, Sabare has gone in for an integrated new plant on 29 acres of land on the outskirts of Karur. All the small mom-and-pop operations that lay scattered were brought under one massive roof, where, through backward/forward integration and SCM, are all now under SAP implementation. This high tech facility of 5 lakh sq. ft. space has 66 looms sourced from Vamatex, Leonardo and Sulzer sewing and finishing lines and every kind of value addition needed for home textile finishing. The plant is a beehive of activity, making table and kitchen textiles, window drapes, pillows, chair pads and bed sheets — all made by German machines.

The workforce has the right productivity-orientation. Karuppiah, the 29-year-old cutter tailor, is happy with the canteen, medical facilities and, above all, the open spaces and temperature-controlled ambient air. V.T. Guru, the EDP man, avers that "Our total strength will be 2,000, of which 780 will be tailors". Mountains of chair pads in bright maroon, butter yellow, tea green and mushroom beige are heaped on the floor, as women stuff the cushion pads with recron fibre, one of the few labour- intensive processes. A whole shift is dedicated to Walmart, one of the major buyers. For these simple workers, it is a matter of pride that their products will adorn US homes.

Kamala, a quality controller, comes with a diploma in textile technology from Karur Polytech. "Karur has many such units," says she. "And, on an average, those who can afford, spend Rs. 60,000 for a course in textiles without hesitation, as employment potential in this field is good, especially for women". Meenatchi, working in the supervisory level, also agrees that Rs. 3,000 as income per month is a good take-home, especially for those who come from agricultural background. She has a diploma in costume designing and dress making. Such units have empowered thousands of women who get to work in humane conditions, and not in sweat shop environs.

The Karur plant makes 20 million metres of table and kitchen line and 2.4 million sets of bed linen per annum. Investment for the plant has been Rs. 52 crore. Regional strengths, based on raw material availability and workforce, apply in the home textiles too. "Regions in the north, like Panipat and Noida, have expertise in value-added and tapestry lines and Sabare needs to be located in those areas, to reap all the economies of scale and skill for those special varieties and value-adds," says Susindran.

Name of the Enterprise: Sabare International Ltd.
Nature of Business Home textiles
Location of the Parent Plant: Karur
CEO and Promoter: Susindran
Current Year's Sales (2005-06): Rs. 200 crore
Major Customers: Walmart, J.C. Penny, Target and Kohls

Most of the cotton-based textile goods are from the south, a hardcore cotton-belt, but blended materials and other decorative items are best sourced from the Delhi region. Panipat rules the roost for rugs, as does Kerala for coir mats. The industry too has evolved on these lines. Sabare has a fully imported production line at Noida to make decorative bedding and pillows, at an investment of Rs. 12 crore. Similarly, it has a 2,00,000 sq.ft. plant at Panipat, with an investment of Rs. 20 crore. In order to have complete control over production and quality, the company has set up its own dyeing and processing complex at Perundurai near Coimbatore for Rs. 25 crore, bringing the total investment to Rs. 109 crore.

Susindran is well aware that mere investments and capacity ramping will not get him places. With all the finance available through venture capital, becoming a large global player is easy enough, but remaining in that slot is a tough act. How is he then confidently projecting Rs. 350 crore sale for 2006-07, and Rs. 500 crore for 2007-08? "I have a solid strategy, to achieve this ambitious projection. A major producer now has to think in terms of total solutions for the retailer — right from product design, to logistics, to SCM, to inventory and meeting seasonal demands. This is where my TRSP emerges as a winning solution". Thus, the retailer will get a completely integrated product line — the total home textile solution. Everything is colour, design and fabric co-ordinated, from bed linen to rugs, drapery and sofa covers. A retailer may have many vendors with large capacities but if he has to source from different plants, it creates delays and uncertainties, and this is not a business model he is comfortable with. "Sabare offers one-stop-shop solutions from my various facilities," Susindran avers. "It is easy for us to scale up to needs from various locations, as we mine the retailer's data and use projection analysis."

Interaction with retailer

The company also has its own product development team, which works closely with the retailer, and this gives a sense of comfort that the producer knows the customers' needs. "We need our own strong product development team, in order to come out co-ordinating 7-8 times," says Susindran. This is the rationale behind establishing a separate SCM team at Atlanta and setting up a design centre there, with an all-American design team. And, how does he resolve the conflict of retailers sourcing from the same company? "The two main areas are product development for each retailer and the ongoing relationship of a retail support team," Susindran explains. "As each retailer's support team is distinct, TRSP ensures that the entire process flow for each retailer is different. It is easy to differentiate, because the basic direction comes from retailers, such as Target, Penny, Walmart, Kohls," he adds.

"But TRSP is not just some marketing or SCM jargon. It is not about giving the best product at a lower cost, and become another typical manufacturer, even if you are world class. TRSP has a long journey. One has to get the SCM side absolutely right on target and then integrate production to that, understand consumer needs and be there for the retailer at every contact point. For example, take setting up of 10 lakh sq. ft. of bedding line. It needs strong investment and proven talent, backed by good design team. I am good at setting up world class facilities. But here, understanding the consumer is the true challenge, and it needs an in-depth study of the retailer's data," Susindran concludes. He is all praise for the way the Martha Stewart line has grown.

The going in home textiles is not getting as smooth as the bed linen or as cushy as the seat pads that Sabare makes, with the US companies now dictating retailer margins and setting up plants in Third World countries, like South America, China and Indonesia. Pakistan has also retained its strong position and the FDI inflows into that country reflect how strong it is – from \$26 million in 2002-03, its earnings went up to a whopping \$39 million for 2004-05.

Perhaps Susindran has found the right approach in partnering US retailers on their own terms. And his TRSP model may just give that edge to a player, to be reckoned with in the post-quota scramble for market share.

Annexure - 2

ERP COMPETENCY CENTRE

A competency centre is crucial for the success of ERP (Enterprise Resource Planning) project. To avoid the diminishing returns from ERP, companies should start the process of creating a Centre just before the first "Go Live" milestone has been reached. And, as additional modules are implemented, the Centre should be upgraded, and its scope must be expanded at each stage.

Tailored to meet the specific needs of an enterprise, such a Centre's functions should include:

- A support desk, for first-level support and a single contact-point for problem-management.
- Contracts administration, for a central licences and contracts management-system.
- Development requests co-ordination, serving as a single interface with the developers.
- A knowledge-centre on ERP, for the benefit of all parts of the company.
- Business support, owning the group's standards for processes, templates, and data.
- Technical support, for optimising systems administration, applications customisation, and interfaces support.
- The on-going development of new business processes, and the integration of core ERP modules with additional business packages.
- Internet training, for all users and processes, functionality and ERP.
- Testing of all new releases.
- Project assistance, for the implementation and upgradation of projects.

The benefits of the ERPC centre are as follows:

- Real systems ownership, by establishing a shared vision of building and sustaining long-term business differentiation.
- Increased revenues, by building unique business processes around customers.
- Increased retention of key project staff, by making the Centre a prestigious unit to work in.
- Increased leverage of ERP knowledge, by focusing on the data available and sharing it.
- Enhanced opportunities for business collaboration, by encouraging greater standardisation of module-configurations, data-definitions, and business processes.
- Faster propagation of package knowledge, by serving as a single point of contact.
- Reduced attrition-costs for expert internal ERP resources.
- Reduced dependence on external consultants, by the greater use of internal resources.

- Reduced licence — and maintenance — fees, by eliminating a value contract with the ERP vendor.
- Faster ERP-upgradation across multiple sites, by leveraging the knowledge gained from the implementation of the first one.
- Reduced training and consulting fees from vendors, if negotiated up-front.

The centre's activities should be coordinated with the ERP project. An organisation serious about the competence of its ERP cannot do without the creation of an ERP Compency Centre.

In fact, such a Centre can serve as a permanent pool of expertise that will help the implementation, enhancement, and maintenance of the business processes and systems built by the ERP system.

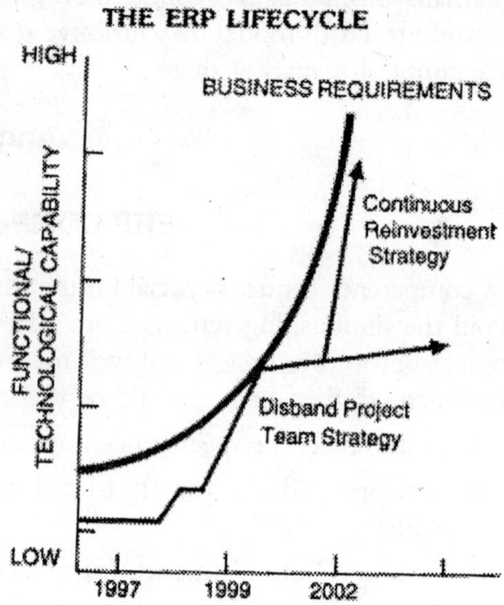

SPICY SUCCESS STORY

The Perfect Blend

With its new blends, new packaging and innovative marketing practices, Everest has outpaced its competitors

The name is Everest and the claim of being at the top is no less lofty even though made in a third party voice. "We are told that we are number one in the country," states Sanjeev Shah, partner of S. Narendrakumar & Company and son of the founder Vadilal Shah, who started the Everest brand of spices almost 40 years ago. The brand, much to the discomfort of its closest competitors, stands taller than the tallest, Everest promoters claim. Just like the Mount Everest.

Mahashayji of the Delhi-based Mahashian Di Hatti — who are equally well known all over the world for their famous branded spices MDH — wouldn't even grudgingly like to concede that position to his Mumbai-based competitors. He thinks MDH brand of spices, launched soon after the Partition in 1947, is the best in every respect — taste, quality and market positioning. MDH has a greater reach in the north Indian market, where it has dominated for over 50 years. Yet many think that Everest has made inroads even in the north and eastern parts of the country with its aggressive marketing campaign on television channels and print medium, which is pan-Indian in its nature and flavour rather than a region-specific one. "There's a tug-of-war between the two principal competitors in the branded spices category," says Chunilal Mehta, a leading spice dealer at Mirchi Galli in Mumbai's Zaveri Bazar area. But right now, what goes in favour of Everest is the fact that for several years it has been featured as one of the top 101 super brands by Superbrands India.

"All this is fine," explains Sanjeev Shah, "but even as branded players we still belong to a very small segment of organised players (Rs. 1,200 crore) in the country's huge spices market estimated to be around Rs. 25,000 crore. The very size of the market makes us all very ambitious, and there are more than 300 companies across the country that market spices with their own brand names, and want to hit the big league somehow or the other in the same way as some of us have done it."

But branding and packaging alone do not make the be-all and end-all of a product. The real story lies behind the understanding of the ingredients that are worked upon to create a distinctive taste, flavour and aroma. Moreover, what works in favour of a product is, getting that unique blend of recipes from different regions to satisfy the taste buds uniformly.

"Everest has been doing precisely that," says Sanjeev Shah. "We have been cross-experimenting with recipes from the north Indian homes with south Indian homes, and *vice versa.* Add to it the purity of the ingredients which also becomes the hallmark of all our products." With a 30 per cent market share until 2002, an ORG-MARG Retail audit, placed Everest as the number one brand in its category. Between 1998 and 2002 Everest sales grew by 107 per cent. It has maintained the lead though the percentage has now come down to around 24 per cent with more and more players entering the branded segment. Everest has been closely followed by MDH with 20 per cent market share. The other brands such as Badshah and MTR are far behind, with 5 and 2 per cent of market shares, respectively.

According to industry estimates, with the evolution of the category the spice industry has been seeing a growth rate of 15 per cent on a year-on-year basis mainly due to the growing popularity of ready-to-add spices. With 175 stock keeping units (SKUS), Everest maintains the lead with 1,200 distributors in equal number of towns, 36 C&F depots and 5 lakh outlets, with regular usage in more than 2.2 crore households across the country. According to Superbrands India study, Everest became a leader because of its single minded focus on quality. It has achieved this position through years of research, creating the right blend. Coupled with innovativeness, Everest has outpaced its competitors in terms of new blends, new packaging and innovative marketing practices.

The Birth

Until 1966, Vadilal Shah, a 26-year-old shopkeeper used to sell loose dry fruits and spices from his 200 sq. ft. shop at Mirchi Galli in Zaveri Bazar. The shop gave the family a comfortable living with each member, which comprised four brothers, allowed to draw up to Rs. 600 per month for household expenses. A chance observation of how milk masala was made in a friend's house sparked the idea of making milk masala. Remembers Vadilal Shah, "I saw how the friend's family members were trying to put the various ingredients together to make milk masala. I also realised at that instant that if the masala ingredients were put together and sold in a packaged form, it could be a good business proposition. At least, one could try and see."

The next morning, Vadilal gathered all the spices at home and experimented with the thought. "The first sample turned out to be really good," he says. He immediately concocted the stuff, packaged and advertised it on a black board with a chalk. It instantly caught the attention of housewives who used to buy spices at his outlet. "Within the next few months," recalls Vadilal, "our milk masala had become an established commodity." He immediately chose the name Everest, got it registered, and started selling milk masala under its brand name. At the same time, he observed that housewives bought masalas with great diligence to blend in their kitchen. This drew him deeper into making of blended spices. He started experimenting with combinations of condiments and grew confident that he had a few blends that would be readily accepted.

A couple of years later, he launched another three blends — Everest *garam* masala, Kesari milk masala and tea masala in Mumbai — which became hot favourites. While his store sold basic spices, he also ventured into blending and packaging them which have now grown to more than 40 varieties of blended spices. To market them he bought a three-wheeler, packed it with his blends and accompanied his driver-cum-helper all over the town. He often faced ridicule from his fellow businessmen, but the following years established him as a businessman of vision. "I could see that the packaged blended spices had great future in this country," says Vadilal Shah with great pride.

The Conquest begins

Being the first in the packaged blended category, and having conquered the Mumbai and Pune markets in the '70s, Vadilal Shah and his elder son Sanjeev decided to venture out of Maharashtra. Sanjeev, who masterminded the brand's presence in other states, realised that the Kolkata business was relatively poor. "Our sales there were horribly low, even though Kolkata was a huge market," says Sanjeev. So, one day he boarded a train to Kolkata, and did some initial market survey. "I realised the city would give us huge business," he adds. He immediately advertised in some local newspapers seeking salespersons for marketing Everest products. "We got some really good people there, who were keen to help us in distributing and marketing our products," he says. "The next two years were very rewarding as the brand started making its presence there and in the eastern India market."

Since then Everest as a national brand has been straddling the Indian food condiments category. The changing needs of Indian families too have helped the category to grow in an

unprecedented manner. Everest spices are sold in two categories: basic and blended. Both the segments cater to masses, though the packaged blended spices attract more customers in metropolises and larger towns. "This segment is growing at a fast pace," says Rajeev Shah, Vadilal's younger son who takes care of the production facilities.

With almost 1,000 employees and three manufacturing facilities in Mumbai, the company has implemented state-of-the-art management information systems, owns highly automated production facilities and built a formidable distribution set up to ensure that the products are available across all the retail outlets in India and abroad. Everest masalas cater to a vast Indian diaspora and NRIs in the UK, USA, the Middle East, Australia, Canada and Southeast Asian countries..

For creating brand recall value in the consumer mindset, the company was the first to use TV as a strong communications medium way back in 1982 when colour TVS made their appearance in the country. "We understood that richness of spices could be conveyed only through colour and we quickly exploited it," says Sanjeev. The company also used emotional quotient such as *"Maan ke baathon ka swaad"* which when roughly translated says, 'only a mother can make such food'.

"The perfect blending of masalas has done all the magic in growing the brand," says Vadilal Shah with a tinge of pride. Right now, the company is at the top for its commitment to its products and consumers. "We need not diversify into other businesses at all," says Sanjeev Shah. "What's the need? We already see a much larger potential in this business itself. It's going to be growth story all the time." So, what's the need to diversify at all? What's the need, really?

❑ ❑ ❑

It starts with the Bid Idea. Gets enriched by custome: response. Gathers pace with design. Progresses to prototypes. And, ultimately, draws in the entire value chain, the visionary presents the benchmarks from India's product development wizards.

THREE

The Concept of Entrepreneurship

Introduction

A decade is not even a punctuation mark in human history, much less in an ancient country like India. Yet the 1990s were a defining decade for the Indian economy and in particular for corporate India. Though its spirit plagues us even today, the licence raj was officially dismantled and the lives of many changed dramatically.

The journey of India Inc. is, above all, the journey of its men and women — those who lead the charge into the new era of competition and globalisation. We have accordingly divided these entrepreneurs into four sections: The Recreators, Pathbreakers, The Pioneers, and The Gamblers.

The first is a generation of entrepreneurs who had the foresight to adapt their old family run business to the modem era. The next group laid the foundation for new business opportunities during the final years of the command economy and saw the fruition of their unrelenting efforts during the 1990s. They were followed by another generation of nimble entrepreneurs who quickly used the social and economic changes of the 1990s to make their fortunes. The final category consists of a brash, new breed of entrepreneurs who see opportunities in new life-styles and global marketplaces. They might make it big — or they might burn.

New Dynamism

Entrepreneurship introduces a critical element of dynamism into an economic system. It is no coincidence that the world's leading economy, the USA, is believed to be the most entrepreneurial society in the world. The process of globalisation and liberalisation has introduced two sets of changes — the first is the obvious introduction of dynamism into the system through the process of globalisation. While new opportunities have opened up in international markets, the bar has been raised in the domestic market through international products and services being available to Indian consumers. The domestic market will no longer be lower-risk. It will force Indian entrepreneurs to regain their spirit of innovation.

The more subtle change is social: Increase in literacy levels, greater consumer awareness, enhanced media penetration, and basic changes in family structure. These changes are bound to result in a higher level of entrepreneurial activity in future.

In keeping with the demands for greater innovation in Indian enterprises, several have fundamentally redesigned structures. There are no easy answers to how the rate of change in entrepreneurial activity can be increased. The solutions to eliminate some of the structural constraints to entrepreneurship are really no different from the solutions to driving higher economic growth rates. Entrepreneurship extends beyond a conventional business and economic perspective. Creativity, innovation, and bringing a vision to life are as much entrepreneurial activities in a social sphere — and have the same impact on society as does business entrepreneurship to the economy.

Indians have always been entrepreneurs: We have all heard about businesses growing from father to son or the rags-to-riches story in conventional industry. But recently, there has been a shift in the nature of Indian entrepreneurship. It has come to stand for something that is out of the box and globally oriented. It began with the infotech revolution a decade ago. Now all the signs point to another industry joining this new wave of Indian enterprise. Venture capitalists and economic forecasters believe biotechnology is India's next big thing, its new IT.

A Complex Phenomenon

The concept of entrepreneurship is a complex phenomenon. Broadly, it relates to the entrepreneur, his vision and its implementation. The key player is the entrepreneur. Entrepreneurship refers to a process of action an entrepreneur (person) undertakes to establish his/her enterprise. It is a creative and innovative response to the environment.

Entrepreneurship is, thus, a cycle of actions to further the interests of the entrepreneur. In this chapter, the concept of entrepreneurship and the related issues are analysed, and discussed.

One of the qualities of entrepreneurship is the ability to discover an investment opportunity and to organise an enterprise, thereby contributing to real economic growth. It involves taking risks and making the necessary investments under conditions of uncertainty and innovating, planning and taking decisions so as to increase production in agriculture, business, industry, etc.

Entrepreneurship is a composite skill, the result of a mix of many qualities and traits. These include imagination, the readiness to take risks, ability to bring together and put to use the other factors of production, capital, labour, land, as also intangible factors such as the ability to mobilise scientific and technological advances.

A hard practical approach is necessary to be able to implement and manage a project by securing the required licences, approvals and finance from governmental and financial agencies. The personal incentive is to make profits from the successful management of the project. A sense of cost consciousness is essential for the long-term success of the enterprise. However, both are different sides of the same coin. Entrepreneurship lies more perhaps in the ability to minimise the use of resources and to put them to maximum advantages. Without an awareness of quality and desire for excellence, consumer acceptance cannot be achieved and sustained. Above all, entrepreneurship today is the product of teamwork and the ability to create, build and work as a team. The entrepreneur is the maestro of the business orchestra, wielding his baton to which the band is played.

THE SIX PILLARS OF ENTERPRISE GOVERNANCE

In this global age, leaders in the business world can come from anywhere. The best ideas will dominate, regardless of their national origins. It is in this competitive global regime that the best hopes and aspirations of India rest.

A well-run enterprise embraces and practices a sound Predictability-Sustainability-Profitability-De-risking (PSPD) model. A good forecasting system for sales based on data gathered ensures predictability.

Sustainability is achieved by motivated sales people who make sales happen; by production people ensuring that quality products are delivered on time; and by billing and collecting on time.

Every enterprise must focus on high profitability in order to ensure the best returns for its shareholders. Indeed, profitability is crucial for the long-term success of a corporation.

The enterprise must have a good de-risking approach that recognise, measure and mitigates risk along every dimension. Take them you must, but carefully thought-out risks.

Enterprise governance is focus on maximising shareholder value while ensuring fairness to all stakeholders. In these days of free following global capital, in order to attract capital, corporations have to adhere to the best global standards of enterprise governance.

The foundation of enterprise governance philosophy is the belief that it is better to lose crores of rupees than to act in ways that make one lose a night's sleep.

It is a good practice to under-promise and over-deliver, it is best to deliver bad news to the stakeholders proactively. This creates goodwill as they understand that ups and downs are inevitable in ever business. What they value is honest and open management.

Quick progress comes in an environment that respects competence, where there is competition and where there are no prejudices, infoscions (those associated with Infosys) have respect our competitors and a sense of humility about what we have achieved. The success is generally ephemeral. We are only as good as the results we produce and we believe in a long-term approach: our strategies and policies reflect that.

The enterprises have an important duty to contribute to society. No enterprise can sustain its progress unless it makes a difference to its context. The six pillars of enterprise governance are:

- I want to emphasise the importance of being trustworthy in your dealings. It is on such foundations that great organisations are created.
- Fear is natural, but do not let your actions be totally governed by it. Just as fear may sometimes be the voice of your institution, it might also be an invitation to explore yourself and the world.
- A supportive family is the bedrock upon which lives and careers are built.

- Learn how to manage yourself separating the merits and demerits of a decision from the accompanying feelings. Infoscions call this 'being transaction-oriented'.
- Live your life and lead you career in a way that makes a difference to your society.
- Follow your bliss. All else will follow.
- So, choose a worthy dream for yourself. Go after it confidently but always ensure that you are following your bliss.

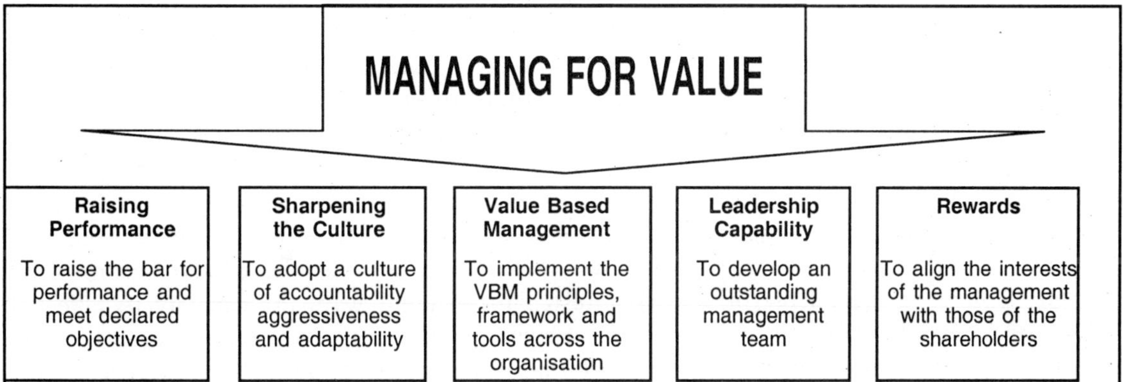

Source: Cadbury Scheme 2006.

Empowering Entrepreneurship

In the new competitive environment, it is necessary to grow out of a mindset that thinks only of control. Organisations have to learn to treat their employees not as mere implementors of decisions, but as entrepreneurs — thus, entrepreneurs — who can all contribute to the growth of the company. But entrepreneurial freedom is more than just the decentralisation or delegation of work.

Treating employees as entrepreneurs means both the ownership of work as well as opportunities for self-management. Not only does an entrepreneur has more freedom, he also has greater responsibility for successful performance. Thus, to stimulate entrepreneurs, organisations must develop systems that combine rewards for creativity and risk-taking with accountability for performance.

Treating support functions as profit centers which charge for the services they render to the line function — has at least three advantages. First, it makes these functions more accountable for their performance. Second, since the line functions pay for their services, they will make more specific demands on them, and, lastly, it will stir entrepreneurial initiative, which is often dormant in support functions.

Finally, the appropriation of the free-market model to the small-scale world has critical imitations for the role of the entrepreneur in a enterprise. To build an empowered and entrepreneurial organisation, intrapreneurs must learn to adopt a hands-off approach. In a liberalised organisation, the role of the intrapreneurs is akin to that of a venture capitalist who supports and strategies organisational initiatives without interfering in the day-to-day management of the enterprise. Without this strategic shift, it is impossible for an organisation to derive the full benefits of liberalisation.

What is Entrepreneurship?

Entrepreneurship is the propensity of mind to take calculated risks with confidence to achieve a predetermined business or industrial objective. In substance, it is the risk-taking ability of the individual, coupled with correct decision-making. When one witnesses a relatively large number of individuals in generation after generation of a particular community, who engage themselves in the industrial or commercial pursuits and appear to take risks and show enterprise, it is acknowledged to be a commercial class. The 'commercial class' is a myth just like that of the so-called 'martial race.' There are neither for all-time, martial races nor commercial classes. Communities, which once appeared to be martial in spirit have, in later periods, emerged as mercantile societies. Those who were once more concerned with and relished trade, are seen later in history to have taken to the profession of the sword. Today, it is quite evident to anyone that national communities which have developed world-wide industrial and consequently commercial interests are militarily powerful; nay, great industrial powers have today become super-military powers as well. Enterprise is manifested in different ways the capacity to take risks independently and individually, with a view to making profits and seizing an opportunity to earn more in the market-oriented economy, is the dominant characteristic of modern entrepreneurship. Enterprise, ready for the pursuit of business and responsive to profit by way of producing and/or marketing goods and commodities, to meet the expanding and diversifying actual and potential needs and demands of the customers, is what constitutes the *entrepreneurial essence.* But this kind of sensitivity of enterprising citizen throws up a species of entrepreneurs, that is mostly mercantile in outlook and performance. In underdeveloped countries like India, a new species of entrepreneurs is desirable, because here economic progress has to be brought about along with social justice. Entrepreneurship in India, has, therefore, to serve the national objective. There is an apparent conflict between social objectives and economic imperatives. This conflict has to be resolved first by the individual entrepreneur in his own mind before achieving economic growth. This includes industrial development, as one of the instruments of attaining the social objectives. A high sense of responsibility is thus an essential attribute of emergent entrepreneurship in India.

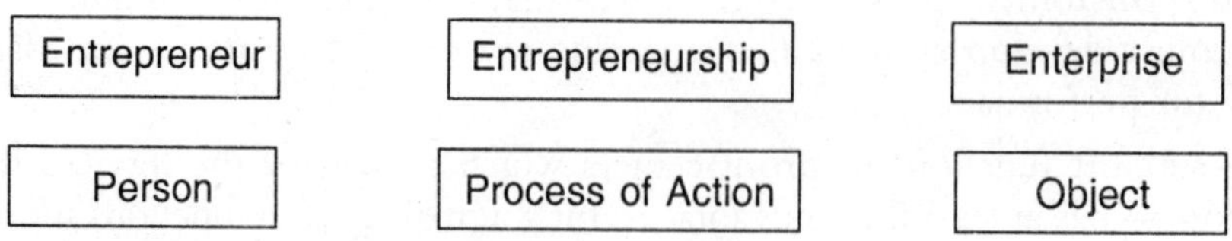

Fig. 1: Concept of Entrepreneurship

Stimulation of Entrepreneurship

Entrepreneurship development is probably one of the most elusive, complicated and perplexing issues in the promotion and growth of small enterprises. Recently, a number of development agencies have been involved, in the process. However, in spite of all these efforts, there have been only a few partially successful programmes and many colossal failures in the field.

The stimulation of entrepreneurship is a function of both internal and external variables. The presence of certain personal qualities in an individual is a requisite. Some of the findings about entrepreneurs in Nepal are as follows:

(*a*) Mainly there are two types of entrepreneurs: the Government and private individuals.

(*b*) In a family-run business, the entrepreneur is owner as well as manager. Entrepreneurs are frequently found to have parents who were engaged in business-related occupations. Membership in certain communities (Mewass, Marwadies, Gurung etc.) is highly correlated with entrepreneurship.

(*c*) Many people who migrated from the hills to the southern part of the country (Terai) and returned have become entrepreneurs and

(*d*) In the family business, a change is taking place. Now educated young members are becoming entrepreneurs rather than heads of the family who are generally old.

Definition

Entrepreneurship is a multi-dimensional function defined differently by different authorities. Centillion was the first to use the term 'entrepreneur.' He portrayed an entrepreneur as one discharging the function of direction and speculation. J.B. Say, moving along in the French (Centillion) tradition, was the first to assign the entrepreneur a position in the economic process. According to him, an entrepreneur's function is to combine the factors of production into producing an organism. But to Adam Smith, the father of political economy, the entrepreneur was a proprietary capitalist, a supplier of capital and at the same time, a manager, intervening between labour and the consumer. Adam Smith also treated him as employer, master, merchant and undertaker, but explicitly identified him with the capitalist. Schumpeter was decidedly the first economic thinker to have assigned the entrepreneur a key role in the process of economic development.

As per **Casson** entrepreneurship consists of an eccentric evaluation of economic events which other people are unwilling to support. As per **Janil** and **Stevenson**, "Entrepreneurship is a process by which individuals — either on their own or inside organisation-persue opportunities without regard to the sources they currently control." Although English classical economists failed to recognise entrepreneurship as a moving force towards the development of an economy but some of them like Israel Kirzner and Mark Casson did have their strong views about entrepreneurship. As **Kirzner** puts it, "Entrepreneurship means alertness towards profit opportunities."

Friedrich Von Hayek (1899-1922) **Ludwig Von Mises** (1881-1973), Keynes defined entrepreneurship and assigned a role played by entrepreneurship. Thus, entrepreneurship came up as a theory which has ability to mobilise the resources and combine them to initiate change in production.

In other words, entrepreneurship means the function of creating something new, organising, coordinating and undertaking risk and handling economic uncertainty. Higgins defines the term as, "Entrepreneurship is meant the function of seeing investment and production opportunity, organising an enterprise to undertake a new production process, raising capital, hiring labour, arranging for the supply of raw materials and selecting top managers for day-to-day operation of the enterprise."

According to Peter Drucker, "Entrepreneurship is neither a science nor an art. It is a practice. It has a knowledge base. Knowledge in entrepreneurship is a means to an end. Indeed what constitutes knowledge in practice is largely defined by the ends, that is, by the practice." Entrepreneurship is considerably less risky, if the entrepreneur is methodical and does not violate elementary and well-known rules.

Innovation and entrepreneurship are thus needed in society as much as in the economy, in public service institutes as much as in business. It is precisely because innovation and entrepreneurship are not 'root and branch' but 'one step at a time', a product here, a policy there, a public service yonder; because they are not planned but focussed on this opportunity and that need; because they are tentative and will disappear if they do not produce the expected and needed results; because, in other words, they are pragmatic rather than dogmatic and modest rather than grandiose — that they promise to keep any society, economy, industry, public service or business flexible and self-renewing.

Thus, entrepreneurship is a complex phenomenon. "Some think of entrepreneurs primarily as innovators, some chiefly as managers of enterprise, some as bearers of risks and others place major emphasis on their function as mobilisers and allocators of capital." In the Indian context, however, an entrepreneur may at best be defined as a person (or a group of persons) responsible for existence of new business enterprises.

In Schumpeter's system, entrepreneurship is essentially a creative activity. The entrepreneur is the innovator who introduces something new into the economy. The innovation may be a method of production, not yet tested by experience in the concerned branch of manufacture, or a product with which consumers are not yet familiar, or a new source of raw material or a market hitherto unexploited or other innovations in the strict sense of the term.

According to him, entrepreneurs are business leaders and not simple owners of capital. They are men of vision, drive and talent, who spot opportunities and promptly seize them for exploitation. It will not be out of place to mention here that the innovators concept of entrepreneurship cannot exclusively be depended upon in underdeveloped countries. In these countries business leaders who promote many large and small enterprises and adapt western techniques of production and distribution to the prevailing conditions in their own industries are entrepreneurs of no mean significance. They may not be innovators in the true sense of the term but they are men of great vision and effective industrial leaders who transform the economic landscape of their countries. People like Jamshetji Nusserwanji Tata, M. Visvesvarayya, G.D. Birla, Jamnalal Bajaj, Laxmanrao Kirloskar and other visionaries, builders and thinkers laid the foundation for a modern industrialised India. Professor Bert F. Hoselitz calls them *imitative entrepreneurs,* and regards their existence as quite purposeful in a mixed economy. "Coupled with all historical experiences of Western Europe, it appears to be safe to assume", he writes, that "small and medium-scale entrepreneurs are likely to play an important role in developing countries for several decades, provided these developing nations permit a private sector of enterprise in the industrial, commercial and financial field at all."

Besides, in South-East Asian countries, at the pre-take-off stage, the need is for more promoters, risk-takers and business organisers than for innovators. In the emerging economies, employment creation is a far more immediate goal for entrepreneurs than technological innovation. As Professor Jan Tinbergen points out: "The best entrepreneur to any developing country is not necessarily the man who use much capital, but .rather the man who knows how to organise the employment and training of his employees. Whoever concentrates on this is rendering a much more important service to his country than the man who uses huge capital."

Box - 1

ENTREPRENEURSHIP

From a humble, but profitable, canteen in Hostel at IIT Bombay to three successful start-ups (including Aspect Development, which was sold to i2 technologies in 1999 for $ 9.8 bn), to a fourth, Symphony Technology Group— the beat never slows for Romesh Wadhwani, nor does his quest to make others step to this drummer. When a man of such tremendous entrepreneurial spirit-not to mentions personal wealth-pledges "many millions" of his fortune of build an entrepreneurial network in India, it's not something to be taken lightly. The vehicle of his dream is the Wadhwani Foundation.

Romesh's reasoning is simple: If the Indian diaspora in the US can start about 30% of the companies in Silicon valley, why can't Indians in India do the same thing? The end result isn't just personal success, it's also the creation of hundreds and thousands of much-needed jobs." The divide between social and for-profit entrepreneurship is superficial," says Laura Parkings, executive director of the Foundation. "So many of the skills required are the same."

It's this belief that will fuel the Foundation's three-fold attack on the risk-averse attitude of Indians. The beginning is from education. The '01 Global Entrepreneurship Monitor noted that "the prevalence rate (of entrepreneurial activity) is lowest among those that do not have any formal education and significantly higher among those with professional degrees." It goes on to suggest that the inclusion of entrepreneurship curricula at all levels of education in India, particularly for professional degree programmes may stimulate start-up activity.

That's where the National Entrepreneurship Network (NEN) comes in NEN builds on the premise that high quality entrepreneurial education and research can increase the success of individuals in all fields. "The purpose of the NEN is to make it possible for millions of Indians like me to start and build large and successful business all over India, in all kinds of industries; businesses; that create join for tens of millions of professional workers," says Romesh Wadhwani. To sow the seed of enterprise, the Foundation is launching a competition to select five Indian academic institutes to form the base of entrepreneurial network. In five years, "we hope to have entrepreneurship development centres in 100s of institutes." The competition will begin with a by-invitation list of 250 institutes, to be pruned to five. Thirty semi-finalists will first submit plans for proposed activities like curricula development, courses, skill-building exercises, networking events and entrepreneurial activities. These will be studies by a panel of judges which includes HSBS's Naina La Kidwi, Sunil Mittal of Brahma, Harsh Mariwala of Marico, and Jaithirth Rao of Mphasis among others. Each of the five will receive non-financial support and seed funding of $10 to 50,000. Each will have a year to develop further proposals for entrepreneurial activity, depending on which they will be eligible for funding of $250,000 to $1m. "Introducing entrepreneurship as a viable career choice for all sectors is very important," says Laura. Adds Mr. Wadhwani. "The key here is to train managers, engineers and others to be entrepreneurs, to encourage them to take risks in the expectation of large rewards, to teach them the tools and help them find the talent and resources they need to succeed, and to provide access to mentors and role models to guide them."

To this end, the contest will include hotel and Mphasis, fashion and design, and technology and management institutes.

Alongside, IIM Bangalore has been roped in to conduct the National Entrepreneurship Survey (NES), NES will attempt to understand the barriers to entrepreneurship and prioritise the conditions needed for such activity to thrive, "For instance," explains Laura," how important was a knowledgeable Diaspora to the success of Indians in the Silicon Valley." Or how seminal are issues like venture capital, infrastructure, FDI or educational levels of the labour force. Executed annually, NES will seek to build a systematic knowledge base and be a resource for developing policies that encourage and support entrepreneurship.

Finally, the foundation plans to set up a Global Entrepreneurship Forum to bring together researchers, entrepreneurs, policy makers, NGOs and funding agencies among others. Not only will the forum provide a platform for discussion of the issues affecting emerging markets, it also hopes to inform and influence policy, and while the Wadhwani Foundation doesn't expect financial returns, this is not charity. "In every venture there is a bottom line. It's about creating value," says Laura.

ENTREPRENEURSHIP: SOME IMPORTANT DEFINITIONS

Joseph Alois Schumpeter (1883-1950)	: Schumpeter described entrepreneurship as a process to shatter the status quo through new combinations of resources and new methods of commerce.
Richard Cantillon	: Entrepreneursip is a matter of foresight and willingness to assume risks, which is not necessarily connected with the employment of labour in some productive process.
Leon Walrus	: Entrepreneurship is not itself a factor of production, but rather a function that can be carried on by an agent.
William Diamond	: Entrepreneurship is equivalent to 'enterprise' which involves the willingness to assume risks in undertaking an economic activity particularly a new one.
Jaffrey A. Timmons	: Entrepreneurship is the ability to create and build something from practically nothing. A human creative activity.
Janil and Howard Stevenson	: Entrepreneurship is a process by which individuals — either on their own or inside organisation — persue opportunities without regard to the sources they currently control.
Isrel Kirzner	: Entrepreneurship means alertness towards profit opportunities.
Arthur H. Cole	: Entrepreneurship is the purposeful activity of an individual or a group of associated individuals, undertaken to initiate, maintain or aggrandise profit by production or distribution of goods and services.
Everett E. Heggins	: Entrepreneurship is meant the function of seeking investment and production opportunity, organising an enterprise to undertake a new production process, raising capital, hiring labour, arranging supply of raw materials, finding site, introducing a new technique and commodities, discovering new sources of raw materials and selecting top managers of day-to-day operations of the enterprise.
Peter F. Drucker: (1909-2005)	: Entrepreneurship is neither a science nor an art. It is a practice. It has knowledge base. Knowledge in entrepreneurship is a means to an end. It is not just about making money. It is about imagination, flexibility, creativity, willingness to think concessionally readiness to take risks, ability to mobilise agents of production and capacity to see change as an opportunity. It is also about marrying passion and process with a good dose of perseverance.
M. Low and J.MacMillans	: Entrepreneurship is the creation of an innovative economic organisation (or network of organisations) for the purpose of gain or growth under conditions of risk and uncertainty.
H. Aldrich and C. Zimmer	: The definition of entrepreneurship include more than the mere creation of a business; in also includes the generation and implementation of an idea.
Robert Ronstadt	: Entrepreneurship is the dynamic process of creating incremental wealth. The wealth is created by individuals who assume the major risks in terms of equity time, and/or career commitment or provide value for some product or service.
Robert D. Hisrich	: Entrepreneurship is the process of creating some thing new with value by devoting the necessary time and effort, assuming the accompanying financial, psychic, and social risks and receiving the resulting rewards of monetary and personal satisfaction and independence.
John J. Kao	: Entrepreneurship is the attempt to create value through regulation of business opportunity, the management of risk-taking appropriate to the opportunity, and through the communicative and management skills to mobilise human financial and material resources necessary to bring a project to institution.
Robert K. Lamb	: Entrepreneurship is that form of social decision which is performed by economic innovators.
V.R. Gaikwad	: Entrepreneurship connotes innovativeness, an urge to take risk in face of uncertainities and an intution.
Mussleman and Jackson	: Entrepreneurship is the investing and risking of time, money and effort to start a business and make it successful.

(Contd.)

(Contd.)

H.N. Pathak	:	Entrepreneurship involve: (*i*) perception of an opportunity (*ii*) organising industrial unit, and (*iii*) running the industrial unit as a profitable, going and growing concern.
The Global Entrepreneurship Monitor:	:	Entrepreneurship, the process of planning, organising, operating, and assuming the risk of a business venture is now a maintstream activity.

The culture of entrepreneurship is deeply rooted: entrepreneurs are celebrated role models, failure is seen as a learning experience and the entrepreneurial career option is regarded as attractive. In to-days economic environment, entrepreneurship is a key component of globalisation.

ENTREPRENEURSHIP: SOME OBSERVATIONS

Saras Sarasvathy	:	Entrepreneurship is about having guts and passion that no one in the world can be taught. "The desire to 'make something happen' — the 'fire in the belly' cannot be taught — but in a country like India it exists on every street corner and bus stop — and if the desire exists, however small the spark, the rest of it can be taught.
Howard H. Stevenson	:	Entrepreneurship means far more than merely getting a business started. It is a never ending process that includes identification of opportunity, marshaling of required resources, exploitation of opportunity, and harvesting.
James Alsner	:	Entrepreneurship is a way of managing that occurs in organisations large or small, youthful or experienced. The three elements that are required for organisational success, careful definition of opportunities, understanding of required resources, and skills in negotiating for these resources.
Steven Wheeler: Walter McFarland Art Kleiner	:	What sorts of leaders are most effective? Creative, experimental risk takers like Richard Branson? Charismatic, domineering battlers like Lee Iacocca? Ruthless pursuers of performance like Jack Welch? The writers argue that while the quality of individual leadership matters, over time, the leader's capability is shaped by the capabilities of the full organisation. To build an organisation in which executives will flourish, the best leaders pay close attention to the design of the elements around them. They articulate a lucid purpose, create effective leadership teams, prioritise their initiatives carefully, redesign organisational structures and, most importantly, integrate all these tactics into one coherent strategy.
Subroto Bagchi	:	Entrepreneurship can be deeply rewarding. The richness of experience and sheer self-confidence you get by starting a small shop is sometimes larger than running a huge department for an established entity. This is because entrepreneurship is the most hands-on thing you will ever do Nothing about entrepreneurship is a spectator sport. Many things in a well paid job in a large organisation could well be. Entrepreneurship is a creative process. When done successfully, it can give you the highest sense of accomplishment possible. That sense of accomplishment is next only to delivering and raising your baby.
Kishore Biyani	:	Entrepreneurship is more a state of mind. If you think you have the self-belief and the tenacity to pursue your dreams, you must become an entrepreneur. Be prepared to face a lot of challenges alone. Most successful entrepreneurs did not start their career working for blue-chip companies. Having a great work experience doesn't prepare a person entrepreneurship. Nor does an MBA degree. While these will definitely help you understand business better, neither of these will be adequate enough for becoming a successful entrepreneur.

Kishore Biyani
CEO, Future Group

(Contd.)

(Contd.)

Laura Perkin	: Entrepreneurship is global. To encourage a culture of entrepreneurhip among the upcoming generation catch them young by promising to support start-ups in a big way.
Thomas J. DeLong	: The rules of the game are changing for entrepreneurs. The integrated entrepreneurship model is built on four management activities: getting direction, gaining commitment to the direction, execution, and setting a personal example.
Rob Goffee Gareth Jones	: Entrepreneurship today takes guts, knowledge, skill and insight. It can be as risky as it is rewarding. Ron Goffee and Gareth Jones argue that effective leaders entrepreneurs are authentic: they deploy individual strengths to engage followers hearts, minds, and souls. They are skillful at consistently being themselves, even as they alter their behaviours to respond effectively in changing contexts.
Narendra Kumar	: Entrepreneurship is all about passion, risks insight, vision, courage, guts, knowledge, skills, decisions and more about innovative products, practices strategies and management.
Jane Wei-Skillern	: Putting entrepreneurship in the social sector to tackle problems in healthcare, education and poverty alleviation has emerged as a new tool. Solving these problems is not just a matter of mobilising more resources to the field, but also developing entirely new models and ways of achieving sustainable mission impact.
BARD	: Many great leaders have turned to the Bard for inspiration. His characters portray several leadership models that are popular in the world of management today: leading from the front, charismatic leadership, leadership by force, leadership inaction, and a leader who puts one foot in front of the other to meet the new challenges of every moment. Leadership is pragmatic and resolute. He is a man of authority.
Aditya Mittal	: Entrepreneurship is a state of mind and can be applied to any number of different fields. Entrepreneurship is critical as it helps to prevent stagnation by challenging traditional thinking and drives progress and development that can bring about long-term positive change. Everyone has the potential to be entrepreneurial in their thinking & approach.
Thomas J. DeLong, Jack Gabarro and Robert J. Lees	: The integrated entrepreneurship model has four critical elements: direction setting; securing partner and associate commitment to this direction; facilitating strategy execution and setting a personal example of behaviour. In the face of new challenges, entrepreneurship is becoming more complex and intreguing.
Dr. N. Radhakrishnan, NCAT State University	: 'Innovation is a necessary component of entrepreneurship, but it's not necessarily a result of all innvoation. Entrepreneurs need innovators at all stages of a start-up but not vice-versa,' Dr. Radhakrishnan emphasises the need for innovators and entrepreneurs to work together.
Ram Shriram	: Entrepreneurship is not just about having a good idea and a vision. But it's more about great execution as successes come with great execution. So what does great execution mean? Hiring great people, building right partnerships and more importantly than doing the right things success for a start-up, it is in figuring out the things not to do. This keeps you focused and finally making sure that you make the right choices in terms of capital *i.e.,* making sure the right kind of people invest in you.

Box - 2

MY BEST LESSON IN LEADERSHIP

Whats the secrete to building a great organisation? How do you sustain consistent growth, profits, and service in an industry that can, literally, change overnight? And how do you build a culture of commitment and performance? I can answer all that in two words: and be Yourself.

That's both a simple and a profoundly difficult goal. It means spending less time building an organisation in which personality counts as much as quality and reliability. Southwest Airlines has the reputation being the wild-and-crazy guy of commercial aviation. Yet, in many ways, we are the most conservative company in our industry. We have always paid as much attention to our financial fitness in good times as in bad. But you can't lead by just the numbers.

At far too many companies, when you come into the office, you put on a mask. Your look different, talk different, and act different, which is why most business encounters are bland and impersonal. But we try not to hire people who are humourless, self-centred, or complacent. So, when they come to work, we want them — not their corporate clones. They are what makes us different from other airlines and in most enterprises, different is better.

Culture defines personality: If you create an environment where people truly participate, you don't need control. They know what needs to be done, and they do it. We're not looking for blind obedience. We're not looking for blind obedience. We're looking for people who, on their own initiative, want to be doing what they're doing because they consider it to be a worthy objective. They know that our company's success rests with them — not with me.

Personality is a strategy: Over the years, we've developed not only a different strategy, but also a different strategic planning-process. Basically, we just don't do it. In an industry where a two-week plan is likely to become obsolete, to spend days debating whether we're to serve Trenton, New Jersey, in 2005 is a meaningless exercise. So, rather than trying to predict what we'll do, we try to define who we are, and what we want in terms of market niche, operational strategy, and financial health. Obviously, you manage a $25 billion company differently than you do a $25 million company. But you change practices — not principles. You remember that systems are not masters. And that nothing comes ahead of your people.

Working for a worthy cause: Because our low-fare strategy is central to who we are, our employees are enormously cost conscious. But you need to spend more time on the intangibles than on the tangibles to create that kind of buy-in. W're not afraid to talk to our people with emotion. One of our managers once said: "The important thing is to take a brick-layer and make him understand that he's building a home" So, we constantly hold up examples of customer-experiences and employee-efforts to make a difference.

Building employee-partnerships: Our most important tools for building employee-partnerships are job-security and a stimulating work-environment. And, as it turns out, providing job-security imposes additional discipline because, if your goals is to avoid lay-offs, you hire sparingly. But it's not enough to try to assure people a job; equally important is allowing them to feel liberated when they come to work. To foster problem-solving and co-operation, for example, we have the Walk-a-Mile programme, in which any employee can do another's job for a day.

Training is another way you forge partnerships. Our most important training is in how to lead. My best lesson in leadership came during my early days as a trial lawyer. Wanting to learn from the best, I went to see 2 of the most renowned litigators in San Antorio try cases. One sat there, never objected to anything, was very gentle with witnesses, and established a rapport with the jury. The other was an aggressive, thundering help raiser. And both seemed to win every case. That's when I realised that there are many different paths. That's true of leadership as well.

People with different personalities, different approaches, and different values succeed not because one set of values or practices is superior, but because their value and practices are genuine. And when you and your organisation are true to yourselves — when you deliver both results and a singular experience — customers can spot it from 30,000 feet.

Herb Kelleher

Aspects of Entrepreneurship

As a catalytic agent the entrepreneur has to change the mindset of the workers so that the latter accepts radical changes in system structure and processes which the organisation is contemplating to introduce in order to compete with the rivals. What is most important is to change the key value, beliefs and norms established and accepted by workers.

There is a strong need for basic cultural change in the organisation that stresses productivity, quality, speed, innovation, customer orientation and empowerment. This calls for impressing certain fundamental changes at the top level. These include helping the latter in envisioning and defining its philosophy, values and beliefs.

As a developer, entrepreneur has to play a pivotal role in developing among the employees requisite knowledge, skills and suitable attitudes and improve their performance.

By imparting need based training and assigning jobs to the individuals best suited for them, using motivational techniques, creating manpower, configurations to boost the operational ability of individuals and by designing individual careers, the entrepreneur can ensure fuller utilisation of human resource potentials of the organisation.

As a facilitator, role of entrepreneur will be to foster an invigorating climate of mutual trust and confidence between the organisation/enterprise and the workers through a high degree of empowerment and recognition, openness, authenticity, internal and external equity and collaboration and team work. This will obviously lead to behavioural changes in the right direction.

Entrepreneurship, it is commonly believed, is enormously risky. And, indeed, in such highly visible areas of innovation as high-tech microcomputers for instance, or biogenetics — the casualty rate is high and the chances of success or even of survival seem to be quite low.

But why should this be so? Entrepreneurs, by definition, shift resources from areas of low productivity and yield to areas of higher productivity and yield. Of course, there is a risk they may not succeed. But if they are even moderately successful, the returns should be more than adequate to offset whatever risk there might be. One should thus expect entrepreneurship to be considerably less risky than optimisation. Indeed, nothing could be as risky as optimising resources in areas where the proper and profitable course is innovation, that is, where the opportunities for innovation already exist. Theoretically, entrepreneurship should be the least risky rather than the most risky course.

There are also enough individual entrepreneurs around whose batting average in starting new ventures is so high as to disprove the popular belief of the high risk of entrepreneurship.

Entrepreneurship is "risky" mainly because so few of the so-called entrepreneurs know what they are doing. They lack the methodology. They violate elementary and well-known rules. This is particularly true of high-tech entrepreneurs. To be sure, high-tech entrepreneurship and innovation are intrinsically more difficult and more risky than innovation based on economics and market structure, on demographies, or even on something as seemingly nebulous and intangible as *Weltanschauung* — perceptions and moods.

Thus, apart from economic, social, psychological, cultural factors affect and influence entrepreneurship. Entrepreneurial culture is both moulded by all cultures in the society in a distinct manner. As a leader, it gives direction and leads to the right path to success.

Importance of Entrepreneurship

From classical economics to the post-Keynesian analysts, the role of the entrepreneur has been surveyed and observations, theories and pronouncements advanced. Not only were pure economists involved in this endeavour, but also prominent social theorists such as Marx, Weber, Sombard and Veblen.

In general, contemporary economists agree that the entrepreneur is a business leader and that his role in fostering economic growth and development is a pivotal one. At present, however, there is no consensus at to what constitutes the essential activity which makes the entrepreneur a crucial figure, while some economists have identified the basic entrepreneurial requirements of production resources, the provision of capital or the introduction of innovations. Professor, James R. Omps of the International Institute of Entreprenology, Honolulu, Hawaii, in his paper entitled *"Entreprenology, the Critical Factor in Nation Development"*, has this to say:

"In all crisis situations, there is one critical factor. There is one factor in each situation that can be cited as being the straw that broke the camel's back! In listing some of today's possible critical factors, such familiar words and phrases as limited natural resources... food... energy all would emerge. A question may be phrased thus:

"What is the critical factor?"

Over-population?

Food shortages?

Energy shortages?

Lack of technology? or

All of the above?

"Many factors have been proposed ... and yet is it possible that the most critical factor has not been recognised? What is this factor that has either been stifled or-totally ignored? It is a relatively untapped source... that of qualified individuals with peculiarly unique aptitudes for innovation... for change, aptitudes, in other words, for using present day technology in ways yet unheard of or perhaps even unthought of. The critical factor is a dire shortage of the appropriate economic innovator and implementor... the Entreprenologists."

In the words of A.H. Cole, entrepreneurship is the purposeful activity of an individual or a group of associated individuals, undertaken to initiate, maintain or organise a profit-oriented business unit for the production or distribution of economic goods and services.

McClelland describes the innovative characteristics of the entrepreneurial role. The entrepreneurial role, by definition, involves doing things in a new and better way. A businessman who simply behaves in a traditional way is not an entrepreneur. Moreover, an entrepreneurial role calls for decision-making under uncertainty. If there is no significant uncertainty and the action involves applying known and predictable results, then entrepreneurship is not at all involved.

McClelland, like others, identified two characteristics of entrepreneurship. First, doing things in a 'new and better way.' This is synonymous with the innovative characteristics mentioned by Schumpeter and secondly, decision-making under uncertainty, *i.e.,* risk as identified by Cantillon. McClelland more explicitly emphasised the need for achievement or achievement-orientation as the most directly relevant factor for explaining economic behaviour. This motive is defined as a tendency to strive for success in situations involved and of one's performance in relation to the same standard of excellence.

In other words, entrepreneurship means the function of creating something new, organising and co-ordinating and undertaking risk and handling economic uncertainty. Higgins defines the term thus, "Entrepreneurship is the function of seeing investment and production opportunity, organising an enterprise to undertake a new production process, raising capital, hiring labour, arranging for the supply of raw materials and selecting top managers for the day-to-day operation of the enterprise."

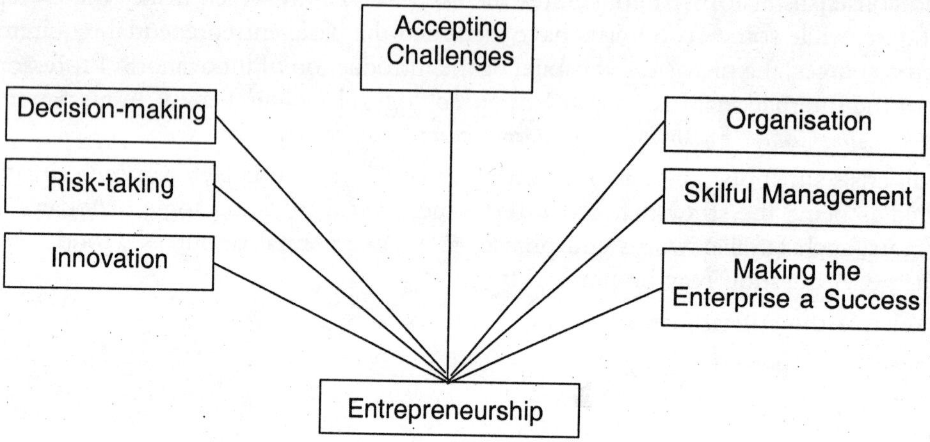

Fig. 2: Characteristics of Entrepreneurship

According to Peter Drucker, "Entrepreneurship is neither a science nor an art. It is a practice. It has a knowledge base. Knowledge in entrepreneurship is a means to an end. Indeed what constitutes knowledge in practice is largely defined by the ends, that is, by the practice." Entrepreneurship is considerably less risky, if the entrepreneur is methodical and does not violate elementary and well-known rules.

Innovation and entrepreneurship are thus needed in society as much as in the economy, in public-service institutes as much as in business. It is precisely because innovation and entrepreneurship are not 'root and branch' but 'one step at a time', a product here, a policy there, a public service yonder; because they are not planned but focussed on this opportunity and that need; because they are tentative and will disappear if they do not produce the expected and needed results; because, in other words, they are pragmatic rather than dogmatic and modest rather than grandiose — that they promise to keep any society, economy, industry, public service or business flexible and self-renewing.

Thus, entrepreneurship is a complex phenomenon. "Some think of entrepreneurs primarily as innovators, some chiefly as managers of enterprises, some as bearers of risks and others place a major emphasis on their function as mobilisers and allocators of capital." In the Indian context, however, an entrepreneur may at best be defined as a person (or a group of persons) responsible for existence of new business enterprises.

PROMINENT ENTREPRENEURS

Azim Premji

As long as IT is the flavour of the month, the flag-bearers of the sector will remain on top of the power stakes. He is also the richest man in India.

AZIM PREMJI
Chairman & CEO, Wpro Ltd.
Net worth: $17.1 billion

Ratan Tata

Still on top: The best-known Indian business group. Tata, is still the most written about and is well thought of

Much of the corporate world wrote him off earlier. But he has brought unexpected dynamism in the group today. The Indica would have been enough to ensure his place in Indian business history. But he has done much more.

Sunil Mittal

His power comes from his proximity to power. Plus, of course, he heads the largest private sector mobile service provider in India.

SUNIL BHARTI MITTAL
Bharti Group
Networth: $9.5 billion

N.R. Narayana Murthy

N.R. NARAYANA MURTHY

People listen when he talks, particularly appreciative over-seas audiences. In that sense, he is less the chief mentor at Infosys and more an ambassador for Brand India. In the country, some of his ideas on corporate governance and CEO responsibility have not been very welcome to his peers. But he is ahead of his times.

Deepak Parekh

He's a man who knows everybody worth knowing. He's been on practically every panel worth being a member of. He's the honest broker when things are broke beyond repair.

DEEPAK PAREKH

THE WORLD LEAGUE

Global Business Leaders Outside the US

1. John Browne, bp, UK.
2. Nobuyuki Idei, Sony, Japan.
3. Shoichiro Toyoda, Toyota Motor, Japan.
4. Jurgen Schrempp, Daimler Chrysler, Germany.
5. Josef Ackermann, Deutsche Bank, Germany.
6. Li Ka-Shing, Hutchison Whampoa, Hong Kong
7. Silvio Berlusconi, Mediaset, Italy.
8. Claude Bebear, axa, France
9. Jorma Ollilia, Nokia, Finland
10. Carlos Ghosn, Nissan Motor, Japan
11. Abdullah Jum'ah, Saudi Aramco, Saudi Arabia
12. Yun Jong Yong, Samsung Electronics, Korea
13. Peter Brabeck-Letmathe, Nestle, Switzerland
14. Bernard Arnault, Ivmh, France
17. Azim Premji, Wipro, India.
19. Zhang Ruimin, Haier, China.
20. Martin Sorrell, wpp, UK.

Source: Fortune.

TIMELESS TITANS

The Most Powerful Businessmen of All Time

Matthew Boulton (1728-1809)
Powered industrial revolution

Andrew Carnegie (1835-1919)
Carnegie's steel built America

Walt Disney (1901-1966)
Mega media blueprint

Henry Ford (1863-1947)
Democratised transportation

Edward H. Harriman (1848-1909)
Proto-turn-around artist

Henry J. Kaiser (1882-1967)
Fathered the HMO (health maintenance organisation)

Ray Kroc (1902-1984)
Founding father of fast-food nation

William Lever (1851-1925)
Invented "the Brand"

Henry Luce (1898-1967)
Mass media pioneer

J.P. Morgan (1837-1913)
Saved Wall Street

Alfred Nobel (1833-1896)
Invented dynamite

John D. Rockefeller (1839-1937)
Spawned global energy industry

Meyer Amschel Rothschild (1744-1812)
International financier pioneer

Alfred P. Sloan (1875-1966)
The perfect organisation man

Gerald Swope (1872-1957)
Wove capitalism's safety net

Sakichi Toyoda (1867-1930)
Smarter machines sage

Sam Walton (1918-1992)
Perfected mass retailing

Aaron Montgomery Ward (1843-1913)
'No Store' retailer

Thomas J. Watson Jr. (1914-1993)
Wired corporate America

Josiah Wedgwood (1730-1795)
Invented celebrity endorsements

Source: Forbes.

Features of Entrepreneurship

The main features of entrepreneurship are as follows:

1. **Economic:** It involves the creation and operation of an enterprise.
2. **Creative:** It involves innovative process. A catalytic agent.
3. **Purposeful:** It is a goal-oriented activity seeking to earn profits.
4. **Risk bearing:** Risk is an inherent and inseparable element of entrepreneurship.
5. **Organisation:** It involves organisation building capabilities.
6. **Human Relations:** Ability to work with other people and signing responsibility is a key to success.
7. **Flexibility:** Flexibility is the hallmark of a successful entrepreneur.
8. **Innovation:** Entrepreneurship is an innovative function.
9. **Skills:** It calls for special skills to handle the situation as it unfolds.
10. **Values:** It is an attempt to create value recognition of business opportunities to bring a project to fruition.

Thus, entrepreneurship is a multi-dimensional concept. It is an art as well as a science.

Creation of a Dream

Creating a dream gives entrepreneurs the energy and desire to become involved in its implementation and to be willing to change. During the formulation of the dream, everyone participates (including the leaders), and this allows people to start seeing each other in a different light. How long they will maintain their commitment depends upon (*i*) how well the organisation's leaders function in their new role of facilitating resolution of the needs or issues that are at variance with the dream, (*ii*) how clearly the leaders articulate and share information about the business needs and (*iii*) how well the leaders openly acknowledge their willingness to change, in whatever fashion, to attain the dreams.

The process of creating dreams should be tailored to the situation with the objective of having the entire organisation ultimately share the dream. In a large organisation, there will be many dreams formulated by interdependent parts of the organisation. At some point, these should be integrated into a total organisational dream. We have found that creating a dream in a bottoms-up manner where all organisational levels participate in some fashion is better than a tiered, top-down approach.

Box - 3

DREAMS UNLIMITED

For industries a change in the environment does not change the basic task. The challenge is two-fold — build a range of services and a truly global workforce. The basic task is really five-fold:

- Execution excellence is everything.
- Rally the organisation around a powerful vision.
- Do not let the enthusing culture binding the organisation get diluted as we grow rapidly.
- Continuously enhance value for our customers.
- Continuously enhance value of the people who have chosen to work with us.

The vision articulated by the entrepreneurs is:

- Business leadership
- Customer leadership
- People leadership, and
- Brand leadership.

Towards this end, create a workplace culture which is open, a political and rooted in values.

Dreams are unlimited. Opportunities are plenty and only really great people will build great organisations.

Brijmohan Lal Munjal
Hero Honda

To illustrate the content of a typical dream, let us look at the leadership portion of one from a Honeywell factory, which evolved as follows:

Leadership should be the ability of those leading work units (managers, supervisors, engineers, technical support and group leaders) to create an atmosphere of acceptance, openness and trust that will properly motivate members of the work units.

Interpersonal competence should be the ability to relate to people in a considerate and effective way.

This means that the leader:

1. Cares —

(*a*) Gives positive feedback for a well done job.

(*b*) Shows confidence in employees.

(*c*) Is fair and objective, not vindictive.

(*d*) Practices what is preached; does not ask for something that he or she would not be willing to do.

(*e*) Has a down-to-earth, person-to-person approach; acts as part of a team and

(*f*) Is compassionate and understanding; creates an atmosphere of acceptance and trust.

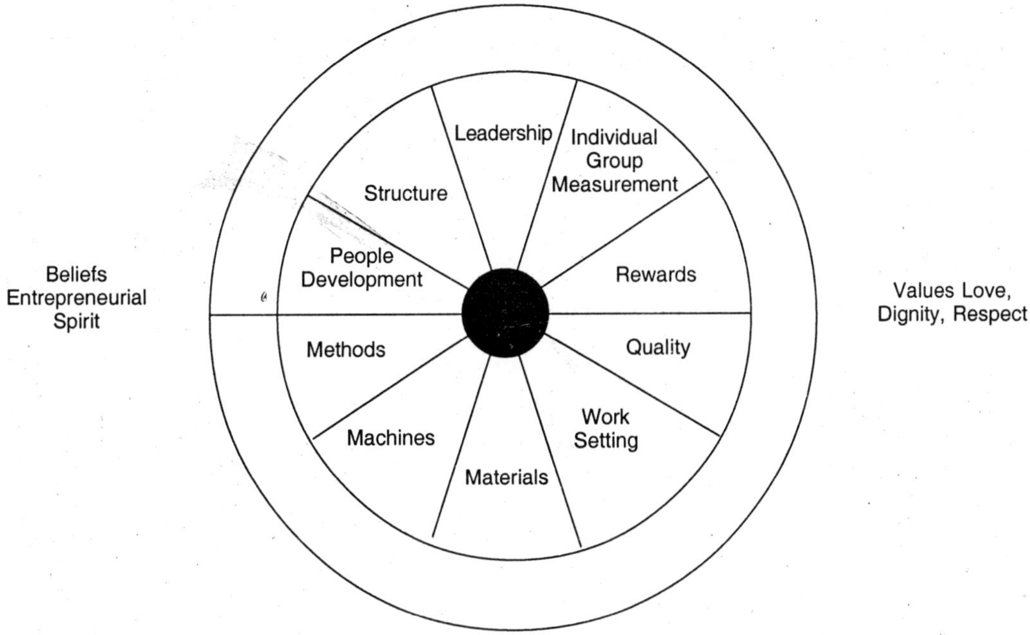

For optimal productivity and quality of work life.

Fig. 3: Basic Elements — Entrepreneurial Involvement

2. Skillfully communicates —

(*a*) Listens actively.

(*b*) Clarifies priorities.

(*c*) Is available.

(*d*) Links management with employees, employees with management, and employees with each other. Communicates effectively with all people on all shifts through all levels of the organisation.

(*e*) Provides feedback for both good and bad work.

(*f*) Talks openly and gives straight answers about what is happening.

3. Guides, inspires —

(*a*) Encourages advancement.

(*b*) Gives direction to the work unit.

(*c*) Is proud of loyal and supportive of employees.

(*d*) Has a sense of vision — a dream that is blend with employees' dream.

(*e*) Projects a positive attitude.

(*f*) Is courageous.

(*g*) Sets a good example; is friendly, not moody.

(*h*) Enjoys his or her work and

(*i*) Keeps promises, plows through red tape.

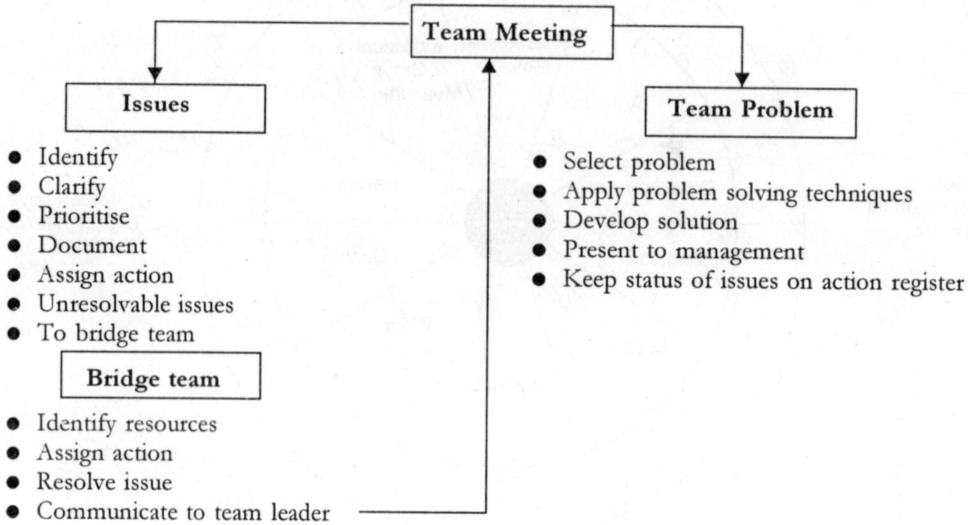

Fig. 4: Team Process

Administrative competence should be the ability to achieve organisational goals within the bound of the business constraints and policies and procedures. This means that the leader:

1. Understands his or her job.
2. Understands employees' jobs:
   (*a*) Utilises people's skills effectively.
   (*b*) Is concerned with employees' work and the workflow.
   (*c*) Stands up for and shows confidence in employees.
3. Takes immediate action:
   (*a*) Does not ignore problems.
   (*b*) Follows up on promises.
   (*c*) Gets tough when necessary.
   (*d*) Takes action to remove poor performers.
   (*e*) Assures that the next in command knows his role and has authority to act and
   (*f*) Provides proper human resources for all shifts and all levels of an organisation.

Change for present life style	*From new enterprise*
Work environment Disruption	**Desirable** 1. Cultural 2. Subculture 3. Family 4. Teachers 5. Peers **Possible** 1. Government 2. Background 3. Marketing 4. Financing 5. Role models

Fig. 5: Decision for a Potential Entrepreneur

Entrepreneurial Decision

Entrepreneurial decisions occur despite recession, inflation, high interest rates, lack of infrastructure, economic uncertainty etc. Each of these decisions is a personal human process that, although unique, have some common characteristics. The impulse to change his/her life style and create something new and an inner urge to do something worthy, are the forces behind these decisions. At times, perhaps even more stimulation for change comes from a negative force-disruption. At times, the available opportunities force a decision in individuals to take up entrepreneurial work, like all process it entails movement from something to new something.

What causes this change due to the work environment or disruption to result in a new company being formed instead of something else? The decision to start a new company occurs when an individual perceives that it is both desirable and possible.

The perception that starting a new company is desirable results from an individual's culture, sub-culture, teachers, family and peers A culture that values an individual who successfully creates a new business will spawn more company formations than one that does not. For example, India places a high value on being your own boss, individual opportunity, being a success and making money — all aspects of entrepreneurship. What is more, many different sub-cultures that shape value systems are operating within a cultural framework. More importantly, these subcultures support and even promote entrepreneurship. Thus, entrepreneurial decision making has more bearing on the sociological, cultural, sub-cultural, psychological and political environment, while satisfaction and adequate rewards are the optimistic goals.

Phases of Entrepreneurship Development

Broadly, entrepreneurship development consists of the three following phases:

(a) **Initial Phase:** Creation of awareness of entrepreneurial opportunities based on survey.

(b) **Development Phase:** Implementation of training programmes to develop motivation and management skills.

(c) **Support Phase:** Infrastructural support of counselling and assistance to establish a new enterprise and to develop existing units.

Box - 4

CEO SURVIVAL KIT

Digital devices rule Chugh's life. Not surprising. His company helps machines talk to one another.

Cellophone: nokia 6210. It is my constant companion, as my wife says. I largely use it for phone calls — and SMS, especially during long, laborious meetings.

Laptop: Toshiba Tecra 8100 — It is the key to my survival. I use it in the office, in flight, any time I am away from home, at least three to four hours a day. I have dispensed with the desk-top PC. (After all) our business runs off the net.

PDA: I rely on my good old Palm IIIxE. I store schedules when I travel, and some spreadsheets. A true friend away from home.

Telephone: Cisco 7960 IP phone. Just one integrated infrastructure. No complex manuals, just simple English.

Manoj Chugh, CEO, CISCO India

Causes of Slow Growth

Entrepreneurship growth is slow in India and that of women's entrepreneurship is still slower and negligible due to discouraging social factors such as unfavourable family background, lack of education, dual role of women, lack of aptitudes and training, absence of individualistic spirit, lack of freedom to choose a job according to ability, influence of sex, caste, kinship, custom and family burden etc. All these retarding causes are due to the unfavourable socio-economic conditions and tradition-bound society.

The *economic factors* retarding entrepreneurship growth are inadequate infrastructural facilities, shortage of capital and technical know-how, inadequate transport and communication facilities, absence of cheap and regular supply of power and raw materials. These constraints exist more in rural areas. The *environmental factors* discouraging entrepreneurship are unstable state governments, lack of security, absence of ideal market conditions and business education and corruption in administration.

Entrepreneurship Stimulates

A variety of social, economic, political and cultural factors are stimulating entrepreneurial activity and thus generating more robust economic development. These stimulants are as follows:

1. An increasing focus on capital formation. Availability of capital is a stimulant to an entrepreneur to start a new firm and/or give birth to a new idea.
2. The ability to transform scientific and technical developments through new institutional development is a second stimulant.
3. A third stimulant is the supportive government programmes.
4. Availability of required training and inputs is the fourth stimulant.
5. A collaborative relationship between business and research and their direct attempts to transfer technology to the market place may provide stimulus to a number of entrepreneurs who seek the opportunity to commercialise their ideas.
6. Finally, an endeavour to create an environment conducive to innovation will provide a much-needed stimulant to entrepreneurial activities.

The innovation centre provides technological evaluation, entrepreneurial assessment and other related assistance to entrepreneurs.

FOSTERING ENTREPRENEURSHIP

Fuelling ambtions and dreams. Help'ng insightful, imaginative business ideas glide smoothly over tough passages, breathing life into promising business ventures. Encouraging foresight and drive complementing acumen and enterprise with a steady flow of resources. *For effective* management, it is *imperative to foster and stimulate entrepreneurship and industrial culture to accelerate the process of industrialisation.*

Innovation is success in business and especially in the small-scale industry, innovation is the path to success. This is widely understood by small, medium and large companies alike. Innovation is particularly important for an operating system so that information can flow without hindrances.

Strategic Phases of Management

- Calibrate strategies constantly with board members.
- Share the company's progress towards set objectives with employees.
- Award employee stock options on a case-by-case basis.
- Stimulate growth by tapping employee's experience and abilities.
- Prepare written short-term and long-term plans.
- Ensure collaborative decision-making among the top management.
- Turn between two and five top managers into entrepreneurs.
- Add to the number of management levels only as sales grow.
- Establish entrepreneurial competencies in finance, marketing, and operations and
- Involve the board of director in all matters of management.

Entrepreneurship and Economic Growth

Economic development of any region is an outcome of purposeful human activity. Men assume various roles in the development process, namely, as organiser of human capital, natural material resources, worker and consumer. He stands at the centre of the whole process of economic development. According to Schumpeter, economic development consists of "employing resources in a different way" in doing a new combination of means of production. The entrepreneur locates ideas and puts them into effect in the process of economic development.

According to Baumol, an entrepreneur is a Schumpeterian innovator and something more than a leader. The entrepreneur, according to him, occupies a crucial place in the process of economic development.

Schumpeter further says that economic growth depends on the rate of applied technical progress (*i.e.,* innovation) and rate of technical progress in the economic field which in- turn depends on the supply of entrepreneurs in the society. Thus, entrepreneurs becomes the agent of change of society.

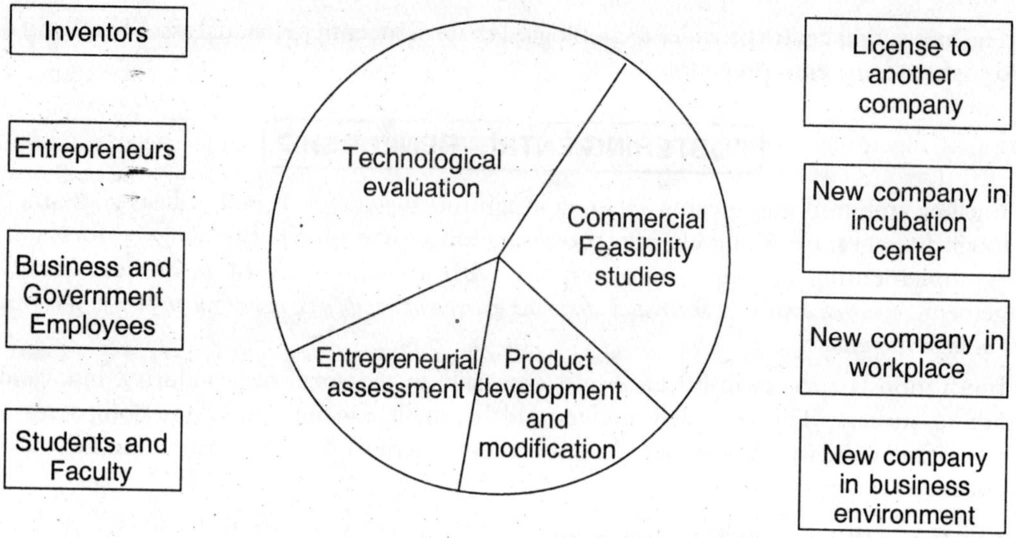

Fig. 6: Innovation Center

In the Schumpeterian model, entrepreneur is an innovator, and the supply of 'innovative entrepreneurs" depends on the necessary social and economic overheads. These economic and social overheads are very poor in backward regions which cause a short supply of entrepreneurs. In this connection, we can refer to David McClelland who explained the development of entrepreneurship in terms of human motivation to achieve or need for achievement (n Ach.). McClelland's hypothesis is that a society with a generally high level of achievement will produce more energetic entrepreneurs, who in turn accelerate the process of economic development.

In the Indian context, entrepreneurship has yet another dimension. An entrepreneur may not necessarily be an "innovator" but an "imitator" who would copy the organisation, technology, products of innovators from other developed regions. His role as imitator is likely to be guided and controlled by the various constraints and conditions peculiar to his area of operation and the factors under which he conducts his minimal modest industrial activity.

Other special scientist, notably Max Weber, have talked of the importance of entrepreneurship and expressed the view that creative and entrepreneurial energies are generated by the adoption of exogenously supplied beliefs which in turn produce intense efforts in occupational pursuits and accumulation of productive assets leading to the manufacture of goods and services. According to him, entrepreneurs are a product of the particular social conditions in which they live and it is the society which shapes the personality of individual entrepreneurs.

John Kunkel believes that the behavioural pattern of individuals is important for development and such a pattern can be influenced by external stimulus so as to alter it in the manner we want it. In other words, if we want more people in society to behave as entrepreneurs, we can bring about such behaviour on their part by appropriate alterations in the social environment so as to influence them to take to entrepreneurial pursuits. Like Weber, Cocharan and Young underscore the importance of society in shaping the entrepreneurial personality and consider that ingredients in the emergence of entrepreneurs are cultural values, role expectations, social tensions and inter-group relations in society.

The entrepreneurs are an important source of economic development. It is, therefore, suggested that there must be a motivational training programme to develop entrepreneurs and measures to be taken to modify the environment to stimulate entrepreneurial behaviour among individuals. There are thinkers who believe that the "Schumpeterian entrepreneurs are needed in underdeveloped countries for rapid economic development." Entrepreneurs are to be innovators who must change the production function and bring about rapid development. It is only through entrepreneurs that substantial development can be brought about.

In a mixed economy, the government tries to remove the evil of monopoly capitalism by placing some restrictions. It may curb the growth of monopolies and introduce workable competition which is essential for the optimum use of the available resources. Mixed economy tries to solve the problem of distribution of goods and services in a better way than the capitalist economy. The government tries to level up the incomes of the poor people and level down those of the rich people. This is done by fiscal measures, fixation of minimum wages and salaries, and improvements in the environment by the people.

The role played by an entrepreneur is significantly important in a mixed economy as it permits the growth of both the public and the private sector. In the private sector, profit motive acts as an incentive to the entrepreneur and market mechanism plays its own role and this establishes the role of entrepreneur in the mixed economy.

Entrepreneurship has great importance in various economic systems. It is all the more important under capitalism and mixed economy where not only the responsibilities of entrepreneur in production and distribution are recognised but the objective of growth of business and profit maximisation is also attained. Therefore, the importance of entrepreneurship stands beyond challenge in every economic system except under socialism where it appears in a different form. Yet, entrepreneurship prevails in all economic systems in one form or the other.

Small-scale Industries as Seed-beds of Entrepreneurship

Small-scale industries contribute significantly to the strengthening of the industrial structure, many articles can be produced economically on a small-scale, with some even more economically than on a larger scale. Efficient small-scale can be linked with large enterprises in complementary relationship, *e.g.,* sub-contracting. One of the most obvious benefits of such relationship is that it expands the industrial bases by efficiently utilizing resources, scarce or otherwise.

Also, small-scale industries may serve as seed-beds of entrepreneurship. They serve a newly industrialising county not only by their output of goods but also by functioning as a nursery of entrepreneurial and managerial talent. The almost infinite diversity of products and services that may be developed and produced by the small-scale industry sector also demands a commensurate development of skills — a desirable basis for long-term development of a diversified industrial structure in the region. Already skilled technicians, foremen and workers are induced, motivated and are often able to set up their own small-scale industrial enterprises. Generally, they offer the most promising means of promoting entrepreneurship among the people from different walks of life, especially those with limited financial resources and scant technical and managerial experience, thus establishing a wide base for rapid industrialisation. This role of small-scale industries is of decisive importance in any economy, where the industrial structure consists of a few large-scale and medium-sized industries (many of which are foreign-owned) on the one hand,

and of large number of traditional industries such as artisans, handicrafts and cottage industries on the other.

The lack of a middle group of modern small-scale industries is a factor of an imbalance in the industrial structure. Such a lack also contributes to the stagnation of the economy as a whole. As a general rule, neither the government nor foreign investors are interested in owning and operating small-scale establishments. Therefore, to promote small-scale industries is to promote rural industrial private enterprise, specifically to create a new class of indigenous industrialists throughout the countryside.

Small-scale industries play a useful role in regional development and industrial dispersal. Indeed, one of the pivotal problem confronting many countries in the world today in the task of social modernisation is how to disperse sources of economic activities so that development should become general, rather than concentrated in larger cities and capital. In a country that sanctions free enterprise, the movement of economic activities cannot easily be directed as the government would want it to be. Instead, we witness the tendency of capital to centralise itself in already developed areas.

Factors Influencing Entrepreneurship

Peter Heydernann, the Science Counsellor in the U.S. Embassy here, is very much impressed with the role the small businesses play in the process in innovation in the U.S. economy. He explained how "incubators" are used successfully in the United States to encourage small entrepreneurs.

The problem is how best to help small entrepreneurs translate the results of laboratory research into marketable products, to transform a new scientific concept into a commercial product. Simply put, "incubators" are very basic facilities offering shared secretarial services, space for conducting a retail or manufacturing business, and a few simple machine tools. But, and this is very important, incubators offer advice and consultation on subjects with which the most budding entrepreneurs are unfamiliar: business and finance planning, market development and government regulations. Incubators have indeed greatly helped small manufacturers to develop new products. Recent studies show that such enterprises are the main source of innovation in the U.S. industry.

The idea of incubators of technology is relatively new, "five or six years old," says Heydemann. This is because until recently it was felt that the U.S. industry would forever remain in the forefront, without any competition. But things changed rapidly. So, realising that "the 600-plus national laboratories could not possibly service all the one-and-a-half million or so small entrepreneurs," individual American states took it upon themselves to help local industry through their technology support and development organisations.

Incubators are very often attached to state university systems as universities have much of the technical and non-technical information that needs to be fed to the entrepreneurs. Moreover, state universities have increasingly come to believe that apart from their traditional role, they must also promote industrial activity in their areas of operation.

State authorities in turn help by enabling businessman cut through red tape, provides low-interest loans to develop prototypes, undertake market research and generally assist in bringing a new product to the consumer. "Some notion of the magnitude of this support can be had from the fact that last year alone, the federal and state governments together spent more than $2,000 million in encouraging small businesses." Many private sector companies also provide incubator facilities, though at a comparatively higher cost.

Another important aspect of incubators is that experts do not make any business decisions for their clients. "They only provide guidelines and advice on product development, engineering, pilot production and in identifying markets.

Among the businesses in which incubators are making a significant contribution, says Heydemann, "are light manufacturing in mature technologies, retail and wholesale trade and, finally, research and development in emerging technologies."

The success rate of incubators has been salutary in the number of new jobs created, the enlarged tax base for state revenues and in the export manufactures. In short, incubators are bringing new vigor and vitality to America's industrial renaissance and are once more giving the country a competitive edge.

NEW ENTREPRENEURSHIP AVENUES

At the turn of the Millennium, *Time* magazine in its 'Visions of the 21st century' gave clues to the emerging professions on the horizon. Here are some.

Tissue Engineers

Radical discoveries and inventions in medical science would make it possible to 'manufacture' human organs including intestines, bladders, liver, heart and kidneys. Remember, man-made human skin is already available in the market, with artificial cartilage not far behind.

Gene Programmers

Scientists are beginning to feel that it is possible to alter human genes by re-writing computer code. Soon, doctors would use 'gene therapy' to prevent numerous diseases including deadly cancers.

Pharmers

This term seems a combination of farmer and pharma, wherein biotech experts will raise crops and livestock that have been genetically engineered to produce therapeutic proteins.

Frankenfood Monitors

In order to satisfy the planet bulging with humans, scientists are working to genetically create foods that would require less 'gestation period' (rapidly-growing fish) or withstand varied climates (freeze-resistant fruits). The danger; these hybrids may wipe out the natural food chain, and hence the accompanying occupation: Eco-sciyts.

VANISHING TRIBE

Jobs that would disappear

Stock Brokers	Automobile Dealers
Post and Mail Careers	Insurance Agents
Real Estate Brokers	Teachers
Printers	Stenographers
CEOs	Orthodontists
Prison Guards	Truckers
Housekeepers	Railroad Employees
Telegraph Operators	Boiler Makers
Cobblers	Blacksmiths
Switchboard Operators	Fathers

Sources: *Time* magazine, May 2000,US Bureau of Census and Churn: The Paradox of Progress by Michael COx and Richard Alm.

Data Miners

These are already a reality, with a number of companies and professionals engaged in extracting useful bits of information from mountains of data. Data miners will thrive in an age of information explosion.

Hot-line Handymen

The online detection and advice concerning PC and related failures will be extended to most of the home electronics. Remote diagnostics will take care of these, and where personal touch is still required, it will be provided by videophone.

Virtual-Reality Actors

A change from 'couch potatoes' to 'mouse potatoes' means new characters and newer stories, which will keep the needs busy and entertained. And as the mouse clicks rise, so would the bank balances of New Age actors and scriptwriters.

Narrowcasters

The broadband industry will concentrate on personalised content and would become increasingly narrowcasting. The advertisers will develop tools and technologies to communicate directly to individuals and the idea of mass markets would take a backseat, at least for certain personal consumption luxuries.

Turing Testers

Owing its origin to British mathematician Alan Turing, the New Age would witness the withering away of difference between human intelligence and machines in every sphere of existence. The simulators would be used not only over phone to communicate with customers but also write personalised e-mails.

THE NEWCOMERS

Fastest Growing Occupations, 2002-2012

Occupation	*Projected Growth (%)*
Medical Assistants	59
Network systems and data communication analysts	57
Physician assistants	49
Social and human service assistants	49
Home health aides	48
Medical records and health information technicians	47
Physical therapist aides	46
Computer software engineers, applications	46
Computer software engineers, systems software	45
Physical therapist assistants	45

Source: US Department of Labour, Washington D.C., February 2004.

Socio-Economic Origins of Entrepreneurship

The entrepreneurial activity at any time and place is governed by varying combination of socio-economic, psychological, cultural and other factors. The empirical studies have identified the following socio-economic factors:

1. Caste/religion
2. Family background
3. Level of education
4. Level of perception
5. Occupational background
6. Migratory character
7. Entry into entrepreneurship
8. Nature of enterprise
9. Investment capacity
10. Ambition/motivation

The entrepreneurs who launched their enterprises during 60s predominantly came from mercantile and allied backgrounds. However, a slight tilt in favour of occupations which traditionally have been unconcerned with entrepreneurial activity, *viz.*, general serviceman, technicians, business executives, doctors, lawyers and the like was noticeable among entrepreneurs emerging for the first time after Independence. The main springs of entrepreneurship have been the traditionally trading castes of Hindu and Jain Banias from Gujarat, Rajasthan and Chettiars of Tamil Nadu. Besides, the new springs of entrepreneurship developed among other communities like Brahmins all over the country, especially the South, Naidus of the South, Patels of Gujarat, Kayasthas of West Bengal, Sikhs, Khatris and Aroras of Punjab making entrepreneurship a widespread phenomenon.

More and more people with high academic attainments started joining the ranks of industrialists, especially the professionals holding qualifications in engineering, law, medicine, cost and chartered accounting. The newer entrepreneurs have a larger proportion of their floatations in the traditional sector, but these professionals have by and large preferred to make their investments in modern sector. The technicians in particular among both old and new entrepreneurs have entered industries in the modern sector having a bearing of their academic qualifications. The traditionally trading communities of Hindu and Jain Banias have relied on modern sector more than others. Intrerestingly, among the regional communities the South Indians have preferred their promotions in traditional sector more than the Gujaratis and Marwaris have.

Barriers to Entrepreneurship

A large number of entrepreneurs particularly in the small enterprises fail due to several problems and barriers. Karl H. Vesper has identified the following entrepreneurship barriers:

1. Lack of a viable concept
2. Lack of market knowledge
3. Lack of technical skills
4. Lack of seed capital
5. Lack of business knowhow
6. Complacency — lack of motivation
7. Social stigma

Table 1

BARRIERS TO ENTREPRENEURSHIP

ENVIRONMENTAL HELPS	BARRIERS
1. Market Contacts	A. Lack of Viable Concept
2. Local Incubator Companies	B. Lack of Market Familiarity
3. Capable Local Manpower	C. Lack of Technical Skills
4. Technical Education and Support	D. Lack of Seed Capital
5. Supplier Assistance and Credit	E. Lack of Business Knowhow
6. Local Venture Capitalists	F. Complacency. Non-motivation
7. Venture-Savvy Bankers	G. Social Stigma
8. Capable Local Advisors	H. Job "Lock-ins." "Golden Handcuffs"
9. Entrepreneurial Education	I. Time Pressure, Distractions
10. Successful Role Models	J. Legal Constraints, Regulation Red Tape
	K. Protectionism Monopoly
	L. Patent Inhibitions

Source: Karl H. Vesper, *Entrepreneurship and National Policy* (1983). Walter E. Heller International Institute for Small Business.

8. Time pressure and distractions
9. Legal constraints and regulations
10. Monopoly and protectionism
11. Inhibitions due to patents

Vesper lists certain entrepreneurial factors that help to reduce the effect of these barriers. Table 1 depicts how this happens:

Environment for Entrepreneurship

The entrepreneurs do not appear spontaneously. While the other factors of production are at last, in principle, available for hire but enterprise is not. It has to come from different vocations. Even the educational system in most of the developing countries is designed in such a way as to create more job-seekers. To sum up, entrepreneurs appear to have been motivated by a combination and interaction of the following factors of environment:

1. Socio-economic environment;
2. Family background;
3. Standard of education and technical knowledge;
4. Financial stability;
5. Political stability and government policy;
6. Caste and religious affiliation;
7. Availability of supporting facilities;
8. Achievement motivation; and
9. Personality and personal skill.

The environmental factors may be summarised as follows:

1. Entrepreneurship is not influenced by single factor but is the outcome of interaction and combination of various environmental factors.
2. By changing the environment, society can be recreated.
3. It is the 'desire to make money' that drives one to start an industry rather than the amount of money one possesses, and
4. Encouraging government policy and social recognition influence a person to become an entrepreneur. Educationist must think of modifying the educational system so as to produce more job-creators rather than just job-seekers.

WORK CULTURES OF THE PAST AND THE FUTURE

Work Culture of the Past	Work Culture of the Future
• individualism	• communitarianism
• independence	• interdependence
• autocracy	• democracy
• humanity against nature	• humanity part of nature
• unsustainable production	• sustainable production
• unsustainable consumption	• sustainable consumption
• patriarchy	• gender equality
• intercultural intolerance	• intercultural tolerance
• interreligious intolerance	• interreligious tolerance
• conflict resolution by confrontation	• conflict resolution by negotiation
• reliance on defence	• reliance on security
• reliance on rational intelligence	• reliance on emotional intelligence

Growth of Entrepreneurs

In terms of benefiting the people, the development of small and medium-scale industries and businesses offered many advantages. Most important perhaps, amid the mounting unemployment, are the small and medium enterprises which generate more jobs and often use labour-intensive methods of production. Industries and business of smaller size also promote better income distribution and development of entrepreneurship and general skills, in addition to such broader benefits such as rural industrialisation and increased export earnings.

One of the most potentially fruitful areas of human resources development for small and medium-sized enterprises is the training of entrepreneurs and managers. Such training programmes should be as well rounded as possible, covering not only the basis of business, technology and so forth but also helping the trainees to identify their aptitudes, motivating them, encouraging innovative thinking and helping to develop personalities and attitudes geared for success. Indeed, small industries and businesses are ideally suited for capitalising on entrepreneurial skill, initiative and talent and thus assisting in building as dynamic private sector in the developing countries.

The growth in the number of small entrepreneurs has been encouraging. The small-scale sector has grown in volume from 16,00 units in 1950 to over 18 lakh units by the end of 1989. The range of items produced by the small-scale sector ranges from consumer goods to high precision items.

Not only has the number of entrepreneurs grown over a period of time but the scope of entrepreneurship is also getting broad-based. Earlier, for a large proportion of firms in India, the basic unit of entrepreurship was the extended family. This tendency is now getting diluted. A study conducted a few years back by the Economic and Scientific Research Foundation (ESRF) indicates that out of a sample of entrepreneurs studied by them, around 1/5 were managers and engineers before they turned entrepreneurs. It was found that around 57 per cent of the new entrepreneurs in starting small-scale units were motivated by the experience that they had gained from the previous employment. Entrepreneurship in these cases was not necessarily in-born but largely acquired.

Though impressive in certain ways, the development accomplished so far, as indicated before, is inadequate and far from satisfactory when set against the needs, as also the existing vast potential. In fact, according to Prof. Herbert Giersh, a noted economist, there is no shortage of entrepreneurial talent anywhere in the world, but the actual numbers depend on the demand conditions, *i.e.,* the demand permitted, induced or actively provoked by the socio-economic structure and the politico-economic environment. According to him, a mixed capitalistic economy such as ours offers scope for development of entrepreneurial talent not only in the private sector but also in the government sector.

Box - 5

THE ENTREPRENEUR: OTHER DEFINITIONS

Quesnay recognized a rich farmer as an entrepreneur who manages and makes his business profitable by his intelligence and wealth.

Adam Smith described entrepreneur as a person who only provides capital without taking active part in the leading role in enterprise.

Richard Cantillon considered all persons engaged in economic activity as entrepreneurs.

Jean Baptiste Say opined that the entrepreneur was a person endowed with the qualities of judgement, perseverance and a knowledge of the world as well as of business. The entrepreneur shifts economic resources out of an area of lower and into an area of higher productivity and greater yield. The definition included the concept of bringing together the factors of production.

French tradition regarded an entrepreneur as a person translating a profitable idea into a productive activity.

Karl Marx regarded entrepreneur as a social parasite.

Joseph A. Schumpeter (1883 – 1950) recognised person who introduces innovation changes an entrepreneur. He treated entrepreneur as an integral part of economic growth. The fundamental source of equilibrium was the entrepreneur.

Frank Young describes entrepreneur as a change agent.

Noah Webster thinks entrepreneur is one who assumes the responsibility of the risk and management of business.

Francis A. Walker observes that the true entrepreneur is one who is endowed with more than average capacities in the risk of organising and coordinating the various other factors of production.

Peter F. Drucker defines as entrepreneur as one who always searches for change, respond to it and exploits it as an opportunity. Innovation is the specific tool of entrepreneurs, the means by which they exploit change as an opportunity for a different business or service.

Arthur Dewing conceptualised the function of the entrepreneur as one that promotes idea into business.

Clarence H. Dantrof considers entrepreneur as a person who makes decision under alternative courses of action.

Entrepreneur has become the focal point in economic activities. He is viewed as an initiator of action, a stimulant of socio-economic change and development.

Robert D. Hisrich says, "The person who is going to establish a successful new business venture must also be a visionary leader – a person who dreams great dreams. Although there are many definitions of leadership, the one that best describes the needed intrepreneurial leadership is: A leader is like a gardener. When you want a tomato, you take a seed, put it in fertile soil, and carefully water under tender care. Your don't manufacture tomatoes, you grow them."

Martin Luther King said, "I have a dream, and thousands followed in spite of overwhelming obstacles. In order to establish a successful new business venture the entrepreneurial leader must have a dream and work against all obstacles to achieve it."

Entrepreneur is one who distinguishes as a person who undertakes to organise, manage and assume the risk of running a factory and/or a business or an enterprise.

(Contd.)

(Contd.)

Entrepreneurship is neither a science nor an art. It is a practice. It has a knowledge base. Knowledge in entrepreneurship is a mean to an end. Indeed, what constitutes knowledge in practice is largely defined by the ends, that is by practice.

According to *Everett E. Haggen*, an entrepreneur is an economic man who tries to maximise his profits by innovations. Innovations involve problem-solving and the entrepreneur gets satisfaction from using his capabilities in attacking problems.

According to *David McClelland:* "An entrepreneur is someone who exercises some control over the means of production and produces more than what he can consume in order to sell (or exchange) it for individual (or household) income."

An entrepreneur, as defined by *Robert E. Nelson,* is a person who is able to look at the environment, identify opportunities to improve the environment, Marshall resources and implement action to maximise those opportunities.

According to *J.K. Galbraith*: "An entrepreneur must accept the challenge and should be willing hard to achieve something."

Albert Shapcro observes that the entrepreneur takes initiative organises some social and economic mechanisms, and accepts risks of failure.

Karl Vesper affirms that the entrepreneur is seen differently by economists, psychologists, business persons and politicians. Robert C. Ronstadt considers that the wealth is created by individual who assume the major risks in terms of equity time, commitment and value for some product service.

Akhouri M.M.P describes entrepreneur as a character who contributes innovativeness, readiness to take risk, sensing opportunities, identifying and mobilizing potential resources concern for excellence, and who is persistent in achieving the goal.

The term entrepreneur contain notions of newness, innovation, vision, organising, creating wealth, mobilising resources, risk taking and achievement. A driven source of economic development

Not every new small by siness is entrepreneurial or represents entrepreneurship. To be entrepreneurial, an enterprise has to have special characteristics over and above being new and small indeed entrepreneurs create developing something different, they change or transmute value.

Laura Parkin: Entrepreneurs are both born and made while some people are born with natural talent and risk tolerance. Entrepreneurship is a discipline and entrepreneurship skills can be learned by every one.

According to *David Ricardo,* the foremost motive of a risk taker is to amass capital and capital accumulation is the sine quanin of economic development.

John Stuart Mill viewed the world entrepreneur as organizer who is paid for his non-manual type of work.

Leonwalrus pointed out that entrepreneur is the coordinator of basic factors of production. He treated 'entrepreneur' who combines other factor such as land, labour and capital.

Carl Menger (1840-1921) considers the entrepreneur as the change agent who transforms resources into useful goods and services, often creating the circumstances that lead to industrial growth.

Frank H. Kright points out that entrepreneurs are a specialised group of persons who bear risk and deals with uncertainty.

Mark Cassons opines that an entrepreneur is a person who specializes in taking judge mental decision about the coordination of scarce resources.

Max Weber states that the entrepreneurs are a product of particular social condition in which they are brought us and it is the society which shapes individuals as entrepreneurs.

A. David Silver Described the entrepreneur as energetic, single minded and having "a mission and clear vision bear she intends to create out of this vision of product or service in a field many have determined is important to improve the lives of millions.

Entrepreneur can do anything with passion and enthusiasm. Enthusiasm is the yeast that makes his hopes rise to the stars. Enthusiasm is the spark in his eye the swing in his gait, the grip of his hand, the insistible surge of his will and his energy to execute his ideas. Enthusiasts are fighters, they have fortitude, and they have strong qualities. Enthusiasm is at the bottom of all progress. With it there is accomplishment. Without it there are only alibis.

Henry Ford created the manufacturing miracle that launched a modern era in industry.

Table 2

THE RELATIONSHIP BETWEEN ENTREPRENEUR AND ENTREPRENEURSHIP

Entrepreneur (PERSON)	Entrepreneurship (ACTION/ACTIVITY)
Administrator	Administration
Able	Ability
Aimer	Aim
Analyser	Analysis
Adopter	Adopting
Accelerator	Accelerating
Accountant	Accounting
Builder	Building
Balanced	Balancing
Believer	Belief
Brilliant	Brilliance
Bold	Boldness
Creator of value and trust	Creativity
Character	Values
Considerator	Consideration
Courageous	Courage
Communicator	Communication
Competitor	Competitive, Competence
Capitalist	Capital-venture, seed, working. Confidence/long-term etc.
Confident cultured	Collaborative culture
Dreamer	Dreams
Designer	Designs
Director	Direction
Decision-maker	Decision-making
Delegator	Delegation
Dominant player	Focussed
Educator	Education
Empowerer	Empowerment
Excellor	Excelling
Ethical	Ethics
Facilitator	Facilitating, Fostering
Foresighter	Foresight
Futurist/Farsighted	Futuristic
Goal-setter	Goal-setting
Growth-Fixer	Growth-oriented
Humble	Humility
Honest	Honesty
Human	Humanity
Initiator	Initiating, Initiative
Investor	Investing/Investment
Innovator	Innovation
Immitator	Immitating
Inspirer	Inspiring
Integrator	Integrity
Ignitor	Igniting
Immaginator	Immagination, Immagining

Intellectual (Driven by values)	Intelligence
Informer	Information
Knowledged	Knowledge
Leader	Leadership
Leverager	Leveraging
Learner	Learning
Mentor	Confidence building/Fostering
Motivator	Motivation
Marketier	Marketing
Net-worker	Net-working
Nurturer	Nurturing
Organiser	Organisation, Organising
Opportunist	Opportunities (Taking advantages of opportunities)
Planner	Planning
Programmer	Programming, Actions
Producer	Production
Performer	Performance
Partner	Partnership
Positioner	Positioning
Packager	Packaging
Promoter	Promotion
Passion-player	Passionate
Risk-bearing	Risk-taking
Responsible	Responsibility
Re-Inventor	Re-Inventing
Re-Engineerer	Re-Engineering
Skilled	Skills
Striver	Striving
Strategist	Strategy
Salesman	Selling
Talented	Talent
Trainer	Training
Trend-setter	Trend-setting
Technologist	Technology
Transformer	Transformation
Venturist	Venturing
Visionary	Vision
Visualiser	Visualisation
Wealth-creator	Wealth creation
Wizard	Specialist, Strategist, Diplomatic

Problems

The task before the national leadership today is to industrialise a predominantly agricultural society, where capital is scarce and labour is plentiful. Again, modem industry implies a style and a method of work which are quite at variance with the traditional culture and modes of social behaviour in the underdeveloped countries. So, the whole structure of society has to undergo a considerable structural and institutional change commensurate with the needs of the situation.

The gap between the indigenous arts and even the improved crafts, on the one hand, and imported and also indigenous technology, on the other, is wide enough and is further widening day after day with the explosion of innovative research. Furthermore, the economy has been historically and unavoidably polarized between a few mighty industrial centres and the far-flung rural areas. With all the progress during the two decades and a half, the national economy is beset with all kinds of shortages and scarcities of inputs, most vital to new entrepreneurs, when they launch their small or tiny units. Besides, they have, at times, to contend and compete with well established small, medium or large industrial units in the same lines of production. Newly emerging industries, particularly those of the first-generation entrepreneurs, even in the underdeveloped economies, are slowly but certainly tending to become high investment industries and the entrepreneurs have to battle against the formidable force of hostile elements, such as (*i*) erratic shortages of raw materials, (*ii*) flourishing black market, (*iii*) prices rigged up by monopolists, (*iv*) administrative maldisribution, (*v*) gaps between official promise and performance, (*vi*) inefficiency of industrial management, (vii) irresponsible attitude to work, (*viii*) rising cost of capital and credit, (*ix*) deficient and arrogant institutional banking, (*x*) inadequacy of common service, (*xi*) primitive wholesale and retail trade outlets and others. New entrepreneurship in India has to be cherished in this environment.

Box - 6

NOW CONSIDER THIS

When defining a new role for education, executives should ask themselves the following questions:

What should be on our learning agenda?

- Key concepts that underpin our values and beliefs.
- Key capabilities to be developed in live initiatives.
- Key conditions that must be in place for performance.

Which initiatives have the potential for big impact?

- Initiatives that are high value-at-stake.
- Initiatives that are high on our corporate agenda.
- Initiatives in which it is important to reinforce high standards.

Which experiences offer opportunities for simulation and learning?

- Issues that span multiple business units.
- Business cases that highlight difficult trade-offs.
- Potential scenario that are likely to be encountered.

What do we need to get started?

- A clear learning agenda.
- Alignment around business and educational priorities.
- The right experience to execute.

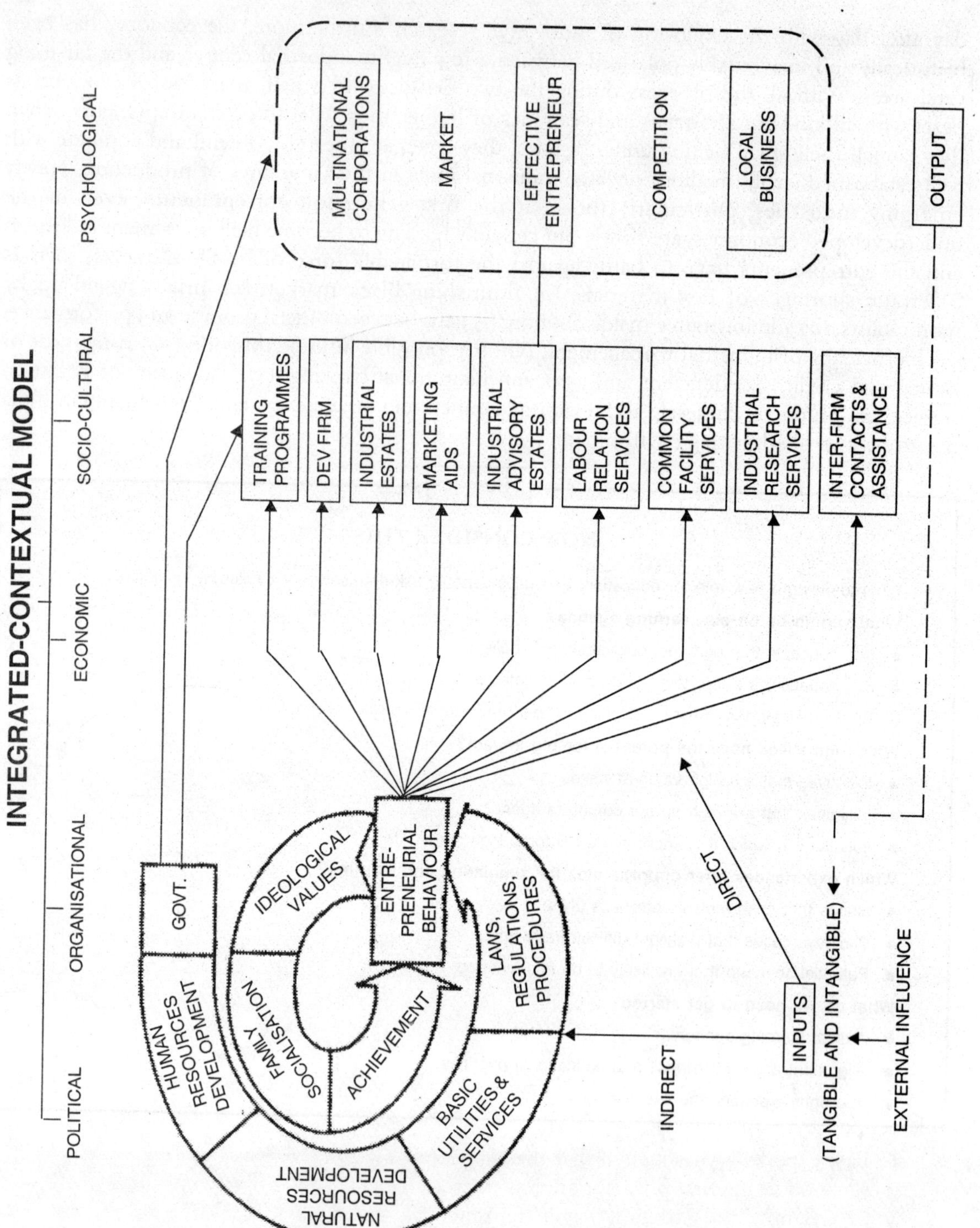

Fig. 7: A Model of Factors Influencing the Emergence of Entrepreneurship

Box - 7

ENTREPRENEURSHIP BEYOND BORDERS

The ability to spot opportunities and do business beyond borders is increasingly becoming the defining trend that will separate the entrepreneur from the rest. Government deregulation is opening national borders for commerce. Trading and investing beyond national borders is now common and is either the salvation or the death knell of the Indian economy. We have an enviable domestic market and that in itself is a threat unless domestic enterprises shake themselves out of their comfort zones and gear up to face the pressures of competition from across the border, now made easier, thanks to the World Trade Organisation (WTO).

India and other developing countries will continue to oppose and seek amendments to the WTO proposals that prohibit developing countries from following the same policies that developed countries pursued to make their domestic enterprises internationally competitive. But the WTO threats are real. The trick, if one is to survive and prosper, will be to identify emerging threats before they become real and then prepare for them. It will be equally important to learn to spot opportunities before they arise, and take advantage of them. Success comes to those who are able to take advantage of opportunity. Alexander Graham Bell said: "When one door closes, another door opens; but we often look so long and so regretfully upon the closed door that we do not see the ones that open for us." In business, opportunity knocks once; it usually does not lean on the doorbell.

Competition from across the border will affect high-cost producers, and perhaps even decimate entire industries, especially in the small-scale sector. India already finds itself in a situation of jobless growth. Where will new jobs be generated?

However, the alternative for job-seekers is to create their own jobs. Entrepreneurship in India (outside of family-controlled businesses) is largely necessity-based, not opportunity-driven. Entrepreneurs in this country have traditionally not been looked up to as role models. It is still widely believed that you cannot become a successful entrepreneur in this country without bending the rules. But this view is slowly changing, thanks to the success of Indian entrepreneurs in the infotech industry. They have fired the imagination of a whole new generation, and entrepreneurship is now a desired career option. Industries where entrepreneurship has flourished are IT, drugs, and pharmaceuticals.

The comparable advantage of developing countries will expand beyond low labour costs. This trend is a clear warning to those who are basking in the comfort of apparent demand for their products and services. If the industry is so complacent, then where is the opportunity for innovation?

The present stage of entrepreneurship development programmes as a factor contributing to the industrialisation of backward and other areas needs a proper direction and organisation for making it more effective and purposeful. The contribution of entrepreneurship development programmes is very uneven among different region and definite programmes need to be chalked out to bring about some degree of uniformity and upgradation. Before these problems are tackled, some important issues need immediate attention, for example: (*i*) structure and composition of entrepreneurship development programmes; (*ii*) areas of operation; (*iii*) Fixing of priorities; (*iv*) follow-up; (*v*) spatial dispersal of the entrepreneurship development programmes; (*vi*) training and (*vii*) financing pattern.

Apart from these, some of the operational problems experienced in the course of implementing the entrepreneurship development programmes are listed below:

1. Past experience has shown that the supporting agencies/organisation either tend to be slipshod in the first phase or are less interested in the third phase which means that the programme fails to tap the entrepreneurial potential of the area or the trained entrepreneurs do not receive the support and counselling which they need most.
2. Most of the existing support organisations meant for maintenance operations are not for innovative functions. There is also an element of cynicism. A reorientation in the attitude of supporting organisations is called for.

3. Poor investment on the part of institutions as also trainees and wrong selection of target groups contributed largely to the failure of the number of entrepreneurship development programmes.
4. Experience reveals that entrepreneurial failures are mostly due to incompetence and poor management.
5. It is also said that there is an inability to identify the needs of institutions and differences of opinion prevailed amongst the practitioners and also amongst trainees.
6. It is also stated that there is a low institutional commitment for local support to the entrepreneurs. There is also a very low level of involvement in the marketing of the products of units.
7. Non-availability of various input, *i.e.,* raw materials, power etc., and infrastructure support, combined with poor follow-up by the primary monetary institutions resulted in the failure of entrepreneurship development programmes.
8. It is also states that there is ill-planned training methodology, inconsistency in the programme design, its content, sequence and theme and that the focus of the programme is not clear.
9. Training institutions do not have much concern for the objective of identification and selection of entrepreneurs and the follow-up after training.
10. Some institutions are still debating whether to have a proper identification and selection of entrepreneurs for preparing successful entrepreneurs.
11. Those involved in and concerned with selection and follow-up-activities have either limited manpower support or a narrow linkage with other support agencies.
12. It is also said that there are no standard curricula even in terms of broad modules being adopted by interventions.
13. A majority of institutions engaged in the entrepreneurship development programmes are themselves not convinced of what they are doing as the task is delegated by the government. As a result, the social objective aimed at is not achieved.
14. Perpetual ambiguity in the objectives of entrepreneurship development programmes seems to have percolated to the grass roots level with significant deterioration in terms of content and interest.
15. In has also been realised that absence of an appropriate industrial and commercial climate coupled with lack of information and access to relevant technology as acted as a great handicap and
16. Mechanical implementation of entrepreneurship development programmes, as is happening in many cases, will not solve the problem. The mechanical approach may help them (entrepreneurs) to initiate the entrepreneurial development activity but they may not be able to manage and expand it successfully.

COMMON MINDBLOCKS AGAINST ENTREPRENEURSHIP

To even those with a strong urge to start their own business, it seems ludicrous to give up a job in a comfortable atmosphere, with full benefits and generous bonuses. The fact is, it's still a job — and you still wonder, every day, what it'd be like to work for yourself, not someone else. The following are the five common mental hurdles you must leap over to realise your dream.

You don't have a lot of money in the bank

That's a very good reason to shy away from quitting your job, isn't it? But that just means you need to get a financial plan together. Consult with a financial planner who can help you map out personal and business finance goals. Some local colleges and community centres even offer workshops and classes on financial planning, usually at a minimal cost, so take advantage of them.

Someone mentions the words "business plan" to you, and you stare blankly

A business plan is not the be-all, end-all of starting a business. But it's pretty important. Some think they don't need a business plan if they aren't planning on seeking financing from outside sources. But even if no one but you ever sees your business plan, it's still important. It helps you put your goals in focus and create a written plan of action for your business. It's almost like a detailed to-do list. Plus, you never know where your business will take you. You might get started and find out you need more money than you thought, and that's where that handy business plan comes in.

You don't know anything about bookkeeping

Go ahead and admit it — it's very freeing. Admitting you don't know everything will only make you successful later, because it means you'll have the courage to ask for help. Get all the advice and mentoring you can at this stage. There's no shame in consulting with an accountant, an attorney, a long-time veteran in the field, and so on.

You're not sure you have the dedication it takes to stick with it

There's a simple way to solve this problem: Don't start a business doing something you don't like. If you hate getting up early, starting a coffee shop or a bakery is not for you. If you get impatient around children, don't start a child-care centre or anything else kid-related. You have to love what you're doing when you start a business, or you will not stick with it. It's no different than working in a job you hate.

You're afraid of selling

That's a big one, because if you're an entrepreneur, you're also a salesperson — that is, unless you figure out a way to bring a top-notch salesperson onto your team from the get-go. Chances are, you don't have the money for that yet, so perhaps a better alternative is to psych yourself up to sell. If you believe in your product or service, you'll find the confidence to sell it.

Now quit stalling, and get to work. You've got a business to start.

(Adapted from Microsoft's Small Business Centre website)

Obstacles Inhibiting Entrepreneurship

There are a variety of obstacles which inhibit entrepreneurship: An unwillingness to devote organisational abilities to business purposes, restrictive effects of customer and tradition, lack of response to monetary incentives, low status of businessmen, high risk involved in new enterprises, absence of vertical mobility in the social structure, market imperfections which deny potential entrepreneurs the resources they need for organising new production units, and arbitrary changes in the administration of laws by the government; all of which make the environment too uncertain for entrepreneurs. N.H. Leff has put it as follows: "Absence of entrepreneurship (in LDCs) is generally attributed to alleged socio-cultural rigidities."

Robert L. Garner has observed that "development is a state of mind. People have to develop themselves before they can change their physical environment and this is a slow process... it involves change in relations between classes and races. It requires improvement of governmental organisations and operations; the extension of social institutions, schools, courts and health services. Habits of thoughts and conduct are the most stubborn obstacles to development."

Motivation, abilities and a congenial environment, which promote entrepreneurship, are lacking in India. If the motives and abilities are weak, then it becomes all the more essential to have a more congenial environment. But in India the right environment is also lacking. The stimulation of entrepreneurial abilities is a complicated long-term sociological problem. The social organisations represented by such major institutions as caste, joint family, rural village, and school are more favourable for the development of entrepreneurship. In India all these are not conducive to the development of entrepreneurship.

In underdeveloped countries, the functions of a person in entrepreneurial capacity include innovation, promotion, capital provision and risk-bearing, management, assembling materials and labour.

He lacks the help of markets for components, materials, labour, capital markets which have already standardised products and trained workers. He also lacks the communication network, specialised industrial newspapers and magazines. Sociologists and anthropologists distinguish many types of family in terms of who lays down the law and where the newly married couples live. The vertical family under which young adults continue to live with one set of parents after marriage and contribute earnings to a common pool, has a distinctly inhibiting effect on many of the factors affecting economic development such as mobility, saving, risk-taking, even willingness to work more for higher rewards.

Labour supply curves may bend backwards with respect to wage increases because of limits on economic aspirations, or because the personal incentive is dulled by the necessity to contribute all the work while sharing its fruits. The incentive to take risks in entrepreneurship is blunted in the same way. The institutional framework of a community determines the scope of an individual's efforts. If the institutions are favourable, willingness to make efforts is encouraged and grows; and if this willingness is strong, institution will be remodelled to accommodate these changes.

If religious attitudes and institution encourage discipline, hard work, efficiency, honesty and thrift among its followers, the social climate will impel people to apply their minds to increasing productivity to acquire wealth and to improve their social prestige and power. Most religions, as prevailing in India, consider the existing order of the universe as sacred and try to make people believe that. Ethical beliefs discourage the spirit of enquiry, experimental and scientific outlook among members of the society. A religion which permits and encourages rationality and a scientific attitude is conducive to technological improvements and dynamism in social relations and social attitudes. A desire to discover the causes of things is the most effective motivating force behind inventions, discoveries and innovations in physical, as well as in social spheres.

Box - 8

THE WINNERS

When disaster struck Manohar Krishna, it struck hard. He lost his job, his wife had just given up her job to look after their newborn, and the couple was suddenly asked to vacate their flat. It would have been easy to get frustrated but the Krishnas were made of sterner stuff. Leaving their child in Krishna's brother's care in Mumbai, the couple moved in with friends as they tried to make sense of their lives.

With an enthusiastic accomplice in former colleague Pankaj Malhotra, Krishna decided to set up shop on his own, "We saw our job loss as an opportunity to try out our own ideas", recalls the 38-year old. With about Rs. 2 lakh pulled in primarily from provident fund savings, the two set up Kam Marketing, to sell a plethora of products, including lawn mowers, shoeshine machines and mail-openers.

A Pipedream come true

People find their destines in the most unusual places. This man found his in a clogged drainpipe.

— Naren Karunakaran

(15 July 1998)

Business: drain cleaning systems.
Company: Kam Avida
Launched: 1991
Starting capital: Rs. 2 lakh
Turnover in 1998: Rs. 4 crore.

The search for the perfect product finally ended at Chennai's TTG Industries: the 'Retrieve', a manual drain cleaner. Krishna took up the Pune agency: "I knew that towns everywhere had innumerable choked drains. That meant an opportunity."

In March 1991, they got their first break. The Air Force station in Pune had been struggling with a blocked pipeline for over a month. Krishna took the Retriever over a demo, and was rewarded with a Rs. 12,000 purchase order. In three months, Kam had sold 10 drain cleaners and bagged the agencies for Mumbai and Gujarat. That first full year, Kam's revenues were an impressive Rs. 12 lakh. By year three, they had logged Rs. 1 crore, with a client list that included hotel chains, large corporates and municipal corporations.

At this point, Krishna realised that if TTG withdrew the product, they would be struck again. That's when they roped in Porusasp Dadchanji, a former Merchant Navy engineer, and reinvented themselves as Kam Avida Enviro Engineers Pvt. Ltd. The company began to manufacture a range of drain cleaning systems, from manual units to massive truck-mounted units that cost Rs. 4.20 lakh. In fiscal 1998, revenues touched Rs. 4 crore and markets expanded to Europe Kam had arrived.

Intoxicating as growth is, Krishna's biggest reward is still the heartfelt thank you that comes when the drain finally clears up with a satisfying gurgle.

THE VIEW FROM UP THERE

Adventure-tour operator Rani Puri, the only woman in adventure tourism, has made it to the top in more ways than one. An avid trekker from childhood, she worked at sita travels and Cox & Kind's for seven years before getting frustrated with a schedule that mean she could not trek anymore. She decided to quit and get out on her own.

Puri launched Rucksack Tours in 1986, and for several months, did nothing but dash off letters to all former clients and hope for a response. Then, Puri took her most resolute plunge into business by investing every last paisa in a small office. The 200 sq. ft. office cost Rs. 1.8 lakh. At this point, Puri was fighting several battles — doubts in her ability to succeed, her family's fears and the gender bias prevalent in the market.

The first booking came in 1987, and earned her Rs. 2 lakh. Within a year of launch, turnover had touched Rs. 4 lakh. Former colleague Shashank Gupta, later her husband, joined her now and they set about growing the business. By 1994, turnover had touched Rs. 70 lakh. And Puri feels great about being the woman on top.

The Success of Entrepreneurship

The success of entrepreneurship and enteprise solely depends on innovation, technological advancement and systematic commercialisation for the good of the society. The significance of entrepreneurship as one of the important keys to economic development hardly needs to be emphasised where motivation is present among the people, and entrepreneurial energy acts as stimulant where motivation is lacking, it acts as lubricant.

The development of entrepreneurship in backward and rural areas with a view of broad-basing their existing skills and utilising local raw materials would help attain the growth rate visualised for the industry.

Hitherto much as we wanted to spread small and rural industry in backward and rural areas, the efforts have not been as intensive as we propose doing in the coming years.

Development of local skills, productive utilisation of local raw materials and wastes, and encouragement to entrepreneurs in backward and tribal areas are new directions of future small industry development. In this programme, it is employment and not investment which is an important criterion, so that the facilities of confessional finance and capital subsidy made available to the backward and tribal areas would reach a larger number of persons and thereby provide larger employment. The generalised assistance programmes so far worked out has to be given an appropriate shape according to the condition of the backwardness or tribal social structures of the area. Where necessary, the scheme may have to be modified so that the plan allocations earmarked for the development of backward and tribal areas are utilised.

If enterprises are to expand, entrepreneurship should also develop. If entrepreneurship is important, then organisations and society might find ways to encourage it. Both the enterprise and entrepreneurship need to be nurtured, supported, cultivated, developed and built up. These infrastructural institutional support provide a strong impetus to the development of new enterprise. More importantly, supportive entrepreneurial climate with a 'can do' attitude among the educational service and the professional consultants combined with assistance in training, finance, venture capital, research and development, government incentive and subsidies and local advisory services be created.

Entrepreneurial Management

Entrepreneurship is not "natural", it is not "creative." It is work. Entrepreneurship and innovation can be achieved in any business. But they must be striven for. They can be learnt, but they require effort.

Specifically, entrepreneurial management in an existing business requires policies and practices in four major areas:

1. "The organisation must be made receptive to innovation and willing to perceive change as an opportunity rather than as a threat. It must be organised to do the hard work of the entrepreneur. Policies and practices are needed to create an entrepreneurial climate.
2. Systematic measurement or at least appraisal of a company's performance as entrepreneurs and innovator is mandatory, as well as built-in, learning to improve performance.

3. Entrepreneurial management requires specific practices pertaining to organisational structure, to staffing and managing, and to compensation, incentives and rewards.
4. There are some "don'ts", things not to do in entrepreneurial management:
   (*a*) not to mix managerial units and entrepreneurial ones, and
   (*b*) innovative efforts that take the existing business out of its own field are rarely successful. Innovation should not be "diversification."

A business that wants to be able to innovate, wants to have a chance to succeed and prosper in a time of rapid change, has to build entrepreneurial management into its own system. It has to adopt policies that create throughout the entire organisation the desire to innovate and the habits of entrepreneurship and innovation.

The Next Big Leap

By the first phase of liberalization, modern management practices began to establish themselves in some family-run firm. As society and the economy changed, it was no longer enough to keep old firms going: it was obvious they needed to be recreated to fit the new moulds.

The biggest warning to the business family was served by the rise of the Indian middle class. With new money and new desires borne on satellite television, new markets were created by a rising tide of entrepreneurs. Many were people who came from communities not previously known for entrepreneurship. They were sons of austere middle-class clerks, bankers, professionals and farmers.

The first wave of entrepreneurship spread to small towns where business folk churning out things like bicycle parts and gaskets began to reach out to the world beyond. They created some of the markets we take for granted today: from housing finance to cheap television sets to private airlines. They were pathbreakers.

But the flaws of liberalisation also meant that to be really successful, the new breed of entrepreneur need to know how to work the system. The result is that many of the people who came out of nowhere since the late 1980s excel at schmoozing their way to the top.

It is time for all of India's entrepreneurs, new and old, to shrug off the chains — perceived or otherwise. While there are a lot of infrastructural problems that must be solved, there is no denying the fact that we need to do much more ourselves. Thinking global is not just about setting up operations in other countries or acquiring companies. It is about having the passion, the zeal, the confidence to beat anybody and everybody, whether at home or in the new markets beyond our shores.

Every point of growth that we witness today is qualitatively better than all the growth we witnessed in the era since Independence. That's because everything the Indian entrepreneur achieves today is in the face of increasing competition.

Vision for Future

The entrepreneurship that contributes in a modest way to critical economic and social needs of the country and always strive to attain global leadership in all of its major initiative. This is the vision for future.

Pursuing this vision, over the next few years, entrepreneurs will pursue a strategy of:

- Reinforcing competitive advantage of existing business through new capacities and synergistic acquisitions.
- Scaling sizeable opportunities in the core sectors.
- Forward integrating into retailing transportation fuels and creating new customer experiences.
- Addressing the significant information and communications market opportunity in India and in the world.
- Leverage its strong balance sheet, cash flows and managerial capacity to create value by adding new capacities, acquisitions and turnaround of under performing assets.
- Developing strategic alliances in technology and product-market domains with global majors.
- Fostering new higher education institutions for knowledge creation and sharing.
- Leveraging its formidable strengths beyond Indian borders.
- Reorienting the best practices to enhance productivity and quality (Q).
- In addition to manufacturing products venture into developing manufacturing systems.
- From having a manufacturing orientation to providing technical solutions.
- From being an intermediate goods producer to being a final goods and services provider.
- From licensing technology to developing technology.
- From being an intellectual property user to an intellectual property creator.
- In addition to operating in India to being a global company.
- From building financial equity to fostering social equity.

This change will entail creating new organisational competencies such as:

- Creating a customer-centric organisation.
- Developing new products and technologies.
- Exploring and producing new products to meet the new generation's expectations.
- Fostering and sustaining globally oriented management talent.
- Training the human resources to harness the opportunities.
- Encouraging intrapreneurship.
- Focusing on Research and Development for sustainable development.
- Imbibing new technology to enhance the value of the product.
- Focusing on business ethics in managing the enterprises.
- Managing customer-oriented supply chains.
- Developing and protecting intellectual capital.
- Managing strategic technology and product-market relationships.
- Managing diversity in businesses, technologies, export markets and people is the primary challenge for Reliance, as it marches ahead in realising its vision.

Conclusion

Entrepreneurship is an attitude of mind which can take risks but calculated ones; a true entrepreneur is one who can see possibilities in a given situation where others see none and has the patience to work out the idea into a scheme to which financial support can be provided. It is one of the catalytic activities fostering initiative, promoting and maintaining economic activities for the production and distribution of wealth. The stimulation of entrepreneurship is a function of both internal and external variables. In developing countries, there is no dearth of ideas, but there is a real scarcity of men with the right blend of vision and practical sense to become successful entrepreneurs. The objective of the programme is to identify such people and to provide them with the support needed to make them a success. They then become 'demonstration models' to the community; and once the right climate is generated, entrepreneurship becomes a way of life.

Industrial growth in a country is achieved through a 'mix' of large and small industries; the entrepreneurship for the former comes through the large companies often in collaboration with the multinationals. Simultaneously, economic growth also depends upon the level of development and use of information systems in the country.

In fact, the small-scale industry sector is considered as an ideal nursery for the rapid growth and development of entrepreneurship. But, alas, there are only a handful of entrepreneurs in the true sense of the term in this sector. The men who will set up small industry units have to come from within the country and the community; they are 'local' in the true sense and their success, therefore, has a much greater impact on generating the right climate for successful entrepreneurship.

Programmes for developing entrepreneurship must recognise that, ultimately, the change they seek to induce is attitudinal; it is more than just providing information, land or money. It is to provide new goals so that a motivated young person is no longer content to take up a secure job which will assure him a modest income, but seeks bigger challenges in setting up and running his own business. The risks are greater but so are the rewards, both in a monetary sense and psychologically, in the feeling of confidence and pride it generates in the person. It is through the effort of such persons that a small industry can become a dynamic sector of the economy and hence, the effort made to develop such persons is well worth the money and labour. The need of the hour is the growth of entrepreneurship in the country to accelerate the process of economic growth. According to Peter Drucker, the entrepreneurial strategy is as important as purposeful innovation and entrepreneurial management.' In a way society-needs entreprenurship on a normal, steady and an ongoing basis. Just as management has become the specific organ of all contemporary institutions, and the integrating organ of our society and of organisations, so innovation and entrepreneurship have to become an integral life-sustaining activity in our organisations, our economy and our society.

This requires of executives in all institutions to make innovation and entrepreneurship a normal, ongoing, *everyday activity, a perceptive in their own work and in that of their organisation. Entrepreneurship is the cornerstone of the emerging economic scene in the world.*

CASE STUDIES

Sarda Plywood

'To be the best rather the biggest.'

Sarda Plywood was incorporated by a young, innovative entrepreneur Shri P. D. Chitlangia way back in 1964. He was a great visionary and envisioned that wood would be a scarce raw material in furture. Therefore, he started the production of plywood and block boards. He set up the first factory of the Group at Jeypore (Assam), in the timber rich havens of the Northeast.

Durobord was the flagship brand of the company. Buoyed by the huge commercial success of this brand, the company grew from strength to strength, and slowly but surely captured the plywood market in India, with strongholds in northern and western India.

In the late 1980s the mantle of responsibility shifted from Shri P. D. Chitlangia to his two sons Jaydeep Chitlangia and Sudeep Chitlangia. Both of them were hands-on practitioners and well versed with the market dynamics, and the demands of the consumer. It was under their expertise that the company started manufacturing brand, which encompassed wide areas of application. Whatever the product or service the emphasis was always on quality.

Through the years, Sarda has instituted their very own demanding performance standards, realising that quality is solely defined from the customer's perspective. This single focus commitment of providing the consumer with the finest quality plywood at a reasonable price has held the company in good stead over the years. All products are manufactured using state of the art technology, are ISI certified, and made to go through stringent quality control tests. Every stage of the manufacturing process is painstakingly supervised and rigid quality control tests are applied, to ensure excellence in the final product.

In 1996, the Supreme Court ruling dealt a severe blow to the company. At that point of time the company was the single largest veneer factory in the country, and the sudden closure of the factory was a huge setback for its proprietors. During the next few years, the company regrouped and opened a state of the art factory at Rajkot and an ancillary unit at Nagpur.

Today the Sarda Group has spread its roots far and wide in the country. From its humble beginnings in the Northeast, the Group has blossomed into a diversified business group, encompassing several manufacturing activities. It has a plethora to brands under its umbrella, which have over the years created a niche for themselves in their respective segments. Durobord, Pumaply, Duroply, Natures' Signature to name just a few. Moreover, all these products are made from 100 per cent imported raw materials.

As the new millennium unfolds, Sarda Plywood looks forward with confidence, and the past merely hints at the accomplishments they are confident of seeing in future.

Vista Flooring

Vista Levoler is a leading interior fashion products manufacturer, which offers a great variety of creative opportunities. It believes in meeting the high and ever changing demand of its customers, innovation and introduction of new products and concepts. One can choose from a wide range of stylish floorings from Vista Floor Fashions which is a trusted household name in the creation of innumerable outstanding products available in a variety in natural wood designs, which are easy to install and maintain. A commitment towards providing complete solution in the field of interior factions, it has introduced Vista laminated wooden flooring.

Vista laminate wooden flouring gives a warm, natural, classy, and a distinctive look to interiors. It is made of high density fiber board, with high performance melamine laminate, and high abrasive silica for wear resistance on the top and melamine polymer film to back it. Vista is the lone laminate flooring that comes with unique underlay material **"Hush Factor"**, a special engineered material that reduces the noise level by absorbing sound, in interiors. Thermal resistance helps to keep interiors cool in summer and warm in winters. The flooring is available in two ranges: the Classic collection comes with 12 decors at a cost of Rs. 140 per sq. ft. (for heavy residential and moderate commercial applications) and the Royal collection with six decors at a cost of Rs. 160 per sq ft. (for heavy residential and general commercial applications).

Vista recently launched Vista Valls laminate wooden ceiling and wall paneling with Vista Exotic, the economy range of laminate wooden flooring. The products cost around Rs. 111 per sq. ft.

These latest products are meant for new constructions and renovations of both residential as well as commercial use. In the commercial sector, the products meant for clubs, hotels, restaurants, auditoriums, small offices, conference halls, gymnasium and aerobic centres. Happy shopping!

A ONE-WOMAN REVOLUTION, SEWA

Businesswoman of the Year

When a group of women workers from the informal sector in Ahmedabad dared to form a union in the early 1970s, little did they know that they were penning history. Even as cynics scoffed, these women went ahead to set up the Self Employed Women's Association (Sewa). They were led singularly by the courage and conviction of Ela Bhatt, the founder general secretary of the association. What began then as a trade union in small numbers is today the country's largest primary union with over seven lakh members. It is revered as one of the exemplary economic revolutions of the world and Elaben had since build over 18 innovative market institutions for the women of India.

These institutions have been instrumental in providing market access to thousands of small and medium businesswomen in India. They epitomise a Utopian blend of grandness of scale coupled with social values and viable financial principles.

Ela Bhatt

One may call Sewa a trade union for record's sake. But more than that, it is a movement which imbibes the essence of the labour movement, the women's movement and the co-operative movement. As is rightly said. It is 'difficult to imagine a solution to a problem which people think does not exist.' However, Elaben defined the quandaries of vendors, hawkers, junk-smiths, garment makers *et al.* and charted the path for their deliverance. In her own words, "Capital formation at the grassroots is a must for women to gain equal access and stake in national wealth building. These institutions save, pool, transfer and generate wealth for and with women."

To know the institutions better, Elaben has built a business development federation of 86 women's service co-operatives with an annual turnover of Rs. 18 crore. She has built six district producers' federations of 1,200 self-help groups covering three lakh rural women workers and a co-operative saving bank of two lakh women entrepreneurs, with a turnover of Rs. 400 crore. There is also a maternal and health insurance programme covering one lakh home-based producers and other women; a national trade facilitation centre for 40,000 agriculture and non-farm rural women; a direct market outlet for 35,000 women artisans, with a turnover of Rs. 60 crore; and women's banking services in 18 states reaching 80,000 women with a Rs. 30-crore credit each year through 150 NGOs. There is a quality improvement network of 17 key micro-credit providers in India, a women's business development service and so on. Not surprisingly Ms. Bhatt was conferred the Millennium Lifetime Achievement Award by FICCI, a representative body of trade and industry, in '00.

Trained in English literature and law Ms. Bhatt taught at SNDT University before moving on to head the women's wing of the Textile Labour Association (TLA) during the 1960s. TLA's original purpose was to assist women belonging to households of mill workers and was focused largely on training and welfare activities. On an appeal from women workers, it was decided to set up a trade union for self-employed women and Sewa was born in December 1971. Sewa later moved out of the aegis of TLA and is today perhaps a larger entity than its parent.

Awards like the Ramon Magsaysay Award for 'Community Leadership' in 1977; the Susan B. Anthony Award for National Integration in 1982; the Right Livelihood Award for Changing the Human Environment in 1984; and the Women in Creation Award from Alliance de Femme of Paris in 1990 have all celebrated the vision of Ms. Bhatt. She was awarded the Padmashree in 1985 and Padmabhushan in 1986.

ENTREPRENEUR OF THE YEAR

You could just call him 'Mr Indian Coffee.' Better known for setting up the country's first fine coffee-cafe chain under the Cafe Coffee Day banner, he is today present in every phase of Indian coffee — from cultivation to consumption. The cuppa you drink at Cafe Coffee Day could be from berries that grow on the 5,000 acres his family owns in the coffee growing heartland of Karnataka. And they may have been processed in the family's own curing works.

He set up India's first fine coffee cafe on Bangalore's Brigade Road in 1996. Today, there are 125. In 1995, he started retailing coffee through 30 outlets where beans were roasted and ground before the consumer. Today, there are 350. He is one of India's leading coffee exporters, shipping out around 20,000 tonnes a year under the holding company Amalgamated Bean Coffee Trading (ABCL). His latest foray is into the packet filter-coffee market.

Even for such a stimulating beverage, that's a lot of coffee. His family has been growing coffee for 120 years, but it's 42-year-old V G. Siddhartha who has gone places with the berry. *His philosophy:* value-add at every stage.

The liberalisation of coffee-marketing India, which began in 1992, gave Siddhartha an opportunity he was hungry for. For 50 years from 1942, coffee growers had to pool their beans with the Coffee Board, a system which mitigated against quality upgradation. In 1992, growers were permitted to sell up to 20% of their produce under an internal sales-quota. That process gained momentum and by 1996, pooling with the Coffee Board was phased out.

Siddhartha was quick off the mark. In 1993, he set up ABCL. Within a few years, ABCL had become one of the country's leading coffee exporters, helped by the boom in global prices following the mid-1994 frost in Brazil, the world's leading coffee producer. India's coffer-export business took off, through a bulk of shipments was in a bean and green form. Coffee is, however, one of the most price-volatile commodities globally. To insulate against this, Siddhartha realised he had to brand coffee. In 1995, ABCL launched what were then known as Coffee Points where the customer in Bangalore and Chennai could buy freshly ground and roasted coffee. In 1996, he launched the first fine coffee cafe on Bangalore's Brigade Road combining coffee drinking with surfing the net.

Today, the business model is no longer just an internet-and-coffee-based one. Everything is focused on the youth market in an attempt to live up to Cafe Coffee Day's promise that 'A lot can happen over a cup of coffee!'.

Through its four divisions — exports, vending machines, retail points, and cafes — ABCL has helped pioneer India's coffee revolution. The 10-year-old ABCL, which ended its first year of operations with a turnover of Rs. 10 crore, crossed the Rs. 200-crore mark for, 02-03 and expects to touch Rs. 250 crore for the current fiscal. If net profits have not risen in tandem (Rs. 1 crore for the first year of operations to Rs. 3 crore for this fiscal), it could be due to the frenetic pace of expansion over the past 30 months. However, Siddhartha feels numbers alone cannot convey the excitement of these years.

Annexure - 1

CODE OF BUSINESS PRINCIPLES

Standard of Conduct

We conduct our operations with honesty, integrity and openness, and with respect for the human rights and interests of our employees. We shall similarly respect the legitimate interests of those with whom we have relationships.

Obeying the Law

Companies and employees are required to comply with the laws and regulations of the countries in which we operate.

Employees

The Enterprise is committed to diversity in a working environment where there is mutual trust and respect and where everyone feels responsible for the performance and reputation of our company. We will recruit, employ and promote employees on the sole basis of the qualifications and abilities needed for the work to be performed. We are committed to safe and healthy working conditions for all employees. We will not use any form of forced, compulsory or child labour. We are committed to working with employees to develop and enhance each individual's skills and capabilities. We respect the dignity of the individual and the right of employees to freedom of association. We will maintain good communications with employees through company based information and consultation procedures.

Consumers

The Enterprise is committed to providing branded products and services which consistently offer value in terms of price and quality, and which are safe for their intended use. Products and services will be accurately and properly labelled, advertised and communicated.

Shareholders

The Enterprise will conduct its operations in accordance with internationally accepted principles of good corporate governance. We will provide timely, regular and reliable information on our activities, structure, financial situation and performance to all shareholders.

Business Partners

The Enterprise is committed to establishing mutually beneficial relations with our suppliers, customers and business partners. In our business dealings we expect our partners to adhere to business principles consistent with our own.

Community Involvement

The Enterprise strives to be a trusted corporate citizen and, as an integral part of society, to fulfill our responsibilities to the societies and communities in which we operate.

Public Activities

The Enterprise is encouraged to promote and defend their legitimate business interests. Unilever will co-operate with governments and other organisations, both directly and through bodies such as trade associations, in the development of proposed legislation and other regulations which may affect legitimate business interests. Unilever neither supports political parties nor contributes to the funds of groups whose activities are calculated to promote party interests.

The Environment

The Entrepreneur is committed to making continuous improvements in the management of our environmental impact and to the longer-term goal of developing a sustainable business. Unilever will work in partnership with others to promote environmental care, increase understanding of environmental issues and disseminate good practice.

Annexure - 2

WEALTH AND LEGACY

Immortality can be bought; Alfred Nobel used his 'WILL' to do it. What would Bill Gates do? Would the world's richest man use his 'will and final testament' as the ultimate software tool to empower the human individual? Would his claim to global leadership, eventually, be less about the man-machine interface, and more about the mind he devotes to his legacy?

Gates' is a mind that has given him $46.6 billion (over Rs. 2 lakh crore) in just a quarter of a century. He owns about a tenth of Microsoft. He has three children, Jennifer, Rory and Phoebe — and he intends leaving them $10 million (Rs. 45 crore) each in his will. About 0.02 per cent, each. "I don't think it would be very useful for my children if they learn about life having so much money," Gates is on record as saying. The man also hopes to give away most of his wealth during his own lifetime, to make the world 'measurably healthier'. Here's a businessman, you'd think, who considers his own do-good efforts more effective than anything 'the people' can undertake. But in 2001, Gates intervened with a resounding 'No!' in the debate raging in the US over whether 'estate tax'-by which the government takes more than half a wealthy person's wealth upon demise-should be abolished. Pay the country back, he urged, for enabling your wealth. "A hypothetical case may illustrate what I mean: suppose two foetuses are summoned to appear before God, and he tells them that they are the next two births on Earth and will go-one to Ethiopia and one to the US. He goes on to say that his treasury is running a bit low, and he wants them to help replenish it, so he is going to auction off the opportunity to be born in the US. He asks each of them to write down and hand him a sheet on which they set forth the per cent of the net worth they will have when they die which they will commit to bequeath to God's treasury. He promises that the one who writes down the highest number will be born in the US. Would either of them put down a number as low as 55 per cent?"

A cleverly reasoned argument. But of obvious US-conception, ironically. In poor countries, giving children a headstart is needed just to give them a global 'equal start'. So, will Gates' notions of a good legacy win a global following? It's still open to debate. Hypothetically, it would take something that can resound with true intellectual power for long after he's gone.

Innovation

In our scientific innovation to meet consumer needs we will respect the concerns of our consumers and of society. We will work on the basis of sound science, applying rigorous standards of product safety

Competition

The Entrepreneur believes in vigorous yet fair competition and supports the development of appropriate competition laws. Unilever companies and employees will conduct their operations in accordance with the principles of fair competition and all applicable regulations.

Business Integrity

The Entrepreneur does not give or receive, whether directly or indirectly, bribes or other improper advantages for business or financial gain. No employee may offer, give or receive any gift or payment which is, or may be construed as being, a bribe. Any demand for, or offer of, a bribe must be rejected immediately and reported to management. Unilever accounting records and supporting documents must accurately describe and reflect the nature of the underlying transactions. No undisclosed or unrecorded account, fund or asset will be established or maintained.

Conflicts of Interests

All employees are expected to avoid personal activities and financial interests which could conflict with their responsibilities to the company. Unilever employees must not seek gain for themselves or others through misuse of their positions.

Compliance-Monitoring-Reporting

Compliance with these principles is an essential element in our business success.

Annexure - 3

POLICY OPTIONS TO PROMOTE ENTREPRENEURSHIP

The OECD recently conducted an in-depth study of the policies that foster entrepreneurship in five countries — Australia, The Netherlands, Spain, Sweden, and the United States. The following presents some of its broad policy guidelines that can be applied to developing countries as well. Each country needs to examine how these could best be applied within its own situation.

Broad Policy Guidelines

Examine the overall institutional framework within which economic activity takes place in order to establish whether it provides maximum scope for entrepreneurship to flourish. In particular:

- Identify and dismantle remaining barriers to competition which limit the incentives of enterprises to innovate and perform more dynamically. Promote competition in all sectors of the economy, including the provision of public services. Provide effective protection of intellectual property.

- Allow scope for flexible employment contracts to be negotiated, with remuneration arrangements and working conditions that are well adapted to the needs of dynamic enterprises. Relax employment protection measures that inhibit restructuring or discourage entrepreneurs from taking on new workers.
- Examine the costs of complying with government-imposed administrative or regulatory requirements and identify where reductions could be made, either by removing the requirements to comply or by reducing the administrative burden involved (including through better coordination among various government agencies).
- Examine the overall effects of the tax system on entrepreneurship, and identify features that discourage entrepreneurs or the financing of entrepreneurial activity. Ensure that the tax system is transparent and that compliance is straight forward.
- Review and simplify the registration procedures required to create a business. Ensure that firms are able to close quickly should they wish to do so.
- Ensure that personal bankruptcy legislation provides an appropriate balance between encouraging risk-taking and protecting creditors.
- Re-examine the effects that social insurance provisions may have on encouraging or discouraging would-be entrepreneurs.

Ensure that specific programs designed to foster entrepreneurship operate as part of an integrated and coherent strategy that complements the framework conditions. In particular:

- Avoid policies that stem from a too-narrow definition of entrepreneurship (*e.g.*, that entrepreneurship is only about start-ups or only about high-technology) and which may divert attention from getting the broader economic policy settings right.
- Widen the target population for entrepreneurship programs, where possible, to attract the participation of women, the young and minorities.
- Undertake regular and comprehensive evaluation of programs, and ensure that evaluation findings are acted on.

Improve the effectiveness of entrepreneurship programs by drawing on the knowledge of local level of government. In particular:

- Ensure that resources for programs to foster entrepreneurship are decentralised where appropriate in order to better tailor programs to the specific needs of an area and its business.
- Provide regular opportunities to exchange information at a national level on the experiences of local authorities in designing and implementing entrepreneurship programs.
- Seek to identify and implement low-cost and effective programs with minimal distortionary effects on market incentives. For example:
- Promote public awareness of entrepreneurship and examine the role the education system could play in developing entrepreneurial skills and attitudes.

- Increase opportunities for the unemployed to create their own jobs through self-employment schemes.
- Facilitate networking among firms in order to foster a culture of mutual cooperation and risk-taking
- Promote the entrepreneurial non-profit sector by contracting-out where possible the delivery of public service that meet pressing demands in economic and social development.

OECD, *Fostering Entrepreneurshjp,* 1998. pp. 28-30. Used with permission of OECD.

❐ ❐ ❐

"Embarking upon 'new combinations' of the factors of production — which he succinctly terms innovation — the entrepreneur activates the economy to a new level of development. the concept of innovation and its corollary development embraces five functions: (1) introduction of a new good, (2) introduction of a new method of production, (3) opening of a new market, (4) conquest of a new source of supply of raw materials and (5) carrying out of a new organisation of any industry..."

FOUR

Theories of Entrepreneurship

Introduction

The concept and theories of entrepreneurship evolved over more than two centuries have undergone major changes. Yet the concept of entrepreneurship is not clear. As the concept of entrepreneurship is complex in its content, it is influenced by not only economical aspects, but also by sociological, political, psychological, ethical, religious and cultural values. The concept also bears, testimony to courage, creativity, determination, networking, hard working etc. Over the years the social scientists have interpreted the phenomenon of entrepreneurship differently in accordance with their perception and economic environment.

A coordinated and comprehensive theory of entrepreneurship is yet to come. Meanwhile let us understand the important theories of entrepreneurship propounded by social thinkers during the last two centuries.

The distinctive features of entrepreneurship over the years are:

1. Innovation,
2. A function of high achievement,
3. Organisation building,
4. Group level activities,
5. Managerial skills and leadership,
6. Gap filling,
7. Status with drawal,

8. Entrepreneurial supply, and
9. Entrepreneurship — an emerging class

Entrepreneurship as a process has and is undergoing changes in keeping with the continued 6 changes in different fields. In keeping with these changes, different theories of entrepreneurship have been evolved by different thinkers at different times. It is a continuously evolving process of *change*.

Entrepreneurship in Developing Countries

Among the many definitions of the entrepreneur, that which distinguishes him as a person who undertakes to organise, manage and assume the risk of running a factory is the one generally adopted in the region. Small enterprises, like entrepreneurship, cannot be defined specifically. The concept is variously understood in different countries depending on the prevailing economic and social conditions. Generally, the definition is based on two criteria: *quantitative*, which includes the size of the company in terms of number of workers, consumption of energy, capitalisation or value of sales; and *qualitative*, which refers to the organisation and management of the enterprise, methods of production or influence on the market.

Entrepreneurship Stimulants

A variety of social, economic, political and cultural factors are stimulating entrepreneurial activity and consequently generating economic development. These stimulants are as follows:

1. An increasing focus on capital formation. Availability of capital is a stimulant to an entrepreneur to start a new firm and/or give birth to a new idea.
2. The ability to transform scientific and technical developments through new institutional development.
3. The supportive government programmes.
4. Availability of required training and inputs.
5. A collaborative relationship between business and research and their direct attempts to transfer technology to the market place will be an opportunity for entrepreneurs who commercialise their ideas.
6. Finally, an endeavour to create an environment conducive to innovation will provide a much-needed stimulant to entrepreneurial activities.

Entrepreneurship and Economic Growth

Economic development of any region is an outcome of purposeful human activity. Men assume various roles in the development process, namely, as organiser of human capital, natural material resources, worker and consumer. He stands at the centre of the whole process of economic development. According to Schumpeter, economic development consists of "employing resources in a different way", bringing in a new combination of means of production. The entrepreneur looks for ideas and puts them into effect for economic development.

According to Baumol, entrepreneur is a Schumpeterian innovator and something more than a leader. The entrepreneur, according to him, occupies a crucial place in the process of economic development.

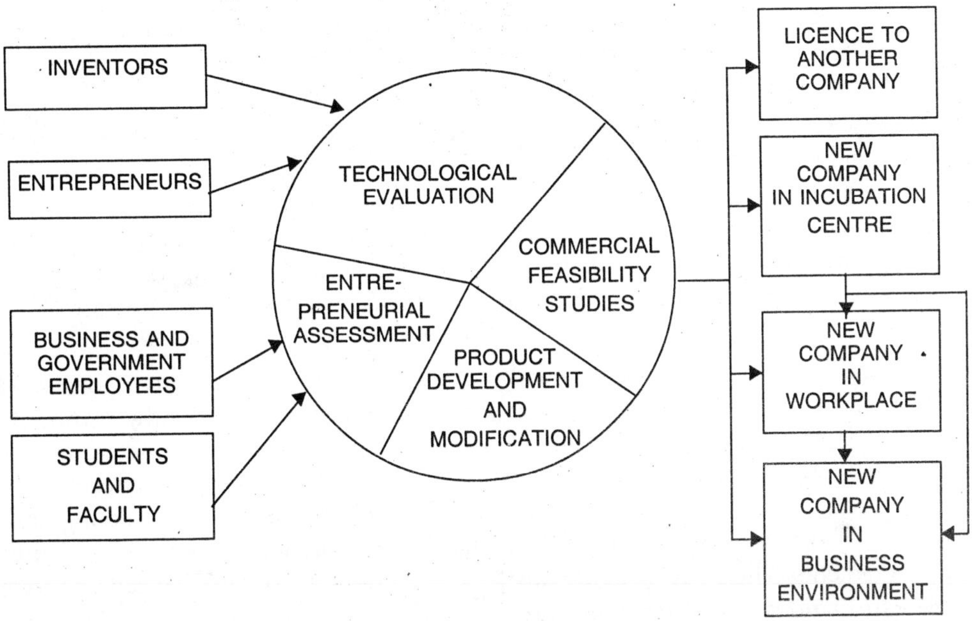

Fig. 1: Innovation Centre

Joseph A. Schumpeter (1934) for the first time put the human agent at the centre of the process of economic development and assigned a critical role to entrepreneurship in his theory of economic development. According to Schumpeter "Entrepreneurship is essentially a creative activity or it is an innovative function. The process of innovation may be in the form of *(a)* Introduction of new product, *(b)* Use of new method of production, *(c)* Opening of new market, *(d)* The conquest of new source of supplying raw material or *(e)* A new form of organisation." Hence he depicted an entrepreneur not only a premier agent of production who brings together all factors of production but also provides a sound management and control for the survival as well as the growth of the production unit.

Schumpeter further says that economic growth depends on the rate of applied technical progress (*i.e.,* innovation) and rate of technical progress in the economic field which in turn depends on the supply of entrepreneurs in the society. Thus, the entrepreneur is the agent of change in society.

In the Schumpeterian model, entrepreneur is an innovator, and the existence of "innovative entrepreneurs" depends on the necessary social and economic overheads. These economic and social overheads are very poor in backward regions which cause a short supply of entrepreneurs. In this connection, we can refer to David McClelland who explained the development of entrepreneurship in terms of human motivation to achieve or need for achievement (n Ach), his hypothesis is that a society with a generally high level of achievement will produce more energetic entrepreneurs, who in turn will accelerate the process of economic development.

In the Indian context, entrepreneurship has yet another dimension. An entrepreneur may not necessarily be in innovator "but an "imitator" who would copy the organisation, technology, products of innovators from other developed regions. His role as an imitator is likely to be guided and controlled by various constraints and conditions peculiar to his area of operation and the factors under which he conducts his minimal modest industrial activity.

Other social scientists, notably Max Weber, have talked of the importance of entrepreneurship and expressed the view that creative and entrepreneurial energies are generated by the adoption of exogenously supplied beliefs which in turn produce intense efforts in occupational pursuits and accumulation of productive assets leading to the manufacture of goods and service. According to him, entrepreneurs are a product of the particular social conditions in which they live and it is social conditions in which they live and it is the society which shapes the personality of individual entrepreneurs.

John Kunkel believes that the behavioural pattern of individuals is important for development and such a pattern can be influenced by external stimulus so as to alter it in the manner we want it. In other words, if we want more people in society to behave as entrepreneurs, we can bring about such behaviour on their part by appropriate alterations in the social environment so as to influence them to take to entrepreneurial pursuits. Like Weber, Cocharan and Young underscore the importance of the role society plays in shaping the entrepreneurial personality and consider the scarce ingredients which are essential in the emergence of potential entrepreneurs cultural values, role expectations, social tensions and inter-group relations in society. Entrepreneurs are an important source of economic development. It becomes imperative that there exists a motivational training programme including measures to modify the environment to stimulate entrepreneurial behaviour among individuals. There are thinkers who believe that the "Schumpeterian entrepreneurs are needed in underdeveloped countries for rapid economic development" is only through entrepreneurs that substantial development can be brought about.

Entrepreneurship and Economic Systems

Entrepreneurship includes the existence of the spirit of venturing into new enterprises through innovations, creation and translation of such spirit into reality in the various fields of industry and commerce by individuals with entrepreneurial qualities and with an intense desire for accomplishment or achievement in this field.

Entrepreneurship plays an important role in the economic system, which determines the nature and scope of this field. Economic systems grow and take shape under the influence of industrial policy, economic policy, and the socio-political and cultural ideas of the people. Entrepreneurship gives a fillip to new organisational forms and the economy has to adjust to these demands. However, changes in the structure of the economy bring about economic reforms which determine other factors affecting the economy. Economic systems is a basic structure of capitalism, socialism and mixed economy in which a certain level of entrepreneurship is found.

Capitalism: Capitalism has 'freedom' as its landmark. Free enterprise, freedom to save or to invest, free and healthy competition, lack of the dominance of central plan and consumer's sovereignty are the main features that distinguish capitalism from other economic systems. In a free enterprise economy, the problem of what to produce is solved by the price mechanism. The goods are bought and sold in the market at a price which is freely determined by the equality between demand for and supply of goods with reference to the cost of production. It is for this reason that entrepreneurship fully commands a price and market mechanism. On the basis of this, the entrepreneur also has the controls of the production and distribution of goods by mobilising the resources to maximise his profit. Profit motive is the main aim of the entrepreneur in a free market mechanism under capitalism. He also distributes the goods according to the different market conditions both in domestic and overseas markets and therefore, we find he is a competitor or monopolist or a monopolistic competitor in the home market. Besides, he is a cut-throat competitor in the overseas market where he allocated the amount of goods and determines the price according to his capacity to unload goods — a special case of discriminating monopoly.

Socialism: Private entrepreneurship does not contribute much to an economic system but it becomes the responsibility of the economic and financial experts in the Central Authority to strategise the exploitation of resources and organise an equitable distribution of goods without any profit motive but for the social good.

Entrepreneurship exists in the form of a body consisting of the representatives nominated by the government to frame the plans for the proper mobilisation of resources, their allocation and re-allocation so that most of the resources channelised towards industries of national importance. It is therefore, for entrepreneur who has a complete control over the resources, the production of the goods according to the needs of the people and their distribution in the internal *vis-a-vis* external market. As socialism is contrary to capitalism or mixed economy, all such responsibilities are not shared by the private entrepreneur and hence his role under socialism is negligible.

Mixed Economy: The entrepreneurs also play an important role in the production and distribution of goods in a mixed economy. The basic characteristics of this economy is that the government undertakes the production of mostly capital goods while the production of consumer goods is left to the private enterprises and hence they are equally responsible for the uplift of the people because they produce not only luxuries and comforts but also goods of basic requirements of the people. Like a capitalist economy, mixed economy also tries to solve the basic problems with the help of the price mechanism. But where the price mechanism fails to achieve the desired result, the state tries to intervene in order to find a better solution to the various problems. When the problem of production is not solved satisfactorily by the private entrepreneur, the state tries to increase the production of essential goods and discourages that of less essential or non-essential goods. It does so by producing defence goods itself as also some basic goods like iron, steel and cement etc. and also by encouraging the private producers to increase the production of essentials like food, clothing, housing etc. In a mixed economy, the government does a good deal to encourage the production of most essential goods and in case their production still lags behind, it may itself undertake their production and increase it by giving it top priority in its economic programme.

In a mixed economy, the government also tries to remove the evil of monopoly capitalism through restrictions. It may curb the growth of monopolies and initiate workable competition which is essential for the optimum use of the available resources. Mixed economy tries to solve the problem of distribution of goods and services in a better way than the capitalist economy. The government tries to level up the incomes of the poor people and level down those of the rich people. This is done by fiscal measures, fixation of minimum wages and salaries and improvements in the environment by the people.

The role played by an entrepreneur is significantly important in a mixed economy as it permits the growth of both the public and the private sector. In the private sector, profit motive acts as an incentive to the entrepreneur and market mechanism plays its own role. This establishes the role of entrepreneur in the mixed economy.

Entrepreneurship has great importance in various economic systems. It is all the more important under capitalism and mixed economy where not only the responsibilities of entrepreneur in production and distribution are recognised but the objective of growth of business and profit maximisation is also attained. Therefore, the importance of entrepreneurship stands beyond challenge in every economic system except under socialism where it appears in a different form. Yet, entrepreneurship prevails in all economic systems in one form or the other.

AN ENTREPRENEURIAL PERSPECTIVE

17th century	:	Undertakers of risks of new enterprise, bore the risks of profit or loss.
1755 Richard Cantillon (A French Economist)	:	An entrepreneur is a person who pays a certain price for a product to resell it at an uncertain price, thereby making decisions about obtaining and using resources while consequently assuming the risk of enterprise.
1776 Adam Smith	:	Entrepreneur is an individual who undertook the formation of an organisation for commercial purposes.
1803 Jean Baptist Say (French Economist)	:	Entrepreneur is one who possessed certain arts and skills of creating new economic enterprises.
1848 John Stuart Mill (1806-1873)	:	Entrepreneur is the 'fourth factor' of economic endeavour and the ultimate owner of a commercial enterprise.
1871 Carl Menger (Austria) (1840-1921)	:	The entrepreneur is the change agent who transforms resources into useful goods and services, often creating the circumstances that lead to industrial growth.

In the 19th century, entrepreneurs were the "Captains of Industry" the risk takers, the decision makers, the individuals who aspired to wealth and who gathered and managed resources to create new enterprises.

1934 Joseph Alois Schumpeter: (1883-1950) (Austrian)	:	The entrepreneur seeks to reform or revolutionise the pattern of production by exploiting an invention or more generally, an untried technological possibility for producing a new commodity or producing and old one in a new way, by opening up a new order for products.... Entrepreneurship, as defined, essentially consists in doing things that are not generally done in the ordinary course of human routine.

1984 Robert Ronstadt	:	Entrepreneurship is the dynamic process of creating incremental wealth. This wealth is created by individuals who assume the major risks in terms of equity, time, and/or career commitment of providing value for some or product or service. The product or service itself may or may not be new or unique but value must somehow be infused by the entrepreneur by securing and allocating the necessary skills and resources.

Theories of Entrepreneurship

Theories of Entrepreneurship are broadly classified into economic, psychological, sociological and cultural.

The static approach of the emerging Neo-classical school did not readily accommodate a concept with such dynamic connotations as entrepreneur. Alfred Marshall, for example, laid much more stress on the routine activities of management and superintendence than he did on the innovative activity of the entrepreneur.

The phenomenon of entrepreneurship development has been viewed, explained and interpreted differently by social scientists. Among those who have stressed on the routine activities of management and superintendence than he did on the innovative activity of the entrepreneur.

The phenomenon of entrepreneurship development has been viewed, explained and interpreted differently by social scientists. Among those who have stressed on the psychological aspects as contributing to entrepreneurial success are Joseph Schumpeter, McClelland, Hagen and Kunkal.

Entrepreneurship is inhibited by the social system, which denies opportunities for creative facilities. "The forces of custom, the rigidity of status and the district of new ideas and of the exercise of intellectual curiosity, combine to create an atmosphere inimical to experiment and innovation." The theories of Weber and Cochran in this context are mainly sociological in nature.

Briefly, the concepts of entrepreneur and entrepreneurship have been investigated from economic, social, political, cultural and managerial points. The development of this understanding is summarised in Table 1.

Table 1

DEVELOPMENT OF ENTREPRENEURSHIP THEORY AND TERM ENTREPRENEUR

The word "entrepreneur" is derived from the French verb entreprendre. It means "to undertake". Or go between.

4th BC Kautilya	:	Most successful enterprises owes to entrepreneurs ability to work in team work to achieve various goals in spite of ups and downs. Capable men, thus, will finally convert the whole idea into an 'amazing balance sheet'. The final leap may come in any manner-a big order, a turnaround client or a big financial investor. But one needs to carry on these trails — a hundred times.

(Contd.)

(Contd.)

The root of any business lies in its core value system, its philosophy. Capable men will certainly convert the ideas into wealth. Just continue doing it.

In the early 16th century, the French attributed this term to people who organised and/or led military expeditions. All those people who were responsible to find new land were also called "entrepreneurs".

Middle Ages: actor and person in charge of large scale production projects.

17th Century	:	Person bearing risks of profit (loss) in a fixed price contract with government.
1725: Richard Cantillon	:	Person bearing risks is different from one supplying capital.
1776: Adam Smith:	:	Entrepreneur is an individual who undertook the formation of an organisation for commercial purposes. He is a person with unusual foresight who could recognise potential demand for goods and services.
1797: Beaudeau	:	Person bearing risks, planning, supervising, organising, and owning.
1803: Jean Baptiste Say:	:	Separated profits of entrepreneur from profits of capital. The entrepreneur is one who possessed certain skills and arts of creating new economic enterprises, yet a person who had exceptional into insight into society's needs and was able to fulfill them.
1840: John Stuart Mills	:	Elaborated on the necessity of entrepreneurship in private enterprise. The term *entrepreneur* subsequently become common as a description of business founders and the fourth factor of economic endeavour in economic literature.
1871: Car L Mender (1840-1921)	:	The entrepreneur is the change agent who transforms resources into useful goods and services that lead to industrial growth.
1876: Francis Walker:	:	Distinguished between those who supplied funds and received interest and those who received profit from managerial capabilities.
1921: Frank H. Knight	:	The man who earns profits by taking risks in an uncertain future and sell the output is an entrepreneur.
1934: Joseph Alois Schumpeter	:	Entrepreneur (1883-1950): ship is often a subtle force, challenging the order of society through marginally small changes. It is a process of creativity and innovation.
1952: Hoselitz Bert F	:	Uncertainty bearing ...... Co-ordination of productive resources.....introduction of innovation and provisions of capital.
1956: Frederick Harbison	:	Skill to build organisation by harnessing the new ideas of different innovators.
1958: Eserett E. Hessen	:	An economic man who tries to maximise his profits by innovations.
1959: Cole Arthur H	:	Purposeful activity to initiate maintain or organise a profit oriented business of economic goods and services.
1961: David McClelland	:	Motivation to achieve foster the entrepreneurial activities in society entrepreneur is an energetic moderate risk taker.
1964: Peter Drucker (1908-2005)	:	Entrepreneur maximises opportunities through systematic innovations. Entrepreneurship is a practices.

(Contd.)

(Contd.)

1975: Albert Shapero	:	Entrepreneur takes initiative, organises some social-economic mechanisms, and accepts risk of failure.
1980: Karl H. Vesper	:	Entrepreneur seen differently by economists, psychologists, business persons, and politicians.
1982 MARK Casson	:	Decisions and Judgements about the co-ordination of scarce resources.
1983: Gifford Pinchot	:	Intrapreneur is an entrepreneur within an already established organization.
1984: Robert C. Ronstadt	:	A dynamic process of creating incremental wealth by assuming the major risks in terms of equity, times and commitment of providing value for products or services.
1985: Robert D. Hisrich	:	Entrepreneur is the process of creating something different with value by devoting the necessary time and effort, assuming the accompanying financial, psychological, and social risks and receiving the results – rewards of monetary and personal satisfaction.
1985: Gartner, W.	:	Creation of new organizations.
1989: Stevenson H. Roberts M., & H. Grousbeck	:	The pursuit of opportunity without regard to resources currently controlled, but constrained by the founders previous choice and industry related experience.
1990: Vasant Desai	:	The entrepreneur brings in overall change through innovation for the maximum social good. Human values remain sacred and inspires him to serve society. He has firm belief in social betterment and he carries out this responsibility with conviction. In the process, he accelerates personal, economic as well as human development. The entrepreneur is a visionary and an integrated man with outstanding leadership qualities. With a desire to excel, the entrepreneur gives top priority to Research and Development. He always works for the well-being of the society. More importantly, entrepreneurial activities encompasses all fields/sectors and fosters a spirit of enterprise for the welfare of mankind.
1995: M. Hart, H. Stevenson & J. Dial	:	The Pursuit of opportunity without regard to resources currently controlled, but constrained by the founder's previous choices and industry-related experience.
1999: P.R. Brahmanand	:	The concept of entrepreneurship represent economic, sociological psychological and cultural aspects of sustained development. The entrepreneur is a doer and innovator.
2004: Nandan Nilekani	:	In essence, entrepreneurship is about dreaming the impossible and helping followers to achieve the same. Moreover, the dream has to be built on sound and context invariant values to sustain the enthusiasm and energy of people over a long time. Further set direction to create a shared vision, encourage execution excellence, embrace inclusive meritocracy to build a globally best-in-class leadership team that delivers outstanding business value in every customer engagement.

(Contd.)

(Contd.)

2005: Sunil Bharati	:	For the Indian-bred entrepreneur, the path to sustained excellence is one that requires willingness to change, learn and excel. Most entrepreneurs exhibit a balanced combination of education and entrepreneurial drive with an eagerness to change and innovate. No doubt, they will be able to play a vital role in contributing to our country's development. As many more entrepreneurs spread their wings and explore new horizons, the fundamental focus must remain unchanged — seek the best in every domain and put to the service of the customer. Let this core thought continue to drive the spirit of entrepreneurship in India. If the economic environment becomes global oriented, it is certainly not difficult to achieve the dream and vision.
2006: N.R. Narayana Murthy	:	Entrepreneurship is an agent of change. Entrepreneurship built and sustained on the true set of value system is ready for the marathon race in the global economy. Innovation conductivity, fairness, frankness, ethics conscience and transparency are the core values of entrepreneurship.
2007: Richard Strozzi-Heckler	:	Entrepreneurial is a practice that can be developed and trained for enterprise. An entrepreneur methodically built fluency and muscle through the regular exercise of disciplines that require simultaneous physical and mental effort.
2008: Mansi Tiwari	:	As technology changes and global connectivity improves, entrepreneurship means that the entrepreneur not only has to ensure profits for all shareholders, he has to fix problems, tap new markets, bring cutting edge ideas to the table, and lead cross-cultural teams. The person has to be passionate, empathetic, sharp and inspirational at the same time.

Entrepreneurship has taken on new meaning and greater challenges in the last decades. The real skill is learning how to influence through commitment, loyalty and trust, rather than through mere compliance or, at worst coercion.

Factors Influencing Entrepreneurship

Peter Heydemann, the Science Counsellor in the U.S. Embassy here seems much impressed with the role the small business play in the process of innovation in the U.S. economy. He explained how "incubators" are used successfully in the United States to encourage small entrepreneurs.

The problem is how best to help small entrepreneurs translate the results of laboratory research into marketable products, to transform a new scientific concept into a commercial product. Simply put, "incubators" are very basic facilities offering shared secretarial services, space for conducting a retail or manufacturing business, and a few simple machine tools. But, and this is very important, incubators offer advice and consultation on subjects with which the most budding entrepreneurs are unfamiliar: business and finance planning, market development, government regulations. Incubators have indeed greatly helped small manufacturers to develop new products. Recent studies show that such enterprises are the main source of innovation in the U.S. industry.

Heydemann said that the idea of the incubator technology is "five or six years old,." This is because until recently it was felt that the U.S. industry would forever remain in the forefront without any competition. But things changed rapidly. So, realising the "the 600-plus national laboratories could not possibly service all the one-and-a-half million or so small entrepreneurs," individual American states took it upon themselves to help local industry through their technology support and development organisations.

Incubators are very often attached to state university systems as universities have much of the technical and non-technical information that needs to be fed to the entrepreneurs. Moreover, state universities have increasingly come to believe that apart from their traditional role, they must also promote industrial activity in their areas of operation.

State authorities in turn help by enabling businessmen cut through red tape, provide low-interest loans to develop prototypes, undertake market research and generally assist in bringing a new product to the consumer. "Some notion of the magnitude of this support can be had from the fact that last year alone, the federal and state governments together spent more than $2,000 million in encouraging small business." Many private sector companies also provide incubator facilities, though at a comparatively higher cost.

Another important aspect of incubators is that experts do not make any business decisions for their clients. They only provide guidelines and advice on product development, engineering, pilot production and in identifying markets.

Among the businesses in which incubators are making a significant contribution, said Heydemann, "are light manufacturing in mature technologies, retail and wholesale trade and, finally, research and development in emerging technologies."

The success rate of incubators has been salutary in the number of new jobs created, the enlarged tax base for state revenues and in the export of manufactures. In short, incubators are bringing new vigour and vitality to America's industrial renaissance and are once more giving the country a competitive edge. It remain to be seen how useful it will be in the context of Indian entrepreneurs.

For Illustration

Mr. Ashok Birla (1939-1990) displayed a restless urge to get going, to get things done. He was ever-sensitive to innovation with a quest for new ideas. His vigorous energy combined with a certain gambler's instinct, led him to pursue every potentially profitable venture. It was this zest to explore the unexplored which created an image of an unabashed entrepreneur willing to invest in risky off-beat ventures.

Always ahead of his time, he sensed the coming of a financial revolution and sought to be in its forefront by seeking to promote an offshore mutual fund — five years before the Unit Trust of India floated its first country fund. Foreseeing the national crunch in power generation, he introduced portable diesel-based gensets on which farmers and small shopkeepers could depend to tide them over critical periods of power shortages.

After a short training stint under the supervision of his uncle, Mr. Basant Kumar Birla, Mr. Ashok Birla built a cluster of companies into a dynamic Rs. 320-crore group.

The sales of Zenith Ltd., his flagship company, which was a mere Rs. 30 crore in 1977-78 when Mr. Birla took over, soared to Rs. 269 crore in 1980-90. Under Mr. Birla's leadership, the company changed from a single product manufacturer to a multi-product, multi-dimensional conglomerate and became India's 74th largest company. Earlier, just out of college, he had nurtured Bharat Commerce from a Rs 2-crore company into a Rs. 56-crore concern.

Mr. Rajan Pillai, (1943-1997) London-based Indian engineer turned an entrepreneur, had brought in one swoop with this a group of four lucrative biscuit and snack food companies in Singapore, Hong Kong, Malayasia and New Zealand under Pillai's belt. The group's combined sales are approximately Rs. 640 crore and net fixed assets in excess of Rs. 200 crore, which include Britannica Industries, India and English Biscuit Manufacturers, Pakistan. Rajan Pillai was an international success.

In 1973, Rajan and his father, who was by then one of the biggest exporters of cashew from India, decided that one member of the family should be abroad. Rajan was one chosen. Relying on some 'contacts', Pillai embarked for Singapore to launch the 20th Century Foods, a salting operation using raw cashew nuts imported mainly from Kerala. But before leaving India, Rajan made a clean break — he redistributed amongst his six sisters and sole brother his inherited wealth, then amounting to about Rs. 5 lakh and relinquished all rights to the family business.

The 20th Century Foods was set in a joint venture with the Inchcape group. A food processing factory in the nuts and nut-related industry was set up in 1973, in the Jurong Industrial Estate, which was marshland in those days. Rajan secured financial assistance and land on easy lease terms from the Singapore Economic Development Board, being one of the first few to set up a factory there. Soon he started shipping branded consumer products (cashews in cans and pouches) to the neighbouring countries. Later, he extended the product line to peanuts, pistachio and almonds to the markets to the Far East, Japan, the Pacific Rim and the Middle East, all in a span of five years.

The products sold under the 'Ole' brand name found wide acceptance. But this did not save the company from cash flow problems. The profits Rajan Pillai made went into paying off the loans from the Citibank and the Bank of India in Singapore. Clearly, working capital shortage and the bane of entrepreneurship threatened to wipe out the young fortune-seeker.

Cash losses started mounting and the company went into a tailspin. But Pillai's experience with the company laid the foundations for what was destined to be a rewarding career. "20th Century Foods is largely responsible for what I am today", he said. To combat the chronic shortage of capital, the young Pillai had started expanding the factory by taking in some local Singaporians as shareholders.

Big Break

In spite of the trials and tribulations, the shift to Singapore was Pillai's big break. Certainly he had not started with nothing in Singapore. On the contrary, by this time he was in a successful family cashew and shipping business. But there were other equally successful and rich businessmen in Kerala in the export trade. But no one had turned that base into an international, organised marketing and production company.

Pillai's success was due to the fact that he had clearly understood how business was organised and conducted in the West. This was the reason why he was able to capitalise on his base. In every instance, he had been able to merge his business into a bigger operation and eventually to gain control of the larger entity. It is this that had set him apart from most other Indian businessmen.

In 1978-79, Pillai convinced Standard Brands, a leading US public company and the largest nut producer, to join him in his venture. Pillai sold 74 per cent of his stake to Standard Brands. The company was renamed 20th Century Standard Brands and he became the working chairman, as is almost a custom in the West when a businessman merges his successful small company into a larger company. In 1980, Nabisco Foods merged with Standard Brands. After the merger, Pillai had sold out his balance holding. Once again, the new management retained Pillai as working chairman. "The senior people quickly saw in him an aggressive entrepreneurial trader", says an insider and in 1985 he was moved to London to head the Nabisco Commodities, a trading company.

Modern Concept

The term "entrepreneur" in the modern sense came into usage in the late 18th century with the advent of the Industrial Revolution in England. It was during this period that people developed inventions and made an appreciable amount of discoveries in a variety of productive occupations. Their innovative behaviour engaged them in doing new and useful things or old things in an improved way. The invention of colour photography and colour television, for example, were the responses of innovative efforts of the individual who conceived the idea, developed it and pursued it to its ultimate success. These innovators came to be known as entrepreneurs.

Critical Analysis

From the above theories we can see that Schumpeter and McClelland have given primary importance to the individual. While Schumpeter has stressed on innovativeness or creativity of the individual as an important determinant of enterpreneurship, McClelland stresses more on the internal factors, specifically, the need for achievement. Though not according any importance to culture *per se,* however, he has dealt with one product of culture, *viz.,* the need for achievement, extensively. Weber has touched upon the belief system which is part and parcel of culture and which has a great influence in determining the individual's behaviour in every aspect of his life — be it religious, social or economic. In Weber's view, certain belief system sanction economic endeavours, while others do not. Hagen views economic development as a process of technological change which is brought about by technological creativity of individuals in society. Granting the significance of psychic factors, Young lays greater emphasis on the nature of the groups, groups' assistance and co-ordination. Like Weber and McClelland, Cochran also speaks in different terms but explicitly, of cultural values and social structure (which include role expectations and social sanction) as playing a vital role in economic development. He identifies three important elements: (*a*) individual attitudes towards economic activity; (*b*) social sanctions; and (*c*) skills needed for the job (of a technical and social nature). While Young considers psychological factors and value system as passive, Kunkel argues that they do really matter and comes close to Cochrans view of social structure as contributing to entrepreneurship development. By and large, the underlying current and emphasis in all theories seems to be the man and his personality, influenced by the culture in a given society.

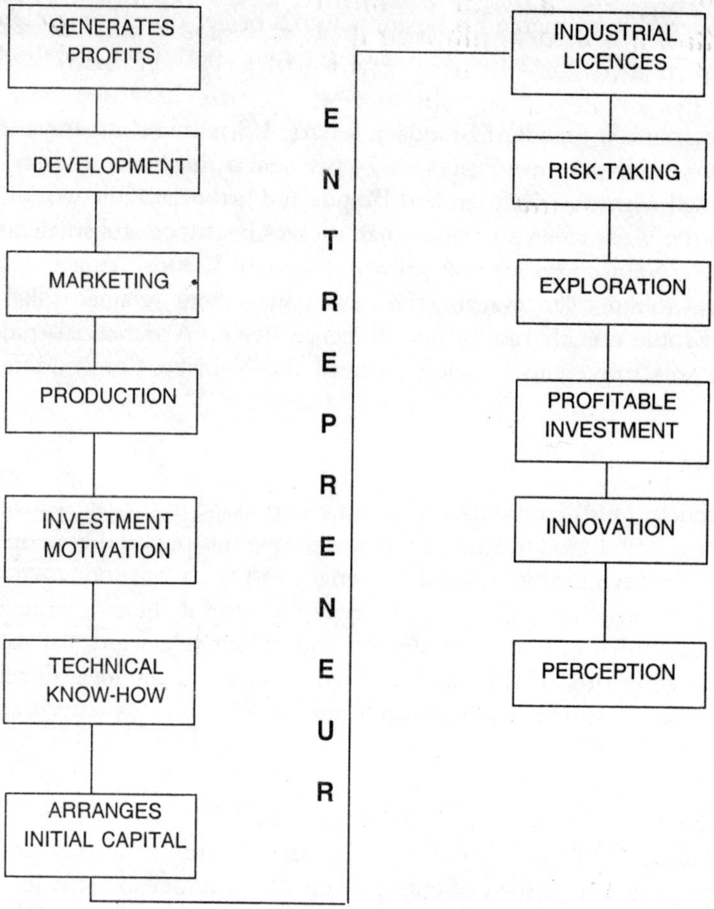

Fig. 2: Flow Chart of an Industrial Entrepreneur

Conclusion

Major theories and expositions from Cantillon to Kirzner view the entrepreneur as performing various functional roles as risk taker, decision maker, organiser or co-ordinator, innovator, employer of factors of production, gap seeker and input completer, arbitraguer, etc. in spite of the diverse roles portrayed, certain common themes could be identified. All the theories ascribe a functional role to the entrepreneur in the productive process and entrepreneurial rewards are explained by the degree of success attained by fulfilling that function, rather than by a purely proprietary claim on income by virtue of mere asset ownership. Again, all the theories have been grounded against the backdrop of a capitalist society and as such the functional roles performed by the entrepreneur is determined within the capitalist paradigms of production and distribution.

The varied theories evolved over more than two centuries have thrown up the concept of intrapreneur as a logical evolution of entrepreneurship in corporations. The intrapreneur is a professional with entrepreneurial skills. The concept of enterpreneurship will certainly undergo a change with the advancement of technology, information technology in particular. The evolution of entrepreneurship is a continuous process.

The entrepreneurial bug is spreading faster than ever. A host of challenges — as with adventure, worth the effort. After all, Indians are historically seen to be risk-avers and old habits are hard to break. However, a generation of role models like NR Narayana Murthy, Jerry rao, Kiran Majumdar, Shaw, Captain Gopinath and others have taken some of the bite out of entrepreneurship. At the same time, they have shown that business and professionalism can go hand-in-hand.

The trick then is to encourage entrepreneurial activity among the professional classes, while at the same time equipping them to create profitable, scalable business ventures that contribute to economic growth. "We believe that entrepreneurs can be trained. It's a question of reducig the possibility of failure and also giving a certain comfort factor to financiers.

FIVE

Economic Theories of Entrepreneurship

Introduction

Economic theories may be deemed useful for a number of reasons. It throws light on the origin of ideas, concepts and evolution of the thought processes. It traces the historical sources and sequence of controversies. It helps to separate the contextual and time specific portions of the subject from the permanent and enduring components. In a discipline with many schools of thought it assists in the choice of specific approaches to the subject.

Economics, in the post-fifties diversified its content in keeping with the changing economic, political, social and cultural environment and its impact on the economy. In many areas new concepts and approaches have emerged and old concepts and approaches have been refined.

Economics has now become more of a science than before. It has also branched into numerous specialisation. In the process it has become increasingly a collection of concepts, techniques and models.

Economic theories relating to entrepreneurship can be visualised, as Schumpeter did, as a linear development from the implicit marginalism in Ricardo, the matrix of production transactions as in Quesnay's *tableau economique*. Most of the theories are directly and/or indirectly connected with the main theme.

The Study of Economics

The study of economics is to study people and that makes it complex indeed. Economics is a study of economy inter alia, the management of household, the administration of the material resources of an individual, community and country, industry and business, money, financial markets and banking, organisation, direction, management, control, price, cost, profit, economic growth economic development, inflation, stagflation, depression, incentives, policies, programmes and the people.

People is both a productive agent and consumer. As a productive agent, it relates to personality, behaviour, skills, aptitudes, dreams and entrepreneurship.

State plays a unique role in shaping the economy that is beneficial to the large segment of the people.

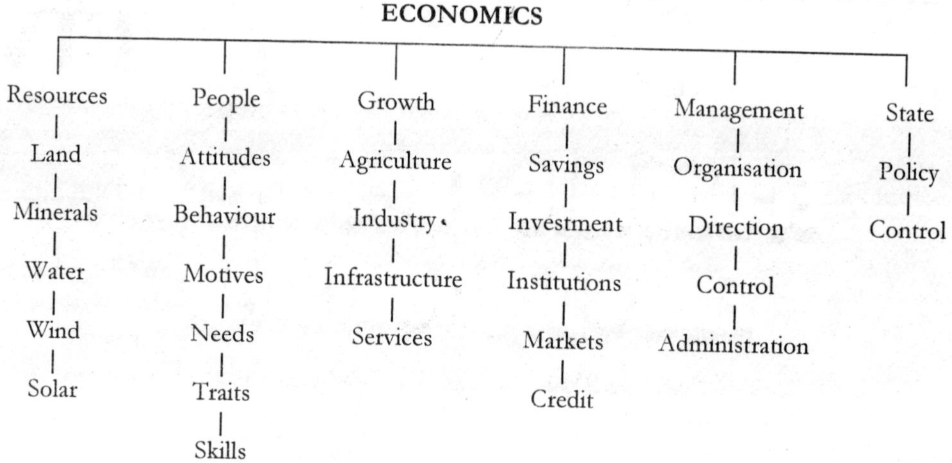

Fig. 1: Study of Economics

Source: Indicative Graphic.

Such a characterisation of economics from a theoretical physicist might strike one as curious, perhaps even ironic. But the truth is that economics is frustratingly complex in ways that physics is not — profoundly awkward ways that can affect its very development and impact.

Physics, of course, can be difficult. Physicists are continually breaking objects down into their constituent parts and creating idealised scenarios (frictionless ramps, spherical planets, and so on) to assess the primary causes of the phenomenon in question and uncover all-encompassing laws.

Economists, meanwhile, face a much more arduous task. The systems that economists study — large populations in widely dissimilar societies — are hardly the simple, abstract systems of fundamental physics. Studying the dynamics of systems of thousands, if not millions, of basic quantities (in this case, people) naturally involves a very different sort of analysis than trying to determine the structure of one central building block — a proton, say. Still, this sort of difficulty is neither unique to economics nor intractable. One encounters precisely the same issue in thermodynamics, where it is defacto impossible to know precise details (position, momentum) about any one of the millions of atoms in a gas. Physicists circumvent this impediment by recognising higher level laws and structures involving properties of the system (pressure and temperature) that can be connected, statistically to the individual constituents (atoms). Similarly, economists have devised meaningful distinctions between the microeconomics of individual choices and the macreconomics of aggregate economic systems.

People-oriented

Without people, economics is simply non-existent, non-sensical. One obviously can't study the wealth of nations or the consumption of goods and services without tacitly assuming that there are humans to produce and consume the goods.

The fact that economics is so inextricably tied to people, however, gives rise to several unique consequences.

- The hope that one can discover an all-encompassing law of economics becomes rather dim when one recognises the diversity inconsistencies and evolution of both individuals and societies.
- Economics is intrinsically political. Our economic system requires a certain political framework in which it can perform, while the politicians are entrusted with implementing key economic notions.

In a modern liberal democracy, where policy is always, typically decided with an eye towards the anticipated reaction of the electorate, economic theory must to some extent first be embraced by a largely economically illiterate audience before it can actually be implemented.

Take free trade. Virtually all modern economists favour free trade and oppose market-distorting subsidies. There seems little doubt that the vast majority of individuals, rich and poor, would benefit from a drastic reduction in trade subsidies across the board.

Yet the world is hardly a free-trading panacea, and is perhaps lurching in a rather different direction. Why? Because, at some level, the economists have not been able to persuade the populace of the merits of their case.

First, she has to delve into the human psyche in develop a meaningful way of understanding individual decisions, then she has to somehow generalise this process across countless regional and cultural divides; finally, and hardest of all, she has to find a way of obtaining widespread popular support of her ideas below they can bring any tangible benefits, so as to actually implement them.

Superstring theory, by comparison, is a walk in the park

Economists's View

In economic analysis, entrepreneurial functions are supposed to be directed towards the materialistic objective of maximisation, though its foundations may be of a high order such as spiritual, patriotic, social, psychological or ethnic, entrepreneurial activity is a form-giving activity — giving form to the wishes of the society, to ideas, to the efforts of factors and to the raw material to be processed.

J.B. Say states that to rationally combine the forces of production into a new producing organisation is the function of the entrepreneur. J.S. Mill lists superintendence, control and direction as entrepreneurial functions.

Superintendence

To assemble the means, turn out maximum at minimum cost and to supervise the work.

Control

The flow of goods, use of finance, utilisation of machinery and the activities of subordinates.

Direction

An entrepreneur is a goal-oriented person; he has to keep the organisation constantly on the path to his objective. His is an activity of producing in the present what the future will demand. Mill also emphasised managerial and administrative functions of an entrepreneur according to Marshall. Organisation-building capacity is the most critical skill expected of an entrepreneur according to Marshall. Mill assigns to the entrepreneur the functions of risk-bearing, innovation and management. To Cantillion, an entrepreneur is an uncertainty-bearer buying at a fixed price and selling at an uncertain one.

Some Other Views

Kirzener viewed the entrepreneur as a disequilibrating force. It is the alertness to unnoticed opportunities which creates a tendency of the ever-circular flow of equilibrium. Harvey Leibenstein states, "Entrepreneur is an individual or group of individuals with four major characteristics. He connects different markets; he is capable of making up marker deficiencies (gap-filling); he is input complete and he creates or expands time-binding, input-transforming entities (firms)."

To Schumpeter, innovation is the sole function of an entrepreneur. It covers the introduction of new goods, a new method of production, a new market, a new source of supply of raw materials or half-manufactured goods and a new organisation of any industry for the creation of monopoly position or breaking it. The function of the entrepreneur is to reform or revise the pattern of production. So, Schumpeter has given a social context to the activity, a psychological objective to be attained and a functionality spearheading development of the community. Lazarfeld as also Meier and Baldwin concur with Schumpeter.

B.F. Hoselitz reports, "The primary function of entrepreneurship is the investment of time, capital and energy in economically significant pursuits; the emphasis is on decision-making in its various aspects." Harbinson enumerates four functions: the undertaking or managing of risks and handling of economic uncertainty; planning and innovation; co-ordination, administration and control routine supervision. Ability to build organisation is, perhaps, Harbinson adds, the most precious of all entrepreneurial skills. Redlich's threefold division of functions is: (1) capitalist — employing the factors and buying raw material, setting up the organisation; (2) managerial — innovation, supervision and co-ordination of productive activities; and (3) entrepreneurial — decision-making. Benjamin Higgins lists seeing opportunities for introduction of new techniques, new products and exploitation of new resources and organising factors of production into an enterprise to take advantage of these opportunities as essential for economic development.

B.C. Tandon discusses the function of an entrepreneur in a developing economy in the context of economic, legal, political and cultural environment. Accordingly, the entrepreneur must possess (*a*) capacity to assume, risk and self-confidence; (*b*) technological knowledge, alertness to know opportunities, willingness to accept change and ability to initiate; (*c*) ability to marshall resources; and (*d*) ability of organisation and administration. He has to have tact, patience, sagacity, power of observation and ability of discrimination. He should have capacity to pick and choose associates and subordinates and wisely delegate authority to inspire loyalty. He must be able to multiply "himself" effectively. Tandon describes entrepreneur as an "ideal-type" rather than as "social-type." Knight identifies entrepreneurship with control and responsibility.

Economic functions described above isolate the entrepreneur from the economic environs, social milieu and political ethos in which he functions. Maximisation is taken as the pole star in his voyage. It seems to be conveniently assumed that he is abundantly provided with all the resources and the market readily absorbs what he put into it. Reality is, however full of bottlenecks and hurdles which are ignored in the above-mentioned works. Small industry is a natural habitat of the entrepreneur where his role is like that of a stoker who keeps the fire burning. Economic functioning takes no notice of this.

Development involves not merely economic changes but also social and institutional ones; in many underdeveloped countries. It calls for new sets of values and new concepts of society and government. No path to development is likely to be smooth. Infrastructure is the root of economic development.

Box - 1

Milton Friedman was around for nearly a century. He was a visionary a humanist and a liberal. The Noble Laureate economist shaped the philosophies of Ronald Reagan (USA) and Margaret Thatcher (UK) like all other grand intellectuals, Friedman thought beyond his own times. This was true in the case of India also.

Just like any great thinker, Friedman represented a simple and easy idea at the core of his entire thought. His was a passionate belief in personal freedom combined with a conviction that free markets were the best way of co-ordinating and bringing together the activities of dispersed individuals to the mutual enrichment. In one form or the other, all over the world, this is recognised as an essential tenet of economic management of enterprises as well as nations today.

Milton Friedman
July 31, 1912 - Nov. 16, 2006

Economic Growth & Economic Development

Economic growth has been widely accepted by the economists as a major goal of national policy, both in the industrialised countries and in countries that are developing. The concept of economic growth has almost become commonplace in the economic studies, particularly in those of underdeveloped countries.

In fact, economic growth is a complex process which, despite the intensive study, is still not understood in its true perspective. It was only in the period since World War II the concept received wide publicity and recognition. In his commentaries on *The Social Framework — An Introduction to Economics*, (1960), Prof. J.R. Hicks, observes that, "There is indeed no single index which is a perfect measure of economic growth; in order to see whether an economy is growing properly, we need to look at far more things than can possibly be expressed in a single figure." He preferred national income to consumption as a better measure'. In a conventional sense, economic growth has been defined as progress in per capita income measured in the currency units of constant purchasing power. Strictly speaking, growth which results from more complete utilization of capacity is easier to achieve and less fundamental than growth which involves actual expansion of an economy's capacity. Some economists have defined economic growth as a relation between the rates of increase in capital and the working force, on the one hand, and in population, on the other, such as that per capita output (not necessarily consumption) is rising. Under this contention, the composition of investment would steadily change. Prof. Rostow is of the opinion that the process of economic growth be regarded as entry on a relatively brief time interval of two or three decades when the economy progresses automatically. While, Prof. Ragnar Nurkse states that, "The technical physical productivity of capital can be realised in economic terms only through balanced growth, enlarging the aggregate size of the market and increasing individual investment incentives all round".

In many cases economic development and economic growth are used to express the same view point. But, economic growth is a term used to evaluate development during a period of time, whereas development as such is a continuous process. Here again, economists have noticed that the less developed countries quite generally regard development as a process to be planned and guided by the State. State participation in the process of economic development has been over-weighted, numerous special-purpose subsidies and incentives are provided by the State to encourage particular aspects of development. Again, it has been accepted that the take-off into self-sustained growth requires a society to be prepared to respond actively lo new possibilities for productive enterprise; and it is likely to require political, social and institutional changes which will both perpetuate an initial increase in the scale of investment and result in the regular acceptance and absorption of innovations. In recent years, economic growth has also been linked with social progress. The accelerated economic growth *inter alia* brings with it social progress, *i.e.,* increase in mass well-being, expansion of employment and reduction of income disparities, the essential prerequisite for this development being the absence of factors causing social injustice, namely, inflation, growth of monopolies and other instruments of perverse income transfer.

Industrial Entrepreneurship

The industrial entrepreneurship is the vital force in industrialization and economic development. Development and Growth of Entrepreneurship is directly related to the economic development of particular region. In the broadest sense economic development is influenced by and its basis revolves around, industrialization, *i.e.,* the correlation exists.

The theory of economic development has been the focal point for the economists. It has been the matter of concern for the economists, ever since the days of Adam Smith David Ricardo, J.S. Mill, Schumpeter and others. Adam Smith, the foremost classical economist did not assign any significance to entrepreneurial role in economic development in his monumental work. *An Enquiry into the Nature and Causes of the Wealth of Nations,* published in 1776. Smith extolled the role of capital formation as an important determinant of economic development. The problem of economic development was largely the ability of the people to save more, and to invest more. According to him, ability to save more is governed by improvement in productive powers of labour, and this increase in productivity is due to the division of labour. Smith regarded every person as the best judge of his own interest, pursuing it to his own advantage. Thus, opposing the intervention of government in industry, he advocated the policy of *lassiez faire* in economic affairs. David Ricardo identified only three factors of production, *viz.,* machinery, capital and labour, among whom the entire produce is distributed us rent, profit and wages respectively." Ricardo appreciated the virtues of profit in capital accumulation. According to him, profit leads to savings of wealth, which ultimately goes to capital formation. Thus, in both the theories of economic development, economic development seems to be automatic and self-regulated.

The 6 Opportunities

	Estimated market size ($ bn.)	*Where*	*Who*	*How much**
Semiconductor	235	Bangalore, Mumbai, Hyderabad	Cosmic Circuits, Softlin, Ittiam Moschip, inSilica, Powai Labs	75-100
Telecom & Software products	200	Bangalore, National Capital Region	Elina Networks, Read Ink, Wilcom Subex Azure Systems, Novatium	60-100
Wireless & Communication	200	National Capital Region Mumbai, Bangalore	MobiApps, Coruscant Tech, ACL Wireless, ARE Technologies	50-100
Gaming & Animation	65	Mumbai, Hyderabad, Thiruvananthapuram, Bangalore, Chennai	Nazara Technologies, Dhruva Interactive, Indiagames, Toonz Animation	60-90
Consumer Internet & Mobile	13	Mumbai, Bangalore	OnMobile, Naukri, Shaadi, Burrp, Redbus, JiGrahak, Webaroo	200-250
Software-as-a-service (SaaS)	6	Chennai, Bangalore	AdventNet, Webex, Atlantis Computing, Vembu Technologies	20-30

* $ million invested till date; Investment figures are estimates of ventures fund investments. Figures for market size pertain to the international market.
Source: BW Research.

Making Silicon Valley in India

The environment for technology entrepreneurship is slowly beginning to take shape in the country

The Start-up Stages

4 Growth & Expansion
Funding: $3 million-10 milion **Objective:** A full market launch **Investors:** Growth-stage VCs

3 Testing & Validation
Funding: $250,000-1 million **Objective:** Test the product in the real world **Investors:** Early-stage venture funds

2 Prototype
Funding: $100,000-250,000 **Objective:** Shape blueprint for the final product **Investors:** Seed funds, angel investors

1 Pre-product
Funding: $50,000-100,000 **Objective:** Shape an idea into a proof-of-concept **Investors:** Mostly founders and their families

Incubators: Pioneered by Stanford University in Silicon Valley, the concept was first adopted in India by the IITs in Mumbai and Chennai. They provide pre-product-to-prototype stage infrastructure — typically put in pre-seed capital for a minority stake. Faculty members sit on the boards as mentors. Others in India include Nirma Labs in Ahmedabad and NSRCEL in Bangalore. Successes include Herald Logic, Myzus and Midas Communications.

Academia: Entrepreneur-academia linkages are second nature in Silicon Valley. In India, IIT-Bombay, IIT-Madras and NSRCEL have taken the initial steps. Professors are now beginning to collaborate with entrepreneurs to bring cutting-edge research to market. Some of the mark include IIT-Bombay's Girish Kumar (Wilcom) and IIT-Madras's Ashok Jhunjhunwala (Rajesh Jain's Novatium).

Government: Its role in developed markets is that of an enabler through policy and regulation. In India, state governments have active funds — Kitven (Karnataka), GVFL (Gujarat) and APIDC (Andhra Pradesh). A better model is the STPI project in Bangalore, which is setting up an incubator for tech startups. Venture capital regulations in India also need to become more entrepreneur friendly.

Venture capitalists: Bring in the critical seed and early-stage money to give start-ups a head start. India's big disadvantage is that it does not have local VC sources; 90 per cent of VC funds in India are funded by US-based institutions. So, most VCs play in the $1 million-10 million deal space. Seed funds are virtually non-existent. Funds like Band of Angels, Erasmic and The Seed Fund are trying to bridge the gap.

Social networks: Social networking is at the heart of the SiliconValley success. In India, forums like BarCamps, TiE entrepreneur workshops and business plan contests have started gaining ground in the past nine months. BarCamp Delhi in March 2006 kicked off this phenomenon in India. The TiE-Draper contest saw two startups being seed funded — Vegayan Systems and NCE Technologies.

Professional services: Again in the Valley, a battery of lawyers, bankers, accountants and recruitment firms focus specifically on technology start-ups. They are often key movers behind networking events. In India, people like SVB Global and Nishith Desai Associates have moved into plug the gap. SVB Global, for instance, now sees about 30 prospective deals go through its offices every month.

Earlier Concept

In the beginning, the attitude of the classical economists was very cold towards the use of this term or towards its role in economic theory. Boulding writes that "in classical economics the firm is a shadowy entity, and the entrepreneurs even shadowier ...or at least shady when is not shadowy". Besides, the classical economists discussed Economics under the condition of perfect competition and thus they were of the opinion: "why bother at with the entrepreneur or his remuneration since in the long run and under perfect competition he is going to disappear or at least be changed into a sort of General Manager."

Adam Smith, though greatly influenced by the physiocrates and by Cantillon, gave little importance to the entrepreneurial activities of leading and directing in his analytic scheme of the economic process. He did not use the word entrepreneur but instead repeatedly talked, about the employer, the master, the merchant, and the undertaker. He seems to be of the opinion that capitalist economy ran of itself, by what is popularly known as the "Invisible hand" in conditions of *Laissez Faire*. Thus, study shows from Adam Smith to Marshall, the economists made no efforts to define or include entrepreneurship in their economic literature. Adam Smith regarded private profit as the sole motive which determined the owner of any capital and enabled him to employ it in any productive activity. According to him the fundamental economic determinant of growth in the rate of the capital formation. Ricardo too had the same to say. He stated that accumulation is governed by two factors — ability to save and will to save. The first depends upon the amount of surpluses, *i.e.*, 'net income' of the economy, and the will to save depends upon the rates of profit. Ricardian profit is affected by the changes in the wage rate as he considers profits as a residual, over and above wages on that portion of land which yields no rent. Changes in profits or wages affect each other. Unlike Smithian economy, the Ricardo system no longer expands or decays strictly according to its rate of investments.

Therefore, underdevelopment can be remedied by changing the exogenous policy variables, *i.e.*, socio-cultural environment and technological improvements. Alfred Marshall too not only followed Smith-Ricardian path but reaffirmed it by treating profit as a single-indifferential income flow.

From Cantillon to Marshall Entrepreneurial concept was treated in the same manner and elevated entrepreneurship to the fourth factor of production, though this function was identified by different names. Nothing was done on the supply side of this factor of production. Moreover, all these economists considered entrepreneurship in the context of stationary equilibrium but all of them failed to recognise it as a force in economic development.

It has been found rather difficult to give a precise definition to economic growth and development. In fact, the term 'economic growth' and 'economic development' is used interchangeably. But certain economists like Schumpeter and Mrs. Ursala Hicks have made a distribution between the two terms. Economic development refers to the problem of underdeveloped countries and economic growth to those of advanced countries. Development, according to Schumpeter, is discontinuous and spontaneous change in the stationary state, which permanently alters and displaces the equilibrium state previously existing, while growth is a gradual and steady change in the long run which comes about by a general increase in the rate of savings, and proper planning. The simplest distinction is sometimes made by saying that, the rising of income levels is generally called economic growth in rich countries and in poor ones it is called economic development.

But despite these apparent differences, some economists like Meir and Baldwin, Arthur Lewis, used these terms to be synonymous. The words 'development' and 'under-development' are used in so many ways, that their precise connotation is often baffling. Economic development essentially means a process of change. But, at the same time, it is very difficult to define precisely the phrase 'economic development'. Perhaps it is easier to say what economic development is not.

Although, a number of economic theories can be related to the concept of entrepreneurship, entrepreneurial role, production, profit, the following theories of greater relevance to the subject of entrepreneurship enuntiated by the economists from time to time are:

Management and the Society of late, management is increasingly becoming an area of interest to society at large, the work provides insight into: Management as Social Function and Liberal Art. Management is the critical determining factor of the organisation. Its task is to help people perform in concert and to make their strengths effective and their weaknesses irrelevant. Because it deals with action and application, and is validated by results, management is a technology. But, because it additionally deals with people, their values, and their growth and development, management is concerned with, and has an impact on, social structure and the community. Thus, it is also a humanity. Given these characteristics, management is what has been traditionally called a liberal art. It is 'liberal' because it deals with fundamentals of knowledge, self-knowledge, wisdom, and leadership. It's an 'art' because it is concerned with practice and application.

The Dimensions of Management. To enable the institution to function and contribute, management must perform three equally important tasks: (1) establish the specific purpose and mission of the institution (in the business enterprise, this means economic performance); (2) make work productive and the worker effective; and (3) manage social impacts and social responsibilities.

Management's New Paradigms

(1) Management is the specific and distinguishing aspect of any and all organisations. (2) There is no one right type of organisation; there is only the right organisation for the task at hand, (3) Management's goal must be to make each individual's specific strengths and knowledge productive: thus, its task is not to manage people, but to lead them. (4) The real foundations for management policy are not technology and end use but customer values and the decisions customers make concerning the distribution of their disposable incomes. (5) Because the economic chain brings businesses together into genuinely equal partnerships, the scope of management must be redefined to encompass the entire economic process beyond the legal entity of the individual enterprise and beyond national boundaries. (6) Management must exist for the sake of the institution's results (which reside only on the outside) and organise the institution to attain those results. (7) Management must be operational and focus on results and performance across the entire economic chain.

Adapting to change

Change management is like a three-legged stool. The first dimension is mindset change. The second is same form of structural change. This includes eliminating or restructuring leaderships responsibilities and restructuring the organisation.

Finally, the most critical change is the reward system. This includes positive incentives to induce behaviour in the direction the company wants to go and negative incentives to discourage behaviour that perpetuates the status quo.

Most companies only focus on one of the three elements of culture change or go through these steps sequentially. However, for truly successful change management, companies must coordinate and execute all three dimensions of change in parallel.

So, the key question is how change has to be brought about, not necessarily who is responsible for it. Here are some strategies that have worked well:

1. Identifying a smart, fast-rising executive who is a few levels below the CEO and then rapidly moving them around the company as preparation for assuming the top job.
2. Appointing as CEO an outside board member who is already a CEO at another company.
3. Taking the company private *via.,* a leveraged buyout. The private equity firm appoints a team to fix the problem, after which the company is often taken public again.

Anticipatory management is a proactive approach for shaping and controlling ones destiny in a changing market. It is most needed and works best when the external environment is undergoing rapid and discontinuous change.

Trends that are anticipated can be planned for and competitive advantage accrues to firms that do so better and earlier than their competitors.

THE CONTRIBUTION OF HRD SUBSYSTEMS TO DEVELOPMENT DIMENSIONS

Development Dimension		*HRD Subsystems*	
	Training	*Career planning*	*Potential appraisal and development*
Individual	Feedback and coaching performance	Rewards	
Individual in the present role	Performance appraisal	Training rewards	Feedback and performance coaching
Individual in regard to likely future role	Potential appraisal and development	Training	Performance appraisal, feedback and performance coaching
Dyadic relationships	Feedback and performance coaching	Performance appraisal	Training
Teams and teamwork	Organisation development	Training	Team rewards
Collaboration among different units/teams	Organisation development	Training	
Self-renewing capacity and health of organisation	Performance appraisal	Organisation development	Training

Therefore, it is imperative that leaders try to anticipate environmental changes and proactively position the company to be even more successful under those altered conditions than it has been under the status quo. This calls for a realignment of the company with the new environment, followed by the engagement of the company with the new environment facing the company.

BATTLE CRY

Management Lessons from the Indian Army

- The army believes in the doctrine of the "Warrior and a Winner". In the battlefield, the "Winner Takes it All" and there's no space for the second-best.
- The army rewards failure. Only leaders who have the courage to swim against the tide make mistakes. No good officer is written off for making mistakes or taking initiative that goes awry as ingenuity and creativity are important to improve processes.

- The army believes that no plan survives the first engagement, howsoever brilliant it is. Changes have to be incorporated after the enemy faces the first offensive and counters it. It is important to be dynamic and flexible in decision-making.
- The army believes that money can't bind an individual to an organisation. The ethos, work culture and scope to achieve satisfaction are more important.
- Army leaders follow the dictum, "Know the way, show the way and go the way."
- The army follows the "directive style of command" where junior leaders don't have to look over their shoulders at every stage of the battle. Flexibility and individual empowerment are important and bureaucracy doesn't work in the battlefield.
- The army doesn't quantify productivity and the system of motivation is not based on monetary considerations. Esprit de corps, camaraderie, regimental pride, act as motivators.
- The army recruits through trial by fire and at the boot camp where the best and fittest survive. Many officers leave the Army midway as they can't be promoted or are not the best.
- In the battlefield, speed and boldness is more important than perfection. Indecisiveness can be a fatal flaw. An average decision taken on time can carry the day while a brilliant decision that came late can result in defeat. The key is to pre-empt the enemy.
- The army believes sending its officers back to school to keep them updated. A high-flying officer goes to top-notch defence colleges every two to three years.

Brief discussion of Economic Theories of Entrepreneurship are made in the following pages.

The economic theories are:

1. Theory of Economic Development — Joseph Alois Schumpeter
2. Theory of Opportunities and Innovation — Peter F. Drucker
3. Theory of Change — Frank W. Young
4. X-efficiency Theory — Leibenstein
5. Theory of Growth — Robert Solow and Paul Romer
6. Regressions
7. An Economic Theory — Mark Casson
8. Theory of Incentives — Papnek & Harris
9. Harvard School Theory — Arthur H. Cole
10. Theory of Profit — Frank H. Knight
11. Theory of Profit Optimisation
12. Theory of Adjustment of Price — Kirzner
13. Theory of Market Equilibrium — Hayek
14. Management Grid — Robert R. Blake

Theory of Economic Development

Schumpeter's theory of entrepreneurship is a pioneering work of economic development. Development, in his sense, implies that carrying out of new combinations of entrepreneurship is basically a creative activity.

Joseph Alois Schumpeter (1883-1950) thus writes: "The entrepreneur in an advanced economy is an individual who introduces something new in the economy — a method of production not yet tested by experience in the branch of manufacture concerned, a product with which consumers are not yet familiar, new source of raw material or of new markets and the like." Schumpeter further states that entrepreneur's function is to "reform or revolutionise the pattern of production by exploiting an invention or more generally, an untired technological possibility for producing a new commodity..."

In his views, the concept of new combination leading to innovation covers the following five cases:

(*i*) The introduction of *new goods*, that is the one with which consumers are not yet familiar, of a new quality.

(*ii*) The introduction of *new method of production,* that is yet to be tested by experience in the branch of manufacture concerned which need, by no means, to be founded upon a scientifically new discovery and can also exist in a new way of handling a commodity commercially.

(*iii*) The opening of a *new market,* that is a market into which the particular branch of manufacture of the country in question has not previously entered, whether or not this market has existed before.

(*iv*) The conquer of a *new source of supply of a raw material* or semi-manufactured goods, again irrespective of whether this source already exists or whether it has first to be created.

(*v*) The carrying out of *the new organisation,* of any industry like the creation of monopoly position through fructification or breaking up of a monopoly position.

Schumpeter had outlined the investment process as a means in generating productivity changes. He also distinguished between risk and uncertainty. And, the course of the maximum rate of profits can be altered favourably by innovation.

In the case of a developing economy like ours, the concept is being understood differently. Entrepreneur in a developing economy is one who starts an industry (old or new), undertakes risk, bears uncertainties and also performs the managerial factions of decision-making and co-ordination. He also puts the new process based on technological research into operation. Even if he imitates any technique of production from a developed economy, he is called an entrepreneur. In point of fact, entrepreneurship in developing economics is one form of labour that tells the rest of the labour what to do and sees to it that it gets things done. Unlike in the developed industrial world, emphasis is not put (nor is there any need for it) only on "Schumpeterian innovations" in the case of developing countries.

Schumpeter's entrepreneur only exists if the factors of production are combined for the first time. To him, maintenance of a combination is not entrepreneurial activity. As such, he differs from the theory of Rent enunciated by Ricardo. Ricardo included the term "entrepreneurial ability" as an independent factor of production. To Ricardo, profit is the reward for entrepreneurial ability.

The carrying out of the above-mentioned combinations, Schumpeter calls *enterprise* and the individual who carries them out he calls *entrepreneur.* In view of the above, Schumpeterian theory of entrepreneurship has got the following features:

Box - 1

PROLOGUE: WHO HE WAS AND WHAT HE DID

If capitalism was the most influential single economic and social force of the 20th century (and continuing today), there is no better guide to understanding its power and complexity than famed economist Joseph Schumpeter, for the first time put the human agent at the centre of the process of economic development and assigned a critical role to entrepreneurship in his theory of economic development. According to Schumpeter "The Entrepreneurship is essentially a creative activity or it is an innovative sanction."

— *Joseph Alois Schumpeter*

"Without innovations, no entrepreneurs; without entrepreneurial achievement, no capitalist propulsion." Schumpeter wrote this during the Great Depression of the 1930s. Many smart people of that time believed that technology had reached its limits and capitalism had passed its peak. Schumpeter believed the exact opposite, and of course he was right.

Economist Joseph Schumpeter was perhaps the most powerful thinker ever on innovation, entrepreneurship, and capitalism. He was also one of the most unusual personalities of the 20th century, Schumpeter, who assessed capitalism as an expression of innovation, human drama, and sheer havoc — all going on it once. He told of capitalism in the way most people experience it; as consumer desires aroused by endless advertising; as forcible jolts up and down the social peaking order; as goals reached, shattered, altered, then reached once more as people try, try again. For capitalism, and for Schumpeter personally, nothing was ever stable. Uproar was their only music.

Like nearly everyone who has thought deeply about capitalism, Schumpeter came away with mixed feelings.... Schumpeter abhorred some of the banalities of business culture and reversed the artistic attainments of the Old World. He knew that creative destruction fosters economic growth but also that it undercuts cherished human values. He was that poverty brings misery but also that prosperity cannot assure peace of mind....

He applied his immense energy to analysing and explaining capitalist innovation not only for other experts but sometimes for the non-specialist. From the compelling story of his life and work, a reader can grasp the basic mechanism of the capitalist engine about as well as from a whole shelf of textbooks. The subject is momentous, and its full social mechanism quite intricate. But its economic essence is not very complicated. As Schumpeter himself wrote in 1946, at the beginning of his long article on capitalism for the Encyclopaedia Britannica, "A society is called capitalist if it entrusts its economic process to the guidance of the private businessman. This may be said to imply, first, private ownership of non-personal means of production...second, production for private account, *i.e.*, production by private initiative for private profit." He went on to say that a third element is "so essential to the functioning of the capitalist system" that it must be added to the other two.

This third element is the creation of credit. The core ethos of capitalism looks constantly ahead and relies on credit and launching new ventures.

Excerpts from 'Prophet of Innovation: Joseph Schumpeter and Creative Destruction'.

1. Distinction between invention and innovation: Schumpeter makes a distinction between innovation and invention. Invention means creation of new things and innovation means application of new things into practical use. An innovator is an enterprising person who applies inventions in order to make new combinations and thus manufactures new goods for better profits. An inventor is the producer or creator of ideas whereas the innovator implements these ideas. An innovator is the entrepreneur who converts these ideas into commercially-viable projects. Thus, an innovator always stands a step further than the inventor in exploiting the new ideas commercially.

While proceeding towards economic development, each economy carries innovations. During 1967-68, the technological breakthrough in agriculture by the Government of India for introduction of HYV seeds, mechanisation in agriculture are the glaring examples of innovation. Similarly, e-commerce evolution of CAD, CAM and the growth of stock company are examples of innovation.

2. Emphasis on entrepreneurial functions: Schimpeter has given emphasis on the role of entrepreneurial functions in economic development. In his views, development means basic transformation of the economy that is brought about by entrepreneurial functions. Entrepreneurs are motivated intellectual class of people and the prime movers of economic development. They foresee the potential opportunity and constantly try to explore it. They are distinguished from rest of the population because of their latent capacity to perceive and mobilize resources. Thus, one of the most important functions of an entrepreneur is to mobilise such resources which are known as **5 Ms** in modern management, *i.e.,* Man, Material, Money, Machine and Method, etc. can be properly co-ordinated by the entrepreneur to maximise profit from his own venture thereby leading to economic growth.

3. Presentation of disequilibrium situation through entrepreneurial activity: The entrepreneurial activity represents a disequilibrium situation, a dynamic phenomenon and a break from the routine or a *circular flow or a tendency towards equilibrium.* Entrepreneurs, therefore, plunges into innovative activity to which they are new.

According to Schumpeter. 'While he swims with the stream in the circular flow which is familiar to him, he swims against stream if he wishes to change its channel. What was formerly a help becomes a hindrance. What was familiar datum becomes an unknown. Where the boundaries of routine stop, many people can go no further and the rest can only do so in a highly variable manner". This is why carrying out new combinations is an object of special kind of function.

4. Entrepreneurship in relation to three corresponding pairs of opposites: Schumpeter determines entrepreneurship and entrepreneurial character by three corresponding pairs of opposites:

(*i*) By the opposition of two real process — the circular flow or the tendency towards equilibrium on one hand and a change in channels of economic routine or spontaneous change in the economic data arising from within the system on the other.

(*ii*) By the opposition of two important apparatus, statistics and dynamics.

(*iii*) By the opposition of two types of conduct, which following reality, we can picture as two types of individuals — mere managers and entrepreneurs.

5. Characteristic motives of the entrepreneurial conduct: In his theory, Schumpeter deals with the question *of* characteristic motives of entrepreneurial conduct. Although he tries to indicate the *psychology of entrepreneur,* he believes that none of the results to which our analysis is intended to lead stands or falls with psychology of entrepreneur or could be vitiated by any errors in it.

6. Entrepreneurial dream and the will to found a private kingdom: Entrepreneurial motives are governed by the will power to conquer for establishing private kingdom. The motives of creating things and applying these things into practice inspire the entrepreneur to undertake innovation. According to Schumpeter, "Dream and the will to found a private kingdom, will to conquer and finally 'the joy of creating and getting things done or simply of exercising ones energy and ingenuity" are the motives that inspire the innovative entrepreneur to undertake innovation.

SCHUMPETERIAN INNOVATIONS

In the above models we can permit Schumpeterian innovations/unitations more or less an ongoing process, though innovations may be occurring at somewhat discrete time intervals. The level of product per worker will be going up continuously. This means that though the population growth rate is given and unchanged, the output growth rate can become higher than the population growth rate. This means that the long-term interest rate will be higher than in it would be in the absence of innovations/imitations as a continuous process. As the innovations imply an upward drift in the savings and in the savings to income ratio, with innovations-imitations sequence through time, the savings ratio will be ruling higher than in their absence.

To the extent that the savings to income ratio can be jacked up to a higher and higher level and in developing countries with a huge backlog of past technological change to be absorbed, the catching up process can be accompanied by a sustained higher savings to income ratio along with a sustained higher growth rate of output though the population growth rate is constant or even is going down. This probably may explain the high growth rates in many Asian countries. To the extent that international trade and the opening up of the economy contributes to the above process of upward movement of investment to income ratio and access to newer and newer technologies, the growth rate can be sustained higher than the population growth rate. These processes can go along with a continuous improvement in the ratio of human capital to labour.

Even with a given population size and a given population growth rate, the process of absorption of disguised unemployed may take a long period and the output growth rate can be sustainedly higher for this reason. We can combine this factor with the absorption/growth of technology, the continuing gains of trade and the rising ratio of human capital to explain the higher growth rates, which have also been sustained in many developing countries in the recent 2 to 3 decades. The rising ratio of human capital to labour may explain why these high growth rates have also seen a rising proportion of services in national income. It may be noted that development economics of developed countries never showed up these growth rates.

Critical Evaluation

Schumpter's theory of entrepreneurship is criticized on the following grounds:

(*a*) The theory has broadened the scope of entrepreneurism in the sense that it has included the individual businessman along with the directors and managers of company who actually carry out new combinations known as innovative functions. It is considered narrow because individuals, though operate successful business enterprise but lacks innovation.

(*b*) *Schumpeter's* innovating entrepreneur represents the enterprise with R and D and innovative character. But developing countries lack these types of entrepreneurs.

(*c*) *Schumpeterian* theory of entrepreneurship gives too much emphasis on innovation. It excludes the risk taking and organizing aspects of entrepreneurship which are equally important from the point of view of enterprise building.

(*d*) Schumpeter's entrepreneurs are large scale businessmen who introduce new technology, methods of production, etc. But in underdeveloped countries entrepreneurs who start their business generally do not have a large scale business enterprise in the beginning. Further, they also prefer to operate on traditional technology. These countries actually need more imitative entrepreneurs than innovating entrepreneurs because of structural imperfections. That's why underdeveloped countries compel the entrepreneurs to start small scale enterprises which are already tested.

(*e*) Schumpeter remained silent about as to why some economies had more entrepreneurial talent than others. According to him an individual is an entrepreneur only when he tries new combinations to produce new things and to innovate. He ceases to be an entrepreneur the moment he establishes himself in running the business effectively. Thus, view of Schumpeter is quite unrealistic and questionable.

However, despite the above criticisms. Schumpeterian theory is regarded as one of the best theories in the history of entrepreneurial development.

Theory of Opportunities and Innovation

Peter Drucker (1910-2005), the man who saw tomorrow, was one of the prophets of entrepreneurship. Drucker in his 1954 work Practice of Management integrated the two schools — Fredrick Taylor's Scientific management ad Mary Parker Follets work on motivation, which was branded as the humanistic school — depicting management as "a distinct function, managing as specific work, and being a manager as a distinct responsibility." At the same time, Drucker also highlighted the role of innovation and entrepreneurship, and the notion of corporate responsibility.

Peter Drucker defines an entrepreneur as one who always searches for change, responds to it, and exploits it as an opportunity. Entrepreneurs innovate.

Box - 2

Drucker had little real interest in management and was almost derisive at the idea of it being a scientific discipline. For him what mattered was what management could do, and he was clear about this: it was to create a functioning responsible society.

Drucker's preferred term for himself was a social ecologist, studying how societies function and how to make them work better. His interest in corporations stemmed simply from the fact that he saw them as the best means to achieve this. Drucker believed businesses and free markets were the best way to achieve a good society, but he was no automatic acolyte of business. In recent years, he attacked exploding corporate salaries and management share options which he felt were almost inevitably instruments of corruption. From the nineties onwards much of Drucker's work was actually outside the business sector, with non-profit organisations (to ensure that his services weren't taken for granted he would charge them his usual fee, which he would then donate back to them).

But its important to note that for Drucker corporations were the means and not the end, hence his readiness to turn against them when he felt they had abandoned their responsibilities to society. It's a view of management that the gurus might spurn, but might find more acceptance in these days of increased interest in questions of corporate social responsibility. These were the areas that Drucker spent much of his last years in and it seems like in this, just as surely as when he saw the rise (and later collapse) of Japan or the importance of independent boards of directors, he will be the real management visionary.

Peter Drucker
(1910-2005)
Social Commentator, Philosopher, Visionary and above all the father of modern management

Mr. Peter Drucker has aptly observed that, "Innovation is the specific tool of entrepreneurs, the means by which they exploit changes as an opportunity for a different business or a different service. It is capable of being presented as a discipline, capable of being learned, capable of being practised. Entrepreneurs need to search purposefully for the sources of innovation, the changes and their symptoms that indicate opportunities for successful innovation. And they need to know and to apply the principles of successful innovation."

Systematic innovation, according to him, consists in the purposeful and organised search for changes and in the systematic analysis of the opportunities such changes might offer scope for economic and social innovation.

Entrepreneurship and innovation are not inborn characteristics. These are competencies that an organisation can learn. Here, Drucker showed how to combine managerial practices with the acts of innovation to create and institutionalise entrepreneurship.

According to Drucker, three conditions have to be fulfilled:

1. Innovation is work. It requires knowledge. It requires ingenuity. It makes great demands on diligence, persistence and commitment.
2. To succeed, innovation must build on their strengths.
3. Innovation always has to be close to the market, focused on the market, indeed market-driven.

Specially, systematic innovation means monitoring six sources for innovative opportunity,

The first three sources lie within the enterprise, whether it be a business or a public service institution or within an industry or service sector. They are, therefore, visible primarily to people within that industry or service sector. They are basically symptoms. But they are highly reliable indicators of changes that have already occurred or can be made to occur with little effort. These four source areas are:

- The unexpected — the unexpected success, the unexpected failure, the unexpected outside event.
- The incongruity — between reality as it actually is and reality as it is assumed to be or as it "ought to be."
- Innovation in industry structure or market structure that catches everyone unawares.

The second set of sources for innovative opportunity, a set of three, involves changes outside the enterprise or industry:

- Demographic (population changes).
- Changes in perception, mood and meaning.
- New knowledge, both scientific and non-scientific.

Principles of Innovations

According to Drucker, the principles of innovation require a few 'dos' and a few 'don'ts.' He also enumerates what he calls "conditions."

The 'Dos'

1. Purposeful, systematic innovation begins with an analysis of opportunities. It begins with thinking through what he has called the sources of innovative principles.
2. Innovation is both conceptual and perceptual. The second imperative of innovation is to go out to look, to ask, and to listen.
3. An innovation to be effective has to be simple and it has to be focused. It should do only one thing, otherwise it confuses. If it is not simple, it won't work.
4. Effective innovations start small. They are not grandiose. They try to do one specific thing.
5. A successful innovation aims at leadership.

The 'Don'ts'

1. The first is simply not to try to be clear. Innovations have to be handled by ordinary human beings. In other words, anything too clear, whether in design or in execution, is almost bound to fail.
2. Do not diversify. Innovations that stray from a core are likely to become diffuse. They remain ideas and do not become innovations.
3. Finally, do not try to innovate for the future. Innovate for the present.

According to Drucker, three conditions have to be fulfilled. All three are obvious, but often go disregarded:

1. Innovation is work. It requires knowledge. It often requires great ingenuity. When all is said and done, innovation becomes hard, focused on purposeful work, making very great demands on diligence, on persistence, and on commitment.
2. To succeed, innovators must build on their strengths.
3. Finally, innovation always has to be close to the market, focussed on the market, indeed market driven.

Drucker believed entrepreneurship, business (individual enterprises) and free markets were the best way to achieve a good society.

Drucker had eminent sense of genealogy, pedigree and structure of assumptions, the categories that constitute the basis of any domain of knowledge. He was also sensitive to the limits of knowledge. At a time when people were demanding a science of leadership, Drucker insisted on sticking to management. He felt management was sociologically grounded and democratic, possessing the prose of an everyday world. The purpose of an organisation he claimed was in "making common man, do uncommon things 'Leadership he felt was irrational, unpredictable, in fact, undecipherable.

Peter F. Drucker opined that "an entrepreneur is one who always searches for change, responds to it and exploits it as an opportunity." He laid emphasis on two important factors — innovation and resource — that led to emergence of entrepreneurship. According to him, innovation is the real hub of entrepreneurship which creates resource. A thing is regarded as resource when its economic value is recognised. For example, mineral oil was considered worthless until the discovery of its use. Similarly, purchasing power was considered an important resource by an American innovative entrepreneur who invented instalment buying.

Box - 3

EMERGING INDIA HOLDS INNOVATIVE SOLUTIONS FOR GLOBAL MALADIES

Innovation, technology and entrepreneurship have played an important role in the contemporary world to expedite the process of social and economic development.

To drive innovations and encourage inventive practices India needs to focus on the following:

- Change mindset to a more rational and scientific thinking in government, administration, universities, science and technology laboratories, schools and homes.
- Use technologies related communication, biotech, nanotech and alternative sources of energy to expedite the process of modernisation and meet basic human needs related to water, sanitation, food, shelter, education and health.
- Develop new cost-effective products and services in collaboration with public/private partnership to create new business models which are scalable to improve access and affordability.
- Create a new eco system to integrate resources and improve interactions between universities, industries, laboratories, financial institutions and markets.
- Innovate ways to modernise age-old processes that the British Raj left behind along with the license raj, controls and confusion. It is time to innovate, new ways and means for government to interface with citizens with simplicity, transparency, clarity and accountability at federal, state, district and taluka levels.
- Bring young talent to the mainstream of highei education and science and technology activities in the country.
- Focus on indigenous development with local expertise on local problems with local content of local relevance.
- Ensure that all development activities, products, services etc. are globally competitive, scalable and sustainable.
- Respect and promote intellectual properties, parents, copyrights, trademarks in order to integrate the Indian economy with the global economy.
- Recognise that the world over the best brain are busy solving the problems of the rich who really do not have problems to solve. Problems of the poor at the bottom of pyramid are far more challenging, complex and demand special efforts and attention. Solving their problems is of the greater consequence and it offers many more opportunities to innovate.

In my judgement India is uniquely placed to appreciate and understand the problems of the emerging markets and bottom of the pyramid and therefore it has the ability to provide global leadership for innovative solutions.

For instance, India has the ability to understand that water requires a great deal of sophisticated technologies related to satellite imagery, geo-hydrological surveys, Geological Survey of India (GIS) mapping desalination plants, water testing laboratories, access iron removal methods and many other technology capabilities related to chemistry, physics, electronics etc. The key is to blend the most sophisticated technologies of satellite and software, fiber optics and biotech, nanotech and solar cell tissue culture and stem cell research to address the fundamental human requirements.

Unfortunately many of the modern technologies have focused on value addition to the needs of the rich and ignored the real mass of people at the bottom of the pyramid.

Indian cost structure, at least at this stage of development, provides unique opportunities to deploy high-end talent to solve low-end problems with hi-tech solutions.

For India and the rest of the world, the great source of hope lies in the country's 550 million people below the age of 25 who are unencumbered by outdated thinking and are eager to learn new technologies and innovate to make a difference.

The key challenge is to re-engineer knowledge institutions and infrastructure now to respond to their needs for the future and create new eco systems to allow and encourage them to innovate and excel globally.

Box - 3

A NATION OF INNOVATORS

These Innovations have made all of us proud.

- **Sulabh**

Set up in 1970, Sulabh revolutionised sanitation practices in India. Developed a scavenging-free two-pit pour-flush toilet (Sulabh Shauchalaya), it uses innovative on-site human waste disposal technology. Its pay-and-use public toilets (popularly known as Sulabh Complexes) with bath, laundry and urinal facilities are used by about 10 million people everyday. It also produces biogas and biofertiliser in excreta-based plants. The organisation reportedly clocks a turnover of about Rs. 100 crore a year.

- **Mumbai's Dabbawalas**

Mumbai's *dabbawala* service (a unique way of delivering lunch boxes) is 114 years old and serves 175,000 customers with an efficiency and precision that won "6 sigma" rating (accuracy being 99.39 per cent). A 5,000 strong *dabbawala* face (including a few woman, too) uses handcarts, fast and slow local trains, and strong wooden racks to reach the *dabbas*, or lunch boxes, to their customers.

Prof. Robert John Aumann
Nobel Laureate (Economics)
on "Game Theory-Applications"

- **Operation Flood**

It's the biggest success story in the country's cooperative movement and one of the biggest in the world. Launched in 1970. Operation Flood was a brainchild of Verghese Kurien. The foundation of Operation Flood are the village milk producers' cooperatives, which procure milk and provide inputs and services, and make modern management and technology available to members. It transformed India from a milk-deficit country to the largest milk producer in the market.

The teNet Group at IIT Madras: A brainchild of Ashok Jhunjhunwala, a Professor at IIT Madras, TeNet group's biggest contribution is the cor DEXCT technology. corDECT is a WLL standard aimed at providing converged services — voice and data — at an affordable price to the masses, irrespective of the location. It simplifies last-mile connectivity and enables wireless remote access. It has also spun off — with faculty, student and alumni involvement — a series of firms that are engaged in a range of activities from IT product development to provision of technology-based services.

- **Gaining Critical Mass**

Indian companies are the most active innovators among Rapidly Developing Economies

India	1,018
Russia	1,000
China	980
South Africa	566
Brazil	525

Figures are US patent filings between 1999 and 2003.

Source: Confederation of Indian Industry — Bostan Consulting Group report dated December 13, 2005.

- **The Key to Innovation**

The country can encourage the spirit of originality by:

- Doing away with rate learning;
- Revamping the bank credit system;
- Encouraging venture capitalists;
- Giving tax breaks to indigenous innovations; and
- Ushering in a strict patent regime.

According to Drucker, successful entrepreneurship involves the following things:

(*a*) Value and satisfaction obtained from resources by the consumer are increased.

(*b*) New values are created.

(*c*) Material is converted into a resource or existing resources are combined in a new or more productive configuration.

(*d*) Entrepreneurship is the practice that has a knowledge base.

(*e*) Entrepreneurship is not confined to big business and economic institutions, it is equally important to small business and non-economic institutions.

(*f*) Entrepreneurship behaviour rather than personality trait is more important to enhance entrepreneurship.

(*g*) The foundation of entrepreneurship lies in concept and theory rather than in intuition.

Thus, Drucker has given his views that "an entrepreneur need not be a capitalist or an owner. A banker who mobilizes other's money and allocates it in areas of higher yield is very much an entrepreneur though he is not the owner of the money.

Box - 5

INNOVATIVE ENTREPRENEURS

They just went ahead and did it

Dr. Charudutt Mishra: Thirty-four-year-old Mishra, the scientist who helped save the snow leopard from extinction by involving local people in conservation efforts, won Britain's top conservation prize, the Whitley Gold Award in 2005. Mishra has been working in a Himalayan village, just south of Ladakh, to successfully address the twin problems of declining wild prey and the human-snow looped conflict, both of which threaten the existence of the beautiful predator.

Sarath Lakshman: All of 16 years old, this plus-two student developed SLYLUX, a user-friendly version of Linux two years ago. Which was hugely appreciated by the global freeware community.

Veena Gunduvalli: This Hyderabadi is the founder and chief strategic officer of Emagia, a leading cash-flow management company with offices In the US and Hyderabad. In recognition of her entrepreneurial skills and business leadership In founding Emagia, she was conferred the Trallblazer of the Year 2002 award by the Forum for Women Entrepreneurs (FEW), US.

Sandeep Pandey: He is the founder of Asha, an NGO which supports education and livelihood projects for poor children in India and helps Dalits overcome caste barriers. Pandey bagged the Ramon Magasaysay award in 2002 in the Emergent Leadership category for his work towards improving the lives of the poor and under-privileged by tapping the resources of Indians living abroad. The 35-year-old activist is an IIT-ian with a doctorate from the University of Berkeley in California.

Sekbar Raghavan: A physicist based in Chennai, Raghavan has dedicated his life to rainwater harvesting (RWH). Long before governments started thinking of RWH, this man did. He gave up his teaching job at Madras University to start Rain Centre, campaigning for RWH. He was awarded the Ashoka Innovator for the Public Fellowship in Washington.

Rajendra Singh: Rajendra Singh (48), a zamindar's son from Dola village of Meerut district in Uttar Pradesh landed in Kishori, a drought-stricken hamlet in the Alwar district of Rajasthan on his watery adventure in the Summer of 1984. During the next five years he revived traditional means of water harvesting across the country to alleviate water scarcity. He won the Ramon Magasaysay award in 2001. Today over 14,000 check dams are built to harvest water.

The Coming of Entrepreneurial Society: Innovation and entrepreneurship are needed equally in society, the economy, in public-service institutions, and in business. For, they keep society flexible and self-renewing, without violence or economic catastrophe, but with purpose, direction, and control. This requires that executives in all institutions make innovation and entrepreneurship an ongoing, everyday activity (*i.e.,* practice) in their own work and in the work of the organisation.

Tryst with the Virtues of Innovation

In an era of rapid change, innovativeness becomes the lifeblood of business. Innovation is essential not just for businesses built on new technology and discoveries in the life sciences, but also for established industries.

My own experience seems to show that innovation and creativity thrive best in certain emotional and social climates. So to verify that innovation is as important as everyone claims and to discover the ideal innovative environment, I investigated what others have said about it. In this column, we look briefly at innovation itself, but focus mostly on the organisational climates that foster it.

Innovation Myths

Vijay Govindarajan

There is a great opportunity for Indian companies to emerge as fierce global players. If they have to succeed in closing their "innovation gap", they had better avoid the common innovation myths and innovation barriers.

1. Innovation is the CEO's job.
2. Listen to the customer.
3. Companies should spend a lot more time trying to generate breakthrough ideas.
4. Innovation is a battle between a maverick and a corporate bureaucracy.
5. Planning is irrelevant for innovation because so much is unknown.
6. Innovation and discipline are oxymorons.
7. There are generalisable principles that companies can use to drive innovation performance.
8. Innovation requires new products.
9. Innovation requires technological breakthrough.
10. Innovation should take place through "skunk works" far away from established business.

Innovation Barriers

Based on extensive discussions and interviews with hundreds of executives in *Fortune 500* corporations, I have identified five barriers that prevent large and established companies from engaging in breakthrough innovations. Indian companies will do well to overcome these barriers.

Barrier 1: Too much focus on current operations
Barrier 2: Lack of a "tolerance for failure" culture
Barrier 3: Not embedding innovation as an organisational capability.
Barrier 4: Too much of a silo mentality
Barrier 5: Lack of a global mindset.

Profit by Innovation

Live out of your imagination, not your history – **Stephen Covey**

The dictionary definition of innovation is (1) the introduction of something new, or (2) something that deviates from established doctrine or practice. If a business succeeds with an established product or process, why change it? The answer is quite obvious: If your business doesn't change or improve its products, the competition will and in ways that will make their products and services more appealing than yours.

The link between profitability and innovation is well-established by business common sense and through many scholarly studies. In the year 2000, a Price Waterhouse Coopers study showed that top innovators may earn more than 75% of their revenue from new products and services, which did not exist 5 years ago. And as you might expect, poor innovators earn poorly from new products and services, 10% or less according to the same study.

With or without the PWC study, business recognises that innovation is a must. A search for "innovation" on the Harvard Business Review's website yields 1744 articles, 49 of them written in the last 3 months. A 1998 survey of 400 American companies found that 70% mentioned innovation in their mission statements or goals. And yet, many of these companies have neither a system to manage innovation nor a climate to foster it. Let's look ever so briefly at the climate.

And the Ideal Innovative Climate is...

Innovation is the specific instrument of entrepreneurship — the act that endows resources with a new capacity to create wealth — ***Peter Drucker***

In 1983, Goran Ekvall did a pioneering study of innovativeness for the Swedish Council of Management and Organisational Behaviour. This and other subsequent studies identified 9 – others identify 10 – organisational factors, which foster innovation:

- *Trust and openness:* Creating safe places to explore dangerous truths and different views
- *Challenge and involvement:* Being emotionally engaged and committed
- *Freedom:* Having the space and responsibility to make your own choices
- *Idea time:* Having the time before acting to think things through
- *Idea support:* Finding the necessary resources to give new ideas a try
- *Playfulness and humour:* Creating a relaxed atmosphere
- *Absence of conflict:* Putting in place 'rules' that encourage consensus building and dialogue
- *Debates:* Engaging in lively discussion of the pros and cons of an issue or solution
- *Risk taking:* Making it OK to think the unthinkable or try new things and be allowed to fail.

The PWC study mentioned above similarly identified innovative organisations as those that (1) consider trust to be the most significant factor influencing their success, (2) harness diversity across viewpoints in generating ideas and making decisions, (3) recruit and develop people that challenge the status quo, and (4) establish a balanced relationship between the contributions of leaders and followers at all levels.

Recent conversations with Jonathan Huxley, co-founder and CEO of the very successful internet startup Enterprise Plc, and Mike McKeever, VP of Corporate Business Development at the telecom company Qwest as it grew from USD $230,000,000 to USD $4,000,000,000 annual revenue in 4 years, affirm the importance of these organisational climatic ingredients. And my own experiences at internet startups and large companies alike validates these factors through their presence or absence, but especially those of trust, freedom, playfulness, debate and risk-taking. Any team that I have been part of or have lead and that can be described with these 5 words has, by my personal measure, been innovative and productive. The PWC survey is in agreement with this view: It lists the capabilities of "fostering a creative working environment" and the closely related "balancing leadership and followership" as two essential factors required in all highly innovative companies.

⌘ What's in it for Me?

Innovation distinguishes between a leader and a follower — **Steve Jobs**

In order to cultivate the spirit of innovation, these studies, surveys, and experiences show that an organisation must forever strive to value each of its members as an individual and promote a climate in which Ekvall's nine factors can truly flourish. And since according to Ekvall, nearly two-thirds of employee behaviour can be directly attributable to behaviours of the leadership team, you as a leader in your own business have to own the responsibility, and must yourself live the recipe for innovation. In conclusion, to use the words of R. W. Emerson, famous 19th century philosopher and poet, "Trust men and they will be true to you; treat them greatly and they will show themselves great."

⌘ Which category do you fall in

Different leadership and followership models and how do they function

Nature of the contract	Leader archetype	Follower archetype	Now the leader works with the diversity	Potential for useful novelty in outcomes	Impact on empowerment
Unilateral	Tyrant	Drone	Trends to ignore	Low	Compliance
Consultative	Benevolent dictator	Supporter	Uses a source of new ideas to support their own		
Consensual	democrat	Equal	Helps others to combine their different ideas and co-create		
Anarchic	Rebel	Independent agent	Creates the environment for synergistic working	High	Commitment

Box - 6

NATURE, SHOW US THE WAY

Nature knows it all. If human kind wants to survive, it better learn and adopt nature's ways of preserving things. That's what 'biomimicry' is all about — the science and art of emulating nature's best biological ideas to solve human design problems sustainably.

VOILA!

> Inspiration > Adaptation

The nests of fungus-growing ants avoid flood damage and create uniform microclimates via necklace-like or tree-like architecture.

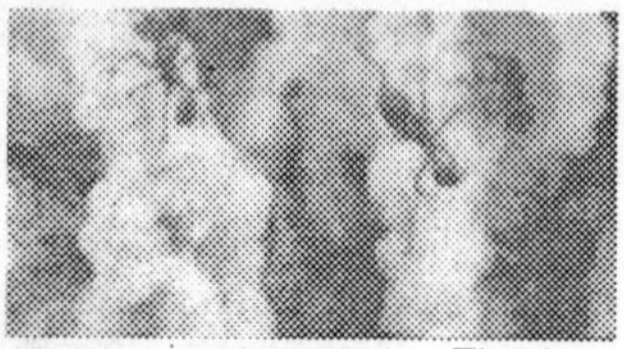

Biomimetic Application Ideas

- Building design for underground homes
- Mushroom farming
- Maintaining a uniform microclimate

The head of a shipworm bores circular burrows in wood thanks to raspy, rotating shells.

Biomimetic Application Ideas

- Tunneling device
- Closure technique (pallets) could be used for packaging

The metacarpal bone of a horse has a hole structure which helps it to avoid structural weakness

Biomimetic Application Ideas. This can be used for increasing the strength of aeroplanes, boats, automobiles and other structures that have holes for wiring or fuel and hydraulic lines. (A quick rule of efficiency in the aerospace industry is that one pound of weight saved in a plane can save 10 pounds of fuel.)

Australian frogs of the genus Notaden protect themselves from insect bites by secreting a glue that gums up the insect's mouth!

Biomimetic Application Ideas

Glue that works in moist environments, is flexible, and porous. Could be uses other than medical.

Nature is an amazing laboratory, it provides us techniques and ideas on how to live life in a sustainable manner — be it through photosynthesis, self-assembly, natural selection, self-sustaining ecosystems, eyes and ears and skin and shells, talking neurons natural medicines, and more. Now it is upto us how smartly we employ these techniques. The question is: are we even thinking on those lines.

Let's take a look at one of these categories: materials. Right now, we use what's called "heat, beat, and treat" to make materials. Kevlar, for instance, the stuff in flak jackets, is our premier, high-tech material. Nothing stronger or tougher. But how do we make it? We pour petroleum-derived molecules into a pressurized vat of concentrated sulphuric acid, and boil it at several hundred degrees Fahrenheit. We then subject it to high pressures to force the fibres into alignment as we draw them out. The energy input is extreme and the toxic byproducts are odious.

Nature takes a different approach. Because an organism makes materials like bone or collagen or silk right in its own body, it doesn't make sense to "heat, beat, and treat." A spider, for instance, produces a waterproof silk that beats the pants off Kevlar for toughness and elasticity. Ounce for ounce, it's five times stronger than steel! But the spider manufactures it in water, at room temperature, using no high heats, chemicals, or pressures. Best of all, it doesn't need to drill offshore for petroleum; it takes flies and crickets at one end and produces this miracle material at the other. In a pinch, the spider can even eat part of its old web to make a new one.

Imagine what this kind of a processing strategy would do for our fibre industry! Renewable raw materials, great fibres, and negligible energy and waste. We obviously have a lot to learn from an organism that has been making silk for some 380 million years.

Theory of Change

Frank W. Young conducted the Thematic Appreciation Test (TAT) on a group of entrepreneurs. The test revealed the tendency to describe the situation as a problem to be solved, an awareness of pragmatic effort required, confidence in their own ability to solve the problem and a tendency to take the viewpoint of each individual in turn and analyse the situation as he might see it before suggesting an outcome.

Young's theory is a theory of change based on society's incorporation of reactive sub-groups. A group becomes reactive when the following three conditions coincide:

(*i*) When a group experiences low status recognition;

(*ii*) 'When denied of access to important social networks; and

(*iii*) When the group has better institutional resources than other groups in the society at the same level.

Frank W. Young said instead of individuals, groups with higher differentiation have the capacity to react. He designed 'reactiveness' or 'solidarity' as the degree to which members of the group create, maintain and project a coherent definition of the situation, and differentiation is defined as the diversity, as approach to coherence of the social meanings maintained by the group. When a group has a higher degree of institutional and occupational diversity, relative to its acceptance, it tends to intensify its internal communication which gives rise to a unified definition of the situation. To improve their symbolic position in the larger structure they find a way which allows mutual understanding despite the differences in the occupation and family status. Such pressures bear not only on social, political and theological factors but also on economic factors. Some members of the solidarity groups excell at combining resources like labour, capital etc. in new ways and they become entrepreneurs.

Though young did not come out with a new definition, he accepted Schumpeterian definition. But he has postulated a casual sequence where transformation codes are developed by the solidarity groups to improve their symbolic position in the larger structure and become entrepreneurs.

Young's theory is a theory of change based on society's incorporation of reactive sub-groups. A group will become reactive as per Young's theory, when the three conditions coincide. The conditions are firstly, when a group experience low status recognition, secondly, when the denial of access to important social networks and thirdly when the group has better institutional resources than other groups in the society at the same level.

X-Efficiency Theory

The Late Harvey Leibenstein propounded the theory of X-efficiency.

This theory, originally developed for another purpose, has recently been applied to analyse the role of the entrepreneur. Basically, X-efficiency is the degree of inefficiency in the use of resources within the firm: it measures the extent to which the firm fails to realise its productive potential.

He borrowed this term from military literature, where between two equal armies, if one army is successful while the other is not, the success is attributed to "X-Efficiency". A mixture of various factors not generally recognised in technical literature is said to account for "X-Efficiency." Leibenstein used this concept in order to challenge the mainstream paradigm of economic theory. In this paradigm households and firms are deemed to be rational agents always trying to maximise utilities or profits in the context of given constraints of resources etc. Leibenstein explored the reasons for the absence of full efficiency and built up a theory, which may have some relevance for conditions in countries like India and to their low economic performance through history.

The first reason is the dominant prevalence of past customs and conventions in the matter of economic relations. Though with modernisation, contract must displace custom it may take a long time for this to come about. The sheer possibility of material improvements for both parties through contracts is not a sufficient condition. Individuals and organisations must be ready to give up past customs and face oppositions and hostility for breaking tradition. This is all the more so in an economy in which religious, caste and tribal, mores and practices continue to exercise their sway. Society does not necessarily value economic efficiency as more important than upward mobility in the social sphere. This even though everyone recognises that full scope for economic efficiency may lead to more production as a result of which there can be more for everyone. The problem here is material betterment is not the single-most criterion. Another way by which the past customs and mores etc. limit the scope for economic advance is in the sphere of population control. We have to depend upon the slow effects of improvements in education to convince people of the need for fertility control. The demographic lag is unnecessarily long in countries like India. Probably many examples can be given of X-Inefficiency due to the rigidity in the sociological and related spheres. The speed of Sanskritisation is rather slow under these conditions. The defeat of the class concept by the caste concept in India and such countries has to be deeply probed. The reasons for the defeat may have something to do with the sociological rigidities against which radical Marxism simply bet its wings in vain.

The second reason suggested by Leibenstein pertains to inertia. When inertia prevails economic agents do not respond to incentives, at least in the measure expected. Inertia itself may be due to morbidity or to excessive belief in exogenous, external chance determinants of the life-course of human beings. The latter are not able to perceive any definite and dependable relation between their own efforts and response and results. Hence, human beings tend to place faith in supernatural forces. The passive economic agents in the sphere of the availing of material opportunities and challenges is very conspicuous in some States in India like Bihar.

A third reason mentioned by Leibenstein pertains to the incomplete contracts because of the difficulty in the specification of required responses in a quantitative manner. This is specially so in regard to the relation between wages and efficiency. The parameters of efficiency cannot be specified except in very simple cases. Hence workers can get away with less work than is generally expected by the employers. In governmental organisations and in services only few persons may be putting their best efforts whereas the laggards will be profiting by the excellent work of the few. This is the case of medicine and teaching. Full and adequate work may not be performed education *vis-a-vis* the parallel tutorial system is a standing example how in colleges teachers do not put in their best efforts. It is so difficult to specify the teaching responsibilities. Consequently society as a whole spends more on education for obtaining given results than is strictly necessary. If we treat the electorate as entering into a contract with the political parties for fulfillment of the manifestos and for efficient administration, the institutions for enforcing the contract even assuming that the contract can be clearly specified. The accountability of governments will be better if contracts can be clear and there are penalties for not fulfilling them.

According to Leibenstein, entrepreneurial functions are determined by the X-efficiency which means the degree of efficiency on the use of resources within the firm. The theory has got the following features:

1. Routine entrepreneurship: While propounding the theory, Leibenstein identified two broad types of entrepreneurship. First type of entrepreneurship is known as routine entrepreneurship, which is intertwined with the important functions of management of the business.

2. New entrepreneurship: The second type of entrepreneurship is new entrepreneurship, which presumes innovative entrepreneurship. This entrepreneurship is characterized by aggressive assemblage of information and the analysis of results derived from sound combination of factors.

3. Twin roles of entrepreneur: Harvey Leibenstein pointed out that there always exists some deficiencies in the production function or input-output relationship. These deficiencies or gaps exist because all the inputs in the production function cannot be marketed. So Leibenstein highlighted the twin functions of entrepreneur, namely:

(*i*) Gap filling

(*ii*) Input completing

While executing the entrepreneurial functions, the entrepreneur has to mobilize all the inputs to derive the final output. But some inputs like motivation and leadership are vague and their outputs is questionable. Thus, it is the function of the entrepreneur to marshall all the inputs to increase the efficiency of the existing methods of production to earn profit.

4. X-efficiency factor: As it is known that X-efficiency is the degree of inefficiency in the use of inputs within the firm, it is the measuring rod to know the extent of deficiencies the firm incur in its production function. X-efficiency arises because either the resources of the firm are not properly utilized or they are wasted

According to Leibenstein, the supply of entrepreneurship is governed by input completing ability and inadequate motivational state.

For a given set of inputs, productive potential is identified with the point on Neo-classical production frontiers. X-efficiency arises either because the firm's resources are used in the wrong way or because they are wasted, that is, not used at all.

Leibenstein identifies two main roles for the entrepreneur. The first role is input completion, which involves making available inputs that improve the efficiency of existing production methods or facilitate the introduction of new ones. The role of the entrepreneur is to improve the flow of information in the market.

The second role, gap filling, is closely asking to the arbitrage function emphasised by Kirzner. Leibenstein provides a very vivid description of gap filling, visualising the economy as a net made up of nodes and pathways.

The economic agents are neither rational nor work to seek the highest utility levels and profits. Leibenstein however provided place for external stimulus, shocks and pushes as a probable way out. This is one reason, a very important reason, why conditions of competition, free entry and free exit, flexibility, full mobility, employment contracts with renewable tenures, recall facilities in politics, public interest petitions, ethical rules with scope for penalties, hire and fire in labour matters for micro-level inefficiencies, probe-oriented and fearless media, etc. are all important.

An important issue, which Leibenstein probably missed is the relative unimportance of materialist goals *per se* in society's norms. Within the total well-being complex, the economic domain may be played down in the socio-political systems and traditions. Even if we assume rationality and utility maximisation, their spheres may be limited. Consequently, societies may not perform as well in the economic sphere as economist may desire.

Students of the history of Indian economic thought would recollect that Mahadev Govind Ranade during the last decade of the 19th century had put out more or less similar reasons for the then low development of India in the economic sphere. Ranade had argued that the structure of socio-economic institutions then prevalent had together worked towards the economic backwardness of India. Leibenstein was aiming at a general theory of backwardness through his X-Inefficiency analysis. Ranade wanted the State to be the economic crane to lift the economy out of its backwardness. Leibenstein did not go to the policy aspects. It would be interesting if the above brief discussion of the analysis of causes for X-Inefficiency are examined in detail and quantitative weights are attached to different causes. This perhaps is a task of major research. We could then work out the link between Ranade and Leibenstein, truly one of the original thinkers in the area of the theory of economic underdevelopment.

Theory of Growth

Modern growth theory, which built on the Harrod-Domar model, was born in 1956 with Robert Solow's famous papers. The "new" growth theory, born with Paul Romer's Papers in 1986.

A Recipe for Growth

To enjoy strong GDP growth, developed economies need, as a priority, policy frameworks that encourage competitive intensity. This means lifting product market regulations, enabling firms to achieve economies of scale, easing land-use restrictions, promoting competition in their often neglected domestic service sectors, and encouraging labour market flexibility.

Growth theory can be viewed as the attempt to formalize the equations of motion or aggregate output, and growth empirics can be viewed as the related effort to estimate these equations of motion, including the "impulse response functions" showing how output responds to various shocks (for example, policy, institutions, geography, prices',' and technical change). The answer to the question "what happens to output growth when trade barriers or inflation are reduced" could, in principle, have a single theoretical and empirical answer. If France and Nepal can both be treated as water in a liquid state, then it is conceivable that a theory and empirics of growth that treat France and Nepal as both generic countries is adequate. I regard it as much more likely that growth dynamics are characterized as equations of motions within states and equations that determine transitions across states.

Growth Theory: Old and New

Growth Theory (as we shall understand it) has no particular bearing on underdevelopment economics, nor has the underdevelopment interest played any essential part in its development.

— John Hicks, Capital and Growth, 1965

Dozens of brilliant (and thousands of amateurish) "new growth theory" papers later, it is hard to re-create the enthusiasm with which "endogenous growth" was first greeted in academic and policy circles in the early 1980s. At that time, growth theory was still dominated by Robert Solow's model, now known as the "exogenous growth" model, and was stuck, badly stuck. By 1971, Solow could write that everything that could be said with his growth model had been said. And what was said was not that nothing could be said with certainty but that, with certainty, nothing could be said by the model. In the model (and all its variants), equilibrium or steady-state growth rates of per capita output were driven by technical progress — but these models, as constructed, could say nothing about the determinants of technical progress. This point is often misunderstood but is important to understanding just how badly cornered the profession was and, hence, how excited it was about new growth.

The Solow model did not assume that technical progress was exogenous — that is, determined outside the model. Rather, the model made the assumptions necessary to produce a model of an economy with a dynamic equilibrium, a path to which, in the long run, the economy would settle down. The implication of those assumptions was that technical progress had to be exogenous to the model. The technical problem is that the assumptions necessary to produce a model with an equilibrium implies that payments to the standard factors of production — labour and capital — exhaust the total product. Nothing is left over to pay entrepreneurs or innovators. But if innovators cannot be paid at all in equilibrium (given the assumptions of the model), then nothing — including policy of any kind — can affect their incentives to innovate. This problem of reconciling purposive economic innovation that results in greater productivity of all factors (such innovation obviously exists and is a key to the success of capitalism) with formal economic models (which could adequately model this phenomenon) was long standing. It was clearly recognised by Joseph Schumpeter and Frank Knight, but Solow's clean algebra and exposition just made it stark.

The best macroeconomic models circa 1980 said national policies could affect the level of incomes but they could not affect steady-state growth. Meanwhile, microeconomic analysis of sector reforms — for example, in trade, privatization, or the financial sector — produced estimates of the level effects of policy changes that were typically only small fractions of GDP. This marriage — of a macroeconomics in which long-run growth rates were driven by technical progress that was independent of national policies to a microeconomics in which policy reform could produce only small efficiency gains in levels — was a stable but increasingly unhappy one. The marriage was stable because both the macro and micro outcomes were not "assumptions" but were technically driven features of their respective analytical approaches.

Into this unhappy marriage of macro and micro came new growth theory models. One of the reasons the marriage was unhappy was entirely technical and internal to the discipline of economics: couldn't economists produce a model that had both purposive innovation and a steady state? Romer (1983) used advances in techniques of modelling "non-competitive" equilibrium (in which factor payments do not exhaust product) to produce new models that did just that. In this new class of models, since innovation could be driven by incentives, national policies could influence not only the level of income but also countries' steady-state growth rates — that is, the very long run rates.

A second reason the marriage of macro and micro was unhappy was external: its inability to explain obvious facts about the world (for instance, that levels of income did, in fact, differ by orders of magnitude) or to provide policy guidance. Therefore, the spirit (if not the actual technical rigor) of new growth models was quickly put to use in the policy world to justify policy reform based on its impact on growth. Structural adjustment as a response to negative economic shocks emphasized the need to restore short-run macroeconomic stability and raise growth rates, with the promise that postshock and poststabilization levels of income would be much higher.

While the contribution of the new growth models to the internal logic of the economics discipline has been lasting, the bloom came off the rose of the explicit use of new growth models for policy purposes in developing countries relatively quickly. Nearly everything about the first-generation growth models was at odds with the needs of developing country policymakers. The new growth literature focused on the very long run and on incentives for expanding the

Box - 7

MANAGEMENT INNOVATION

In a market where talent is largely a commodity and can be bought anywhere, the secret sauce is creating an environment in which you push that frontier out, in which you can steadily raise the returns on human capital. The combination of technology and talent is a powerful catalyst for value creation, but to take advantage of the web's capacity to help us aggregate and amplify human potential in new ways.

Gary Hamel

The opportunity is substantial. Against the backdrop of the digital age's dramatic technological change, ongoing globalisation, and the declining predictability of strategic planning models, only new approaches to managing employees and organising talent to maximise wealth creation will provide companies with a durable competitive advantage.

There's something intriguing about the phenomenon of management innovation. Almost by definition, it is hard to do... But when a company does have the courage to innovate in this way, the very same qualities are what makes the innovation hard for competitors to copy.

Research on management innovation has suggested the following a few important factors.

Become a management innovator: Just as you need a physical R&D lab to do technological innovation, you need awareness and dedicated resources to take management innovation seriously. Very few companies do this at the moment.

Create a problem-solving culture: When employees are faced with an unusual problem or challenge in the company, what is their typical reaction? Do they resort to a standard solution that has already been endorsed by competitors? Or do they look deeper, see the problem in new ways and start to hypothesise about new ways of solving it? Only the latter path can lead the company toward management innovation.

Seek out analogies and exemplars from different environments: If your challenge is to become more resilient, try looking at highly resilient social systems, such as parliamentary democracies, cities or faith systems. If the problem is one of increasing the motivation of employees, then look at the Scouting movement, or Open Source Software. Benchmarking your competitors is not going to do the job.

Build capacity for low-risk experiments: Rather than letting new and questionable ideas loose on the entire organisation, try an experimental approach where each innovation can be tested with a limited number of people and for a limited period of time. We have seen companies run one-day experiments with genuinely valuable outputs.

Make use of external change agents to explore your new ideas: While you need to own your innovation activities, there is value in selectively making use of outsiders as sources of new ideas and analogies, and as sounding boards and sense-makers.

technological frontier — not particularly useful for most developing countries, whose primary interest was in restoring short- to medium-term growth and accelerating technological catchup by adopting known innovations. In the end, Hicks was not only right but also prescient about the irrelevance of new growth to the "underdevelopment interest."

Empirical growth research; short and long

I just ran four million growth regressions.

— Xavier Sala-i-Martin

New growth theory and empirical research into growth have the same relationship as lightning and a forest fire. Although lightning may start the fire, where the fire goes and how much it burns are determined by the condition of the forest, not its origins. New growth theory legitimized a research agenda — including growth regressions — focused on the correlates of national growth rates that has continued long past the relevance of the original spark. In fact, nearly all growth regressions today, while they place growth of output on the left-hand side as the variable to be explained, are arithmetically equivalent to "levels" regressions that do not depend on new growth theory at all. Of course, from a policy viewpoint; this is irrelevant. The relevant question is what actions can be taken to spur more rapid economic growth over the relevant horizon. The answer to this question does not depend at all on whether the growth impact is a steady-state gain (and, hence, an infinitely large-level impact) or just a big enough impact on levels to accelerate growth rates.

As they have evolved, growth regressions have moved toward the "short" (using panel regression techniques) or the "long" (which goes back to regressions on the level of income, which is, after all, the same as the longest possible growth rate). Let us review these two strands separately.

Growth regressions: the short: Growth regressions have proved a very useful extended investigation into the correlates of medium- to long-run growth. From the original growth regressions, which used single cross sections with 20 to 30 year growth rates and ordinary least squares, to the latest use of panel data with 5 and 10 year growth rates and more sophisticated estimation techniques, the growth regression literature has added to the stock of knowledge about the correlates of growth with various policy and non-policy variables. However, in the end, as an instrument for informing policy, regressions have suffered five exhausting, if not mortal wounds.

First, growth regressions never satisfactorily resolved the "symptoms versus syndromes" problem. They could establish the relationship between particular observable empirical variables ("symptoms") and growth but could only rarely move convincingly from those observed associations to specific recommendations on how to tackle the underlying causes of the emergence of the symptoms. For example, suppose one finds that a high black market premium is associated with lower growth. Is this an indicator that trade policy was awry, that there were macroeconomic imbalances, or that the country was unable to respond to adverse trade shocks? Or was it just an indicator of general dysfunction? Hence, although it was clear that there was something about a country's external policies that affected growth and triggered a syndrome of misguided inward orientation, even two decades into trade liberalisation, prominent scholars are still debating exactly what that something is and how best to address it.

Second, growth regressions were widely seen as producing estimates of gains from policy reform that were orders of magnitude larger than the microeconomic estimates of those gains — without any particularly convincing economic explanation. As trade theorists like T.N. Srinivasan and Jagdish Bhagwati consistently pointed out, the justification of trade reform based on growth regressions was a dubious exercise indeed, compared with the firmer groundings in theory and microeconomic empirics such reforms already had. The growth regression literature in field after field (trade, tax and expenditure, and finance) has had a very difficult time reconciling micro and macro evidence.

Third, growth regressions have a tough time dealing with the huge differences in country experiences. Establishing a correlation between economic output and some variable, say, corruption, on average across countries is only the very beginning of wisdom. Is the effect proportional to corruption as measured? Or does it follow a different relationship? Is the effect stronger in democracies than in non-democracies? In poorer than in richer countries? In more open than in less open countries? In reality, the growth regression is only a crude approximation that indicates the average impact of corruption, but it does not provide the information policymakers really want — the specific impact in a particular country. This inability to tackle country differences head-on led to differing results about one set of growth determinants (for example, external orientation) depending on sample, period, technique, and the other variables included — creating a general skepticism about the reliability of all growth regressions.

Fourth, growth regressions cannot predict turning points — either accelerations or decelerations — and we know that developing country growth rates have these turning points. The growth regression approach is much better at identifying the longer-run (30-years or more) determinants of growth than at predicting the very short run ones. In part, this is because the short-run volatility of many growth determinants is simply too small to play much of a role in explaining growth changes. For instance, while few doubt that human capital is vital for long-run development, it evolves so smoothly that it can explain at best.

Regressions

In economics, correlations are common. But identifying whether the correlation between two or more variables represents a causal relationship is rarely so easy. Countries that trade more with the rest of the world also have higher income levels — but does this mean that trade raises income levels? People with more education tend to have higher earnings, but does this imply that education results in higher earnings? Knowing precise answers to these questions is important. If additional years of schooling caused higher earnings, then policymakers could reduce poverty by providing more funding for education.

To help answer these types of questions, economists use a statistical tool known as regression analysis. Regressions are used to quantify the relationship between one variable and the other variables that are thought to explain it; regressions can also identify how close and well determined the relationship is. These days, running thousands of regressions has become commonplace and easy — although that was not always the case — and, in fact, it is difficult to find an empirical economic study without a regression in it. Other fields, including sociology, statistics, and psychology, rely heavily on regressions as well.

How to run a regression

To illustrate how a regression works, let's take a closer look at the problem of trying to determine the returns to education. The government collects data on people's education level and their subsequent earnings. But people go to school for a variety of reasons — some find it easier to learn than others or are just more motivated to stay in school longer. Others may be successful pursuing nonscholastic careers and may still achieve high earnings. These varied reasons for attending school may affect earnings, making it difficult to know whether the correlation between schooling and earnings represents a causal relationship or is driven by some other factor. People who find it easier to learn in school may also find it easier to learn on the job, resulting in higher earnings. Thus, the positive correlation between higher earnings and education levels may reflect innate aptitude, rather than the effects of education.

Before a regression is run, a theoretical model can help explain how and why one "dependent" variable is determined by one or more "independent" or "explanatory" variables. If an individual's earnings depends on his or her level of education is an example of a simple model with one explanatory variable. A corresponding regression equation, assumed to be linear, would look like:

$$Y = a + bX$$

On the left-hand side is Y, our dependent variable, earnings. On the right-hand side are a, our constant (or intercept), and b, our coefficient (or slope) multiplied by X our independent (or-explanatory) variable, education. The regression says in algebra that "earnings depend only on education and in a linear way"; the other explanatory factors, if there are any, are omitted.

But what if we think that the world is much more complicated and that a variety of factors might explain the impact of education on earnings? In that case, we would run a multiple-variable regression, which would look like:

$$Y = a + b_1X_1 + b_2X_2 + \ldots$$

Now, we have several X variables to help explain Y earnings — like ability, intelligence, age, education, marital status, and parental education. The b coefficients simply measure the impact of each of these variables on earnings, assuming the other variables are constant.

Smarter Is richer?

Let's try running a regression on the basis of the theory that hourly wages (our dependent variable) depend on the level .of education (our explanatory variable). We'll assume that another possible explanatory variable — aptitude, as measured by intelligence quotient *(IQ)* tests — has no effect on wages separate from any effect it may have through education. We plug in all of the data on earnings and education levels. We run the regression and find:

$$Y = 5.40 + 1.06\ EDU$$

The b coefficient tells us that an additional year of education is associated with a \$1.06 increase in the hourly wage. And for those with no education (EDU = 0), the constant indicates that the average wage is \$5.40 per hour.

But what if we put IQ in the equation — that is, assume that earnings depend on both the level of education and IQ? We plug in the data on IQ test results and find:

$$Y = 5.40 + 0.83EDU + 0.00\ IQ$$

We learn that individuals who performed better on IQ tests also had higher hourly wages. Moreover, while the impact of education on wages remains positive, it is about 27 per cent smaller than if we hadn't included IQ results (the 27 per cent comes from the difference in the coefficients: 100(1.06-0.83)/0.83). The implication is that we previously overestimated the effect of education on wages because we did not take into account the influence of IQ, which is correlated with education.

Potential pitfalls

Despite their benefits, regressions are prone to pitfalls and often misused. Take the following four leading difficulties.

Omitted variables: It is necessary to have a good theoretical model to suggest variables that explain the dependent variable. In the case of a simple two-variable regression, one has to think of the other factors that might explain the dependent variable. In our example, even when IQ is included, the correlation between education and earnings may reflect yet some other factor that is not included. That is, the individuals in the sample may still be different in some "unobserved" way that explains their subsequent earnings, possibly through their education choices. Individuals from wealthy families usually have better access to education, but family wealth may also create more connections in the labour market, leading to higher earnings. Thus, parental wealth may be another variable that should be included.

Reverse causality: Many theoretical models predict bidirectional causality — that is, a dependent variable can cause changes in one or more explanatory variables. For instance, higher earnings may enable people to invest more in their own education, which, in turn, raises their earnings. This complicates the way regressions should be estimated, calling for special techniques.

Mismeasurement: Factors might be measured incorrectly. For example, aptitude is difficult to measure, and there are well-known problems with IQ tests. As a result, the regression using IQ might not properly control for aptitude, leading to inaccurate or biased correlations between education and earnings.

Too limited a focus: A regression coefficient provides information only about how small changes — not large changes — in one variable relate to changes in another. It will show how a small change in education is likely to affect earnings but it will not allow the researcher to generalise about the effect of large changes. If everyone became college educated at the same time, a newly minted college graduate would be unlikely to earn a great deal more because the total supply of college graduates would have increased dramatically.

An Economic Theory

Mark Casson, in his book **The Entrepreneur — An Economic Theory,** a functional definition of the entrepreneur and considered why the entrepreneurial function is so valuable. He emphasised that the demand for entrepreneurship stems from the need to adjust to change, and that the supply of entrepreneurship is limited firstly, by the scarcity of the requisite personal qualities, and secondly, by the difficulty of identifying them when they are available. He suggested that there are four main qualities which are crucial for a successful entrepreneur of which one — imagination — is almost entirely innate. The other three qualities may be enhanced. The problems encountered in screening for these qualities, and in enhancing the ones that are deficient have a number of important implications for the development of a successful entrepreneurial career.

Most of the studies of entrepreneur make no attempt at proper definition. It may be said quite categorically that at the present moment, there is no established economic theory of entrepreneur. The subject area has been surrendered by economists to sociologists, psychologists and social scientists. However, his theory of entrepreneurship deals with the functional behaviour of entrepreneur and his qualities which are crucial for his success His theory has got the following features:

1. Demand-supply relationship: He has explained the theory using the economic jargons like demand and supply. These twin market forces act as the crucial parameters for entrepreneurial activities. According to M. Casson, the demand for entrepreneurship stems from the need to adjust to change and the supply of entrepreneurship is limited by the scarcity of the desired personal qualities.

2. Identification of qualities: To become a successful entrepreneur, Mark Casson identified some important qualities. According to him, qualities of a person drive him to take up entrepreneurial initiative and these qualities are mostly innate. He gives example of a quality which is crucial for a successful entrepreneur — the quality of imagination.

The theory reveals that in the development of successful entrepreneurship the following things are to be followed:

(*a*) The demand for entrepreneurship need to be adjusted as per the changing needs of the time.

(*b*) The deficient qualities of the entrepreneur should be made good by personal care.

Thus, according to Mark Casson, an entrepreneur is a person, who specialises in taking judgemental decisions about the co-ordination of scarce resources.

Theory of Incentives

Economists like Papanek and Harris have propounded that when certain economic conditions are favourable, entrepreneurship and economic growth will take place.

According to these two economists, economic incentives are the integral factors that have induced entrepreneurial initiatives. The main features of their theory are depicted as under:

1. Economic incentives: Entrepreneurial development is a function of economic incentives. This is one of the basic traits which drives the entrepreneur to take up entrepreneurial activities and to bring about success.

2. Link between economic gains and the inner urge: According to the above economists, the link between a person's inner urge and desired economic gains play a pivotal role for development of entrepreneurial competencies. The inner drives coupled with the hope of getting pecuniary benefits can give rise to entrepreneurial development.

3. Economic gain — sufficient condition: Theory of entrepreneurship, advocated by Papanek and Harris, reveals that entrepreneurs have got spontaneity in their willingness for undertaking diverse types of entrepreneurial activities because of economic gains. Thus, economic gain is considered as the sufficient condition for the origin of entrepreneurial initiatives in the economy.

Harvard School Theory

According to the Harvard School (Cole, 1949) entrepreneurship comprises any purposeful activity that initiate, maintain or develop a profit-oriented business in interaction with the internal situation of the business or with the economic, political and social circumstances surrounding the business. This approach emphasised two types of activities: the organisation or co-ordination activity, and the sensitivity to the environmental characteristics that affect decision making. Another exposition of the Harvard tradition is that of Leibenstein (1968) who emphasised activities such as searching and evaluating economic opportunities, mobilising resources necessary for the production process, connecting different markets and creating or expanding the firm.

Harvard School contemplated that entrepreneurship involves any deliberate activity that initiates, maintains and grows a profit-oriented enterprise for production or distribution of economic goods or services, which is inconsistent with internal and external forces. The following points portray some important features of Harvard School theory.

1. Internal forces: These forces refer to the internal qualities of the individual such as intelligence, skill, knowledge experience, intuition, exposure etc. These forces influence the entrepreneurial activities of an individual to a great extent.

2. External forces: These forces refer to the economic, political, social, cultural and legal factors which influence origin and growth of entrepreneurship in an economy. As such, entrepreneurial activity needs an environment conducive to its growth and development.

A.H. Cole, who had taken untiring pain in setting up Entrepreneurial Research Centre at Harvard University, speaks of the impact of the following environmental conditions which govern the emergence of entrepreneurial class:

- Stable government
- External security, protection from war, invasion, etc.
- Internal security, protection from internal strife and revolution, protection of person and property under law and the assurance of legal process in disputes.

3. Emphasis on two types of entrepreneurial activities. The Harvard School theory gives emphasis on two types of entrepreneurial activities, namely:

(*i*) Entrepreneurial functions like organisation and combination of resources for creating viable enterprises.

(*ii*) The responsiveness to the environmental condition that influences decision-making function.

At the initial stage the functions are mostly performed by the entrepreneurs all by themselves. Later, as the enterprise grows, the number of employees also grows, and the need for highly trained and skilled labour arises. The problems of relations with labour, labour unions, suppliers, customers, government become more complex. At this stage it becomes necessary to delegate a number of decisions to the subordinates. But as the powers delegated are of a routine nature, his central functions remain those of decision making, capital structure, diversification, and relations with the outside agencies, etc. Arthur H. Cole has described the entrepreneur as a decision maker:

"1. The determination of the business objectives of the enterprise and the change of those objectives as conditions require or make advantageous;

2. The development of an organisation including efficient with subordinates and all employees;
3. The securing of adequate financial resources, the relations with existing and potential investors;
4. The requisition of efficient technology equipment and the revision of it as new machinery appears;
5. The development of a market for the products and the devising of new products to meet or anticipate consumers' demand; and
6. The maintenance of good relations with public authorities and with society at large."

While interpreting the views expressed by different economists in context of the underdeveloped countries the functional analysis of the entrepreneurs becomes complex, since he has to perform a host of other activities, against the odds. As in the advanced capitalist countries he cannot be merely a 'promoter', everywhere.

The functions of an entrepreneur with reference to the undeveloped countries include a wide range of activities, say "In underdeveloped countries the functions of a given person in entrepreneurial capacity include innovation, promotion, capital provision and risk-bearing management, assembling materials and labour.

Besides, Leibenstein of Harvard School opined that the following activities are also equally important from the standpoint of entrepreneurship.

(*a*) To search and evaluate economic opportunities.

(*b*) To master the process of mobilizing resources to accomplish the goal.

Despite its stress on the human factor in the production system, the Harvard tradition never explicitly challenged the equilibrium-obsessed orthodox economic theory. This was challenged by the neo-Austrian School who argued that disequilibrium, rather than equilibrium, was the likely scenario and as such, entrepreneurs operate under fairly uncertain circumstances. The essence of entrepreneurship consists in the alertness of market participants to profit opportunities. A typical entrepreneur, according to Kizner (1979) is the arbitrageur, the person who discovers opportunity at low prices and sells the same items at high prices because of inter-temporal and interspatial demands.

Theory of Profit

Fran. H. Knight (1885-1972) in his book *Risk, Uncertainty and Profit* propounded the theory of profit. He points out that entrepreneurs are a specialised group of persons who bear risk and deals with uncertainty.

Knight's theory has the following features:

1. Pure profit: Knight identified entrepreneurs as the recipient of pure profit. Pure profit refers to the reward for bearing the cost of uncertainty.

2. Situation of uncertainty: Uncertainty, according to Knight, is identified with a situation where the probability of alternative cannot be determined either by a prior reasoning or by statistical inference.

3. Risk-bearing capability: Risk bearing implies assuming the responsibilities of loss or gain that may occur due to unforeseen contingencies of the future. According to Knight, an entrepreneur is the person who willingly carries on those responsible activities which are neither insured nor salaried.

4. Guarantee of specified sum: While undertaking the responsibility of the business enterprise, entrepreneur guarantees interest to leader, wages to employees and rent to the landlord. Thus, specified sums of money are guaranteed by the entrepreneur for the assignment made to them. However, the supply of entrepreneurship depends upon the following three factors as per his opinion:

(*i*) Ability of the entrepreneur

(*ii*) Willingness of entrepreneur

(*iii*) The power to extend guarantees to others.

5. Identification of socio-economic and psychological factors: Knight identified the social, economic and psychological factors which infiuence the supply of entrepreneur since entrepreneurial motivation and abilities are long-run problems. Economic, social and psychological factors should be combined to promote entrepreneurship.

6. Use of consolidation technique to reduce business uncertainty: Knight's entrepreneurs specifically commit their capital and bear the resultant risk and uncertainty. He argued that business uncertainty can be reduced by using the technique of consolidation to increase the profit. Through the help of consolidation in which individual instances are pooled total uncertainty can be reduced.

7. Self-confidence: Self-confidence is the most important factor which is essential for the entrepreneur to undertake risk and to determine the level of profit. However, Knight felt that uncertainty defied definition as every uncertain condition was unique and depended on a number of imponderables in the market place. The elasticity of supply of self-confidence is an important factor that determined the level of profit and size of the entrepreneur.

Knight identifies the entrepreneur as a recipient of pure profit. Pure profit, according to him, with regard to the entrepreneur, is bearing the costs of uncertainty. He identifies uncertainty with a situation where the probabilities of alternative outcomes cannot be determined either by a *priori* reasoning or by statistical inference. A *priori* reasoning is simply irrelevant to economic situation involving a unique event.

Knight argues that business uncertainty can be reduced through 'consolidation.' Consolidation is to uncertainty what insurance is to risk; it is a method of reducing total uncertainty by pooling individual instances. The elasticity of the supply of self-confidence is the single most important determinant of the level of profit and the number of entrepreneurs.

The Theory of Profit Optimisation

Profiteering as an economic function, has to be understood as a concept distinct from profit. Profit, as enunciated by Pigou, is a particular species of monetary gain — a monetary gain secured in a particular way. To make a profit, in the sense relevant here — implies performing a middleman's or an entrepreneur's function, hiring the services of other men or buying goods from other men, and selling the products or the good and obtaining, as a reward, the difference between outlay and receipt.

If the difference exceeds a socially acceptable limit, and that by questionable methods, it is a case of profiteering.

For the purpose of a realistic economic analysis we have to shelve the principles governing perfect market competition, and have to reckon with the forces of imperfect competition, duopoly, monosony and oligopoly, monopolistic competition and black market.

Before we analyse the economic process of profit-making and, in that context the theory of maximisation, and finally of profiteering, it is necessary to appreciate that it would no longer suffice to assume merely that the demand and supply curves exist, and that some are elastic and some inelastic, or that some rise and some fall. If we do not appreciate it, we shall reduce the study of economic phenomena of today's market situation to the simplicity of the concept of bilateral trade.

The assumption of perfect competition on which much of the supply and demand analysis is based must also be scrutinised. Perfect competition is rare — and, in a real sense, does not exist anywhere outside the imagination of the economists. Over large areas of economic life, other systems of market relationships are of great importance.

Let us first indicate the principle of the profit-making process in a market of imperfect competition, as was done by the post-Chamberlain economists. Very briefly, the profit-making under imperfect market conditions is determined by what is called the dynamics of a marketer.

In the marketing of a product or a service, the larger the savings in a profitable succession of transformations of the product or the service (or in short, the investment), the greater the total profit.

But this is not all. The play of these savings is restricted, or even determined, by the nature and extent of market imperfection and the presence and delineation of risks and uncertainty.

According to the theory of profit optimisation, marginal conditions in the market will lead to optimisation of production in relation to its total marketable cost components, so that the maximum average revenue for minimum average cost is achieved. In any case, this will be one of the ends of the economic functions of a marketer under imperfect competition in his endeavour to optimise profit.

Profit maximisation, or profiteering, is conditioned by the "principle of increasing risk and uncertainty", as Kalechi calls it. With an increase in the potential of risks on the investment co-efficient, profits will increase or decrease to the extent of the risk that is taken.

In the long run, a small industry can survive only if it can make enough profit to pay a return on the capital after making adequate and necessary provisions. Profit, is the outcome of the operations of all small-scale industries and, in the ultimate analysis, of profit planning. Profit can be expressed as an earning per share, a return on the capital employed or a return on a shareholder's capital. There are difficulties in expressing all the three and in making comparison with the competitors in the field.

It has now been recognised that the old theory of profit maximisation is not strictly valid in the present-day Indian context because of the developmental role which the small-scale industry is called upon to play in the context of its socio-economic obligations, although in the long run it has to be a profitable proposition if it has to survive in the fiercely competitive world of today. The central objective, therefore, should be a judicious combination of profit with achievements on the socio-economic front. Some economists refer to this as profit with growth. For our purpose, we shall assume that what small-scale industries are primarily striving for is improved profitability rather than maximisation of profit as an end in judicious combination of profit with achievements on the socio-economic front. Some economists refer to this as profit with growth. For our purpose, we shall assume that what small-scale industries are primarily striving for is improved profitability rather than maximisation of profit as an end in itself.

The accent ought to be on efficiency. The domestic economy today is strong and growing at a satisfactory rate. What is needed is to impart to it a degree of efficiency. It is on the foundation of a strong and efficient domestic economy that we can build our industrial as well as export effort. This should be the cornerstone of our medium term strategy.

A variety of social and economic factors are stimulating entrepreneurial activity and thus generating more robust economic development. These factors include an increasing focus on capital formation, changing institutional relationship, supportive government programmes, a reassessment of intellectual quality, and new approaches to innovations.

THE AGONY... AND ECSTASY... OF PROFITS!

Lets face it. There is something about money that makes the world go round. Your pay cheque, bonus, annual increment, stock option and other incentives, all revolve around money. The exotic holidays that you share with your family, the exquisite gifts that you buy for them, the swanky car that you *vroom* around in... everything! Of course, there's that school of thought that money can't buy everything. Yet, along with religion and sex, money is perhaps that something that humanity has always coveted, fought for, despaired over and even killed for. In a modern society, no matter what distorted, perverted or adapted brand of capitalism or socialism it practices, money matters!

In any modern society, those are entrepreneurs and corporations that can be said to be the fountainheads of money. Adam Smith recognised this over 200 years ago, when he published The *Wealth of Nations* Hundreds of economists, thinkers and philosophers have since explained how profits generated by entrepreneurs and corporations have transformed modern societies. Sure, the government in any modern nation state is perhaps the biggest employer so far. Sure, the government fixes the rules of the game for corporate gladiators to fight it out. Sure, too

Marshall Goldsmith

Andrew Campbell

Srikumar S. Rao

Steve Tappin

much of greed is bad. Yet, as the collapse of Soviet Union proved irrefutably, the profit motive is intrinsic to man; and to deny and suppress it has never yielded desired results. Adam Smith called it self-interest. But for a modern corporation, positive and ethical greed and a consistent track record of profits are the only way to earn the respect of stakeholders. An ethical company that's not very profitable will not survive for long. For that matter, a profitable company that discards all ethical norms too wont survive very long. Think Enron, WorldCom and many others.

One of the key reasons for the US emerging as one of the greatest powers in world history is because of a societal consensus that the pursuit of profits is a legitimate activity. The US military and the seemingly irrational policies of the Bush administration have made America by far the most disliked nation in the world. Yet, how many of us have walked away from Microsoft, Google, Intel, Reebok and dozens of other American brands and companies just because we happen to dislike Uncle Sam? Many analysts during the 1980s predicted the end of American dominance in the world of business because nations like Japan and South Korea were driving American manufacturing literally out of business.

Forget going out of business, exploiting cross-border cost competencies, American companies now completely dominate even the world of information technology and services. And this will be the century of information technology. A society that recognizes the value of distributed entrepreneurship, regardless of geographical boundaries, is bound to consequently profit exorbitantly. On the cynical wave, people who regard the quest for money, profits and corporate success as unworthy goals could well ask themselves a few questions. Could Sabeer Bhatia have made $400 million in India? And, despite the wealth of intellectual prowess in India, how is it that companies like Google, eBay, My Space & Yahoo all have American origins?

Profits matter. The pursuit of profit matters even more. In a medieval society, people whispered, gossiped about and envied the most successful warriors and knights. In modern society, the entrepreneur and the CEO have replaced the *Samurai* and the knight at the top of the popularity charts. In the latest ranking of 100 most powerful women in the world released by Forbes, Indian

Ram Charan **John Kotter**

born CEO designate of Pepsi, Indira Nooyi, is ranked well above India's most powerful woman Sonia Gandhi. And before her ouster, Carly Fiorina of HP was routinely ranked as one of the most powerful women in the world. There has always been a nagging feeling in societies that encouraging the pursuit of profits increases inequalities and creates social divisions that end up destroying the social order. In fact, Karl Marx based his entire edifice of Marxism and Communism on the belief that the capitalist will always exploit the worker and keep denying him his dues till the revolution of the proletariat overthrows Capitalism. Exactly 110 years ago, Henry Ford, who otherwise never treated his workers fairly by any standard, demolished this belief by making cars that even his workers could afford. And, a few years ago, the feisty entrepreneur and promoter of CNN, Ted Turner, stunned the world by giving away almost one billion dollars — virtually his entire fortune — to charity. Recent events have made even that gesture pale in comparison. Bill Gates and Warren Buffet have together committed more than $50 billion of their wealth to fight poverty, disease and illiteracy in the third world. Google has gone one step ahead. It has started a charity with a $1 billion corpus that will operate like a corporation - earning profits even as it tackles some of the ills that plague the world. You can be sure that these huge funds won't disappear into the pockets of corrupt third world politicians and bureaucrats but actually make a difference.

Clearly, profits can do a lot of good. But they can also do a lot of harm. It all depends on how you define profitability. The best business thinkers have always maintained that corporations must pursue profits in a manner that will reward the investor in the long run. Yet, modern American corporations seem to be in the grip of what is now called the tyranny of the Wall Street, where the quarterly profits of the company, and daily share price movements, matter more than its long-term health. In fact, many thinkers and analysts agree that it is this totally perverted definition of profit that has triggered the excesses that led to scandals like Enron, WorldCom and Home Depot, to name just a few. Profits, like happiness, can be disruptive when it is fleeting. If corporations take profits as a quarterly fling and not a long-term relationship, they will always end up in trouble — destroying shareholder wealth in the bargain. India has begun to celebrate the success of entrepreneurs and corporations. The billion-dollar question is, will India Inc. also be overwhelmed by the tyranny of Dalal Street?

Theory of Adjustment of Price

Israel M. Kirzner, the noted economist, has coined the theory of adjustment of price. According to him, the essential entrepreneurial element is the alertness to information rather than its possession alone. He contends that those entrepreneurs who have the superior telescopic faculty keep themselves all the while alert to confront any disequilibrium in the market.

His theory has got the following features.

1. Adjustment of price: The chief role of entrepreneur is based upon the adjustment of price in the market. He contemplates that prevalence of wrong price in the market may reduce the profit of the entrepreneur. In this case, the buyer may pay higher price or seller may accept a lower price which may give rise to opportunities for profit. Further, if different opportunity for profitable arbitrage between the two segments of the market. Thus, adjustment of price is the chief role of the entrepreneur.

2. Alertness To disequilibrium: According to M. Kirzner, entrepreneur possessing superior foresight are alert to disequilibrium. Alertness enables the entrepreneur to intervene in the market by changing the price. Thus, economy in purchase and profitable selling results in economic gains.

For Kirzner, the adjustment of price is the main role of the entrepreneur. If the wrong price prevails in the market, then an opportunity for profit is created somewhere in the market if a frustrated buyer or seller is willing, respectively, to pay a higher price or accept a lower one. Then, again, if different prices prevail in the same market, there is scope for profitable arbitrage between the two segments of the market.

According to Kirzner, alertness to disequilibrium is the distinguishing characteristic of an entrepreneur. Alertness enables some individuals to intervene in the market by changing the price while other individuals simply respond by changing their buying and selling plans in lieu of the new price.

Kirzner further maintains that the primary role of economic theory is to explain behaviour in terms of purposeful human action, and to consider to what extent purposeful human actions can interact to produce unexpected outcomes. To pursue the analysis of entrepreneurship further would be to go beyond the limits of the agenda of this piece. Anyone who believes that the entrepreneurs is predictable has an incentive to himself intervene in the market process, and so become an entrepreneur.

To Kirzner, this provides a satisfactory basis for asserting the inherent upredictability of the entrepreneur. It suggests that no predictor can be anything but an entrepreneur, and so makes a predictive theory of entrepreneurship impossible.

Theory of Market Equilibrium

Frederick von Hayek (1889-1992) propounded the theory of market equilibrium. His main contribution to entrepreneurial theory is to identify the absence of entrepreneurs in neo-classical economics which is associated with the assumption of market equilibrium.

According to Hayek, the services of entrepreneur can be of following types:

(*a*) To combine the means and resources together for production.

(*b*) To undertake the entrepreneurial function of planning, scheduling and decision making.

(*c*) To guarantee a fixed rate of income, profit and interest which will go to entrepreneur as the reward for his services.

In view of the above, the theory of market equilibrium can be depicted clearly under the following points:

1. Postulate of full equilibrium: According to Hayek, postulate of full equilibrium resembles the postulate of full information. Full information presupposes the fact that there is no need for further information to modify the decision.

2. Acquisition and communication of knowledge: Hayek emphasised the role of acquisition and communication of knowledge in his theory for adjustment towards equilibrium.

3. Market as the medium of communication: Markets are the crucial media which help the entrepreneurs to communicate their creative ventures or discoveries to others. Thus, they move towards the desired level of sales to arrive at equilibrium.

Hayek's main contribution to entrepreneurial theory is to point out that the absence of entrepreneurs in Neo-classical economics is intimately associated with the assumption of market equilibrium. According to Hayek, the equilibrium postulate is equivalent to a postulate of full information; not full information in the sense of a complete information theory about every conceivable thing, but full information in the sense that no further information is needed in order to modify anyone's decisions.

For him, the empirical content of economics relates to the process of adjustment towards an equilibrium. This process involves the acquisition and communication of knowledge. He visualises a world in which there is a continuous process of discovery. Markets help people to communicate their discoveries to others and learn of discoveries, thereby moving towards a sale of equilibrium.

The Management Grid

THE MANAGERIAL GRID

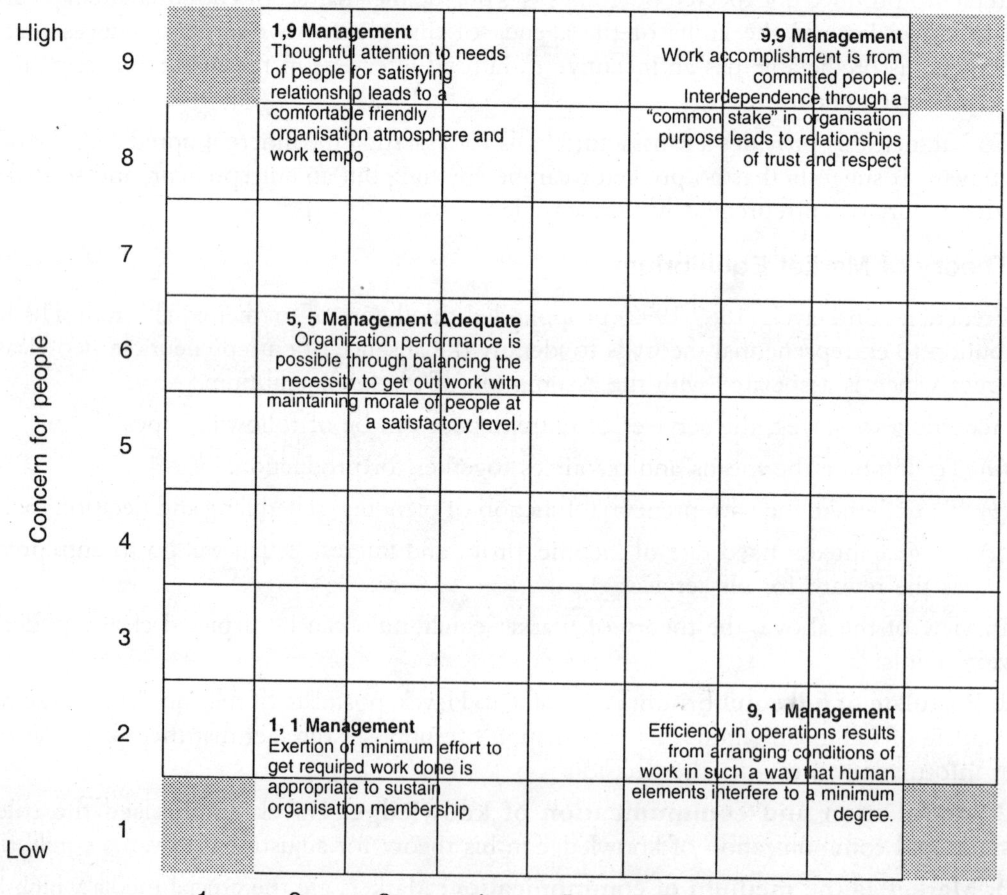

M/s. Robert R. Blake and Jane S. Moulton, who are psychologist and behavioural researchers created the Management Grid to promote enthusiasm for experimentation and innovation and learn from interaction with others.

The authors have devised a graphical system called the "Managerial Grid" to illustrate the various styles of Management.

Managerial Grid

The Managerial Grid results from combining two fundamental ingredients of managerial behaviour. One is concern for production, the other is concern for people. Concern for production can be combined with concern for people in various degree. The term 'production' can refer to the number of good research ideas, the number of accounts, the volume of sales, the quality of service given or of major policy decisions taken and such other things that contribute to efficient working of an organisation. Concern for people similarly includes all concern for friendship, for personal commitment to tasks, for someone's self respect, for equitable payment and so on. For the sake of simplicity, only the following five combinations are considered:

(*i*) Maximum concern for production and minimum concern for people.

(*ii*) Maximum concern for people and minimum concern for production.

(*iii*) Low concern for production as well as for people.

(*iv*) Equal concern for production and people.

(*v*) High concern both for production as well as people.

What is the Grid?

The Grid is an 81-squared framework on which styles of behaviour can be plotted on the horizontal axis of the Grid, which ranges from 1 to 9, with 9 representing high concern for output and 1 low concern for output. On the vertical axis, 9 represents high concern for people and 1 low concern for people.

Maximum Concern for Production, Minimum for People

9,1 management, or 'task management', focuses overwhelmingly on production. A manager is acting as taskmaster, who expects schedules to be met and the people to do what they are told; no more and no less. He is a disciplinarian. Produce or perish is his directive principle. He directs and he expects others to follow his instructions strictly. This leaves hardly any scope for participation or even expression of one's views. Anything that goes wrong will be viewed as due to some mistake. The organisation functions in a mechanical manner and creativity is stalled. Human talent is wasted.

Maximum Concern for People, Minimum Concern for Production

The 1,9 managerial style or country club management as it has been called, emphasises solely concern for people. It does not push people for production because of the attitude that one can lead a horse to water, but cannot make it drink. People are encouraged and supported, and their mistakes are overlooked because they are doing the best they can. The firm is run as a big happy working group like a social club. Tea breaks for instance, may be quite generous and the formal rule is "no work discussions during breaks". The management's prime objective is to avoid conflict and tension. People are easy-going like the boss. New ideas receive scant attention and support as they are likely to disturb the tranquil atmosphere.

To sum up, the work tempo is easy and comfortable. There is, however, no challenge to people's abilities. Work goes on in a routine manner. The group, not the individual, is the basic unit of the organisation. The important values are friendliness, harmony and comfort. The boss is like a kind big brother. Some work naturally gets done. Its ultimate end may be the complete closing of a non-competitive unit.

Low Concern for Production as Well as People

A1, 1 configuration results in 'impoverished management'. It is difficult to imagine an organisation surviving for long under such a management, but such a trait is frequent enough in individual managers and supervisors. Planning is almost non-existent. People are free to work as they like. They are expected to solve their own problems. Supervisors act as messengers. There is no target, no compulsions to achieve something concrete. The approach typically reveals the frustration of someone, who has been passed over for promotion, shunted sideway, or has been performing a routine job for years.

Equal Concern for Both Production and People

The middle of the managerial grid shows the dampened pendulum style. This style of management aims at balancing the two requirements. It views them as conflicting and therefore none can be maximised. Subordinates will be taken into confidence in the matter of planning. Similarly, the progress of work will be reviewed in periodical meetings, but there will not be rigid insistence on attainment of plan targets. The organisation is modest in its aims as it tries to avoid conflict-and uncertainty. It is therefore not truly creative and innovative. To sum up, the organisation remains so bureaucratic that people are taken into confidence only in a limited way. It is but natural that creativity is drained and the organisation is impoverished.

High Concern for Production as Well as People

9, 9 style is termed team management, which shows high concern for production and high concern for people and does not accept that these concerns are incompatible. The team manager seeks to integrate people around production. Morale is task related. People satisfy their own need through the job and working with others, not through incidental sociability in the country club style. The Manager's responsibility is to see to it that work is planned and organised by those with a stake in it and not necessarily by himself. Team is task-oriented. It is creative and morale is heightened through successful team work under conditions of mutual trust, support and respect. The function of the boss is to develop such teams. He acts as an advisor, consultant and coach. He inspires, guides and teaches.

The long-term benefits of this style of management are considerable. It increases the profitability of the organisation. Relationship between trade unions and management improve. The entire organisation is invigorated. It becomes innovative. Genuine human needs are fulfilled through organisational work and interpersonal relations developed along healthy lines.

To sum up, this is by far the best style of management. It promotes full human development and utilises human talent and energy fully. In the process, it achieves the highest level of production and creativity. An organisation can reach this ideal condition only gradually.

The Grid approach has achieved remarkable success in North America, Europe and East Asia. It is equally successful in different types of work such as production, sales R and D as well as in different types of organisations.

Theory of Organisation

Decision making is one of the most important managerial activity in any business organisation. The fundamental theory of organisation also talks about decision making as one of the primary purposes behind the evolution of organisations. An organisation offers a structure and comparatively better managed data and information base for making decisions that serve corporate goals. And hence the shift from purely personal decision making to organisational decision making, though finally a decision is seen as being made at a particular managerial level.

Managerial decision making is a complex phenomenon, with a variety of factors influencing the final decision. The psychological factors in decision making are discernible to keen observers and researchers, though the decision makers may not be conscious of the same.

FRAMING

Every decision is mad in a frame of situation or a frame of events where there is an element of precedent and an element of antecedent.

Frames are created within paradigms, personal and organisational. Shifting organisational paradigms offer new opportunities as organisations begin to see their businesses and related problems in a different perspective and frame. Market orientation or customer orientation, a paradigm shift, has enabled many organisations to look at marketing from a totally new angle. This has enabled them to redesign/reengineer their business processes to suit the customer and market rather than suit the organisation and its employees. This is a direct consequence of seeing the business situations in totally new "frames" in which problem solutions are created. Within the organisation, framing of problems or phenomenon at corporate level, *e.g.,* is mostly different than the operating managers' whose problem frames are devoid of any conceptual context. It therefore happens frequently that corporate decisions regarding many business problems fail to solve the problems at the operating level, apart from the disagreements that precede the implementation of these decisions. Framing is also in the context of a manager's personal motive and the organisation's compulsions. A manager, who plays a defensive game, creates a different type of frame of a particular situation, where a decision is required while an aggressive manager works in a different frame altogether. The sub-conscious constructs of the manager affect the framing which gives him the unwritten, "self talked" description of the situation in which he is operating. The frame comprises his psychological needs in order to commend himself to himself as also to the world. The frame enables the manager to either "break-out" of a situation by making a decision or to "stay and fight" in the situation to assert himself. The former type of manager takes transfer decisions which enable him to off-load the burden and the pressure to others for making the decision effective. The later type of manager owns and retains the decision implementation with himself without rescinding the responsibility for decision implementation.

Even within these frames, a manager operates with responsibility or irresponsibility. This naturally influences the effective implementation of a decision leading to the ultimate effectiveness or otherwise of an organisation.

Though decision making is always a focused activity that gravitates to an individual manager or a small group of managers, in some cases, where group decision making is assiduously followed, "shared frames" are used by the decision makers. In every organisation, its history, culture, values and perceptions about the nature of its business and success signposts create shared beliefs and acceptances that generate the "shared frames". Problem diagnosis and available options are therefore seen through these frames and all other decision options that an outside observer/ expert is able to see are not visible to the inside managers. Information that fits the frame is readily accepted and used while other information and data is either rejected as irrelevant or is relied on only marginally.

Weber's Theory of Industrial Location

The Weber's theory of industrial location is based on the following basic assumptions:

(1) The materials used by an industry can be classified into ubiquitous and localised materials.

The ubiquities are those raw materials which are available everywhere, like brick, clay and water. The localised materials are those which are available in certain localities only, like minerals, fuel etc.

The localised materials are further divided into (*i*) weight-losing or gross materials and (*ii*) pure materials. The weight losing materials are those which considerably lose weight during the manufacturing process (*e.g.,* coal and other minerals), as opposed to pure materials like cotton or wool.

(2) The situation and size of places of consumption are given, with the market comprising a number of separate points.

(3) There are certain fixed labour locations and labour is immobile. Wage rates may vary from location to location but in each location supply of labour is unlimited at the given wage rate.

Weber's theory divides the factors influencing industrial location into the following two:

(*i*) The general regional factors of transport and labour costs. These general regional factors are regarded as the primary causes affecting industrial location.

(*ii*) The local factor of 'agglomerative' or 'deglomerative' forces regraded as the secondary causes responsible for redistribution of industries.

The location of an industry is determined by the interaction of the two sets of factors.

The limitations of the Weber's theory of industrial location are:

1. The theory is based on three wrong assumptions about labour supply;
2. Transport cost depend on the mode of transport, nature of goods etc.;
3. Location and size of markets may vary with changes in the economy;
4. Non-economic factors also exert important influence on industrial location;
5. The theory ignores the role of capital and entrepreneurship in industrialisation; and
6. The classification of materials is not proper.

THE 'ESCAPE VELOCITY' STRATEGY

Entrepreneurs who try to scale up typically run out of cash and are forced to bring in outside investors, thus, diluting their ownership. Fortunately, there is a straightforward solution: achieve 'escape velocity', a phrase that physicists use for the speed at which a rocket goes into orbit. Understanding the strategy is simple, but finding a practical solution for your company can be frustratingly elusive. When a company figures out how to design a sales process where the cost of acquiring a customer is less than the immediate contribution of that customer to profits, it can grow sales to an arbitrarily large number, requiring no further investment or dilution of existing investors.

Attaining escape velocity means growing sales dramatically without having to push more cash into the company. For example, if each new customer generated a gross margin of Rs. 100 in his first order, and it cost less than Rs. 100 to convert that prospect into a customer (via an ad campaign or sales commission), then the customer essentially paid for himself. The company invested Rs. 100 to acquire the customer, and got the money back immediately. That same Rs. 100 can be rotated many times to get a thousand customers, a million customers, or an arbitrarily large number of customers.

Most companies find that customers take time to pay off the cost associated with acquiring them. In fact, customer loyalty is a preoccupation of CEOs because they know that if they don't hang on to a customer for several years, the company would actually lose money during the life cycle of that relationship. The trick is to get the customer to pay for himself as soon as possible, which can be measured by comparing the cost per conversion (ad budget divided by number of conversions) against the gross margin earned in the customer's first order (or first set of orders). There maybe several ways to achieve this — increasing prices while at the same time increasing the ad budget or by improving the effectiveness of the ads while reducing the cost of goods sold. Experimentation is essential, as the right solution tends to evolve over time through trial and error.

Several forces are allowing companies to scale up quickly without the help of venture capital. These include the declining prices of hardware and bandwidth, the easy availability of open source software, and the ability to generate income via online ads. Meebo, a Web-based instant-messaging service, was getting over 50,000 logins per day within a month of its launch in September 2005 — and was funded with only $2,000 from the credit cards of the founders. With such a small capital base, the only way to scale up was by quickly figuring out a solution to the escape velocity puzzle.

One of PSi's portfolio companies also had the good fortune of achieving escape velocity. The company is now adding a customer almost every day by carefully monitoring the effectiveness of its advertising, and weeding out poorly performing ads, which are easy to identify as each ad points customers to unique websites and toll free numbers. As a result of constant adjustments, the number of new customers generated for each rupee spent on advertising has gone down steadily over the past year. In addition, the company has worked hard to maintain margins by improving productivity and focusing on a segment of the market that other players have ignored. Although the company's client base has doubled over the past year, its cash position has actually improved.

Like sailors testing the wind and adjusting their sails, entrepreneurs make many adjustments before their company 'catches the wind' and achieves escape velocity. Some companies never experience this bliss, but succeed anyway, fuelled by the cash from investors. While there will always be a role for venture capital, entrepreneurs who can figure out how to get customers to finance sales growth will be less dependent on venture capital, and will, thus, secure the right to own more of their company.

BRANDS AS MARKETING PEARLS

In the mid 1800s, after the steam engine had powered its first train, the US Patents Office put up a board that said "Since everything that has to be invented has been invented this office may consider closing down in the near future. The world's most profound inventions have, in fact, been made 100 years after trial notice was put up. These have changed the world we live and have inspected our lives in dozens of different ways.

The spin offs of these inventions and discoveries — have been products that have brought joy to millions of people. As markets developed and competition grew, the very nature of these products changed. The joys of owning a product that brought convenience to its purchaser were soon replaced with selecting a product that introduced price to ownership. Things bought in known bags — like baguettes — were no longer enough. This development which simply followed human nature was in itself not an insightful discovery. But it did bring about an intense search for that "little extra" to woo the customer. In turn this resulted in the development of strategic thinking and what is now commonly known as marketing strategies. Products were on their way to becoming brands.

The story of the development of brands is as fascinating as the evolution of the steam engine itself — the invention that had the US Patents Office in despair. The reason why brand development is a fascinating study is because brands cover hundreds of categories each with several price points. In every one of these sub-divisions is a brand that has a stirring story to tell. The lowly bidi, you can be sure, has outstanding brands, as do private jets. The sheer magnitude of this landscape and the fact that each has dealt with a different genre of people with differen wants and different idiosyncrasies would suggest literally thousands of case studies that have pitted wonderful minds against each other.

Brands, however, are a rich nation's and a rich people's indulgence. This explains why the USA has several thousand brands and Somalia so few. It also explains why brand development in India is a recent phenomenon. Not so long ago, even in urban India, people bought 2 kilos of rice in a bag made from a forgotten edition of a newspaper today many of them reach out for 2 kilos of Kohinoor and 10 kilos of Pillsbury instead of 10 kilos of flour. But some products by their very nature come pre-packaged. This simply means they come with a brand name. Consider toothpaste or cement. You are unlikely to buy toothpaste loose or 400 kilos of loose cement. In the scheme of things you buy one tube of Colgate and 10 bags of ACC cement, You are also unlikely to buy components and build your own truck, So, you buy an Ashok Leyland.

The problem with many pre-packaged brands has been that for most owners of these "brands', the brand was simply the name that needed to be put on the pack. The thought that the name had value or the pack was identified by it — as their sons and daughters were — never crossed their minds. Products that started with an advantage simply lost it by a vision that was profoundly narrow

But this was not true of commodities such as textiles or shoes. Much of the Indian market simply purchased shirting or trousering or bought a shoe made by a roadside cobbler. The fabric — within a pre-determined budget — was purchased because it seemed to have a good hand feel, colour or print and the shoe, because it served an immediate purpose.

In defence of manufacturers of these commodities would be the compelling reason that brand building also requires a distribution channel. Flury's in Kolkata or Wenger's in Delhi are great local brands but they will never have a national following unless they are available nationally. This requires several things from the intellect- marketing-, sales-, advertising- and media strategies — and one important contribution from the bank-money.

The roadside cobbler is unlike to come up with either and the owner of the textile mill that manufactured the fabric with a good hand feel has unaccountable inertia that says, L couldn't care." The logic was overpoweringly simple; if I am making money why fool around with creating an expense head? The philosophy "if it is not bust why repair it" has been the bane of Indian brand development for time memorial. Supported by an audience that, without demur, accepted rubbish was simply the encouragement to perpetuate poor quality.

THE PYRAMIDAL MODEL OF THE BRAND

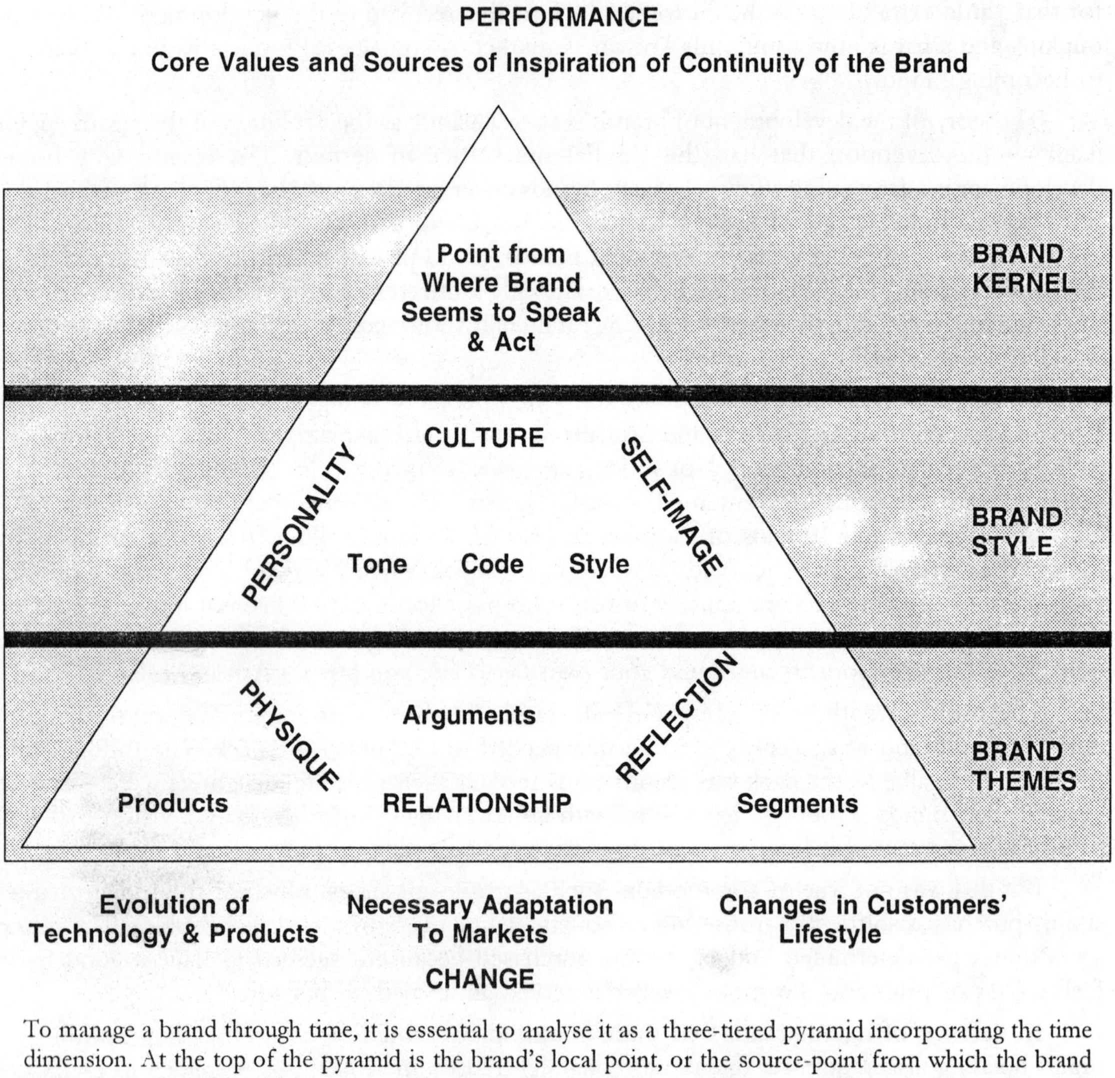

To manage a brand through time, it is essential to analyse it as a three-tiered pyramid incorporating the time dimension. At the top of the pyramid is the brand's local point, or the source-point from which the brand seems to speak and act. This source-point must be known, but most remain unspoken of and invisible. It is the brand's deep identity, its core value. As such, it is permanent over the long run.

In the middle of the pyramid, we have the style and codes of the brand. Etymologically speaking, it is the stylus with which one writes and leaves one's mark and imprint. As one's signature, the style — a brand's specific means of conveying a message — is a reflection of the brand's core identity.

The lower stage of the pyramid relates to the communication themes, the brand's current advertising positioning. The customers look at the brand bottom-up. They discover it by its products, its themes, and the style of its communication.

The advantages that come with brand development of course rest with just a few. Much of the commodity market simply remains a commodity market; over a period of time it fades away — only to emerge in another Mali or Somalia or Chad. So, today, as people have evolved they go out and buy a Raymond or a Reid & Taylor suit length; instead of an S, M or I, T-shirt they buy a ColorPlus or a Wills Life Style. And a Bata shoe instead of a local make.

Talking of shoes, the handmade Chinese stuff was pretty good. But since handmade by its very nature is restrictive and production limited, the probability of these ever becoming serious brands is unlikely. Brand development obviously also requires production capacities.

India, today is divided into two very distinct parts. Urban India which has shown a remarkable propensity to and brands will continue to live side by side in an uneasy truce.

It may be several decades before an integration of these two faces of India is made — for the nation is huge and disparities real. For a man who has just seen his first telephone and spoken to a faceless voice across a huge chasm, the need for a brand to replace 2 kilos of rice is a long way away. He is happy to use a lantern to light his home instead of a Crompton Greaves bulb, reetha to clean his clothes instead of Nirma, a local paste to help heal a wound instead of Boroline, smoke from burning leaves and twigs to drive away mosquitoes instead of Good Knight and nothing instead of Jockey. The Economic Times, Canon cameras, movies on HBO and Barista are not even on the horizon. Neither for that matter is Kerala Tourism — nor sadly, Kamasutra.

In truth, it's not the 250 million strong middle income but the 750 million who reside in India's 586,000 villages that have caused international flutter. Of course it's not happening tomorrow. Every one of the companies that is eyeing this segment is a long-term player, willing to wait — even help in their upliftment. Clearly, as the benefits of economic development percolate downward numerous opportunities will manifest themselves and hundred of brands will join the fight for share of the pocket. Some will survive, some will fall and several will be badly bruised. In this churn of evolving market the positions of brands will change from year to year and from village to village. Multiply this excitement by hundreds of categories and several price points in each and you are looking at one of the most stimulating exercises for the mind.

India, at the bottom of the rung also happens to be at the beginning of the long cycle of brand development. From the marketers perspective it'd be interesting to understand why some brands succeeded while others failed; to learn important lessons from their strategies; to discover their bitter struggle toward off competition; to comprehend the true nature of their achievements to grasp the depth of the brand values and indeed, to know things we thought didn't exist in their lexicon.

Superbrands is perhaps, the world's foremost compendia of case studies on the most outstanding brands in a country. Over the years it has gained immense respect.

WORK HARD, LEAVE THE REST TO A DIVINE PLAN

Saaz Aggarwal looks at two young individuals and tracks their lives as they move from jobs to entrepreneurship.

Anu Malhotra and Preetal Swami had always dreamt of running their own businesses. Anu had worked for several years for a multinational company in Mumbai, while Preetal, after stints with organisations in various parts of the country, was now number two at a smaller private limited firm in Chennai.

Anu and Preetal often felt that the efforts and ideas they put in at work were bringing a lot of benefit to others but hardly any to themselves. They felt that they would never get the kind of wealth and prestige that they deserved unless they set up on their own. They also felt constricted by the corporate hierarchy and realised that it was only as independent entrepreneurs that they would really be able to do things their own way.

In addition, the whole idea of entrepreneurship — of conceiving a vision, of following one's own path to implement it, and of all the adventures doubtless in store was immensely appealing. About 10 years ago, they finally took the plunge and started enterprises of their own.

Things went well for Anu right from day one. She chose a business with which she was familiar, and it grew like a dream. Clients of her organisation, familiar with her competence and style of working, brought their custom to her. She knew the market, the workforce, vendors and industry best practices all very well, and they hung together.

Preetal picked a line which had just begun to throw opportunities into the market. Initially working on software services for retail organisations, her company began to develop their own product in the field.

BASIC STRENGTHS

- Spirit of adventure, the common sense to anticipate turbulence, the resilience to retain your balance when it occurs, and the fortitude to stick to your mission regardless.
- A viable business idea, with a clear vision of the outcome you intend to achieve.
- Intimate knowledge of your field: Ground-level logistics, clarity and insight on business processes and industry best practices, sufficient experience to forecast future trends, and the ingenuity to innovate as you go along.
- Excellent presentation skills which will bring you funding and talent, and assist in building your brand.
- Seasoned problem-solving skills as well as the skill to convert threats into opportunities.
- The ability to manage people, money, change, and — most important — your own moods.

As a pioneer in organised retail in this country, she not only learnt a lot, but her special visionary skills helped her create an organisation which became a market leader with a strong brand Identity. However, being an untested field, funding was a problem and Preetal soon ran into financial difficulties.

Today, seven years later, Anu's business process outsourcing business is thriving. She employs 350 people and caters to three tier-2 European clients.

Preetal, meanwhile, was unable to sustain her business and accepted an acquisition bid from a larger software firm with relief. Today, much in demand by head hunters and recognised nationwide as an expert in her domain area, she has settled into a highly paid job through which she was able to service the debt her company had raised in around 18 months.

Here are some of the lessons on wealth, prestige and freedom, the mirages of entrepreneurship, that this experience gave them:

Wealth

Anu: "I've learnt that real wealth is less about money and more about attitude and lifestyle. So many people have a lot of money — far more than they could spend in their lifetime — but they're miserable, unhealthy, and weighed down with bad relationships."

Preetal: "As my business grew, I was often unable to pay staff salaries on time. There was a very strong feeling of gazing up at the sky, praying as the dark clouds approached, that this time they would bring rain! I came to believe that there was some kind of divine plan, and the best that any one could do was to honour opportunities with hard work and enterprise, but that the results could never be predicted.

"When people talk to me about savings, about investment, I feel amused. I have learnt that this type of security is illusory, and I take refuge instead in the certainty of an existence in whose plan we are all provided for."

Prestige

Ann: "I think prestige has to do with how you feel about yourself, and it is this which projects on how others feel about you. So to achieve prestige, we should build our self worth — perhaps by learning how to relax and enjoy being alive, and to spend time doing things which one is good at, and therefore likely to achieve success at."

Preetal: "I agree. But I've also learnt that one can do this both in your own business as well as while working in an organisation."

Freedom

Anu: "Freedom! Are you joking? I dream of the moment I'll be free from all this! Here I am, juggling market expansion against existing customer requirements, employee attrition rates, vendor quality issues and supercilious queries from my investors... I'm answerable to so many people — the only freedom I have today is to choose my operational strategies!"

Preetal: "My fixed monthly pay packet gives me an exhilarating freedom that I missed for years! Besides, I've also found that, by bringing your own resources and ingenuity, your own individual genius to the job, you achieve much of the satisfaction of entrepreneurship without its rugged rock face aspects."

Integrated Model of Entrepreneurship Development

The present stage of entrepreneurship development programmes as a factor contributing to the industrialisation of backward and other areas needs a proper direction and organisation for making it more effective and purposeful. The contribution of entrepreneurship development programmes is very uneven among different regions and definite programmes need to be chalked, out to bring about some degree of uniformity and upgradation. Before these problems are tackled, some important issues need immediate attention, for example, (*i*) structure and composition of entrepreneurship development programmes; (*ii*) areas of operation; (*iii*) fixing of priorities; (*iv*) follow-up; (*v*) spatial dispersal of the entrepreneurship development programmes; (*vi*) training of trainees; and (*vii*) financing pattern.

Box - 5

ENTREPRENEURSHIP BEYOND BORDER

The ability to opt opportunities and do business beyond borders is increasingly becoming the defining trend that will separate the entrepreneur from the rest. Government de-regulation is opening national borders for commerce, Trading and investing beyond national borders is now common and is either the salvation or the death knell of the Indian economy. We have an enviable domestic market and that in itself is a threat unless domestic enterprises shake themselves out of their comfort zones and gear up to face the pressures of competition from across the border, now made easier, thanks to the World Trade Organisation (WTO).

India and other developing countries will continue to oppose and seek amendments to the WTO proposals that prohibit developing countries from following the same policies that developed countries pursued to make their domestic enterprises internationally competitive. But the WTO threats are real. The trick, if one is to survive and prosper, will be to identify emerging threats before they become real and then prepare for them. It will be equally important to learn to spot opportunities before they arise, and take advantage of them. Success comes to those who are able to take advantage of opportunity. Alexander Graham Bell said: "When one door closes, another door opens: but we often look so long and so regretfully upon the closed door that we do not see the ones that open for us." In business, opportunity knocks once; it usually does not lean on the doorbell,

Competition from across the border will affect high-cost producers, and perhaps even decimate entire industries, especially in the small scale sector, India already finds itself in a situation of jobless growth. Where will new jobs be generated?

However, the alternative for job-seekers is to create their own jobs. Entrepreneurship in India (outside of family-controlled businesses) is largely necessarily-based, not opportunity-driven. Entrepreneurs in this country have traditionally not been looked up to as role models, It is still widely believed that you cannot become a successful entrepreneur in this country without bending the rules. But this view is slowly changing, thanks to the success of Indian entrepreneurs in the infotech industry. They have fired the imagination of a whole new generation, and entrepreneurship is now desired career option. Industries where entrepreneurship has flourished are IT, drugs, and pharmaceuticals.

The comparable advantage of developing countries will expand beyond low labour costs. This trend is a clear warning to those who are banking in the comfort of apparent demand for their products and services. If the industry is so complacent, when there is the opportunity for innovation?

Apart from these, some of the operational problems experienced in the course of implementing the entrepreneurship development programmes are listed below:

1. Past experience has shown that the supporting agencies/organisation, either tend to be slipshod in the first phase or are less interested in the third phase which means that the programme fails to tape the entrepreneurial potential of the area or the trained entrepreneurs do not receive the support and counselling which they need most.
2. Most of the existing support organisations meant for maintenance operations are not for innovative functions. There is also an element of cynicism. A reorientation in the attitude of supporting organisations is called for.
3. Poor investment on the part of institutions as also trainees and wrong selection of target groups contributed largely to the failure of the number of entrepreneurship development programmes.
4. Experiences reveal that entrepreneurial failures are mostly due to incompetence and poor management.
5. It is also said that there is an inability to identify the needs of institutions and differences of opinion prevailed amongst the practitioners and also amongst the trainees.

6. It is also stated that there is a low institutional commitment for local support to the entrepreneurs. There is also a very low level of involvement in the marketing of products of the units.
7. Non-availability of various inputs, *i.e.,* raw materials, power etc., and infrastructure support combined with poor follow-up by the primary monetary institutions resulted in the failure of the entrepreneurship development programmes.
8. It is also stated that there is ill-planned training methodology, inconsistency in the programme design, its content, sequence and theme and the focus of the programme is not clear.
9. Tanning institutions do not have much concern for the objective of identification and selection of entrepreneurs and the follow-up after training.
10. Some of the institutions are still debating whether to have a proper identification and selection of entrepreneurs for preparing successful entrepreneurs.
11. Those involved in and concerned with the selection and follow-up activities have either limited manpower support or a narrow linkage with other support agencies.
12. It is also said that there is no standard curricula even in terms of broad module being adopted by interventions.
13. A majority of the institutions engaged in the entrepreneurship development programmes are themselves not convinced of what they are doing as the task is delegated by the government. As a result, the social objective aimed at is not achieved.
14. Perpetual ambiguity in the objectives of entrepreneurship development programmes seems to have percolated to the grass-root level with significant deterioration in terms of content and interest.
15. It has also been realised that absence of an appropriate industrial and commercial climate coupled with lack of information and access to relevant technology has acted as a great handicap and
16. Mechanical implementation of entrepreneurship development programmes, as it is happening in many cases, will not solve the problem. The mechanical approach may help entrepreneurs to initiate the entrepreneurial development activity but they may not be able to manage it and expand it successfully.

Abdul Aziz Mahmud prepared an integrated Model in 1974 to explain the process of developing effective indigenous entrepreneurs to take up and accelerate the process of economic growth and development.

According to his model the creation of effective entrepreneurs is influenced by political, economical, socio-cultural, psychological and organisational forces in the society. Each one of these factors influence directly and indirectly the creation of entrepreneurs, making them effective in their chosen entrepreneurial activity for the betterment of the society.

Each one of these components play a crucial role in this process. They are complimentary to each other. It is this integrated approach to entrepreneurship sustains economic development.

The model prepared by Abdul Aziz Mahmud is presented in the Chart illustrated in the following figure.

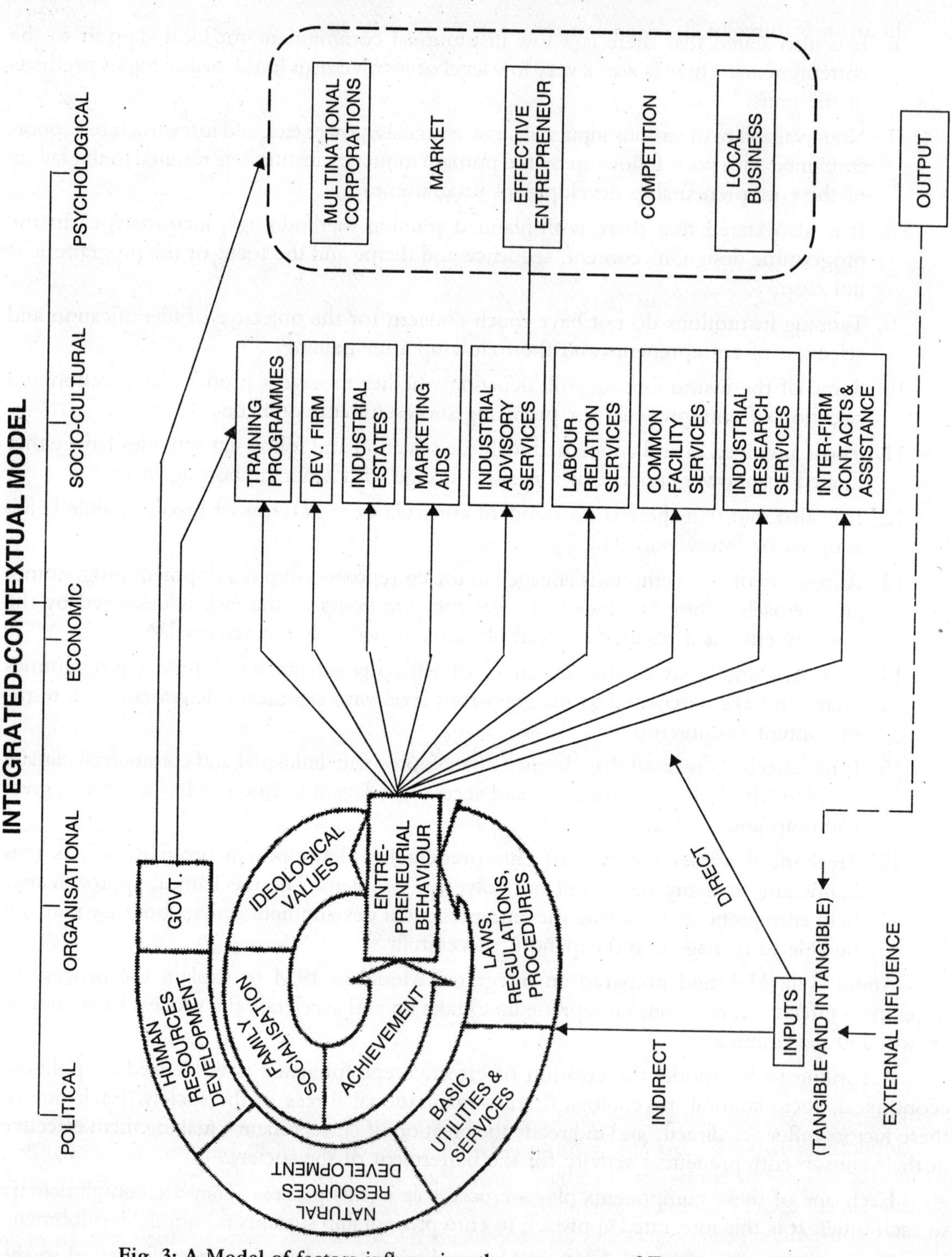

Fig. 3: A Model of factors influencing the emergence of Entrepreneurship

Source: Adapted from Adbul Aziz Mohumud Developing Effective Indigenous Entrepreneurs. *Malaysian Management Review*, April 1974, Vol. 9, No. 1.

The main features of the model are:

1. Family background, role models and a supportive relationship encourages independence and achievement.
2. Personal characteristics skills, leadership traits, creativity, opportunism, and intuition distinguishes one from the another.
3. Motivation, achievement and profit encourages entrepreneurship.
4. Government plays a unique role in promoting industrial research, multinational cooperation and entrepreneurial training facilities.
5. Globalisation and competitive environment to change and economic activities.
6. Entrepreneurial behaviour promotes development of new ventures, basic infrastructure and training.
7. Innovation and development of new concepts, ideas and services received a big boost.
8. Laws, regulations and procedures sets a new venture in process.
9. Economically it means new products/services, profit, employment opportunities, income generation, standard of living stands enhanced.
10. In the process, organisation culture, work culture become operative.

This integrated model explain the multi-disciplinary process of entrepreneurship. It merits attention of all students of entrepreneurism and entrepreneurship.

THE 4Ps

❐ Product ❐ Price ❐ Promotion and ❐ place.

— ***Philip Kotler***

Trying to exchange business cards with Philip Kotler, the father of marketing, is quite an experience. Instead of giving you his, he will autograph yours and give it back. No one seems to mind — the card with 'P Kotler' scribbled on it with a stubby pencil will probably be preserved for posterity. Few people in the world of management achieve the kind of rockstar status Kotler enjoys. Marketing executives in some European countries celebrate Kotler Day once a year. One country even released a postage stamp in his honour.

Economic theory

But the man who became a marketing icon didn't enter the discipline by design Economics was his first love. But "having grown up in the lower middle class, I saw a big difference in income and wealth, and saw some people suffering," he says. This prompted him to understand income distribution more closely. And in the 1960s Kotler slowly meandered his way into marketing.

"Economics makes very simple assumptions that every consumer will maximise utility and every producer is greedy enough to do what is profitable. So I got interested in fleshing out what I still think is economics — the marketplace," he says. What started as an exploration of issues about how consumers make choices and how producers figure out who they want their customers to be, soon resulted in his seminal book, *Marketing Management.*

Marketing textbooks then were not based on scientific evidence. "The market needed a more decision-oriented book drawing from four fields: organisational theory, consumer psychological theory, mathematics and economics," he says. The book went on to become a bible on B-school campuses.

That was 1967. A lot has changed since then. The book's 13th edition will be out soon. In addition, Kotler has written more than 35 books, covering themes as diverse as nation brands, marketing for the service industry marketing for congregations like churches and even a book on social marketing. His latest biggie is the concept of holistic marketing — a concept that states that marketing decisions in one area should be consistent with decisions in other areas. The idea is to take virtually everything Into account for marketing — customers, employees, other companies, competition and society.

But is Kotler losing his magic touch?

More than anything Kotler is known for popularising the 4P model of marketing or the marketing mix — that marketing needs to be driven by product, pricing, promotions and place. The 4Ps have ruled the marketing world for three decades. No one is quite sure though about who originally came up with the 4Ps: Kotler or Jerome McCarthy another leader in marketing thought.

But over the last few years the 4Ps have drawn flak. "The 4Ps model is plateauing because it lays too much emphasis on product and promotions," says Jagdish Sheth, a well-known marketing guru and professor at Emory University's Goizueta Business School.

Practitioners agree, Pepsi India CEO Rajeev Bakshi says, "The 4Ps are far too basic a framework for today's complex world where each of the 4Ps needs to be sub-segmented." Take promotion. At that time it stood for a 30-second commercial. Today it also means managing work-of-mouth promotion and creating more interactivity around your brand through communities, for instance. Similarly, there weren't too many choices in packaging at that time and pricing was also unidimensional. As for place, the number of distribution channels that a company can use today has exploded.

"You need to build in more customer centricity in marketing today" says sheth, who has proposed a new framework called the 4As of marketing which look at things from the customer's point of view (availability access, affordability and awareness).

Kevin Lane Keller, a branding expert and professor at Tuck School of Business, who co-authored the 12th edition of *Marketing Management* with Kotler, says: "The 4Ps are an Incomplete view of how marketing works in today's dynamic environment." He thinks It needs to be replaced with the holistic marketing framework.

Kotler, on his part, is unfazed by the criticism. "The 4Ps, are still relevant," he says emphatically But he has realised that they will not work on their own. "I have already decided that they should be encased in a larger vision of marketing that centres on the term of 'value'," says Kotler. "Essentially the job of the marketing people is to create value, communicate value and deliver value." This is a concept that will show up in the next edition of *Marketing Management.*

But what about other academics who are coming up with new models to rival the 4Ps? Sheth's 4As, for Instance? "The 4As precede the 4Ps framework. It doesn't dispense with it. So make a product that is available, easy to acquire etcetra etcetra. But okay, I still have to make the product, the pricing, the place and the promotion," says Kotler.

Even the holistic marketing framework hasn't gained too many followers. Says Sheth, "The concept has immense potential. But for it to be implemented companies need massive internal reorganisation. He doesn't suggest ways to do that and I am not sure they will take the risk of doing this." The marketing head of a consumer durables company says that holistic marketing is far too complicated and gets into the nitty-gritty of "organisational delivery". "Instead Kotler should have made the 4Ps more customer-centric by taking an outside-in view," he says. What he means is simple: the 4Ps assume that the manufacturer controls supply. Instead, companies must hook up with all the links in the chain to revise their marketing model. For instance, for the product they can rope in suppliers, trawl through blogs to pick up insights, and speak to consumers. Then they can reconfigure R&D to design that. They need to do similar work on the other Ps.

Will Kotler meet his equal?

Kotler's critics accuse him of constantly "repackaging his old Ideas" and presenting them as new. Since the 4P framework is drawing flak, would it be fair to say that the Kotler reign is over? A top-league professor at one of the best international business schools, says, "When someone comes up with a new idea, he is viewing things through a prism. Just because someone else looks through the prism from another angle, it doesn't mean that Kotler will become Irrelevant."

The fact remains that given the breadth of Kotler's work, marketing will probably not see such a dominant figure again (See 'Young Kotlers'). "He came along when there were few other marketing writers out there and he has created worldwide impact across a broad range of marketing topics. There will be other writers with huge impact. But not so much in the breadth of contribution," says Keller.

In recent years, various people have added more Ps — Passion, People, Packaging, Process, Public relation, Public opinion, process, passion, product design and promotion, Placement, politics and some persons have converted 4Ps into 4Cs — customer, value, customer cost, customer convenience and customer communication.

However, Philip Kotler's 4Ps has still relevance to all organisation.

"Young Kotlers' or rising stars in the world of marketing

Will the world of marketing see another figure as dominant as Kotler? Perhaps not. The way academic research is currently structured, young professors are being forced into narrow research areas. They lack the overarching view that Kotler had. He says, "The problem with young people is that they can make their career only if they become well-known as specialists. The tenured track system really forces them to be a leader in a specialised part of marketing." But he does identify a handful of people who he thinks have great potential.

Kevin Lane Keller (Tuck School of Business): "This is the first time someone else worked with me to write the new edition of Marketing Management. He has already risen as a branding expert."

Nirmalya Kumar (London Business School): "We co-authored an article called *Market Driving Firms*. He is a real comer — he is writing four books at the same time. I think he's great."

Kash Rangan (Harward Business School): "He has written a new book on distribution, *Go To Market.* It is probably one of the best distribution books ever."

V. Kumar (University of Connecticut): "He is very technical. He measures customer lifetime value. I would watch him."

Greg Carpenter (Kellogg School of Business): "He is managerial."

James Anderson (Kellogg School of Business): "A broad specialist,' he really loves B2B, which is such a big area. But he is really strong. He has published 8-10 articles in HBR and a book."

Box - 6

HOLISTIC MARKETING

The holistic marketing framework enables management to answer the following questions. How can a company identify new value opportunities? How can a company efficiently create more promising new value offerings? How can a company use its capabilities and infrastructure to deliver the new value offerings efficiently?

Because markets are dynamic and competitive, management needs a well-defined strategy for value exploration. Developing such a strategy requires understanding the connections and interactions among three spaces: the customer's cognitive space, the company's competency space, and the collaborator's resource spaces. To exploit a value opportunity, the company needs value creation skills. Marketers need to identify new customer benefits from the customer's cognitive space, utilise core competencies from its business domain, and select and manage business partners from its collaborative network.

To be able to deliver value requires substantial investment in infrastructure and capabilities. The company must become proficient at customer relationship management, internal resource management, and business partnership management. Customer relationship management allows the company to discover who its customers are, how they behave, and what they need or want. It also enables it to respond appropriately. To respond effectively, the company requires internal resource management — to integrate major business processes within a single family of software modules. Finally, business partnership management allows [it] to handle complex relationships with its trading partners to source, process and deliver products....

Crafting the Competitive Platforms

The nine building blocks in the holistic marketing framework constitute a strategic foundation for crafting four key competitive platforms for establishing corporate and business strategies.

1. *Market offerings platform:* The first set of basic building blocks — cognitive space, competency space, customer benefits and business domain — gives management strategic insight for developing market offerings.
2. *Business architecture platform:* The next set of basic building blocks — competency space, resource space, business domain and business partners — guides management in reconfiguring the business architecture, which is made up of several value chains.
3. *Marketing activities platform:* The next set of basic building blocks — customer benefits, business domain, customer relationship management and internal resource management — helps management formulate its marketing activities to support the market offerings.
4. *Operational system platform:* The final set of basic building blocks — business domain, business partners, internal resource management and business partnership management — provides strategic insight for designing the operational system.

LOYALTY MODEL

Marketers have been indulging in varied practises to sustain the loyalty of the consumers and lure them too.

Loyalty programmes have a simple logic to provide customers an incentive to spend more. And in keeping with that logic, retailers, service providers, telecom services, financial services and many other companies, have been doling out loyalty cards with associated rewards. Their aim is to retain what they hope will be high-spending customers.

Horns of a dilemma

Loyalty programmes are a double-edged sword. On the one hand business gurus tell us that a loyal customer is an investment. Reward her with points and she will keep coming back to spend more. But retailers that have a huge bank of unredeemed points often consider it a liability and not investments. The immediate reaction tends to be to bring down the value of the points to reduce the liability. But could it simply be that the company got the maths wrong?

A formula gone wrong?

Well, here's how it works in India: Most loyalty programmes are based on the model followed by the credit card industry, where 1% - 2% reward points is the norm. But the thing is — the economics of the credit card business does not allow anything more.

Besides, people make many more purchases on their credit cards than they are likely to make at any single retail outlet. In a year, an average family spends between Rs. 50,000 to Rs. 1.5 lakh through credit cards. Even a 1% reward on that would work out to between Rs. 500 to Rs. 1,500 — that's large enough to give a higher notional value to the 1% reward point.

The irony here is that, a few years ago, a leading MNC bank reported up to 65% unredeemed points. Yet, unfortunately the credit card model has become the bench mark for everyone else, irrelevance notwithstanding.

Promises, promises

Now consider this. If a shopper gets only 2% of the purchase value as reward, she would have to buy things worth Rs. 25,000 to collect a mere 500 points. Given an industry norm of 1 point equals Re. 1, it works out to Rs. 500. Recently there were reports of a major retailer shaving off 30 paise from that "one rupee". A drop to 70 paise means a 30% drop that is, Rs. 350. So as a loyal member, I spend Rs. 25,000 and at the end I get a mere Rs. 350 gift. Is that really winning over loyalty? Probably that's why the Indian consumer is so apathetic towards such programmes and why we have loyalty programmes either closing down or forever restructuring themselves.

FAST FACTS

- Up to 50% reward points remain unredeemed because memberships lapse.
- Almost 50% - 60% of programme members tend to spend less and less on the company's products.
- Almost 40% - 50% are the low spenders. Having earned the points, they are unable or unwilling to use their points.

Perceptions

Indian companies need to create novel strategic management approaches. It comes as much as from the limitations in transplanting approaches developed in other contexts as from the possibilities of doing business in a fast growing economy. This also implies that we need to break new ground in terms of evolution processes.

The concept of strategic configuration is based on the realisation that strategy and the organisation design of a company are symbiotically related in many aspects. The aspects need to not only be in fit with the context but also among themselves internally, and better still be mutually reinforcing — as if in a living being. For instance, the strategy of high growth through diversification needs to be backed by the organisation design of divisional structure, profit centre based planning and review systems, decentralising style of top management and a culture of openness and risk taking. Strategic configuration of a company, as analogous to an organism, can be handily extended to visualise strategy as akin to brain, structure as bone frame, plans and procedures as nervous system, and managerial style and organisational culture as personality traits and soul.

Drawing on the overwhelming evidence that the strategic approaches of a company are influenced almost equally by the patterns acquired along the path of evolution till now and the trends in its emerging landscape, a new analytical technique can be developed. It juxtaposes the implications of the nature of evolution with that of future trends, to analyse the context. This technique can be used in consonance and be superimposed on others, such as SWOT, strategic planning matrices, industry attractiveness, and competitor analysis.

We used the new 'imperatives' technique to analyse the context of Indian companies as a genre. From a suitably chosen horizon, extending about a decade into the past and into the future, we found five evolutionary and five emerging imperatives in the context of Indian companies. And in the context defined by these imperatives, there were four viable and effective configurations. The outcome was startling, as rarely do the positions of focus vs diversification and of primary attention on domestics overseas markets, are equally and simultaneously attractive in a context. The new analytical technique equips Indian companies to assess their context in a far more holistic manner, covering the past and future and the macro, industry and resource scenarios, to outline better informed and clearer approaches.

In the context of individual Indian companies, the concepts of configuration and the imperatives technique are creditably appropriate to outline possible strategic configurations that best fit with its specific context. Four generic configurations of 'India-focused', 'India — a diversified', 'global-focused' and 'global-diversified', can act as a useful guide. For instance, a leading Indian cement company identified three possible configurations for the future — of becoming 'India diversified inorganic materials company' or 'a cement multinational', besides continuing as 'India cement focused' company. Similarly, a shipping company toyed with the new strategic configuration of becoming 'an integrated global shipping' vs 'India diversified' company.

This brings us to the question of 'how', or the process of a company evolving, either into the most effective state of existing configuration or into the newly chosen one. Notably, here the organism analogy of configuration breaks down a bit, as unlike living beings, company's can move from one configuration to another. There are two processes by which the configurations evolve, namely of transformation and momentum. The transformation process is evidently deliberate and quantum, involving replacing one or more aspects of strategy and organisation design. It requires enormous amount of energy and conviction, and generally driven by the quest for markedly superior performance or new opportunities. Some aspects such as new competitive capabilities and organisation culture, take relatively longer to put in place. However, changes in business portfolio and in organisation structure and management systems, which are faster to carry out, can be used to signal irreversibility and to engineer and catalyse slower changes.

Once a majority of the aspects of desired configuration are in place, the momentum process get going. It will not only speed up slower moving aspects but also engender mutually reinforcing routines. Change will move on its own momentum and generally be incremental. One of finest examples is Ranbaxy in mid-1990s, when it moved from 'India-focused' to 'global-focused' configuration. The strategy of drug discovery and overseas expansion was pushed forth by the implementation of new international geographies based structure and the research oriented and outward looking managerial style of Parvinder Singh. In a couple of years, the momentum settled in, and the company went to register and sustain vastly improved growth and profitability for nearly a decade.

The understanding of evolution in the terms of transformation and momentum, and more importantly the linkages and sequentially *vis-a-vis* the momentum, is another insight that is valid in the Indian contest. Transformation and momentum in evolution, along with the concept of configuration and the imperatives technique, are an adequate toolkit for Indian companies to chart original and path breaking strategic management approaches.

LOYALTY MATRIX

Loyalty segmentation

Shep Hyken

Customers can be categorised into four segments, based on their responses to attitudinal loyalty and behavioural loyalty.

Truly loyal customers are those who are high on attitudinal as well as behavioural loyalty. These customers not only like dealing with the service provider but are also highly likely to continue using their services in the near future. The higher the truly loyal percentage, the better for the organisation.

Accessible customers are those who like dealing with the service provider but are not very likely to use their services in the future. Customers could be Accessible for a number of reasons. They may seek better value, differentiated services with the changing market scenario and intense competition.

Trapped customers are those who are not happy dealing with the service provider and yet are forced to continue using the service provider in future.

High risk customers are those who do not like dealing with the service provider and have decided to switch to another service provider. This tends to be a lead indicator of future churn.

THE POWER OF LOYALTY

Ted Levitt, senior professor at Harvard Business School, says that the function of every business is to get and keep customers. Consequently, it is also the function of every employee of every business to do the same. Knowing how to keep existing customers happy is key to a company's continued success. Studies have also proven that it is much more expensive to attract a new customer to a business than to keep an existing one.

To build customer loyalty, here are six universal points.

- Create a demanding customer. Creating one means that if your customers were to go to your competition, they would not just expect but demand the same level of service that they get from you. Anything less from the competition reinforces that the customer made the right choice to do business with you. In other words, you have spoiled your customer.
- Find out if you are doing a good job and if there are problems, react quickly. Your customers are not likely to tell you if there are problems. Numerous studies have shown that complaining customers do not complain. TARP (Technical Assistance Research Program) was commissioned by the White House Office of Consumer Affairs to survey customer satisfaction. They found that an average business only hears from 4 per cent of unhappy customers. The other 96 per cent don't complain — at least not to the places they did business. While the study was conducted a number of years ago, current independent studies show similar findings. Your ultimate goal should be to try and find any problems before the customer complains.

- Make sure your customers know they made the right decision to do business with you. Educate and reinforce that they have made a good choice. If you do something different than the competition, make sure the customer knows about it. I remember buying meat from a grocery store. The butcher proudly held up the steak he was selling me and said, "Look at that! Is that a beautiful piece of meat or what? Did you know that we trim the fat around the steak to just 1/8 of an inch? You won't find that at the competition! Thanks for shopping with us." It is your opportunity to standout.
- Guarantee your products or services. Personally stand behind everything you do. Customers do not do business with a company, they do business with the people who represent the company. If a customer has a problem, and you are the person that received it, it is your responsibility to see it through. Do not just push it off to someone else. You may not make the final decision, but you are there at the end when it is made.
- Recognise that there may be others in the 'buying process' that should be made to feel appreciated. These people might also be involved in the buying process, such as an assistant, a secretary or even a committee, but may not be the person or people you are dealing with day to day. Even if the assistant or secretary is not involved in the buying decision, they are still part of the team. Do not forget to show appreciation for these people as well.
- Do not ever forget to say thanks! It can be face to face, over the phone or via written thank you notes. Customers like to feel appreciated.

Work toward implementing these and you will find a higher success rate in keeping your existing customers and creating moments of magic.

LOYALTY MATRIX

	The first...		... and the last	
PRODUCTS				
Apparel	Allen Solly	67	UCB	49
Sportswear & accessories	Planet Sports	61	Adidas	53
Air conditioner	LG	59	Carrier	51
Television	Samsung	57	BPL	46
Washing machine	Videocon	57	BPL	49
2-Wheelers	Hero Honda	60	LML	44
4-Wheelers	Ford and Honda	55	Tata Motors	49
Refrigerator	LG	53	Electrolus	48
FINANCIAL SERVICES				
Insurance	LIC	59	ING Vysya & Max New York	45
Credit cards	AM EX	58	Citibank	45
Retail banking	SBI	57	ABN Amro and BOB	45
Housing loans	SBI	55	ICICI	49
RETAIL & SERVICE				
Fast food joints	Pizza Hut	62	Domino's	48
Coffee outlets	Café Coffee Day	57	Barista	49
Airlines	Kingfisher	55	Air Deccan	35
Lifestyle & fashion store	Westside	54	Globus	39

Figures are the loyalty score of the brands

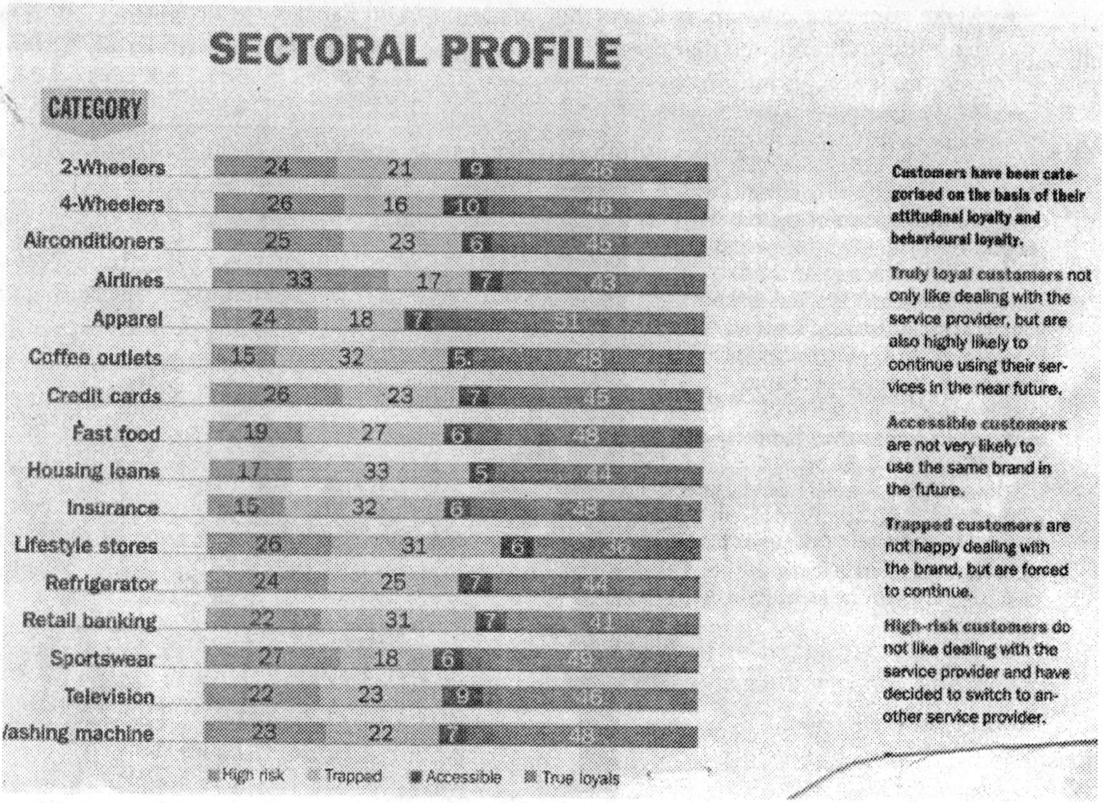

The Loyalty Pyramid

But it need not be like that. Smart programme managers globally have created sophisticated techniques to predict which 'loyal' consumers are going to drop out. They then proactively assign residual value to the truly loyal members. Instead of killing the lapsed points and their value, they reassign value somewhere else. What this means is, creating a tiered loyalty structure, where the top 20% members get higher points.

The reasons for doing this are fairly strong. Top-end members spend proportionately much greater than the lower tier members, even though at the beginning of the programs the spends may have been similar.

A large retailer reported that out of a total of 1.5 lakh members, the skew was clearly noticeable with only 15,000-20,000 spending greater than Rs. 25,000 or more, as against the national average of Rs. 8,000. It therefore makes sense to move part of the rewards to the better and more profitable members by carefully restructuring the potentially dead points.

Furthermore, it is now a well established fact, proven by many surveys, that on an average a frequent shopper is a member of at least three such programs with different retailers. A rationally structured loyalty programme could be a way to get an increased "share of his wallet".

Data has also shown that loyalty members tend to be more educated, involved and more discerning customers. The higher they go up in the loyalty 'pyramid', such profiles get even stronger.

Many large retailers in the US have actually given up to and sometime beyond 8%-10% of bill as rewards to their best customers.

A good loyalty programme is one that lets members see value per point beyond the commercial par value, that is 1 point equals 1 unit currency.

Many loyalty programmes have, with smartly carved rewards structure, given up to 50% more value per point (read as 1 point equals Re 1.50). This is what makes a loyal customer feel good about the program.

It is a matter of assigning notional values that have far reaching implications. Redemption improves sales. But unredeemed points hit bottom-line. Unredeemed points also do not belong to anyone after validity expires.

This surely calls for programme restructuring to provide a greater value to potential winning customers.

THE MILLENNIAL VALUE CHAIN

Among the factors that will impact the ay companies have traditionally done business are changing value expectations, fragmentation of demand, and the convergence of technologies. This is bluming the boundaries between traditional business entities and creating global brands. Indian companies will be subject to intense competition this millennium. They will have to push the boundaries of productivity to enter markets and survive. Consequently, we can expect a change in the manager's role. Technology will increasingly take care of mundane processes and reduce managerialisation.

The characteristics of management are:

1. The e-management
2. Orientation towards shareholder value
3. Strategic perspective
4. Lateral thinking
5. Responsiveness
6. Global competitiveness
7. People management
8. Courage in decision-making
9. Logistic management
10. Corporate governance

"21st century leaders and managers must rethink 20th century process. These processes must focus on core practices. I believe four critical areas will have a significant impact on a 21st century organisation. These are: grass root education, fire prevention, direct interaction, and effective globalisation. These concepts could apply as easily to the non-profit organisation as to a transnational or a government organisation."

Subir Chowdhury, towards the future of management

"Managers have to embrace a very different management philosophy, grounded in an alternative set of assumptions about both individuals and institutions, this philosophy leads to some very different beliefs about the role of the company in society, about the relationship between employers and employees, and about the functions of management. It posits a very different moral contract between the individual, the company, and society."

Sumantra Ghoshal, Chris Barrtlett and Peter Moran, Value Creation

"Consider the global market as a pyramid of consumers based on economic strength. The new and emerging opportunity in countries such as China, India and Brazil is in the lower-income segments: Tiers 2, 3, and 4 serving these markets will dramatically influence the management process in transnationals. This market demands a fundamentally different type of capability. Firms ought to be able to rethink the price performance relationship."

— C.K. Praharlad, Emerging work of Managers

"Business strategy means multi-dimensional and multi-local thinking. Globalisation creates a world business elite — an English-speaking, highly-educated business class — but that managerial class must understand the differences among markets and nations while rising above them. Thus tour of the macro-environment points to the forces creating a need for innovation everywhere. To succeed, business must tap the power in brainpower"

Rosabeth Moss Kanter, Kaleidoscope Thinking

"Speed will become a major determinant of organisational success. Judgements about television programmes, clothing styles or movies will be made much more quickly. Product life-styles will shorten and the first-mover advantage will become even more important. With speed comes the requirement for the agility to change, adopt, and learn more quickly. Speed means changing from a mindset of accuracy to one of innovation.

Peter Lorange, Ultra-rapid Management Processes

"In contrast to the traditional organisation design process, where organisational structures and system are derived from a predefined strategy. The design of the customised workplace will seek to balance what matters of the im (its strategy) with what matters for individuals (their life strategies). Thus, the individual in the 21st century organisation will reclaim some control over fundamental aspects of her workers"

– Hamid Bouchkhi and John R. Kimberly, the customised workplace

❑ ❑ ❑

"Intelligence and knowledge ensure the success of individuals without any regard to the consequence of the success. The survival of society and organisations depends on the wisdom and not only on the intelligence of individuals who form a part of it. Intelligence is not rare to find in today's world. This ability to learn, analyse and derive solution-options can be commonly found in people. What is not common is the ability to apply wisdom and choose the true option. Failure to look beyond immediate needs, self-centred interests, short-sighted objectives and reluctance to think in a larger perspective, will create pathways to defeat."

SIX

Socio-Cultural Theories of Entrepreneurship

Introduction

Entrepreneurs play an important role in the development of society. For example, the use of Jeans in America has created the demand for it throughout the world. Similarly, Coca Cola has been accepted as a social drink. The introduction of the television has provided the society a means of information and entertainment. The society has accepted the innovations of such entrepreneurs as Gillet, Wright Brothers, and Henry Ford. The inventions of these great entrepreneurs of the history has revolutionised the life style of people in the society.

Modern business studies have a distinct entrepreneurial discipline: The approach to the study of entrepreneurship is multi-disciplinary. It impinges on such areas as demography, economic anthropology, business history, politics, sociology, psychology, marketing and finance. That is why entreprenpurship development becomes an integral part of the overall economic, social and industrial development of a country. This is what makes the identification and management of entrepreneurial functions a highly complex exercise.

Thus, entrepreneurship, the *de facto* barometer of overall economic, social and industrial growth has brought revolutionary changes in the society. It is the *sine quo non* of a nation's progress which has facilitated large-scale production and distribution. It has widened the area and scope of the marketing of goods and services. Perhaps it is for these reasons that the small business sector has been given priority in our national development programmes, for entrepreneurship flourishes when the size of business remains relatively small and viable.

There seems to exist a relationship between society and entrepreneurial talent. This is a relative importance of some social conditions that influence the stability and development of new institutions. In an essay entitled Democracy in Asia, Past and Future, published in the 20th Volume of For Eastern Survey, R. A. Scaliapio has drawn attention to how the stress of international political economic tensions has aided the transition in the entrepreneurial behaviour. Over the period of time it has been proved that for the proper development of entrepreneurship, state protection is a necessary input. Thus, it can be viewed as a function of social, political and economic structure.

Environment for Entrepreneurship

The entrepreneurs do not appear spontaneously. While the other factors of production are at last, in principle, available for hire but enterprise is not. It has to come from different vocations. Even the educational system in most of the developing countries is designed in such a way as to create more job-seekers. To sum up, entrepreneurs appear to have been motivated by a combination and interaction of the following factors of environment:

1. Socio-economic environment;
2. Family background;
3. Standard of education and technical knowledge;
4. Financial stability;
5. Political stability and government policy;
6. Caste and religious affiliation;
7. Availability of supporting facilities;
8. Achievement motivation; and
9. Personality and personal skill.

The environmental factors may be summarised as follows:

1. Entrepreneurship is not influenced by single factor but is the outcome of the interaction and combination of various environmental factors.
2. By changing the environment, society can be recreated.
3. It is the 'desire to make money' that drives one to start an industry rather than the amount of money one possesses and
4. Encouraging government policy and social recognition influence a person to become an entrepreneur. Educationist must think of modifying the educational system, so as to produce more job-creators than just job-seekers.

Knowledge Plays an Important Role in Entrepreneurship

There are three kinds of knowledge:

Tacit Knowledge: Insights and context from the mind, what the knower "knows". Knowledge, that is difficult to articulate or represent. This is the stuff that you pick up at water cooler/cafeteria.

Embedded Knowledge: Organisational understanding manifested in process manuals, products and services. This can be made available through the KM system, or through various directories, which people maintain on their servers.

Explicit Knowledge: Knowledge represented in artifacts like books and documents.

There are five pillars of KM that, have technological and non-technological solutions.

- **Business Intelligence** uses concepts of data Mining
- **Collaboration:** Groupware, working with people.
- **Knowledge Transfer:** Distance Learning or computer-based training.
- **Knowledge Discovery and Mapping:** Document management and categorisation of essential prerequisite.
- **Expertise:** Expert Networks, like the knowledge networks, etc.

CULTURE

Globalisation, fuelled by technological advancement, is the order of the day. Trade and tourism flourish across the entire canvass of the globe, bringing together people of varied cultures, values, languages and religions. Success in such a multinational environment, with its concomitant challenges and problems, is largely a function of one's cross cultural sensitivity. So what is cross-cultural sensitivity? It is the ability to read into and interpret culturally-rooted situations and contexts with flexibility and openness. It refers to the appreciation of cultural nuances and the ability to react to and handle such situations with intelligence and finesse.

Cross-cultural ignorance or insensitivity can lead to situations ranging from the comical to the more serious, resulting in trauma, loss of business and failure at the negotiation table.

What is Culture?

Culture is an anthropological term that is applicable to organisations too. *It represents a pattern of beliefs and behaviours that have been learned from other members of the society, It is, in its broadest sense, the cultivated behaviour, i.e.,* the totality of man's learned experience which is socially transmitted or more briefly behaviours acquired through social learning. It is most frequently described as custom and includes both actions, man-made objects called artifacts and also ideas. Culture of an organization plays a significant role in the area of motivation and the level of economic rewards. Organizational culture also influences the level of commitment to work on the part of the members.

Culture is a symbolic integration of individual behaviours in a large system. The system may be country, or an organization, or a particular unit or society. As every system has subsystem, every culture has its subcultures. There is a great divergence of views among anthropologists as to a proper definition of culture. One classic and comprehensive definition of culture, however, is given by Taylor long back who views culture as "the complex which includes knowledge belief, art, law, custom and any other capability and habits acquired by man as a member of the society.' The concept of culture can be applicable to the study of organisations, leadership, entrepreneurship and influence work culture.

Definition of Culture

There are very varying definitions of *culture*. Culture, in its broadest definition, "refers to that part of the total repertoire of human action (and its product) which is socially, as opposed to genetically, transmitted." A very popular definition is that of Edward Burnett Taylor: "Culture of civilization is that complex whole which includes knowledge, belief, art, morals, law, custom, and other capabilities and habits acquired by man as a member of society." Clyde Kluckhohn has defined culture very simply as 'the total life-way of a people."

The concept of culture is used to distinguish human societies from animal groups. The customs, ideas, and attitudes shared by a group, which make up its culture are transmitted from generation to generation by learning processes rather than biological inheritance. Adherence to these customs and attitudes is regulated by systems of rewards and punishments peculiar to each culture. Language and other symbolic media are the chief agents of culture transmission, but many behaviour patterns are acquired through experience alone. A pattern of cultural universals is found in all societies. It includes such human institutions as social organisation, and material culture (tools, weapons, clothing). Societies are differentiated according to the degree of complexity of cultural organisation. Basically, each human group has its own distinctive culture but a complex society may contain subcultures determined by national origin religion, or social status. The spread of culture traits through direct or indirect contact among groups is called diffusion. A culture area is the territory within which a certain configuration of culture traits is to be found. The two theories of culture that have dominated anthropological thought in the 20th century are the structural-functional theory derived from Bronislaw Malinowski and the pattern-process theory derived from Franz Boas. Structural-functional theory focuses on social structure, while pattern-process theory emphasizes cultural patterns. Each theory attempts to explain all aspects of culture, and each is applied to all cultures. All anthropologists, however, recognise certain broad evolutionary sequences in the cultural history of mankind, particularly in the technological and economic spheres.

On the basis of the various definitions of culture, Francis Merill formulates the concept of culture as follows. Culture, he says,

(*a*) is the characteristically human product of social interaction;
(*b*) provides socially acceptable patterns for meeting biological and social needs;
(*c*) is cumulative, for it is handed down from generation to generation in a given society;
(*d*) is meaningful to human beings because of its symbolic quality;
(*e*) is learned by each person in the course of his development in a particular society;
(*f*) is, therefore, a basic determinant of personality; and
(*g*) depends for its existence upon the continued functioning of society but is independent of any individual group.

Culture consists of both material and non-material culture. Material culture involves man-made things *e.g.*, automobiles, television, mobile, computers etc. and man-made alterations in the environment. Non-material culture refers to the intangible beliefs, philosophies, values, habits, customs among the members of the organisation or society.

In short, culture is the sum total of social behaviour, environment. It includes knowledge, beliefs, ideals, values and preferences.

Organisation's Culture

Culture and share values (ideology and shared culture): Webster says that culture is the integral pattern of human behaviour that includes thought, speech and action and depends on man's capacity for learning and transmitting knowledge to succeeding generations. Most elements of a culture take a long time in their evolution and equally as long to change. An organisation has a mission when its culture fits with its strategy. Culture enables organisation to function as a collective unit. The cultural glue consists of strong norms and values that heavily influence the way people behave, how they work together and how they pursue the goals of the organisation. Values are the beliefs and, moral principles that lie behind the company's culture. Values give meaning to the norms and behaviour standards in the company.

To strengthen an organisation's culture, a set of values, behaviour characteristics, procedural rituals, and role models for the professionals working in an organisation, should be identified. Structure reflects the organisation of work into roles. The roles may be in professionals working in an organisation, should be identified. Structure reflects the organisation of work into roles. The roles may be in production, finance, marketing, personnel etc. The structure of the organisation embodies the fundamental division of labour, describes the nature and duties of the jobs to be done, and aggregates them into groups, or business.

Leadership Culture

The new economic era that's going to continue at least into the first quarter of the 21st century, if not throughout the century, is driven by the globalisation of markets, competition and a faster-moving environment. In such a situation, we need to think about leadership culture which act as *anchors* to help us adapt to change.

The two core elements of the new adaptive corporate culture are, first, that the management group deeply, honestly, sincerely values the various players in the corporate drama. And not just themselves. In other words, they highly value the basic constituencies that support their business, starting with customers — but not ending with customers — and going right through to suppliers, employees, and stockholders. As a result, they look outwards, not inwards. They really do care about customers. They really do care about their stockholders. They really do care about their employees. That single characteristic is enormously important in producing flexible and adaptive cultures. Cultures that tend to be anchors on change are cultures where what managers implicitly value most of all are managers. Where you have an inward focus and a lot of self-interest.

The second core characteristic of healthy cultures is that initiative and leadership are truly valued and encouraged at every level in the organisation. Not just at the top, but at the middle and lower levels too. In change-anchoring cultures, leadership tends to be valued not much at all. And if it is tolerated, it is tolerated only at the very top of the organisation.

The combination of these two core characteristics — a deep concern for the basic constituencies outside the management that make up the enterprise and leadership up and down the hierarchy — gives you an incredible capacity to navigate in a turbulent environment because people are not just turned inwards, looking at themselves but they are focused outwards, looking at the basic constituencies, starting with customers, where the real action is. The when they see problems or opportunities, which they will it's not just up to one or two people to do something, as it is when the whole centre of initiative for leadership is invested in one or two people. Instead, it's possible for hundreds or even thousands of people to initiate action to solve the problems or take advantage of the opportunities.

It is the combination of these two characteristics that can help you adapt remarkably well in a rapidly-changing environment and to outperform even financially stronger competitors by significant amounts. Because, first you have got all the eyeballs lacing outwards, so you can spot things changing faster, and then you have got so many sources of initiative inside the organisation to do something about it. And this makes it possible even for an aircraft carrier to be relatively maneuverable in a very volatile environment.

Vision for Future

The entrepreneurship that contributes in a modest way to critical economic and social needs of the country and always strive to attain global leadership in all of its major initiative. This is the vision for future.

Pursuing this vision, over the next few years, entrepreneurs will pursue a strategy of:

- Reinforcing competitive advantage of existing business through new capacities and synergistic acquisitions.
- Scaling sizeable opportunities in the core sectors.
- Forward integrating into retailing transportation fuels and creating new customer experiences.
- Addressing the significant information and communications market opportunity in India and in the world.
- Leveraging its strong balance sheet, cash flows and managerial capacity to create value by adding new capacities, acquisitions and turnaround of under performing assets.
- Developing strategic alliances in technology and product-market domains with global majors.
- Fostering new higher education institutions for knowledge creation and sharing.
- Leveraging its formidable strengths beyond Indian borders.
- Reorienting the best practices to enhance productivity and quality (Q).
- In addition to manufacturing products venture into developing manufacturing systems.
- From having a manufacturing orientation to providing technical solutions.

Meaning of Entrepreneurial Culture

Culture consists of tangible man-made objects, such as automobiles, clothing, furniture, buildings, and tools and intangible concepts such as laws, morals, and knowledge. In addition, culture includes the values, character, qualities, skills acceptable within the particular society.

Culture in a society is learned and is passed on from one generation to the next. Culture is nurtured, fostered and promoted.

A culture is usually divided into sub-cultures based upon geography or such human characteristics as age or ethnic background.

What accounts for the rise in civilisation is not the external resources such as markets, minerals or factories but the entrepreneurial spirit which exploits the resources — a spirit found most often among businessmen entrepreneurs.

Entrepreneurial culture thus implies vision, values, norms and traits that are conducive for the development of the economy.

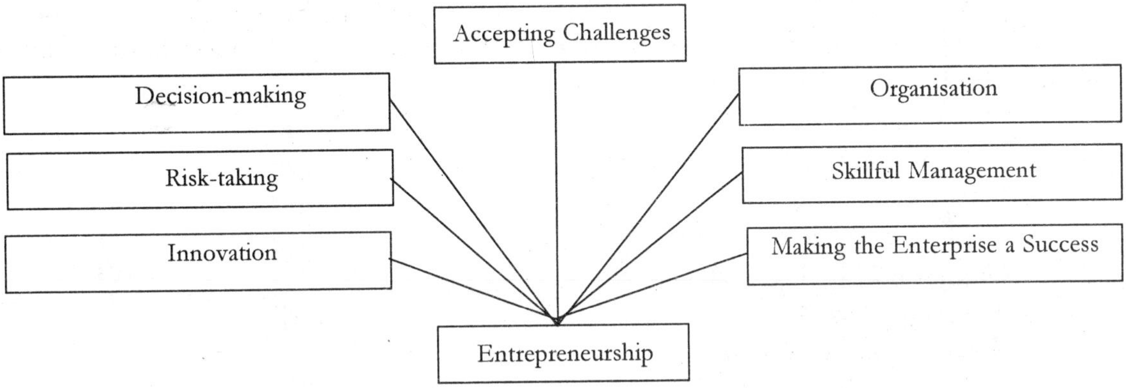

Fig. 1: Characteristics of Entrepreneurship

An entrepreneur has been described as a person who organises, manages and assumes resistibility for a business or an enterprise. The entrepreneur could therefore mean to be an individual who perceives the profitability in production of goods or service, and organises accordingly. In effect he is a vital contributor to the bottomline of the venture. Can there be entrepreneurs without owner-worker status or amongst the organisational workforce who are compensated by fixed emoluments unrelated to the productivity and profitability? Certainly yes, in the light of the fact that the growth and prosperity of individuals is inextricably interwoven with the success and sustenance of the organisation.

The emerging market environment and globalisation is challenging every organisation and every person in the organisation to consider, evaluate and bring about changes in thinking, vision and action. And the changes that need to be brought about should facilitate organisations in becoming competitive, profitable and sustainable.

The world is on the threshold of economic history and it is no longer adequate if the organisation just makes profit or generates surplus — the output has to be maximum from the grassroots level onwards so that the entire organisation shows a healthy growth. Each individual has to become a unit of production in himself and has to assume full responsibility of the assigned task with the philosophy of producing positive results and contributing, not only in full measure, but substantially to the overall good and growth of the organisation. The new setting accelerates transformation to ensure optimum utilisation of the resources — men, money and materials — provide a distinctive contribution to the organisation's prosperity and keep evolving strategies for a sustained competitive edge. And as an entrepreneur one has to review, evaluate and assess one's performance and take decisions.

Instilling such transformation even amongst the most articulate person with a contemporary outlook is not an easy task. Human beings by nature, habit and practice are used to a way of working and any change that is envisaged ushers in a sense of insecurity simultaneously with the change process. This can possibly be overcome by accepting that in today's dynamic society, changes are inevitable, frequent and the rapidity and profundity of changes can even be overwhelming.

Socio-Economic Origins of Entrepreneurship

The entrepreneurial activity at any time and place is governed by varying combination of socio-economic, psychological, cultural and other factors. The empirical studies have identified the following socio-economic factors:

1. Caste religion
2. Family background
3. Level of education
4. Level of perception
5. Occupational background
6. Migratory character
7. Entry into entrepreneurship
8. Nature of enterprise
9. Investment capacity
10. Ambition/motivation

The entrepreneurs who launched their enterprises during 60s predominantly came from mercantile and allied backgrounds. However, a slight tilt in favour of occupations which traditionally have been unconcerned with entrepreneurial activity, *viz.*, general serviceman, technicians, business executives, doctors, lawyers and the like was noticeable among entrepreneurs emerging for the first time after Independence. The main springs of entrepreneurship have been the traditionally trading castes of Hindu and Jain Banias from Gujarat, Rajasthan and Chettiars of Tamil Nadu. Besides, the new springs of entrepreneurship developed among other communities like Brahmins all over the country, especially the South, Naidus of the South, Patels of Gujarat, Kayasthas of West Bengal, Sikhs, Khatris and Aroras of Punjab making entrepreneurship a widespread phenomenon.

More and more people with high academic attainments started joining the ranks of industrialists, especially the professionals holding qualifications in engineering, law, medicine, cost and chartered accounting. The newer entrepreneurs have a larger proportion of their floatations in the traditional sector, but these professionals have by and large preferred to make their investments in modern sector. The technicians in particular among both old and new entrepreneurs have entered industries in the modern sector having a bearing of their academic qualifications. The traditionally trading communities of Hindu and Jain Banias have relied on modern sector more than others. Interestingly, among the regional communities the South Indians have preferred their promotions in traditional sector more than the Gujaratis and Marwaris have.

Table 1

COMPARISON BETWEEN THE ENTREPRENEURIAL CULTURE AND ADMINISTRATIVE CULTURE

	Entrepreneurial Culture		*Administrative Culture*	
Dimensions	*Characteristics*	*Pressures*	*Characteristics*	*Pressures*
1 Strategic orientation	Driven by perception of opportunity	Diminishing oppor-tunities Rapidly changing technology, consumer economics, social values and political rules	Driven by controlled resources	Social contracts Performance measurement criteria Planning systems an cycles
2. Commitment to seize opportunities	Revolutionary with short duration	Action orientaton Narrow decision windows Acceptance of resources risks Few decision constituencies	Evolutionary with long duration	Acknowledgement of multiple constituencies Nagotiation about strategic course Risk reduction Coordination with existing resource base
3. Commitment of resources	Many stages with minimal exposure at each stage	Lack of predictable resource needs Lack of control over the environment Social demands for appropriate use of resources Foreign competition Demands for more efficient resource use	A single stage, with complete commitment out of decision	Need to reduce risk incentive compensation turnover in managers Capital budgeting systems Formal planning systems.
4. Control of resources	Episodic use or rent of required resources	Increased resource specialisation long resource life compared with need Risk of obsolescence Risk inherent in the identified opportunity, Inflexibility of permanent commitment to resources.	Ownership or employment of required resources	Power, status and financial rewards Coordination of activity Efficiency measures. Inertia and cost of change industry structures.
5. Management Structure	Flat, with multiple Informal networks	Coordination of key noncontrolled resources. Challenge to hierarchy Employee's desire for independence	Hierarchy	Need for clearly defined authority and responsibility Organisational culure. Reward system. Management theory

Source: Howard H. Stevenson and David. E. Gumpert, "The Heart of Entrepreneurship." *Harward Busines Review* (March-April 1985).

Social Choice

The social choice approach, as generally understood in the tradition of Pareto Bergson and Arrow, proceeds by treating the community's aggregate welfare as a function of the welfare of each individual taken separately. Each individual is supposed to make his choices out of alternative programmes, policies and projects on the basis of the net effect of each on his own well-being. Each individual's preferences has the same weight as those of every other individual. Just as each individual prefers one commodity bundle out of several alternative, given his income and preference schedule in regard to alternative programmes etc., he follows the same procedure. The society is deemed to consist of a finite number of individuals.

Kenneth Arrow has been involved in contributions both to the theory of social choice and to, along with Debreu, the pure theory of value.

Arrow has also made important contributions to the analysis of several social and policy issues like health and medical care; he has tried to examine the implications of learning by doing; he has also thrown considerable light on information theory and its bearing an uncertainty. In what follows, we touch upon his work on Social Choice theory and on aspects of his work on General Equilibrium.

The Significance of Sociology

While psychology examines more of the workings of the human mind, why individuals think and behave as they do; sociology tends to examine groups of persons (societies), communities, and nations. Sociology is the scientific study of human social behaviour, interaction between humans, social institutions, and social organisations/structures. Sociology examines the relations between all aspects of social life (social facts and problems) in modern industrialised society, but with special emphasis on class, race, and gender. The term sociologist often accompanies people in the academic field who have advanced degrees in sociology.

Sociology gives one of the best perspective of the society, understanding of human relations and culture. It is open to a diversified range of specialisation both in the public and private sector. Further, it enables one to understand problems of society, organisations and gives a macro-perspective. Sociologists also often work in tandem with specialists in other fields, which gives rise to the growth of much interdisciplinary knowledge and action.

Man is a social animal. Being social to him is both natural and necessary. The nature of the 'society' has remained the same from times immemorial; instincts or in built capacities determine the patterns of their organisation. Organisational change is indeed a continuous process. In this, man has interwoven the cultural fabric to enrich human society. These social bearings have reflected in his socio-economic development pursuit and cultural enrichment. Therefore sociology is often described as the science of society. The subject does indeed focus on society, but there are many other disciplines which also cannot be considered in isolation from society.

— Activities such as production, distribution and consumption

— The subject matter of economies

— take place within the social framework. Likewise political science, psychology are also interwoven with sociology.

ANTHROPOLOGY

An anthropologist traces the origin and evolutionary development of management by studying the changed physical characteristics and cultural, social institutions. Class 12 in Arts or Science stream and follow it up by BA/MA/BSc/MSc in Anthropology.

Aptitudes required:
One should have interest in History, various cultures, tribes and communities and so forth. Careful record-keeping, attention to details, analytical reading and clear thinking are essential aptitudes for this field. Critical thinking and strong skills in oral and written expression are also necessary.

Institutes:
- University of Delhi
- Mumbai University
- University of Pune
- Bangalore University

Specialisations in Postgraduation:
- Physical Anthropology
- Archaeological Anthropology
- Socio-Cultural Anthropology
- Linguistic Anthropology

Further Scope:
- Academics
- Corporate sector
- Non-profit organisations
- Government jobs

Researched and developed by Disha Counselling Center

Three major functions appear to be implicit in the emerging concept — normative, evaluative, and operative. While the three are necessarily interrelated, each has its own complexities. To invest reality into the ideal of social development it is essential to attend to all the three functions.

The normative function is the most essential, although it is perhaps the most complex and difficult.

The social inadequacy of economic growth is visible in some of the richest countries of the world. It is evident that affluence, While solving some problems, also generates a new and wide range of baffling problems. Disenchantment with the culture of affluence often finds expression in dissent and protest, in anomie and alienation, and in endeavours towards the development of counter cultures and new Utopias. Many of these affluent societies have not been able to find a solution to the problem of inequality. In any case, their spiralling per capita consumption of world resources will have to encounter severe limitations sooner or later. First, the developing countries will demand an increasing share in it, necessitating cuts in the consumption levels of the affluent nations. Secondly, a reduction in this high consumption of resources will have to be effected because of the growing recognition of the hazards of resource exhaustion alongwith the associated problems of ecological imbalances and atmospheric pollution. These and other related problems have already generated some serious criticism of the industrial society and several blueprints of the post-industrial society are currently being worked out.

The developing societies are still facing the spectre of poverty; only small sections of them have attained the affluence of the developed countries. In general, their developmental efforts notwithstanding, they find that the gap between the developed and the developing is widening and that as years go by it is likely to be still wider. Their elite, which is the trend setter and a reference model for the lower strata of society, follows 'international styles' of high living. Thus, despite their poverty these societies also cherish and promote consumerism. This distorted perspective leads to lopsided priorities in developmental planning. Individual consumption for the few often gets precedence over investment in social services for the many. The Third World appears to be chasing a mirage. Failures in performance lead to frustration and anger; vendors of instant solutions and magical cure-alls get temporarily worshipped as prophets. But prosperity continues to elude it. In the process, the crisis of distribution gets heightened. A thoughtless imitation of the model of affluent societies leads to the perpetuation of social injustices.

An institutional revolution, involving radical value change, is indicated in both the affluent and the non-affluent societies. The dimensions of the problems facing the two types of societies are different and as such they will have to choose different paths for solving their problems. However, both will have to redefine their social objectives and both will have to opt for some self-limiting choices according to the dictates of their environmental requirements.

The experience of two decades and a half of unimpressive development activity in the Third World necessitates serious rethinking regarding both the social objectives of planning and the strategies of implementation. Some major shifts in approach are imperative. These shifts will have to be from high consumption to relative austerity; from goods to services; from self-oriented values to society-oriented values; and from present-orientation to present/future-orientation.

The counter-productive and dysfunctional aspects of conspicuous consumption are all too evident. The mounting revulsion against the basically unjust and unequal system of distribution compels a thorough going modification of the system. The United States, with 6 per cent of the world's population, consumes about 35 per cent of its resources. The ideal, for the Third World at any rate, is austerity — a self-chosen state of relative poverty. If this ethos is created the emphasis will shift from goods to services, more appropriately from personal consumption to collective welfare. Rather than concentrate on self-needs, the individual will merge them into the needs of the society. The re-awakened social conscience will lay stress on a common and ordered way of life characterized by justice, equality, and fair play. Over-concentration on present-bound and proximate goals can have, in the long run lethal effects. Thus, it will be essential to relate time-bound programmes to a future that one visualizes. This will involve consideration of the ultimate nature of the human community; anticipation of future needs; and setting up conflict-resolving, consensus-building, and problem-solving mechanisms.

The quality of life would depend on conceptualising the human need-structure in a new perspective and on making adequate provision for it. It is difficult to offer an inventory of needs that would respond adequately ' to diverse cultural demands and aspiration levels; yet, it is essential to achieve a measure of consensus in regard to them. In any event, the need-structure will include:

1. **Survival needs,** with provision for food, shelter, gainful employment, preventive and curative medicine, and, protection of life and property;
2. **Societal needs,** involving promotion of communityness and social cohesion, creation of effective conflict-resolving and consensus-building mechanisms, and evolving and enforcing norms of social discipline;
3. **Welfare needs,** including measures that offer a fair deal to the weak, the disabled, the handicapped, and the vulnerable;
4. **Psychic and cultural needs,** including provision for personal freedom and privacy, leisure and its creative utilization, and equal opportunity for advancement and general development;
5. **Adaptive needs,** requiring mechanisms for scanning the social, cultural, psychological, and physical environments as well is for identifying and effecting modifications necessitated by changes in these environments; and
6. **Progress needs,** involving sharpening of problem-anticipating and problem-solving capabilities, growth of scientific and technological research, and development of human engineering skills.

The survival needs will require a basic alteration in distributive values and the reward system. They will also require a curb on individual consumption and an extension and enrichment of social services The societal needs assume growth of social consciousness, restructuring of statuses and roles, and a major human engineering effort with accent on co-operation, consensus, and discipline. The welfare needs seek to offer protection to the weak and the vulnerable, but in operationalising them care will have to be taken to ensure that they do not indirectly contribute to the growth of parasitical sections in society. The psychic and cultural needs cover difficult and slippery terrain. The effectiveness of programmes geared to them will be judged by their success in finding an alternative reward structure that de-emphasizes material gains. Even in a predominantly society-oriented value system it would be essential to ensure a measure of autonomy for the individual. Leisure is a necessity, but it can be used towards non-and even anti-social ends. Channels for its utilisation in a manner that one gets fulfilment out of it are essential. Such channels should ideally provide for a diversity and wide range of interests. Adaptive and progress needs will make these kinds of demands — skills in environmental surveillance, foresight regarding problems that are likely to come up, and innovative capability to find solutions to them through scientific, technological, and behavioural research.

For evolving a proper normative structure of social development and for evaluating the trends of change several steps will be necessary. They will include a balanced and reliable assessment of the contemporary social situation, an in-depth examination of major problem-areas, and scientific forecasts of possible trends. This can be done by developing a series of social indicators.

The quantitative measurement of development in several policy-areas — distribution and range of inequality, especially in respect of food and housing, education, public health, deviance and public order, population growth, and so forth — is relatively easy. But their qualitative dimensions are difficult to handle. How does one assess the inputs and outputs qualitatively?

What should be the priorities and scale of inputs? Does the eradication of poverty only mean increase in income? Or, do we also have to ensure that increased incomes are utilised in a desired direction? Are higher literacy rates and a quantitative increase in the number of those receiving advanced education is sufficient indication of social development? Or, do we have to go also into the qualitative aspects of education? Such nagging doubts and questions arise for each major policy area. The attainment of the stipulated social objectives such as the ethos of austerity, social cohesiveness and integration, satisfaction through non-material regards, and urge for excellence will be still more difficult to measure. Simple quantitative indicators are, thus, instruments of limited utility. To enhance their, predictive and prescriptive powers it is essential to evolve techniques that translate quality into quantity. This cannot be done without certain significant value assumptions.

A meaningful programme of social development will require a series of reliable social indicators. They will be invaluable for an accurate reporting on the contemporary state of society, for identifying trends of change and for anticipating problems and crises,' and for suggesting policy leads and strategy modifications.

The new design for living, aimed at ensuring social development, must be a workable Utopia. The strategy to operationalise it must be realistic.

Several difficulties in translating it into reality can be anticipated. First, the entrenched vested interests will oppose the emergence of a new redistributive institutional structure that is a precondition to the implementation of the projected design for living. Second, the value transformation implicit in the scheme will not be easy; established value patterns will most certainly assert themselves. In societies with ancient traditions and a long record of their continuity, every misapplication of science and technology and each failure in the management of social relations is likely to generate atavistic tendencies. Scaly prejudices, developed over generations, are likely to find new rationalizations after enthusiastic promoters. Third, the absence of an international consensus on human goals and mechanisms to defuse explosive tensions will-pose serious threats to a smooth transition from the prevailing chaos to the happy equilibrium sought in the new design for living.

Formidable as the difficulties are, they are not insurmountable. All human societies, in lesser or greater degree, have a reality-adjustment orientation. The inevitable has to be accepted: essential adaptations, in the first instance, arc made. But in an era bristling with contradictions and paradoxes — one in which the gap between aspiration and achievement is widening, where there is growing disenchantment with the established order which is showing every sign of rapid deterioration and which has readied a point where large sections of the population have become ungovernable reality — adjustment in the natural course does not appear feasible. To avert the impending peril, innovative processes addressing themselves directly to the crises of' our time must be set in motion. Mankind has done so several times in the past, though on a smaller scale. The problems in the contemporary context are infinitely larger and more complex; they are beyond palliatives. Far-reaching institutional and value changes are indicated.

Textbook panaceas have failed to work; cook-book recipes at best can touch only the fringe of the enormous problems. Purposive thinking and resolute political action alone can save the situation. The society's response is likely to be positive if the overt and covert dimensions of the contemporary crisis can be explained to it and a viable and convincing alternative is put before it. Egalitarianism and social justice are not impossible ideals: redesigning man's future through institutional revolution and value transformation is well within the realm of possibility. But this would require reflection and action. Sociology can make a valuable contribution towards providing understanding regarding major issues of public policy.

Sociology should be viewed as an adventure. It should provide understanding about the social order in which we live and about the forces that shape and mould it. It should also suggest paths of action to ensure the emergence of new social patterns that eliminate the contradictions and tensions that have created serious imbalances in contemporary society and posed a threat to its survival. Imaginatively pursued, the study of sociology can enable us to understand the condition and predicament of man; it can also help in finding solutions to the pressing problems and dilemmas of society.

Sociologists' View

Sociologists consider the entrepreneur as a role performer corresponding to the role expected by the society. Wishes of the society are exhibited through customs and taboos, rewards and restraints, ethnic values and child-rearing practices, nationalistic attitude and patriotic inculcations and protestant ethics. He is conditioned by the social milieu to which he belongs. According to Peter Marris, to assemble or reassemble from what is available, very concrete independent of imagination, to see what others have missed, sensitivity to business and social environment, zest in industrial development and entrepreneurial courage are the factors that make an entrepreneur. According to Flavia Derossi, co-ordination at every stage — inception, maintenance and expansion — is the function of an entrepreneur. She feels an entrepreneur needs two qualities: (1) Optimistic outlook that there is a possibility of change, the environment can be mastered and he himself can introduce the required change. He finds difficulties challenging and stimulating; he thrives on them. (2) In a share as dynamic industry, new problems are seized upon as opportunities for testing one's own capabilities.

Sociologists and anthropologists distinguish many types of family in terms of who lays down the law and where the newly married couples live. The vertical family under which young adults continue to live with one set of parents after marriage and contribute earnings to a common pool, has a distinctly inhibiting effect on many of the factors affecting economic development such as mobility, savings, risk-taking, even willingness to work more for a higher price. Labour supply curves may bend backward with respect to wage increases because of a limit on economic aspirations or because the personal incentive is dulled by the necessity to contribute all the work while sharing its fruits. The incentive to take risks in entrepreneurship is blunted in the same way. The institutional framework of a community determines the scope of an individual's efforts. If the institutions are favourable, willingness to make effort is encouraged and grows; and if this willingness is strong, institutions will be remodelled to accommodate themselves. If religious attitudes and institutions encourage discipline, hard work, efficiency, honesty and thrift among its followers, the social climate will impel people to apply their minds to increasing productivity to acquire wealth and to improve their social prestige and power. Most religions, as prevailing in India, consider the existing order of the universe as sacred and try to make people believe like that. Ethical beliefs discourage the spirit of enquiry, experimental and scientific outlook among the members of the society. A religion which permits and encourages rationality and scientific attitude is conducive to technological improvements and dynamism in social relations and in social attitude. A desire to discover the causes of things is the most effective motivating force behind inventions, discoveries and innovations in physical as well as in social spheres.

Motives, abilities and a congenial environment, which promote entrepreneurship, are lacking in India. If the motives and abilities are weak, then it becomes all the more essential to have a more congenial environment. But in India the congenial environment is also lacking. The stimulation of entrepreneurial abilities is a complicated long-run sociological problem. The social organisations represented by such major institutions as caste, joint family, rural village, and school are more favourable for the development of entrepreneurship. In underdeveloped countries, the functions of a given person in entrepreneurial capacity include innovation, promotion, capital provision and risk-bearing, management, assembling materials and labour. He lacks the help of markets for components, materials, labour, capital markets which have already standardised products and trained workers. He also lacks the communications network, specialised industrial newspapers and magazines.

Social scientists notably Max Weber, have talked of the importance of entrepreneurship and expressed his view that creative and entrepreneurial energies are generated by the adoption of exogenously supplied belief which in turn produce intense efforts in occupational pursuits and accumulation of productive assets leading to the manufacture of goods and services. According to him, entrepreneurs are a product of the particular social conditions in which they live and it is the society which shapes the personality of individual entrepreneurs.

John Kunkel believes that the behavioural pattern of individuals is important for development and such a pattern can be influenced by external stimuli so as to alter it in the manner we want. In other words, if we want more people in society to behave as entrepreneurs, we can bring about such behaviour on their part by appropriate alterations in the social environment so as to influence them to take to entrepreneurial pursuits. Like Weber, Cochran and Young underscore the importance of society in shaping the entrepreneurial personality and consider that ingredients in the emergence of entrepreneurs are cultural values, role expectations, social tensions and inter-group relations in society.

Psychologists' View

Among psychologists, Frank Young describes an entrepreneur as a change-agent. K.L. Sharma maintains that entrepreneurs are men who exhibit qualities of leadership in solving persistent professional problems; but those persons likewise demonstrate eagerness to seize unusual opportunities. They have a business gambler's itch. T.V. Rao and Udai Pareek describe entrepreneurship as a creative and innovative response to the environment. The entrepreneur is goal-oriented rather than means-oriented. He must not only have a high capacity for risk-taking but must also have a high capacity for risk-sustaining which is a function of a high degree of self-confidence.

In sum, the foregoing description of the functions of an entrepreneur presents the profile of a functionary. Economists present him as a perceiver of otherwise unnoticed opportunity, an organisation builder, adapter of new profitable activity and beneficiary thereof. Sociologists present him as a personality moulded by various practices of social enforcement and values imbibed in him. Psychologically, entrepreneurship is a vigorous application of the person's energies towards long-cherished goals.

Large firms, both large industrial undertakings and multinational units — are now such a dominant form of business enterprise in most countries that we are sometimes likely to forget that this is a comparatively recent development. The Industrial Revolution was accomplished largely through small-scale industries — entities with modest capital, a few score workers at the most, owned and managed by a single individual or family. In fact, industrialisation made its warily beginning in the small sector. Really large-scale organisations emerged slowly, and their explosive growth did not take place until the first half of the present century. In spite of rapid growth of large enterprises and multinationals and the scale of economics, in recent years, however, there has been renewed interest in and appreciation of the value of small and medium enterprises, and efforts have been made to encourage them and create a better climate for their successful operations in the hope that they would reduce the nation's dependence on imports and promote greater decentralisation of economic activity in the country. At the same time, it may be possible for individual entrepreneurs to achieve a greater sense of identity with local community. This apart, the small-scale sector has been given due importance in the developing countries on account of their employment potential.

Ethics as a Value

Ethics has been defined as a code of conduct, rules or principles or as a reflection of culture, etc. It is also described as the branch of philosophy dealing with values relating to human conduct concerned with the human character. *The Fontana Dictionary of Modem Thoughts* describes ethics as the branch of philosophy that investigates morality and in particular, the varieties of thinking by which human conduct is guided and appraised. It would thus appear ethics enunciates the use of practices which have certain values and principles ingrained in them. However, the ethics of management is much wider a concept than mere avoidance of complicity, corruption, pinching and purloining.

It is a widely accepted belief that decisions involving ethics have extended consequences, uncertain probabilities, mixed outcomes, multiple options and far reaching implications. Should an individual be concerned with ethics? He has his own aims and objectives, ambitions and aspirations and a mission and vision. And, to be, one has to succeed in life either by hook or crook! Possibly in sustained success lies the purpose of all his activities. Pareto's optimality enshrines 'it would be impossible to make any single person better off without making some other person worse off'. Every individual survives and thrives on the support of the people and the society at large and in case, the people and the society withdraw their support, his very existence will be endangered. How can it be appropriate that one can unabashedly continue to pursue his enlightened self interest sacrificing moral values, principles of good conduct, and behaviour, without caring for the interest of others.

In a civilised society ethical aspects cannot be brushed aside and the primary responsibility to set standards devolves on the shoulders of enlightened and privileged citizens. Everyone must at all times, while setting objectives, conceptualising strategies and taking decisions, accord due consideration to ethics and the impact that will be experienced by others and the society at large.

None can possibly ensure that others in the society, the organisation and even the family would not envy, grudge or view, with scepticism the success of an individual. The severity of the feeling can, however, be minimised in case, in the process of achieving success, ethical standards have not been undermined. In fact, there is a strong possibility of goodwill being generated even in the hearts and minds of the competitors, if the standards of ethics are complied with.

The disregard of ethics cannot be condoned for too long except at the risk of the disintegration and dissolution of civilised society, the evolution-of which has taken thousands of years and the toil of our innumerable ancestors. We owe it to our birth, survival and blessedness that we conduce to improving the order of the society and one method could be our conformity to ethics.

Converting this vision into an opportunity and thereafter into achievement demands more than theoretical formulae and quick fix. The leaders who achieved this are the ones who do things first, sometimes even before others dream of them. Fortunately leaders are made, not born.

Corporate Values

Balancing the spirit of the entrepreneur with the reality of big business take more than a single simple policy or strategy. What is required is a flexible, dynamic structure that pays heed to the importance of the people within and is based on a value set that is clear and agreeable to all.

Lotus Employee Handbook, therefore, devotes a full page to our corporate values, placing importance on the attributes of honesty, ethics, fairness and integrity, as well as on teamwork, co-operation, creativity and initiative and on having a sense of humour.

Be a leader, not just a manager: Leadership begins with setting examples in terms of personal characteristics, like honesty and fairness.

Be a facilitator: Management should demonstrate a commitment to communication throughout the organisation. This means being accessible, and listening to people in the lower realms of the organisation.

Be deliberate: When calling and conducting meetings (the greatest time-waster in companies), be result-oriented. Use firm agendas and strive for specific objectives.

Be explicit: In assigning responsibility, get people to take responsibility for small tasks as well as for a big projects.

Be decisive: If someone isn't working out, and you have exhausted all possibilities, break quickly and cleanly. Indecision can be bad for everyone.

If these attributes are combined with sincerity and integrity, the result should be a business culture that stimulates innovation and *esprit de corp* at every corporate level, whether developing a new product, building a new headquarters, or contributing to the neighbouring community.

For people in communications and creative business it is major breakthrough, because it puts a powerful weapon into the hands of the people who develop concepts: the ability to execute those concepts so that they can be evaluated and appreciated by peers and by clients. The dream is to make information accessible and understandable to more people by bringing the benefits of computing closer and closer to the individual.

FACTORS IN COMPARATIVE TECHNOLOGY DEVELOPMENT

Factors	*Timing factors*		*Accumulation factors*	*Overall factors*	
	Time and environment	*Social system and policy*	*Economic, industrial and technological traditions*	*Natural and geographical conditions*	*National character*
Supply factors	Contemporary level of world technology development — innovations active or inactive? Competition with neighbouring countries Competition with advanced countries	Social system and government leadership — led by the government or the private sector? — centralised or decentralised?	Level of industrialisation — quality and quantity of technical manpower — development or ancillary industries and small firms Presence of traditional technology Relative to agriculture	Resource endowments Land area and climae — closed or open, to sea? — transport conditions?	Values — labour experience or logic? — aesthetic senses — inward or outward looking? Behaviour principle — group or individual?
Demand factors	Contemporary stae of the world economy — growing or stagnating? International commercial relations	Linkages with market	Market size — income level and distribution opopulation Market characteristics — quality of demand? — export-oriented?	Markets — homogenous or regional?	Characteristics of demand — conservative or progressive? — aesthetic sense

Cultural Essence

By culture we mean that complex whole which includes knowledge, belief, art, morals, law, custom, and other capabilities and habits acquired by man in a society. Two terms are key to the concept culture: history and shared phenomenon. With regard to the first, it may be stated that cultural mores of a society are passed on from generation to generation. The second key term which is basic to culture implies that the cultural ethos are shared among the members of a society.

Having known the meaning of culture, we may attempt to define organisational culture. Organizational culture (or its sister term corporate culture) has been defined as the philosophies, ideologies, values, assumptions, beliefs, expectations, attitudes and norms that knit an organisation together and are shared by its employees.

The following ten characteristics help us understand the nature of culture better. When these characteristics are mixed and meshed, we get the essence of culture.

1. **Individual Initiative:** The degree of responsibility, freedom, and independence that individuals have.
2. **Risk Tolerance:** The degree to which employees are encouraged to be aggressive, innovative, and risk-seeking.
3. **Direction:** The degree to which the organisation creates clear objectives and performance expectations.
4. **Integration:** The degree to which units within the organisation are encouraged to operate in a co-ordinated manner.
5. **Management Support:** The degree to which managers provide clear communication, assistance and support to their subordinates.
6. **Control:** The number of rules and regulations, and the amount of direct supervision that is used to oversee and control employee behaviour.
7. **Identity:** The degree to which members' identify with the organisation as a whole rather than with their particular work group or field of professional expertise.
8. **Reward System:** The degree to which reward allocations are based on employee, performance criteria in contrast to seniority, favouritism, and so on.
9. **Conflict Tolerance:** The degree to which employees are encouraged to air conflicts and criticisms openly.
10. **Communication Patterns:** The degree to which organisational communications are restricted to the formal hierarchy of authority.

Creation of Culture

Culture is essentially learnt. What applies to the learning process applies to culture too. Basically, an organisational culture forms in response to two major challenges that confront every organisation: (1) external adaptation and survival, and (2) internal integration.

External adaptation and survival have to do with how the organisation will find a niche in and cope with its constantly changing external environment. External adaptation and survival involve addressing the following issues:

- **Mission and strategy:** Identifying the primary purpose of the organisation; selecting strategies to pursue this mission.
- **Goals:** Setting specific targets to achieve.
- **Means:** Determining how to pursue the goals, including selecting an organisation structure, and reward system.
- **Measurement:** Establishing criteria to determine how well individuals and teams are accomplishing their goals.

Internal integration has to do with the establishment and maintenance of effective working relationships among the members of an organisation. Internal integration involves addressing the following issues:

- **Language and concepts:** Identifying methods of communication and developing a shared meaning for important concepts.
- **Group and team boundaries:** Establishing criteria for membership in groups and teams.
- **Power and statuses:** Determining rules for acquiring, maintaining, and losing power and status.
- **Reward and punishment:** Developing systems for encouraging desirable behaviours and discouraging undesirable behaviours.

Theories of Entrepreneurship

The concept of entrepreneurship is as old as civilisation while the theories of entrepreneurship have been evolved during the last two centuries.

Sociologists suggest that entrepreneurship can be conceptualised as a social movement and entrepreneurs exist not only in the economy but also in other spheres of society as well. S.M. Lip set argues that cultural values deeply affect entrepreneurship and the level of economic development. Mark Granovetter points that family influences the entrepreneurial activities. He emphasises on the role played by society and family in growth of entrepreneurship

To a psychologist, entrepreneur is a person driven by certain forces — the need to obtain or attain something, to experiment, to accomplish or perhaps to escape the authority of others. Motives, achievement, status, satisfaction govern the entrepreneurs more than money or wealth.

According to Fredrik Barth, entrepreneurship has essentially to do with connecting two spheres in the society between which there exists a difference in value.

Socio-cultural theories emphasise on varied and vivid aspects of entrepreneurship.

The socio-cultural theories discussed in this chapter are as follows:

1. Theory of Religious Belief — *Max Weber*
2. Theory of Entrepreneurial Supply — *Thomas Cochran*
3. Theory of Group Level Pattern — *Frank Young*
4. Theory of Social Change — *Everett E. Hagen*
5. Theory of Personal Resourcefulness — *Bygrave & Hofer*
6. Theory of Entrepreneurial Supply — *John H. Kunkel*

7. Theory of Culture — *Bert F. Hoselitz*
8. Stroke's Theory
9. Theory of Cultural Values
10. Conceptual Model
11. Walker on Entrepreneurship
12. Frederic Harbison on Entrepreneurship
13. Peter Kilby on Entrepreneurship
14. Social Responsibility.

Theory of Religious Belief

Max Weber has propounded the theory of religious belief. According to him entrepreneurism is a function of religious belief and the impact of religion shapes the entrepreneurial culture. He emphasized that the entrepreneurial energies are exogenous supplied by means of religious belief. The central feature of Weberian theory of social change, therefore, consists in his treatment of the *protestant ethic* and the *spirit of capitalism*. However, the important elements of Weber's theory are discussed further.

1. Spirit of capitalism: In the Webrian theory, spirit of capitalism is highlighted. We all know that capitalism is an economic system in which economic freedom and private enterprise are glorified, so also the entrepreneurial culture. Spirit of capitalism, therefore, is the guiding factor which guides the entrepreneur to get engaged in activities that can bring about more and more profit. Thus, the profit motive character coupled with the attitude towards acquisition of money urges the individual to start new venture.

2. Adventurous spirit: Weber also made a distinction between spirit of capitalism and adventurous spirit. According to him, the former is influenced by the strict discipline whereas the latter is affected by the free force of impulse. Entrepreneurship culture is governed by both these factors. According to Max Weber, the spirit of capitalism can be grown only when mental attitude in the society is favourable in capitalism.

3. Protestant ethic: According to Max Weber, the spirit of capitalism can be grown only when mental attitude in the society is favourable to capitalism. This attitude can be provided by protestant ethic irrespective of the cultural background, personality type of the individual and the experiences in the society. According to Max Weber, Hinduism lacks this sort of mental attitude which acts as a stumbling block is their way to entrepreneurship.

4. Inducement of profit: Weber introduced the new businessmen into the picture of tranquil routine. The spirit of capitalism intertwined with the motive of profit resulted in creation of greater number of business enterprises thereby leading to a complete reorganisation of industrial sector. The principle of low prices and large turnover was the mechanism of the entrepreneurs to reap profit. So this motive of profit guided the protestant ethic to become entrepreneurial which was not found among the Hindus.

In fact, this theory suited the British rulers, who desired in encourage European entrepreneurship in India. This theory was vehemently criticized by many researchers because of the following unrealistic assumptions which Max Weber highlighted.

(*a*) There is only one system of Hindu value.

(*b*) The Indian community internalised those values and translated them into daily routine.

(*c*) These values remained immune to and insulated against external pressures and change.

But rapid growth of entrepreneurship and emergence of a large number of entrepreneurs in the post-independence era proved that Hinduism is neither a stumbling block nor a demotivating religious belief to the spirit of capitalism and to the spirit of adventure to start innovative enterprises.

In support of Max Webers theory of religious belief, one can draw lessons from India. Since Independence, however, India's industrial development has been sustained largely by the domestic entrepreneurship. The inadequate supply of entrepreneurship in those regions, which lack significant industrial activity is mainly due to the uneven regional distribution of industries in the country. Majority of the studies deal with entrepreneurship in large scale manufacturing sector. The social origins of the entrepreneurs seem to have attracted most of the attention of the investigators in the field, till recently. Gadgil and Medhava's studies conclude that the caste system and its obligations tend to reduce occupational mobility, and technical change. But then, their studies related to an earlier period of industrialisation of the country. Hazlehurst in his study notes that refugee entrepreneurs tend to be more innovative than local entrepreneurs. Berna finds that economic factors are more important than the sociological factors in explaining entrepreneurial activity. Singh's study discloses that the public enterprises are characterised by low profit and savings rates, which may partly be due to the lack of entrepreneurial skills in the public sector. Sareswara Rao and Nafziger, while studying the small industry in Visakhapatnam, established that even in a comparatively backward area, the socio-cultural features of the traditional Indian society are no longer standing in the way of the development of modern entrepreneurship. Sarveswara Rao, V. Lakshmana Rao and Siva Prasad in their study of trading sector found little utilisation of the institutional credit facilities. Certain interesting facts about the emerging investors in East Godavari district are brought about by the Government of Andhra Pradesh, in collaboration with Administrative Staff College of India (ASCI), Hyderabad.

McCrory's study is confined to small enterprises in a North Indian Town, whereas Berna's study centred round the medium scale engineering enterprises in Chennai and Coimbatore cities. The UNESCO's studies covered small enterprises in selected regions like Mumbai, Howrah, Delhi, Rajkot, Hyderabad and Ludhiana. B.C. Tandon argued that the rate of entrepreneurial change is a function of human factor and one can bring about a change in the effectiveness of an enterprise by improving the human Factor.

Gangadhar Rao has brought a realistic approach to the evaluation of industrial estates as a device to encourage entrepreneurship in India. Millman's study of the Marwari caste revealed the possibility of communal customs providing for apprenticeship in which youngsters could learn techniques of business and, in due course of time, they could well, become entrepreneurs. Lamb noted that Parsis, Gujaratis and Marwaris had monopolised industry even after independence and that they are mostly concentrated in Bombay and Bengal. Sharma found that the relationship between the background of entrepreneurs and their sources of initial capital was important. He established that new springs of entrepreneurship had developed in the non-trading, and non-financing communities. Sharma held that there were four stages of entrepreneurial development, *viz.*, entry manufacturing, finding of market, establishment of business and expansion of the firm.

He observed that types of family background showed relations with these stages. Harris made his study of a single entrepreneur, J.N. Tata and considered economic, educational, and political status of the family as the prime determinant of entrepreneurial development.

There is no doubt in establishing the fact that there have been certain forces which have brought about a tremendous forceful flow of entrepreneurs, thereby building the pillars of industrial development of the country. The study shows that different policies and reasons have contributed to the growth of entrepreneurship. However, the Government has been the most important single contributor.

Entrepreneurial Heritage

During the planned period the dominance of the traditional entrepreneurial communities continued. Though figures point towards a relative decline in the contribution of private sector, yet an in-depth study shows an overall growth of private entrepreneurs to be significant. The major contributor has been the Marwari Community, followed by Gujaratis and Parsis. In general, all other major communities too are coming forward with Punjab as the leading State.

Theory of Entrepreneurial Supply

The theory, propounded by Thomas Cochran, centres round the sociological aspect of entrepreneurial supply. Beginning with the premise that fundamental problems of economic development are non-economic, he emphasizes on the cultural values, role expectation and social sanctions as the key elements that determine the supply of entrepreneurs. The basic elements of Thomas Cochran's theory are depicted further.

1. Entrepreneur as a society's modal personality: According to T. Cochran, entrepreneur is neither a supernormal individual nor a deviant person but is a role model of the society representing modal personality. This personality is a composite of the person, his skills, styles and motives.

2. Modal personality as a derivative of social conditioning: The entrepreneur, being the Chief Executive of his business, plays a social role. The role is partly shaped by the modal personality that is a derivative of social conditioning of his generation. Further, innovation and invention go together with the type of conditioning in the society.

3. Role expectations and entrepreneurial role: Cochran pointed out that in corporate organisations, senior officers or the Board of Directors have well-defined expectations. They are known as defining group and entrepreneurial role is closely defined by them. According to him, "Primary cultural factors operating on the personality of the executive and the defining of his role by those involved must accommodate to some degree to the necessities of the operation to be carried out".

4. The type of childrearing and schooling and its influence on intrinsic character of the executive: According to Cochran, the executive's 'inner character is conditioned by the childrearing and schooling common to the cultural legacies. He contemplated, "This relatively simple framework of an entrepreneurial role defined by personality of the actor, the expectations of the groups with power to sanction deviations from expected behaviour and the operational needs of the function to be performed subsumes all the social or cultural factors."

5. Dynamics of entrepreneurs and thrust upon the social factors for the major changes: According to Cochran, the demonstration of this model of dynamics of entrepreneurs gives thrust upon the social factors for the major changes. He pointed out that the model is based upon the American Economic History which proves that American economy has experienced major changes during 19th century due to entrepreneurial dynamism. The changes are ascribed to the following factors:

(*a*) Quick adoption of mechanical devices in the first half of the 19th century.

(*b*) Growth of professional management in the corporate sector that started in the second half of the 19th century.

(*c*) Widespread application of mass production techniques in the 19th century.

In each of these major transformation, the social factors operating through entrepreneur appear to be well marked. Under the above backdrop, Cochran pointed out that individual's performance as entrepreneur is governed by the following elements:

(*a*) Attitude of the entrepreneur towards his own occupation.

(*b*) The role expectation held by sanctioning groups.

(*c*) The operational requirements of the job.

In fact, both the first and the second elements are determined by the societal value whereas the last element is governed by the changes over a period of time in extraneous parameters such as population, technology, consumer demand, tastes and preferences of the customers, etc.

Theory of Group Level Pattern

Frank Young, in his theory, *A Micro-sociological Interpretation of Entrepreneurship,* points out that entrepreneurial initiative is a function of group level pattern. Young has elaborately analysed the shortcomings of psychogeneric interpretation of entrepreneurship and suggested a causal sequence where transformation codes are developed by the solidarity groups to improve this symbolic position in their larger structure and thus become entrepreneurs. The theory has the following important features:

1. Deficiencies in psychogenic mediation model: Prior to depicting a microsociological interpretation of entrepreneurship. Young deals with the shortcomings of psychogenic mediation model. While stating that development is an organisational phenomenon, he points out the deficiencies to explain the emergence of new kind of organisation. He states, without exception, that they are mute on the question of how individual tendencies, special abilities, unusual motivation or perception of particular opportunities is transformed into emergent property that is social organization. According to Young, "Of entrepreneurs in particular, imitative time taken by the development process are some of the demerits of psychogenic interpretation of entrepreneurship."

2. Solidarity groups: Frank Young regarded the solidarity groups as the main agencies for building entrepreneurship. He interprets individual level entrepreneurism as the under side of group level pattern. He maintains that entrepreneurial characteristics are found in clusters, ethnic communities, occupational groups or politically-oriented factions. According to Frank Young: "Of these groups, those who show a certain reactiveness or solidarity define the degree to which members create, maintain a coherent definition of their situation that size upon the rhetoric of religion or politics as a vehicle for expressing their deviation view of the world."

3. Disregarding single-handed concept of entrepreneurship: Young disregards the claim that entrepreneur works single handedly or solely. According to him, entrepreneurial activity is the product of family background, experience and exposure of the individual as a member of the group and as a reflection of general values. Thus, entrepreneur as a member of a particular group does not work alone. In his own words, he is simply the most visible member from an economic point of view what is typically a cluster of families whose activity is mutually reinforcing and co-ordinated by a coherent outlook on the world.

4. Reduction of complex economic problems: The solidarity of entrepreneurial groups induces a number of economic problems that crop up in case of individual entrepreneur. This effort is likely to reduce the economic problems through the device of recombination of factors related to the production, higher standards of labour, search for new resources, technology and markets and a more effective management of money and time. As such, the entrepreneur builds confidence which he derives from the concept of solidarity in a pragmatic manner by the solution of economic and social problems.

Young conducted a Thematic Apperception Test (TAT) on a group of entrepreneurs. The following findings are derived from the test:

(*a*) The test revealed the tendency to depict the situation as a problem to be solved.

(*b*) An awareness of pragmatic effort required.

(*c*) Confidence on their ability to solve the problems.

(*d*) Willingness to take the views of each individual in turn and analyse the situation as he perceives before suggesting any outcome.

To be more clear, Young discussed the sociogenic explanation of solidarity structure of entrepreneurial supply.

5. Incorporation of reactive sub-groups: In his theory, Frank Young, incorporated the idea of reactive sub-groups which play the most important role in enterprise creation. According to Young, a group becomes reactive when three important conditions coincide. They are very much helpful to the entrepreneurial supply. These conditions are as follows:

(*a*) When low status recognition is found in a group.

(*b*) When access to important social networks is denied.

(*c*) When the group has better institutional resources than other groups in the society at the same level.

In fine, Young's theory of entrepreneurial supply is a function of group level pattern which gives emphasis on the concept of solidarity clusters, ethnic communities and above all the groups.

According to Psychologists, entrepreneurship is most likely to emerge when a society has sufficient supply of individuals possessing particular psychological characteristics.

The main characteristics are:

1. an urge to do something
2. dare to dream big and strive to fulfill a dream.
3. passionate about an intuitive idea.
4. an institutional capacity to see things in new way.

5. a visionary who visualises the future.
6. energy of will and mind to overcome fixed habits of thought.
7. capacity to withstand social opposition and
8. high confidence for achievement. These characteristics motivate and drives people towards entrepreneurial/intrapreneurial activities.

THE INDIAN BRIGADE THAT RULES THE WORLD

	CITIGROUP	PEPSICO	VODAFONE	HARTFORD FINANCIAL	ADOBE SYSTEMS
	Vikram Pandit CEO	**Indra Nooyi CEO**	**Arun Sarin CEO**	**Ramani Ayer CEO**	**Shantanu Narayen CEO**
Fortune 500 rank	8	63	95	82	NA
HQ	US	US	UK	US	US
Industry	**Banking**	**Food Drink & Tobacco**	**Telecom Services**	**Property Casualty Insurance**	**Software and Services**
Founded	1812	1965	1984	1810	1982
Operations	**100 Countries**	**200 Countries**	**24 Countries**	**Japan, Brazil, Ireland, England, Canada**	**NA**
Employees	Over 300000	Over 168,000	Over 60,000	30,000	6,667
Turnover/Revenues	**$147 bn**	**$35 bn**	**$51bn**	**$27 bn**	**$3 bn**
Profits	$22 bn	$6 bn	$38 bn	$3 bn	$0.5 bn
Assets	**$1.9tr**	**$30 bn**	**$22 bn**	**$327n**	**$6 bn**
Market value	$247 bn	$103 bn	$147 bn	$30 bn	$23 bn

Theory of Social Change

Everett E. Hagen, in his work *"Theory of Social Change: How Economic Growth Begins* (1964), meditates on its psychological explanation. His creative personality is an individual characterised by a high need for achievement, order and autonomy. He views the entrepreneur as a creative problem solver interested in things in the practical and technological realm, and driven by a duty to achieve.

Hagen considers the withdrawal of status, of respect, as the trigger mechanism for changes in personality formation. Status withdrawal occurs when members of some social group perceive that their purposes and values in life are not respected by the groups in the society they respect, and whose esteem they value. Hagen postulates four types of events which can produce status withdrawal—

- Displacement of a traditional elite group from its previous status by another traditional supply physical force.
- Denigration of valued symbols through some change in the attitude of the superior group.

- Inconsistency of status symbols with a changing distribution of economic power.
- Non-acceptance of expected status on migration to a new society.

Everett Hagen (1962), while describing the process of change in any society as the transition to economic growth searched for the causes of the transition. He states that the transition to economic growth has been very gradual and typically occupies a period of several generations. He suggests that growth has been led not by individuals randomly distributed throughout a society but disproportionately by individuals from some distinctive group. He identified 'creative innovation' or 'change' as the fundamental characteristic of economic growth.

Hagen, after analysing the traditional societies, maintains that the position of authority are granted in such societies not on the basis of individual 'ability' but on the basis of his 'status'. Hagen postulated a sequence of the formation of creative and authoritarian personalities.

Since the traditional society has great stability, the forces required to disrupt it must be equally powerful. Of course such change may occur in the same generation but it is more likely to be an inter-generation change. Hagen's ties or group emerge when the members of some social group experience what he calls, "the withdrawal of status respect." The "withdrawal of status respect" may occur when traditionally alike group is displaced by force from its previous status by another traditional group, or when any superior group changes its attitude towards a subordinate group or on migration to a new society.

The theory exhorts the following features which presumes the entrepreneur's creativity as the key element of social transformation and economic growth:

1. Presentation of the general model of the society: The theory reveals a general model of the society which considers interrelationship among physical environment, social structure, personality and culture.

2. Economic growth: product of social change and political change: According to Hagen, most of the economic theories of underdevelopments are inadequate. He viewed entrepreneur as a creative problem-shooter who brings about economic development which is mingled with political and social changes.

3. Rejection of follower's syndrome: Hagen rejected the idea that the solution to economic development lies in imitating western technology. So the follower's syndrome on the part of the entrepreneur, is discouraged. This is because the technology is an integral part of socio-cultural-complex, and super-imposition of the same into different socio-cultural set-up may not deliver the goods.

4. Historic shift as a factor of initiating change: Hagen, in his book *How Economic Growth Begins,* depicts historic shift as the crucial force which has brought about social change and technological progress thereby leading to the emergence of entrepreneurial class from different castes and communities. The historic shift caused some groups of the lesser elite, who previously held commanding position in the social hierarchy, feel that they were no longer valued and regarded. As a result of this, their inner urge was kindled to take up entrepreneurial venture through personality formation and thus they become competent enough to take up any kind of venture.

5. Withdrawal of status respects as the mechanism for rigorous entrepreneurial activity: Closely consistent with the historic shift it is the social group that plunges into rigorous entrepreneurism which experiences the status withdrawal or 'withdrawal of status respect'. According to Hagen, they are a group of individuals, creative and alienated from traditional values, driven by a gnawing burning drive to prove themselves (to themselves as well as to their fellows) seeking for an area in which to do — preferably an area in which they can gain power and in some symbolic way they can vent their rage at the elites who have caused their troubles. Their inner urge will culminate into entrepreneurism disregarding their traditional values and turning to innovative entrepreneurship. The role of lesser Samurai as innovators and entrepreneur in Japan's industrial revolution is a glaring example of status withdrawal.

Whenever there is any withdrawal of status respect, it would create response and personalities of the following four types:

(a) **Retreatist :** He who continues to work in the society but remains indifferent to his work and position.

(b) **Ritualists :** He who adopts a kind of defensive behaviour and acts in the way accepted and approved in his society but with no hopes of improving his position.

(c) **Reformist :** Is a person who forments a rebellion and attempts to establish a new society.

(d) **Innovator :** He is creative individual and is likely to be an entrepreneur.

Schumpeter and Hagen have much in common so far as analysing the growth process is concerned and Hagen's "creative personality" is also characterised by McClelland's high need for achievement.

Hagen's analysis fails to give policy measures for backward countries which are striving for economic development as he is identifying 'status withdrawal' as the casual factor in emergence of creative personality and status withdrawal by force cannot be contemplated in a democratic set-up.

Theory of Personal Resourcefulness

The root of entrepreneurial process can be traced to the initiative taken by some individuals to go beyond the existing way of life. The emphasis is on initiative rather than reaction, although events in the environment may have provided the trigger for the person to express initiative. This aspect seems to have been subsumed within 'innovation' which has been studied more as the 'change' or 'newness' associated with the term rather 'proactiveness,' This tendency to take initiative has been approached from different directions at various stages in the development of theory in entrepreneurship. For instance, Bygrave and Hoffer (1991) talk of the importance of human volition, Carland *et al.* (1984) define an entrepreneur as one who 'establishes' an organisation, or Schumpeter (1949) talks of the agent who consciously disturbs the stationary process to take it in a new direction. They all reflect on the primacy of individual initiative. Studies of entrepreneurial traits related to this aspect of behaviour, such as internal focus of control (Brochaus, 1982), capability to take personal risks (Gasse, 1985) and positive approach to work and problems, without excessive fear of failure, seeming from strong belief in favourable future (Kuratko & Hodgetts, 1989) — all lend to a strong sense of personal resourcefulness (Kanungo & Misra, 1992) through which entrepreneurs take up and deal with non-routine tasks and situations. Hence, 'personal resourcefulness' in the context of this paper is the belief in one's own capability for initiating actions directed towards creation and growth of enterprises. Such initiating process requires cognitively mediated self regulations of internal feelings and emotions, thought and actions as suggested by Kanungo and Misra (1992).

Personal resourcefulness is a critical factor for the growth and development of entrepreneurship. The theory of persons resourcefulness has got the following implications as far as the supply of entrepreneurs is concerned in the society:

1. Cognitive function: The present theory presupposes the activities undertaken by the individuals who require cognitively mediated behaviour like emotions, sentiments, inner feelings, thoughts and actions. In these situations, entrepreneur is fully appraised of the situation and knowledge which is shaded by risk and motivational involvement.

2. Human aspects of psychology: Different authors have given their different opinions on human aspects of psychology. For example. Bygrave and Hoffer highlight the significance of human volition. Schumpeter pointed out entrepreneurship as innovator while Carland gives emphasis on organization building for entrepreneurship development. In Schumpeter's words, entrepreneurship is influenced by the following traits:

(*a*) will to power (*b*) will to conquer (*c*) will to excell
(*d*) will to achieve (*e*) will to change (*f*) will to innovate
(*g*) will to succeed (*h*) will to serve

Thus, studies examining factors have brought out the fact that more provisions of economic input, may not itself guarantee success in entrepreneurial ventures, organisational and psychological factors also still remain a subject of further investigation.

Box - 1

SUPPLY OF PERSONNEL TO GUIDE BUSINESS

The elevation of Nagpur-born Vikram Pandit as CEO of the world's largest financial institution has cast the spotlight on foreign-born head honchos in the American corporate world, with the conspicuous realisation here that 15 of the Fortune 100 companies are run by foreign-born executives.

Even more striking is that three of the 15 are of Indian-Origin, with perhaps an equal number in the larger Fortune 500. Pandit r. w heads the list as CEO of Citigroup, which is ranked 8th in the Fortune 100, followed by Indra Nooyi at Pepsico, which is ranked 63rd. Ramani Ayer is CEO of Hartford Financial Services, which is 82 in the Fortune 100.

All three were born in India and took the familiar route to the US to study — Pandit to Columbia University, Nooyi to Yale and Ayer to Drexel University.

The shift towards appointing foreign-born CEOs reflects, in part, the focus that companies place on foreign markets that companies place on foreign markets for growth.

Ironically, it even quoted a business school academic of Indian-origin reflecting on the trend.

It's absolutely nothing wrong with the US, but our population here is only 300 million. Imagine two billion people from the outside start getting a decent education and going through the pipeline. Well, we are going to encounter more of them who rise to the top.

Pandit, Nooyi and Ramani further the pioneering road taken by Vinod Khosla, Kanwal Rekhi and other Silicon Valley Indians who became the first CEOs of Indian-origin in the 1980s.

Most India-born executives readily acknowledge their debt of gratitude to a society that emphasizes industry and hard work and honed their survival skills if nothing else.

In contrast to the US corporations' worldwide search of the best executive talent, with the suggestion that immigrants may have decisively broken the glass ceiling Indian companies, many of them closely held, are still leery of hiring foreign CEOs.

Some of the more prominent examples of bucking the tradition is the hiring by Jet Airways of the Australian Wolfgang Prock-Schauer as CEC. Another breakthrough is the Hawaiian Raymond Bickson, CEO of Indian Hotels who has successfully expanded the Taj Hospitality business worldwide, including in the US.

Source: Times of India, 12.12.2007.

Behaviouristic Model

Another theory of entrepreneurial supply is the Behaviouristic Model propounded and elaborated by John Kunkel in 1965. His behavioural model is concerned with the overtly expressed activities of individuals and their relations to both past and present, and surrounding social structures and physical conditions.

The determinants of an individual's activities are to be found largely in the conditioning procedures, both deliberate and accidental, to which he has been subjected in the past, and in the sets of reinforcing and discriminating stimuli which have become part of his behavioural claims and are part of the present social context.

The selected elements of social environment are amenable to change. Kunkel's theory is based upon experimental psychology, identifying sociological variables as the determinants of entrepreneurial supply.

John H. Kunkel advocated the theory of entrepreneurship supply. According to him, psychological and sociological variables are the main determinants for the emergence of entrepreneurs. He contemplated that entrepreneurial talent can be found in minorities, religious, ethnic, migrated, displaced elites and these minorities have supplied most of the entrepreneurism in the society. Entrepreneurism can be dependent upon the following structures in the economy:

- Demand structure
- Limitation structure
- Labour structure
- Opportunity structure.

1. Demand structure: It implies economic demand with relation to changes in economic development and government policies. Demand structure can be augmented with the help of material rewards which can influence entrepreneurial behaviour.

2. Limitation structure: It is originally socio-cultural in character. In this structure, entrepreneur is regarded as the most deviant individual in the society and that's why the society restricts specific activities that influence all members in the society.

3. Labour structure: It refers to the supply of skilled and willing labour. The structure is governed by a large numbers of factors such as racial stock, available job-alternatives, traditionalism, mobility of labour etc.

4. Opportunity structure: It is the most important structure governing the supply of entrepreneurs. The structure refers to the technological and "managerial skills, information about techniques of production, market structure and supply of capital.

Thus, J.H. Kunkel in his behavioural model depicted that entrepreneurial supply is concerned with overtly expressed activities of individuals and their relations to the previously and presently surrounding social structure and physical conditions. This behavioural model is based upon the following premises.

1. Man's internal state — beyond objective analysis: Man's internal state is beyond the scope of presently available means of measurement and objective analysis and so knowledge about this is of less significance so far as the explanation and prediction of behaviour is concerned.

2. Conditioning procedure, determinant of individual activities: The behavioural model of Kunkel depicts that the determinant of an individual activities are to be found largely in the conditioning procedure both deliberate and accidental to which he has been subjected in the past and in the sets of reinforcing and discriminative stimuli which become part of his behavioural chains and are part of present social context.

3. Behavioural approach and human spirit: This model does not deny the existence of human spirit. According to Kunkel, "This approach simply dues not make use of these concepts in analysis of behaviour because of their ambiguities. It also does not depreciate the internal stage of the man."

4. Model contrast with psychogenic approach: This behavioural model is in quite contrast with the psychogenic approaches. According to Kunkel, to change man's activities one need not concern oneself with altering values, one need to change only certain elements of the operant conditioning context of which all men at all times are an integral part.

5. Role of ambiguous and inadequate concepts: In his model, Kunkel indicates the ambiguity and inadequacy of some concepts like values, personality and attitudes. He points out that any sociological analysis will be inadequate if the above ambiguous concepts are given much importance in a society.

Keeping in view the above concepts, some writers point out that the spiritualism, philosophy of renunciation and asceticism are the stumbling blocks to the economic development of India. But Kunkel gives his opinion quoting Srinivas, Singer and Lambart who attributed India's development to existing social and political institutions rather than to the values and religious attitudes.

Theory of Culture

Bert F. Hoselitz (1952) states that, "a person who is to become an industrial entrepreneur must have additional personality traits to those resulting from a drive to a mass wealth. In addition to being motivated by the expectations of profit he must also have some managerial abilities and more important he must have the ability to lead. Hoselitz maintains that, financial skills have only a secondary consideration in entrepreneurship. According to him, managerial skills and leadership are the important facets of entrepreneurship. To strengthen his argument, he quotes the history of French and German industrial establishments of the early 19th Century where the former were men with mechanical skills rather than financial skills. Hoselitz's analysis of entrepreneurship naturally suggests a method for the development of entrepreneurship which depends upon allowing the maturation of development of personalities whose predominant orientation is in the direction of productivity, working, creation, and creative integration along with establishment of social institutions which create a favourable environment for the establishment and existence of independent individual enterprise. Hoselitz has also said that only a strange desire to make profit is not enough to succeed in becoming an industrial entrepreneur. He added one more characteristic to entrepreneurship, namely, liquidity of wealth. The commodity with which a money lender deals is acceptable to every one but an industrial entrepreneur creates his own commodity and its acceptability is uncertain. Therefore the entrepreneur assumes more risk than those in trading and lending profession.

Hoselitz explains that the supply of entrepreneurship is governed by cultural factors, and culturally minority groups are the spark-plugs of entrepreneurial and economic development. In many countries, entrepreneurs have emerged from a particular socio-economic class. He emphasizes the role of culturally marginal groups like the Jews and the Greeks in medieval Europe, the Lebanese in West Africa, the Chinese in South Africa, the Indians in East Africa in promoting economic development. Hoselitz's theory of entrepreneurship supply can be viewed from the following standpoints which are cultural in nature:

1. Hypothesis of marginal men: Hoselitz formulated the Hypothesis of marginal men who are the important reservoir of entrepreneur development. According to Hoselitz, marginal men because of their ambiguous position from a cultural or social statement are particularly suited to make creative adjustments in situations of change and in the course of this adjustment process, they develop genuine innovations in social behaviour.

2. Emphasis on the functions of managerial and leadership skill: Entrepreneurial talents can be brought about in a society by the individuals who possess extraordinary managerial and leadership skills. Hoselitz noted that a person who is to become an industrial entrepreneur have additional personality traits to those resulting from a drive to amass wealth. In addition to being motivated by the expectation of profit, he must also have the ability to lead.

3. Contribution of specific social classes: The theory reveals that in several countries entrepreneurial talents are found in persons having particular socio-economic background. For example, contribution of the precedent ethic of the west is significant in so far as the growth of a new class of industrialists is concerned. In Britain, the United States and Turkey, ranks of entrepreneurs were filled from commerce, Samurai in Japan, Family pattern in France, Yoruba in Nigeria, Kikiyu in Kenya, Christians in Lebanon, Halai Memon industrialists in Pakistan, Marwaris and Parsis in India are considered to be the dominant social classes in the field of entrepreneurship.

Stoke's Theory

Stoke's theory portrays that entrepreneurship is likely to emerge under specific social sanctions, social culture and economic action. According to Stoke, socio-cultural values channel economic action. He suggests that personal and societal opportunities and the presence of requisite psychological distributions may be seen as conditions for an individual movement to get changed into industrial entrepreneurship.

Theory of Cultural Values

The key elements in Thomas Cochran's theory are cultural values, role expectations and social sanctions. In his theory on the process of economic development, entrepreneurs are not seen as being deviant or super normal individuals but rather as representing society's model personality. This model personality is moulded by prevailing child-rearing practices and schooling common to a given culture. The performance of a businessman, according to him, will generally be influenced by three factors: (1) his own attitude towards his occupation; (2) the role expectations held by the sanctioning groups, and (3) the operational requirements of the job. The determinants for the first two factors are the society's values. Changes over time in such variables as population, technology, and institutional drift will impinge on the role structure by creating new operational needs.

Development in any walk of life has always depended, to some degree, on individual qualities of entrepreneurship. The success of planned efforts made by some countries in developing local entrepreneurs demolished the contention that an entrepreneur is a rare character, that entrepreneurship is not restricted to those who are gifted with certain qualities at birth. It can also be developed. It is precisely this conviction that has led to careful studies on entrepreneurship from economical, psychological and sociological perspectives, as well as steps to identify and develop entrepreneurship. As observed, every theorist has looked at the entrepreneur and entrepreneurship on the basis of his perception, and therefore, can at best provide only a limited view of entrepreneurial phenomenon.

THEORY OF BRAIN POWER AND TEASER

Maslow's hierarchy of needs is history. Drawing on the latest on neuroscience research, author David Rock explains why a pat-on-the-back works just as well as a pay hike and why people stay loyal to an organisation they perceive to be fair.

David Rock

David Rock is one of the management Gurus who are looking to neuroscience to explain the limits and the power of the human brain Rocks SCARF model provides with more nuanced and cost-effective ways to expand the definition of reward. The theory of Brain Power and Teaser explain the cost-effective rewards in effecting loyalty to an organisation they perceive to be fair.

Drawing on published research in the field of neuroscience and backing this up with interview with some leading scientists, Rock delves into the working of the human brain to explain why we're so easily distracted, why multi-tasking is so difficult, why we make mistakes when we're over-stressed as well as under-stressed and why those brilliant insights don't come to us as often as we would like them to.

Take the example of all those exhausting distractions in the form of phone calls, e-mails waiting in the inbox or the mind just wandering when it should be focusing on the work at hand. A study published in October 2005, found that the average employee spends an average of 11 minutes on a project before being distracted and it takes him 25 minutes to return to the original task. So how do we avoid distractions? Rock's advice is to consciously inhibit internal distractions by clearing the mind ahead of a difficult task and avoid external distractions by switching off the cell phones.

This is something most people would know intuitively, but Rock's contribution lies in his neurological explanation of how deadly distractions can be to performance. Making decisions and solving problems relies on the prefrontal cortex of the brain, just behind the forehead. It's the last region to develop in human evolutionary history and though it makes up just 4% of the brain's volume, it chews up a big quantity of energy. In fact, its best quality thinking lasts for a limited time and any distraction can be extremely damaging. People are much more willing to absorb and digest this idea when it's put to them scientifically. Don't underestimate the power of language. Even when it's something fairly obvious, you need to communicate it right.

Understanding how your brain works helps control stress, even if it's only through the mechanism of "oh well, that's just my brain." But Rock's more practical insights are on how we can use the findings of neuroscience to collaborate with other people. Here, he presents the research done by Naomi Eisenberger of UCLA, which demonstrates how "social pain" works very much like physical pain in that both involve activity in the dorsal portion of the brain's anterior cingulate cortex. This refutes the well-entrenched concept Maslow's hierarchy of needs, which says social needs follow physical needs like food and shelter. The brain reacts to being ostracised like it does to a physical blow. The idea that social threats and rewards are on par with physical threats and rewards is a new one and contradicts established ways of thinking:

Rock lists five social factors that trigger threat or reward responses in our brains: status, certainty, autonomy, relatedness and fairness (acronym: SCARF).

The battle for status is an age-old one, but it offers an explanation as to why people often react to words of praise as they would to a purely economic incentive like a pay hike.

Uncertainty or "not knowing what's going to happen next" can be even more debilitating than the threat of loss of status, diminishing memory and disengaging people from the present. Which is why it becomes important for leaders to share organisational plans, especially those that directly affect their people.

Autonomy is probably one of the more subtle social rewards and leaders need to be conscious of how it works. Part of it is eschewing micro-managing and giving people control of how they wish to work. When faced with an impasse, it's also about helping people to work things out for themselves rather than telling them what to do, even if they've asked for your suggestions.

Relatedness and fairness often go a long way in explaining why many people stay on with an organisation even when they have higher paying job offers elsewhere. Many organisations today also harness the brain's need for fairness by involving employees in corporate social responsibility projects — playing even a small part in creating a more just society can be very rewarding.

Economists have always defined incentives in material terms, but economic incentives work only when people perceive them to be supporting their social needs.

Leaders themselves are not immune to the SCARF dynamic. In fact, it's amplified in top positions since leaders are constantly required to deal with the threats of uncertainty, of diminished relatedness with colleagues and the loss of status on account of adverse reports on their performance in the media and elsewhere. Many people reaching senior positions need coaching because they've spent so much of their careers planning and thinking strategically that they've forgotten how to use that other part of the brain that is to do with knowing yourself and other people.

Kao's Conceptual Model

J.J. Kao in his book, *Entrepreneurship, Creativity and Organization,* has developed a conceptual model of entrepreneurship. The model is represented in Fig. 2. This is otherwise known as *The ECO Analysis Framework* (ECO stands for Entrepreneurship, Creativity and Organisation)

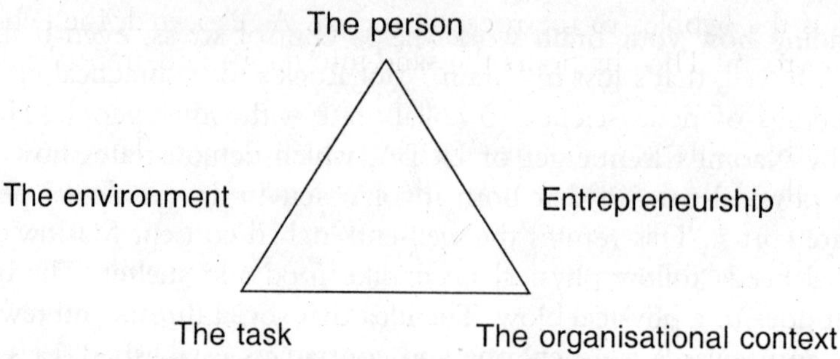

Fig. 2: The ECO analysis framework

According to Kao, entrepreneurship and creativity result from the interrelationship of the following three elements as shown in Fig. 2.

- The person
- The task
- The organisational context.

Element I: The most important element is the person. New ideas are not generated or implemented by organization or technology but come into being through efforts of dedicated people. So for entrepreneurial talent, it is important to understand people's personality, skills, motivation, levels of experience and psychological preferences.

Element II: The task is what a group of people or organisation does. Tasks may be determined by an individual's personality or private vision. They are shaped by organizational strategy and influenced by the external environment. The task includes perceiving of opportunities of resources and providing leadership qualities appropriate for entrepreneurial growth.

Element III: *The organisational context* is the immediate setting in which creative and entrepreneurial work rolls place. Factors like organizational structure and systems, the definition of work rolls and group culture affect significantly the nature of the creative or entrepreneurial environment.

Finally, the above elements exist in an environment which refers to the outside world surrounding the organisation. Environment includes in it the available resources, infrastructure, competitive pressures, social values, rules and regulations and state of technology. Environment too can facilitate or impede creative and entrepreneurial endeavour.

As such, the environment influences the enterprise creation significantly and the most successful entrepreneur is one who adapts himself to the changing needs of the environment and makes it hospitable for the growth of his business enterprise.

ROCK SOLID ADVICE

A philosophy professor is teaching his class. He has brought with him an empty glass jar, some rocks, some pebbles and a box of sand. Wordlessly, he fills up the jar with the rocks, and asks his students if the jar is full. They agree it is.

Next, he adds the pebbles to the rocks in the jar. As expected, the pebbles settle into the spaces between the rocks. Then he pours the sand into the jar and, immediately, the sand covers everything else.

"Now," says the professor, "Think of this jar as your life. The rocks are the important things — your family, your partner, your health, your children — anything that is so important to you that if it were lost, you would be nearly destroyed. The pebbles are the other things that matter, like your job, your house, your car. The sand is everything else. The small stuff.

"If you put the sand into the jar first, there is no room for the pebbles or the rocks. The same goes for your life. If you spend all your energy and time on the small stuff, you will never have room for the things that are important to you.

DREAM THEORY

Learn to use your dreams to help resolve issues and even as warnings of imminent problems, advise experts.

A dream is the experience of envisioned images, voices or other sensations during sleep. Scientists believe almost all humans dream with approximately the same frequency. Even those who rarely recall dreams report having them if awakened during rapid eye movement (REM) sleep.

Did you Know?

- In a typical lifetime, a person spends about 6 years dreaming (about 2 hours each night).
- Though animals dream, their capacity to dream varies from one species to another. Some animals cannot dream at all.
- Dreams have sometimes been like real life communications from one person to another, especially loved ones.
- Dreaming profound dreams with a religious or spiritual content has led to the dreamer converting from one religion to another. This is a recorded fact.

We've all spent hours wondering exactly what a dream to trying to tell us. Intrigued by a recurring dream, we've spent many a waking moment trying to decipher it.

Dreams unlock the mysteries of life. Rather apt then that dream therapy is emerging as a scientific tool for emotional well-being. Says Madhu Tandon, dream-interpreter and author of *Dialogue with Dreams,* "You can use your dreams to help you heal emotionally. Your dreams can indicate emotions, moods and conflict. They will guide you and give you answers. "

Dream therapy links the mysterious inner world of the mind and the outer physical world of waking life. In ancient Greece, more than 300 dream temples were built to heal the sick. In fact, Newsweek reports that technology and brain scientists are discovering how we can benefit from our dreams. Lucid dreaming is the process in which the person takes his/her conscious awareness (conscious mind) into the dream state to receive guidance or insight on a particular subject or problem. "While sleeping, the dream ego is less afraid of a threatening situation. So, there's less resistance to confrontation with these figures or situations. Using lucid dreaming, you can get in touch with places, times, situations or persons important to you. When you go to sleep tell yourself that you'd like to see a solution to your problem. And slowly, the answer will unfold before you like a film. Individuals themselves can interpret their dreams best.

No wonder then that Rosalind Cartwright, chairman of psychology at Rush University Medical Centre in Chicago believes that when it comes to understanding human behaviour, dreaming is a way of storytelling.

It helps us learn who we are, where we're going and how we're going to get there," she says. According to Tandon, telepathy is strong while dreaming.

Entrepreneur is a dreamer. Dreams helps the entrepreneur in many ways.

At times dreams not only perceives the business opportunities but also helps in idea, generation, creativity, innovation taking right decision at right time, relieving stress, business planning ways and means of mobilising resources, but also helps in problem solving at a critical time by showing right direction.

Dreams provide right solutions, strengthens self-confidence, self-esteem as well as self-worth, at times, forewarns of dangers/crises.

According to psychologists, dreams enhance creativity, capability and courage of entrepreneurs at times of need.

If you pay attention and recall your dreams, they can guide you." She suggests.

Agrees astrologer-turned-dream interpreter, Namita Vadehra, "Dreams can be used as a tool for psychic interpretation. They help you predict what's going to happen in the future. I've always felt that the dreamer can best identify with the emotions and situations in the dreams. If you wake up feeling uneasy, try to recall the dream immediately. Nightmares reflect that we need to face up to our fears and inner conflicts."

Currently, dream researchers are trying to understand the connection between sleeping and waking. They're using dream science to treat depression, post-traumatic stress, anxiety and a whole range of other problems. Psychologists are studying dreams to learn how both ordinary people and great artistes resolve problems in their life and work by "sleeping on them".

Psychiatrist Dr. Avdesh Sharma adds, "If you have recurrent dreams, they can reveal what's going on in your mind. If someone is depressed, dreams can indicate the area of conflict or stress. Dreams are like having a built-in therapist." Today, psychologists are applying modern technology to probe the content of dreams. A computer-based approach called content analysis is being used to interpret the colours in dreams. The study has found that red means action, excitement and desire: blue equals calmness, tranquillity and harmony, while black connotes fear, anxiety and intimidation.

So, the next time you have a technicolour dream, pay close attention — you might just get a glimpse into your future!

For over a year now, I've been relying on my dreams to show me the right direction. Recently, I got an offer for a business tie-up in Europe. But, I wasn't too sure. Fortunately, I dreamt that this deal was favourable for me and I accepted it. In retrospect, I can say that I did the right thing!

— **Puja Nayyar,** *Fashion Designer*

Dreams are fascinating. But at times, they can be spooky top. I had been pondering over a problem for many days and finally, I came up with a solution. Soon after that, I dreamt of a much better option. But, it was too late, I really wish I had this dream just a few nights earlier!

— **Rajeshwari Sachdeva**, *Performer*

Walker on Entrepreneurship

According to Walker, entrepreneur is a person who organizes and co-ordinates the various agents of production. He points out that the true entrepreneur is one who is in possession of above average ability for organizing and co-ordinating the resources. But in a country, the supply of *'true entrepreneur'* is limited. Entrepreneurs are endowed with different levels of organizational skill and co-ordinating capacity. Thus, entrepreneurs with higher level of competency are more successful and effective in earning superior rewards in terms of profit in comparison to their counterparts.

Frederick Harbison

Frederick Harbison states that the organisation building ability is the most critical skill needed for the industrial development. According to him, entrepreneurship means the skill to build an organisation. Harbison spots the crux of the entrepreneurship in his ability to multiply himself by effectively delegating responsibilities to others. Unlike Schumpeter, Harbison's entrepreneur is not an innovator but an organisation builder who must be able to harness the new ideas of different innovators to the rest of the organisation. Such persons are not always the men with ideas or men who try new combinations of resources but they may simply be good leaders and excellent administrators.

Harbison's definition of entrepreneurship lays more stress on the managerial skills and the creativity so far as organisation is concerned. His definition, as it appears is not far from Schumpeter's concept of innovation. It also allows creation of new organisation as innovation and Harbison also emphasises the organisation building ability. But Harbison maintains that the ability to create an organisation is the most crucial skill which facilitates the economic use of other innovations. If this skill is absent then other innovations fail to stimulate economic development.

Harbison did not propound any theory of entrepreneurship but he has made very interesting observations relating, to entrepreneurship as a factor of economic development He viewed organisation-building as the most critical skill needed for economic development as it facilitates the use of other innovations. He laid emphasis on the individual's organisational skill, creativity and ability to plan and initiate changes . He suggested that entrepreneurship should be treated as a resource which has both qualitative and quantitative dimensions.

Harbison categorized the functions of modern entrepreneurs in the following ways:

(*a*) Undertaking and managing of risk and the handling of economic activity.

(*b*) Planning and innovation.

(*c*) Co-ordination, administration, time control.

(*d*) Routine supervision.

In small enterprises, the above functions are performed by a single individual. But according to Harbison, all the persons who perform entrepreneurial function in a large organization are characterised as Managerial Resources. He pointed out that the efficacy of business organisation depends upon the following factors:

(*a*) Dynamic and innovative entrepreneurs

(*b*) Dynamic organization with creative thinkers who can plan and initiate changes.

Thus, the organization builder must be able "to harness the new ideas to select and develop persons who can properly manage enthusiasm in the accomplishment of objectives, multiply himself by efficiently delegating responsibilities."

However, Harbison emphasized that organisation is more than a summation of particular abilities of certain individuals. It is more than the statistical aggregate of managerial personnel. Organisation connotes a constellation of functions in a common undertaking.

Keeping in view the organizational importance, Harbison stated a few tentative hypotheses on entrepreneurship and organization. The propositions are given below:

(*a*) Large expenditures for equipment and machinery are likely to be quite unproductive unless there is a corresponding investment in organisation.

(*b*) Organization is probably the principal factor determining the productivity of labour, assuming that capital and natural resources are constant.

(*c*) "Because of non-economic factors (managerial persons may be guided in their decision making by consideration other than profits such as power, social prestige, ability to help friends and relatives which the success brings) which determine in part the behaviour of human beings as managerial resources, all organisations are probably inefficient in effecting the optimum of combination of economic resources which is theoretically possible." All the same, the ability to build organisation is perhaps the most precious of all entrepreneurial skills and thus, those who can achieve success in this very critical area, may be the ones who most nearly fulfil the role of true entrepreneur.

Peter Kilby on Entrepreneurship

Peter Kilby is a famous author on entrepreneurship. In his book *Entrepreneurship and Economic Development*, he has attempted to study the entrepreneur in greater detail and gave a comprehensive list of activities critical to entrepreneurial success in the context of an underdeveloped country.

1. Exchange relationship

(*a*) Perception of market opportunities.

(*b*) Obtaining control of scarce resources.

(*c*) Purchasing inputs.

(*d*) Marketing the product and responding to competition.

2. Political administration

(*a*) Dealing with bureaucracies (concessions/licences, etc.)

(*b*) Management of human relations within the firm.

(*c*) Management of customer-supplier relationship management and control.

(*d*) Financial management.

(*e*) Production management (control by written records, supervision, co-ordinating input flows with orders, maintenance)

3. Technology

(*a*) Acquiring and overseeing assembly of the factory.

(*b*) Industrial engineering (minimizing inputs with a given production process).

(*c*) Upgrading product and product quality.

(*d*) Introduction of new production techniques and products.

Peter Kilby proceeds to empirically assess the differential role performance of entrepreneurs on the basis of evidence from contemporary underdeveloped countries. He draws evidence from the studies made by himself, J.J. Berna, J.J. Carole, T.C. Cochran, J.R. Harris, G.F. Papamek, A.P. Alexander, ILO missions and others. The evidence led him to the following findings. According to him: "Entrepreneurial performance in those roles involving exchange relationships and political administration is vigorous and effective. On the other hand, entrepreneurs typically do not apply themselves with equal intensity or skill to their task in the realms of management control and technology. Deficiencies in these latter areas represent, in many instances, the operational bottleneck to indigenous industrial development."

Though these can be delegated but it depends upon the scale of production, social factors, and entrepreneur's self-efficiency. In an underdeveloped country an entrepreneur lacks the help of the markets for components, materials, labour, capital markets (which have already standardised products and trained workers). He also lacks the communications network *i.e.,* specialised industrial newspapers, magazines, and statistics of the complete structure of the industry collected by the government, and other institutions which provide all the information in the developed countries, say about the sources and availabilities of inputs, nearest and the best possible outlets for outputs.

Types of Entrepreneurs

On the basis of the forgoing analysis, the entrepreneurs can be classified into two groups, viz., on the basis of their functions, and on the basis of the characteristics. The former type reflects the role played by the entrepreneurs in the economic development of a particular country, and latter type reflects the degree, and the manner in which the entrepreneurs respond to the changing economic conditions.

Clarence Danhof, on the basis of his study of American Agriculture, classified entrepreneurs in the manner that at the initial stage of economic development, entrepreneurs have less initiative and drive, and as economic development proceeds they become more innovating and enthusiastic. This suggests a particular type of entrepreneurs that will emerge out in an economy will usually depend upon the levels of development achieved in that particular economy. As such, while an underdeveloped economy will produce shy and humble entrepreneurs, and the developed ones would make the innovating entrepreneurs. On the basis of this theory, Danhof classified entreprepreneurs into four categories.

"The difference between what we do and what we are capable of doing, would suffice to solve most of the world's problems..."
— Mahatma Gandhi

Innovating Entrepreneurs: Innovating entrepreneurship is characterised by aggressive assemblage of information and analysis of results, deriving from a novel combination of factors. Men/women in this group are generally aggressive in experimentation who exhibit cleverness in putting attractive possibilities into practice. One need not invent but convert even old established products or services, by changing their utility, their value, their economic characteristics, into something new, attractive and utilitarian. Therein lies the key to their phenomenal success. Such an entrepreneur is one who sees the opportunity for introducing a new technique of production process, a new commodity, a new market, a new service or even reorganisation of an existing enterprise.

Adoptive or Imitating Entrepreneurs: Imitative entrepreneurship is characterised by readiness to adopt successful innovation inaugurated by innovating entrepreneurs. In other words, imitators follow the innovators later after observing how the latter fare. These groups are also revolutionary entrepreneurs with the difference that they do not innovate the changes themselves. They just imitate techniques and technology innovated by others. Such entrepreneurs are particularly important in developing countries because they contribute significantly to the development of such economies. Imitative entrepreneurs are most suitable for the developing regions because in such countries people prefer to imitate the technology, knowledge and skill already available in more advanced countries.

The reason for the backwardness of the underdeveloped countries lies in the fact that they are deficient in innovating and imitating entrepreneurs when they are found in abundance in developed countries. Men are needed who can imitate the technologies and products to the particular conditions prevailing in such countries. And at times, there is a need of changing and adjusting the new technologies to their special conditions. Such countries, primarily need imitators who are responsible for transforming the system with the limited resources they possess.

Fabian Entrepreneurs: Fabian entrepreneurship is characterised by great caution and scepticism in practising any change. Such entrepreneurs have neither will to introduce new changes nor desire to adopt new methods innovated by the most enterprising entrepreneurs. Such entrepreneurs are shy and lazy. Their dealings are determined by customs, religion, tradition and past practices. They are not much interested in taking risk and they try to follow the footsteps of their predecessors.

Drone Entrepreneurship: Drone entrepreneurship is characterised by a refusal to adopt and use opportunities to make changes in production. Such entrepreneurs may even suffer losses but they do not make changes in production methods. They are laggards because they continue in their traditional way and infields their product loses its marketability of their operation becomes uneconomical they are pushed out of the market.

David Bornstein

Social Entrepreneur

David Bornstein, the exponent of social innovations and entrepreneurship believes that the future belongs to social entrepreneurs. They are news worthy and pose serious threats to the status quo.

In essence they are both the same. However, while the former is concerned about profits, the latter is fanatical about a cause. So much so, that he or she is not happy solving an idea in one village or two villages. Yet at the same time, social entrepreneurs have got to be very systematic, are basically really good people, with a high streak of integrity. And finally, they are really self-effacing-always passing on the credit of their work to the team.

Most of these social entrepreneurs start with a higher base of education with greater access to information, and are more aware of problems around them in this era of the internet. Between 1970 and 1985, adult literacy rates have increased in the developed world from 43% to 60% and there has been a proliferation of the dot orgs too. Finally, there is more opportunity both politically and financially now, than ever before in history. Per capita incomes in free market economies have risen by more than 700% in the 20th century. So essentially, freedom, wealth, exposure, social mobility and greater individual confidence re driving this huge wave of social innovation and entrepreneurship. After all, people are tired with the inefficiency of governments and the indifference of corporates, and want to make a change and this is the case everywhere.

Businesses must also realise that besides the cause, social entrepreneurs also allow them to tap a market which they themselves perhaps can never capture. Secondly, it is beneficial for employees to know that their workplace associates itself not only with profits, but also with social causes, where occasionally they can go and work too. Thirdly, business organisations have developed better competencies to understand a market over the years, developing distribution channels and also identifying target customers for example. They can help social entrepreneurs with these skills. Finally, organisations can also use their strengths to identify social entrepreneurs to associate with. For example, an architectural firm can associate with a person doing work on landscape beautification. An excellent example is how Tata Consultancy Services came forward to associate with Childline to create a nationwide database of destitute children Childnet. It's quite simple-TCS used its software skills, Childline had the cause ready, together both beneficiary earning a good name for a noble cause.

The Serial Entrepreneur

BOT (Build, Operate, Transfer) is a phenomena that wouldn't have happened if it wasn't for the rise of the new age entrepreneur. The new age entrepreneurs today aren't the scions of rich business families diversifying into new areas. They are men and women who have earned their spurs is professionals. Raman Roy had run a similar business in GE and Amex before setting up Spectramind. Sanjeev Aggarwal had worked with motorola and 3 com before he set up Daksh with another entrepreneur Pavan Vaish. Among the younger lot there are well educated ex-execs who have worked with blue chip companies. For example, Transwork's Rizwan Koita, is an ex-McKinsey consultant with an MIT and IIT background. Vision Health-source's Anurag Jain is an ex-Cap Gemini consultant and holds an Michigan University MBA. Indialife Hewitt's Manish Sabharwal is a Wharton MBA.

BOT is an established way of business in highly entrepreneurial societies like the US where serial entrepreneurs abound.

Changing industry dynamics have played an important part in the rise of BOT model in India.

Many entrepreneurs have begun to realise that to grow and compete with big firms, they need scale and size.

Ready buyers, in the form of large companies in the acquisition mode and MNCs who wish to have a foot hold in India have provided a sale exit route for these mid-sized companies.

Venture capitalists have played a significant role in the emergence of the BOT model. Remember that many of these companies are funded by VCs and they have a large say in the future direction of these companies.

The new age entrepreneurs are a different lot. They create world class enterprises. But unlike the older generation of Indian businessmen, they do not hold on to their enterprises (babies) for life.

They believe in a company first attitude and would happily set aside their egos and personal agendas for ensuring the good of their companies. So the decision to sellout, though a painful one, is taken if it helps maximise value for all the shareholders, employees, investors, and clients. "It was a decision taken for the long term benefit of all who mattered," says Koppar of Kshema. And, moreover, they don't have the 'know-all' attitude. "I realised that my strengths lay in building a business — growing the business further need a different set of skill acknowledges India World's Jain, who now runs Netcore Solutions. Most tend to accept this fact and therefore, there are battles after they have sold out the promoters of yore, even stay back within the company, "As long as there's clarity of thought on where you want to take the company and you are clear your role, it's easy," says Koita. And, the entrepreneurial activity accelerates in new pastures.

ENTREPRENEURS FOR THE AGES

They are early colonial traders and 19th century industrialists. Throughout history there have been a handful of people who had the vision to successfully exploit untapped markets. They changed the world in the process. See who they are, what they did, and why they matter today.

— *Business Week*

Estee Lauder

(b. 1907, d. 2004)

Young Estee Lauder, born Josephine Esther Mentzer to immigrant parents in the Corona, Queens section of New York City, began experimenting as a child with skin treatments her uncle cooked up. In 1946, she founded the company that bears her name to sell makeup and perfume in high-end department stores around the world.

Lauder's business philosophy centered on selling products she considered to be of the highest quality, and she used her products themselves as advertisements. Lauder pioneered giving free samples at stores like Saks Fifth Avenue to hook customers. Although Lauder died in 2004, her grandson William still runs the company, with more than 9,000 products and $6.5 billion in sales in 2006.

Key takeaway: Lauder became a giant in the nascent beauty industry by making sure the quality of her products exceeded the expectations of her target market, namely wealthy society women.

Madam C. J. Walker

(b. 1867, d. 1919)

Born the daughter of former Louisiana slaves and orphaned at age 7, Walker developed a homemade scalp lotion to stop her hair loss. She then turned her remedy into a business-and a movement.

Walker's line of hair-and-beauty products geared toward blacks tapped into a market ignored by other businesses because of racism. She also used her clout and fortune to advocate for change, pushing for anti-lynching laws and contributing to civil rights causes. She set an example for generations of entrepreneurs in a time when women were still struggling for voting rights and Brown v. Board of Education was a half-century away.

Key takeaway: The era's ingrained racism left a huge part of the population underserved by the market. Walker profited by making them her customers.

Thomas Edison

(b. 1847, d. 1931)

Edison's relentless innovation made him the most prolific inventor of his time. He got his start as a telegraph operator but soon moved on to refining that technology and creating others that would turn the world on its head: a device to turn power into light, a machine to record and play back sound. Edison's labs were always working on new consumer products — a model familiar to today's crop of innovators like Google and Apple.

But only Edison's business sense allowed him to transform his ideas into enterprises that turned a profit. The Wizard of Menlo Park understood the importance of owning his ideas — he registered 1,093 patents — so he could retain profits on his products and discourage competitors.

Key takeaway: Innovation is Crucial, but new ideas alone will not make a business successful. Ideas need to be focused into products that customers will value.

COMPUTER WIZARD

Sabeer Bhatia, Computer Wizard

(Born, December 13, 1968)

Regarded as one of the poster boys of Indian success story at Silicon Valley, **Sabeer Bhatia** started his journey as a systems integrator at Apple Computers, where along with his colleague Jack Smith, in 1995, he co-founded Hotmail Corporation. They launched pioneering web-based e-mail service Hotmail, which in less than six months attracted over 1 million subscribers. Later on, he sold it to Microsoft. After working for a year for Microsoft, in 1999 he launched Arzoo.com. Arzoo failed with the burst of dot-com bubble. However, in 2006, he relaunched Arzoo as a travel portal which is growing constantly. Along with Shiraz Kanga and Viraf Zack, he also started BlogEverywhere. In 2007, he released an on-line office alternative to Microsoft

Office, called Live Documents, while in 2008, announced the launch of his latest venture SabseBolo.com. He plans to develop a new city in India called Nanocity, a replication of Silicon Valley. Mr. Bhatia has also won several prestigious awards.

Sergey Mihailovich Brin, The 'Search' Expert

Born: August 21, 1973

Sergey Brin co-founded Google with Larry Page. Born in a Jewish family in Moscow that migrated to the US in 1979, Sergey was fascinated by computers from childhood. He met Larry at the Stanford University where they wolted together on a project while pursuing their Ph.Ds. They left studies to focus on their common interest-developing a search engine. They began with BackRub, a search engine named so because it could analyse back-links pointing to a particular website. This technology began gaining popularity on the campus while Sergey and Larry kept improving on it. They bought terabyte of disks (at bargain rates) and set up the first data centre for Google in Larry's room! Initially, they wanted to sell the technology but later at the suggestion of a friend decided to build their own company. Andy Bechtolsheim (a founder of Sun Microsystems) saw their demo, recognised the potential and became the first investor with a $100,000 cheque. Google Inc came into being in September 1998.

Charles Robert Schwab, Jr. The Philanthropic Entrepreneur

Born: July 29, 1937)

Charles Schwab suffers from dyslexia but the disorder did not stop him from establishing one of the largest discount brokerage firms ever. Today, as the founder and CEO of The Charles Schwab Corporation, he is one of the richest persons in his country. Even though Charles still finds reading and writing difficult, he successfully earned a BA in economics from the Stanford University in 1959 and an MBA from the Stanford Graduate School of Business in 1961. He started his professional life as a mutual fund manager and did quite well mostly because of his expertise in finance and excellent communication skills. After spending about a decade in the field, he thought he was ready for bigger things. He borrowed $100,000 and started America's first discount brokerage firm. His business philosophy of making stock market accessible to everybody worked really well. Having achieved great business success, Charles Schwab contributes substantially towards philanthropic activities through his foundation.

Gordon Earle Moore Entrepreneur with his own 'Law'!

(Born: January 3, 1929)

Great entrepreneurs not only contribute through their pioneering work but also provide a guiding principle to the world through their vision. One such man is **Gordon Moore** the co-founder of Intel Corporation. That he co-founded Intel in 1968 would have been enough to rank him amongst the all the time greats. However, the Moore's law, which he propounded in a magazine article in 1965, has also carved his name forever in the world of techno-business. This law has kept the semiconductor industry motivated to deliver increasingly powerful chips while bringing the cost of electronics down. Moore became president and CEO of Intel in 1975, a position he held till he was elected chairman and CEO in 1979. He continued to be the CEO until 1987 and was named chairman emeritus in 1997. Born in San Francisco,. Moore earned a bachelor's in chemistry from the University of California in 1950 and a Ph.D. in Chemistry and Physics from the California Institute of Technology in 1954 .

Li Ka-shing, The Super Asian

(Born July 29, 1928)

He wields tremendous business powers. Not surprisingly, **Li Ka-shing** is often referred to as 'Superman' in Hong Kong. Currently, he is the Chairman of Hutchison Whampoa and Cheung Kong Holdings. Forced to Spend his childhood in the home of a wealthy but arrogant uncle, Li was determined to make it big. He left school after his father's death and started working to a plastics company where he toiled for sixteen hours daily. It was this sheer hard work and determination that helped him set up his own company at 22. He had to borrow money from friends and family but that did not deter him. Being an excellent salesman, he had developed good contacts. This helped him and he never looked back. Though he began with plastics, he ventured into every possible segment spreading his reach as wide as possible. His empire soon engulfed Hong Kong and went beyond through presence in diversified sectors such as electricity, real estate, transportation, telecommunications, shipping, retail, Internet, etc.

Michael Dell, Personalising Computers

(Born: February 23, 1965)

When he first began building personal computers in his university dorm room, **Michael Dell** had little inkling where his small venture would take him. Dell had entered the University of Texas hoping to become a doctor, but at 19 realised that he can build better computers than cure humans. He began building and selling personal computers from stock parts. In 1984, he started his own business, 'PC's limited', with just one thousand dollars. Dell's process allowed customisation of the computers and he sold directly to consumers, thus avoiding the costs of middlemen and store operations. This small business was soon to become Dell Inc., one of the largest companies in the world. In 1992, the company made it to the Fortune 500 list, and Michael Dell became the youngest CEO to head a Fortune 500 company. Dell is also known for his philanthropy; the 'Michael and Susan Dell Foundation' which works towards children's causes, is an initiative of Dell.

Bob Parsons, Master of his Domain

(Born: 1950)

Entrepreneur **Bob (Robert) Parsons** is best known as the Founder of The Go Daddy Group, which comprises three domain registrar and web hosting companies. Born in Baltimore, and raised in difficult financial conditions, Parsons began working even as a child: selling newspapers, working in a factory or pumping gas. His academic achievements during childhood left much to be desired, but this changed once he enlisted in the United States armed forces. His experiences in the Marine Corps gave him the confidence and focus to pursue a degree in accounting after his discharge. He earned his CPA and also taught himself programming by night. Parsons began his career in software selling MoneyCourts, a home accounting programme, through his company, Parsons Technology. In 1997, he founded Go Daddy, and hasn't looked back since. Go Daddy has been voted the "Best Registrar" and the "Most Innovative Company", besides other honours.

Milton Snavely Hershey, The Chocolate King

(September 13, 1857 - October 13, 1945)

Milton Hershey's name has been imprinted on the millions of Hershey's chocolate bars sold around the world every day. Hershey dropped out of school early, and was apprenticed, first to a printer and then to a candy maker. He later started his own candy-making business, which failed. His next two candy businesses also flopped. Despite the failures, he persisted, and eventually struck gold with a caramel recipe. Later on, Hershey ventured into chocolate-making, seeking to mass-produce milk chocolate, which was then a luxury product. He perfected his own formula and set up a factory to mass-produce the confectionery. Hershey was known for his employee welfare initiatives. He financed the building of an entire community around the factory, quite different from the drab industrial towns of the day. He set up a charitable foundation for meeting the education needs of Hershey residents and also funded the building of a teaching hospital.

According to Traits

Another interesting approach to classify and understand personality is the trait. A personality trait is understood as being an enduring attribute of a person that appears consistently in a variety of situations. A trait differentiates one from another in a relatively permanent or consistent way. A trait of an individual is abstracted from his behaviour, and serves an useful 'unit of analysis' to understand personality.

Entrepreneurial traits influence and shape the entrepreneurial skills and the entrepreneurial activities. Traits are broadly grouped into two distinctive groups — positive and negative traits. The following chart shows the classification of entrepreneurs in accordance with positive/negative traits. The classification is suggestive and not comprehensive.

TRAITS

Positive

Able entrepreneur
Achiever entrepreneur
Adaptable entrepreneur
Adventurous entrepreneur
Ambitious entrepreneur
Aspiring entrepreneur

Negative

Arrogant entrepreneur
Careless entrepreneur
Complacent entrepreneur
Corrupt entrepreneur
Cunning entrepreneur
Egoistic entrepreneur

Authoritative entrepreneur
Brave entrepreneur
Brilliant entrepreneur
Caring entrepreneur
Cautious entrepreneur
Charming entrepreneur
Charismatic entrepreneur
Catalyst entrepreneur
Committed entrepreneur
Confident entrepreneur
Congenial entrepreneur
Creative entrepreneur
Credible entrepreneur
Cultured entrepreneur
Daring entrepreneur
Dedicated entrepreneur
Dreamer entrepreneur
Dynamic entrepreneur
Efficient entrepreneur
Empathetic entrepreneur
Empowering entrepreneur
Encouraging entrepreneur
Enterprising entrepreneur
Ethical entrepreneur
Experimental entrepreneur
Exploring entrepreneur
Flexible entrepreneur
Friendly entrepreneur
Focussed entrepreneur
Hardworking entrepreneur
Honest entrepreneur
Humanitarian entrepreneur
Humble entrepreneur
Icon entrepreneur
Innovative entrepreneur
Intelligent entrepreneur
Intuitive entrepreneur
Judicious entrepreneur
Levelhead entrepreneur
Logical entrepreneur
Loyal entrepreneur
Mentoring entrepreneur
Meticulous entrepreneur
Motivated entrepreneur
Reclusive entrepreneur
Resilience entrepreneur
Restless entrepreneur
Righteous entrepreneur
Rolemodel entrepreneur
Sincere entrepreneur
Sensitive entrepreneur
Fraudulent entrepreneur
Gambler entrepreneur
Gorgin entrepreneur
Greasing entrepreneur
Greedy entrepreneur
Grumbling entrepreneur
Harsh entrepreneur
Jealous entrepreneur
Lazy entrepreneur
Manipulator entrepreneur
Mean entrepreneur
Miscreant entrepreneur
Miser entrepreneur
Naughty entrepreneur
Notorious entrepreneur
Quarrelsome entrepreneur
Perverse entrepreneur
Rigid entrepreneur
Rogue entrepreneur
Ruthless entrepreneur
Scoundrel entrepreneur
Selfish entrepreneur
Superboss entrepreneur
Unscrupulous entrepreneur
Worst entrepreneur

Skilled entrepreneur
Softspoken entrepreneur
Strategist entrepreneur
Supportive entrepreneur
Tactful entrepreneur
Tough entrepreneur
Trusting entrepreneur
Transformer entrepreneur
Understanding entrepreneur
Visionary entrepreneur
Wise entrepreneur
Zealous entrepreneur

SOCIAL RESPONSIBILITY

Entrepreneurial development is the key to achieve all-round economic development through acceleration of industrial and entrepreneurial activities. Entrepreneurship, therefore, will flourish in an atmosphere which is favourable for enterprise building — politically, economically and socially. In the context of new economic scenario where liberalization, privatisation and globalisation are glorified, the responsibilities of business have undergone radical changes. Ethical discipline plays a great role in the changing environmental conditions. Entrepreneurs have to follow the ethical norms of the business in the society. As such, social responsibility implies responsibility of the entrepreneur towards smooth operation of the society by efficient utilization of national resources for greater interest of the people.

To remain in business on a sustainable basis, an entrepreneur has to exercise his responsibilities to the society in the following ways:

1. **Responsibility of the entrepreneur towards conservation of national resources:** The first and foremost social responsibility of an entrepreneur is to efficiently conserve and utilize national resources for the public good.
2. **Responsibility towards owners/shareholders:** An entrepreneur is responsible to safeguard the capital invested by the shareholders and the owners of the enterprise. He should ensure that they get adequate dividend from their investment.
3. **Responsibility towards customers:** An entrepreneur has to satisfy his customers by the following two ways:
   (*i*) Providing quality products to the customers.
   (*ii*) Charging reasonable and affordable price for the product.
4. **Responsibility towards employees:** Social responsibility of an entrepreneur is to provide adequate measures to make the employees contented in all respects so as to encourage them to contribute their best. The responsibility of an entrepreneur towards the employees may include the following:
   (*a*) Providing at least minimum wages to the employees.
   (*b*) Providing conducive working environment for good work culture.

Corporate Social Responsibility

Corporate Social Responsibility initiatives, if included in strategic business planning can achieve desired business goals. To operationalise responsible business practices — human resources, finance and time are involved. Investments in responsible business practices leads to benefits like enhanced brand image, employee retention, reduced operational costs and increased community support.

Corporate Social Responsibility begins with a trigger. The process normally begins with a trigger or an event that requires management attention and action. This attention can come from a product, workplace crisis, from external pressures or from inner values and principles. The trigger motivates management to take required steps for initiating CSR action in the company. Motivated management formulates CSR policy and describes the vision and mission statement of the company. Written CSR policy will ensure common understanding amongst board of members and will define how much and what a company wants to achieve that will ensure effective implementation. To implement CSR policy, management should form a core group or a committee. The core group would be responsible to plan, execute, monitor, evaluate, report and communicate the progress and impact of CSR programmes. The core group will be responsible to identify the resources, execute planned activities and sustain the commitment for motivation to responsible business practices. The CSR core group must identify the focus area of the company. The focus area will be based on the CSR policy, vision and mission of the company.

To Survive and Prosper

Privately held businesses (PHBs) are adopting corporate social responsibility (CSR) policies not just to save the planet but because they are having to in order to survive and prosper. According to the latest Grant Thornton International Business Report, 65% of PHBs cite recruitment and retention pressures as their main CSR driver, closely followed by cost management concerns (63%), suggesting that controlling costs is not only good for business but also good for business ethics.

While multinational companies may engage in CSR activities to manage their reputation, PHBs are focussing on the basics making themselves are more attractive as employers and suppliers.

Alex MacBeath, global leader of privately held businesses says, "The individuals who own PHBs have a speed advantage over the multinationals, however, as their ethical policies can be adopted much more quickly than within the more complex structure of larger companies. The PHBs that introduce ethical business practices quickly and efficiently will survive and prosper, as they will secure the skilled workers and the future contracts with the multinationals."

The concept of Corporate Social Responsibility (CSR) in India has witnessed a substantial evolution in the new millennium. The shift from basic, random efforts to structured, well-planned, focused initiatives has made a considerable difference in the effectiveness of CSR agendas as well as their perception.

While highlighting the correlation between CSR and corporate profitability has contributed to the transformation so far, the thrust will now be on ensuring inclusive growth and linking CSR with good corporate governance and best business practices. With a major change envisioned in terms of attitude and approach, the overall significance of CSR is expected to see a major rise in the near future.

CSR is an effective business tool that provides returns in the long-term to both civil society and the industry. There is a need to bridge the gap between corporate governance and CSR, make CSR activities more accountable as well as more effective, further improve delivery systems and update the laws relating to these issues.

What is CSR?

Corporate Social Responsibility has been influenced by two major concepts — stakeholder model, wherein it is recognised that good business practice entails engaging all stakeholders in company's business. So good business is not only seen as maximising shareholder value but also stakeholder value. The other concept is triple bottom line, where companies would no longer be judged by the conventional single *i.e.*, financial bottomline, but also on their performance in social

QUOTE UNQUOTE

Corporate social responsibility is a hardedged business decision. Not because it is a nice thing to do or because people are forcing us to do it... because it is good for our business.

— **Niall Fitzerald, Former** *CEO, Unilever*

Social obligation is much bigger than supporting worthy causes. It includes anything that impacts people and the quality of their lives.

— **William Ford** Jr. *Chairman, Ford Motor Co.*

In my view the successful companies of the future will be those that integrate business and employees' personal values. The best people want to do work that contributes to society with a company whose values they share, where their actions count and their views matter.

— **Jeroen van der Veer,** *Committee of Managing Director (Shell)*

Our consumers are very sensitive to social and environmental issues... We have actively engaged with them on these issues in the last ten years and they have become very aware as consumers. They especially ask for information on environmental policies, workers' rights and product safety.

— **Walter Dondi,** *Director of Co-op. Adriatica (Italy's largest retailer)*

Business has a responsibility beyond its basic responsibility to its shareholders; a responsibility to a broader constituency that includes its key stakeholders, customers, employee NGOs, government — the people of the communities in which it operates.

— **Courtesy Pratt,** *Former CEO, Toronto Hydro.*

Courtesy: Pratt, Former (CEO), Toronto Hydro

and environmental bottomlines. CSR can be defined as operating a business in a manner that meets or exceeds the ethical, legal, commercial and public expectations that society has of business. CSR is viewed as a comprehensive set of policies, practices and programs that are integrated throughout business operations and decision making processes that are supported and rewarded by top management. According to European Union, CSR is a concept that an enterprise is accountable for its impact on all relevant stakeholders. It is continuing commitment by business to behave fairly and responsibly, contribute to economic development while improving the quality of life of the workforce and their families as well of the local community and society at large. By expressing their social responsibility, companies are affirming their role in societal and territorial cohesion, quality and environment.

Corporate Social Responsibility is the commitment of business to contribute to sustainable economic development, working with employees and their families, the local community and society at large to improve their quality of life in ways that are good for business and good for development.

ACTION PLAN FOR CORPORATE SOCIAL RESPONSIBILITY

There are several areas of action plan for corporate social responsibility.

Environment and Ecology

- Reduce consumption of energy, water and other natural resources and emission of hazardous substances.
- Establish environment management system.
- Use recycled and recyclable products.
- Increase durability of products and minimise packaging.
- Train staff in environmental issues.

Health and Well Being

- Establish policies to ensure the health and safety of all employees — which are known to employees.
- Involve employees in business decisions that affect them.
- Operate open book policies.
- Consult employees on how to handle a down turn in the business if layoffs are avoidable, offer out placement services, retraining and severance benefits.
- Provide training opportunities.
- Extend training to life management, retirement planning and dependents care.

Diversity and Human Rights

- Work with charities, job centres to redesign jobs to make them accessible to disadvantaged.
- Set the tone in not tolerating sexist, racist, homophobic jokes.

- Support organisations that promote fair trade and human rights compliance.
- Make sure that staff member is aware that there are explicit policies against discrimination, in hiring, salary, promotion, training or termination of any employee on the basis of gender, race, age, ethnicity, disability.

Community

- Encourage employee volunteering in the community, payroll giving and back up with financial contributions and help in kind.
- Make some of the business products or services available free or at cost to charitable products.
- Look for opportunities to make surplus product and redundant equipment available to local schools, charities and community organisations.
- Offer quality work experience for school children and students.
- Collaborate with local teachers to make the activity of business the subject of school project.
- Use business experience to help local school of charity.
- Use marketing budget to associate business with social cause.

Emerging Areas of Corporate Social Responsibility

There are several emerging areas of corporate social responsibility — social responsibility, business responsibility, environmental responsibility and stakeholder involvement.

Areas of social responsibility include — respecting human rights, contributing to social economic development, employee welfare — this includes right to organise, eliminating child labour, non-discrimination, living wage and social security, training, safety, health and well-being, lifelong learning, empowerment of employees etc. Consumer protection includes right to information. Respect for national sovereignty and local communities for multinationals. Sharing resources with underprivileged communities. Investing in sustainable development programmes for the community.

Areas of environmental responsibility include — respect for environment and environment friendly technologies. Use, conservation and discharge of energy, material and water in eco-friendly manner. Adopting preventive and precautionary measures for environment pollution control. Rectifying environmental damage at source. Treating waste before disposing it. Preservation of biodiversity. Promoting and implementing an environmental policy for sustainable energy and environment.

Areas of business responsibility includes — compliance with tax laws and other regulations, investing in developing science and technology, fostering ethical trade practices, regulating supplier's CSR practices and distributor's CSR practices and transparent financial reporting. Areas of corporate social responsibility include extension of principles and ethical values enshrined in organisation to all its stakeholders such as authorities, customer groups, business partners and external influences.

Compliance of CSSR

"The purpose of corporation is to do as much good as we can, everywhere for everybody concerned... and incidently to make money" — **Henry Ford**

A sample compliance checklist for CSR would include:

Company CSR Management Involvement

1. Does the company have separate department/cell for CSR initiatives?
2. Does the company produce an annual sustainable CSR report?
3. How does the vision of company integrate CSR issues?
4. How does the organisation propose to meet future economic, environmental and social challenges?

Marketplace: Products/Services/Business Operations

1. Give the unique selling features of products highlighting following points — innovative issues, ensuring safety, ensuring health issues.
2. Has the company conducted a feedback survey to gauge public perception/customer satisfaction of its products/services/business operations, to assess the social and environmental impact of its activities.
3. Does the company have management system that addresses customer redressals/ grievances.
4. Does the company adhere to any specific ethical standards for its advertising campaigns?

Workplace CSR Practices

1. Does the company have a CSR policy/policies.
2. Does the company have a policy on any of the following: HIV/AIDS, Child labour, employment of disabled, business ethics, environment, quality?
3. What active steps are taken to increase awareness of company policies among employees?
4. Is your company an equal opportunity organisations?
5. Have any special measures been taken to improve gender representation in the organisations?
6. What are the indicators used in monitoring the implementation of policies?

Governance and Legal Issues

1. What steps are undertaken by the company to enhance corporate governance in the organisation?
2. Are issues like transparency integral to fulfillment of CSR policy?

3. Has the company been involved in litigation involving breach of corporate law in the past four years?
4. Have any managers .been convicted of illegal activities?
5. Has any demand been pending against the company from any tax and or any revenue authorities?
6. Has the company complied with SEBI corporate governance guidelines?

Employee Welfare/Human Resource Practices

1. Does the company have clear employee guidelines concerning recruitment, termination, career development and performance appraisals?
2. What are the motivational incentives provided by the company to its employees?
3. What are mechanisms installed to identify training needs of employees?

Labour Relations/Health and Safety Measures

1. Has the company faced labour disputes (strikes, dharnas, lockouts) and what are the average number of work days lost?
2. Does the company report on labour practices?
3. What are the steps taken to monitor the implementation of fair labour practices?
4. What employee welfare programmes are organised by the company?

Social and Community Initiatives

1. Is there an established trust/foundation/NGO set up by the company to implement social activities?
2. What are the key positive impacts provided by the companies which benefit the community?
3. What strategies has the company adopted to undertake developmental activities for marginalized/underprivileged/poor communities?
4. What is the mode of dialogue for NGOs, local governments and local communities?
5. What percentage of annual profits is allocated as funds for community development works?
6. What are the kinds of partnerships that are created with civil society/NGOs for social development? — Healthcare/Education, literacy promotion/improving rural infrastructure/community development.
7. Does the company encourage employee giving for imparting skills to local community, secondments and time off for employees?
8. How are social projects monitored and reported?

Measuring Corporate Social Responsibility

Measuring CSR initiative is important to ensure effective implementation of planned strategy and to determine future action plans. Each company can design measuring strategies based on their selected CSR focus areas. There are several ways to measure impact of CSR initiatives — community initiatives, workplace initiatives, environmental initiatives and marketplace initiatives.

Measurement of Community Initiatives

1. Cash value of community support as a percentage of pre-tax profit.
2. Impact of evaluations carried out on community programmes.
3. Project progress.
4. Perception measures.
5. Positive and Negative media comments.

Measurement of Workplace Initiatives

1. Workplace profile
2. Staff absenteeism
3. Legal non-compliance
4. Staff grievances
5. Staff turnover.

Measurement of Environment Initiatives

1. Overall energy consumption
2. Water usage
3. Quantity of solid waste produced
4. Use of recycled material
5. Environment impact.

Measurement of Marketplace Initiatives

1. Number of product complaints regarding products and services.
2. Advertising complaints upheld.
3. Complaints about late payment of bills.
4. Upheld cases of anti corruptive behaviour.
5. Customer satisfaction levels.
6. Customer retention.

Corporate Social Entrepreneurship

The traditional philanthropy practised by your company is good. But you may be squandering an opportunity to create true strategic value, both social and financial, through your relationships with civil society. Corporate Social Entrepreneurship (CSE) is a process aimed at enabling business to develop more advanced and powerful forms of Corporate Social Responsibility (CSR)… Because CSE expands the core purpose of corporations and their organisational values, it constitutes fundamental change that can be particularly threatening and resisted. Furthermore, it pushes the corporation's actions more broadly and deeply into the area of social value creation where the firm's experiences and skill sets are less developed. The disruptive social innovations intrinsic to the CSE approach amplify this zone of discomfort.

Values-based leadership, the synergistic generation of social and economic value, and strategic cross-sector alliances are key ingredients to achieving a sustainably successful business. For companies to move their corporate social responsibility (CSR) activities to the next level, they need to rethink their current approaches to CSR, tapping into the creativity of each individual. Like all entrepreneurship. CSE is abut creating disruptive change in the pursuit of new opportunities. It combines the willingness and desire to create joint economic and social value with the entrepreneurial redesign, systems development, and action necessary to carry it out.

Corporate social entrepreneurship combines values, skills, vision to create enterprises/services of economic and social value for the betterment of the society on an ongoing basis. The wealth created by entrepreneurial design and system development is ploughed back to the enrichment of the society. Profit and social good accelerate the economic growth.

CSE is based squarely on values, systems, entrepreneurial design and common threads. The design of CSE is as follows:

1. Be audacious in your vision.
2. Focus on what you know best.
3. Trim flab to achieve operational excellence.
4. Good governance makes business sense.
5. Develop leaders from within.
6. Forge stronger partnerships with your supplier base.
7. Pursue quality with zeal.
8. Innovate to create value for customers.
9. Give back to the society.
10. Give Indian edge.
11. Imbibe strong value and build them among your workers. The value includes technical, economical, social, psychological services and social benefits that accrue to customers and the society.
12. Inculcate work culture in the organise.
13. Delegate and build healthy relations with the stake holders.
14. Stress on education, technology and skill development.
15. Plan well and design the management process.

In fact, best entrepreneurs score higher on corporate social responsibility. Certainly CSE brings in a greater credibility to Corporate Social responsibility and ensures continuity in social good along with accelerated economic growth.

Annexure - 1

THE BUSINESS OF GIVING

Corporate Social Responsibility is about managing issues that affect any corporate house's business reputation. It also means responding to the growing needs and concerns of different stakeholders.

Henning Holck-Larsen
4-7-1907 to 27-7-2003

VALUE PROPOSITIONS

- Companies responsive to the demands of all of their stakeholders are better equipped to achieve long-term financial success;
- Helps cutting costs;
- A viable brand building exercise
- Spurt in sales and customer loyalty
- Enhanced productivity and quality
- Increased market pie
- Competitive edge
- Environmental sustainability
- Business alliances

The protagonists holding on to the view that globalisation has its discontents too have often been at odds with those who think otherwise. In view of the corporate houses worldwide raking in moolah riding on the wave of the global economy, and the increasing public concern about business activities coupled with a decline in trust of the stakeholders, the need for reinventing corporate philosophy is gradually gaining ground world over. The need is fuelled more by a significant increase in the expectations of a wide range of stakeholders that include consumers, employees, investors, communities, and governments regarding corporate houses' commitment to socially responsible business practices. As a natural corollary to these concerns is the corporate social responsibility (CSR) that is becoming a progressively more important component of good business practice with corporates increasingly pitching in for social cause.

CSR is like social investment which the corporate houses make. In other words, CSR is a set of voluntary actions that business houses undertake to address both their competitive interests and the interests of society. It's about how business takes account of its economic, social and environmental impacts in the way it operates, thus maximising the benefits and minimising the downsides. The concept of CSR, however, goes beyond the philanthropic gestures, *i.e.,* donating money to good causes at the end of the financial year. Rather it's an all year round responsibility that companies accept for the environment around them, for the best working practices, for their engagement in their local communities and for their recognition (read reputation).

"The concept of corporate social responsibility owes its origin to the economic transformation which the U.S. was undergoing in the beginning of the last century. There were growing demands from the media and pressure groups to the corporate big-wigs to share a part of their profits for social cause," says Abhishek Chaturvedi, business development manager of Jiva group, based in Faridabad. The onset of Rockefeller Foundation and Ford Foundation on the scene was the upshot of this pressure campaign, he adds. The Switzerland-based World Business Council for Sustainable

Development, a coalition of 160 international companies united by a shared commitment to sustainable development with members drawn from more than 30 countries, says as an engine for social progress, CSR helps companies live up to their responsibilities as global citizens and local neighbours in a fast-changing world.

CSR can be broadly categorised into two based on the nature of its application in different geographical settings. In the U.S. CSR has been defined much more in terms of a philanthropic model. This model explains that companies make profits and then they donate a certain share of the profits to charitable causes. It is seen as tainting the act for the company to receive any benefit from the giving. On the other hand, the European model is much more focused on operating the core business in a socially responsible way, complemented by investment in communities for solid business case reasons. In other words, in the European model social responsibility becomes the underlying aspect of the company's chase for profit, which eventually enhances the company's competitiveness and maximises wealth creation in society. An instance of how social and environmental performances of corporate houses are considered side by side with financial performance is best visible in China's Shenzhen city government's recent pronouncement that it may refuse to award contracts to companies that do not meet their social responsibilities. This is the first indication of how CSR is influencing decision makers in China, the global economic powerhouse.

❐ ❐ ❐

"Motivation theories provides a great deal of insight into the reasons that different individuals exhibit different behavioural patterns in an organisation." Leadership is behaviour and not about holding a position. People, who claim to be leaders in business are not chosen by their followers. They are selected by those above them and are expected to lead people by controlling them which is positionship and not leadership. Being chosen to manage a group does not qualify one as leader until the behaviour creates an environment of trust, commitment and service to followers.

To create a wining team, a leader should promote independent thinking in his people, encourage new ideas, show willingness to take risks, and inspire excellence and loyalty among his subordinates. Leaders must never forget the following when they run their organisaitons. We are what we repeatedly do. Excellence, then, is not an act, but a habit.

SEVEN

Motivation Theories of Entrepreneurship

Introduction

What makes people work? Why some people perform better than others? Perhaps one of the biggest questions confronting organisations today is the 'people' question. In fact, if you dig very deeply into any problem you will get to people. But how do we motivate, employees to achieve the goals of an organisation and at the same time satisfy the needs of employees. How to tap the latent human capability in organisation endeavours? Managers encounter an interesting problem here. The manager is responsible for completing a task. However, a manager alone cannot complete the task. The contributed efforts of subordinates are necessary and vital. A manager must stimulate people to action to accomplish the desired goals; he must fuse the varied individual human capacities and powers of the many people employed into a smoothly working team with high productivity. How do we get people to perform at a higher than 'normal' per cent of their physical and mental capacities and also maintain satisfaction? This is the challenge of motivation.

Motivation is an indispensable function of management. When man is at work, he cannot be forced to work like a machine. He is a human being who has his dignity, self-respect, values, sentiments and aspirations apart from the economic status. Under such circumstances the efficiency of the enterprise is related not merely to the efficiency of sophisticated machines installed but more importantly upon the satisfaction and the spontaneous desire of man to put his mind and heart into the work. This spontaneous urge to involve in work is not merely related to monetary awards or assignment of position or the direction to perform the duty or even the fear of punishment but to the mechanics and system of motivation.

The Concept

Motivation is an inspirational process which impels he members of the team, to pull their weight effectively, to give their loyalty to the group, to carry out properly the tasks that they have accepted and generally to plav an effective part in the job that the group has undertaken). It is the process of indoctrinating employees with unity of purpose and the need to maintain harmonious relationships among people. Managers cannot change people; they can only change behaviour.

Motivation encompasses complex aspects of human behaviour to which contribution has been made by sociologists, social anthropologists, psychologists and business executives. This concept has its roots in motives within a person which induce him to behave in a particular manner. Generally speaking, the concept of motivation is by and large psychological which "relates to those forces operating within the individual employee or subordinate which impel him to act or not to act in certain ways" —

'Motivation refers to the way in which urges, drives, desires, aspirations, strivings or needs direct, control or explain the behaviour of human beings."

This is a deep-seated definition of Motivation. It includes three things:

(*i*) The urges, drives, desires, aspirations, strivings or needs of human being influence human behaviour.

(*ii*) The factors which influence human behaviour — psychological, sociological, economic or managerial.

(*iii*) The efficiency of such behaviour — this may be tested by the resultant action. Whether this behaviour has directed, controlled or implemented the desired action.

If the entrepreneur feels motivated his behaviour will bring about the desired action.

Ability refers to skill and competence of the person to complete a given task. However, ability alone is not enough. The person's desire to accomplish the task is also necessary. Organisations become successful when employees have abilities and desire to accomplish given tasks.

Motivation in simple terms may be understood as the set of forces that cause people to behave in certain ways. The framework given in Fig.1 helps us to understand the nature of motivation better.

The framework (Fig. 1 comprises six steps. Motivation process, as shown in the Fig. 1, begins with the individual's needs (step 1). Needs are felt deprivations which the individual experiences at a given time and act as energizers. These needs may be psychological (*e.g.,* the need for recognition), physiological (*e.g.,* the need for water, air, or food), or social (*e.g.,* the need for friendship). These deprivations force the individual to search for ways to reduce or eliminate them (Step 2).

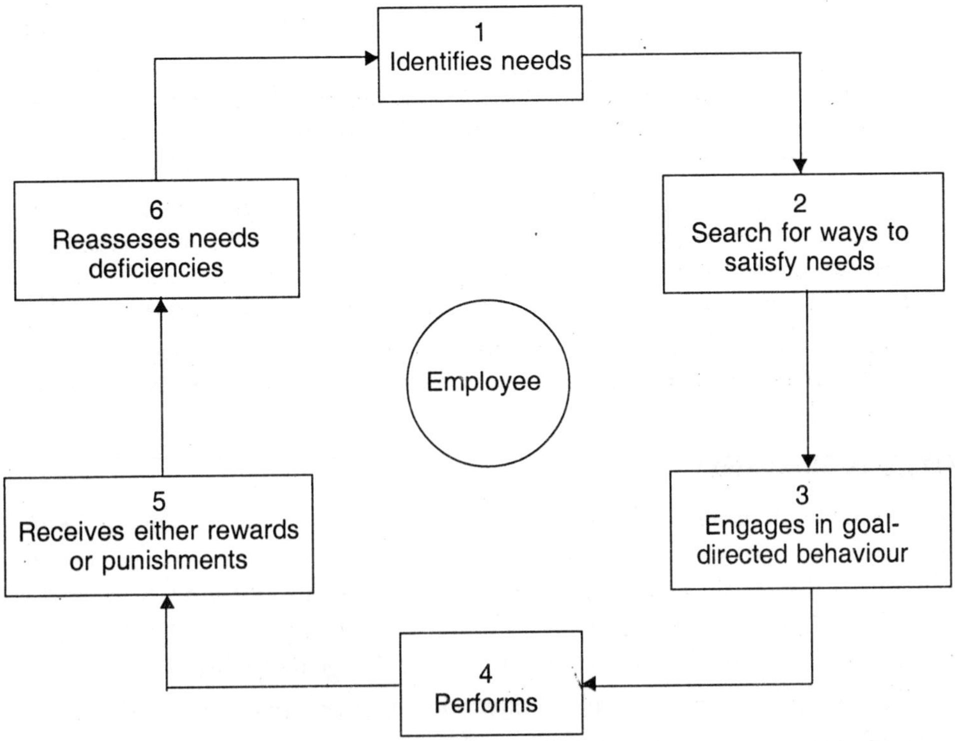

Fig. 1: Framework of Motivation

Motivation is goal directed (step 3). A goal is a specific result that the individual wants to achieve. An employee's goals are often driving forces and accomplishing those goals can significantly reduce needs. For example, some employees have strong drives for advancement and expectations that working long hours on visible projects will lead to promotions, and greater influence. Such needs and expectations often create uncomfortable tension within these individuals. Believing that certain specific behaviours can overcome this tension, these employees act to reduce it. Employees striving to advance may seek to work on major problems facing the organisation in order to gain visibility and influence with senior managers (step 4). Promotions and raises are two of the ways that organisation seek to maintain desirable behaviours. They are signals (feedback) to employees that their needs for advancement and recognition and their behaviours are appropriate (step 5). Once the employees have received either rewards or punishments, they reassess their needs (step 6).

Importance of Motivation

Interest in the topic of motivation in work organisations has escalated dramatically in recent years. Several factors appear to account for the prominence of this topic as a focal point of interest.

1. Managers and organisational researchers cannot avoid a concern with the behavioural requirements of an organisation. Every organisation needs people (in addition to physical and financial resources) in order to function.
2. Motivation as a concept is pervasive and a highly complex activity that affects and is affected by a host of factors in the organisational milieu.
3. Organisational effectiveness becomes to some degree a question of management's ability to motivate its employees, to direct atleast a reasonable effort toward the goals of the organisation.
4. As technology increases in complexity, machines tend to become necessary, yet insufficient vehicles of effective and efficient operations. In other words, it becomes necessary for an organisation to ensure that it has employees who are both capable of using and willing to use the advanced technology to achieve organisational goals.
5. Many organisations are now beginning to pay increasing attention to developing their employees as future resources (or talent bank) upon which they can draw as they grow and develop.

Nature of Motivation

In terms of its derivation, the word motivate means to move, to activate. In this general sense, anything, that initiates activity whether external or internal, is motivating. Today, the term means a lot more than this. Motivating is the work of a manager performs to inspire, encourage and impel people to take required action. Some of the widely quoted definitions are given below:

1. Motivation is a predisposition to act in a specific goal-directed way.
2. The immediate influences on the direction, vigor and persistence of action.
3. Steering one's actions toward certain goals and committing a certain part of one's energies to reach them."
4. How behaviour gets started, is energized, is sustained, is directed, is stopped and what kind of subjective reaction is present in the organism while all this is going on."

All these definitions contain three common aspects of the motivation process: What energizes human behaviour? What directs or channels such behaviour? How this behaviour is maintained or sustained? The process of motivation is characterized by the following:

(a) Motivation is an internal feeling: Motivation points to energetic forces within individuals that drive them to behave in certain ways and to environmental forces that trigger these drives.

(b) Motivation produces goal-directed behaviour: (Motivation has got a profound influence on human behaviour, it harnesses human energy to organisational requirements) There is the notion of goal orientation on the part of individuals, their behaviour is directed towards something.

(c) Motivation contains systems orientation: It considers in those forces in the individuals and in their surrounding environments that feedback to the individuals either to reinforce the intensity of their drive and the direction of this energy or to dissuade them from their cause of action and redirect their efforts.

(d) Motivation can be either positive or negative: Positive motivation or the carrot approach, offers something precious to the person in the form of additional pay, incentives, praise etc., for satisfactory performance. Negative motivation or stick approach emphasizes penalties while controlling performance (reprimands, threat of demotion).

(e) Motivation means bargaining: Behaviour is what people DO. Motivation is WHY they do it. Barnard explained motivation in the form of 'inducements-contribution' theory." It focuses on workers and organisations endeavouring to find what payouts (inducements) to workers in exchange for what degree of cooperation (contributions) from workers will be satisfactory to both parties. The problem of motivation then becomes one of arriving at compensation to workers that will coax them the output that is required."

(f) Motivation is a complete process. Five reasons can be provided in support of this statement:

(*i*) First, motive is a hypothetical construct. It cannot be seen. Often we observe individuals putting a great deal of overtime. We cannot definitely state whether they are doing it because of additional income they receive or simply because they enjoy their work.

(*ii*) Individuals may have a host of needs that are continuously changing, and, sometimes, in conflict with each other. As a result, it becomes exceedingly difficult to observe or measure motivation with certainty.

(*iii*) People satisfy their needs in many different ways. A salesman may work hard to earn money; a second salesman may be spurred by his achievement motive and so on. By simply observing sales persons in action it is not easy to differentiate between these groups.

(*iv*) Promoting an employee to a new and more challenging task may intensify the drive to work harder in anticipation of the next promotion. Thus, gratification of a particular need may gradually lead to an increase in its intensity.

(*v*) Finally, goal-directed behaviour does not always lead to need satisfaction.

(g) Motivation and satisfaction are related but not synonymous concepts: (Motivation is the drive to satisfy a want or goal. It is concerned with goal-directed behaviour. Satisfaction refers to the contentment experiences when a want is satisfied). The term 'satisfaction' is used to analyse outcomes already experienced by an employee. Satisfaction is a consequence of rewards and punishments associated with past experience.

Motivation Process: A Generalized Model

The basic building blocks of a generalized model of motivation are: (*i*) behaviour (*ii*) motives (*iii*) goals and (*iv*) some form of feedback, as shown below.

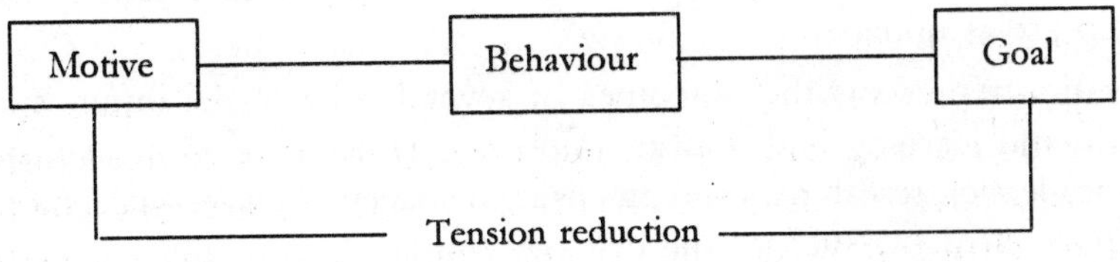

Fig. 2: Motivation Process: A Generalized Model

Behaviour: All behaviour is a series of activities. *Behaviour is generally motivated by a desire to achieve a goal.* At any moment individuals may indulge in multifarious activities like walking, talking, eating and the like. They switch over from one activity to another activity swiftly. In order to predict and control behaviour managers must understand the motives of people.

Motives: *(Needs/drives/wants). Motives prompt people to action.* They are the primary energizers of behaviour. They are the 'whys' of behaviour; mainsprings of action. They are largely subjective and represent the mental feelings of human beings. They are cognitive variables. They cause behaviour in many ways. They arise continuously and determine the general direction of an individual's behaviour.

Goals: Motives are directed toward goals. Motives generally, create a state of disequilibrium, physiological or psychological imbalance, within the individuals. *Attaining a goal will tend to restore physiological or psychological balance. Goals are the ends which provide satisfaction of human wants.* They are outside an individual; they are hoped for incentives toward which needs are directed. One person may satisfy his need for power by beating his wife and children, another by kicking subordinates and a third by becoming the president of a company. Thus, a need can be satisfied by several alternate goals. The particular goals chosen by an individual depends on four factors: (*i*) the cultural norms and values that are instilled as one matures, (*ii*) one's inherited, biological capabilities, (*iii*) personal experience and learning influences and (*iv*) mobility in the physical and social environment.

The Starting Point

Need is the starting point of motivation. A satisfied need does not motivate an individual. It is only the unsatisfied need which creates tension and stimulate drives within the individuals for the satisfaction of the need and reduction of tension. The efforts or actions initiated by the individual will yield results which will lead to satisfaction of need or removal of tension. Classical theorists and scientific management thinkers were of the opinion that people were mainly interested in maximising economic gains as they were primarily concerned with satisfying their basic needs of food, water, air, shelter etc. Thus, they tried to link up performance and productivity with monetary rewards or incentives. F.W. Taylor, father of Scientific Management proposed Differential Piece rate system for motivating workers to work at their level best. The traditional thinkers were mainly concerned with the monetary reward and were treating human beings as mere machines, which do not have any inner feelings or emotions. Under Hawthorne Experiments it was proved that there was no direct relationship between productivity and economic rewards.' Money is an essential condition but not a sufficient one for motivating people to work. Human beings are not machines and they have also social and psychological needs.

Various researchers are actively engaged in finding answer to one basic question *i.e.,* What motivates people? or what makes them work? Various theories have been propounded by different experts to focus attention on this basic issue. Prominent and relatively more relevant to entrepreneurship are as under:

- Motivation represents the outcomes of several behavioural inputs such as perception, attitude and learning and it is an important concept receiving considerable attention from academics, researchers and practising managers. In its essence, motivation comprises important elements such as the need or content, search and choice of strategies, goal directed behaviour, social comparison of rewards, reinforcement, performance and satisfaction.

- The increasing attention paid towards motivation is justified because of several reasons. Motivated employees come out with new ways of doing jobs. They are quality oriented. They are more productive. Any technology needs motivated employees to adopt it successfully.
- Several approaches to motivation are available. Early theories are too simplistic in their approach towards motivation. For example, advocates of Scientific Management believe that money is the motivating factor. The Human Relations Movement posits that social contacts will motivate workers.

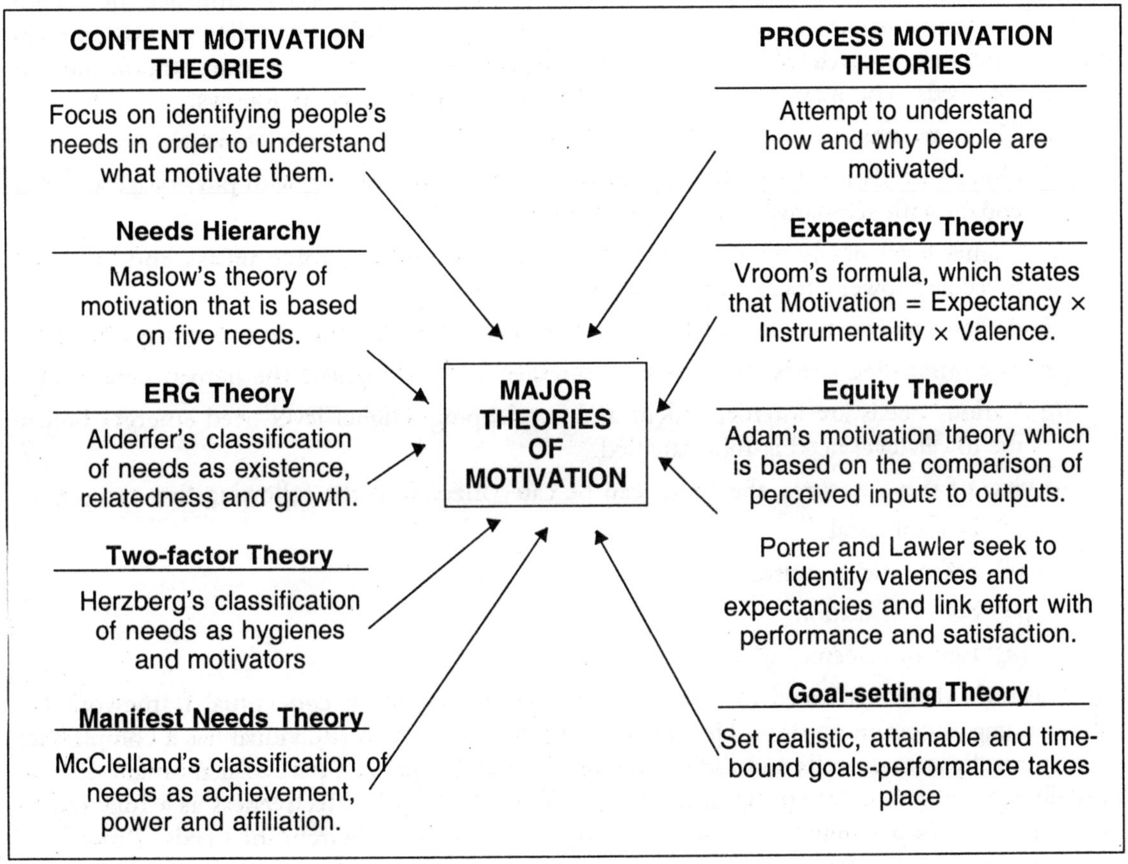

Fig. 3: Motivational Theories

The distinctive features of the following motivational theories are discussed.

1. Need Hierarchy Theory (Maslow)
2. ERG Theory (Clay Alderfer)
3. Two-Factor Theory (Fredrick Herzberg)
4. Expectancy Theory (V.H. Vroom)

5. Theory of X vs. Y (Douglas McGregor)
6. Goal Setting Theory
7. Achievement Motivation Theory (David C. McClelland)
8. Psychoanalytic Theory — Sigmund Feud
9. Social Learning Theory
10. The Humanistic Approach.

MASLOW'S NEED HIERARCHY THEORY

Abraham H. Maslow, an eminent American psychologist, propounded a general theory of motivation named *Need Hierarchy Theory.* This theory is important enough to influence the human behaviour in many aspects as per the satisfaction of human needs. According to him, human needs are complex, interrelated and everchanging in nature and thus, there exist stratification or hierarchy of needs. The main features of this theory can be depicted as follows:

(*a*) The inner urge to fulfil needs is the fundamental factor in entrepreneurial motivation.

(*b*) Human needs form a particular structure of hierarchy starting with physiological needs ending with self-actualisation needs via other needs.

(*c*) Higher-level needs do not become an active motivating force unless and until the preceding lower-order needs are satisfied.

(*d*) As soon as one need is satisfied, another need crops up and this process continues.

(*e*) The unsatisfied needs are the basic ingredients which regulate the human behaviour.

(*f*) Various needs are interdependent and overlapping. Higher-level need emerges before the lower-level need is fully satisfied.

In view of these features, the needs can be categorized into the following five categories:

(*i*) Physiological

(*ii*) Safety and security

(*iii*) Social affiliation

(*iv*) Ego or esteem.

Maslow's theory is based on human needs. He developed a conceptual framework for understanding human motivation. He was of the opinion that every individual has a complex set of exceptionally strong needs and the behaviour of an individual at a particular moment of time is usually determined by his strongest need. He defined a person's effectiveness as a function of matching man's opportunity with the appropriate position of hierarchy of needs. Process of motivation begins with the assumption that the behaviour, atleast in part, is directed towards the achievement or the satisfaction of needs. Maslow feel that the 'needs have a definite sequence of domination'. Second need does not dominate till first need is reasonably satisfied and third need does not dominate until first two needs have been reasonably satisfied. Man is never fully satisfied, if one need is satisfied the other will arise and so on. Once a need or certain order of needs is satisfied, it ceases to be a motivating factor. Maslow stated that human beings have five basic levels of needs, which they tend to satisfy in a hierarchial manner. He proposed that human needs can be arranged in a particular order from the lower level needs to the highest level needs. This hierarchy of human needs can be shown in the following figure.

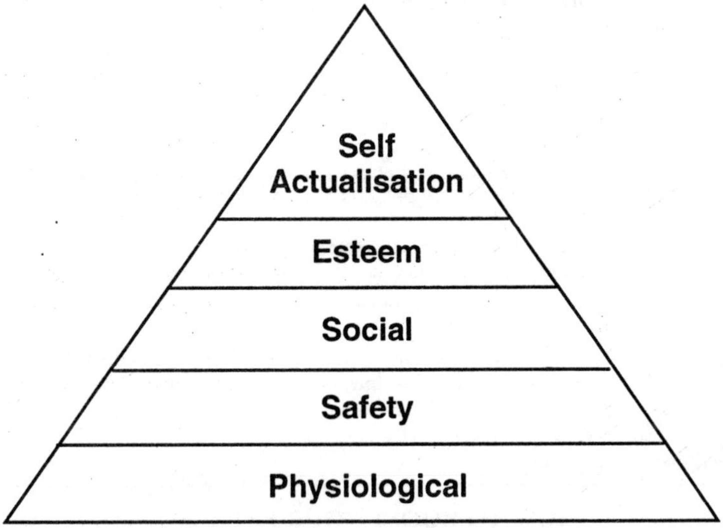

Fig. 4: Maslow's Need Hierarchy

According to Maslow, an individual shall graduate to a higher need only after his lower order needs have been satisfied.

These five needs can be discussed as follows :

(i) Physiological Needs: These needs are basic and are related to survival and maintenance of life. These needs comprise of food water, air, shelter, clothing and other necessities of life. The first priority of human beings is to acquire these basic necessities of life and then move to second level of needs.

(ii) Safety and Security Needs: After satisfying physiological needs, human beings aim at satisfying safety and security needs. Human beings are not content with just satisfying present physiological needs, they want to make provision for the same for future also. They want job security, personal body security, security of source of income, provision for old age, insurance against risk's etc. Entrepreneurs just like other human beings are guided by all these factors.

(iii) Social Needs: Man is a social animal and wants to belong to a social group where his social and emotional needs for love, affection, warmth and friendship are satisfied. An entrepreneur too is interested in conversation, exchange of feelings & grievances with fellow entrepreneurs, his employees and others. He wants to belong to others and expects that others should belong to him *i.e.,* the feeling of belongingness.

(iv) Esteem Needs: These needs include self respect, self confidence, recognition, appreciation, prestige, power & control. These are also known as egoistic needs and affect prestige and status of individuals. Entrepreneur derive status and respect through their ownership and control over their business.

Box - 1

IMPORTANCE OF SELF ESTEEM

Having high self-esteem is very important. It pays to have a positive attitude and value yourself. Be convinced of your abilities and competence; believe in yourself and recognise your strengths. Self-esteem is important for normal psychological development. You have to believe that you can achieve what you want to, and that you deserve happiness and joy.

High self-esteem can act as a cushion against feeling of rejection, disappointments and failures. Being confident helps you take up challenges. A person with high self-esteem will be able to look people in the eye, which in turn gets a positive response from others. Besides, such persons are less likely to engage in self-destructive behaviour like alcohol and drug abuse, violence and crime.

A negative self image often leads to feelings of helplessness, powerlessness and at times, even depression. Lacking clear direction and goals makes it difficult to take up initiatives and trying anything new or challenging.

- Believe in yourself and recognise your strengths.
- High self-esteem can act as a cushion against the feeling of rejection, disappointments and failures.
- Examine the circumstances that make you feel low, and try to understand the reasons for them.
- Always set achievable goals for a specific time frame. Success is the best esteem booster.
- Listen to others' point of view and solicit feedback.
- Sit back, Idled and analyse your acts.

HOW TO BOOST YOUR ESTEEM

- Exploring what self-esteem means to you and its effects on your behaviour and actions can be helpful in identifying the causes of esteem.
- Examine the circumstances that make you feel low, and try to understand the reasons for them.

  If you are not fairing well in your job, think about what's holding you back. Why are you unable to put in your best? The reasons could be anything from your boss, a disturbing colleague or even a complete dislike for the work you are doing! Think about solutions to the problem. Ignoring a problem will not give you the solution. You could probably have a chat with the colleague or if you think you aren't enjoying the work, there are ample of other opportunities to think of.
- Always set achievable goals for a specific time frame. Failing to deliver often leads to low self esteem. So, next time, be practical and set competent deadlines that you can meet. Do not commit to something you know you cannot achieve. First, assess the tasks at hand, and the deadlines you have set for these tasks. Success is the best esteem booster.
- Be organised and clear about what you want to do. In a demanding situation, think, prioritise and take a call before you act. For example, if you have to choose between two offers, analyse the pros and cons of both before you decide. Ensure that you don't regret the decision later.
- Regularly, take up tasks that you're good at. If you are good at sketching, come up with something creative. It adds to the 'feel good' factor. Show it to your friends. The appreciation you get will help boost yourself. Listing down activities and challenges that can act as esteem builders is very helpful.
- Always take responsibility for your actions, especially those that purposefully enhance your self-image. Nevertheless, even if you make a mistake, accept it. It leaves a positive impact on others.
- Listen to others' point of view and solicit feedback that can be helpful as a means of gauging your own performance or establishing your own system of ranking. It is important to be open to criticism. Accept negative feedback in a positive manner. Think of it as a step towards improvement. Criticism contributes to overall growth and development of an individual.
- Giving yourself enough time and space is very important. Sit back, reflect and analyse your acts. When something goes wrong, instead of analysing what went wrong, think about what went right.
- Taking calculated risk can be a win-win situation as it boosts your self-esteem. Taking a risk in one area and succeeding can have an impact on other areas of life.
- Changing something about yourself can make you feel better. Buy yourself new clothes, don a new look, hang out with friends, take a break and pamper yourself. Accomplishing something small that you have been avoiding, making a list of your strengths can enhance self-esteem.
- Last but not the least, do not hesitate to visit a counsellor to help you boost your self esteem. It is important to talk about your concerns.

(v) Self-actualisation or Self-fulfilment needs: This is the ultimate goal and involves realising one's potentialities for continued self development. After other needs are fulfilled a man has the desire for personal achievement. He want to do something which is challenging and since this challenge gives him enough push and initiative to work. It is beneficial to him and the society. The sense of achievement gives him psychological satisfaction. An entrepreneur can achieve self actualization in being a successful entrepreneur.

For the development of entrepreneurship last three in the hierarchy *i.e.,* social, esteem and self-actualisation are more important.

Maslow was of the opinion that people put emphasis on lower-level needs and then proceed to higher-level needs in a step-by-step approach. Satisfied need ceases to be a motivator while unsatisfied needs regulate an individual's behaviour.

Merits of the theory

The merits of Maslow's theory are as follows:

(*a*) This theory is easy to understand.

(*b*) This theory is generally applicable to a wide range of culture.

(*c*) This theory is capable enough to explain how needs influence human behaviour and motivate the human beings to chalking out their work plans.

(*d*) This theory gives an opportunity to the entrepreneurs and the managers to understand the needs of the people at different levels and to motivate them according to their needs.

Criticism

Maslow's Need Priority Model of motivation has gained extensive popularity because of its simplicity and logical explanation. This theory also explains how human behaviour differs in two similar situations. Nevertheless, there is little impartial support for it because its proposition could not be vigorously tested through empirical research. However, the theory is widely criticised for the following reasons:

(*a*) The theory does not give any scientific explanation or tool for measuring needs.

(*b*) The theory gives an oversimplification of human needs and motivation.

(*c*) Not everyone strives for higher-level needs.

(*d*) The hierarchy of needs is not always fixed. It varies from person to person, place to place and time to time. For example, in case of creative people like singers, artists, etc., self-actualisation need may be a dominant force even before the lower-order needs are fulfilled. Similarly, the need priorities of the same individual may change over a period of time.

(*e*) Motivation and needs are not directly linked. The same need may lead to different types of behaviour in different individuals.

(*f*) Deprivation of needs may not necessarily motivate, it may cause depression also.

Inspite of the criticism; Maslow's theory has a commonsense appeal for all managers and entrepreneurs. The theory provides a deep insight into the concept of need and its relation to human behaviour.

Evaluation of the Theory: Advantages of the ERG theory are as follows:

- First, The ERG theory is more consistent with our knowledge of individual differences among people. Variables such as education, family background and cultural environment can alter the importance or driving force that a group of needs holds for a particular individual. The evidence demonstrates that people in other cultures rank the need categories differently, for instance, natives of Spain and Japan place social needs before their psychological requirements. This would be consistent with the ERG theory. The ERG theory, therefore, represents a more valid version of the need hierarchy.
- Second, although there is some evidence to counter the theory's predictive value, most contemporary analysis of work motivation tends to support Alderfer's theory over Maslow's and Herzberg's. Overall, the ERG theory seems to take some of the strong points of the earlier content theories, but is less restrictive and limiting.

Disadvantages of the theory are as follows

The theory does not offer clear cut guidelines. The ERG theory implies that individuals will be motivated to engage in behaviour which will satisfy one of the three sets of needs postulated by the theory. In order to predict what behaviour any given person will be motivated to engage in would require an assessment of that person to determine which of the three needs were most salient and most important to that person. The individuals would then be predicted to engage in behaviour which would lead to the attainment of outcomes, with the capacity of fulfilling these salient needs.

Research on Alderfer's modifications to Maslow's theory has been supportive. Both laboratory and field studies have generated support for Alderfer's three categories and their hierarchical fulfillment relationship. Other studies have supported Alderfer's seemingly paradoxical contention that strength of need will increase when a need is either highly satisfied or highly unsatisfied.

Alderfer's theory appeared to be encouraging for organisations seeking to motivate employees.

Evaluation of the Theory

Comparatively, ERG theory received more support than Maslow's, but many problems remained unsolved. The psychological and/or physiological basis of needs was still unclear and nebulous. The question why do people engage in behaviour that is seemingly unrelated to need fulfillment theory has also not achieved any significant breakthrough. The unanswered questions which are still being raised are:

- Can managers "instill" certain needs, to motivate employees?
- Are employees who are trying to satisfy existence needs less productive than employees striving to satisfy growth needs?
- What advice can an employee be offered for improving his performance on the basis of his needs?
- The theory although failed to be of much practical value, stimulated further thoughts and efforts in research in this area.

ERG Theory: A modification of Maslow's need hierarchy was proposed by Clay Alderfer. Alderfer's views on motivation arose from the results of questionnaires he gave to over 100 employees at several levels in a bank. Alderfer's work led him to propose that there are three (rather than Maslow's five) primary categories of human needs. These categories are:

(a) Existence: The basic physiological needs (hunger and thirst) and protection from physical danger.

(b) Relatedness: Social and affiliation needs and the need for respect and positive regard from others.

(c) Growth: The need to develop and realise one's potential.

By establishing these broader categories of human needs, Alderfer retained the idea of a hierarchy of needs, but offered a less rigid version of Maslow's "satisfaction-progression" hypothesis. For example, since Maslow's social and esteem needs are together in Alderfer's ERG model under the umbrella of "relatedness" needs, neither takes fulfillment precedence over the other.

Where Maslow proposed "satisfaction-progression" model, Alderfer came out with "frustration-regression" hypothesis. If fulfillment of a higher order need is blocked — if something prevents the higher — order need from being fulfilled — an individual's attention will regress back towards fulfillment of needs lower in the hierarchy. For instance, if relatedness needs are relatively fulfilled but growth — need fulfillment is blocked, an individual's attention will return to fulfillment of relatedness needs. Besides, Alderfer's ERG theory assumes that growth needs become more rather than less important as they become fulfilled.

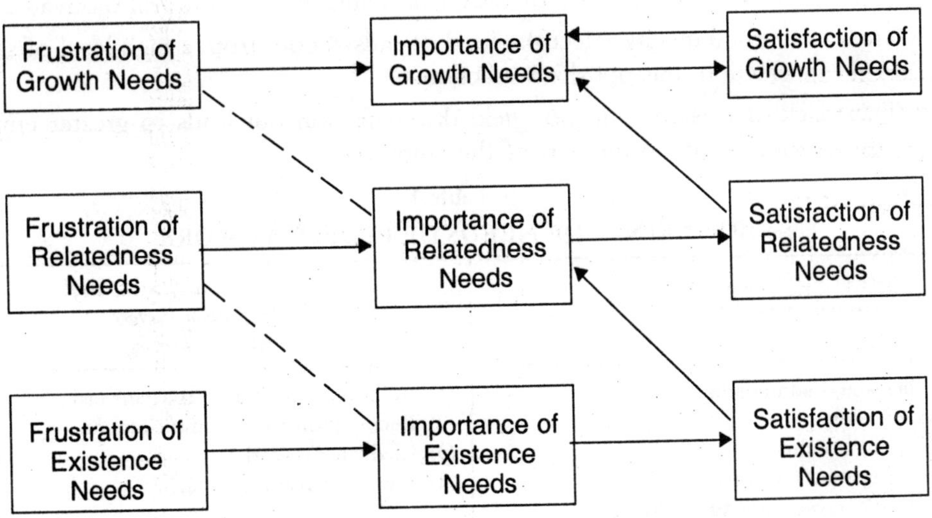

Fig. 5: Two Key Components of ERG Theory:

Satisfaction — Progression and Frustration-Regression

(*Source:* Richard M. Hodgetts, *Organisational Behaviour*, MacMillan, 1991, p. 134).

Two-factor Theory of Herzberg

It is the last of the content theories we are discussing in this part of the chapter. It differentiates itself in a separate sub-category from need theories in that it treats 'need' somewhat differently from them.

The theory is also known as Motivation-Hygiene theory. It was originally developed by Fredrick Herzberg with the help of his associates in the late 1950s as a theory of job-satisfaction. It was adopted by him as a motivational theory later. We shall concentrate on the contributions and controversies regarding Herzberg's theory as a motivation theory at present.

Statement of the Theory: The essence of the theory may be stated as follows:

Human needs are grouped into two sets — one the maintenance needs, and the other, the motivation needs.

Maintenance needs relate to factors in the job situation (extrinsic to the job). These factors are noted as "dissatisfiers". They have the following characteristics:

(*a*) If they *exist* in a work environment in high quantity and quality, they yield no dissatisfaction.

(*b*) Their *existence* does not yield satisfaction nor do they *motivate.*

(*c*) Their *lack* of existence would, however, result in *dissatisfaction.*

Motivation needs relate to factors inherent in job (intrinsic to the job) itself. These factors are noted as "motivators". They have the following characteristics:

(*a*) Their existence yields a sense of satisfaction and they are the real motivators.

(*b*) Their extent and quality affect the level of satisfaction, from a high level of satisfaction to no satisfaction, but not dissatisfaction.

(*c*) Their lack of existence do not yield dissatisfaction but leads to greater emphasis on maintenance needs on the part of the employees.

Table 1

TWO KINDS OF NEEDS OF PEOPLE AT WORK

Hygiene or Maintenance Factors *Environmental Needs*	*Needs intrinsic to work itself* *Motivation Factors* *(Real motivators)*
(1) Policies and administration (2) Supervision (3) Working conditions (4) Interpersonal relations — Boss, Peer, Subordinates. (5) Money — Wages, Salaries. (6) Status and Security. (Negative feelings towards the job)	(1) Achievement of an important task. (2) Recognition for accomplishment. (3) Challenging work. (4) Increased responsibility. (5) Opportunity for growth and development (Positive feelings towards the job).

Comments

(1) Herzberg calls factors leading to dissatisfaction as 'Hygiene or Maintenance' factors. If absent, these make employees feel exceptionally bad. Note that they are extrinsic, *i.e.,* they come

from outside the person. When they are adequate, they merely prevent dissatisfaction. These factors correspond to Maslow's lower level needs. (2) Factors leading to satisfaction are termed as motivators. They are the causes of job satisfaction. If present, these make employees feel exceptionally good. Note that these factors are intrinsic. *i.e.,* they come from inside the person. They lead to motivation when you build them into the way you manage. (3) Theory X assumptions of human beings lead to Herzberg's hygiene factors or dissatisfiers mentioned above. (4) Theory Y assumptions of human beings lead to Herzberg's satisfiers or motivators. (5) Herzberg's approach to motivation is applicable to affluent or richer countries. (6) According to two-factor theory of

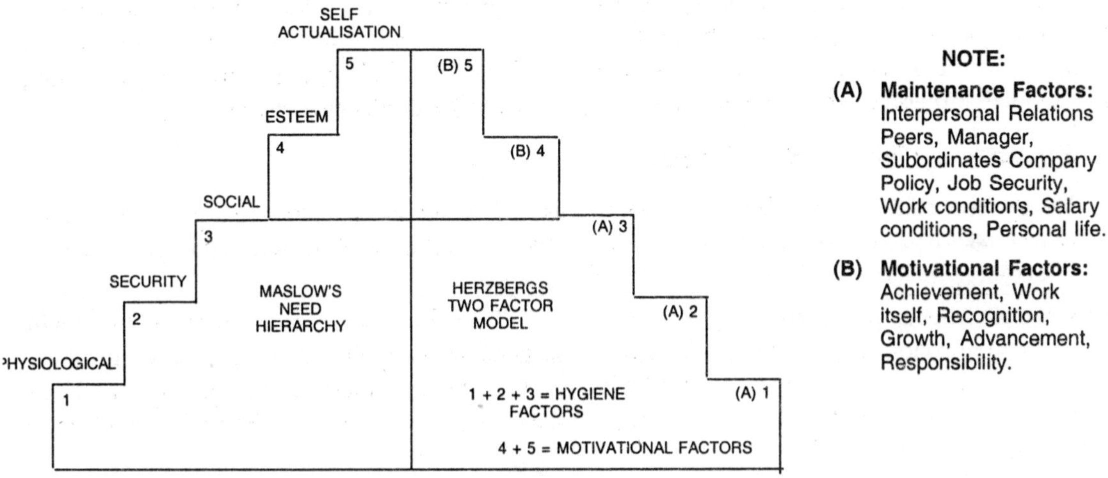

Fig. 6: A Comparison of Maslow and Herzberg Models

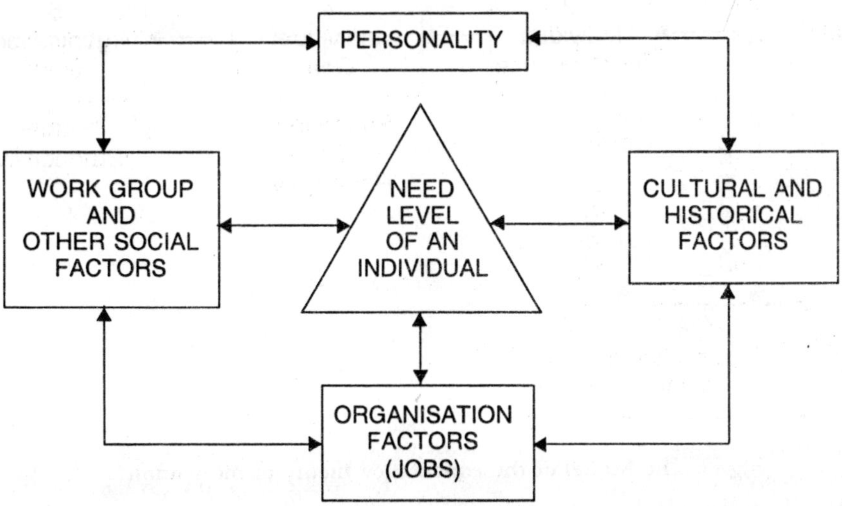

Fig. 7: Forces influencing Human Behaviour (Motivation)

Note: The major factors leading to the development of a hierarchy of needs for any person are dynamic and mutually interacting. Each acts on the person's need hierarchy and on all the others.

motivation developed by Herzberg, money is a hygienic factor and not a motivator. In India, however, money is still a motivator. (7) It should be noted that improving work environment, raising wages and salaries, offering social security, maintaining good human relations, etc., cannot achieve greater output, efficiency, and productivity under Herzberg's approach to motivation. Of course, we may have the result in the form of peace, less conflict, but no satisfaction or motivation. In Herzberg's terms, satisfaction is equal to motivation. No satisfaction, means no motivation. Unhygienic environment creates dissatisfaction. Hygienic environment, fair wages, means no dissatisfaction.

Maslow refers to needs and motives. Herzberg deals with goals and incentives necessary for satisfying these needs. Money and benefits satisfy needs at physiological and security levels. Interpersonal relations and supervision satisfy social needs. Challenging work, responsibility, growth, development satisfy needs at esteem (ego) and self-actualisation levels.

Expectancy Theory of V.H. Vroom

Vroom combined a number of variables into his theory. He emphasized the role of expectation in motivating the employees of an enterprise to higher levels of individual performance or productivity.

Vroom's theory gave stress on five elements. These five elements interact in the chain. Activities or behaviour of a worker is linked to the goal of an organisation. The diagram given below demonstrates the inter-relationships between the five variables: (1) Individual activity or behaviour; (2) Organisational reward; (3) Individual performance; (4) Individual goal; (5) Organisational goal.

Force (Motivation) = Expectancy × Valance (attitude/incentive).

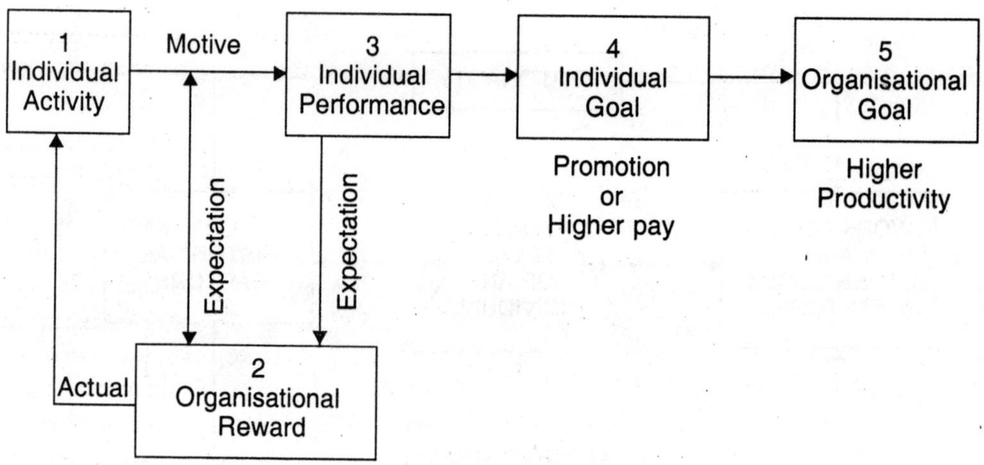

Fig. 8: The Model of the expectancy theory of motivation

The working of the chain of five variables:

1. The individual activity leads to individual performance through motivation.
2. The individual performance seeks (expects) organisational reward,
3. The organisational reward (actual) conditions the activities of the individual.

If an individual wants to be promoted (personal goal), his motivation to perform well is directly influenced by the degree to which he believes high productivity (the goal of the organisation) will assist him in being promoted. Thus, the more a person is convinced that promotion is both desirable and likely to result from the good performance, the greater will be his motivation to increase his productivity.

Activity, motive and performance are the three components of the total chain and these variables form a loop which works in a circular manner either strengthening or weakening the direct movement of the chain ⟶ (Activity – Motive – Performance).

There is also a subloop, (Activity – Motive – Reward) within the main loop,. The activity is linked to motive through reward — expected and actual reward.

Please note that the individual performance is directed to accomplish the individual goal. Then again, the organisational goal must be reached, through the individual goal. This link clearly points out that the individual objective should match or coincide with the organisational (managerial) goal. Similarly, group goals must match with the enterprise goals in order to secure high group performance, and thereby high productivity.

Vroom's theory takes into account the person's expectations regarding the accomplishment of the task. If a person sees that effort will lead to accomplishing task and if that person sees that accomplishing task leads to important outcome (such as satisfying a need for a status, pay raise, promotion, recognition, etc.), then motivation takes place and the person is induced to show the maximum performance productivity.

Individual performance is conditioned by the expectation of its contribution to his personal goal. Thus, it is clear that productivity or high performance is not an end but it is merely a means to an end (the end is personal goal).

If the employee is convinced and strongly believes (expects) that his performance will lead to achievement of his goal, *i.e.,* his expected reward and advancement, he shall be motivated to put in maximum efforts and achieve the planned performance.

The chain of high performance — high reward — rising degree of motivation, will be continued as long as the expected performance or contribution secures accomplishment of the personal goal, i.e., expected reward.

Vroom's theory is in line with the concept of harmony of objective and it fits with the fundamental principle of leadership, *viz.,* integration of organisational objective and individual goal for getting optimum performance or productivity. Individual goals can be harmonised with organisational objective. This is the challenge to leadership. Vroom's theory of motivation is completely in agreement with the entire system of management by objective. Theory Y of McGregor also emphasises the integration of individual and organisational objectives.

If the interest of the group (to which an individual belongs) is against organisational goal of high productivity (for example, the group feels that moderate productivity will help larger employment), productivity may not really improve through monetary reward (productivity bonus) or through satisfaction of other traditional needs indicated in Maslow's need hierarchies. The need for harmony of individual group goal and organisational objective, clearly indicates the importance of informal organisation and the need to integrate formal an informal organisation goals. Vroom's theory is also a contingency model of motivation.

Motivation Model of Smith and Cranny

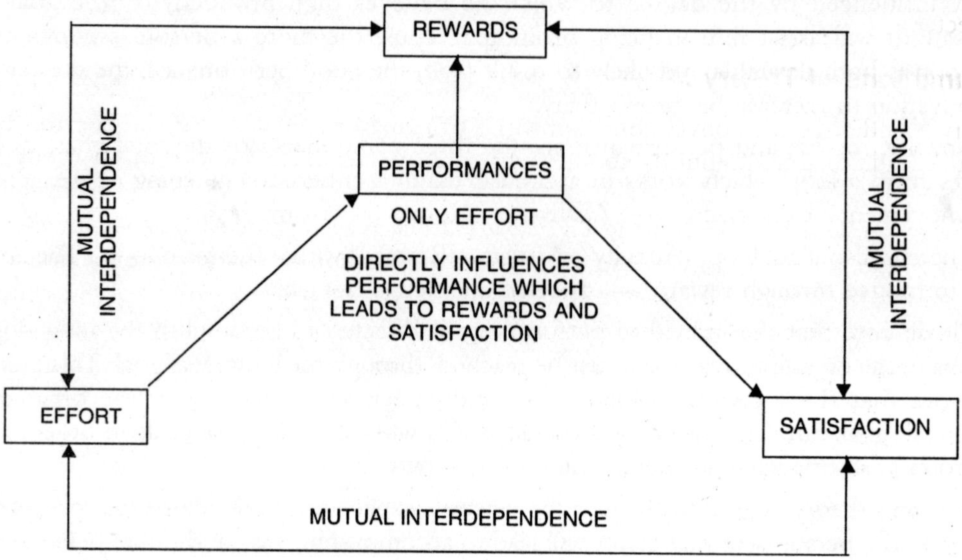

Fig. 9: Expectancy Model of Motivation: Smith and Cranny

Smith and Cranny have proposed a simple three way relationship among: (1) effort; (2) satisfaction; (3) reward — the three variables in the process of motivation. Each variable occupies the corner of a triangle. Each variable has a causal effect on the other, either individually, or in combination. For instance, praise or appreciation from a manager (reward) may lead to enhanced satisfaction or morale, or a satisfied employee doing the job very efficiently may invite praise or recognition from the manager.

The real key to this model lies in the concept of effort. Performance is affected only by effort, not by reward or satisfaction. Performance occupies the central area of the model. Performance can influence both the rewards and satisfaction; but it in itself can be influenced only by effort.

This model is easy to understand and apply. It emphasises that manager's responsibility is to administer rewards but it clearly points out this alone does not have a direct impact on performance. Effort satisfaction after rewards are interrelated and also interdependent. But it is only effort (not reward or satisfaction) that directly affects performance.

Note: Human relations advocates thought that satisfaction causes better performance. This model points out that performance causes satisfaction rather than the other way round.

Theory X Vs. Theory Y (Human Behaviour)

Assumptions about People: Douglas McGregor in his *The Human Side of Enterprise* has developed two theories to explain human behaviour and two sharply opposite concepts of leadership and management style for motivation and human behaviour which he calls Theory X and Theory Y. Essentially, Theory X builds on the lower order of human needs. Theory Y assumes that once these are met, they no longer can act as motivators. Human behaviour is based on the three interrelated assumptions: (1) Behaviour is caused. (2) Behaviour is motivated. (3) Behaviour is goal directed.

Assumptions of Theory X

Theory X indicates the conventional approach to managerial motivation and control. It is based on the traditional assumptions about human behaviour, *i.e.*, behaviour of an economic man. Theory X visualises the workers as inherently lazy, passive and unambitious. The assumptions of human behaviour under theory X are given below: (1) The average human being has an inherent dislike of work and will avoid it if he can. (2) Because of the human characteristic of dislike of work, most people must be coerced, controlled, directed, motivated by fear or threat of punishment or threat of unemployment to get them to put in adequate effort toward the achievement of organisational objectives. Some kind of carrot and stick or club has to be held over their heads to make sure that they do work as per plans. (3) The average human being prefers to be directed, wishes to avoid responsibility, has relatively little ambition, and wants security above all.

These negative assumptions underlie the assembly line and mechanisation of people as well as processes. The world is supposed to be full of peons and messengers and managing them is largely a matter of vigilance and strict supervision. Management merely thinks of catering to their physical and safety needs with some fringe benefits, keeping the implied threat of punishment or unemployment handy in case of need.

Theory X is built on the least common human denominator the factory "Hand' of the past, who could be hired and fired, used and discarded just like any other commodity by management. The management adopted the carrot and stick technique for human motivation. Theory X represented the autocratic managerial style. The leadership practices attributed to the Scientific management advocates are thought to be based on the Theory X assumptions. The customary management pyramid describing superior-subordinate relationship reflects Theory X.

Theory Y

The central principle of organisation based on Theory X is that of direction and control through autocratic and/or bureaucratic management, *i.e.*, through the exercise of authority-responsibility indicated by the chain of command and the scalar principle. Theory X is associated with mental sickness, while Theory Y with mental health. Theory X believes in negative motivation, while Theory Y believes in positive and intrinsic motivation. Theory X believes In bureaucracy, while Theory Y believes in democracy. Mentally healthier people will opt for Theory Y while sick will prefer Theory X.

Assumptions of Theory Y are derived from facts of life uncovered by objective behaviour and research. It recognises the interdependence of the leader and the led and reflects the current scientific understanding of what people at work are really like — organisational behaviour or dynamic nature of people.

Assumptions about people: Theory X	Assumptions about people: Theory Y
(1) People are by nature indolent. (2) They lack ambition, dislike responsibility, prefer to be led. (3) They are self-centred, indifferent to organisatlonal needs. (4) They are by nature resistant to change. (5) They are not very bright and lack creativity.	(1) People are ambitious. (2) They seek responsibility. (3) They are dynamic and flexible. (4) They recognise and accept organisational goals. (5) They are intelligent and possess creative potential.
We have conservative style of management under Theory X assumptions.	We have liberal style of management under Theory Y assumptions.

Assumptions of Theory 'Y'

(1) The expenditure of physical and mental effort in work is as natural as in play or rest: Work, if meaningful, should be a source of satisfaction and it can be voluntarily performed. There is no inherent like or dislike of work. A man develops an attitude towards it on his personal experience with it.

(2) Man will exercise self-control and self-direction in the service of objectives to which be is committed: External control or threat of punishment is not the only means of motivating people to work and achieve company goals. Authoritarian methods are not the only methods for getting things done. There is nothing inevitable about them, and their undesirable side effects do not have to be tolerated.

(3) Commitment to objectives is a result of the rewards associated with their achievement: The most significant of such rewards, *e.g.,* the satisfaction of ego and self-development needs, can be the direct result of effort directed toward company objectives. People select goals for themselves if they see the possibility of some kind of reward, be it material or purely psychic (mental). Once they have selected their goal, they will pursue it even without close supervision and control.

(4) The average human beings, under proper conditions, do not shun responsibility, but learn not only to accept responsibility but also to seek it.

(5) The capacity to exercise a relatively high degree of imagination, ingenuity, and creativity in the solution of organisational problems is widely, not narrowly distributed in the population. Management cannot monopolise initiativeness and creativity.

(6) Under conditions of modern industrial life, the intellectual potentialities of people are only partially utilised. In reality, men and women have unlimited potential.

The psychological foundations on which these assumptions rest, include the well-known formulation of hierarchy of human needs developed by A. H. Maslow. Theory Y represents democratic or participative management. It is an invitation to innovation. After having satisfaction of basic needs, people tend to be motivated by higher level needs and by the intangible rewards offered by those needs. It is these motivating forces that Theory Y management proposes to tap. In other words, Theory Y management aims at integrating goals of individual workers with those of the enterprise and at making the job the principal means through which each member can enlarge his competence, self-control, and sense of achievement. In such an atmosphere. Theory

Y holds that the employees (operatives and executives) are likely to identify with the goals of the organisation because the organisation identifies with their goals. The operative, the manager and the organisation are seen as mutually supportive. In effect the organisation is set into motion by the motivation of its various members, whose individual contributions combine to achieve overall company goals. Theory Y is a challenge to enlightened management to provide the right atmosphere for the development, motivation, the full use of human resources which have immense potential. Theory Y points out that management can create self-propelled, self-disciplining kind of organisation wherein the satisfaction of one's activated needs occurs as an integral part of the process of achieving the company's goals. Theory Y emphasizes integrative leadership, *i.e.,* democratic and participative leadership where the manager will be more of a coach and counsellor, less of a commander, supervisor or a judge. Direction and command have outlived their utility under Theory Y management.

Once the manager recognises the worker as potentially energetic, self-disciplined, aspiring, self-responsible, and innovative, (Theory 'Y'), then he can construct a work situation that features: (1) general supervision, (2) active participation of labour in decision making process. (3) job enrichment, (4) job rotation, (5) work group autonomy, and (6) management by objectives, all designed to enlist the employee's higher level needs such as egoistic and growth needs (esteem and self-realisation) as principal motivators. Management wants the individual to participate in setting goals for himself and for the organisation in an integrated manner. Theory Y management can work wonders under the following conditions: (1) People are literate, well-informed, intelligent competent to participate in management with zeal and enthusiasm to satisfy their higher level wants, particularly psychic wants. (2) People have duly and reasonably satisfied their basic needs such as physiological needs, safety needs, as well as social needs, according to their general standard of living. Once, they have no burning economic problems, only non-financial incentives become important motivators. Such conditions are prevalent in the affluent countries like the U.S.A., the U.K., and many other European countries.

In undeveloped or developing countries, national income is low, standard of living is low, poverty is universal, population may be, too large, people are illiterate and ignorant, labour is unorganised. Under such conditions, as long as the stomach is semi-empty, what is the use of igniting higher level wants. In such countries 70 p.c. of human energy is essential just to keep the body and soul together and to solve the problem of physical survival. To such people satisfaction of egoistic wants is just an unrealisable dream. In India due to poverty God is food. Financial incentives are naturally greatest motivators or satisfiers. Belly must be satisfied before brain.

In a developing country like India, however, gradually we are witnessing favourable conditions (particularly for knowledge workers) for Theory Y management. But for a few decades at least, we cannot practice the ideals of Theory Y on a large scale. At present, there are lakhs of people in India who need external discipline from a manager for getting things done through them. Till then, we may have to tolerate conventional managerial style *viz.,* Theory X with suitable and necessary modifications, *e.g.,* recognition of human factor in industry, consultative management, use of non-financial incentives particularly for managerial group, etc.

As a long-term goal, Theory Y or Management by Integration of individual and organisation goals should be ideal to be nourished by managers. Economic development is only a means to an end, the end being all round development of every human being. No doubt the journey is very tedious. The road is long, steep and also slippery. We have to go through clouded atmosphere. However, there is no substitute for democratic management based on the assumptions of Theory Y. Theory Y also fits in admirably into the systems concept and approach now being applied to business. Industrial organisation is a socio-technical system. It Is also an open, organic system. Five M's (men, money, materials, machinery and management) as well as social, economic political and cultural forces, constitute the inputs. The outputs are products, services and rewards to the members of the business system. It can be definitely said that Theory Y offers motivators such as achievement, recognition, status, the work itself, creativity, and higher responsibility. It can develop a better lovable, admirable and matured person. Human resource management prefers Theory Y.

Theory Y suggests a new style of managing by integration and self-control. Individual objectives should be integrated with organisational objectives.

The "new organisation" breaks free of this engineering heritage. In "Results", a recent book by two Booz Allen Hamilton consultants, Gary Neilson and Bruce Pasternak, the authors talk about "the DNA of living organisations". Corporate DNA, they suggest, consists of "four basic building blocks: decision rights; information; motivators; and structure". These combine in different ways to make more than the sum of their parts, expressing distinct identities or personalities. McKinsey's Lowell Bryan also talks about "the personality of the firm."

This switch, from Lego to DNA, echoes one of the best-known classifications of corporate culture ever made. In "The Human Side of Enterprise", originally published in 1960, Douglas McGregor, a Harvard academic, divided management styles into Theory X and Theory Y. Theory X was the classic command-and-control type of management, the authoritarian style which (McGregor wrote) "reflects an underlying belief that management must counteract an inherent human tendency to avoid work." This is the world that Frederick Taylor observed, and the world that organisation man was designed for.

Theory Y is the antithesis of X. 'It assumes that people will exercise self-direction and self-control in the achievement of organisational objectives to the degree that they are committed to those objectives'. Theory X is bent on devising the right sticks with which to prod work-shy labour; Theory Y looks for the carrots that will induce them to stay.

McGregor's dichotomy has been hugely influential in management thinking ever since his death in 1964. The new organisation lies firmly at the Theory Y end of his spectrum. It challenges employees, in his words, "to innovate, to discover new ways of organising and directing human effort, even though we recognise that the perfect organisation, like the perfect vacuum, is practically out of reach."

McGregor himself came to believe that neither management style in its pure form could work successfully. Firms would find a balance between the two that would shift over time to fit new circumstances. But the new organisation is beginning to prove him wrong. Companies are coming to realise that knowledge workers, who have been identified as the creators of future wealth, thrive only under Theory Y. Theory X is becoming extinct — just like organisation man himself.

Behavioural Signs

Over the years, there is a paradigm shift in customer behaviour. As a natural corollary — Robert Lauterborn thinks that it is time to blow away integrated marketing communication and focus on integrated customer behaviour management.

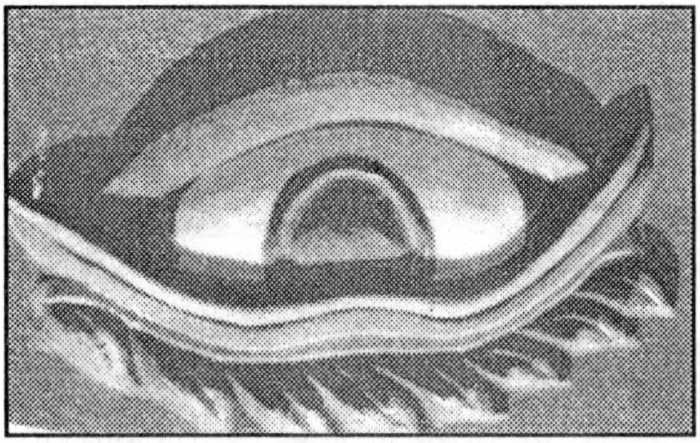

Integrated marketing communications — IMC, in short — was a label that Don Schultz, Stan Tannenbaum and I stuck on to a process a decade ago in a book titled *Integrated Marketing Communications: Pulling it Together and Making it Work*. What we thought we were describing, was a strategic problem-solving approach, a new way of thinking and working, a banner under which multiple functions could march together in lockstep to accomplish a business objective accountably.

Instead, what IMC has come to mean to many people is little more than 'two-from-Column A one-from-Column B' media selection. IMC is too often perceived even by the authors of some subsequent textbooks as simply making sure that PR efforts are in synch with advertising placements.

We've battled to get out of this box for too long. Maybe its time to blow it all away and rebuild. Let's start with a new name: ICBM. Integrated Customer Behaviour Management.

Here's the thinking that fuels the ICBM concept:

- Profitability is a function of customer behaviour.
- Any programme launched without specific, measurable behavioural objectives is doomed to veer off course.
- Marketing and marketing communications are investment functions, and the return on investment is a computation based on the incremental revenue that results from altered customer behaviour.

Here's how to launch the ICBM Process:

1. What core business objective does the company want to achieve? What is the net value of success to the company?
2. Exactly whose behaviour needs to be changed for these results to happen?
3. Exactly what do we want these people to do, and why should they do it?
4. How do we engage them in a dialogue over time to make it happen?
5. How will we measure success? How will we demonstrate a return on the investment?

Some readers may squint at the fourth point and say, 'Aha, here's where he's talking about IMC.' But of course, that's the problem. IMC has been pigeonholed as an end-of-the-food-chain function that only kicks in at the tactical level and then only deals with communication issues.

So maybe the vision of IMC is too limited. ICBM integrates everything that impacts customer behaviour. Product development to meet customer needs more precisely. Packaging that communicates with equal precision. Pricing that reflects the value the customer perceives in the product, compared to other ways to satisfy the need or want. A distribution scheme that makes it convenient for the customer to buy. Channel management, sales management, financing, CRM, TQM, Six Sigma and whatever else needs to be happening to change how the customer thinks and behaves, plus the timing of it all and the dialogue around it, internal and external — all of that is part of ICBM. And, yes, the multidimensional, interactive, continuously measured communication package that connects the brand or product and the customer, because that's what makes the whole process lift off and stay in orbit.

IMC as it was designed, works. But we need to blow away the misconceptions that keep the IMC concept from making the contributions it could to marketers and agencies alike. Integrated Customer Behaviour Management. Sounds a lot more powerful, doesn't it?

GOAL SETTING THEORY

Goal setting is one of the most effective and widely practised tools of motivation. Goals are the immediate or ultimate objectives that employees are trying to accomplish from their work efforts in organisations. Goal setting is the process of motivating employees by establishing performance goals. That goal motivates any individual is an established fact. We tend to relax and slacken our efforts if we are not clear about what we want to achieve. A student does not do well in an examination if he or she does not keep a target in mind — target may be a first class or securing distinction. An individual may not rise in personal life if he or she does not have clear career goals. It does not mean that performance of an individual is nil in the absence of a goal. The theory emphasises that with clear goals performance tends to increase.

Why goals motivate employees? There are at least five reasons which explain the correlation between goals and motivation.

First, they lead employees to compare their present performance with the goal. To the extent that individuals fall short of the goal, they feel dissatisfied and work harder to attain it — as long as they believe that it is possible for them to do so.

Second, when individuals succeed in reaching a goal, they feel competent and successful; such feelings are desirable and can serve as a strong incentive to extra effort.

Third, the existence of a goal clarifies what level of performance is required. Once this level is established, individuals can focus on developing effective strategies for attaining it.

Fourth, the theory calls attention to the important role of self-efficacy — individuals' beliefs about their ability to perform at given levels. If people do not have confidence in themselves, their effort and performance will decrease. In contrast, if they conclude that they can reach the goal, motivation and performance will be enhanced.

Finally, goal setting theory indicates that goals will guide behaviour only when they are accepted by the self and by others. If others concerned do not accept the goals, performance of an employee will not increase. Similarly, if the goal is not acceptable to the self, its effect on the behaviour of the person will be minimal.

Goals need to fulfill certain requisites if they were to impact employee behaviour.

One requirement is that goals must be specific. Specific goals lead to higher output than do vague goals such as "Do your best". Acceptance of the goal and commitment towards its achievement will have effect on employee behaviour and satisfaction. Similarly, organisational support towards goal attainment supported by individual abilities and traits leads to goal realisation. As a result of performance, a person receives various intrinsic and extrinsic rewards, which in turn, influence satisfaction.

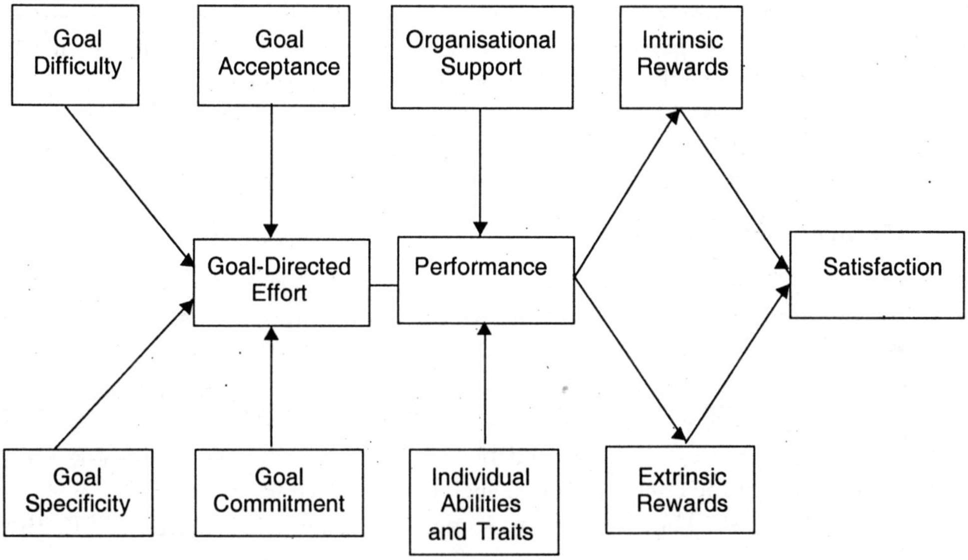

Fig. 10: Goal Setting Requisites

(***Source***: Gregory Moorhead and Rieky W. Griffin, *op. cit.*, p. 362).

Goal setting theory is a very powerful technique of motivation. When used correctly, carefully monitored, and actively supported by managers, goal setting can improve performance. However, neither goal setting nor any other technique can be used to correct every problem.

Achievement Motivation Theory

The Achievement Motivation theory provides a final content 'theory of motivation. The theory has been advocated by David C. McClelland and his associates. It was in the late 1940s that David C. McClelland and his friends began to study three needs that motivate human behaviour-power, affiliation and achievement. McClelland believes that each person has a need for all the three (as well as for others) but that people differ in the degree to which the various needs motivate their behaviour.

It is not only the desire to achieve but the favourable environment which translate the desire into reality. The above motivational factors were significantly influenced by certain assisting factors like family environment (business family), technical knowledge (through education or past employment), training and Government incentives. Entrepreneurs from business families enjoyed financial support, former employees had social contact, engineers were having technical competence. It was, therefore, difficult to single out any particular motivating factor. However, income, social recognition and other 'pull' factors strongly induced people to start industry. Moreover, most of the entrepreneurs were self motivated.

An entrepreneur is an agent who has to perform several functions to mobilize and utilise resources and to create market. He ventures into an uncertain future to exploit the potentiality that exists. Therefore, entrepreneurship is a very risky proposition. Some people leave very cosy jobs to start their own enterprises. Some merchants who are earning well put their hard-earned money at stake in manufacturing. Technologists and engineers start their own industry instead of going for safe jobs. All these persons have high achievement motivation. Like all achievement-oriented people, they want to take personal responsibility, tend to persist in the face of adversity, tend to take moderate risks and like to know the results of their efforts. They are innovative and full of interpersonal competence. According to McClelland, they are unusually creative, having high propensity of risk taking capacity and a strong need for achievement.

The Achievement Motivation

David McClelland has developed an Achievement Motivation Theory. According to this theory an individual's need for achievement (N Ach) refers to the need for personal accomplishment. It is the drive to excel, to strive for success and to achieve in relation to a set of standards. People with high achievement motive like to take calculated risks and want to win. They like to take personal responsibility for solving problems and want to know how well they are doing. High achievers are not motivated by money *per se* but instead employ money as a method of keeping sure of their achievements. Such people strive for personal achievement rather than the rewards of success. They want to do something better and more efficiently than it has been done before.

Need for achievement is simply the desire to do well, not so much for the sake of social recognition or prestige but for the sake of an inner feeling of personal accomplishment. It is this need for achievement that motivates people to take risk. People with high need for achievement behave in an entrepreneurial way. Need for achievement stimulates the behaviour of a person to be an entrepreneur.

The following psychological factors contribute to entrepreneurial motivation:

1. Need for achievement through self-study, goal-setting and inter-personal support.
2. Keen interest in situations involving moderate risk.
3. Desire for taking personal responsibility.
4. Concrete measures of task performance.
5. Anticipation of future possibilities.
6. Energetic or novel instrumental activity.
7. Organisational skills, etc.

Some societies produce a larger percentage of people with high need achievement. Entrepreneurship becomes the link between need achievement and economic growth.

McClelland considers the need for achievement to be most critical to a nation's economic development. He held that a strong 'inner spirit' in individuals to attain is a measurable variable arising from a need, which the individual develops mainly in childhood and seeks to satisfy throughout his life. This 'inner spirit' which he called need for achievement, if higher, would produce more energetic entrepreneurs capable of generating rapid economic development." High need for achievement or ambition motivates an entrepreneur to take risks, work hard, find new things, save more, reinvest the savings in industry and so on. The limited empirical evidence supports the hypothesis that need for achievement contributes to entrepreneurial success.

Behavioural Pattern of Entrepreneur

Entrepreneur's need of self-actualisation manifested in the need for achievement (N-Ach) which forces him to create something new; a new product, a new order, a newer way of doing things and a newer standard for himself and the society. He is a competitor of himself. He sets his own standards by competing with himself and in the process continues to set newer standards by beating his own past performance overtime. He is never satisfied with the present and always look ahead for more challenging jobs. The behavioural pattern of these high achievers, as observed empirically, may be summed up in the following paragraphs:

1. He acts out of desire and not out of necessity. He is preactive and not reactive in nature. He hardly adapts himself to a situation but influences the environment to suit his designs. If he is an entrepreneur he will create the demand for his product; if he is a writer he will force people to think his own way.
2. He feels himself emotionally attached to his activities. But this attachment continues so long as the goal is not achieved on a new project. The transitory period between the two is characterised by restlessness and a feeling of void.
3. He constantly insists on quick feed-back of the results of his actions. He must know how he is doing and he must know it fast.
4. He is a marathon runner and does not settle for a hundred metre race, that is why he often operates from a high risk position as it appears to the outsiders. But to him it is a moderate risk. (This point was elaborated in the theory developed by McClelland, Atkinson etc. all who tried to prove from their studies of various countries that high achievers prefer to operate from intermediate risk situations.)
5. He is very active professionally but lazy in his personal appearance. This will be reflected by his casual dresses; unkempt hair and even unpolished shoes. This casualness enables him to work even in minimum physical facilities and amidst lot of wordly constraints. He has minimum of Maslow's "Lower order needs."
6. He is conscious about time, committed to his work, efficiency and achievement. He dislikes waste and abhors drunkenness.
7. He is not a complaining child but a brooding "Little professor". His "adult" is very strong which gives him a keen sense of analysing the present and future realities. This two ego status are predominant in a high-achiever which are complementary to each other. His "little professor" hits an idea and his "adult" translates the idea into a reality. He is, however, a benevolent "parent" when dealing with his subordinates.
8. He has a 'tendency to go straight to the top man in an organisation to get his job done. If he is working in an organisation this behaviour of his creates disorder and stir in the organisation till it is decentralised to make room for him. He loves to deal in one-to-one basis and abhors bureaucratic levels.

9. In an organisation he will have tremendous following from below, mixed feelings in the line, strong feelings in intermediary level and mostly "adult" feeling at the top depending upon whether the structure is vertical or horizontal.
10. He has a tendency to take up more than one job at a time to avoid the feeling of void once one is done.
11. He acts and learns. He does not reject an idea before being thorough with it.
12. He is hopeful about future. He sees opportunity in crisis.
13. He accepts responsibility for his actions.
14. He may not have a brilliant academic career. Being a marathon runner, academic attainments were never his objectives. These are just tools for him for the attainment of his goal.
15. He is however, a voracious collector of information but not a "bookish type." He scans everything from almanac to theory of relativity and store every bit of information in his brain which may become uniquely useful in a particular situation.

The Model

Any behavioural model for entrepreneurial development must, therefore, take care of proportionate development of both Need for Power and Need for Affiliation in relation to the high priest — Need for achievement.

The model will thus look the following:

$$M = \text{N-Ach} + \text{N-Pow} + \text{N-Aff} \qquad \ldots(1)$$

Or Entrepreneurial motivation (Mo) is the additive function of three need variables. In this model N-Pow and N-Aff have fixed proportional relationship with N-Ach (which for sake of simplification may be denoted as m_{ea})

Hence, $\text{N-Pow} = K_p \cdot m_{ea} = m_{ep}$

and $\text{N-Aff} = k_f \cdot m_{ea} = m_{ef}$

which means that if N-Ach (m_{ea}) score of an entrepreneur is 20, his N-Pow (or entrepreneurial power need - m_{ep}) should be 20 kp and N-Aff (or entrepreneurial affiliation need - m_{ef}) score will be 20 kf. The model can therefore be recast in the following form:

$$Mo = (m_{ea} + m_{ep} + m_{ef}) \ldots\ldots \qquad \ldots(2)$$

Need for achievement (m_{ea}) being the vital motivational ingredient of entrepreneur and the guiding force, its score shall be highest amongst all his motivational needs followed by the scores of (m_{ep}) and (m_{ef}). Constants k_p for N-Pow and k_f for N-aff can be derived empirically from the study of motivational data of successful entrepreneurs, both present and past. These constants can also be established by Stochastic method and then tested for their validity.

As m_{ea} or entrepreneurial need for achievement is the biggest and guiding variable in terms of which both m_{ep} and m_{ef} re developed, theoretically the model can be presented 'in a right-angled triangle where m_{ea} is hypotenuse; m_{ep} is the base and m_{ef} — the perpendicular as below:

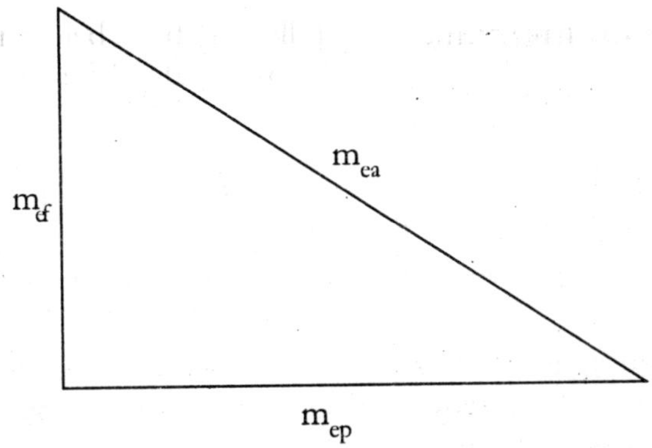

Then the control equations will be:

$$(m_{es})^2 = (m_{ep})^2 + (m_{ef})^2 \text{ ....} \qquad \ldots(3)$$

$$\text{and } k_{p2} + k_{f2} = 1 \text{ ....} \qquad \ldots(4)$$

because k_p and k_r are both proportional to hypotenuse m_{ac}.

Geometrically speaking, with a given hypotenue there could be a number of such right-angled triangles and an ideal form can be determined for each class of entrepreneurs where $(m_{ep}) > (m_{ef})$; the base (m_{ep}) and perpendicular (m_{er}) being determined automatically for the given hypotenuse (m_{ea}).

If the measurement scale is reduced to one it will be further observed that:

$$M_o = m_{ea} + m_{ep} + m_{ef}$$

The additive is less than three because it is difficult to find all the three motivational needs in equal degree in an individual and more so, it is an impossible psychological situation for a successful entrepreneur.

With the help of the model it will be possible to determine the degree of need for power and need for affiliation for a given score of need for achievement of a potential entrepreneur. Suitable training inputs can then be provided to increase or reduce the need variables to make the motivational profile of an entrepreneur effectively workable. For this purpose entrepreneurial motivational score (M_B) must satisfy all the conditions on the right hand side of the equation and none of the need variables will have any zero value.

Although, McClelland has shown, N-Ach of an individual can be increased, it can be increased only upto a certain extent depending upon his past and present life situation.

However, in case of some entrepreneurs Mo is higher than others but both may be successful in the relative magnitude of their ventures. Some may build up large corporations but others may be equally successful in small and medium ventures. The variation is due to the variable in the degree of mea, which, however, is the predominant variable in both the two classes of entrepreneurs. It is possible, therefore, with the help of this model, to identify the separate potential entrepreneurs in terms of their existing and potential mea and impart the desired quantity of training inputs to raise or reduce their needs, for making them successful entrepreneurs.

Developing Achievement Motives

McClelland and his associates have made specific suggestions for developing a high achievement need. They are:

(*a*) Give employees periodic feedback on performance. This will provide information that will enable them to modify or correct their performance.

(*b*) Provide good models of achievement. Employees who are "heroes" should be available for others to emulate.

(*c*) Arrange tasks so that employees can pursue moderate challenges and responsibilities. Avoid tasks that are either extremely difficult or extremely easy.

(*d*) As much as possible, employees should be able to control their own destiny and imagination. They should be trained, however, to think realistically and positively about how they will accomplish goals.

Though McClelland placed emphasis on n-Ach motives, he also studied need for power and affiliation.

Need for Power (nPow): The employees exhibiting the needs for power derive satisfaction from the ability to control others. Actual achievement of goals is less important than the means by which goals are achieved. Satisfaction is derived from being in positions of influence and control. Individuals with a high nPow derive satisfaction from being in positions of influence and control. Organisations that foster the power motive tend to attract individuals with a high need for power (for example, military and political organisations).

Need for Affiliation (nAff): Individuals exhibiting this need as a dominant motive derive satisfaction from social and interpersonal activities. There is a need to form strong interpersonalties and to 'get close' to people psychologically. If asked to choose between working at a task with those who are technically competent and those who are their friends, high nAff individuals will choose their friends.

Needs of individuals and their work preferences are summarised in Table below:

Table 2

WORK PREFERENCES OF PERSONS HIGH IN NEED FOR ACHIEVEMENT, AFFILIATION AND POWER

Individual Needs	*Work Preferences*	*Example*
High need for achievement	Individual responsibility Challenging but achievable goals Feedback on performances.	Field sales person with challenging quota and opportunity to earn individual bonus.
High need for affiliation	Interpersonal relationships Opportunities to communicate.	Customer service representative Member of work groups subject to group bonus plan.
High need for power	Control over other persons attention; Recognition.	Formal positions of supervisory responsibility; Appointment as head of special task force or committee.

Empirical Tests for the Theory

MeClelland, through extended studies of his postulates, found along with others that achievement motivation is not as stable a personality characteristic determined exclusively by childhood experiences as he originality thought it to be. Further investigations and experimental applications established that *achievement motivation can be learned.* Such learning has been brought about through special training programmes. It is also recognised that a person's achievement motivation may increase because of being placed in a position in which some extent of achievement motivation is expected and rewarded. A number of studies tend to support the basic premise of the theory. Relationships between n-Ach and various indices of entrepreneurial success have been usually found to be moderately too highly positive. Research data also tends to suggest that success of companies is related to high achievement motivation of their executives.

- Achievement motivation can be learned.
- Special training programmes help to attain high n-Ach.
- Studies support the basic premise of the theory.
- High n-Ach is related to entrepreneurial success.
- Success of companies is related to high n-Ach of executives.

Although McClelland implied that staffing an organisation with people having a high achievement motivation leads to a highly successful and competitive organisation rather than the placement of people in highly competitive jobs or organisations, which leads to achievement related behaviour, the research data seems to suggest that, while both occur, the weight is more in favour of the reverse.

- Situations demanding competition and achievement lead to achievement related activity more than the recruitment of high n-Ach people in the organisation:

Evaluation of the Theory

Like any other theory on motivation, McClelland's theory too has been criticised, criticisms often being unfair. In the first place, the critics question whether motives can be taught to adults. Considerable psychological literature suggests that the acquisition of motives normally occurs in childhood and is very difficult to change once it has been established. McClelland, however, counters that there is strong evidence from politics and religion to indicate that adult behaviour can be drastically altered in a relatively short time.

The second criticism of this theory questions the contention that the needs are permanently acquired. McClelland is the only theorist who argues that the needs can be socially changed through education and training. Opponents contend that the change may be only temporary similar to the one which occurs at an evangelistic meeting or a political rally.

The third criticism relates to the methodology used by McClelland and his associates to advocate the theory. These researchers used the famous Thematic Apperception Test (TAT) of Murray as the main tool to determine basic needs. While projective technique — as TAT have many advantages over structured questionnaires, the interpretation of responses is more subject to research's bias.

On the positive side, it may be stated that the findings of McClelland highlight the importance of matching the individual and the job. Employees with high achievement needs thrive on work that is challenging, satisfying, stimulating and complex; they welcome autonomy, variety and frequent feedback from supervisors. Employees with low achievement needs prefer situations of stability, security and predictability, they respond better to considerate than to impersonal high-pressure supervision and look to the work place and co-workers for social satisfaction. McClelland's research also suggests that managers can, to some extent, raise the achievement need level of subordinates by creating the proper work environment — permitting their subordinates a measure of independence, increasing responsibility and autonomy, gradually making tasks more challenging and praising and rewarding high performance.

Thus, McClelland's work seems to have numerous practical applications at least in the economic realm. It would appear that the current problem is to concentrate on the development of an environment that will support the desired need, be it affiliation, power or achievement, or to change the need to fit the environment. The essence of the theory is that

$$\text{Individual needs} + \text{responsive work environment} \xrightarrow[\text{create}]{\text{can}} \text{work motivation and job satisfaction}$$

McClelland rated the achievement motivation of different countries on the basis of ideas related to need for achievement contained in the children's stories. This has come to be known as *n*-factor rating. He established a correlation between *n*-factor rating and the prosperity of the countries a generation ahead. The criterion of *n*-factor rating was the inherent concern for achievement or the non-induced achievement motivation.

McClelland found that achievement motivation was lower among people of underdeveloped countries than among those of developed nations. Even in USA, about ten per cent of the people were actually high achievers. It is the low level of aspirations or ambitions that explains the lack of enterprise in underdeveloped countries. Ambition is the lever of all motives and "aimless life is a goal-less game". Ambitions motivate men, activise them, broaden their vision and make life meaningful. Ambition is an index of one's resourcefulness. The ambition builds up achievement pressure in the individual and provides the basis for McClelland's *n* factor. Ambition is the lever of all motives. The initiative and intentions of an individual are directed by his ambitions. It is the ambition that electrifies man's actions. Therefore, what matters is not merely the people but their aspirations and the means to achieve the goals. Therefore, it is the duty of leaders and teachers to build up ambition into the minds of the young people. However, ambitions differ from greed and windfall. Greed results in disaster and windfall makes one a speculator. Sometimes, personal ambitions may come in the way of family aspirations or national aspirations. Unfulfilled ambitions are passed on to the next generation who may chase the goal with redoubled effort and vigour. Thus, ambition nourishes the achievement motivation and brings economic growth. The biggest obstacle to economic progress in countries like India is perhaps the limited ambition of people. The initiative of an individual is directed by his ambitions which nourish the entrepreneurial spirit and bring about economic development. Hence, what matters is not merely the people and their talents but their aspirations. However, ambitions differ among individuals on the basis of the environment in which they are born and brought up. Galbraith J.K. also attributed the backwardness of many Asian and African countries to lack of ambition.

Thus, the theory of achievement motivation provides a deep introspection to the human behaviour in general and entrepreneurial behaviour in particular. It also glorifies the necessity of the Achievement Motivation Training (AMT) as an important tool for achievement of needs.

Keeping in view the above needs, 'n-Ach', 'n-Pow' and 'n-Aff', David McCelland has pointed out that these factors, especially 'n-Ach' are responsible for entrepreneurial development. The following analysis can reveal the impact of need for achievement in accelerating entrepreneurial urge among individuals.

McClelland pointed out the twin important characteristics of entrepreneurship that govern the economic behaviour of a person to become entrepreneurial. They are:

(*i*) Doing things in a novel and excellent manner

(*ii*) Decision making under uncertainty.

According to this theory, 'n-Ach' or need for achievement refers to the need for personal accomplishment by the person through excellence. This category of persons is fond of shouldering personal responsibility. They are generally moderate risk takers and try to be winners all the time. High achievers aim at personal achievement rather than the reward of success. Persons with high need for achievement behave in the entrepreneurial way.

While some controversies regarding the order of causation remain, achievement motivation as a concept has been found useful to explain and understand important work behaviour. High achievers, for instance, have been found to stay on the job longer than low achievers. High achievers also have been found to respond to criticism with better performance than low achievers. Also, desirable managerial behaviours are typically displayed by achievement oriented managers. On an overall analysis, however, the theory has a very limited practical value today, as it is realised that personality traits such as needs explain far less of the variance in behaviour than do the characteristics of the situation. Even allowing for the usual discrepancies in reliability and validity of need measures, often situations appear to be more important to be understood and assessed for understanding work behaviour.

The Kakinada Experiment

Assuming need for achievement plays a vital role in promoting economic growth, McClelland has tried to induce achievement motivation in adults and provide them with an urge to improve their lot because uninduced achievement motivation results in long waiting before it bears fruit. Such an inducement may help break the barrier of limited aspirations". For this purpose, he conducted experiments with groups of businessmen in America, Mexico and Mumbai. Later, he carried out a full-fledged programme in the Kakinada city of Andhra Pradesh.

Kakinada is a well-developed district town of a population of around one lakh with high literacy and a modest industrial structure. The objective of the programme was to break the barrier of "limited aspirations" by inducing achievement motivation. The project which began in January 1964 consisted of recruiting batches of personnel drawn from business and industrial community of the town and putting them through orientation programme at the Small Industry Extension Training (SIET) Institute, Hyderabad. Fifty-two persons grouped into three batches participated in the programme. The training was designed primarily to stimulate the imagination and encourage introspection into personal motivation and community goals. The achievement development course contained four main items:

1. The individuals strived to attain concrete and frequent feedback.
2. The participants sought models of achievement. *i.e.*, watched those who have performed well and tried to emulate.
3. The participants imagined themselves in need of success and challenge and set carefully planned and realistic work goals.
4. The trainees were asked to control day dreaming by thinking and talk to themselves in positive terms.

The Achievement Motivation Training (AMT) included the following basics which were supposed to be accomplished by the trainees:

(*a*) Goal setting and goal achievement.

(*b*) Emulating the models of the achievement by constant watch and alertness.

(*c*) Attainment of concrete and frequent feedback.

(*d*) Planning carefully the realistic goals through performance appraisal of their own.

(*e*) Converting ideas into opportunities using the positive self-concept and controlling day dreaming.

Thus, the training helped those participants in providing high degree of motivation and subsequently the need for achievement. They displayed a more active business behaviour and took enough stress to accomplish the job. As such, Kakinada experience was considered the most successful experiment so far as the need for Achievement Motivation Training (AMI) is concerned for the benefit of the potential entrepreneurs. This AMT is regarded as a necessary tool for breaking the barrier of limited aspirations among individuals on the one hand and inducing in them high need for achievement on the other. The training also acts as a boost to the risk-taking and decision-making behaviour of the potential entrepreneurs. The n Ach factor or p achievement approach suggests promotion of achievement-oriented ways of thinking to foster economic development in the underdeveloped countries.

- Concept of achievement motivation has been useful to explain work behaviour.
- n-Ach does distinguish between high and low achievers.
- The theory has a very limited value today.
- Study of the situation appears more useful than the study of personality traits like needs.

After two years those had taken the course except for one Mexican case performed better than comparable men who did not take the course. The former made more money, got promoted faster and expanded business faster. In order to assess need for achievement, McClelland used the Thematic Appreciation Test (TAT) which presents the subject with an ambiguous picture. The individual is asked to interpret what he sees and what is happening in the picture. Achievement related themes are then counted and the final score represents the individual's desire for high achievement.

About the results of the Kakinada experiment, McClelland concluded that those participating in the programme displayed a more active business behaviour (51 per cent as against 25 per cent in the control group) and worked longer hours. Significantly he found that caste, traditional beliefs or western ways of life did not determine the mental makeup of a participant. The training as was given at Hyderabad is likely to improve those who have a great yearning to do something and have the opportunity to do so in their business framework.

The Kakinada experiment is being utilised in a number of experiments that have recently initiated technical personnel to set up new enterprises of their own. In Gujarat various State agencies have combined to operate an Entrepreneurship Development Programme to help young people acquire the motivation necessary to become risk-takers. The Gujarat programme has been successful in persuading many persons to set up new enterprises in the small scale sector. It was found that the follow up "package" assistance offered by the State agencies in Gujarat has been particularly instrumental in helping the participants to decide on the enterprise they wish to start. Similarly, in Andhra Pradesh, the Small Scale Industrial Development Corporation Ltd. (APSSIDC) has been assisting technically qualified persons to become entrepreneurs through orientation programmes of the SIET Institute. This is followed by specific assistance of providing developed land specially earmarked for such persons at nominal rates in the technocrats industrial estates.

Based on the experiences in Gujarat and Andhra Pradesh, the Ministry of Industrial Development has recently formulated schemes of helping technical personnel to become entrepreneurs. This programme, which went into operation early in 1971, consists of three months programme at selected centres spread all over the country, followed by financial assistance in terms of a subsidy on the interest on advances taken by the entrepreneurs from the commercial banks so that the net interest paid by the entrepreneur himself does not exceed five per cent. The programme is designed to enable a young person to know the real problems of setting up an enterprise and to work out the feasibility report of his own project. During this period, he is also provided with opportunities to visit industrial establishments in his field of specialisation. Careful screening of the participants is done by the Selection Committee with the State Director of Industries as its Chairman so that the programme would result in a sizable number of new enterprises. It is expected thousands of young persons will be provided with such training in the years to come.

It is realised that entrepreneurship is to be developed from a very young age. In this connection, the Ford Foundation has been conducting a pilot project study under the direction of Eugene Staley. Staley has taken up one district in Maharashtra (Osmanabad) for the pilot study and he is trying to develop a school curriculum that would provide a high degree of motivation among the students. He is introducing success stories drawn from history and legends of the indigenous culture to induce in young minds the sense of "need for achievement" and the desire to do something after they grow up.

Interest in similar programmes is evinced in the USA and UK. In the United States, a Junior Achievement Programme has been working for many years as an educational activity through which 40,000 boys and girls are engaged in making and selling products as an after-school activity. They are helped by 14,000 corporations whose employees act as guides and philosophers of the miniature enterprises. Each company begins its operation when the school opens and dissolves itself after nine months when the vacation begins. With the help of sponsors, a group of students, generally about a dozen, form themselves into a company and then select their own officers and Board of Directors. Since the company will operate for only a year, the products they select are usually easily made such as perfume, jewellery, toys or Christmas decorations. Quite often the product is allied to that of its sponsoring "big brother" company. The money required for operations is raised by each member by selling stock at 50 per cent share. Usually, such shares are sold to adults in the community who are interested in the experiments, but a dividend is declared if the venture succeeds. The students buy their raw materials, manufacture, package and sell their products in the open market. At the end of the year a share-holders report is prepared and the company dissolves itself.

In the United Kingdom, the same idea has been taken up and developed further. The programme is known as the "Young Enterprises" programme and operates normally from September to the following May. Each company consists of 15 to 20 young people and meets once or twice a week for two hours. They are called the Achievers and are in the age group of fifteen years to early twenties. Each young enterprise is assisted by a team of advisers drawn from a local firm. There are usually three advisers in each team — one for general management, one for production and one for sales. An Area Board consisting of leading persons in the region is formed to assist these companies and a full time. Area Director is employed by the Board to recruit Advisers and the Achievers for the centres in the area. A Young Enterprise Centre consists of a small factory providing workshop space and meeting room for the companies. The centre can simultaneously accommodate five companies on one night and can cater for as many as 20 or 25 companies per week.

Making people achievement "oriented or inculcating in them "need for achievement,' is the objective of all such programmes. Thus, efforts are made through such programmes to spread ambition. Ambition is the mother of all motives. The intentions and the initiative of the man are directed by his ambitions. It is the ambition that electrifies man's actions. The common saying — aimless life is a goalless game — emphasises the importance of ambition in life. So, what matters most is not merely the men but their aspirations and what they do to reach their goal. It is the duty of the parents, the teachers and the leaders of the nation to instil ambition into the minds of the people. Naturally, ambitions differ from individual to individual on the basis of personal tastes and temperaments, and family to family and nation to nation, depending upon the circumstances in which they are placed and the priorities which they have set for themselves. Sometimes, personal aspirations come in the way of family aspirations or national aspirations. Whoever it may be, aspirations do change with the changing times and values. For any man, it may not be possible to cherish all his aspirations in his lifetime. So also a nation may not be able to fulfil all her ambitions within a span of 300 or 200 years. But the ambitions aspirations which are unfulfilled are passed on to the next generation who may chase the target with redoubled effort and vigour. So, ambition which nourishes the achievement motivation brings in economic growth, brings in development not merely in one any segment of the economy but it results in total growth.

Box - 2

ACHIEVEMENT

D.B. Gupta's Lupin is a great Indian pharma success story.

While the success of Indian pharma companies has been spectacular in the generic space, some feel that there is a limitation on how far generic companies can grow. (With severe price cutting from other Indian generic firms themselves, margins come quickly under pressure.)

After the sale of Ranbaxy, many feel that Indian generics can only grow this far and no further. And that the decision of the Singh brothers to sell at the top of the market was the best decision.

But others take a different view. They believe that while generics sold on price was the starting point of the Indian pharma industry; the best years are still ahead. First, they point to the growing share of generics in every major market in the world. Even world leaders like Novartis revived the Sandoz brand to capture market share in Western markets. Also they ask why Daiichi would have paid a high price for Ranbaxy. They point out that as in other areas of business, branding, distribution and service play a key role in garnering markets and profits.

Moreover, worldwide, the pharma industry will continue to be a highly regulated industry, with a high emphasis on quality standards and laws against mis-selling. As such, manufacturing at the lowest price is only the first step in the business. They point out that it is for these reasons that Chinese companies that have not gone through the regulatory steps are significantly behind Indian pharma companies. The next step forward is to carve out high technology niches within the generic space. Lupin and one or two others have done this very well.

As in other areas of business other elements have to be considered. These include size, access to capital, availability of skilled people (including those with soft skills like marketing and legal) and of course business savvy and determination. Several Indian companies used the long period of protected home markets and lax patent protection laws to build strong and enviable businesses.

It took seven years for Desh Bandhu Gupta to find the opportunity he was looking for. Meanwhile, he used his time profitably, accumulating on-the-job experience. He worked for four years with Khandelwal Laboratories and two years at May & Baker. In 1968, Gupta decided to do his own thing, a brave decision considering that his capital base was next to nothing — Rs. 5,000! He bought over a defunct company, Lupin Laboratories, for just Rs. 1,000 and sub-contracted the manufacture of drugs to a number of small suppliers. In 1982, he had a sales turnover of just over Rs. 10 crore.

Current status Standing tall

Lupin has grown tremendously to a position of leadership among the country's biggest drug manufacturers. The company's annual results for 2008-09 show that Lupin's sales revenue has grown from Rs. 2,706.4 crore in FY08 to Rs. 3,775.9 crore in FY09 (ended 31 March). Its net profit jumped from Rs. 333.8 crore to Rs. 501.5 crore, which translates into a 50.2 per cent growth among the best in the Indian drug industry that year.

Desh Bandhu Gupta with son, Nilesh: Gen Next

(Cont.)

(Cont.)

Having recorded a three-fold increase in annual sales and even greater growth in net profits in the past five years, Lupin is now preparing itself for another giant leap forward. Its top management is putting together a blueprint known as 'Plan 13' which charts the company's growth plans between now and 2013. "The objective is to maintain the same rate of growth as we have done in the past," says chairman Desh Bandhu Gupta.

Lupin is at the very forefront of successful Indian (Pharma) Companies. Of course, many first generation companies find it difficult to transition to the second or third generation. But Lupin has overcome this hurdle with Gupta's son Nilesh and daughter Vinita firmly placed in the business.

But in business one never says never. And while it is difficult to be certain in business, and there can be unexpected turns in the future, there is every reason to believe that Lupin will continue on its chosen path.

ACHIEVEMENT ORIENTED DRIVE

The desire to achieve is a major source of strength in business, both for individual managers and for the organisations they lead. It generates passion and energy, which fuel growth and help companies sustain performance over the long term. And the achievement drive is on the rise.

We've spent 35 years assessing executive motivation, and we've seen a steady increase during the past decade in the number of managers for whom achievement is the primary motive. Businesses have benefited from this trend: Productivity has risen, and innovation, as measured by the number of patents issued per year, has soared.

In the short term, through sheer drive and determination, overachieving leaders may be very successful, but there's a dark side to the achievement motive. By relentlessly focusing on tasks and goals — revenue or sales targets, say — an executive or company can, over time, damage performance.

The Six Styles of Leadership

In our research, we've identified six styles of leadership that managers and executives use to motivate, reward, direct and develop others. They include:

- Directive, which entails strong, sometimes coercive behaviour
- Visionary, which focuses on clarity and communication
- Affiliate, which emphasises harmony and relationships
- Participative, which is collaborative and democratic
- Pace-setting, which is characterised by personal heroics
- Coaching, which focuses on long-term development and mentoring

The most effective leaders are adept at all six leadership styles and use each when appropriate. Typically, however, a manager defaults to the styles he or she is most comfortable using, a preference that reflects the person's dominant motive combined with the level of pressure in the workplace. People motivated mainly by achievement tend to favour pace-setting in low-pressure situations, but to become directive when the pressure is on.

Recognising Your Motives

David McClelland, the late Harvard psychologist, identified three internal drivers that explain how we behave: Achievement (*meeting or exceeding a standard of excellence*), affiliation (*maintaining close personal relationships*) and power (*influencing or having an impact on others*).

For an overachiever seeking to broaden his or her range, the first step is to become aware of how motives influence leadership style. You can get a good sense of which drive is dominant in you simply by examining the activities you like to indulge in and why.

- People with high achievement drives tend to like challenging projects that allow them to accomplish something new. They also like to outperform people who represent a high standard of excellence and tend to be utilitarian in their communication — often brief and to the point.
- Those high in affiliation are energised by personal relationships. They make heavy use of the phone and e-mail just to stay connected.
- People mainly motivated by personalised power (*those who draw strength from controlling others*) tend to be driven by status and image.
- Individuals mainly driven by socialised power (*those whose strength comes from empowering people*) get satisfaction from helping people feel more capable. They like to advise and assist, whether or not the advice is wanted or needed.

Managing & Exercising Your Motive

Even trickier and more important than recognising an overactive drive to achieve is figuring out how to channel that drive into new behaviours. Dean McAlister, Senior Pharmaceutical Sales Director with Astra Zeneca, found himself promoted to a management position early in his career. He was talented, sincere and hardworking, and at times he drove people crazy.

While he took pride in his high-achievement approach, others saw him as arrogant, impatient and manipulative. "Dean was known for his 3 a.m. e-mails," said one colleague. "That was his normal pace — everything was a priority."

McAlister stayed ahead of the industry's information curve, regularly rising before dawn to study the latest market trends. But by always providing the answers, he stifled the input and creativity of his team members. He didn't realise this until his manager told him. In classic achievement mode, McAlister instantly turned his energy towards transforming his leadership. With the help of a coach, he began studying his own actions, trying to determine why he behaved as he did. He also monitored his behaviour with his team, peers and manager, asking them to give honest feedback.

Much of what he learned was unexpected. At one point, he was describing his daily routine. A deeply spiritual man, McAlister spoke of taking time each day for prayer. When he was asked how much time he spent talking to God and how much time listening, he realised that even in his spiritual life he was focused on his own agenda. "Of course," he groaned, "I'm always talking."

Next, he adopted specific new behaviours. Rather than issue a set of directives on sales targets, for instance, he engaged his team in a detailed discussion on how to achieve the goals. He consciously tried to listen and not jump to conclusions — a continuing struggle, though the behaviour is now becoming more natural with time and practice.

Changing the Culture

Some companies unabashedly create cultures that foster and reward the achievement-at-all-costs mentality. But organisations can redirect their focus and still achieve good numbers,

In the early 1990s, when CEO Louis Gerstner set out to regain IBM's market dominance by transforming the company into a flatter, matrix-driven organisation, he sought managers who would orchestrate and enable rather than command and control. He knew IBM needed to move away from its culture of personal heroics and individual achievement and begin valuing socialized power and managers who paid attention to the greater needs of the company.

As part of that transformation, we assessed the motives and leadership styles of 2,000 IBM managers. We found an achievement-oriented culture in which executives focused on their own departments or divisions, even if doing so had a negative impact on performance in other parts of the organisation.

Among the executives we interviewed, however, was a small, but highly successful group that led very differently. They exhibited a drive to achieve, but they worked through others, created strong teams, provided coaching and focused on increasing the capability of the whole organisation, not just their departments. IBM incorporated these behaviours into a competency model that over the next eight years was used to select, develop and promote leaders.

Of course, a high achievement drive continues to be a source of strength for any organisation. But companies must also learn when to draw on it and when to rein it in. The challenge for managers today, then, is to seek an approach to leadership that uses socialised power to keep achievement in check.

Psychoanalytic Theory

Psychoanalytic theory owes its origin to Sigmund Freud. In his 40 years of writing and clinical practice, Freud, acknowledged as one of the intellectual giants in the history of modern thought, developed (*i*) the first comprehensive personality theory, (*ii*) a method for treating neurotic ills, and (*iii*) an extensive body of clinical observations based on his therapeutic experience and self-analysis.

Freud likened the mind to an iceberg — only a small segment of which protruded above the surface of the water. This small portion of the mind represents conscious experience, while the much larger mass below water level represents the unconscious — a storehouse of impulses, passions and primitive instincts that affect our thoughts and behaviour. It was this unconscious portion of the mind that Freud sought to explore, and he did so by the method of free association. The method requires that the person talks about everything that comes into the conscious mind, no matter how ridiculous or trivial it might seem. By analysing free association, including the recall of dreams and early childhood memories, Freud sought to identify the basic determinants of personality.

Freud saw personality as being composed of three elements — id, ego, and super ego (See Fig. 11). This tripartite division of personality is known as the structural model of mental life, although Freud felt the divisions should be understood as hypothetical rather than as specific 'structures' of personality. Freud insisted that these structures be considered as hypothetical constructs, since the field of neuroanatomy was not sufficiently advanced to locate them within the central nervous system.

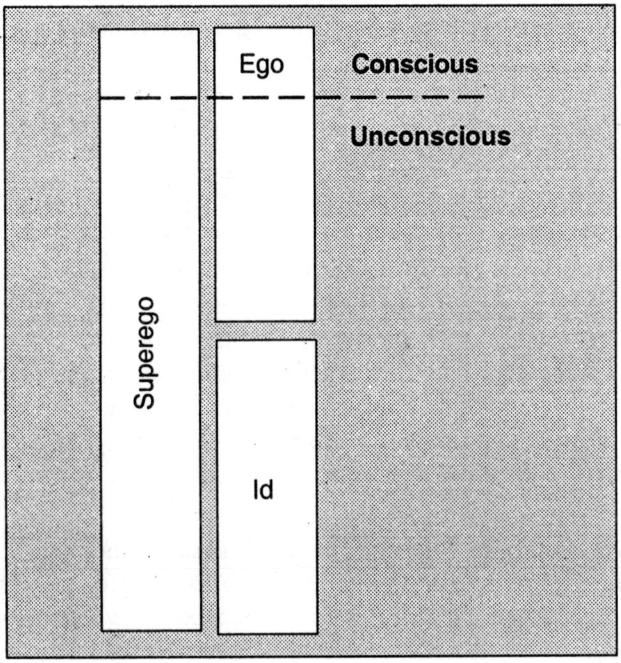

Fig. 11: Level of Consciousness of Id, Ego and Superego

The Id: The word 'id' is the Latin word for 'it' and refers exclusively to the innate component of personality. The id is the mental agency containing everything inherited, present at birth, and fixed in the individual's constitution, especially instincts. It is raw, animalistic, unorganised, knows no laws, obeys no rules, and remains basic to the individual throughout life. Operating on a primitive basis, it is free from all inhibitions. The id, as the original personality system, expresses the primary principle of all human life — the immediate discharge of psychic energy (libido) produced by animal drives (especially sex and aggression) which, when pent up, creates tension throughout the personality system. Immediate tension reduction is called the pleasure principle, and the id obeys it, manifesting itself in an impulsive and irrational manner, regardless of the consequences of its actions for others or its own self-preservation. Furthermore, since the id does not recognise fear or anxiety, it takes no precautions in expressing its purpose — a fact which Freud felt may result in danger for the individual and/or for society.

The id, according to Freud, employs to rid the personality of tension: *reflex* actions and *primary process.* Primary process refers to attempts of an individual to form a mental image of the object that will remove the tension. A hungry man, for example, experiences partial gratification of his hunger by imagining a delicious meal. In reflex actions, the id responds automatically to sources of irritation, thereby promptly removing the tension which the irritant elicits. Examples of such inborn reflex mechanisms are sneezing, coughing, and blinking.

The Ego: Mental images do not satisfy needs. The starving man cannot satisfy his hunger by eating images. Reality must be considered. This is the role of the ego. The ego develops out of the id because of the necessity for dealing with the real world. The hungry man must have food if the tension of hunger is to be reduced.

The Super Ego: In order for a person to function constructively in society, he should acquire a system of values, norms, ethics, and attitudes which are reasonably compatible with that society. The super ego, the third part of the personality, represents the internalised representation of the values and morals of society as taught to the child by parents and others. The super ego judges whether an action is right or wrong according to the standards of society. The id seeks pleasure, the ego tests reality, and the super ego strives for perfection. In Freud's view, the human organism is not born with a super ego; rather, children must incorporate it through interactions with parents, teachers, and other 'formative' figures.

Sometimes, the three components of personality are at odds with each other: the ego postpones gratification that the id wants right away, and the super ego battles with both the ego and the id because behaviour often falls short of the moral code it represents. But more often, in the normal person, the three work as a team producing integrated behaviour. Freud believed that the conflict between the id impulses — primarily sexual and aggressive instincts — and the restraining influences of the ego and the super ego constituted the motivating sources of personality.

Evaluation of Psychoanalytic Theory: The psychoanalytic theory is an improvement over the trait theories. Trait theories try to find the stable dimensions of personality by studying groups of people and much of their data is obtained from self reports — what the individual says about himself or herself. In contrast, psychoanalytic theory is based on the in-depth study of individual personalities.

Psychoanalytic theory has had an enormous impact on psychological and philosophical conceptions of people. The ideas of the unconscious, anxiety, and the childhood causes of adult psychological difficulties have permeated people's views of human behaviour, including their understanding of the cause of their own behaviour.

Freud's emphasis on the unconscious has been partially supported by some of the current research findings of cognitive psychologists. This work has revealed that mental processes about which people are unaware all have an important impact on thoughts and actions. In addition, experimental techniques derived from procedures used to study implicit memory allow the unconscious to be studied in a more scientifically sophisticated manner. The techniques help overcome the reliance of traditional Freudian approaches on single-subject case studies and unverifiable interpretations of dreams and slips of the tongue for support.

The importance of psychoanalytic theory is underscored by the fact that it spawned a significant and enduring method of treating psychological disturbances. For Freud, the basic sources of abnormal behaviour are unresolved past conflicts and anxiety. How to rid oneself of the anxiety produced by the unconscious? The answer, according to Freud is to bring the unconscious to the conscious part. Freud suggested free association and dream interpretation as techniques to probe the unconscious.

Finally, Freud's emphasis on sexual factors led to an awareness of their role in adjustment problems and paved the way for the scientific study of sexuality.

Freud also contributed to the study of organisational behaviour in at least four areas.

(*i*) *Creative behaviour:* For instance, certain stages of the creative processes are unconscious in nature.

(*ii*) *Dissatisfaction:* Certain behaviours of employees such as day-dreaming, forgetting, apathy, rationalisation, and even some sicknesses, disability, and pain are often analysed in psychoanalytic terms.

(*iii*) *Group development:* Descriptions of the stages which groups must go through to become 'mature' are highly psychoanalytic in nature.

(*Iv*) *Leadership and influence:* Freud's great interest in authority and power is reflected in psychoanalytic approaches to the study of the emergence of leadership, the nature of a leader's relationship with his followers, and styles or leadership.

Freud's psychoanalytic theory has been criticized as much as it has been praised. One criticism against the theory is that the approach is not based on empirically verifiable facts. The psychoanalytic elements are largely hypothetical constructs and are not measurable, observable items susceptible to scientific analysis and verification. The id, the ego, and the super ego are primarily a 'black box' explanation of human beings. Hence, the theory fails to reflect clearly human personality and behaviour.

Some critics point out that Freud's theory of personality is based almost entirely upon his observations of emotionally disturbed individuals. It may not represent an appropriate description of the normal, healthy personality. Maslow, the proponent of humanistic psychology, came down heavily on Freud's psychoanalytics. Maslow considered Freudian theory as a one-sided psychology lacking in comprehensiveness since it was grounded on the abnormal or 'sick' part of human behaviour. He felt that psychology had exclusively dwelled on the negative side of human nature (i.e., its frailties and shortcomings), ignoring humanity's strengths and virtues. For example, the nature of graduate students would hardly become evident by exclusively studying high school dropouts. In fact, such a study would be much more likely to discover what graduate students are not like than what they are like. Stated more boldly, Maslow argued that the study of crippled, stunted, immature, and unhealthy persons can yield only a 'crippled' psychology.

About the claim of Freud's theory serving as a basis for scientific study of sexuality, critics point out that Freud overemphasised the role of sex in human motivation. He made his observations during the Victorian period, when sexual standards were very strict, so it was understandable that many of his patients had conflicts centering around sexual desires. In today's permissive society guilt feelings about sex are less frequent, yet the incidence of mental illness remains about the same. Sexual conflicts are not the only causes of personality disturbances — perhaps not even a major cause.

Freud assumed that all human events (actions, thoughts, feelings, aspirations) are lawful and determined by powerful instinctual forces, notably sex and aggression. Thus, human beings are seen as essentially mechanistic, they are governed by the same natural laws that apply to the behaviour of other organisms. In his approach there is no room for concepts such as free will, choice, personal responsibility, volition, spontaneity, and self determination.

Social Learning Theory

Much of human behaviour is either learnt or modified by learning. Through learning one acquires knowledge, language, attitudes, values, manual skills, fears, personality traits, and self-insight. Therefore, a study of the process of learning throws more light on understanding human's activities.

There are two ways of learning: Learning through reinforcement, direct experience, and learning by observing others, also called vicarious learning. For social learning theorists, reinforcement is not always necessary for learning. They believe that since an individual can make use of complex symbolic processes to code and store his observations in memory, he can learn by observing the actions of others and by noting the consequences of those actions.

The social learning theories of personality regard a situation as an important determinant of behaviour.

A person's action in a given situation depends upon the specific characteristics of a situation, the individual's understanding of the situation, and past behaviour in similar situations (or observations of others in similar situations).

The social learning theory focuses on behaviour patterns and cognitive activities in relation to the specific conditions that evoke, maintain, or modify them. The emphasis is on what an individual does in a given situation. Some of the personal variables that determine what an individual will do in a particular situation include the following:

(*i*) *Competencies:* Intelligence ability, social skills, and other abilities.

(*ii*) *Cognitive strategies:* Habitual ways of selectively attending to information and organising it into meaningful units.

(*iii*) *Outcome expectations:* Expectations about the consequences of different behaviours and the meaning of certain stimuli.

(*iv*) *Subjective value outcome:* Even if individuals have similar expectancies, they may choose to behave differently because of differences in the subjective values of the outcomes they expect. Two students may expect that a certain behaviour will please the professor, but for one this outcome is important, while for the other it is not.

(*v*) *Self-regulatory systems and plans:* Individual differences in self-imposed goals, rules guiding behaviour, self-imposed rewards for success or punishment for failure, and ability to plan and execute steps leading to a goal will lead to differences in behaviour.

All of the above variables interact with the conditions of a particular situation to determine what an individual will do in that situation.

These theorists also believe in reciprocal behaviour patterns. A situation is no doubt capable of evoking, maintaining, or modifying the behaviour patterns of individuals. An individual, in turn, is able to mould the condition of a situation. We are not simply passive reactors to situational conditions. Our behaviour influences the 'situations' of life as well as being influenced by them; the relationship is reciprocal. By selectively attending to what is happening, we can prevent certain conditions from impinging on us. And by our actions we can partly create the condition that do impinge; changes in behaviour towards others are usually followed by reciprocal changes in the behaviour of others.

Evaluation of Social Learning Theory: Unlike the trait and psychoanalytic theories on personality, the social learning theory regards situation as an important variable in determining human behaviour. Trait theories assume that personality is consistent so that a person can be characterized according to enduring traits. In other words, behaviour of an individual will be the same irrespective of environmental conditions. However, this assumption may not be correct. After all, actions of the individuals should be in accordance with the demands of the situation.

Psychoanalytic theory assumes that behaviour is influenced by mentalistic (unobservable) concept, namely, the unconscious. B.F. Skinner, one of the social learning theorists, strongly repudiates all explanations of behaviour based on the presumed existence of an inner metaphysical man, the self, the unconscious, or any other hypothetic entity referring to events which 'lie under the skin'. Such mentalists and intrapsychic mechanisms, he notes, originated in primitive animism but persist because there is ignorance of environmental conditions.

Skinner's objection to the use of such hypothetic constructs or inner causes is not that they are inappropriate phenomenon for psychologists to study but rather that they are shrouded in terminology that makes objective definitions and empirical tests impossible. In the history of science, he observes, it has usually been necessary to completely abandon such conceptions rather than modify them to a form which permits empirical study. To explain why a competent student flunks in college, we might easily say 'because he lacked motivation', or 'because he cuts classes due to an unconscious fear of success.' Such hypotheses about the student's dismissal from college may sound like explanations, but Skinner warns that they explain nothing, unless the motives involved are explicitly defined and unless the antecedents of flunking are established.

Social learning theory has made a major contribution to both clinical psychology and personality theory. It has led us to look more closely at the situation that can modify behaviour. Careful application of learning principles has proved very successful in changing maladaptive behaviour.

Social learning theorists have been criticised for over-emphasising the importance of situational factors in behaviour to the neglect of individual differences. They show little interest, for example, in innate differences that may predispose one person to be characteristically passive and slow to respond and another to be excitable and quick.

An individual is regarded as a flexible, malleable, and passive victim of external stimuli — the permanent pawn of environmental fate. Environmental conditions are held to be superior to human nature.

As will be studied later in Maslow's humanistic theory of personality, each individual must be studied, as an integrated, unique, organised whole. Maslow felt that for far too long psychologists had concentrated upon minute analysis of separate events, neglecting the basic aspects of the whole person and his human nature. In a common-place metaphor psychologist studied the trees, not the forest. In fact, Maslow's theory was primarily developed as a revolt against those theories (especially learning) which deal in bits and pieces of behaviour while ignoring the person as a unified whole.

The Humanistic Approach

The humanistic approach to the study of personality includes a number of theories which, although different in some respects, share a common emphasis on man's potential for self-direction and freedom of choice. They are concerned with the 'self and the individual's subjective experiences. The theories stress a man's positive nature — his push towards growth and self-actualization. Their emphasis is also on the 'here and now' rather than on events in early childhood that may have shaped the individual's personality.

Carl Rogers and Abraham Maslow are credited with the humanistic theory of personality. Their views on personality are explained, in brief, in the following paragraphs:

Rogers Self Theory: Roger's approach to personality is described as phenomenological. Phenomenology is the study of the individual's subjective experience, feelings, and private concepts as well as his views of the world and self. For Rogers, behaviour is utterly dependent upon how one perceives the world, that is, behaviour is the result of immediate events as they are actually perceived and interpreted by the individual. Such an approach to personality emphasises the self and its characteristics. Indeed, his theory is often referred to as self theory personality because the best vantage point for understanding behaviour is from the internal frame of reference of the individual himself.

Roger's ideas of human nature, like Freud's, grew out of his experiences in working with emotionally disturbed people. On the basis of his clinical experience, Rogers has concluded that the core of the human nature is essentially purposive, forward-moving, constructive, realistic, and quite trustworthy. He regards the person as an active force of energy, oriented towards future goals and self-directed purpose rather than a creature pushed and pulled by forces beyond his control.

Freud presented us with a portrait of the person with an id and an self unconscious which, if permitted expression, manifests itself in incest, homicide, thievery, rape, and other horrendous acts. According to this view, humanity is basically irrational, unsocialised, and destructive of self and others. Rogers agrees that people occasionally express all kinds of bitter and murderous feelings, abnormal impulses, bizarre and antisocial actions, but he argues that at such times they are not behaving in concert with their inner natures. Thus, the people are functioning as fully human beings, when they are free at experience and satisfying their inner nature, they show themselves to be positive and rational creatures who can be trusted to live in harmony with themselves and others.

Table 3
SUMMARY AND EVALUATIONS OF EIGHT THEORIES OF WORK MOTIVATION

Sr. No.	*Theory*	*Source of Motivation*	*Empirical Support*	*Industrial Applicability*
1.	Need Hierarchy Theory	Five sets of unconscious innate needs arranged in a hierarchical order for potential satisfaction, one at a time.	Weak. Little support for proposed relationships among needs.	
2.	ERG Theory	In effect, Maslow's five needs grouped into three broader sets, arranged not in hierarchy but in continuance, from the most concrete to the most abstract. Order of satisfaction was proposed to be flexile, not fixed.	Moderate strong. Strong support for the existence of three relatively independent needs and people's progression through them. Relationship among needs and the view that satisfied need is a motivator as proposed obtained support.	Very limited. No significant break-through. People also engage in behaviours seemingly unrelated to need fulfillment.

Table 3 *(contd.)*

3. Achievement Motivation Theory	Need for achievement. Specific to achievement motivation.	Weak Moderate. Good support for basic practice of the theory and for relationship between achievement need, and entrepreneurial/executive success. Achievement need was found not to be as stable is personality trait as was originally postulated.	Limited. Special training programmes to improve achievement motivation had positive effect. But achievement motivation seemed to improve more through placement in a demanding position and other environmental factors than because of high achievement need.
4. Two-factory Theory	Two groups of needs, motivation and maintenance, corresponding to two sets of job factors.	Very weak. Distinction between satisfaction and motivation not often conceptually clear. Tests have failed to support the postulate.	Limited. Although overall applicability is limited, it has provided initial basis of job design. Also concept of intrinsic motivation has influenced professional thinking.
5. Equity Theory	The drive to reduce feelings of tension caused by perceived inequity	Mixed. Good support for underpayment inequity, weak support for overpayment inequity.	Limited. Social comparisons are made, but feelings of inequity can be reduced through means other than increased motivation.
6. Reinforcement Theory	The schedule of reinforcement used to reward people for their performance.	Moderate. Ratio reinforcement schedules evoke superior performance compared to interval schedules, but little difference exists among the various ratio schedules.	Moderate. Contingent payment for performance is possible in some jobs, although ethical problems can be present in an organisation's attempt to shape employee behaviour.
7. Expectancy Theory	Relationship among desired outcomes, performance-reward and effort-performance variables.	Moderate Strong. Theory is more strongly supported within the subject than across the subject experiment.	Strong. Theory provides a rational basis for why people expend effort, although not all behaviour is as consciously determined as the theory postulates.
8. Goal-setting Theory	Intention to direct behaviour in pursuit of an acceptable goal.	Moderate -Strong. Performance under goal setting condition is usually superior to condition under which no goals are set.	Strong. Applicability is over a vast range of jobs and not restricted to certain types of people or jobs.

Thus, Rogers has a profound (almost religious) sense of respect for human nature. He posits that human organism has a natural tendency to move in the direction of differentiation, self-responsibility, co-operation, and maturity. The expression of this basic nature allows for the continuation and enhancement of the individual and species.

Thus, basic to Rogers' personality theory are two concepts; self and self-actualisation. The self consist of all the ideas, perceptions, and values that characterise 'I' or 'me'; it includes the awareness 'what I am' and 'what I can do'. Self-concept denotes the individual's conception of the person he is. The self-concept is one's image of oneself. This perceived self (self-concept) influences both the person's perception of the world and his own behaviour.

Self-actualisation, according to Rogers, is the basic motivating force representing the inherent tendency of the organism to develop all its capabilities in ways which serve to maintain or enhance the person. Thus, the primary motive in people's lives is to actualise, maintain, or enhance themselves to become the best that their inherited nature will allow them to be.

Conclusion

All the above theories primarily deal with the motivation of an individual to perform a specific task, which ultimately leads to achievement of a specific goal. So a manager can make use of any one or all of these in order to understand the behaviour/expected behaviour of an employee in particular situations.

Motivation has been defined as "The process of activating the psychological impulses to channelise human behaviour towards accomplishing the desired organisational objectives"

So motivation in the organisational setup can also be defined as the process of drawing a synergy between the personal goals of the individuals and the overall organisational goals and providing an environment where the two complement each other.

Thus it is important for the entrepreneur to know and understand the Goals of Both the Organisation and the individual. Generally, the Organisational goals are well spelled out and so there is no difficulty in understanding them. The biggest challenge for the manager is to know "what drives the individual". With every individual having different preferences this process becomes very complex and complicated one.

Annexure

The Young and the Restless

Culture Gap

"The BPO industry has a unique set of challenges as far as the workforce is concerned. Firstly, there is a sense of disconnect with the people in UK and US, is as far as culture, language, exposure is concerned. The industry has been trying to orient people here to culture is those countries with appropriate training.

Social Stigma

Besides, we're the only service sector, barring the hospitality and the airline industry, that works 24*7. This renders the industry an image of being 'inappropriate' for women and those looking for a serious career. What people don't realise is that this industry is a very good opportunity in an environment when people are constantly trying to automate and get rid of the workforce. If the youth hadn't been absorbed by this industry it would have serious social implications; unemployment is always related to crime rate. Plain graduates can add on to existing qualification and 3-4 years here prepare them for the hospitality or airline industry.

Time Warp

The typical challenge we face in this industry is that we have to change our biological clock, you have to look for a day in the night, that's the only way you'll be happy and look for a night in the day, that's the only way you'll rest. You can't switch on the weekend to a day environment; the life-style has to be consistent. A lot of people have quit due to health reasons. Therefore we insist that employees have to be careful about food habits and sleeping hours. There are obvious roadblocks, like you can't go home at 4 in the morning and expect breakfast. We mitigate this to an extent by providing food at a 24-hours cafe. What is to our advantage is that these people are young, and they're able to adapt.

Walk the Talk

In addition to this there is a concern around culture, these young people right out of college suddenly have the freedom to do what they want all night, so we counsel them on the need to be career oriented. It is important that the senior management display a certain pattern of behaviour, we have to lead by example. We also encourage our leaders to counsel, communicate and mentor as much as possible. We never miss a chance to bond as a family — cricket matches, tug of war. Relationships at workplace is one of the biggest reasons that people don't leave the organisation, according to Gallop.

Tailor Made

Over the years, we have done a good job of designing our training to ensure that it has the right ingredients to quickly orient these people to the culture and kind of work that we are going to be delivering to our clients. We have counsellors who counsel these young adults on how to make a day of night and *vice versa*, food habits, etc.

Dream Big

In the new world of business creative thinking and story telling is the ultimate leadership tool. It's about taking people from where they are now to where they need to be. In one such exercise we have imagined ourselves to be a Fortune company. The best way to get people to venture into unknown terrain is to make it desirable by taking them there in their imaginations.

LEARNING CURVE

"We hope to provide an accelerated growth platform to our employees."

- Generic training — sensitises employees to US/UK culture, orients them to a voice and accent culture.
- Orientation for applications and customer relations.
- Training to maintain work-life balances.
- Leadership training
- Specified operational training
- On-site education.

Chairman Murthy (left) and CEO Nilekani were a study in contrasts as far as their image scores and QoE scores were concerned

Sheen S. Levine has found that often, what gives firms competitive advantage isn't just their repository of sheer knowledge, but their use and encouragement of so-called "performance ties" — those impromptu communications made by colleagues who are strangers, in which critical knowledge is transferred with no expectation of a quid pro quo. "Not many managers even understand that this happens, much less why," says Levine. "They think it's just friends helping friends. But it's not. Usually, people will reach out and connect with colleagues whom they have never met or talked to before. It's not dependent on prior or future favours."

For knowledge to become a real competitive advantage, companies must encourage 'performative ties' — informal flow of information between employees, without expectations of a quid pro quo.

EIGHT

Emotional Intelligence and Effective Leadership

The world is a vastly changed place today. The challenges and complexity we face in our relationships, families, professional lives, and communities are of an entirely new order of magnitude. **Being effective as individuals and organisations is no longer merely an option — survival in today's world requires it.**

"The dogmas of the quiet past are inadequate to the stormy present" — **Abraham Lincoln**

In order to thrive, innovate, excel, and lead in this new knowledge worker age, we must build on and move beyond effectiveness. **The call for this new era in human history is for greatness; it's for fulfillment, passionate execution, and significant contribution.** Accessing the higher levels of human genius and motivation in today's new reality **requires a sea change in thinking; a new mind-set, a new skill-set, a new tool-set, in short, a whole new habit.**

Voice-the unique, personal significance

Two roads diverged in a wood, and I...
I took the one less traveled by,
And that has made all the difference.

— Robert Frost

Introduction

The most effective leaders are alike in one crucial way. They all have a high degree of what has come to be known as emotional intelligence. It's not that IQ and technical skills are irrelevant. They do matter, but mainly as "threshold capabilities", that is, they are the entry-level requirements for executive positions. But my research, along with other recent studies, clearly shows that emotional intelligence is the *sine qua non* of leadership. Without it, a person can have the best training in the world, an incisive, analytical mind, and an endless supply of smart ideas, but he still won't make a great leader.

Emotional Intelligence

The writing is on the wall for the brilliant but bullying boss. Driving ambition and a high IQ might give you a head start in the race for the top but emotional intelligence (El) is essential for medium to long-term success, interpersonal skills have long been valued in the workplace. The concept that emotional intelligence explains the difference between outstanding and average performance is comparatively new. In a recent study, psychologist Daniel Goleman, author of *Emotional intelligence: Why It Can Matter More Than lQ* (Bloornsbury), found that nearly 90% of the difference between star performers in senior leadership positions and average ones was "attributable to emotional intelligence factors rather than cognitive abilities."

Initially sceptical about the value of El, Dr. Malcolm Higgs and Prof. Vic Dulewicz of Henley Management College set out to establish whether it exists, if it can be assessed and developed. They identified seven measurable core emotional skills. They also devised a psychometric test to score managers on the seven factors and identify the areas that need to be worked on.

Seven Core Skills

- Awareness of your feelings and an ability to control them.
- Emotional resilience — the ability to perform consistency under pressure.
- Motivation — the drive and energy to achieve results.
- The ability to take other people's needs into account.
- Influence — persuasive skills.
- Decisiveness — arrive at clear decisions and drive them through.
- Conscientiousness — display commitment to a plan of action and match words and deeds.

According to Gary Cooper, Bupa professor of organisational psychology and health at the University of Manchester Institute of Science and Technology (Umist), "in the workplace it is very important for people in managerial jobs to tap into emotions, to understand people's feelings about change, their fears of redundancy. And it is important that they understand themselves if they are to get ahead. An automaton is going to create a people-unfriendly workplace but good employers sustain a workforce with low turnover and good balance."

Getting in touch with your own feelings and empathising with those of others definitely has benefits which extend beyond the workplace. Says Cooper, "Without El, in the medium to long term you will have a less-balanced personal life and make lots of enemies. A screwed up private life spills over into work life."

Evaluating Emotional Intelligence

Most-large companies today have employed trained psychologists to develop what are known as "competency models" to aid them in identifying, training, and promoting likely stars in the leadership firmament. The psychologists have also developed such models for lower level positions. And in recent years, I have analysed competency models from 188 companies, most of which were large and global and included the like of Lucent Technologies, British Airways, and Credit Suisse".

In carrying out this work, Daniel Goleman's objective was to determine which personal capabilities drove outstanding performance within these organisations, and to what degree they did so. He grouped capabilities into three categories, purely technical skills like accounting and business planning; cognitive abilities like analytical reasoning; and competencies demonstrating emotional intelligence, such as the ability to work with others and effectiveness in leading change.

To create some of the competency models, psychologists asked senior managers at the companies to identify the capabilities that typified the organisation's most outstanding leaders. To create other models, the psychologists used objective criteria, such as a divisions' profitability, to differentiate the star performers at senior levels within their organisations from the average ones. Those individuals were then extensively interviewed and tested, and their capabilities were compared. The process resulted in the creation of lists of ingredients for highly effective leaders. The lists ranged in length from seven to 15 items and included such ingredients as initiative and strategic vision.

When he analysed all this data, he found dramatic results. To be sure, intellect was a drive of outstanding performance. Cognitive skills such as big-picture thinking and long-term vision were particularly important. But when he calculated the ratio of technical skills, IQ, and emotional intelligence as ingredients of excellent performance, emotional intelligence proved to be twice as important as the others for jobs at all levels.

Moreover, his analysis showed that emotional intelligence played an increasingly important role at the highest levels of the company, where differences in technical skills are of negligible importance. In other words, the higher the rank of a person considered to be a star performer, the more emotional intelligence capabilities showed up as the reason for his or her effectiveness. When compared star performers with average ones in senior leadership positions, nearly 90% of the difference in their profiles were attributable to emotional intelligence factors rather than cognitive abilities.

Other researchers have confirmed that emotional intelligence not only distinguishes outstanding leaders but can also be linked to strong performance. The findings of the late David MClelland, the renowned researcher in human and organisation behaviour, are a good example. In a 1996 study of a global food and beverage company, MClelland found that when senior managers had a critical mass of emotional intelligence capabilities, their divisions outperformed yearly earnings' goals by 20%. Meanwhile, division leaders without that critical mass underperformed by almost the same amount. McClelland's findings, interestingly, held as true in the company's U.S. divisions as in its divisions in Asia and Europe.

In short, the numbers are beginning to tell us a persuasive story about the link between a company's success and the emotional intelligence of its leaders. And just as important, research is also demonstrating that people can, if they take the right approach, develop their emotional intelligence.

Self-Awareness

Self-awareness is the first component of emotional intelligence — which makes sense when one considers that the Delphic oracle gave the advice to "now thyself" thousands of years ago. Self-awareness means having a deep understanding of one's emotions, strengths, weaknesses, needs, and drives. People with strong, self-awareness are neither overly critical nor unrealistically hopeful. Rather, they are honest-with themselves and with others.

People who have a high degree of self-awareness recognise how their feelings affect them, other people, and their job performance. Thus, a self-aware person who knows that tight deadlines bring out the worst in him, plans his time carefully and gets his work done well in advance. Another person with high self-awareness will be able to work with a demanding client, she will understand the client's impact on her moods and the deeper reasons for her frustration. "Their trivial demands take us away from the real work that need to be done," she might explain. And she will go one step further and turn her anger into something constructive.

Self-awareness extends to a person's understanding of his or her values and goals. Someone who is highly self-aware knows where he is headed and why; so, for example, he will be able to be firm in turning down a job offer that is tempting financially but does not fit with his principles or long-term goals. A person who lacks self-awareness is apt to make decision that bring on inner turmoil by treading on buried values. "The money looked good so I signed on," someone might say two years into a job, "but the work means so little to me that I'm constantly bored." The decisions of self aware people mesh with their values: consequently, they often find work to be energising.

How can one recognise self-awareness? First and foremost, it shows itself as candor and an ability to assess oneself realistically. People with high self awareness are able to speak accurately and openly although not necessarily effusively or confessionally-about their emotions and the impact they have on their work. For instance, one manager he knew who was skeptical about a new personal-shopper service that her company, a major department store chain, was about to introduce. Without prompting from her team or her boss, she offered them an explanation; "It's hard for me to get behind the rollout of this service," she admitted," because I really wanted to run the project, but I wasn't selected, bear with me while I deal with that." The manager did indeed examine her feelings; a week later, she was supporting the project fully.

Such self-knowledge often shows itself in the hiring process. Ask a candidate to describe a time he got carried away by his feelings and did something he later regretted. Self-aware candidates will be frank in admitting to failure-and will often tell their tales with a smile. One of the hallmarks of self awareness is a self-deprecating sense of humor.

Self-awareness can also be identified during performance reviews. Self-aware people know-and are comfortable talking about-their limitations and strengths, and they often demonstrate a thirst for constructive criticism. By contrast, people with low self-awareness interpret the message that they need to improve as a threat or a sign of failure.

Self-aware people can also be recognised by their self-confidence. They have a firm grasp of their capabilities and are less likely to set themselves up to fail by, for example, overstretching on assignments. They know, too, when to ask for help. And the risks they take on the job are calculated. They won't ask for a challenge that they know they can't handle alone. They'll play to their strengths.

Consider the actions of a mid-level employee who was invited to sit in on a strategy meeting with her company's top executives. Although she was the most junior person in the room, she did not sit there quietly, listening in awestruck or fearful silence. She knows she had a head for clear logic and the skill to present ideas persuasively, and she offered cogent suggestions about the company's strategy. At the same time, her self-awareness stopped her from wandering into territories where she knew she was weak.

Despite the value of having self-aware people in the workplace, my research indicates that senior executives don't often give self-awareness the credit it deserves when they look for potential leaders. Many executives mistake candor about feelings for "wimpiness" and fail to give due respect to employees who openly acknowledge their shortcomings. Such people are too readily dismissed as "not tough enough" to lead others.

In fact, the opposite is true. In the first place, people generally admire and respect candor. Furthermore, leaders are constantly required to make judgement calls that require a candid assessment of capabilities of their own and those of others. Do we have the management expertise to acquire a competitor? Can we launch a new product within six months? People who assess themselves honestly -that is, self-aware people are well suited to do the same for the organisations they run.

Self-regulation

Biological impulses drive our emotions. We cannot do away with them, but we can do much to manage them. Self-regulation, which is like an ongoing inner conversation, is the component of emotional intelligence that frees us from being prisoners of our feelings. People engaged in such a conversation feel bad moods and emotional impulses just as everyone else does, but they find ways to control them and even to channel them in useful ways.

Imagine an executive who has just watched a team of his employees present a botched analysis to the company's board of directors. In the gloom that follows, the executive might find himself tempted to pound on the table in anger or kick over a chair, he could leap up and scream at the group. Or he might maintain a grim silence, glaring at everyone before stalking off.

But if he had a gift for self-regulation, he would choose a different approach. He would pick his words carefully, acknowledging the team's poor performance without rushing to any hasty judgement. He would then step back to consider the reasons for the failure. Are they personal — a lack of effort? Are there any mitigating factors? What was his role in the debacle? After considering these questions, he would call the team together, lay out the incident's consequences, and offer his feelings about it. He would then present his analysis of the problem and a well-considered solution.

Why does self-regulation matter so much for leaders? First of all, people who are in control of their feelings and impulses — that is, people who are reasonable — are able to create an environment of trust and fairness. In such an environment, politics and infighting are sharply reduced and productivity is high. Talented people flock to the organisation and aren't tempted to leave. And self-regulation has a trickle down effect. No one wants to be known as a hothead when the boss is known for her calm approach. Fewer bad moods at the top mean fewer throughout the organisation.

Second, self-regulation is important for competitive reasons. Everyone knows that business today is rife with ambiguity and change. Companies merge and break apart regularly. Technology transforms work at a dizzying pace. People who have mastered their emotions are able to roll with the changes. When a new program is announced, they don't panic, instead, they are able to suspend judgement, seek out information, and listen to the executives as they explain the new program. As the initiative moves forward, these people are able to move with it.

Sometimes, they even lead the way — consider the case of a manager at a large manufacturing company. Like her colleagues, she had used a certain software program for five years. The program drove how she collected and reported data and how she thought about the company's strategy. One day, senior executives announced that a new program was to be installed that would radically change how information was gathered and assessed within the organisation. While many people in the company complained bitterly about how disruptive the change would be, the manager mulled over the reasons for the new program and was convinced of its potential to improve performance. She eagerly attended training sessions some of her colleagues refused to do so and was eventually promoted to run several divisions, in part because she used the new technology so effectively.

I want to push the importance or self regulation to leadership even further and make the case that it enhances integrity, which is not only a personal virtue but also an organisational strength. Many of the bad things that happen in companies are a function of impulsive behaviour. People rarely plan to exaggerate profits, pad expense accounts, dip into the till, or abuse power for selfish ends. Instead, an opportunity presents itself, and people with low impulse control just say yes.

By contrast, consider the behaviour of the senior executive at a large food company. The executive was scrupulously honest in his negotiations with local distributors. He would routinely lay out his cost structure in detail, thereby giving the distributors a realistic understanding of the company's pricing. This approach meant the executive couldn't always drive a hard bargain. Now, on occasion, he felt the urge to increase profits by withholding information about the company's costs. But he challenged that impulse — he saw that it made more sense in the long run to counteract it. His emotional self-regulation paid off in strong, lasting relationships with distributors that benefited the company more than any short-term financial gains would have.

The signs of emotional self-regulation, therefore, are easy to see: a propensity for reflection and thoughtfulness; comfort with ambiguity and change; and integrity an ability to say no to impulsive urges.

Like self awareness, self regulation often does not get its due. People who can master their emotions are sometimes seen as cold fish — their considered responses are taken as a lack of passion. People with fiery temperaments are frequently thought of as 'classic' leaders, their outbursts are considered hallmarks of charisma and power. But when such people make it to the top, their impulsiveness often works against them. In my research, extreme displays of negative emotion have never emerged as a driver of good leadership.

Motivation

If there is one trait that virtually all-effective leaders have, it is motivation. They are driven to achieve beyond expectation — their own and everyone else's. The key word here is achieve. Plenty of people are motivated by external factors, such as a big salary or the status that comes from having an impressive title or being part of a prestigious company. By contrast, those with leadership potential are motivated by a deeply embedded desire to achieve for the sake of achievement.

If you are looking for leaders, how can you identify people who are motivated by the drive to achieve rather than by external rewards? The first sign is a passion for the work itself — such people seek out creative challenges, love to learn, and take great pride in a job well done. They also display an unflagging energy to do things better. People with such energy often seem restless with the *status quo.* They are persistent with their questions about why things are done one way rather than another; they are eager to explore new approaches to their work.

A cosmetics company manager, for example, was frustrated that he had to wait two weeks to get sales results from people in the field. He finally tracked down an automated phone system that would beep each of his sales people at 5 pm every day. An automated message then prompted them to punch in their numbers — how many calls and sales they had made that day. The system shortened the feedback time on sales results from weeks to hours.

That story illustrates two other common traits of people who are driven to achieve. They are forever raising the performance bar, and they like to keep score. Take the performance bar first. During performance reviews, people with high levels of motivation might ask to be 'stretched' by their superiors. Of course, an employee who combines self awareness with internal motivation will recognise her limits — but she won't settle for objectives that seem too easy to fulfill.

And it follows naturally that people who are driven to do better also want a way of tracking progress — their own, their team's, and their company's. Whereas, people with low achievement motivation are often fuzzy about results, those with high achievement motivation often keep score by tracking such hard measures as profitability or market share. I know of many managers who start and end their day on the Internet, gauging the performance of their stock fund against four industry-set benchmarks.

Interestingly, people with high motivation remain optimistic even when the score is against them. In such cases, self-regulation combines with achievement motivation to overcome the frustration and depression that come after a set back or failure. Take the case of another portfolio manager at a large investment company. After several successful years, her fund tumbled for three consecutive quarters, leading three large institutional clients to shift their business elsewhere.

THE FIVE COMPONENTS OF EMOTIONAL INTELLIGENCE AT WORK

	Definition	*Hallmarks*
Self-Awareness	Definition the ability to recognise and understand your moods, emotions and drives, as well as their effect on others	Self-confidence, realistic, self assessment, self deprecating sense of humor
Self-Regulation	The ability to control or redirect disruptive impulses and mood, the propensity to suspend judgement — to think before acting	Trustworthiness and integrity, comfort with ambiguity, openness to change
Motivation	A passion to work for reasons that go beyond money or status, a propensity to pursue goals with energy and persistence	Strong drive to achieve optimism, even in the face of failure organisational commitment
Empathy	The ability to understand the emotional makeup of other people skill in treating people according to their emotional reactions	Expertise in building and retaining talent, cross-cultural sensitivity service to clients and customers
Social Skill	Proficiency in managing relationships and building networks an ability to find common ground and build rapport.	Effectiveness in leading change persuasiveness, expertise in building and leading teams.

Some executives would have blamed the nosedive on circumstances outside their control: others might have seen the setback as evidence of personal failure. This portfolio manager, however, saw an opportunity to prove she could lead a turn-around. Two years later, when she was promoted to a very senior level in the company, she described the experience as "the best thing that ever happened to me; I learned so much from it."

Executives trying to recognise high levels of achievement motivation in their people can look for one last piece of evidence: commitment to the organisation. When people love their jobs for the work itself, they often feel committed to the organisations that make that work possible. Committed employees are likely to stay with an organisation even when they are pursued by headhunters waving money.

It's not difficult to understand how and why a motivation to achieve translates into strong leadership. It you set the performance bar high for yourself, you will do the same for the organisation when you are in a position to do so. Likewise, a drive to surpass goals and an interest in keeping score can be contagious. Leaders with these traits can often build a team of managers around them with the same traits. And of course, optimism and organisational commitment are fundamental to leadership, just try to imagine running a company without them.

Empathy

Of all the dimensions of emotional intelligence, empathy is the most easily recognised, we have all felt the empathy of a sensitive teacher or friend; we have all been struck by its absence in an unfeeling coach or boss. But when it comes to business, we rarely hear people praised, let alone rewarded, for their empathy. The very word seems unbusinesslike, out of place amid the tough realities of the marketplace.

But empathy doesn't mean a kind of "I'm OK, you're OK" mushiness.

For a leader, that is, it doesn't mean adopting other people's emotions as one's own and trying to please everybody. That would be a nightmare — it would make action impossible. Rather, empathy means thoughtfully considering employees' feelings along with other factors — in the process of making intelligent decisions.

For an example of empathy in action, consider what happened when two giant brokerage companies merged, creating redundant jobs in all their divisions. One division manager called his people together and gave a gloomy speech that emphasised the number of people who would soon be fired. The manager of another division gave his people a different kind of speech. He was up-front about his own worry and confusion, and he promised to keep people informed and to treat everyone fairly.

The difference between these two managers was empathy. The first manager was too worried about his own fate to consider the feelings of his anxiety-sticken colleagues. The second knew intuitively what his people were feeling, and he acknowledged their fears with his words. Is it any surprise that the first manager saw his division sink as many demoralised people, especially the most talented, departed? By contrast, the second manager continued to be a strong leader, his best people stayed, and his division remained as productive as ever.

Empathy is particularly important today as a component of leadership for at least three reasons: the increasing use of team; the rapid pace of globalisation; and the rowing need to retain talent.

Consider the challenge of leading a team. As anyone who has ever been a part of one can attest, teams are cauldrons of bubbling emotions. They are often charged with reaching a consensus — which is hard enough with two people and much more difficult as the numbers increase. Even in groups with as few as four or five members, alliances form and clashing agendas get set. A team's leader must be able to sense and understand the viewpoints of everyone around the table.

That's exactly what a marketing manager at a large information technology company was able to do when she was appointed to lead a troubled team. The group was in turmoil, overloaded by work and missing deadlines. Tensions were high among the members. Tinkering with procedures was not enough to bring the group together and make it an effective part of the company.

So the manager took several steps. In a series of one-on-one sessions, she took the time to listen to everyone in the group — what was frustrating them, how they rated their colleagues, whether they felt they had been ignored. And then she directed the team in a way that brought it together. She encouraged people to speak more openly about their frustrations, and she helped people raise constructive complaints during meetings. In short, her empathy allowed her to understand her team's emotional makeup. The result was not just heightened collaboration among members but also added business, as the team was called on for help by a wider range of internal clients.

Globalisation is another reason for the rising importance of empathy for business leaders. Cross-cultural dialogue can easily lead to miscues and misunderstandings. Empathy is an antidote. People who have it are attuned to subtleties in body language; they can hear the message beneath the words being spoken. Beyond that, they have a deep understanding of both the existence and the importance of cultural and ethnic differences.

Consider the case of an American consultant whose team had just pitched a project to a potential Japanese client. In its dealings with Americans, the team was accustomed to being bombarded with questions after such a proposal, but this time it was greeted with a long silence. Other members of the team, taking the silence as disapproval, were ready to pack and leave. The lead consultant gestured them to stop. Although he was not particularly familiar with Japanese culture, he read the client's face and posture and sensed not rejection but interest, even deep consideration. He was right: When the client finally spoke, it was to give the consulting firm the job.

Finally, empathy plays a key role in the retention of talent, particularly in today's information economy. Leaders have always needed empathy to develop and keep good people, but today the stakes are higher. When good people leave, they take the company's knowledge with them.

That's where coaching and mentoring come in. It has repeatedly been shown that coaching and mentoring pay off not just in better performance but also in increased job satisfaction and decreased turnover. But what makes coaching and mentoring work best is the nature of the relationship. Outstanding coaches and mentors get inside the heads of the people they are helping. They sense how to give effective feedback. They know when to push for better performance and when to hold back. In the way they motivate their proteges, they demonstrate empathy in action.

In what is probably sounding like a refrain, let me repeat that empathy doesn't get much respect in business. People wonder how leaders can make hard decisions if they are "feeling" for all the people who will be affected. But leaders with empathy do more than sympathise with people around them. They use their knowledge to improve their companies in subtle but important ways.

Social Skill

The first three components of emotional intelligence are self-management skills. The last two, empathy and social skill, concern a person's ability to manage relationships with others. As a component of emotional intelligence, social skill is not as simple as it sounds, it's not just a matter of friendliness, although people with high levels of social skill are rarely mean-spirited. Social skill, rather, is friendliness with a purpose: moving people in the direction you desire, whether that's agreement on a new marketing strategy or enthusiasm about a new product.

Socially skilled people tend to have a wide circle of acquaintances, and they have a knack for finding common ground with people of all kinds, a knack for building rapport. The doesn't mean they socialize continually; it means they work according to the assumption that nothing important gets done alone. Such people have a network in place when the time for action comes.

Social skill is the culmination of the other dimensions of emotional intelligence, people tend to be very effective at managing relationships when they can understand and control their own emotions and can empathize with the feelings of others. Even motivation contributes to social skill. Remember that people who are driven to achieve tend to be optimistic, even in the face of set backs or failure. When people are up beat, their "glow" is cast upon conversations and other social encounters. They are popular, and for good reason.

Because it is the outcome of the other dimensions of emotional intelligence, social skill is recognizable on the job in many ways that will by now sound familiar. Socially skilled people, for instance, are adept at managing teams — that's their empathy at work. Likewise, they are expert persuaders — a manifestation of self-awareness, self-regulation, and empathy combined, given those skills, good persuaders know when to make an emotional plea, for instance, and when an appeal to reason will work better. And motivation, when publicly visible, makes such people excellent collaborators; their passion for the work spreads to others, and they are driven to find solutions.

But sometimes, social skill shows itself in ways the other emotional intelligence components do not. For instance, socially skilled people may at times appear not to be working while at work. They seem to be idly schmoozing chatting in the hall ways with colleagues or joking around with people who are not even connected to their "real" jobs, socially skilled people, however, don't think it makes sense to arbitrarily limit the scope of their relationships. They build bonds widely because they know that in these fluid times, they may need help some day from people they are just getting to know today.

For example, consider the case of an executive in the strategy department of a global computer manufacture. By 1993, he was convinced that the company's future lay with the Internet. Over the course of the next year, he found kindred spirits and used his social skill to stitch together a virtual community that cut across levels, divisions, and nationals. He then used this *de facto* team to put up a corporate Web site, among the first by a major company. And, on his own initiative, with no budget or formal status, he signed up the company to participate in a annual Internet industry convention. Calling on his allies and persuading various divisions to donate funds, he recruited more than 50 people from a dozen different units to represent the company at the convention. Management took notice; Within a year of the conference, the executive's team formed the basis for the company's first Internet division, and he was formally put in charge of it. To get there, the executive had ignored conventional boundaries, forging and maintaining connections with people in every corner of the organisation.

Is social skill considered a key leadership capability in most companies? The answer is yes, especially when compared with the other components of emotional intelligence. People seem to know intuitively that leaders need to manage relationships effectively; no leader is an island. After all, the leader's task is to get work done through other people, and social skill makes that possible. A leader who cannot express her empathy may as well not have it at all. And a leader's motivation will be useless if he cannot communicate his passion to the organisation. Social skill allows leaders to put their emotional intelligence to work.

It would be foolish to assert that good-old-fashioned IQ and technical ability are not important ingredients in strong leadership. But the recipe would not be complete without emotional intelligence. It was once thought that the components of emotional intelligence were "nice to

NON-VERBAL COMMUNICATION

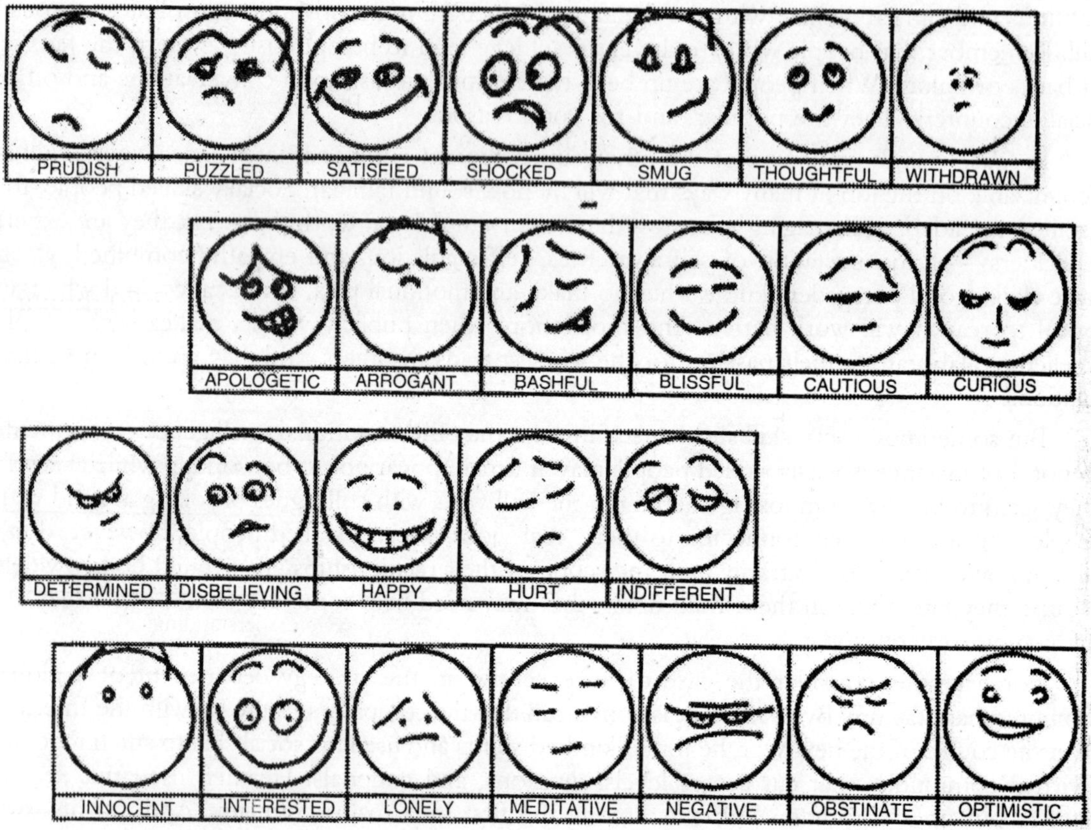

have" in business leaders. But now we know that, for the sake of performance, these are ingredients that leaders "need to have."

It is fortunate, then, that emotional intelligence can be learned. The process is not easy. It takes time and, most of all, commitment. But the benefits that come from having a well-developed emotional intelligence, both for the individual and for the organisation, make it worth the effort.

The four intelligences/capacities of our nature

All of us possess four capacities or intelligences; our physical or body intelligence **(PQ)**, *our mental intelligence* **(IQ)**, *our emotional intelligence* **(EQ)** and *our spiritual intelligence* **(SQ)**. *Developing and using these intelligences will instill with us confidence, internal strength and security, ability to be simultaneously courageous and considerate, and personal moral authority.* It will also impact our ability to influence others and inspire them to find their voice.

Developing the 4 Intelligences/Capacities — A Practical Guide to Action

- **Developing Physical Intelligence (PQ)**
  - — Wise nutrition
  - — Consistent balanced exercise
  - — Proper rest, relaxation and stress management and prevention thinking
- **Developing Mental Intelligence (IQ)**
  - — Continuous, systematic, disciplined study and education
  - — Cultivation of self-awareness
  - — Learning by teaching and doing
- **Developing The Five Main Components of Emotional Intelligence (EQ) through the 7 Habits**

Five main components of (EQ)	*7 Habit*	*Principle*
Self-Awareness	Be Proactive	Responsibility/Initiative
Personal Motivation	Begin with the End in Mind	Vision/Values
Self-Regulation	— Puy First Things First — Sharpen the Saw	— Integrity/Execution — Renewal
Empathy	Seek First to understand, then to be understood	Mutual understanding
Social Skills	— Think win-win — Seek first to understand, then to be understood — Synergize	— Mutual Respect/Benefit — Mutual understanding — Creative Co-operation

- **Developing Spiritual Intelligence (SO)**
  - — *Integrity* (Being true to one's highest values and conscience)
  - — *Meaning* (A sense of contribution to people and causes)
  - — *Voice* (Aligning work with one's unique calling and gifts)

Express Your Voice-Vision, Discipline, Passion & Conscience

When we study the lives of all the great achievers who have had greatest influence on others **— George Washington, Florence Nightingale, M.K. Gandhi, Margaret Thatcher, Nelson Mandela, Mother Teresa etc, we find a striking similarity**. All of them through persistent efforts and inner struggle *have greatly expanded their four native human intelligence or capacities. The highest manifestations of these four intelligences are: for the mental,* **vision**; *for the physical,* **discipline**; *for the emotiona'* **passion**; *for the spiritual,* **conscience**. *These manifestations also represent our highest means of expressing o voice.*

Inspiring Others to Find Their Voice

In everyone's life, at some time, our inner fire goes out.
It is then burst into flame by an encounter with another human being.
We should all be thankful for those people who rekindle the inner spirit

— Albert Schweitzer

The process of inspiring others to find their voice would be summarised as follows:

- **Focus-Modeling and Path finding**
  1. *The voice of influence.* Being a model involves finding your own voice first and then choosing the ATTITUDE of initiative-to expand your influence in every opportunity around you.
  2. *The voice of Trustworthiness.* Modeling character and competence lays the foundation for trust in every relationship and organisation.
  3. *The voice and Speed of Trust.* Modeling also involves developing strong relationship SKILLS that Build Trust and Blending Voices — creating Third-Alternative solutions to your challenges and differences with others.
  4. *One Voice.* Path finding involves creating with others a common vision about your highest priorities and the values by which you will achieve your priorities.
- **Execution-Aligning and Empowering**
  1. *The voice of Execution:* Aligning goals and enabling systems for results.
  2. *The Empowering Voice:* Releasing passion and talent, clearing the way before them and then getting out of the way.
- **Emotional Intelligence and Leadership**

A given sensation can produce quite different emotional effects in different individuals. The key is to use our emotions intelligently, which is just what we mean by emotional intelligence. It is possible for us to make our emotions work for us by using them to help guide our behaviour and thinking in ways that enhance our results. There should not be any pessimism on this count because emotional intelligence can be nurtured, developed and augmented. We can maximise the effectiveness of our emotional intelligence by self-awareness, developing good communication skills, interpersonal expertise and mentoring abilities.

The Competencies of Emotional Intelligence

Competencies are defined as underlying behaviour necessary to the achievement of a desired outcome. Individuals high on emotional Intelligence defer immediate gratification and exhibit self-control m order to optimise pleasure over their lifetime Also, they display enlightened self-interests by engaging in activities that are both pro-individual and prosocial, they feel emotions flexibly and in a manner appropriate to the situation. Successful emotional regulation is a prerequisite for adaptive functioning. To get along with others, we must be able to regulate emotions and how we experience and express these emotions.

Author quotes "Will Slutz" book on FIRO, where he has mentioned that every human being has three interpersonal needs: Inclusion, control and affection. For each of these interpersonal needs, there are three subdivisions. Thus people can be categorised into nine types based on interpersonal needs.

In the second part, the author goes on discussing Leadership Styles and Leaders. He discusses 9 types of leadership styles, their strong and emotional competencies and preferences and Leadership profile. He has quoted lives of leaders and their thought process under different categories to substantiate his understanding.

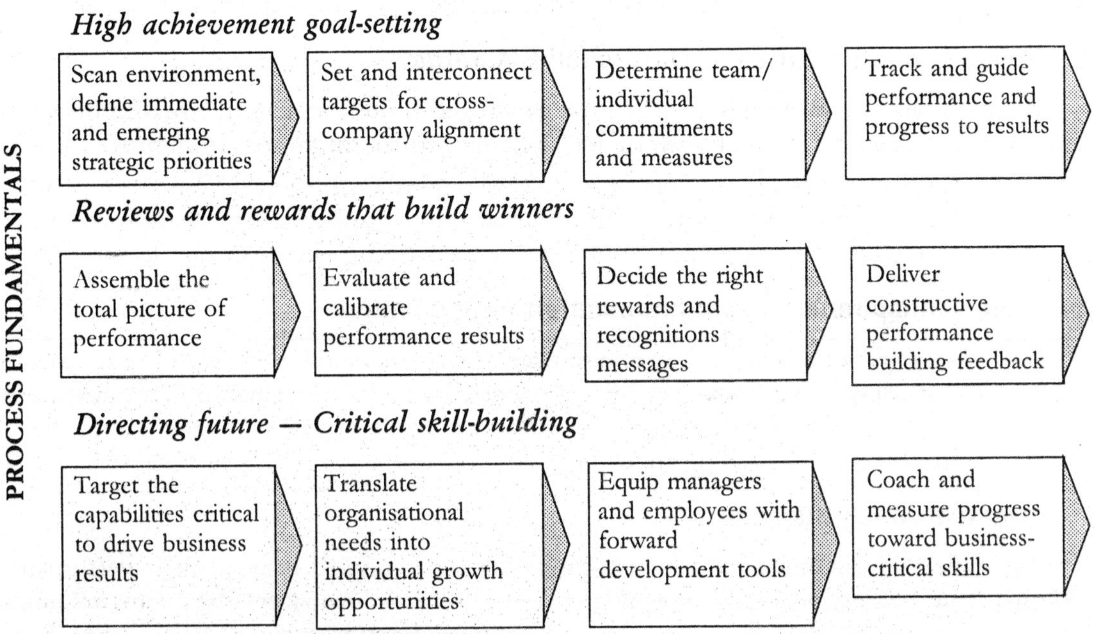

Towards High Performance

Enterprises need to create an environment conductive to creating a high performance workforce.

Hewitt's research has shown that a 'High Performance Workforce' requires its leaders at all levels to be passionate about two key concepts:

- Driving achievement through goal setting, guidance and support they provide to those who are pursuing aggressive goals aligned to the business.
- Driving engagement by creating an environment where people feel successful, valued and an integral part of what the greater team is trying to accomplish.

KRA — Reach for the Stars

High stretch goals that are aligned to achievement of business targets works for India's top performing companies. 68% of CEOs in Hewitt's Best Employers 2007 India study said that they are more likely to reward their managers and employees on these targets.

The Manager as a Coach

One of the biggest enablers to high performance in organisations is the ability of managers to provide feedback and performance coaching. While this may be the intent of most organisations, they are a long way from being able to effectively instil this skill in their managers. Most Indian industry captains complain that their middle management lacks maturity. One witnesses issues of insecurity of team leaders, attrition due to bad people managers and dwindling profits because a recently promoted business manager couldn't train his team to move up the learning curve.

Reviews and Rewards — The Coach'S Mantras

It's important that the ratings as well as the ranking distributions make the solid contributors feel successful, leading performers special and underperformers motivated to improve.

The performance distribution curve can only be applied at the level of large teams. When applied to smaller teams, a performance distribution curve can leave many de-motivated and dissatisfied. A large enough team removes any distortions arising out of smaller teams.

From Transparency to Communication to Motivation

Successful organisations see all their employees as insiders and share not only the goals the organisation is striving to achieve but also share how these goals will be achieved. The transparency helps individuals see for themselves how the goals link to their vision of their job profile. It motivates them to contribute to the stretch goals.

Engineered for Success

These five drivers can go a long way in creating an engaged, aligned high performance workforce. But the trick lies in the implementation. Performance-management systems are critical in driving organisational performance and results. As Larry Bossidy, former CEO at Allied Signal and Honeywell, and the co-author of *Execution: The Discipline of Getting Things Done,* says: "Corporate strategies are intellectually simple; their execution is not. The question is, can you execute? That's what differentiates one company from another."

Conclusion

Emotional intelligence has a greater bearing on effective leadership. Emotional intelligence is much more than intelligent quotient (IQ) and technical skills. The components of emotional intelligence — self-awareness, self-regulation, motivation, empathy and social skill — in turn have a direct bearing on effective performance of leadership. EI enhances the effectiveness of entrepreneurial activities.

❒ ❒ ❒

Leadership is about taking risks. If your life is free of failure, you aren't much of a leader. To succeed, we must attempt new things. Mistakes are not a problem. How one identifies and corrects errors, how one turns failure into a new opportunity, determines the quality and durability of leadership. A crisis allows us the opportunity to dip deep into the reservoirs of our very being, to rise to levels of confidence, strength, and resolve that otherwise we didn't think we possessed.

Leadership also calls for a high degree of confidence. To believe in one's self and to not to be swayed by the emotions of the moment provide the energy to lead. There is a great 'can do' spirit in each of us, ready to be set free. We all have reserves to tap in times of danger. In a crisis, a person's mind can be brilliant and highly creative; true character is revealed.

NINE

Entrepreneurial Leadership

Bill Gates

Mark of a Leader "In the knowledge-based industries, India has the unique advantage of being a quality leader. Just like Japan was able to win in the overseas market with its quality leadership in automobile manufacturing, India has been able to do the same in information technology." — ***Azim Premji, Chairman, Wipro Ltd.***

⌘ Introduction

As this millennium dawned, it was apparent that a new India was emerging very fast. Indian economy is on a fast tract. It is all because of entrepreneurial leadership. The lure of self-employment has drawn hordes of people to venture into entrepreneurial activities. The classic entrepreneurs are often innovative risk takers. A few of them are Ratan Tata N.R. Narayana Murthy, Azim Premji, Ambani, Deepak Parekh, Kumar Mangalam Birla and Kiran Majumdar-Shaw, all of them considered *eminence grises* in India.

In fact, entrepreneurial leadership is the back bone of business, industry, trade, services etc. It encompasses every field in life.

The entrepreneurial leaders have fuelled ambitions and dreams, helping insightful, imaginative ideas guide smoothly over rough passages. Breathed life into promising business ventures, generated employment opportunities gave fillip to trade and services. The entrepreneurial leader's clear vision to give impetus to industrialise and give fillip to Indian talent. With the opening of the economy and globalisation, the information technology revolution, the knowledge sector chose entrepreneur way to serve the world economy in a big way. The BPO, KPO, LPO and HPO are in the fore front.

Everyone has the potential to become a leader within an organsation. Leaders are crucial for survival of an organisation. An organisation running without a leader would fail due to chaos and confusion. However, not every one is able to become a leader as though every individual possesses leadership quality but very few use it. A leader is not necessarily born but can be developed and groomed. Leaders develop more leaders. It is better to develop an organisational culture that facilitates development of leaders. Leadership is an art that needs to be perfected over a given period of time.

Leadership infact is the ability to guide a group toward the achievement of a goal. It is a process whereby one individual influences other group members toward attaining defined group or organisational goals. Leadership and management, though seem to be similar, are two distinct things. The primary function of a leader is to create the essential purpose or mission of the organisation and the strategy for attaining it while the.primary function of management is to implement it. Management is a career while Leadership is a calling. You manage things while you lead people. Management is about arms & hands, Leadership is about head & hearts. Management is about present, Leadership is about future. Managers are known for competence, leaders for creativity. Managerial role is exploitative — do as per situation, leadership is exploratory — create the situation. Leadership concerns with "whys", "whats" and "whens". Management is concerned with only "How". All good bankers may not necessarily be good managers and all good managers may not be good leaders.

Defining Leadership

Some of the common ideas included in leadership definitions include exerting influence, motivating and inspiring, helping others realise their potential, leading by example, selflessness and making a difference. I have given hereunder some well known definitions of leadership.

John C. Maxwell feels that leadership is "ability of the leader to influence others — those who consider themselves followers as well as non followers. Indirectly, it also builds in leadership character, since without maintaining integrity and trustworthiness, the capability to influence others will disappear.

Warren Bennis says "Leadership is a function of knowing yourself, having a vision that is well communicated, building trust among colleagues, and taking effective action to realise your own leadership potential"

According to Peter F. Drucker,

"Leadership is not magnetic personality that can just as well be a glib tongue. It is not "making friends and influencing people" — that is flattery. Leadership is lifting a person's vision to higher sights, the raising of a person's performance to a higher standard, the building of a personality beyond its normal limitations."

Effective leadership is neither charisma nor a set of personality traits. Leadership is work: Effective leaders think through the organisation's mission and then clearly define and establish it. They set goals that are compatible with the mission, they set of priorities, and they set and maintain standards. Effective leaders see leadership as a responsibility rather than rank and privilege, and they hold themselves accountable when things go wrong. They also want and encourage strong associates and subordinates, never viewing their triumphs as threats. Finally, effective leaders earn trust by always acting in congruence with their professed beliefs. Thus, the requirements for being an effective leader are essentially the same as those for being an effective manager.

We quote a few important definitions on leadership from the existing literature. These definitions reveal the essence of leadership.

1. Leadership is *"the process of encouraging and helping others to work enthusiastically towards objectives."*
2. Leadership is *"the behaviour of an individual when he is directing the activities of a group towards a shared goal."*
3. Leadership *"interpersonal influence, exercised in a situation and directed, through the communication process, towards the attainment of a specified goal or goals."*
4. Leadership is *"an interaction between persons in which one presents information of a sort and in such a manner that the other becomes convinced that his outcomes (benefits/costs ratios) will improve if he behaves in the manner suggested or desired."*
5. Leadership is *"both a process and property. The process of leadership is the use of non-coercive influence to direct and coordinate the activities of the members of an organised group towards the accomplishment of group objectives. As a property, leadership is the set of qualities or characteristics attributed to those who are perceived to successfully employ such influence."*
6. Leadership is *"the relationship in which one person (the leader) influences others to work together willingly on related tasks to attain goals desired by the leader and/or group."*

The core points that run through all these definitions and which constitute the essence of leadership are the following:

(*a*) Leadership refers to the ability of one individual to influence others.

(*b*) The influence is exercised to change the behaviour of others.

(*c*) Behaviour is changed through non-coercive means.

(*d*) Change of behaviour is caused with an objective of achieving a shared goal.

(*e*) The person influencing others (leader) possesses a set of qualities or characteristics which he or she uses to influence others, as the opening case indicates.

(*f*) Leadership is a group phenomenon. It involves interaction between two or more people.

(a) Briefly, leadership means a Visionary. Leader, Mentor, Dream Shaper, Inspirer, Challenger, Fierce and fair competitor. Honest, Passionate, Human, Global. Changing the rules of the game. Changing the world. Powered by intellect and driven by values. He is the face of new India.

Thus, the leader selects, equips, trains and influences his follower(s) who have diverse abilities and skills and guides the follower(s) to the organisation's mission and objectives so that they are achieved. The leader achieves this using ethical means and seeks the greater good of the follower(s) in the process. The leader achieves this same state for him/herself as he/she seeks personal growth, renewal, regeneration, and increased stamina through the leader-follower interactions.

The leader should recognise the diversity of the follower(s) and achieve unity of common values and directions without destroying the uniqueness of the person.The leader accomplishes this through innovative flexible means of education, training, supporting and protecting each follower. The leader, thus enables the follower(s) to be innovative as well as self-directed within the scope of individual-follower assignments and allows the follower(s) to learn from his/her/their own, as well as others' successes, mistakes, and failures along the process of completing the organisation' objectives. The leader accomplishes this by building credibility and trust with the followers through interaction and feedback to and with the followers that shapes the followers' values, attitudes, and behaviours towards risk, failure and success. In doing this, the leader builds the followers' sense of self worth and self-efficacy such that both the leader and followers are willing and ready to take calculated risks in making decisions to meet the organisation' goals/objectives and through repeated process steps of risk-taking and decision-making the leader and followers together change the organisation to best accomplish the organisation objectives.

Leadership In Practice

A person can learn Leadership from Army. A leader has to conceive vision, define mission, provide direction, understand people, motivate people, delegate authority, be adaptable to contingencies, create & seize opportunities and finally conquer. The Army compares a leader to a diamond. Just as a diamond requires three properties for formation — Carbon, heat & pressure — successful leaders require interaction of three qualities — character, knowledge & application.

American Army defines leadership in three simple words — "Be, Know, Do". Leadership begins with what the leader must **BE**, the values & attributes, the traits that shape up the leader. A leader has to identify such traits, imbibe them, nurture them, practice them and live them.

The second is **KNOW** — A leader, to be competent, must have certain level of knowledge spread over following four domains

- Interpersonal skills: ability to deal with people.
- Conceptual skills: ability to understand & apply ideas required to do the job.
- Technical skills: know-how to use tools & methods to improve productivity.
- Tactical skills: ability to make or take the right decisions.

The third & most important attribute of leadership is **DO.** Character & knowledge, though essential, are not enough unless you act & do what you must. Actions are the essence of leadership.

BE the leader of character, embrace values and demonstrate leader attributes. Study & practice so that you have the skills to ***KNOW*** your job. Then act and ***DO*** what is right to achieve excellence.

Leadership Styles

Each person has a leadership style that they feel comfortable with. There are different styles of leadership that are required for different situations. Some of them are discussed hereunder.

A Leader needs no introduction

Lt. Lala Juggilal Singhania, The Founder; Lt. Lala Kamlapat Singhania, The Founder; Lt. Sir Padampat Singhania, The Architect; Dr. Gaur Hari Singhania, The Torchbearer; Mr. Yadupati Singhania, The Propagator

An **autocratic** leader tells others what to do and is not receptive to suggestions on ideas and new ways of doing things. As a result, the Group does not experience feeling of teamwork. Such an autocratic style of leadership would not work in case the goal is development of a strong sense of team and in case a team comprises skilled and knowledgeable members. Generally, an authoritarian approach is not a good way to get the best performance from a team. There are. however, some instances where an autocratic style of leadership may not be inappropriate. Some situations may call for urgent action, and in these cases an autocratic style of leadership may be best. Besides, such a style may be warranted in case of limited time or in a situation when the individuals in the Group lack skill and knowledge.

A **democratic leader,** on the other hand, involves group members in planning and carrying out activities and promotes the sense of teamwork. The democratic leader makes decisions by consulting his team, while still maintaining control of the group. A good democratic leader encourages participation and delegates wisely, but never loses sight of the fact that he bears the crucial responsibility of leadership. He motivates his team by empowering them to direct themselves, and guides them with a loose reign. A democratic style of functioning is most suitable in case of availability of plenty of time and in case of a self motivated group with a sense of teamwork or even in case the group is skilled. However, a democratic leader would prove ineffective in case of an unmotivated or unskilled group and a group with high degree of conflict.

The **Laissez-Faire** style of leadership gives little or no direction to group/team members, leaving them to sort out their roles and tackle their work, without participating in this process himself. In general, this approach leaves the team floundering with little direction or motivation. Thus such a leader would fail when there is low sense of team/interdependence, low degree of skill/knowledge in members and when the group expects to be told what to do or awaits a direction. The *Laissez-Faire* technique would be effective only when leading a team of highly motivated and skilled people. Once a leader has established that his team is confident, capable and motivated, it is often best to step back and let them get on with the task. By handing over ownership, a leader can empower his group to achieve their goals.

Transactional Leaders normally believe in giving "Contingent Rewards" implying that the leader will reward the individuals based upon the level of success achieved or goal reached. For example, the harder the task was to complete the more refined the reward would be. Further, such leaders believe in undertaking Management by Exception and hence the manager will actively look for those problem area's that are out of control and need additional support.

Transformational leaders usually display Charisma meaning a rare personal quality through which leaders arouse fervent popular devotion and enthusiasm. It may also be described as a personal magnetism or charm. Transformational leadership focuses on the leaders ability to-provide shared values and a vision for the future of the work group. This would imply identifying and articulating a vision, providing an appropriate model, fostering the acceptance of group goals, maintaining high performance expectations, providing individualised support and providing intellectual stimulation.

Principle-centered leadership is focused on the principles rooted in the unchanging laws that govern human and organisational effectiveness This could easily be restated to imply that godly immutable laws affect all of us. Breaking them causes harm to the organisational success. Often principles kept for a long time becomes character and hence the leadership style changes to **character-based leadership.The** major problem with this is that people usually only briefly embrace principles and shortly thereafter return to their already set behaviours.

Box - 1

THE MAN WHO SAW TOMORROW

Bhai Mohan Singh (1917-2006)

Bhai Mohan Singh's place as the father of the first Indian pharmaceutical multinational is secure in the pantheon of Indian business. He was a descendant of Bhai Gurdas, the personal scribe of the fifth Sikh guru Arjan Dev (hence the title, 'Bhai'), and son of a builder who migrated from Rawalpindi to Delhi during the partition of India in 1947. A young Mohan Singh prospered as a moneylender before taking over Ranbaxy Laboratories in 1952, when its promoters defaulted on a loan.

Thereafter, over the next four decades, he converted the medicine distribution outfit into a manufacturing company and prepared it to go global. He had the vision to perceive the opportunity that the patent laws in force in India at that time offered. His son, Parvinder Singh (who died of cancer on 4th July 1999), may have gone around the world planting Ranbaxy flags, but it was Bhai Mohan Singh who initiated the company into generics by founding, perhaps, India's first reverse engineering pharmaceutical laboratory. In fact, the legacies of Mohan Singh and Parvinder Singh are so intertwined that it is difficult to talk about one without mentioning the other. Both loved the company more than they loved each other.

The year 1993 was the annus horribilis for Bhai Mohan Singh. That year, Parvinder took over the company and Bhai Mohan Singh had to leave. This left him so bitter that he cried before the media. Mohan Singh likened his fate to that of King Lear, and regretted passing on the baton to his son. But the latter wanted to run Ranbaxy according to his own wisdom, and with the help of his trusted lieutenant Davindar Singh Brar.

Mohan Singh spent his last 10 years away from the corporate limelight, watching his estranged son do him proud by making Ranbaxy into one of the world's most formidable generics companies. He was close to his two grandsons and must have been very pleased to see Malvinder Mohan Singh take over Ranbaxy's reins in January 2006. Malvindar, and his younger brother Shivinder, owe it to their illustrious father and grandfather to build on their legacy.

FEROZ AHMED

Value-based leadership focuses on adding value to the entire process. In some instances, this type may overlook the aspect of being the nice guy on the block and rather think about adding value to the leadership process. It is an organisation's responsibility to add quality (value) to each service and product delivered to its customers. Researchers say that a good percentage of Corporate America rates their leaders on their vision for the organisation, and their final performance on that vision.

They have rekindled a new vision to the entrepreneurs of the 21st century. The vision to emerge as a leading entrepreneur of India, devoted to achieving sustainable and balanced economic development through value based services, to excel on the strength of professional innovation, customer orientation, empowerment and enrichment of all stakeholders; and to set an example of enlightened entrepreneurial governance and citizenship.

Core Competitiveness

The liberalisation process in India is at a very interesting stage at the moment; there is enormous growth in the country, yet the full force of global competition is still not being felt. Many of the shackles of the old licence **raj** have been removed and there is tremendous consumer demand. These three forces together make a recipe for extraordinary growth. But the question is whether this growth can be sustained when competition really intensifies? In this competitive backdrop, small industries doing business in India has changed significantly. It is not business as usual.

In the changed scenario, Indian entrepreneur/entrapreneur will be required to have an analytical orientation along with a commitment to introspection and self-development, and enforce learning through uncomfortable situations.

An entrepreneur's task will include:

- Exploiting opportunities that are increasingly becoming global
- Customising at low cost
- Learning to manage and work in highly volatile environments, political and otherwise, and to scale down or scale up operations, according to need
- Learning to become part of the global, intellectual chain
- Being less dependent on governments, the role of which is increasingly being challenged in every sphere
- Realising that a job is no longer an entitlement or a right
- Being able to convert data into knowledge
- Looking at strategy as resource mobilisation and resource leverage
- Developing capacity for knowledge in action
- Developing education, particularly management education, for a framework for sustaining change.

THE DNA OF LEADERSHIP

Developing effective organisational leaders ranks number one on the list of top talent issues globally. So which companies do it effectively? According to brand-new research by the Hay Group and 'CEO' magazine, entitled 'Best Companies for Leaders', Procter & Gamble, PepsiCo, IBM, General Electric and Johnson & Johnson are on top of the heap. The study took inputs on leadership development from over 300 global and regional companies and one of the key findings it came up with was that the best companies for leaders invest heavily in leadership development and do more of "every thing." The report adds that there are six vital factors that account for the differences in number and quality of leaders.

These are:

1. CEO and senior leaders make leadership development a top priority.
2. Leaders at all levels are accountable for creating a motivating work climate.
3. Leadership teams receive training and coaching to help them work together more effectively.
4. Mid-career managers receive job-shadowing opportunities.
5. High-potentials receive objective 360-degree assessments and feedback on their leadership ability early on.
6. Mid-level managers get enough time to take part in leadership development activities early in their careers.

In India too, the subject of developing capable leaders for tomorrow has assumed tremendous importance. Tharuma Raja, GM, Asia Pacific & Thought Leader – Leadership Consulting – Hay Group, says that if left unchecked, the leadership crisis in India could assume alarming proportions over the next 5-7 years. Raja says, "Indian corporations are the last of the block in realising that leadership development and planning in advance for a second line of potential leaders is critical to business success in the medium to long term."

However, the good news is that Indian corporations are making diligent efforts to develop global leaders, such as cross functional team participation, providing targeted feedback, offsite development programmes and coaching. So what differentiates a global leader from a common one? First and foremost, says Raja, is the ability to 'dream big.' Next is being able to predict business changes, deal with uncertainty and being 'driven to succeed'. "The key is that the approach towards leadership development needs to be holistic rather than a on-off approach," he says. India Inc. would do well to keep this particular fact in mind even as it occupies itself with taking big strides forward in the international business arena.

Leadership and Team Building

Leadership is the influence relationship in which one person (the leader) influences others (the led) in a given situation to work together on the related tasks to attain what the leader desires. It is the ability to influence the behaviour of others in a particular direction.

Managerial leadership is that part of a manager's activities by which he influences the behaviour of individuals and groups towards a desired result; it depends upon the skills and personality of the manager to meet the wants needs and desires of the group he leads.

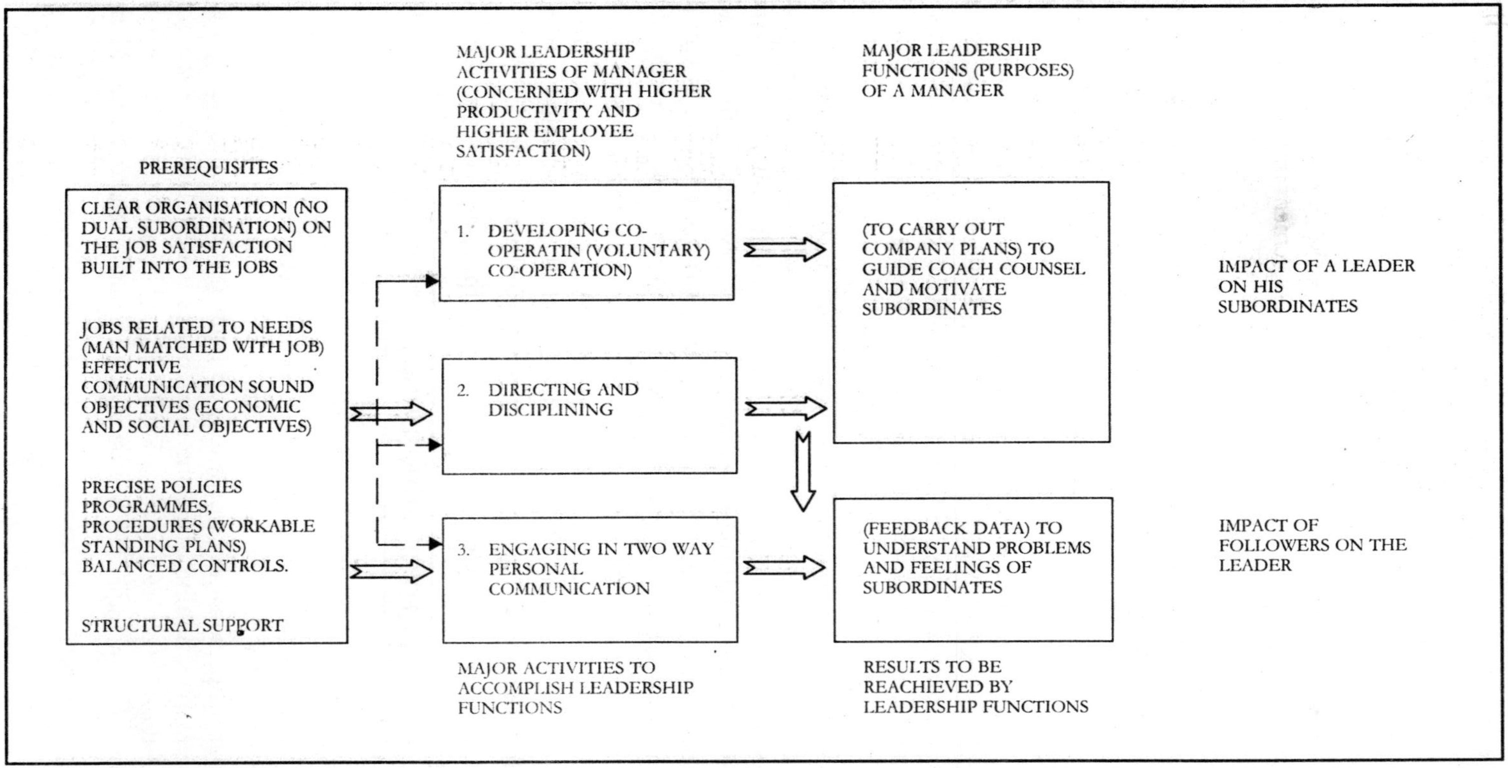

Fig. 1: Elements of Managerial Leadership that foster active interpersonal man-to-man relationship between a manager (leader) and his subordinates (Followers)

Note: *Leadership activities must be backed by a management structure that is in harmony with, and favourable good leadership.*

Leadership Qualities: Leadership is more than personal ability and skill. Although a true leader should have ability, he should also be professionally competent, intelligent and analytical. A good leader should have a sense of fail play, including honesty, integrity and a feeling of responsibility. He must possess initiative and be industrious, diligent and tough-minded. Human sympathy is absolutely necessary. Sympathy, self-awareness (awareness of your preferences, weaknesses and habits) and objectivity are the desirable characteristics of leadership.

Role of Leadership: It is an important element of management that impels others to action. Leadership alone can guide the feeling, thinking and action of other people towards a set objective. We must make a person feel good before we can open his mind. Then we can give him definite ideas or thoughts, and only then, we can motivate him to concrete and specific action — the greatest challenge of all. Leader is the fulcrum on which demands of individuals (or groups) and demands of the organisation are balanced. Leadership can transform potential into a reality. A leader can be a powerful atmosphere creator. Leadership ignites a person's will-to-do and transforms simple desires for achievement into burning passions for successful accomplishment.

What is it that will make some leaders tremendously successful at this while others will fail? First, the capacity to have enough self-awareness and self-esteem to be able to sense when a different repertoire of competencies will be needed, without being threatened by the need to change. In other words, the diagnostic ability to understand what new things are required, or what things should be learned, plus the behavioural flexibility to be able to change.

Number two is to have the boundaries of the organisation sufficiently porous and permeable so that you can spot things. So you have the foresight to see things before the curve, before others do. And the only way you get that is by being in touch with your customers, being in touch with society, being in touch with the outside world, by having the boundaries of the organisation permeable and porous enough to get your information. That's why people at the periphery of organisations are usually the most creative and often the least consulted.

What we are learning is that successful leadership doesn't depend on masculinity or feminity. It's not about being tough or soft, or whether you are assertive or sensitive. It's about the particular organisational culture within which you are embedded, and about having a particular set of attributes which all leaders, both male and female, seem to share.

Leaders need to have a strongly-defined sense of purpose and a sense of vision.

ENTREPRENEURIAL LEADERS

Proving his mettle

Sterlite CEO Anil Agarwal ended 2003 on a high. He capped his successful streak in December with the London float of holding company Vedanta, which raised more than £500 million. That's about his personal net worth too, up from £75 million a year ago. Exciting times are in store. In the market, Sterlite is making a 1:1 bonus issue followed by a rights issue. This money and another Rs. 4,500 crore in international debt will be invested in the non-ferrous metals and optical fibre business in India. He will be giving metals magnate Kumar Mangalam Birla a run for his money.

Anil Agarwal
CMD, Sterlite Group

Ringing up growth

One in every four cellphones in the country is connected by Airtel, which makes Sunil Mittal a frontrunner in the telecom sweepstakes and the only serious contender against the Reliance Infocomm juggernaut. Having called truce with the CDMA enemy, Mittal has much to look forward to. The hike in FDI limit to 74 per cent, spells growth for his capital-starved Bharti Televentures. Also likely — an acquisition here and an ADR issue there. Bharti's bid for airport privatisation, could take the lad from Ludhiana to another frontier in infrastructure.

Sunil Mittal
Chairman & Group MD, Bharti Enterprises

The Age of Ram

For far too long, Tata Consultancy Services, India's largest software services provider and its CEO, S. Ramadorai, have played second fiddle to the more high profile, publicly-listed Wipro and Infosys Technologies (and Azim Premji and N.R Narayana Murthy). Now the age of Ram (as Ramadorai is called) is going to dawn with TCS's long-awaited IPO set to become a reality this year. In the market-cap stakes, TCS is likely to zoom above Wipro and Infosys, grabbing the title of India's most valuable software company. This ULCA alumnus has ably filled the shoes of mentor F.C. Kohli making TCS a $1-billion (sales) enterprise. And now its time to make those TCS drones *crorepatis* at last!

Spinning Gold from Steel

In the steel industry, Lakshmi Mittal is considered the ultimate alchemist. His Gulf Stream IV is always ready to carry this 'Brown Knight of the Rust Belt' to any part of the world to rescue some sinking steel company. But recently, Mittal chose to travel at a more leisurely pace anchoring his luxurious yacht off the West Coast of India. In 2003, Mittal upped his steel capacity from 22 million tonnes to 40 million tonnes, falling 5 million tonnes short to making his LNM group the largest steel maker in the world. Mittal who never lacks acquisition proposals but always waits for the right price to strike a deal is likely to snag the title of steel supremo this year. Yet his globe girdling empire has one piece missing: a presence in India. Will this be the year when that too falls into place.

Indian Number 1: L.N. Mittal's ambitious plans for an India-plant had everyone agog

Working Billionnaire

After a decade of waiting in the wings. Malvinder Singh's all set to take charge at Ranbaxy Labs which is set to end this fiscal year with sales close to $1 billion.

The premature retirement of CEO, D.S. Brar, handicapicked to lead Ranbaxy by Malvinder's late Dad Parvinder Singh, bespeaks a return to family management at the pharma giant. The wellspoken, American educated Malvinder and his brother Shivinder, together own about a third a Ranbaxy's equity, making them the youngest billionnaires. A keen photographer, Malvinder should go all out to prove that he can handle the big picture.

Malvinder Singh
Director, Ranbaxy Labs

Lady Biotech

Come March, India's first biotech IPO will hit the market when Biocon India makes its public debut. Billed as one of the hottest IPOs in the pipeline, the issue will propel Biocon into the big leagues and its pioneering founder Kiran Mazumdar Shaw into the elite billionnaire club. Twenty-five-year-old Biocon (March 2004 sales Rs. 520 crore) is already being spoken of as the Infosys of the biotech sector. On the threshold of a Rs. 500-crore expansion. Mazumdar is all set to launch human insulin in the domestic market.

The Concept

Success of business organisation depends on entrepreneurial leaders like Ratan Tata, Bill Gates, Mittal, Kiran Majumdar – Shaw, Kumar Mangalam, N.R. Narayana Murthy, Nandan Nilekani etc.

The word leadership has been widely used. Yet, entrepreneurial leadership refers to effective leadership in business activities – manufacturing, trade, services and other enterprising activities. *Inter-alia* it is associated with vision, passion, mission, commitment, motive and perseverance.

Kiran Mazumdar Shaw
Chairman & Managing Director,
Biocon India

India's most respected Companies

India's Most Respected Companies is a peer perception survey (2006) conducted by IMRB. The survey assessed the companies on seven parameters, *viz.,* Innovativeness, Quality and Depth of Management, Financial performance, Ethics and Transparency, Quality of products and services, people practices/Talent Management and Global competitiveness. The survey covers seventeen sectors:

- **Auto** Tata Motors is the new No.1.
- **Auto Ancillaries** Naturally, Bharat Forge.
- **Banking & Finance** It's State Bank of India.
- **BPO** Convergys on top, Genpact second.
- **FMCG** HLL retains top billing, ITC second.
- **Food Retailing** McDonald's still No.1.
- **Infrastructure** Still L&T, Tata Steel & BHEL.

- **Insurance** who else but LIC?
- **IT** Need we say it? Infosys, of course.
- **Media & Entertainment** Star still up there.
- **Petroleum** ONGC tops, IOC is second.
- **Pharmaceuticals** Ranbaxy is No. 1.
- **Retail** Shoppers' Stop, followed by Westside.
- **Telecommunications** It's Hutch.
- **Textiles & Garments** Arvind Mills is No.1.
- **Travel & Hospitality** Still Jet Airways.
- **White Goods/Durables** Nokia again.

THE TALLY: TOP 25

Current rank	Prev. rank	Company	Total score	Innovativeness	Quality & depth of management	Financial performance	Ethics & transparency	Quality of products or services	People pratices/ talent management	Global Competitiveness
1	1	Infosys Technologies	18,124.2	2,230.2	2,581.0	2,778.2	2,772.3	2,315.7	2,623.4	2,823.4
2	3	Wipro	10,218.5	1,052.7	1,435.9	1,551.4	1,590.3	1,235.5	1,636.6	1,716.1
3	2	Reliance Industries	9,118.8	1,276.5	1,317.5	1,969.6	1,021.4	1,007.4	1,132.5	1,393.9
4	9	ICICI Bank	8,911.2	1,528.3	1,381.8	1,211.6	1,166.9	1,200.5	1,229.6	1,192.5
5	13	Tata Consultancy Services	8,474.5	822.8	1,232.0	1,210.3	1,445.7	976.6	1,323.3	1,463.8
6	5	Maruti Udyog	7,690.9	1,012.1	1,069.6	1,010.5	1,047.2	1,357.7	1,061.2	1,132.5
7	21	ITC	7,154.2	938.5	1,167.3	1,120.4	1,004.4	943.4	1,116.0	864.2
8	7	HDFC Bank	7,097.9	1,091.9	1,126.3	956.3	1,076.4	1,000.2	1,029.5	817.6
9	12	Tata Motors	6,357.9	647.9	982.8	780.2	1,202.3	997.5	848.2	899.0
10	14	Larsen & Toubro	6,331.8	662.2	924.8	940.0	1,027.5	926.4	937.4	913.6
11	23	Nokia India	6,286.2	1,213.4	700.1	605.6	675.3	1,156.2	887.4	1,048.0
12	26	Bharti Airtel[1]	5,969.4	1,064.6	872.3	902.7	690.0	880.1	822.8	737.0
13	17	Oil & Natural Gas Corp.	5,952.3	687.1	944.9	996.9	836.6	694.3	799.2	993.2
14	8	Jet Airways	5,860.9	978.2	797.1	532.1	689.0	1,086.4	805.6	972.5
15	18	Hero Honda Motors	5,789.3	863.8	763.0	993.0	697.9	915.1	784.4	781.2
16	15	Tata Steel[2]	5,751.9	499.2	846.9	765.0	1,182.6	736.2	850.0	872.1
17	4	Hindustan Lever	4,863.1	629.0	780.0	621.3	716.3	707.8	811.1	597.6
18	11	GCMMF (Amul)[3]	4,659.2	967.7	625.0	450.1	721.9	923.4	527.0	444.1

19	10	Ranbaxy Laboratories	4,433.2	655.9	622.9	692.6	561.7	639.0	630.4	630.7
20	20	Bajaj Auto	4,309.2	689.1	629.2	725.7	551.3	675.9	474.9	563.2
21	24	Citi Bank	4,155.7	746.7	680.4	495.1	412.0	568.3	695.2	558.0
22	16	State Bank of India	3,939.8	451.7	578.9	699.8	703.7	478.7	494.2	532.8
23	6	Dr. Reddy's Laboratories	3,527.2	624.1	495.0	630.1	428.2	432.1	445.3	472.3
24	32	New Delhi Television	3,457.7	618.8	489.8	395.9	417.0	592.1	573.3	370.8
25	22	Indian Oil Corp.	3,431.0	426.0	497.1	574.1	489.7	491.8	480.0	472.3

1 Formerly Bharti Tele-Ventures; 2 Formerly Tata Iron & Steel Co.; 3 GCMMF: Gujarat Co-operative Milk Marketing Federation.

UNPROMPTED TOP 5

Company	*Rank*
Infosys Technologies	1
Tata	2
Reliance Industries	3
Wipro	4
Hindustan Lever	5

Above is the list of India's 25 Most Respected Companies. These corporates made it after having received the highest number of aggregate points across seven parameters.

To the left is the list of the Top 5 Most Respected Companies based on unprompted responses by the respondents of the poll. These results, though almost in sync with the main poll, still manage to throw up some interesting insights.

For example, although Hindustan Lever may have sustained a mighty fall in the main poll, in the unprompted one it manages a respectable showing at No. 5. (The positions of Infosys and Reliance Industries stay unchanged, while Wipro's slips a bit, to No. 4.)

Another fascinating fact that emerges is that people tend to express respect for the Tata Group as a whole and not for any individual Tata company. That is why the table reads just 'Tata'.

Box - 1

THE STORY SO FAR

Gates was born on October 28, 1955, the second of three children in a prominent family in Seattle, USA. His father, William Henry Gates Jr, was a partner at one of the city's most powerful law firms, while his late mother, Mary, was an active charity fund-raiser.

He was introduced to computers at the exclusive Lakeside Preparatory School, where as a teen, he began programming in BASIC computer language on a primitive ASR-33 Teletype unit.

Gates first programmed a computer at 13, creating a class scheduling system for his school. As he gained more experience, he realised the potential that software held to change how humans worked, played and communicated.

(Contd.)

(Contd.)

It was at Lakeside that Gates met Paul Allen, a student two years his senior who shared his fascination with computers.

"Of course, in those days, we were just goofing around, or so we thought," Gates recalled in his 1995 book, *The Road Ahead.*

"When I was 19, I caught sight of the future and based my career on what I saw, I turned out to have been right," Gates wrote.

Working with Allen, Gates went on to drop out of Harvard and founded Microsoft, naming the company for its mission of providing microcomputer software.

Also at Harvard, Gates developed an ebullient friend who shared his love of math and cynical humour. He eventually talked that classmate — current CEO Steve Ballmer — into leaving business school to join Microsoft.

MAKING IT BIG

The big break came in 1980, when Gates and his carelessly dressed young colleagues signed an agreement to build the operating system that became known as MS-DOS for IBM Corp's new personal computer.

Gates realised at an early stage of the PC revolution that software would be more important than hardware, and secured the rights to license the operating system to others, spawning an industry of "IBM-compatible" machines dependent on Microsoft software. The rest, as they say, is history.

Microsoft went public in 1986 in one of the most celebrated offerings of its time. By the next year, the soaring stock made Gates, at age 31, the youngest self-made billionaire.

Rob Helm, director of research at independent research firm Directions of Microsoft, said Gates will go down as one of the greatest businessmen in history like John D. Rockefeller — for better or for worse.

"He's never going to be necessarily a widely admired figure, but someone who created an activity that came to represent a chunk of the American economy."

Box - 2

THE ROAD AHEAD

The announcement by Gates two years ago that he intended to switch from the corporate arena to the world of charity sounded like a cliche. Today, the man faces the challenge of making it real.

Melinda Gates, Warren Buffet and Bill discuss the foundation

"With success, I have been given great wealth," Gates said in June 2006. "And with great wealth comes great responsibility... to see that those resources are put to work in the best possible way to help those in need."

(Contd.)

(Contd.)

That pledge will see Gates take a hands-on role as co-chairman of the Bill and Melinda Gates Foundation, the world's richest charity with a war chest of $37.3 billion — thanks to the generosity of Gates and his close friend, fellow business tycoon, and the world's richest man, Warren Buffet.

The foundation — dedicated to improving health care and fighting poverty in the developing world — is destined to become even richer with both its main benefactors pledging to donate almost their entire fortunes, and to require the foundation to spend all its money within 50 years of their deaths.

THE THREE ARMS

The foundation is split into three units:

The Global Health Programme currently donates some $800 million a year — roughly equal to the annual budget of the UN's World Health Organisation. It plays a leading role in efforts to eradicate polio, fight AIDS and spread the use of vaccines and immunisations.

The Global Development Programme helps fight extreme poverty, with grants that support micro-finance loans, agricultural development in Africa, and the spread of information technology.

Among the biggest projects of the United States Programme are scholarships for high-achieving minority college students, Internet access in libraries, and numerous other educational initiatives.

"We do family planning. We fund research on crops... This whole thing about which operating system somebody uses is a pretty silly thing versus issues involving starvation or death," Gates had said.

He is determined to have a major impact on the world's major problems and has been studying furiously to get familiar with the science behind the issues.

He also brings his clout, vision and business acumen to the table, which could be decisive in pushing forward remedies and cajoling governments that might have different agendas.

"This is good news for the world's poor," said Anne Lynam Goddard, chief of staff of CARE, a US-based non-profit funded by the Gates Foundation. "The Gates come with no political agenda."

TASKS OF LEADERSHIP

- To build vision
- Create Commitment
- Pursue to achieve the desired goal
- Streamline the System
- Draw us the strategies
- Shaping skills
- Strengthening relationships
- Shape us behaviour in order
- Provide solutions
- Help People
- Codify the culture (work & organisation)
- Build up core values
- Set-up benchmarks
- Promote creativity
- Encourage innovation

- Adapt to change
- Draw up of the mission
- Ensure accountability
- Encourage entrepreneurship
- Cope up with the evolving environment.

Some of the most important leadership challenges today are:

1. To select and retain the right people as employees.
2. To give each employee the opportunity to help further the objectives and goals of the company.
3. To give each individual optimal opportunity for self-realisation. Employees should consider it valuable to themselves, their employers and to the society.

The authoritative managers, who see themselves as the power centres on decision-making, are becoming redundant. Leaders who exhibit high tolerance for failure and allow opportunities to experiment, create a culture of achieving better long-term results.

Managers in future will be required to create an information-rich-environment for their employees to excel. This means a paradigm shift from performance and process management to knowledge management.

Giving good information and gathering good information are two vital elements to successful communication. A leader has to create a reciprocal process of communication.

Those managers who "check with everyone first" rather than encouraging independent action from their subordinates create many work place conflicts. Such managers take refuge under slogans like "Quality above all" without really meaning it.

Tomorrow's managers will have to learn to adapt to change, to live with uncertainty, to handle stress and to become skilled co-ordinators, innovators and above all "people's persons". One possible reason for this demand can be rapid technological obsolescence and woefully short product life cycles.

Ancillaries

It's a sector that heralded India's manufacturing revival. It's a sector where even the smaller players have a plan to go global. It's a sector that's got venture capitalists all agog. It's also the sector where Baba Kalyani's word is gospel these days. Any surprises that Bharat Forge is on top?

The reasons behind Bharat Forge's rise to the top — it was ranked third in the previous survey — lie outside India's borders. In the last five years, it has done five deals worth around $115 million, globally. Today it is the world's second largest automobile forgings company, with a stated ambition to be the largest soon, as Kalyani, chairman and managing director of the company, puts it. (Germany's Thyssen Krupp is the largest at the moment.) Moreover, he has been advocating the path of dual shoring for the Indian auto ancillary sector — buy companies or even order books abroad and relocate some of the manufacturing back to India while keeping the rest overseas. It's an approach he has mastered. Little wonder Bharat Forge ranks ahead of its peers in two parameters — 'innovativeness' and 'globalisation.'

Box - 2

KALYANI GROUP

TOWARDS GLOBALISATION

Kalyani: realising his vision

Baba Kalyani's ultimate aim is to become an international supplier in forgings. The people in developing countries are moving out of the polluting, bulk material handling, low-tech labour-intensive industries to sophisticated, clean and high-tech industries. The group is going to be almost entirely integrated, backward and forward. "We will emerge as one of the leading export houses in the country in the next three to fours," hopes founder Neelkanth Kalyani, who strongly believes that the ability to export on one's own merit is the ultimate test of the success of a company.

Baba N. Kalyani, group chairman, is on his way to realising his global vision: of running India's first manufacturing multinational company. With six plants abroad and four companies in India, led by the Rs. 3,085 crore flagship Bharat Forge Ltd., and employing a total of 8,000 people, the group now has its footprint on every continent.

Kalyani: Realising his vision

Current status

Today, the Kalyani group's annual turnover is over $2.4 billion and it has joint ventures with some world leaders such as ArvinMeritor, Carpenter Technology Corporation and Hayes Lemmerz, US, FAW Corporation, China, and Gerdau SA, Brazil. Bharat Forge Limited, the flagship company of the group, is a global forging conglomerate, with a global capacity of over 7,50,000 tpa spread across 12 locations and six countries — four in India, three in Germany, one each in Sweden, Scotland and the US and two in China.

While Bharat Forge and Kalyani are slowly gaining the kind of aura that Infosys and N.R. Narayana Murthy enjoy in IT, the industry isn't about them only. Prior to the ascendancy of Bharat Forge, another company, along with its CEO, was considered somewhat iconic — Sundram Fasteners. It was ranked No. 1 in the last survey and this time round has been dislodged to second position.

Yet, industry watchers argue that Sundram hasn't of late been displaying the kind of well-thought-out aggression that some of the other players are showing and has, therefore, slipped in the perception rankings.

TOP FIVE

Rank	*This survey*	*Last survey*
1	Bharat Forge	Sundram Fasteners
2	Sundram Fasteners	MICO
3	Lucas-TVS	Bharat Forge
4	MRF	MRF
5	MICO	Lucas-TVS

After all, the previous year or two have been mostly about deals that Indian auto-ancillary companies have struck around the globe. Tata Technologies picked up UK's Incat International for $95 million, Ucal Fuel Systems picked up Amtec Precision in the US for $28 million, Sona Koyo bought 21 per cent of Fuji Autotech (France) for $6.15 million and so on.

In all this spate of cross border M&As, besides Bharat Forge, the one other company that has demonstrated plenty of aggression is Amtek Auto, maker of auto components that are used in engine, transmission and suspension systems. This will be a company to watch out for in the future.

Yet, five years ago, very few could have predicted the kind of growth that the sector is showing.

The Indian auto ancillary industry was born in the early 1980s, shortly after Maruti Suzuki set up shop here. But it was only in the late 1990s that the industry was confident enough to take on the world. Years of working with world class car makers (GM, Ford, Hyundai, Toyota, Daimler Chrysler, etc.) helped auto component companies sharpen their engineering and design skills. Those, along with relatively cheap manufacturing costs, have come together to create an almost unbeatable combination.

According to estimates by the Automotive Component Manufacturers Association (ACMA), domestic production increased by 17 per cent in 2005-06 to $10 billion. This marks an almost five-fold increase in the last decade ($2.4 billion in 1997). Exports have grown impressively by 30 per cent to $1.8 billion this year. Its share as a percentage of total output has risen from 12.9 per cent in 2001-02 to 18 per cent this year.

It is estimated that the Indian auto components industry will invest about $1 billion towards ramping up capacities and acquiring newer technologies every year for the next 10 years.

Riding on the buoyancy in the industry and a study by McKinsey &Co., ACMA has set an export target of $20 billion-25 billion by 2015.

Companies such as Ford, General Motors, Fiat and Daimler Chrysler are already sourcing significant volumes of auto components from India every year.

Bharat Forge's is perhaps somewhat representative of how the sector has evolved. It began its export drive around 10 years ago. The natural progression was, as Kalyani puts it, "how do you globalise your company".

"We identified for ourselves three markets — North America, Europe and Asia. And while we said we must have a footprint in each, there must be a bigger emphasis on Europe. In our business, all the technology development happens in Europe. We wanted to be plugged in to the high-end auto business circuit and that's really why we focused on Europe." Says Kalyani.

But the one curious thing is that auto-component manufacturers still aren't cutting the mustard when it comes to the overall rankings. Bharat Forge, the first auto-component company on the overall rankings, debuts at No. 38.

Entrepreneurship leadership is a driving force of the economy. It is truly said that an entrepreneur is a person who converts an innovative idea into business, nurture it and excel as well. In fact, an entrepreneur is a leader who leads the team to success. An effective leadership demands certain unique qualities.

The leader must be competent enough to perform a task better than what his or her followers are capable of. This earns him or her enormous respect from his or her followers. Competence gives robust confidence to the leader about himself or herself and about his or her team. It is the confidence which equips him or her to face any adverse situation with courage. It also enables the leader to kindle hope in his or her followers when their spirits are down, which is usually the case when the organisation is passing through a lean period. A leader needs to be an intellectual. He or she needs to understand not only the intricacies of the immediate task before him or her, but must also have knowledge about the political, economic, social and cultural milieu operating beyond his business. He should also be a visionary to provide a road map to his/her organisation. In short, the success of his business decisively depends upon his/her dynamic leadership, active involvement, passion and commitment to business/organisation.

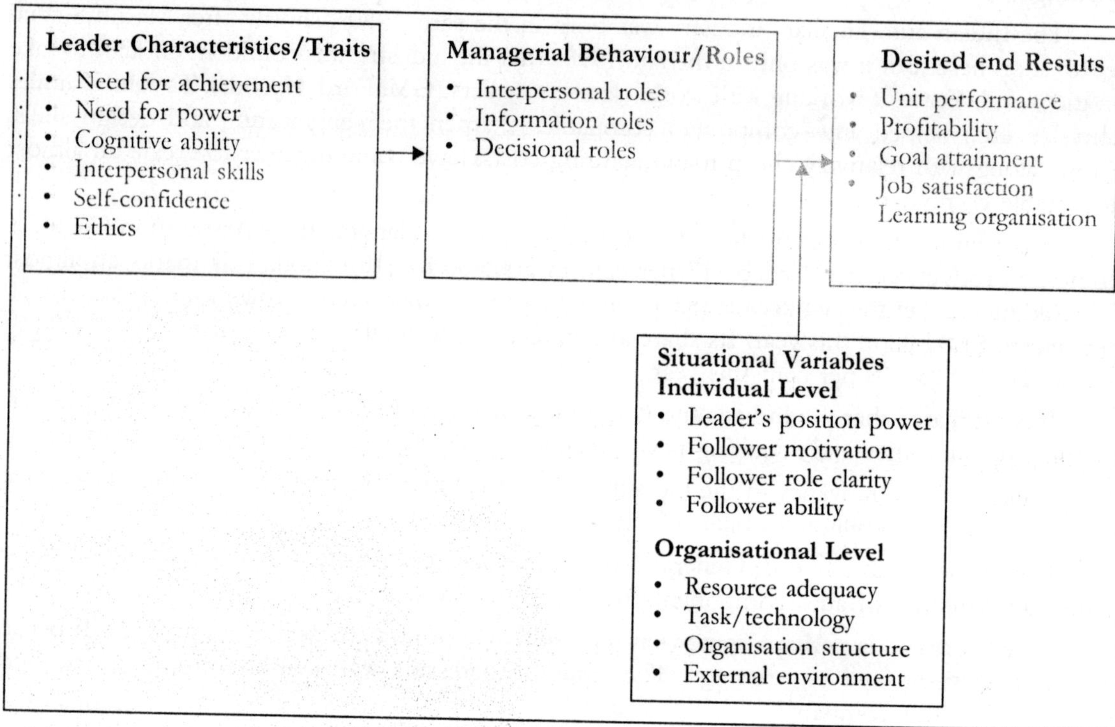

A Conceptual Framework for Understanding Leadership
(***Source:*** Robert Kreitner and Angelo Kinicki, *Organisational Behaviour*, p. 496).

Leadership is also about teaching others to cope with difficult situations. A true leader does not bend in the face of what a crowd demands. He or she bends the crowd to his or her will and make it move in the desired direction. Leaders need to be passionate. Passionate leaders, instead of pushing their followers to monotonously pursue deadlines, constantly create excitement by encouraging them to think, stimulate their intellectual growth and apply new ideas to mundane jobs.

Successful leaders are those who sense the need for change before others and devote all their energies to make that change happen. Good leaders are those that create an open forum for communication with everyone in the organisation, listen to their suggestions and then make the final decision. This open communication creates a sense of responsibility among team members.

In a typical organisation, both leadership and management roles are combined in every individual. Whether one is a leader or manager depends on what role he or she performs at any given time. In fact, backed by leadership traits, an executive is in a stronger position to perform managerial functions that result in desired outcomes. Of course, several situational factors influence how effectively the end results have been obtained.

Leadership is a Mutual Influence Process: The discussion on the nature of leadership till now makes a reader believe that leadership is unidirectional *i.e.,* the leader influencing his followers. It is true that leadership refers to the influence of the leader on followers. At the same time, the characteristics of employees and their tasks do yield influence on the leader. Leadership is, therefore, a mutual influence process.

SUCCESSFUL BUSINESS LEADERS

The successful entrepreneurial leaders of Indian industry, the master geniuses, visionaries, who planned a dynamic and progressive programme by laying a strong foundation of a robust industry and fortified its invulnerable social, cultural and spiritual ramification which have amply stood the test of time. These illustrious entrepreneurs were privileged to give India its present industrial greatness. These men are the visionaries and leaders of the Indian industry.

These illustrious entrepreneurs of Indian industry have fostered the all-round development of industry in India. They have not only opened up enterprises in diverse field and excelled in it, more importantly, fostered the development of entrepreneurship in the country.

Ten Questions Every Leader Ought to be Asking

We are at our best when we catalyse progress — when we create environments that help people, teams and processes do great work together. Here are ten questions you can ask yourself and your team to get catalytic juices flowing:

1. What's the new opportunity that we are not seeing? How might we learn from other organisations, both competitors an non-competitors?
2. How might new trends in how people communicate and work open up new ways to improve our organisation?
3. When a meeting feels flat and perfunctory, what's going on? What's on people minds that they are not saying?
4. What is "my best work" and how can I ensure I do that today? How can I enable my team to do their best work?
5. If we were starting this organisation from scratch, how would we design it?
6. What's the craziest idea that just might work?
7. What are the most irksome/damaging barriers facing me and my team right now and how can I reduce or obliterate them?
8. What is my manifesto (driving philosophy and passion) as a leader and how can I ensure my team understands it?
9. What's possible now that was not possible last year/month?
10. Do I have my team focused on doing the work that matters most?

We are leaders because we make things happen that would not happen without us. We are driven to create, model, and catalyse excellence. We do not maintain. We do not play the victim. We take the initiative to do whatever it takes to make a significant and positive difference and we have more opportunities to do this today than ever.
Source: http://www.managementcraft.typad.com

PETER'S PRINCIPLES ON LEADERSHIP

Box - 3

Laurence Peter

Born: 1919 Died: 1990

Education: Director of Education, Washington State University

Claim To Fame:

A educationist and hierarchiologist, he put forth 'The Peter Principle' according to which, in a hierarchy every employee tends to rise to his level of incompetence.

Author of:

- The Peter Principle
- Why Things Always Go Wrong

Key Concepts:

IThe Peter Principle and Peter's Corollary; which states in time every post tends to be occupied by an employee who is incompetent to carry out its duties, were first formulated for the educational world. Over time though, their applicability to industrial organisations was recognised as well. Though putforth in a humorous tongue-in-cheek manner, it was a depressing thought that if you were good at your job, it was only a matter of time before you were promoted and reached a stage of inefficiency.

Also known for:

Was involved in the management of the Kinetic Sculpture Race where he proposed 'The Golden Dinosaur Award'. This is given to the first sculptural machine to break down completely immediately after the start, to utterly break down immediately after the start.

Quotable Quote:

"The man who is willing to meet you halfway is usually a poor judge of distance."

Leadership is confusing as hell. We might as well say it upfront: There's no one-size-fits-all approach to it. Leadership mantra # 1: It all depends. Think situational leadership — the right person, the right style, for the right situation. Leader for all seasons? In your dreams!

1. **Leaders on snorting steeds (the visionary greats!) are important.** But great managers are the bedrock of great organisations.

2. **But then again, there are times when this cult-of-personality stuff actually works!** Okay, here goes the zigzag, paradoxical path of leadership in freaked-out times. It's true that there are times of genuine corporate peril when no one other than a large-than-life visionary leader can get the job done.

3 **Leadership is confusing as hell.** If we're going to make any headway in figuring out the new rules of leadership, we might as well say it up front: There is no one-size-fits-all approach.

4 **When it comes to talent, leadership doesn't income-average.** It's a favourite one-liner these days: There is no 'I' in team.

5 **Leaders love the mess.** One leader who deserves to be celebrated? That fabulous third-grade teacher your Charlie has — the one who sees each of her 23 charges as unique.

6 **The leader is rarely-possibly never? — the best performer.**

7 **Leaders deliver.** If you're aiming to be a real leader during the next five years, then you need to mimic the pizza man: You' better deliver!

8 **Leaders create their own (peculiar?) destinies.** During the next five years, there won't be room for paper pushers. Only people who make personal determinations to be leaders will survive — and that holds true at all levels of all organisations (including entry level).

9 **Leaders win through logistics.** Vision, sure. Strategy, yes. But when you go to war, you need to have both toilet paper and bullets at the right place at the right time. In other words, you must win through superior logistics. Go back to the Gulf War. After that war ended, the media stories focused on the strategy that was devised by Colin Powell.

10 Leaders understand the ultimate power of relationships. Here's a mind-blowing proposition: War — or business on a wartime footing — is fundamentally a woman's game! Why? Because when everything's on the line, what really matters are the relationship that leaders have created with their people. I recall a Douglas MacArthur biographer who claimed that the one piece of advice that MacArthur most valued (which was passed on to him by one of his military forbearers) was "Never give an order that can't be obeyed." But women already know that. They tend to understand the primacy of massive IIR (investment in relationship), which is one reason why the premier untapped leadership talent in the world today rests with women!

11 **Leaders multitask.** Which element is in the shortest supply today — and tomorrow and tomorrow? Time. The future belongs to the leader who can juggle a dozen conundrums at once. And who is he? I mean she? I just glanced at a lovely book called selling is a Woman's Game: 15 Powerful Reasons why Women can Outsell Men (Avon Books, 1994), by Nicki Joy and Susan Kane-Benson. Take this quick quiz, the authors urge: Who manages more things at once? Who usually takes care of the details? Who finds it easier to meet new people? Who asks more questions in a conversation? Who is a better listener? Who encourages harmony and agreement? Who works with a longer to-do list? Who's better at keeping in tough with others? Now that's what I call multi-tasking! And again: Let's hear it for women leaders!

12 **Leaders groove on ambiguity.** Wall Street is nuttier than a fruit-cake! All of that stuff they teach us in Economic 101 about rational expectations? In the past year, we've seen those 'rational' boys and girls of Wall Street fall in and out of love with whole sectors of the economy the way teenagers with overactive hormones swoon and dive over movie stars. But when Wall Streeters do it, real leaders in real companies feel real effects.

The next five years are going to be an economic roller-coaster ride. That means that business leaders are going to be challenged repeatedly not just to make fact-based decisions, but also to make some sense out of all of the conflicting and hard-to-detect signals that come through the fog and the noise. Leaders are the ones who can handle gobs and gobs of ambiguity.

13 **Leaders wire the joint.** The good-old-boy's network provided a direct way of operating: I'm a vice president, you're a vice president. I want your order, I call you up, I take you out for a drink or a game of golf, and man to man, I get your order.

It doesn't work like that anymore — not when power is diffuse, alliance is ever changing, and decision-making channels are fluid, indirect, and muddy. The game today: Soft-wire the whole joint. The way to make the sale today — or to have influence on any high-impact decision — is to build, nurture, and mobilise a vast net work of key influencers at every level and in every function of the operation.

14 **Leadership is an improvisational art.** The game — hey, the basic rule book — keeps changing. Completion keeps changing. So leaders need to change, to keep reinventing themselves. Leaders have to be ready to adapt, to move, to forget yesterday, to forgive, and to structure new roles and new relationships for themselves, their teams, and their ever-shifting portfolio of partners.

15 **Leaders trust their guts.** 'Intuition' is one of those good words that had gotten a bad rap. For some reason, intuition has become a 'soft' notion. Garbage! Intuition is the new physics. It's an Einsteiniam, seven-sense, practical way to make tough decisions. Bottom line, circa 2001 to 2010: the crazier the times are, the more important it is for leaders to develop and to trust their intuition.

16 **Leaders trust trust.** May long-time business partner Jim Kouzes and his colleague Barry Posner nailed it with a one-word title to their recent book: Credibility (How Leaders Gain and Lose it, Why People Demand It, Jossey Bass Publishers, 1993). In a world gone nuts, we cry out for something or someone to rely on. To trust. The fearless leader may (make that, had better) change his or her mind with the times. But as a subordinate, I trust a leader who shows up, makes the tough calls, takes the heat, sleeps well amidst the furore, and then aggressively chomps into the next task in the morning with visible vitality.

17 **Leaders are natural empowerment freaks.** There are two ways to look at Jack Welch's legacy as a leader. The first is to say that he has created more value for his shareholders

than any other comparable modern-day business leader. Which he has. He has also created more leaders than any comparable modern day business leader.

When we think of Welch, we do not ordinarily think vision. (What is GE's vision? I haven't a clue? "We bring good things to life' ain't it.) We do think rigorous performance standards, empowerment ('Work Out' in GE-speak), leadership, and talent development. Jack Welch, it turns out, is a great manager (see rule # 1).

18 **Leaders are good at forgetting.** Peter Senge's brilliant insight 10 years ago was that companies need to be learning organisations. May campaign 2001: companies need to be forgetting organisations. Enron Corp., which has repeatedly been tagged as the nation's most innovative corporation, is exhibit A as a world-class forgetting organisation. It's not wedded to what it did yesterday. Enron chiefs Kenneth Lay and Jeff Skilling have figured out how to operate like a band of pirates. Got an idea? Don't dally. Go for it while it's an orginal! Doesn't work? Try something else if that doesn't work, fuhgeddaboutit!

19 **Leaders bring in different dudes.** This is a corollary to forgetting. Many leaders are preoccupied with creating high-performance organisations. But to that, I say: Crazy times demand high-standard deviation organisations! This isn't just weirdness for the sake of weirdness. This is weirdness for the sake of variety.

Winning leaders know that their organisations need to refresh the gene pool. That happens when leaders forget old practices and open up their minds to new ones. That also happens — and more effectively — when leaders bring in new people and new partners with new ideas. As a leader, do with your people what Cisco has done so effectively with technology: Acquire a new line of thinking by acquiring a new group of thinkers.

20 **Leaders make mistakes and make no bones about it.** Nobody – repeat, nobody – gets it right the first time. Most of us don't get it right the second, third or fourth time either. Winston Churchill said it best: "Success is the ability to go from failure to failure without losing your enthusiasm." Churchill blew one assignment after another – until he came up against the big one and saved the world.

As times get crazier, you're going to see more – and dumber – mistakes when you make mistakes, you need to recognise them quickly, deal with them quickly, move on quickly – and make cooler mistakes tomorrow.

21 **Leaders love to work with other leaders.** Nortel CEO, president, and VC John Roth says, "Our strategies must be tied to leading-edge customers on the attack. If we focus on the defensive customers, we will also become defensive." Amen. (No: AMEN!) Leaders are known by the people who are cool, pioneering leaders who have customers who are cool, pioneering leaders who source from suppliers who are cool, pioneering leaders — then you'll stay on the leading edge for the next five years. Laggards work with laggards. Leaders work with leaders. It really is that simple.

22 **Leaders can laugh.** Another corollary to the art of leadership and making mistakes: No one's infallible (except for the Pope). In order to survive in these wild times, you're going to make a total fool of yourself with incredible regularity. If you can't laugh about it, then you are doomed. Take it from me. (And if you are a humourless bastard, please do me a favour: Don't immediately march over to your VP of human resources and order, "Ve vill haff humour! Bring me ze funny people!." But do remember the madness of the times. Humour is the best tool you've got to keep your team from going mad. No bull!)

23 **Leaders set design specs.** You can't be a leader over the next five years and not be totally into design. Design specs are the double-helix DNA that sets the tone of the culture and establishes the operating ideas that embody the company. They are your distinguishing characteristics, your brand's brand. If you don't already know how, learn how to speak design. Apple CEO Steve Jobs calls design 'soul'. I say: Design specs = soul operating system.

24 **Leaders also know when to challenge design specs.** Here comes another bloody brain flip. In zany times, design specs (corporate character) must be open to constant re-evaluation. What worked during the past five years may or may not work for the next five years.

25 **Leaders have taste.** It's a big part of the often-subtle topic of design. There is such a thing as good taste. May be a better word is 'grace'. I love this quote from designer Celeste Cooper: "My favourite word is 'grace' — whether it's amazing grace, saving grace, grace under fire, Grace Kelly. How we live contributes to beauty — whether it's how we treat other people or the environment." Leaders who would change our lives don't shy away from words like grace and beauty and taste.

26 **Leaders don't create followers, they create more leaders.** Too many old fashioned leaders measure their influence by the number of followers that they can claim. But the greatest leaders are those who don't go looking for followers. Think of Martin Luther King Jr., Mohandas Gandhi, or Nelson Mandela. They were looking for more leaders in order to empower others – to find and create their own destinies.

27 **Leaders love rainbows – for totally pragmatic reasons.** Another good word gone bad: 'diversity'. The case for diversity during the past 20 years has been that it was the 'right thing to do'. Well, in no-bull times, diversity isn't a good thing, it's an essential thing. It's a good thing; it's an essential thing. It's a survival thing. The case for diversity is the case against homogeneity: When the world is undergoing sudden, unpredictable, dire change, you need to have a diverse gene pool. You need to have multiple points of view. In a heterogeneous time, homogeneity sucks!

28 **Leaders don't fall prey to their own success.** There are a lot of people who have made it really, really big over the past five years. Some of them actually think that

they're responsible for their success, if you can imagine that. But in crazy times, leaders don't believe in their own press clippings. And they never, ever let their organisations get complacent! Read The Paradox of Success: When Winning at Work Means Losing at Life: A Book of Renewal for Leaders (GP Putnam's Sons, 1993), by John O'Neil. He talks about the good qualities that breed monsters. The first one on the list; Confidence breeds a sense of infallibility. Again: Amen.

29 **Leaders never get caught fighting the last war.** It's the age-old problem with bemedalled generals: They're always preparing to fight the last war. The lesson, embedded in history, applies to business. What business are you in? The only answer that makes sense today is, God alone knows! Did you win the war during the past five years? Were you an early adopter of Internet ways? Good for you! The only problem is that the Internet is still in diapers. The old giants are awakening to its potential. What's you next totally new act?

30 **But leaders have to deliver, so they worry about throwing the baby out with the bathwater.** Did I mention that these are paradoxical times? Well, they are. So here's the flip side to the other side: You must execute consistently, while fighting consistency. Years ago, in Liberation Management: Necessary Organisation for the Nanosecond Nineties (AA Knopf, 1992), I called it the 'ultimate leadership paradox'. To be 'excellent' (to deliver profits, provide quality, and satisfy customers), you must be consistent and build a stellar infrastructure-delivery capability. But the single-mindedness that allows you to hit earnings targets and quality goals is a disguised set of blinders that makes you vulnerable to new, oddball threats (consistency = focus = blinders). Love the bathwater! Throw the bathwater out! Go figure!

31 **Leaders honour the assassins in their own organisations.** There's only one reason whey any human being ever makes it into the history books: because he or she remorselessly overthrew the conventional wisdom. Those are leaders. But truly great leaders, the ones who aim to leave a legacy, go to the next level. They consistently seek out and honour the people in their own organisations who want to overthrow their conventional wisdom. Great leaders honour the people who want to depose them, the assassins in their midst. Real leaders, repeat after me: All hail Brutus!

32 **Leaders love technology.** I mean love! L-O-V-E. here's the equation for the next five years: Technology = architect of change. If you don't love (and I don't mean like or tolerate) the technology, it will change you and your company, but you will be the unwitting victim, not the partner of change. Look, you don't have to be a technologist. But you must embrace technology, care for it. It's your friend, your lover. It will be unfaithful at times. It will lead you down dark and dangerous alleys. No matter. It is remaking the world. And you must joyously leap aboard (that's the way love is).

33 **Leaders wear their passion on their sleeve.** There's absolutely no question in my mind: Leaders dream in Technicolor. They see the world in brighter colours, sharper images, and higher resolution. Leadership, in the end, is all about having energy, creating

energy, showing energy, and spreading energy. Leaders emote, they erupt, they flame, and they have boundless (nutty) enthusiasm. And why shouldn't they? The cold logic of it is unassailable: If you do not love what you're doing, if you do not go totally bonkers for your project, your team, your customers, and your company, then why in the world are doing what you're doing? And why in the world would you expect anybody to follow you?

34 **Leaders know: Energy begets energy:** Every successful company, every successful team, and every successful project run on one thing: energy. It's the leader's job to be the energy source that other feed from. But sometimes the leader has no energy. Sometimes the situation is bleak, and the outcome is in doubt. And I say: Fake it! For it is at that critical juncture that having energy is the most essential. So if you gotta fake it, then fake it! Once you kick-start the energy cycle, nature takes over. The energy will start to flow. Benjamin Zander said it best: The job of the leader is to be a 'dispenser of enthusiasm.

35 **Leaders are community organisers.** Let's hear three raucous cheers for Saul Alinksy! (Haven't heard to him? Quick! Go to Amazon. com and buy Rules For Radicals: A Practical Primer for Realistic Radicals [Random House, 1971]. Read it immediately!) It doesn't matter if you're recruiting talent, making a sale, or forging a partnership. Everything you do is the exact equivalent of grassroots organising.

Your title may say that you are the leader but you're running for office every day. Want to pull off that Internet enabled business-process redesign? You've got to get the frontline commitment, the votes! You've got go get your customers to vote for you, yours suppliers to vote for you, your employees to vote for you. How do you get them to do more than just show up? You enlist them and win their votes one damn day at a time.

36 **Leaders give respect.** There's another great book with a one-word title: Respect (An Explanation, Perseus Books, 1999), by Sara Lawrence-Lightfoot. The heart of her message: "It was much later that I realized Dad's secret. He gained respect by giving it. He talked and listened to the fourth-grade kid in Spring Valley who shined shoes the same way he talked and listened to a bishop or a college president. He was seriously interested in who you were and what you had to say." Care. Respect. Leaders care about connecting – because it moves mountains.

37 **Leaders show up.** Legendary, all-powerful sports agent Mark McCormack offers a potent lesson on leadership in one of his books. He insists that, even in the Internet Age (or is it especially in the Internet Age?), it's a worthwhile show of commitment and respect (see rule # 36) to travel 6,000 miles round-trip to consummate a five-minute face-to-face meeting. Hatim Tyabji, who was then the soft-spoken, charismatic CEO of Verifone, once travelled from South Africa to Colorado — on his way to Norway – to give a one-hour presentation at a conference of just 30 people. Why? Because three months prior to that engagement, before all of the other trips had even

been booked, he had promised to be there. I guarantee that people paid uncompromising attention to his one-hour talk, because he showed uncompromising leadership — by showing up.

38 **Leadership is a performance.** According to HP big cheese Carly Fiorina, "Leadership is a performance. You have to be conscious about your behaviour because everyone else is." Leaders spend time leading – which means that they spend time and exert ceaseless effort making sure that they come across with the right message in the way that they walk, talk, dress, and stand. Leadership in not only about action. It's also about acting.

39 **Leaders have great stories.** A performance (see rule # 38) needs to have a script. Howard Gardner wrote about that in his book, Leading Minds: An Anatomy of Leadership (Basic Books, 1995). Effective communication of a story is a key – perhaps the key to leadership.

Why? Because stories are the real thing. They are how we remember, how we learn, and how we visualize what can be. If you want to involve your colleagues in the future performance of your business, then don't just present them with the numbers. Tell them a story. Numbers are numbing. Stories are personal, passionate, and purposeful.

40 **Leaders give everyone a cause.** Corollary to rule #39: What's the point of our story? If you want people to care — really to care — enlist them in a cause that they can care about: being part of the team that will go down in history for inventing the most amazing personal computer that the world has ever seen (Apple's Mac); achieving customer loyalty so intense that it becomes the stuff of legends (Nordstrom); executing a strategy with such precision that proud, old competitors are publicly humbled in the market (Home Depot).

People enlist on behalf of a cause. They do the impossible for a cause. For a business, however, they just work. What's your cause?

41 **Leaders focus on the soft stuff.** People. Values. Character. Commitment A cause. All of the staff that was supposed to be too goo-goo to count in business. Yet, it's the stuff that real leaders take care of first. And forever. That's way leadership is an art, not a science.

If leadership were just about hitting your numbers, about driving the troops to meet their quotas, then leadership would just be a math problem. But leadership is a human mastery.

In these times, as the numbers get harder to hit (or even to understand), and a frustration abets the temptation to be a kick-ass, take-charge, top-down leader, we'll see every quickly who keeps an enterprise energized in the face of adversity and ambiguity. And we'll see who is faced with passive resistance, quiet rebellion, and random acts of insubordination.

42 **Leaders think — make that know — that they can make a difference.** Call it instance optimism. Call it rampant self-confidence. Call it plain stupid. Leaders are convinced that they are going to make a difference. It's not about egotism it's about having a healthy, unquestioning feeling of mattering. And a leader who radiates (good word, 'radiate') a sense of mattering attracts others who share that feeling. And out of that sharing comes a team of people who, by God, will damn well make a difference! Which comes first, the sense of mattering or the ability to matter? Ah, yet another layer to the alchemy of leadership.

43 **Leaders always make time to work the phones.** If you read the books on leadership, there's a strong undercurrent that says that leaders are people of action, charging about on great white steeds! Well, yes. But leaders are also great talkers. Leadership takes an almost bottomless supply of verbal energy: working the phones, staying focused on your message, repeating the same mantra until you can't stand the sound of your own voice – and then repeating it some more, because just when you start to become bored witless with the message, it's probably starting to seep into the organisation. You can't be a leader these days and be the strong, silent type. You have to be an endless talker, a tireless communicator.

44 **Leaders listen intently.** Leaders talk. Leaders listen. That is, the other side of this coin is also true — again. Leaders listen to what the market is saying, to what the customer is saying, and to what the team is saying. No, you don't have to do everything that you constituents demand that you do. But just be showing that you're listening, really listening, you demonstrate the respect that you accord to them (there's that word 'respect' again). Intent tuned-in listening engenders empathy, creates connectedness, and ultimately, builds cohesiveness. When the crap hits the fan, as it inevitably will, those are the qualities that will see you through. Listen while you can, so that you can lead when you must.

45 **Leaders revel in surrounding themselves with people who are smarter than they are.** Now hear this: you will not have all of the answers. More important, you are no longer expected to have all of the answers. Nobody can have all of the answers. What you are expected to do is recruit people – at all levels of your organisation – who do have the answers. These are the folks who lead you to make the right decision about how to deal with an unglued world. These are, ultimately, the people you will be known by. Their accomplishments will be your signature, the measure of your tenure.

If you are confident enough to hire people who are more talented than you are, then you are, then you will be known as an audacious leader. If you hire only people who are not as talented as you are, than you will appear to be weak and insecure. And you will ultimately fail. So you decide. Do you want to be the smartest person in the company? Or do you want to win — and leave a legacy?

46 **Great leaders are great pols.** Time for a reality check. Leadership is not for the lily-livered. Taking the responsibility to lead other into battle whether it's at war or at work – isn't for the faint of heart. It's not just the casualties that you need to be able

to stomach. It's the real world of organisational politics and inside deal making: doing what it takes to get things done. Dwight Eisenhower didn't become president because of his skills as a general, he became a general because of his skills as a politician. I'm not endorsing playing dirty. I'm just telling you that you can't pretend that the game won't get rough and that you can stay above the fray and still be an effective leader. Period.

47 **Leaders make meaning.** John Seely Brown, the former head of ceaselessly innovative Xerox PARC, nailed it, especially for these totally insane times: A leader's job isn't just to make decisions and to make products or services. A leader's job is also to make meaning. Why? Because in times like these, people depend on their leaders to absorb all of the chaos, all of the information, all of the change, and to find some meaningful pattern and compelling purpose in the midst of all of the splatter.

48 **Leaders learn.** The single worst thing that can happen to you as a leader? You exhaust your intellectual capital before you became a leader, you accumulated that capital by going to conference and taking notes. You networked like a lunatic. You kept your eyes and ears open, and you came up with the totally original synthesis that propelled you into the front ranks of leadership. And then you got bogged down in the perpetual politics of implementation and started to dissipate all of that accumulated wisdom. And because you were so damn busy doing, you stopped learning. You became a broken record for yesterday's paradigm. (Hey, it boosted you into orbit). You listened to yesterday's (closed) circle of 'brilliant' advisors. You started to quote yourself! (As I said in In Search of Excellence in 1982….) This is only natural – if you let it happen. Leaders work double overtime to keep it from happening. Learn fast, or get left behind fast.

49 **Leaders……?** I left this one open. You tell me. What is the one key idea for leadership in whacked-out times that you would propose? What's the one-liner that captures the essence of leadership for you? What do you think leaders need to do to win in the next five years?

The best leader is rarely the best pitcher or catcher. The best leader is just what's advertised: the best leader. Leaders get their kicks from orchestrating the work of others – not from doing it themselves.

"Success is the ability to go from failure to failure without losing your enthusiasm," said Churchill, who blew one assignment after another — until he came up against the big one and saved the world. As times get crazier, you're going to see more, and dumber, mistakes. Move on — and make cooler mistakes tomorrow."

Why do we Need Leaders?

John P. Kotter

Leadership is required for mobilising people to handle challenging times. In a world that has no challenges, things are fine and you don't require leaders. In such a world, you don't need to mobilize people for handling any crisis. But unfortunately, in our world, we a have huge number of challenges in the government, non-profit and business sectors; we have many challenges in the developing and the developed world. Hence, we require leadership in our world. In fact, in our world, the need for leadership is more now than ever before. In our current world of business, we cannot afford to restrict leadership to just the top management positions. Every employee, every engineer should rise to a leadership role. They should step in to solve customer problems; they should step in to solve internal company problems. The number of people that we need to provide leadership is huge now. The turbulences in life will never stabilise, and I see the demand for leaders going up steadily.

Almost always leadership produces change. They are always helping people to change their behaviour. The are always focussed on changing systems. Look at Jamshedji Tata, G.D. Birla, JRD Tata, N.R. Narayan Murthy, Azim Premji, Kumar Mangalam Birla – they induced change in Indian business and laid a foundation of entrepreneurial culture.

The Importance of Wisdom

Clayton Christensen
Born: 1952

Successful leadership requires one more element – wisdom. You can be creatively, analytically and practically intelligent. You can be creative and intelligent, but if you are not wise, then it goes sour. Wisdom emphasizes the positive use of knowledge and skills. So, wisdom basically helps in integrating the other aspects of WICS, the application of successful intelligence, creativity and experience towards the attainment of a common good, through a balance of intrapersonal, interpersonal and extrapersonal interests. And all the that means is that you balance your own interests with the interests of other people and the interests of higher order things — it could be your institution, your country, God, whatever, over the shorter and long terms. This means that you care about the long-term outcomes of your organisation or your society as much as you do about the short term goals, through the mediation of values like reciprocity, honesty and sincerity by acting to balance adaptation to your shaping and selection of environments. And that means some of the time you change yourself to fit the environment, some of the times you change the environment to fit you, and some of the times you just get out.

Prof. W. Edwards Deming

The basic idea of the WICS (Wisdom, Intelligence, Creativity Synthesised) model is that leadership is not something that you are born with and it's not an inherited trait, but it's something you decide to do. Good leadership is a decision that builds on a combination of wisdom, intelligence and creativity synthesized. Successful Intelligence is the ability to attain one's goals in life within one's socio-cultural context by capitalizing on strengths and correcting or compensating for weaknesses, by adapting through shaping and selecting environments. It's basically your ability to do what you want to do in your life. Creative ability to come up with the ideas and analytical ability is to see if they're good ideas, and practical ability is to make them work. So, the big decision is to use your intelligence to achieve success in your life by your own standards.

The Ethical side of Leadership: Leaders carry moral authority. Without moral authority, leadership is blind. Survey's of business people around the world show that they rank integrity at the top of the list of essential elements for leadership. The ethics are shared among cultures and religions.

Leadership, at the end of the day, boils down to taking the right decision at the right time. A leader needs to set the direction, get buy-in from the team, and then align the company to achieve the goals. Helping set the balance between short-term and long-term goals, between achieving day-to-day numbers and teamwork is also important.

In addition to leading the team, it is important to have skills in change management, have a more participative style of management and being able to build relationships at all levels. You have strategic and operational relationships. A leader should be able to identify and manage each one of them. I learnt how to juggle between short-term and long-term relationships, between managing our growth goals, and also investing in long-term and high impact projects like Shiksha for school education and Bhasha for enabling technology in major local languages. One needs to have leadership at various levels – operational and strategic. Operational leadership is about here and now. It is about producing short-term results that are visible. Strategic leadership is broader and is more at a change level. An organisation requires both of these.

The fulfillment and satisfaction derived from the hard work, the frustrations and the challenges, the success and, eventually, seeing your team and institution grow and create a broad impact, is tremendous.

THEORIES OF LEADERSHIP

Leadership theories and models which are available in the literature can be broadly classified into three categories having three underlying basic approaches. They also show a chronological transition from highly over simplified to considerably sophisticated approaches. While we shall consider here the major models or theories in each of the categories, we shall also make a brief note on the more recent trends and approaches.

Historically, focus on leadership in theories shifted from one dimension of leadership to another. Early leadership research focused on the leader himself or herself to the virtual exclusion of other variables. It was assumed that leadership effectiveness could be explained isolating psychological, physical characteristics, or traits, which were presumed to differentiate the leader from the other members of the group.

COMPARISON OF AUTHORITARIAN, PATERNALISTIC, DEMOCRATIC, BUREAUCRATIC, LAISSEZ-FAIRE AND AUTHORITATIVE LEADERSHIP STYLES

	Authoritarian	*Paternalistic*	*Democratic*	*Bureaucratic*	*Laissez Faire*	*Authoritative*
1. Policy making	Everything is decided by the leader	Is decided by the leader.	Is decided by the group with the help from leader.	Is decided by another group who represents employer.	Group or individual free to make own decision.	Is decided by leader and the group jointly. Leader has the final say.
2. Techniques, methods and activities.	Is dictated by leader, one at a time.	Material is supplied by leader, advice given wherever needed.	Is determined by group discussion of goals & techniques, helped by technical advice from leader.	Is determined strictly by existing rules & regulations.	Material is supplied by leader — advice given only when asked for.	Material is primarily supplied by leader but group contribution also is obtained. Targets and techniques are jointly decided more often by group discussion.
3. Allotment of tasks and colleagues.	Is dictated by leader.	Is decided by leader.	Primarily they are left to members.	Strictly followed by existing rules and regulations.	Complete non-participation by leader.	Leader actively leads and involves members to participate. Allotment decided more jointly.
4. Praise, criticism and participation in group activity	Leader does not participate. He praises or criticises members at personal level.	Leader occasionally participates symbolically. He praises and criticises members at personal level.	Leader participates symbolically. He praises and criticises members objectively based on facts.	Leader participates according to prescribed rules and regulations and never goes beyond that limit. He praises or criticises on the basis of facts and only does them when rules and regulations demand these from him.	No attempt by leader to appraise or regulate activities of group, no deliberate participation.	Leader exercises his authority to guide and train. He praises and criticises members objectively based on facts related to task performance.

Sources: (1) White, Ralph & Lippit, Ronalt, "Leader Behaviour and Member Reaction" in *Three Social Climates: Group Dynamics,* ed. by Cartwright, D., & Zander, A. Row Peterson and Co., New York, 1956, pp. 585-611; (2) Chatterjee, N.R., *Industrial Psychology,* Sudha Publicatiohs (P) Ltd., New Delhi, 1969, p. 303; (3) Ghosh, P.K., *"Authoritative Supervisory Style and Task Orineted Relationship."* Lecture Notes for Executive Development Programmes, Unpublished, J.B. Inst. of Management Studies, 1978.

AUTHORITATIVE STYLE COMPARED WITH BUREAUCRATIC, AUTOCRATIC, IDIOCRATIC AND DEMOCRATIC STYLE

	Bureaucratic	*Autocratic*	*Idiocratic*	*Democratic*	*Authoritative*
1. Sources of authority	Rules	Self	Individual worker	Group codes	Self and group
2. Goals	Develop system	Develop self	Develop individual	Develop groups	Develop self and group with system viewed as important.
3. Demand on workers	Loyalty	Obedience	Ambition	Teamwork	Compliance through acceptance, commitment, mutual trust and confidence.
4. Supervisory motivation	Security	Self expression	Social contact	Participation membership	Achievement as per commitment.

Source: (1) Ganguli, H.C., *Industrial Productivity and Motivation,* Asia Publishing House, 1961, p. 73. (2) Ghosh, P.K., "Authoritative Supervisory Style and Task-oriented Relationship." Lecture Notes for Executive Development Programmes, Unpublished, J.B. Inst. of Management Studies, 1978.

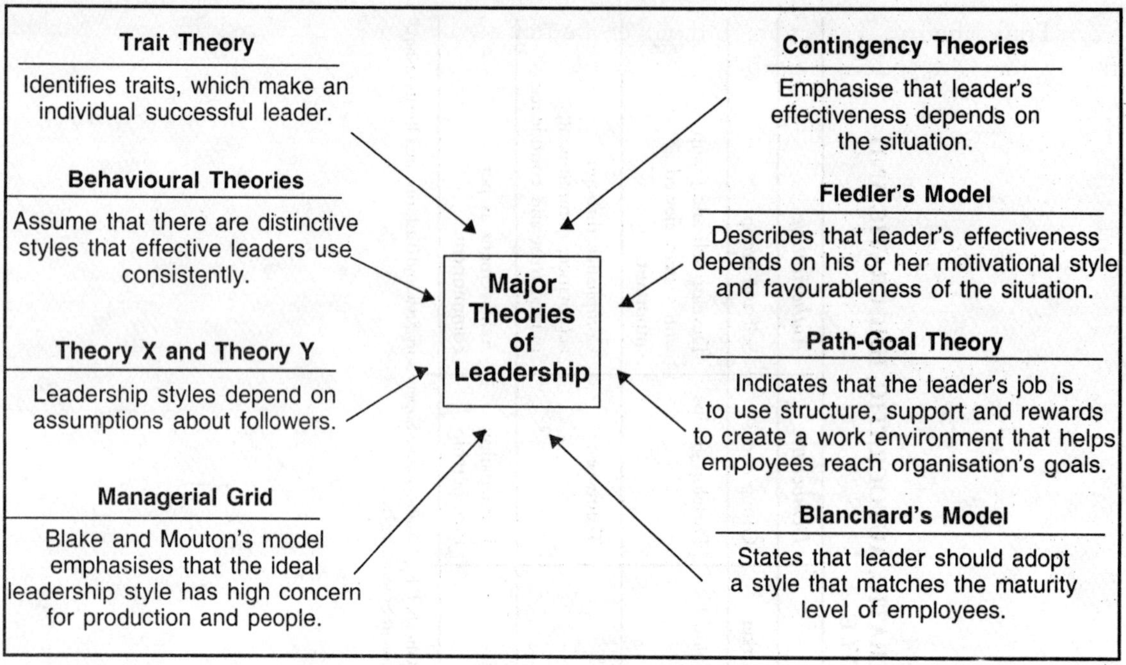

LEADERSHIP THEORIES

A BROAD CLASSIFICATION OF LEADERSHIP THEORIES AND THEIR SALIENT FEATURES

Trait Theories	*Behavioural Theories*	*Contingency or Situational Theories*	*Recent Advances*
Emphasise on Characteristic Traits of leaders	Emphasise on dimensions of leadership Behaviour. (I) Authoritarian and democratic (II) Employee-centred and production centred. (III) Initiating structure and consideration.	Emphasise on situational factors. A and D contingency model. Fiedler's model	The VDL Model Substitutes for leadership
Key traits theory	Managerial Grid.	Normative theories: (a) Path-goal model (b) Decision making	

UNIVERSAL THEORIES

Great man/woman Theory: This theory postulates that great leaders are born, not made. Great leaders possess key traits that set them apart from most other humans.

Trait Theory: It attempts to discover the traits shared by all effective leaders. As per this theory, traits are enduring attributes associated with an individual's make-up or personality. The trait theory says leaders must be Dominant, Intelligent and Masculine. Main problems with Trait Theory is that it deals with perceptions of leadership effectiveness, not actual effectiveness and does not take the situation into account.

Contingency Theories

Fiedler's Contingency Model: A leadership theory that maintains that effective leadership depends on a match between the leaders style and the degree to which the work situation gives control and influence to the leader. Fiedler believed that different situations in an organisations could be classified in terms of favourableness (situational control) determined by 3 factors:

1. Leader-member relations — Degree to which a leader is accepted and supported by the group members.
2. Task structure — Extent to which the task is structured and defined, with clear goals and procedures.
3. Position power — The ability of a leader to control subordinates through reward and punishment.

High levels of these three factors give the most favourable situation while low levels, the least favourable. Relationship-motivated leaders are most effective in moderately favourable situations. Task-motivated leaders are most effective at either end of the scale. Since personality is relatively stable, the contingency model suggests that improving effectiveness requires changing the situation to fit the leader. This is called "job engineering".

The Path-Goal Theory: Path-Goal Theory of Evans and House identifies achievement-oriented, directive, participative and supportive leadership styles. An *achievement-oriented leader* sets challenging goals for followers, expects them to perform at their highest level and shows confidence in their ability to meet this expectation. This style is appropriate when the follower suffers from a lack of job challenge. In *directive leadership,* the leader lets followers know what is expected of them and tells them how to perform their tasks. This style is appropriate when the follower has an ambiguous job. *Participative leaders* consult their followers and seek their suggestions before making a decision. This style is appropriate when the follower is using improper procedures or is making poor decisions. Under *supportive leadership*, the leader is friendly and approachable and shows concern for the followers. This style is appropriate when the followers lack confidence.

Path-Goal Theory assumes that leaders are flexible and that they can change their style, as situations require. The theory proposes two contingency variables, such as environment and follower characteristics, that moderate the leader behaviour-outcome relationship. Environment is outside the control while follower characteristics are controllable. Effective leaders clarify the path to help their followers achieve goals. Research demonstrates that employee performance and satisfaction are positively influenced when the leader compensates for the shortcomings in either the employee or the work setting.

Situational Leadership Theories

Situational Theory presumes that different leadership styles are better in different situations, and that leaders must be flexible enough to adapt their style to the situation they are in. A good situational leader is one who can quickly change leadership styles as the situation changes. **Hersey-Blanchard** theory suggests that leadership style should be matched to the maturity of the subordinates. Maturity is assessed in relation to a specific task and has two parts:

- **Psychological maturity:** Their self-confidence and ability and readiness to accept responsibility.
- **Job maturity:** Their relevant skills and technical knowledge.

As the subordinate maturity increases, leadership should be more relationship-motivated than task-motivated. Leadership can consist of *Delegating* to subordinates (Hands-off leadership), *Participating* with subordinates (Allowing followers to approach the task autonomously but providing emotional support for motivation), *Selling* ideas to subordinates (Explaining and clarifying how work is to be done and attempting to motivate workers) and *Telling* subordinates.

LEADERSHIP THEORIES AND MODELS

Contributor	*Theory or Model*	*Year of Publication of Significant Research*
Taylor	Scientific Management	1911
Mayo	Hawthorne Studies	1933
Barnard	Executive Function	1938
Coch-French	Michigan Studies	1948
Stogdill	Ohio State Studies	1948
Homans	Human Group	1950
Maslow	Hierarchy of Needs	1954
McGregor	Theory X – Theory Y	1957
Tannenbaum-Schmidt	Continuum of Leader Behaviour	1957
Blake-Mouton	Managerial Grid	1964
Argyris	Maturity – Immaturity	1964
McClelland	Achievement Theory	1965
Odiorne	Management by Objectives	1965
Herzberg	Motivation – Hygiene	1966
Likert	Systems 1- 4	1967
Fiedler	Contingency Model	1967
Reddin	3-D Management Style	1967
Olsson	Management by Objectives	1968
Heresy-Blanchard	Situational Leadership	1969
Vroom-Yetten	Contigency Model	1973
House-Mitchell	Path – Goal	1974
Vroom	Expectancy Theory	1976
House	Charismatic Leadership	1977
Burns	Transformational Leadership	1978
Kerr-Jermier	Substitutes for Leadership	1978
McCall-Lombardo	Fatal Leadership Flaws	1983
Greenleaf	Servant Leadership	1983
Bennis-Nanus	Leadership Competencies	1985
Tichy-Devanna	Transformational Leadership	1986
Manz	Super Leadership	1989
Yukl	Integrating Leadership Model	1989
Covey	Principle-centred Leadership	1991

Fisher	Principle Self-directed Work Teams	1993
Johnson	SOAR Model	1994
Pansegrouw	Transformational Model	1995
Gyllenpalm	Organisational Cone	1995
Whetter-Cameron	Empowerment	1995
Tichy	Leadership Engine	1997
Ball	DNA Leadership	1997
Byham-Cox	Empowerment	1998
Fairholm	Value-Based Leadership	1998
Cohen,	8 Universal Laws of Leadership	1998
Ulrich, Zenger, Smallwood	Results-Based Leadership	1999
Wheatley	Leadership and the New Science	1999

(***Source:*** Paul Hersey, *et al, Management of Organisational Behaviour,* Pearson, 2001, p. 87).

The theories of leadership focus on the individual characteristics of successful leaders. According to the theories, leaders possess a set of traits which make them distinct from followers. An attempt must, therefore, be made to identify and measure these traits.

According to Ralph Stogdill, for instance, the successful leaders tend to have the following qualities:

(*i*) A strong desire for accomplishment

(*ii*) Persistent pursuit of goals

(*iii*) Creativity and intelligence used to solve problems

(*iv*) Initiative applied to social situations

(*v*) Self-assumed personality

(*vi*) Willingness to accept behavioural consequences

(*vii*) Low susceptibility to interpersonal stress

(*viii*) High tolerance of ambiguity

(*ix*) Ability to influence other people

(*x*) Ability to structure social interactions.

Next in importance are the behavioural theories which focus on what the leaders do while influencing the behaviour of subordinates. The behaviours of leaders can be acquired. Ohio State University studies and the University of Michigan studies are the research studies conducted in support of the behavioural theories.

Contingency theories (including Fielder's model and the path-goal model of Robert House) stress on the fact that leadership effectiveness depends on situations and not on traits or behaviours of leaders.

Situational leadership theory propounded by Paul Hersey and Kenneth Blanchard, adds a new dimension to leadership, *viz.,* maturity. The theory hypothesizes that the leader's style depends on the maturity level of the subordinate employees.

McGregor's Theory X and Theory Y remind the leaders that contrary to popular belief, individuals are under Theory Y. Accordingly, leaders must adopt participative styles to influence the followers.

The discussion of theories is highly useful to leaders in more than one way. The traits theory underlines that an individual possessing the necessary qualities must be appointed as leader.

LEADER BEHAVIOUR DIMENSIONS

Leader Directiveness

Letting subordinates know what's expected.
Providing specific guidance as to what should be done and how.
Making leader's part in the group understood.
Scheduling work to be done.
Maintaining definite standards of performance.

Leader Supportiveness

Showing concern for status and well-being of subordinates.
Doing little things to make the work more pleasant.
Treating members as equals.
Being friendly and approachable.

Leader Participativeness

Consulting with subordinates.
Soliciting subordinate suggestions.
Taking these suggestions seriously.
Maintaining definite standards of performance.

Leader Achievement-orientedness

Setting challenging goals.
Expecting subordinates to perform at their peak levels.
Showing a high degree of confidence in subordinates.
Constantly emphasising excellence in performance.

Behavioural theories postulate that the behaviour of leaders are more important than their qualities. These behaviours can be acquired unlike traits which are generally inherited.

Today's business is characterised as global, dynamic and customer driven which requires managers to surpass boundries, become accustomed to culture, develop efficient processes an integrate teams. Attitudes, which are important to success of individual rather than just talent, can and will make a difference in people's personal lives and work environment. The organisational costs associated with poor employee attitudes may sternly reduce an organisation's *competitiveness*. Alternatively, employees with favourable attitudes tend to be connected with positive outcomes that organisations need in the fast growing competitive environment. The leader's responsibility is to influence the behaviour of his people in such a way that the goals are achieved. A key challenge for managers, while dealing with employees, is to have concern for their attitudes and feelings. *Every manager*, thus, has to act as *leader* at his work place for influencing and inspiring subordinates to perform their duties *willingly*, *competently* and *enthusiastically* to achieve the organisational goals.

Conclusion

Entrepreneurial leadership has come to stay and thrive. In the 21st century the entrepreneurial leaders with their innovative skills, intelligence, integrity go a long way in throwing up new products, services to accelerate economic growth, all along creating employment opportunities, raising the income level all along. The entrepreneurial leadership initiative rests on three avenues of research legacy leadership, emerging leadership and global leadership. The entrepreneur formulates the vision, sets the direction with clear goals, and helps drive change. In the 21st century innovation, technology, knowledge, special skills, motivations will continue to be the change vehicles of entrepreneurial leadership.

Contingency theories emphasise that the situation in which a leader operates is the most important determinant of his effectiveness. Three contemporary issues on leadership should not be missed by any reader. First one relates to the need for transformational leadership and not mere transactional leadership. The second issue relates to the women as leaders. Surprisingly, women are not inferior to men in skills and abilities but the latter are generally preferred for leadership positions in our male dominated society. The third issue relates to charismatic leadership which is needed when an organisation is introducing a totally new product.

Thus a leader has to analyse the situation and adopt a leadership style that would be able to derive the best possible results from the staff working with him. For this, he should have a fair idea of knowledge and skill level of his employees, their abilities as well as their constraints. The leader has to even use different approaches with two different people among one team as no two persons can be identical. There may be persons who are self motivated and could be given some degree of operational freedom. However, there may be others who need to be motivated and given directions for performing. And still there may be others who need an autocratic leader to get results. Whatever be the leader-follower interaction, the leader has to behave like "Head of Family" and exhibit traits like humility, concern for others, controlled discipline, focusing on the purpose of the organisation and on the well-being of the followers and creating and sustaining peace in the organisation. The crucial aspect is that leaders must be able to change their styles to increase performance.

Like the theories of motivation, leadership theories are also moving from simple to complex. It is not at all surprising to the more complicated models in future. The tragedy is that these models are at the expense of simplicity. Practicing manager, on the other hand, feels to have equipped with a simple, concrete, solutions or models of leadership problems. The manager appreciates simply stated, neatly presented and theoretically sound and empirically justified. Even a complex theory might become 'simple' and 'easy' to do: This 'case of use' Philosophy becomes true when practising managers understand fully well the 'concept' and 'importance' of leadership in helping create healthy organisational climate.

Leadership is situational. The situation is not composed of a small number of fixed parts. The organisation and environment are dynamic. Leaders face a near-infinite set of situations and engage in near-infinite set of behaviours. Therefore, many different combinations of behaviours or styles may be effective in a given situation so that there is no one best way of responding. This being so, the search for invariant truth is an academic exercise and any understanding of leadership should involve a more holistic approach — one that looks beyond superficial behaviours and simplified taxonomies of situations.

It is a dynamic, relational process involving interactions among leaders, members and sometimes outside constituencies. Therefore, the essence of leadership is not the leader, but the relationship. Leadership thinkers Dorwin Cartwright and Alvin Zander agree with this definition.

"Leadership is about moving the group toward its goals by improving the quality of interactions among the members, building the cohesiveness of the group and making resources available to the group. In principle, leadership may be performed by one or many members of the group," they say.

Ultimately, whichever way you define leadership, someone else may do it differently. However, it still remains important that before your organisation or group can move forward, you must come up with a way of thinking about leadership that everyone can agree upon.

Reddin's Three-Dimensional Model

William J. Reddin may be called the apostolic father of the three dimensional theory of leadership. Reddin is the first person to introduce effectiveness dimension which has a pragmatically amorphous meaning so far. In his model, Reddin uses three dimensions of task-orientation, relationship-orientation and the effectiveness. He contends that the manager who exhibits the leadership style inconcinnity with the situation is called effective leader, ineffective otherwise.

Ineffective styles		*Basic styles*		*Effective styles*
Missionary	⟵	Relegated	⟶	Developer
Deserter	⟵	Separated	⟶	Bureaucrat
Autocrat	⟵	Dedicated	⟶	Benevolent autocrat
Compromiser	⟵	Integrated	⟶	Executive

Fig. 2

Taking the Balke and Mouton's managerial grid as a useful platform, Reddin went beyond this by adding effectiveness dimension. He suggests that all the four styles of leadership in the grid are effective or ineffective depending on the situation. The four styles on the upper right are effective as they achieve the output requirements of the manager's job and four styles on the left of the diagram are ineffective. (Fig. 3)

These eight styles show different degrees of effectiveness of the basic styles.

Effective Styles

(a) Executive: *He attaches maximum importance for work and people.* Manager using this style is a good motivator, utilises team effectively, sets high standards and is highly successful in accomplishing goals.

(b) Developer: *He gives maximum importance for people and minimum concern for work.* He trusts people and is mainly concerned with developing them as individuals.

(c) Benevolent autocrat: *He allocates more time for work and less concern for people. He knows what is to be done, how is to be done without causing resentment.*

(d) Bureaucrat: *Here the manager shows minimum concern for both people and work. He wants to control the situation by the rules and often is disliked by subordinates.*

Ineffective Styles

(a) Compromiser: He recognises the importance of both people and work and thus gives a great deal of concern for both, even in situations that require emphasis on any one of these. He is a poor decision maker because of the pressures that are pounced on him.

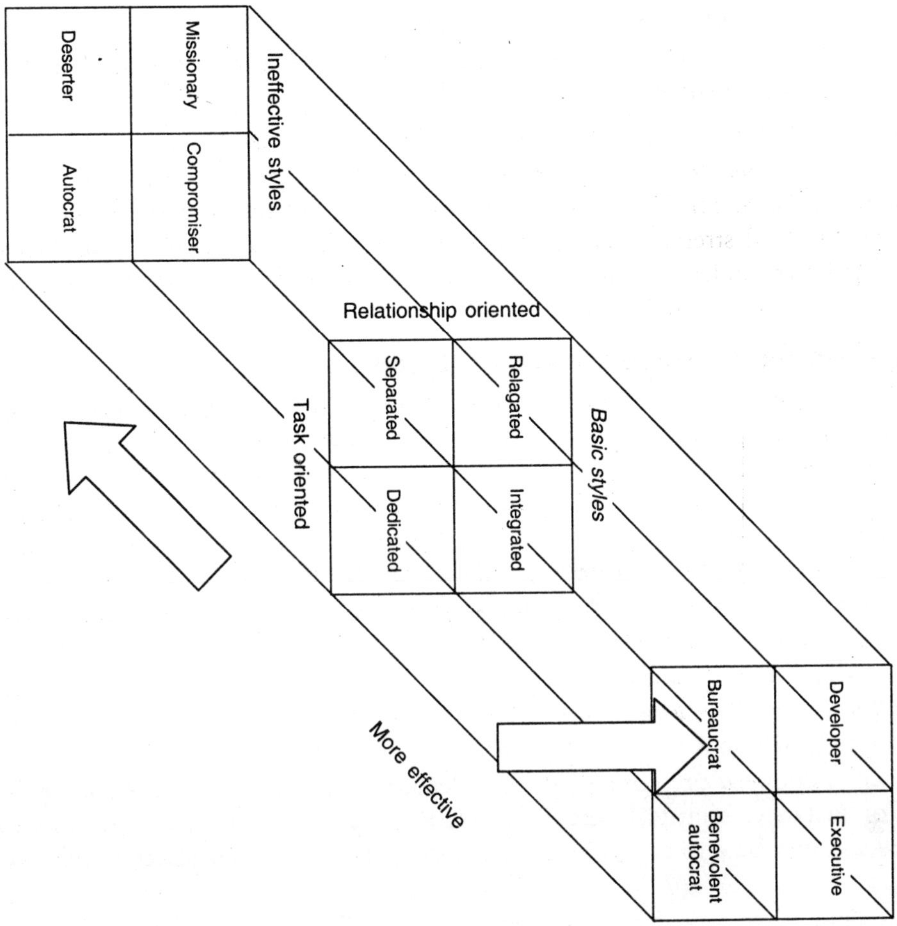

Fig. 3: Reddin's Model of leadership effectiveness

Source: W.J.Reddin, Managerial Effectiveness, McGraw-Hill, New York, 1970, p. 230.

(b) Missionary: He is relationship-oriented where the situation demands otherwise. He is basically do-gooder.

(c) Autocrat: Here the manager is task-oriented where the situation warrants otherwise and his style is inappropriate. Manager is unpleasant and has no confidence in others. He is interested only in the immediate job.

(d) Deserter. Here the manager neither task nor relationship-oriented. Manager is passive and largely escapist.

Reddin maintains that no style is good or bad in itself. It depend on the situation as to which style is best or appropriate. If the basic style is used appropriately it becomes effective, otherwise ineffective.

Reddin maintains that no style is good or bad in itself. It depends on the situation as to which style is best or appropriate. If the basic style is used appropriately it becomes effective, otherwise ineffective.

Reddin's model is appreciated on two accounts.

(*i*) For introducing the effectiveness dimension to the earlier concepts of Blake and Mouton's task-orientation and relationship-orientation.

(*ii*) For integrating the behaviour of the leader with the situation.

Reddin has just tried to provide a variety of styles that may be effective or ineffective depending on the situation. His 3-D approach incorporates all the three theoretical bases — leader, group and situation, and stresses that the manager should have an adaptive style that leads to effectiveness. Reddin's model helps in identifying a particular style a manager is using, but could not explain how a manager can improve his style.

Hersey-Blanchard's Three Dimensional Model

Using Reddin's 3-D management style, Paul Hersey and Kenneth Blanchards went a step further by adopting 'environment' as the effectiveness dimension. As against the attitudinal concepts of task-orientation and people-orientation, they have incorporated behavioural notions (i.e., task behaviour and relationship behaviour) in their three-dimensional model. Their bone of contention is that what is important is not the behaviour that is observed but what is the appropriateness of the observed behaviour to the given situation.

By adding the effectiveness dimension to the task-behaviour and relationship-behaviour dimensions of the earlier Ohio State Leadership model, Hersey and Blanchard tried to integrate the concepts of leadership styles with the situational demands of a specific environment. They suggest "when the style of a leader is appropriate to a given situation it is termed effective, when the style is inappropriate to a situation it is termed ineffective."

In essence, it does not present a single ideal leader behaviour style that is appropriate in all situations. For instance, high-task and high-relationship style is appropriate only in some circumstances and may be a total failure in some other situations. They illustrate this point with an example:

"In basically crisis-oriented organisations such as military or fire department, there is a considerable evidence that the most appropriate style would be high task and low relationship since under combat, fire or emergency conditions success often depends on immediate response to orders. Time demands do not permit talking things or explaining decisions. But once this crisis is over, other styles might become appropriate."

Thus Hersey-Blanchard's three-dimensional model is different from that of Reddin's in two respects:

(*i*) Using environment as an effectiveness dimension.

(*ii*) Using the behavioural notions in the place of attitudinal concepts of Reddin's.

But for these differences, both the models depict the same information; both converge at the viewpoint that leadership is situational.

AN INTEGRATIVE MODEL OF LEADERSHIP

Leadership is replete with many models of leadership effectiveness. But unfortunately no single model is effective enough to include all the variables of leadership. However, a model is proposed by Gibson et al that integrates the most reliable knowledge on leadership.

The integrative model as developed by Gibson includes the following variables:

(*a*) *Leader's awareness of self:* An introspective analysis of one's style of leading is essential for the leader interested in achieving effectiveness.

(*b*) *Group's characteristics:* Leader must diagnose the group's characteristics, such as skills, maturity, norms, size and cohesiveness. He must also assess the groups' future expectations about the rewards, style and tasks.

(*c*) *The individual characteristics:* Leader must be familiar with the complex individual characteristics such as personality, attitudes, perception and motivation. The effective leader must integrate the diverse mix of people in the groups and provide positive leadership in the organisation.

(*d*) *Motivation:* Motivation is the one very important aspect that leader must understand. He should know how to motivate the workers effectively. "Money can motivate some workers to perform better while it is not an effective motivator of other employees." Leader should know who responds to what rewards and how they respond. The answer to this provides guidelines for the appropriate motivational strategy.

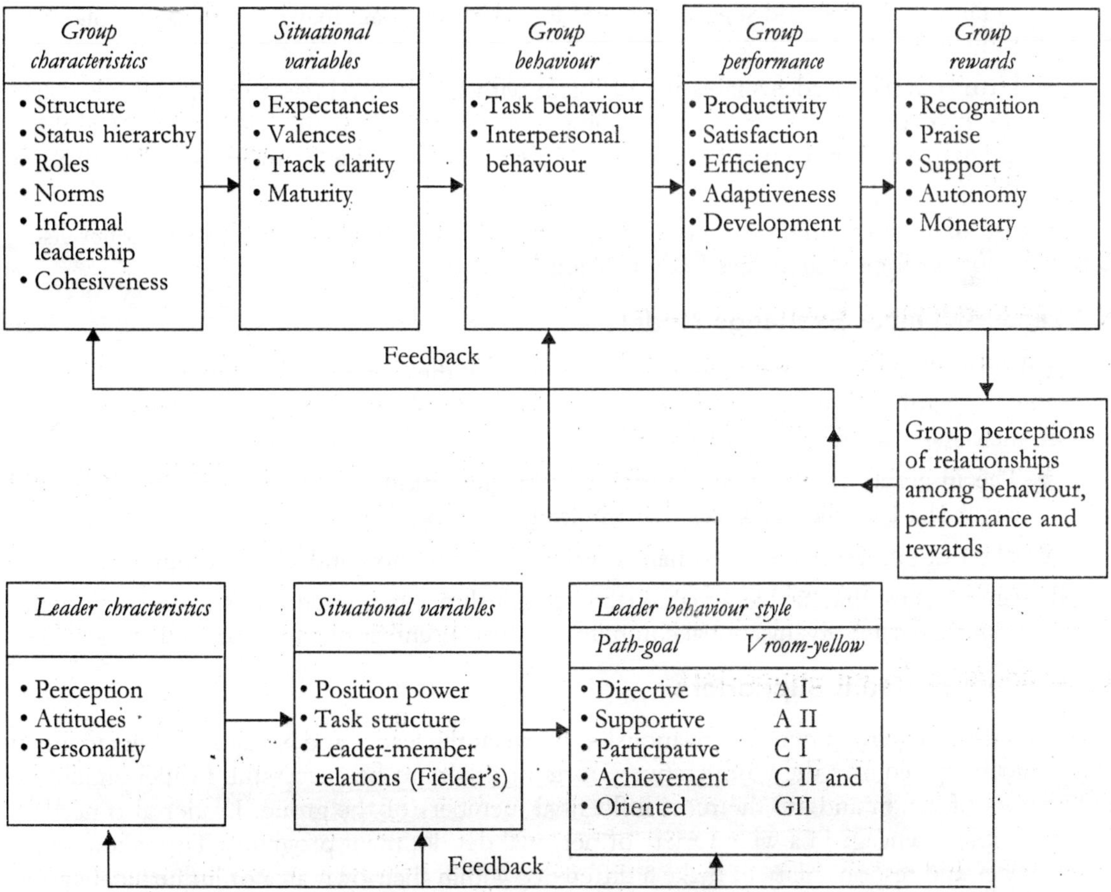

Fig. 4: An Integrative Model of Leadership

Source: Adapted from Gibşon, James L. John, M. Ivancewich and James H. Donally Jr. "Organisations: Behaviour, Structure and Processes", Business Publication inc, Dallas, Texas, Third edition, 1979, p. 226.

Through the integration of these variables we can visualise that while leader influences group behaviour, the group influences the leader in turn. In essence, leadership is viewed as a reciprocal process — leaders and groups influence each other.

Vroom-Yetton Leadership Model

This model suggests the selection of a leadership style for making a decision. There are five decision making styles:

- **Autocratic 1:** Problem is solved using information already available.
- **Autocratic 2:** Additional information is obtained from group before leader makes decision. Info is given in response to leader's request, but followers may not be "in" on process.
- **Consultative 1:** Leader shares the problem with the relevant followers individually, getting their ideas and suggestions without bringing them together as a group. However, leaders decision may not reflect followers' input.
- **Consultative 2:** The leader shares the problem with followers in a group meeting and obtains their ideas and suggestions. Leader's decision again may not reflect the followers' influence.
- **Group 2:** The leader shares the problem with his followers as a group. Group solves the problem with leader simply acting as chair. Together, they generate and evaluate alternatives to try to reach consensus. Leader accepts and implements solution given by the group.

In case of time constraint, a more autocratic approach should be preferred. Otherwise a more participative approach always leads to team spirit.

Leader-Member Exchange Model

A theory that effective leadership is determined by the quality of the interaction between the leader and particular group members. One proposition of this theory is that leaders tend to separate their subordinates into two groups:

- The in-group, or the cadre receive considerably more attention from the leader and larger share of the resources that the leader has to offer.
- The out-group, or the hired hands receive less attention and fewer resources.

Research suggest that having a high quality relationship with a leader is associated with better job performance, greater organisational commitment, less absenteeism and greater job satisfaction.

Leaders as Team Supporters

Leadership requires a two-way relationship between the leader and group members to attain goals. Leadership requires the co-operative efforts of others to be successful. Leader should be the initiators of action and are the most influential members of the group. Leader also need to support people to engage in a wide variety of personal development programs. They should give people power and responsibility to make a difference within their own area of influence. Leaders must respect those people who have the courage to differ and express an alternative point of view. Trend-setting bosses know that when people take control of their own lives they can bring increased value to organisations through increased effort, insights and innovation.

Leadership certainly involves creating a vision and achieving it. A leader has to be visionary and is something that comes from within the individual. Leadership is not positional and does not require formal authority or personal charisma. However, a leader must interact closely with his people and know them well since only then would he be able to decide which style of leadership should be used.

Leading Change

Leadership is all about change management to start with and leading change ultimately. Changes happen whether you like it or not. Change is inevitable. Either you learn to manage it or be swept by it. A leader accepts realities, understands changing environment and tries to excel in the given situation. A better leader, however, leads change in anticipation. A leader should have the courage to change things and should lead by example. A leader should also be bold to reprimand his subordinates for poor performance and should never tolerate behaviour which is not in the best interest of the organisation. He should bring behavioural changes by setting his own example.

RETAIL INDUSTRY IN INDIA — 12 MILLION OUTLETS

Organised (2%)	*Unorganised (98%)*
Corporate backed modern retail formats	Traditional formats of family owned or individual enterprise
Hypermarkets, supermarkets, department stores, convenient stores	Kirana stores, general stores, paan/beedi stores, handcart & pavement vendors
Employs 5 lakh people	Employs 3.95 crore people
Focus on ambience & visual elements	Focus on personalised service
Utilities technology and supply chain management	Not technology driven

VALUE POSITION OF MODERN RETAIL FORMATS

Format	*Definition*	*Value Position*
Supermarkets/ convenience stores	Food & household products	Convenience
Department stores	Multiple product categories, usually life-style driven with apparel accessories predominating	Service & choice
Hypermarkets discount stores	Large stores in big box format, with volume-based discounted prices	Price & Choice
Specially stores/ category killers	Extensive range of products under a single category	Service

REFERENCES

1. Blanchard, Ken and Hersey, Paul, "Great Ideas on Training and Development."
2. Fiedler, Fred, "A Theory of Leadership Effectiveness."
3. Greenberg, J. and Baron R., "Behaviour in Organisations."
4. Hollander, Edwin, "Leadership Dynamics."
5. Johnson, Howard, "A Symposium — a Requirement for Leadership."
6. Schriescheim, Cheser, "Least Preferred Co-Worker Score."
7. Goodworth, C., "The Secrets of Successful Leadership and People Management."
8. Blanchard K., Zigarmi P. and Zigarmi D., "Leadership and the One Minute Manager."
9. Vecchio R.P.: "Organisational Behaviour."
10. D.S. Pugh, "Organisation Theory — Selected Readings."
11. Robert P. Vecchio, "Organisational Behaviour."

Annexure - 1

CREATE MORE LEADERS

Leadership is integral to Entrepreneurship. An entrepreneur continuously seeks to innovate and create value around perceived opportunities. He has the ability to foresee opportunities ahead of the curve, manage risks and create capital — human, financial and social. Leaders must do the same.

Leadership is about making winning contagious; leaders must develop a strategy so that the successes grow not one by one, but exponentially. Also, to generate passion in an organisation, I believe one has to create early wins. It helps to make achievers out of people. The focus must be to build organisations that actively promote innovation, and where structure, management and processes are adapted to gain the required agility, creativity and drive to act profitably upon well-defined opportunities.

The function of a leader is to create more leaders, not mere followers. Leaders have to empower employees to act and deliver on the organisational vision. Leaders need to execute through inspiration and develop net-works through well-aligned relationships. In my judgement, human capital creation focuses on the economic behaviour of individuals and on their accumulation of knowledge and skill, which enables them to increase their and the organisation's wealth and productivity. Sound investment in human capital multiplies individual and collective economic returns and is essential for one's organisation to achieve its goal.

Innovation is a key driver in the fast evolving market dynamics of today. Leading innovation is a challenging process. One needs to encourage expansive, out-of-box thinking to generate new ideas.

I follow an 'easy-tight' leadership style — 'easy' for innovation and 'tight' for execution. And lastly, I believe in 'stretch' — driving the frontiers and inspiring on moving ahead.

Annexure - 2

EMPOWERING THE RETAIL ENTREPRENEUR

Retail is amongst the fastest growing sectors in the country. India ranks 1st, ahead of Russia, in terms of emerging market potential in retail and is deemed a 'Priority 1' market for international retail.

There are about 12 million retail outlets spread across India, earning in the epithet of a "nation of shopkeepers." "More than 80 per cent of these 12 million retail outlets are run by small family businesses, which use only household labour. However, the retail sector in India is highly fragmented and organised retail in the country is at a very nascent stage. In the retail sector, in spite of a 1.07 billion strong population, the target consumer base for most retailers in India stands at about 405 million. Of this, about 30 million have a combined purchasing capacity of USD 230 billion. The country's 6 million 'rich' population shops worth USD 28.36 billion every year.

Traditionally, small-store retailing has been one of the easiest ways to generate self-employment, as it requires limited investment in land, capital and labour. Consequently, India has one of the highest retail densities in the world at 6 per cent (12 million retail shops for about 209 million household). India's peers, such as China and Brazil, took 10-15 years to raise the share of their organised retail sectors from 5 per cent when they began, to 20 and 38 per cent respectively. India too is moving towards growth and maturity in the retail sector at a fast pace.

Creating Entrepreneurs

India's GDP, which currently stands at USD 690 billion is slated to touch USD 740 billion by the end of 2006. India is the world's 4th largest economy as regards in GDP (in PPP terms) and is expected to rank 3rd by 2010, just behind the US and china. The country is on the brink of becoming an economic powerhouse ready to unleash its largely untapped potential for those who are willing to take the right step forward. India's is being considered as a potential marketplace for most of the industries, especially retail.

Franchising & Retail

Globally franchising the #1 marketing and business development format and contributes to over 50 per cent of retail in the US. In India, considering the FDI restriction and the sheer size of the country, franchising remains the only solution. In a country as diverse and large as ours, franchising is bound to grow manifolds. Franchising could be seen as an alternative for India entry or a business development format for Pan-India expansion. It offers a unique opportunity for global companies to grow fast locally.

Entrepreneurship through franchising

India holds the opportunity of being one of the biggest entrepreneurial resource, and significantly contributes to the economic growth. Franchise India has been dedicated to the cause of entrepreneurship through franchising, the single largest format for empowering entrepreneurship. According to the Small Business Administration, less than 5% of all franchise units fall every year. This is compared to 30 to 35% of small businesses which fail within the first year of operation. Franchising further contributing in women entrepreneurship and creating self-employment, in turn contributing 20% of the world GDP.

ENTREPRENEURS FOR THE AGES

They are early colonial traders and 19th century industrialists. Throughout history, there have been a handful of people who had the vision to successfully exploit untapped markets. They changed the world in the process. See who they are, what they did, and why they matter today.

Admiral Zheng He *(b. around 1371, d. 1433)*

Zheng He, a Muslim from southwestern China's Yunnan province, was captured by the emperor's troops as a boy and pressed into Prince Zhu Di's corps of eunuch servants in the 14th century. When the prince became emperor, he charged Zheng He with building a trading fleet to make China an imperial economic power.

The servant-turned-admiral built the vaunted Treasure Fleets, comprising dozens of ships and tens of thousands of sailors, and led them in trade missions across South Asia and as far west as Africa and the Strait of Hormuz in the Persian Gulf. In seven voyages from 1405 to 1433, Zheng He spread China's goods across the world and returned with treasures for the Ming Dynasty. Along the way, Zheng He battled pirates and established trading centers in cities like Calicut, India, during a brief era of Chinese naval dominance.

Key takeaway: Zheng He's journeys matched the risks taken by the boldest entrepreneurs — and the pay off set a high bar for six centuries of risk takers to follow.

Jean D. Rockefeller *(b. 1839, d. 1937)*

Rockefeller started his first business selling grain and other goods before he was 20. He turned to oil a few years after it was discovered in western Pennsylvania in 1859. By buying out refineries around Cleveland and New York after the Civil War, Rockefeller soon dominated the market. Vertical integration was key: His company made its own oil barrels and owned storage and shipping facilities.

Although Standard Oil was later broken up under antitrust laws, Rockefeller had created a modern industry. He stepped back from the business in 1896 to devote himself to philanthropy, endowing the University of Chicago and the Rockefeller Foundation.

Key takeaway: Rockefeller used economies of scale and vertical integration to modernise an industry.

Andrew Carnegie *(b. 1835, d. 1919)*

The Scottish immigrant and weaver's son built a steel empire whose mills churned out the railroads, ships, and structures of post-Civil War America — and created a fortune for himself in the process. Carnegie's quick adoption of the Bessemer process and other techniques to efficiently refine steel enabled him to lower costs and undercut his competitors.

After he sold his steel business to J.P. Morgan for $480 million at the start of the 20th century, Carnegie devoted his life and his wealth to endowing institutions that would let other poor sons of weavers better themselves. His "Gospel of Wealth" became a model for future entrepreneurs-turned-philanthropists like Bill Gates.

Key takeaway: Recognising the innovations that will catalyse an industry means the difference between shutting down the competition and getting shut down.

Benjamin Franklin *(b. 1706, d. 1790)*

Franklin was a prime example of America's entrepreneurial spirit. He started as an apprentice in his brother's print shop and went on to publish the Pennsylvania Gazette newspaper and Poor Richard's Almanac, one of the most widely read books in early America, which was filled with Franklin's aphorisms and proverbs.

Even before the colonies broke with England, Franklin helped create the infrastructure that would allow enterprise to thrive in an independent

America: universities (he founded what would become the University of Pennsylvania), libraries, and the postal system. A writer, publisher, inventor, politician an diplomat, he always considered himself a businessman.

Key takeaway: Franklin's idea that people can improve their lives through their own hard work and enterprise, as he did, continues to encourage the American Dream.

Mayer Amschel Ruthschild *(b. 1744, d. 1812)*

Born in Frankfurt's Jewish Ghetto, Rothschild's banking empire would stretch across Europe, essentially becoming the world's first international bank. He sent his five sons to cities across the continent — to London, Paris, Vienna, Naples, and Frankfurt — where they established banks. The network banked merchants and more importantly, governments, financing the British war against Napoleon.

Rothschild made control of information paramount within the business, even to the point of discouraging his children from marrying outside the family. He created communication channels across Europe, including carrier pigeons, to gather and relay information from one branch of the dynasty to another.

Key takeaway: In an era of nation-states that were just beginning to industrialise, Rothschild created the world's first multinational. Because his company crossed borders, it was not beholden to anyone ruler.

K.K. Kellogg *(b. 1860, d. 1951)*

Kellogg changed the notion of breakfast for a century of Americans when he and his older brother, John Harvey Kellogg, stumbled on a way to make dry cereal while preparing food for patients at the world famous Battle Creek (Mich.) Sanitarium. The company he formed in 1906 quickly became successful corn flakes and other ready-to-eat cereals filled bowls on breakfast tables across America.

Kellogg grasped the idea that kids influence buying decisions — galvanizing the brand's success. As early as 1931, the company sponsored children's radio programmes, tried other forms of national advertising and expanded its operations overseas. In 1930, Kellogg used his wealth to endow the Kellogg foundation.

Key takeaway: Kellogg's accidental discovery, promoted with savvy marketing, transformed the way Americans ate breakfast.

Estee Lauder *(b. 1907, d. 2004)*

Young Estee Lauder, born Josephine Esther Mentzer to immigrant parents in the Corona, Queens section of New York City, began experimenting as a child with skin treatments her uncle cooked up. In 1946, she founded the company that bears her name to sell makeup and perfume in high-end department stores around the world.

Lauder's business philosophy centered on selling products she considered to be of the highest quality, and she used her products themselves as advertisements. Lauder pioneered giving free samples at stores like Saks Fifth Avenue to hook customers. Although

Lauder died in 2004, her grandson William still runs the company, with more than 9,000 products and $6.5 billion in sales in 2006.

Key takeaway: Lauder became a giant in the nascent beauty industry by making sure the quality of her products exceeded the expectations of her target market, namely, wealth society women.

Madam C.J. Walker *(b. 1867, d. 1919)*

Born the daughter of former Louisiana slaves and orphaned at age 7, Walker developed a homemade scalp lotion to stop her fair loss. She then turned her remedy into a business — and a movement.

Walker's lie of hair-and-beauty products geared toward blacks tapped into a market ignored by other business because of racism. She also used her clout and fortune to advocate for change, pushing for antilynching laws and contributing to civil rights causes. She set an example for generations of entrepreneurs ion a time when women were still struggling for voting rights and Brown v. Board of Education was a half century away.

Key takeaway: The era's ingrained racism left a huge part of the population underserved by the market. Walker profited by making them her customers.

Thomas Edison *(b. 1847, d. 1931)*

Edison's relentless innovation made him the most prolific inventor of his time. He got his start as a telegraph operator but soon moved on to refining that technology and creating others that would turn the world on its head: a device to turn power into light, a machine to record and playback sound. Edison's labs were always working on new consumer products — a model familiar to today's crop of innovators like Google and Appic.

But only Edison's business sense allowed him to transform his ideas into enterprises that turned a profit. The Wizard of Menlo Park understood the importance of owing his ideas — he registered 1,093 patents — so he could retain profits on his products and discourage competitors.

Key takeaway: Innovation is crucial, but new ideas alone will not make a business successful. Ideas need to be focused into products that customers will value.

INSPIRING AND INNOVATIVE ENTREPRENEURS

Adding Value in Merchandise

Samuel Moore Walton, founder and former chairperson of Wal-Mart, started his career as a supervisor in the US Army Intelligence Corps. In 1945, after leaving the military, Walton purchased a Ben Franklin variety store with a loan of $20,000. With the concept of discount merchandising, Walton drove up the volume of sales in this variety store. This helped him to open a chain of Ben Franklin sores.

He set up the first Wal-Mart store in 1962 and this was a beginning of a great success story. Within five years of opening, Wal-Mart opened 24 stores across the state of Arkasansas in US. And as of July 31, 2007, Wal-Mart had a total of 4,091 retail units in the US alone. The company also operates more than 2500 units internationally.

Dusting-off Old Practices

James Dyson was an innovator who used his inventions to start his entrepreneurial journey. He started his career with the invention of industrial appliances and went on to open a manufacturing unit for developing dual cyclone cleaners. The Sea Truck, Dyson's first product, was launched in 1970 whilst he was at the Royal College of Art. His next product, the Bailbarrow, was a modified version of a wheelbarrow using a ball to replace the wheel. In the late 1970s, Dyson came up with an idea of using cyclonic separation to create a vacuum cleaner that would not dog and lose suction as it picked up dirt. He picked up the idea of cyclones from the spray-finishing room's air filter in his Ballbarrow factory. Finally, Dyson launched the world's first bagless vacuum cleaner, 'G-Force' pick his product in the UK, as it would have edged the cleaner bag market. So Dyson launched it in Japan through catalogue sales where it won the 1991 International Design Fair prize. He finally obtained his first US patent on the idea in 1986.

Stall to Fast-Food Chain

Ray Kroc started as a multi-mixer salesperson, and this business led him to his largest customers, the McDonald brothers. Dubbed as 'Hamburger King', he was the man behind the making of McDonalds. He was the first businessman to introduce the principles of mass production in a service industry.

Kroc had the competency to recognise popular trends in the form of customer preferences. He identified the market for convenient and cheap dining, and balanced this trend with traditional American foods. Kroc was successful in transforming a highly ritualistic, structured and code-oriented restaurant delivery system into a friendly, fast and reasonable dining service. He also took the entire menu range through a very effective product development process in order to revive the 'nine-item menu' earlier offered by the McDonald brothers. Kroc's ability to master the fast food concept helped him to expand. McDonald globally, turning it into a multi-million dollar business.

Driven by Trends

Dhirubhai Ambani, founder of Reliance Industries Ltd. started his entrepreneurial career by selling fried snacks to pilgrims at Mount Girnar. On completing matriculation. Mr. Ambani moved to Aden in Yemen where he worked as a gas station attendant. He simultaneously also worked as a clerk in an oil company. In 1960, he returned to India and started his first textile mill in 1996 with Rs. 50,000, under the brand name Vimal.

In the late seventies, Mr. Ambani created the equity cult, with more than 58,000 retail investors from rural and urban parts of India, who subscribed to Reliance's IPO. In 1992, Reliance became the first Indian company to raise money in global markets, its high credit-taking in international markets reserved only by India's autonomous rating. His vision and efforts pushed Reliance in feature in the Forbes 500 list and led to the company's expansion into other sectors like petrochemicals, telecom, IT, energy, power, retail, infrastructure services, capital markets and logistics.

Vision Build on Values

Azim Hushim Premji, Chairman, Wipro Technologies, is rated as one of the richest persons in India. Mr. Premji's wealth is estimated at US $17.1 billion. His vision to build an organisation based on values led Wipro to great heights. Wipro initially dealt with cooking oils and consumer products but gradually expanded as a provider of IT and BPO services. Mr. Premji's passion for delivering value to consumers gave birth to world class quality processes. This craying for quality made Wipro the first Indian Company to embrace Six Sigma solutions, becoming the first software services Company in the world to achieve SEI CMM Level 5.

Mr. Premji's success is based on strong beliefs, which include fervour for excellence, building collective self-confidence, team building, creating efficient processes and being patient towards change.

Illustrious but Humble

Pallonji Shapoorji Mistry, Chairman, Shapoorji Pullonji group, is considered to be one of the construction tycoons in India. Over the past years, his determination has earned many firsts for his company Shapoorji Pallonji Co. & Ltd. It has been the first Indian construction company to enter the Middle East in the 1970s, to earn the ISO 9001 Certification and construct two 60-storey residential towers in the heart of Mumbai. Mr. Mistry firmly believes in modern management skills, state-of-the-art technology, innovation and customer satisfaction.

Mr. Mistry's passion for quality and commitment has resulted in the diversification of his company. Today, Shapoorji Pallonji Co. & Ltd. is one of the biggest players in the construction of roads and textile & IT parks. The company is credited with many civil and structural engineering tour de forces like industrial units, hotels, hospitals, residential quarters, townships, water treatment plants, roads, power plants and biotech facilities.

An Apple a Day

Sieve Paul Jobs' vision in the world of personal computers led the entire industry to restructure itself. When he was just twenty-one, with the help of a friend, he built a personal computer called the Apple. Apple was an undergog that took on the big player called IBM. Steve revolutionised personal computing with the launch of the Apple Macintosh computer. This technology was a giant step ahead in the marketability of PCs. PC was once believed to be a government and large corporation's equipment. But with a graphical user interface that made it easier to use. Steve brought computers to every household across North America.

In 1982, Apple went public and this made him a very rich man. However, instead of retiring, he strived further in making Apple a great company. While doing so, he also helped make his other company Pixar into an animation powerhouse that made animated movies like Toy Story and a Bug's Life.

He Did it!

Perhaps the biggest inspirational lesson that entrepreneurs can learn from Philip Knight is in brand building. Phil, as he is popularly known, revolutionised the sports goods industry and in the process created one of the best known global brands. ... Nike. As a young man who was passionate about track and field. Phil was smart enough to see the opportunity in creation of sports goods that could enhanced performance. He started with a small company and transformed it into a multi-billion dollar giant.

Of course, the growth has not been an accident. As an entrepreneur, Phil ensured that he delivered great quality to his customers. He regularly brought innovations in his products, expanded the product offerings and backed it all with great management skills. He also made excellent use of advertising and brand building exercises. Today, he continues to inspire his employees and many budding entrepreneurs. Whenever a list of all time great entrepreneurs is created. Phil's name will certainly feature in it as the man who just did it!

Grit Amidst Gross Circumstances

Christopher Paul Gardner, CEO of stockbrokerage firm, Gardner Rich & Co. has achieved 'big' amidst extreme poverty. Gardner started his career as a hospital corpsman in Navy, but later shifted his career and went on to become a stockbroker. The learning Gardner received from stock brokerage training programmes equipped him enough to start a brokerage firm of his own. In 1987, Gardner started Gardner Rich & co. with a paltry amount. In 2006, Gardner sold a small stake in Gardner Rich in a multi-million dollar deal, which led to expansion of Gardner Rich into Christopher Gardner International Holdings.

His brokerage firm specialises in the execution of debt, equity and derivative products transactions for some of the largest institutions, public pension plans and unions in US, Gardner is an enthusiastic and motivational speaker, addressing survival strategies. He is also an avid humanitarian committed to many noble causes. Briefly, Gardner is a remarkable story of struggle with homelessness and also about his personal struggle of establishing himself as a stock broker while managing fatherhood.

❐ ❐ ❐

"A customer is the most important visitor on our premises. He is not dependent on us. We are dependant on him. He is not an outsider on our business. He is part of it. We are not doing him a favour by serving him. He is doing us a favour by giving us an opportunity to do so."

— Mahatma Gandhi

TEN

Drive Towards Customer Satisfaction

Introduction

Customer satisfaction is a dominant factor in the success of an enterprise. In the service industry where intangible products are to be marketed, the importance of customer satisfaction is all the more significant. The customer has, therefore, necessarily and consistently to be the focal point in all decision-making relating to the policies, programmes and practices of an organisation. While there is a growing need to improve customer service, there is no corresponding motivation at all in those who are required to deliver the service. The motivation will spring only when there is recognition of the worth of the individual, recognition of one's duty to the organisation and above all, a sense of pride in the organisation one belongs to.

The task of management in modern organisations is to get the best out of people so that organisational objectives can be achieved. Many organisations are developing new cultures with flatter, responsive team structures, empowered to take action to meet goals and targets. The ability to influence the behaviour of people is leadership and *customer satisfaction* depends largely on *behaviour of employees* during interaction which reflects;

Customer Satisfaction is not the latest management fad. It has been there in the profitability model of companies right from their inception. Almost all enterprises promise customer satisfaction. Their corporate mission settlements are mostly geared TOWARDS THIS OBJECTIVE. One typical statement is:

"XYZ is committed to providing high quality service and products to assist Customers in making better decisions. If customers have any question or concerns about our products, services or representatives, we want to make sure that these concerns are handled fairly and efficiently".

Box - 1

IN INSURANCE SECTOR

"Creating and managing customer relationships is not about having just a call-center without appropriate strategies, or having just a database of consumers to send direct mail, or establishing just a social relationship with consumer or having an eternal price discount procedure. Both the company and the customer should be willing to stay committed to the relationship based on mutual benefits, if this initiative has to succeed. There is a need for a non-transactional orientation on the part of the marketer, and the willingness to invest in infrastructure. Sustainable customer orientation initiative requires that a company looks at both business and technology throughout the organisation and ensure that disparate areas can work together toward a common goal. For building an integrated relationship channeling strategy, companies need to consider issues like projected demand, organisational integration, responsiveness, rising customer expectations, and transparency. In my view those companies that figure out how to fit all the pieces together — and do it with zeal — will be well positioned to deliver greater value to their customers."

Niru Mehta, Managing Director, Avaya Global Connect

Actuaries also consider this aspect carefully while developing insurance products. In fact, the customer is the source of all revenues. Therefore he or she is the most important person in product development process. Yet most companies underachieve in this vital area, usually for non-implementation of the customer feedback.

The key issue is what customers are telling and what is being listened. For example customer says he wants low premium. That does not necessarily mean that premium has to be decreased to sell the policy. He might imply a premium corresponding to the service level or value of the policy to him. Slight improvement in service levels can make the presumably high premiums affordable.

Many insures are blind to what their customers are telling them. They listen but don't comprehend. Some executives get too enamoured with their own products and internal capabilities. They're invested financially and emotionally in their company infrastructure, research and product development. Others get caught up with the teachings of the latest and greatest customer satisfaction gurus. The result? Carriers deliver what they think the customers want or should have, rather than giving them what they ask for.

Some companies may understand what the customer wants, but they can't or won't deliver it because their organisational structure and way of doing business prevent them from doing so. Many carriers remain inflexible in traditional functional areas, such as underwriting, claims, marketing and loss control. After all, the traditional structure served insurers well for decades and built core competencies in critical bottom-line areas.

Underutilised and unmotivated. Despite these warnings, many executives refuse to act. Are they, as Carlyle notes, waiting for their homes to fall around their ears?

Perhaps, a review of the Harvard Business Review classic, "Marketing Myopia" is in order. Author Theodore Levitt lays out the dire circumstances of filling to keep pace with evolving customer needs and changing market conditions. Much has changed since then, but some timeless lessons haven't.

For one, standing pattern may be disastrous, and incremental change may not be enough. Many insurers consider themselves progressive firms that work to implement change strategies. They were the first to implement quality initiatives. They have re-engineered, restructured, laid-off and are now instituting Balanced Scorecard initiatives. While most entrepreneurs improved their operations through these initiatives, it was only marginally. Why? Their functional structures chained them in.

Consider the example of an enterprise who asks for a single solution from XYZ consultant. The consultant greets the request with, " Love to do that, but I am afraid we can't." Then in trudges the underwriter, loss control officer and, eventually, the adjuster. Each has his or her own mission and boss to answer to. Meanwhile, the agent tries to play conductor and politician. Sometimes it works, but more often than not miscommunication, confusion and delays test customer patience. Unfortunately, functional areas routinely become entrenched, and it becomes difficult for senior management to fundamentally change them.

Of course, any executive contemplating such major structural change is going head-to-head with traditional insurance thinking. Insurance companies' organisational structures have deep historical roots. When asked why their organisations are constructed the way they are, executives offer standard responses. "That's the way companies should be run," says one.

When pressed to elaborate, CEOs cite horror stories about how ill-fated collaborations of marketing and underwriting or marketing and claims led to poor risks being put on the book or excessive claim adjustments.

Service to the Society

Service to the society, at the micro level, means service to customers, present and potential. From this point of view, the prime function of banks can be defined as the creation and delivery of customer-needed services in a customer-satisfying manner. To begin with, therefore, a banker's task is to identify his customer and his needs.

Broadly, a customer can be defined as a user or a potential user of bank services. So defined, a customer would obviously include an account holder, or his representative, or a person carrying out casual business transactions with a bank, or a person who, on his own initiative or on banker's initiative, may come within the banking fold. The problem would really arise in locating or identifying a potential customer. This would call for vision, on the one hand, and the right marketing and developmental attitude, on the other: vision for grasping quickly and intelligently (and with futuristic perspective) the 'heart' of policies and priorities, and the right marketing and developmental attitude for creating, in a planned and organically co-ordinated manner, customers, products and delivery systems. Such 'creation and delivery ' naturally presuppose bank marketing as an active, creative and outgoing process.

Customer Needs

Identification of a customer should be followed by identification of his needs — articulated and inarticulated. Often, the inarticulated needs are like the submerged part of an iceberg, invisible but real and, in fact, of greater relevance and import. Here, too, the 'active' role of the banker would add to his functions yet another dimension, *viz.,* generation of healthy and socially desirable needs. An 'active' banker may not rest with just responding to a customer's needs. He may, by creating awareness through customer education, himself encourage generation of new needs or surfacing of silent needs.

The process of fulfilling customer needs so identified or generated would necessitate tailoring bank services to what the customer wants, rather than making him helplessly accept whatever banks can conveniently provide. This approach has particular relevance in serving a multitude of small customers.

Designing services to suit the requirements of customer is one part of the story. The other part is good delivery, because bad delivery of a perfectly designed service is as disastrous as perfect delivery of a badly conceived service. Both are indicative of poor marketing. The five elements of good delivery could be said to be speed, timeliness, accuracy, courtesy and concern.

Having ascertained customer needs and designed appropriate services and delivery systems to meet them, it is necessary to continually assess and reassess how customers perceive bank services. Good service and good delivery (as perceived by a banker) do not automatically or necessarily lead to customer satisfaction. Maybe, the spirit does not percolate to the lowest operating levels. Maybe, and this is important, customer's perception does not agree with the banker's perception. And, in a service industry, customer's perception is what matters. Or, should matter. Meaningful appraisal of customer service has, thus, to be an essential activity for all banks. Admittedly, such an appraisal is not an easy job. More so, because customer service is an extremely dynamic concept. What is good customer service today may become indifferent service tomorrow, and bad service the next day.

Unfortunately, there has been so far no integrated, unified and organised effort for a study of customer service in all its aspects by banks in India. Even individually, we are afraid, not much attention — at least not on a regular basis — has so far been devoted to this by banks. The low priority given to such appraisal and study might have been due to inadequacy of bank services compared to large unsatisfied demand all these years; banks have been operating in a seller's market. Banks had, and continue to have, ready customers and large waiting lists. Public opinion was also, till recently, not very articulate or organised nor was the total environment conducive to self-improvement measures within banks.

Despite the absence of any regular or comprehensive appraisal of bank services, there is a general consensus that the service presently rendered by banks needs, and is capable of, vast improvement. Bank users criticise and bankers themselves concede, that customer service rendered by banks leaves much to be desired, and, in certain respects, has indeed reached very low levels, both absolutely and in comparison with the past. This can be ascribed to many reasons. Maybe, the enormous branch expansion programme undertaken by banks, along with the ever-widening range of their activities and responsibilities, particularly after nationalisation, has weakened the structural fabric of the organisations. Simultaneously, public expectations have been constantly, often justifiably, increasing, and with the growing public awareness, dissatisfaction over the service rendered by banks has assumed growing expression. The near obsolescence of reward and punishment systems, increasing security available to employees, pressures from powerful employee organisations and managerial deficiencies have all had their impact on the quality of service rendered. In a much broader sense, the atmosphere of indifference and casualness prevalent in the society could not but have had repercussions in banks. It is not our intention here to go into the merits or the relative impact of individual causes. It would be enough to say that bank services need considerable improvement on an emergent basis. And, the time has come for banks to look inward to find out what is the nature and quality of the products they sell, what is the product demanded by the customers and how to go about matching the two.

Fortunately, in recent times there has been some improvement in discipline and attitudes amongst bank employees, as a result of the changed climate. The acceptance of the interim report by the Government also seems to have added to the awareness, on an industry-wide basis, for rendering better customer service.

Assessment of customer service of banks should take into account the following four important, interdependent factors which influence customer service:

- demands on, and expectations from, banks;
- quality and job knowledge of bank personnel;
- attitudes and motivation of bank employees; and
- back-up systems and procedures.

Customer Dedicated Structure

But customers should dictate structure. Functional setups still work for some carriers, if the customer wants functional expertise, then that's what should be delivered. On the other hand, if the customer changes are in order. Many leaders would be wise to follow the immortal words of Ronald Reagan to Mikhail Gorbachev: "Tear down that wall!" That is, the one holding up the functional organisation. The next step is to organize around customers using multifunctional teams, companies now know employees are quite capable of making decisions, teaming up to find customer solutions and doing the right thing for the customer solutions and doing the right thing for the organisation. They just need to be given a proper framework and an incentive for their efforts.

The new structure a company develops will be dictated by the unique nature of its customer base, but there will be some common characteristics. The structure is much flatter than the typical functional hierarchy, with wider spans of control. In this new environment, decision-making is pushed down to lower levels. There are fewer managers, and their roles change. They spend more time hiring, developing and assessing talent. More time is available for communicating and removing obstacles.

Organisation has a Heart

Does this naturally happen out of loyalty and a good work ethic? Yes, it does. People want to do quality work and get satisfaction from a job well done. But usually, people respond even better to good, old-fashioned greenbacks. Insurers who insert team based gain-sharing incentives programs and pay their employees a portion of any additional profit they produce generally see outstanding results. Gain sharing programs are usually based on a formula of sales, expenses and underwriting profits and pay out quarterly to provide short-term motivation. Adjustments can be made for long-term liability lines of business.

Team members will naturally drive their efforts and behaviour toward customer satisfaction and bottom-line profitability. An ownership mentality permeates the team. People cross-train each other to minimize service interruptions. They focus on insureds' needs and wants and find faster, better and cheaper ways to fulfill them. Employees start watching expenses. Training and tools tend to be requested when the benefit outweighs the cost. Team members who don't pull their weight aren't tolerated.

The result? Everyone wins. Customers get what they want. Employees are happier, more productive and better compensated. Profitability increases, and the company's prospects look brighter long-term, liberated from functional silos, organisational structure grows and evolves naturally with changing customer needs and market conditions. Innovation flourishes and gets driven up and down the organisation. Personal agendas diminish. True managers thrive in this new environment, and technical and professional employees are respected more for their efforts.

Fundamental change of this nature is obviously a daunting task. The best way to start is by doing an operational review. This is a thorough and objective analysis of the entire company's operations. Some organizations can do it internally, but most need outside help and expertise to get it done. There are several reasons for this. Outsiders have the critical advantage of having seen the structures and inside workings of many insurers and are experienced in making objective evaluations of a company's operations. They then can make unbiased recommendations for structural changes. These proposals are created in consultation with senior management and implemented with the help of employee teams. Since much can go wrong in the transition, follow-up and monitoring services are highly advised so the company can concentrate on its business operations.

Customer Loyalty

Customer loyalty (return) is worth investing in, only if it can adequately compensate for the customer experience (risk) the company is exposed to. The challenge with customer experience is that it has shifted from being defined only by such tangibles as quality and price to being defined by intangibles such as values, culture, attitude. To deflect the impact of negative customer experience or to influence and induce its positives, companies should invest at intangible and subtle levels by defining customer-centric processes and products with embedded values and culture identities.

Companies offer more of the same products at almost the same price through similar distribution channels, which erodes competitive advantage. When properly implemented customer-centrism is likely to bring back the competitive edge, long-lost with differentiation by quality, price and technology.

Innovation for Sustained Growth

In business where one needs to keep running to be in the same place. Innovation holds the key to a sustained profitable growth. And, in a scenario where customer delight turns to hygiene almost automatically over time, companies need to regularly innovate on different ways of enticing customers — be different, be relevant, be more than your competitors. Truly delight your customers, and listen carefully to them to discover how.

Successful innovations involve identifying the unexpressed needs of customers, understanding the firm's values and unique strengths, inventing easily adoptable customer solutions, and delivering new and timely offerings with high quality standards. Innovations have already started playing the lead roles in designing and delivering unique customer experiences, anticipating customer complaints before hand, aligning customers, value propositions and the brand together and helping delve deep into customer insights.

UP with Technology

Technology has become the most revolutionary asset for transforming the relationship between organisations and their customers, and enhancing the overall experience of buyers. Its active use to improve the interface between the two is a must today.

Technology is creating greater transparencies between organisations and their clients. By helping track customers, it is enabling companies to provide them with better and proactive levels of service. Technology is only going to get bigger and better in the entire customer-vendor relationship.

How to Improve Customer Service?

1. Incompetent and demoralised staff cannot render good service. Hence, training becomes important in order to change employees' attitudes and build up their morale and interpersonal skills.
2. Motivating the staff and showing that the organisation cares and respects the employees is equally important.
3. Introduction of computers to support customer service is of great value to the organisation. It improves efficiency, productivity and the quality of services.
4. Delegation of appropriate authority to employees who deal with customers so as to enable them to take on-the-spot decision.
5. The best way to develop a service strategy is to listen to the customers. Conduct regular customer surveys to improve the services. Communicate with the customers constantly through press advertisements.
6. There has to be greater appreciation of the problems between the customer and the organisation.
7. Setting up of customer service cells to handle complaints/grievances, projects a favourable image of the organisation.
8. Keeping an eye on the competitors and how they handle their customers and their problems can help us to shape the strategy.

9. It may be necessary for the customers to organise themselves into forums and associations so that their voice is heard.
10. In large organisations, complaints/grievances are bound to be received from the customers. What matters is the manner in which these customer problems are resolved. The image of the organisation will improve if these complaints are handled with sympathy, consideration and conciliarly attitude. They can highlight, through proper literature, their limitations and how complaints/grievances would be met for speedy redressal.

An organisation should be more responsive and pro-active in fulfilling the rising consumer aspirations and the changing consumer preferences. A mere policy decision, a directive, or a circular, though necessary, cannot help to bring about improved customer service. Employee conduct must demonstrate to customers at all times, at all levels, a feeling of concern and earnestness in their efforts and approach. Every customer visiting the banks (*i.e.,* branches etc.) should leave the premises bearing goodwill for the organisation (bank). Nothing worthwhile can ever be achieved without total commitment and comprehensive involvement.

Conclusion

Customer service is to put youself in the other man's shoes, and being concerned about him. Customer service covers all aspects of the banking interface — from courtesy to efficiency and speed.

Ted Levitt, of Harvard Business School, widely acclaimed as an authority on marketing, observes in *The Marketing Imagination:* "All emerges should be directed towards satisfying the customer, no matter what.... The purpose of business is to get and keep a customer, or, to use Peter Drucker's more demanding construction, to create and keep a customer....

To do that, you have to do those things that will make people want to do business with you. All other truths on this subject are merely derivative."

Besides, putting yourself on the other side of the table, good customer service hinges on three critical factors:

- to treat each customer as if he is the only "king" you have. Successful polygamy depends upon pretending to each spouse that she is the only pebble on your beach.
- to encompass the interpersonal influences (in the case of industrial products) in the organisational buying behaviour. The users, the influencers, the deciders, the buyers and even the gate-keeper (!) must all perceive satisfaction.
- Evolving strategies to improve the quality of customer service. Serving as a catalyst and a visionary to make the dreams, aspirations and expectations of the banking industry come true.

"THE VALUE DECADE
IS UPON US.
IF YOU CAN'T SELL A TOP QUALITY
PRODUCT AT THE WORLD'S
LOWEST PRICE,
YOU ARE GOING TO BE
OUT OF THE GAME......
THE BEST WAY TO HOLD
YOUR CUSTOMERS
IS TO CONSTANTLY FIGURE
HOW TO GIVE THEM
MORE FOR LESS"

Appendix - 1

ARE YOU A NATURAL LEADER?

Do you have the skills employers look for? Or are you better as a team player rather than a leader? Take our quiz to find out.

1. How significant is status to you?

(*a*) *Very important:* I like to feel like I'm in the top echelon.

(*b*) *Quite important:* It's good to be in with the in-crowd.

(*c*) It's more about the quality of relationships than where you fall within those relationships.

(*d*) *Not very important:* I just want to get on.

2. In your childhood, what was your 'Gang Rank'?

(*a*) *The leader:* feared by all.

(*b*) *The funny one:* adored by all.

(*c*) *The thinking one:* listened to by all.

(*d*) *The geeky one:* noticed by none.

3. At the office do you come up with new ideas and suggestions?

(*a*) *All the time:* I really let everyone know what I think.

(*b*) *Quite often:* but not at all if it would mean upsetting someone.

(*c*) *Often:* being careful of any personal and political issues.

(*d*) *Rarely:* what if it was the wrong thing?

4. A colleague has been criticised for shoddy report writing. Do you —

(*a*) Tell them why they should have known better.

(*b*) Take them out for a drink after work.

(*c*) Offer to proof read their next effort.

(*d*) Avoid them. You've got too much to do as it is.

5. You have just faced some negative feedback. How do you respond?

(*a*) Get angry and defensive.

(*b*) Listen carefully but come away feeling disappointed.

(*c*) Consider what you could change and how you could improve.

(*d*) Sigh and think, "yeah that's me".

6. What does EQ mean to you?

(*a*) *Nothing:* it's a wishy washy management fad that hopefully will soon go out of fashion.

(*b*) It's an excuse to be allowed to a laugh on company time.

(*c*) It's a way of empathising with how your colleagues may be feeling.

(*d*) That you should try to understand your boss's moods.

7. **Faced with a problem to solve, what do you do?**
   (*a*) Come up with one solution and pronounce it correct.
   (*b*) Generate a few possible solutions and ask others what they think.
   (*c*) Brainstorm with a couple of nearby colleagues.
   (*d*) Seek your manager's advice.
8. **Your boss has asked you to do something that is beyond your abilities. Do you?**
   (*a*) Take it on with gusto: you're up to anything.
   (*b*) *Give it your best shot:* making a passing joke not to blame you if it all goes horribly wrong.
   (*c*) *Agree to do the task:* but ask for further direction and assistance.
   (*d*) Stress out, clam up and finally confess that you just don't think you could manage it.
9. **Is delegation...**
   (*a*) *A waste of time:* no one else will be able to do it as well as you so you might as well do it yourself.
   (*b*) An easy way to share the work-load.
   (*c*) An effective way to create new learning opportunities for others.
   (*d*) Something I'm always on the receiving end of.
10. **Change to you means...**
   (*a*) Something to be controlled.
   (*b*) An opportunity where anything could happen.
   (*c*) A chance to make progress.
   (*d*) Something to go along with,

Your Score ...

Mostly A'S

You're a born leader waiting for the right job to come along. You're strong, decisive, and authoritarian. At least that's what you'd like to think. In reality, the situation is different. At best your arrogant, bullish, autocratic approach is seen as old fashioned. At worse, it's ridiculed by peers and management alike. It's best to be less punitive to those who do not see the world as you do, and open up to the talents of those around you.

Mostly B'S

You've got good potential. You support people, listen to others, are lateral and take initiative. All this bodes well for your future only if you overcome a fatal career flaw — wanting to be liked. There is nothing wrong with it, but you do this to such an extent that you want to be everyone's best friend. So, when difficult and direct words are needed your end-up being nice instead. Learn to confront potential conflicts with sensitivity and honesty you will earn more respect.

Mostly C's

Management, here you come. If you want to move up the ranks you've got the ability to do so. You're creative, assertive and empathetic. You easily draw groups together and enjoy heading them. Most promising is the importance you give to bringing out abilities of others. You have high expectations of them and you seem prepared to do what you can to help them realise their potential. Of all management skills, this is the one companies seek out most. Be mindful, however, not to let superficially forceful characters conquer your position.

Mostly D'S

You're smart enough to have figured out that your place is in, rather than at the head of, the team. You listen to ideas, not voice them. You're a solid, reliable, loyal team player, but be cautious, that in your acquiescence to others, you don't become sycophantic. At times, do things your way.

Appendix - 2

ARE YOU GOOD MANAGER?

Take the quiz below and find out whether you are a good manager and how can you become one.

1. You should always praise in ________.
2. Listening is the most important management skill: **True/False**
3. Most managers spend too little time planning: **True/False**
4. You should always discipline in ________.
5. Every employee can benefit from additional training: **True/False**
6. All corporate culture flows ________.
7. Morale is directly related to ________.
8. Employee perceptions become ________.
9. One of the biggest weaknesses of most managers is ________.
10. Organisation direction is one of the biggest employee ________.
11. Money and/or benefits is the number one issue with most employees: **True/False**
12. Most employees feel they receive adequate recognition: **True/False**
13. When you hire under pressure you always ________.
14. One of the major responsibilities of a manager is to motivate their employees: **True/False**
15. One of the biggest employee concerns is management ________.
16. Turnover is the direct result of ________.
17. The best employees come in early and stay late: **True/False**
18. Disagreement from an employee is a: **positive/negative** trait.
19. You can't motivate anyone: **True/False**
20. Managers do not contribute to employee performance: **True/False**
21. Most employees don't care about the company's success: **True/False**
22. Always inspect what you ________.
23. You should solicit employee feedback on all issues: **True/False**

24. You get the behaviour you ________.
25. Good managers hire weaker candidates: **True/False**
26. You should only seek opinions that reinforce your's: **True/False**
27. Keeping a poor employee too long ________.
28. The purpose of negative feedback is to ________.
29. You should always hire attitudes rather than ________.
30. You should delegate ________ and ________.
31. Most managers are good interviewers: **True/False**
32. Organisational goals should be communicated to employees: **True/False**
33. A vision statement is ________.
34. A mission statement is ________.
35. Familiarity breeds contempt: **True/False**
36. Employees like to feel in on things because ________.
37. You should always consult employees when you make decisions that impact them: **True/False**
38. You can manage your organisation from behind your desk: **True/False.**
39. Always delegate activities rather than results: **True/False**
40. Rules and policies should be flexible: **True/False**
41. By not clearly communicating expectations to an employee you ________.
42. It is important to really know your people: **True/False**
43. A lack of empowered employees contributes to ________.
44. Having an open door policy always encourages employees to share issues: **True/False**
45. Employees generally want more training: **True/False**
46. Politics in an organisation is inevitable: **True/False**
47. It is impossible to eliminate rumor and hearsay: **True/False**
48. Arrogance and ignorance are two of the biggest reasons why organisations fail: **True/False**
49. As a manager you should always give the credit and take the ________.
50. When you promote your best employee you will always end up with a good manager: **True/False**

Correct Answers: *(Keep in mind that the answers to some questions are subjective)*

(1) Public. (2) True. (3) True. (4) Private. (5) True. (6) Top-down. (7) Corporate culture, communication patterns, stress levels, management style. (8) Reality. (9) Failure to give timely positive and negative feedback. (10) Issues, concerns, frustrations (11) False. (12) False. (13) Hire beneath your standards. (14) False. (15) Direction. (16) See answer 7 - plus poor hiring, poor training, poor compensation plans. (17) False. (18) Can be both. (19) True. (20) False. (21) False. (22) Expect. (23) True. (24) Reward. (25) False. (26) False. (27) Is a sign of management weakness, sends wrong message to other employees. (28) Change or modify behaviour. (29) Skills. (30) Responsibility and authority. (31) False. (32) True. (33) A statement of direction. (34) Who you are, who your customers are, how you serve them, the business you are in. (35) False. (36) It makes them feel important, it builds trust and respect. (37) True. (38) False. (39) False.

(40) True. (41) Improve their performance. (42) True. 43) Employee apathy, poor performance. (44) False. (45) True (46) True (47) True (48) True (49) Blame or responsibility. (50) False.

Scores

50. Correct answers..... You are the best
45-50 correct answers..... You understand the basics of effective management
40-45 correct answers..... There is hope for you yet.
35-40 correct answers..... .With luck, you may make it as a manager.
30-35 correct answers.... ..You have a lot to learn. Better get started.
30 or less correct answers......You need help big-time.

Appendix - 3

EMPOWERING WORK ENVIRONMENT

Empowering work environment requires a set of values and beliefs that must be embraced and practiced by all levels of management. This quiz tests your readiness to accept on empowering work environment by evaluating the degree to which you hold these values.

1. **In evaluating/recommending three candidates for promotion into a middle level managerial position, you believe:**
   A. Past achievements
   B. The person's ability to coach, train, and lead a high-performance team
   C. The candidate's ability to fit in with the current middle management team
2. **You are composing next year's budget. What criteria do you use to determine allocations for training employees?**
   A. Fund business and leadership training for managers.
   B. Fund literacy and basic skills training for hourly and non-exempt employees.
   C. Fund basic business and leadership training for all employees.
3. **Whose feedback should be considered when evaluating manager's performance?**
   A. Collect feedback from everyone — the manager's boss, subordinates and peers and any customers and/or suppliers who do business with the manager.
   B. Only the manager's boss and key leaders with whom the manager interacts
   C. Management performance appraisals should be eliminated.
4. **You have made a very costly error that has resulted in extensive budget reductions for your department. How do you explain the reductions to your group?**
   A. Explain that the budget has been cut
   B. Explain the whole truth up front
   C. Create a reason that the employees would be likely to tolerate to explain why the budget was cut

5. Your organisation invested heavily in a new technology. In implementing the changes you:

A. Get input from the technology experts and your management team
B. Have the plan developed by one of your managers and, if appropriate, have the union representative work with the manager.
C. Bring together a team of individuals who will be directly affected by the technology

6. When evaluating a department's performance, how much importance should be placed on individual performance; how much on the team's effort?

A. Individual accomplishment - 20% and team accomplishments - 80%.
B. 100% on individual accomplishment.
C. 80% on individual accomplishment and 20% on team accomplishments.

7. You have been asked to reduce your department's budget by five per cent. Which of the following items would you cut?

A. Training expenses.
B. Your salary and the salary of others
C. Employee Recognition Awards.

8. You have been asked to identify the obstacles to implementing an employee-empowering environment at your company. Where do you start?

A. With a study to determine the obstacles
B. With the employees
C. With the systems and practices controlled by management

9. Which of the following best depicts how the role of the front line supervisor will develop in an employee-empowering environment?

A. The role of the supervisor will change and expand to include providing direction, developing teams and team members
B. The supervisor will control and decide all the important decisions
C. The role of the supervisor will be greatly reduced.

10. How would you describe the employee empowering work environment?

A. It is something for hourly employees.
B. It is a system based on shared values.

11. How long will take to implement an employee-empowering environment?

A. 2 to 3 years
B. Longer than 3 years and less than 10
C. More than 10 years

12. How do you typically refer to the people you work with?

A. As individuals, associates, and teammates
B. As managers and subordinates
C. As supervisors, labour, and support

13. Which of the following are true about the employee-empowered environment?

A. The biggest barriers are created by rank and file.
B. The biggest barriers are created by management, primarily first-level supervision.
C. The results are quick and quantifiable after the process is implemented.

Answers:

Question 1:	A = 0,	B = 10,	C = 5
Question 2:	A = 5,	B = 0,	C = 10
Question 3:	A = 10,	B = 5,	C = 0
Question 4:	A = 5,	B = 10,	C = 0
Question 5:	A = 0.	B = 5,	C = 10
Question 6:	A = 10,	B = 0,	C = 5
Question 7:	A = 0,	B = 10,	C = 5
Question 8:	A = 5,	B = 0,	C = 10
Question 9:	A = 10,	B = 5.	C = 0
Question 10:	A = 5,	B = 10,	C = 0
Question 11:	A = 0,	B = 5,	C = 10
Question 12:	A = 10,	B = 0,	C = 5
Question 13:	A = 0,	B = 10,	C = 5

Your Score

105-130 points : You are ready to embark upon the journey required to create and maintain an employee empowered environment. Your belief in high performance teams and leadership shines through your recognition of the value of training, development, and employee respect. It is now time to create an environment that encourages all employees to achieve their maximum potential. You don't have to wait for anyone; start by removing the barriers that prevent employees from exercising judgment and creativity in their work.

80-100 points : You're not quite ready; your predominant values are the traditional views on management and management practices. To change, expand your own awareness, skills and information: Learn to be a leader, coach, trainer, and team builder. Develop high-performance teams with high-performance team members. Find small successes within your organisation and build upon them. Create a participative setting. Provide support to those in your organisation who are true beilevers in this type of culture.

Less than 75 points : You may be interested in employee empowerment because it is a fashionable thing to do. If so, rethink your strategy. Any attempt to "fake it" will be met with employee mistrust and disdain.

The Entrepreneurship Ecosystem

Professor Daniel Isenberg of Bebson College has developed a 13-pillar eco-system that nurtures, sustains and create an environment conducive to entrepreneurship. The 13-pillars are:

01 Leadership
02 Government
03 Culture
04 Success Stories
05 Human Capital
06 Financial Capital
07 Entrepreneurship organisations/Non-Government institutions
08 Educational Institutions
09 Infrastructure
10 Economic Clusters
11 Networks
12 Support Services and
13 Early Customers.

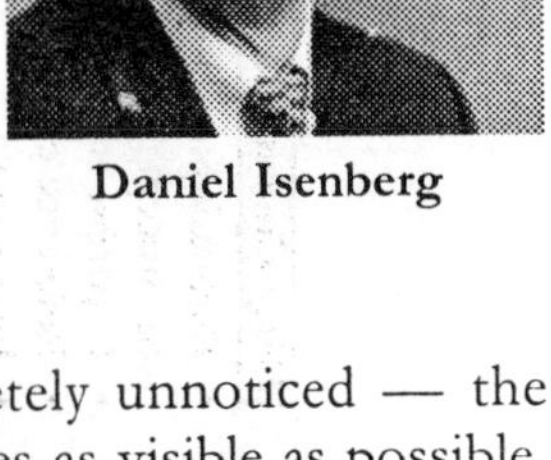

Daniel Isenberg

There are some support systems that traditionally go completely unnoticed — the entrepreneur's own network, the role of media in making success stories as visible as possible, early customers. And that's where the support of the large corporates comes in handy. You'd think naturally that the big companies would be threatened by the small start-ups, but entrepreneurship is very important for them because it is one of the ways in which they get access to innovative services and products: a lot of the innovation comes from the upstarts. The smart ones recognise that the young start ups with high ambition can actually make them more competitive.

THE ENTREPRENEURSHIP ECOSYSTEM

Early Customers
- Early adopters for proof-of-concept
- Expertise in productizing
- Reference customer
- First reviews
- Distribution channels

Leadership
- Unequivocal support
- Social legitimacy
- Open door for advocate
- Entrepreneurship strategy
- Urgency, crisis and challenge

Government
- Institutions. e.g., investment, support
- Financial support. e.g., for R&O, jump start funds
- Regulatory framework incentives. e.g., Tax benefits
- Research institutes
- Ventures-friendly legislation. e.g., Bankruptcy, contract enforcement, property rights, and labour

Support Services
- Legal
- Accounting
- Investment bankers
- Technological experts, advisors
- Board members

Networks
- Entrepreneur's networks
- Diaspora networks
- Multinational corporations

Economic Clusters
- Critical masses of companies
- Country specific reputation
- Doman-specific skills
- Technology

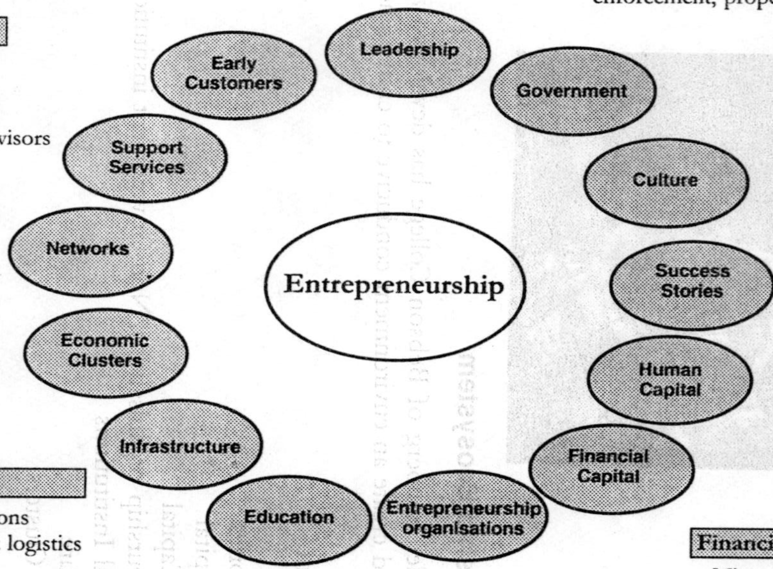

Culture
- Tolerance of risk
- Innovation, creativity, experimentation
- Social status
- Ambition, drive, hunger

Success Stories
- Visible successes
- Wealth generation for founders
- International reputation

Human Capital
- Skilled and unskilled
- Serial entrepreneurs
- Later generation family

Infrastructure
- Telecommunications
- Transportation & logistics
- Energy

Educational Institutions
- General degrees (professional and academic)
- Specific entrepreneurship training

Non-Government Institutions
- Entrepreneurship promotion in non-profits
- Business plan contests
- Conferences
- Entrepreneur-friendly associations

Financial Capital
- Micro-loans
- Angel investors, friends and family
- Zero-stage venture capital
- Venture capital funds
- Private equity
- Public capital markets
- Debt

APPENDICES

Passion Works Wonders

ECONOMICS OF TRUST

What is the cost of trust? After all, trust is an important element in business. Trust is like a pot of money. When we do something for other people, we put money in the pot. When they do things for us, they take money out of the pot. The problem is that when we act in an untrustworthy manner, we are fined a huge amount and we can even become bankrupt. And when trust is lost, it requires an even larger investment over a period of time to restore.

Individually, we have trust capital with the people around us, which determines how much they trust us and how quickly they will act to help us when we ask things of them. Companies and groups also have trust capital within them, which is the aggregate trust levels of the people within the company. There is also an external trust capital, which approximates to the internal levels. This is the brand value of the company, which is the aggregate of the trust placed in the company by all of its external stakeholders, including customers, shareholders and suppliers.

CONUNDRUM

What should you do when faced with uncertainty of two environments? Suppose, however, that we are uncertain about which environment we are in but the uncertainty will resolve over time. In this case, there is a strong argument for delay. Imagine, for example, that there are 100 doors before us. We can enter any door but once we enter, it will be costly to exit. If we don't decide then over time we learn a little bit about what is behind each door. If our uncertainty to begin with is small, we know that behind each door is more or less the same thing, then learning has little value and we should decide now (assuming some modest cost to waiting). But if our uncertainty is large then learning has a lot of value and we should delay our decision until some of our uncertainty has been resolved.

Changing the Rules of the Game: Successful latecomers...

What happens when your company enters a mature market? Obviously, it is tough to find a foothold, Ichijo, an expert on Toyota, offers some clues from the company's European market entry. The answers lie in thinking beyond existing methods, innovation and extreme customer focus. When Toyota entered the European market, it challenged the traditional Toyota way of doing business with the launch of the Aygo minicar. "It decided to enter the hugely competitive minicar segment, even after several competitors withdrew due to lack of sales and profits — existing assumptions of the business model had to be changed."

INDIAN GDP GROWTH

Year %	*Rate of Growth*	*Year* %	*Rate of Growth*
1981-82	6.0	1996-97	7.3
1982-83	3.1	1997-98	4.8
1983-84	7.7	1998-99	6.5
1984-85	4.3	1999-2000	6.1
1985-86	4.5	2000-01	4.4
1987-88	3.8	2001-02	5.8
1988-89	10.5	2002-03	4.0
1989-90	6.7	2003-04	8.5
1990-91	5.6	2004-05	7.5
1991-92	1.3	2005-06	9.0
1992-93	5.1	2006-07	9.2
1993-94	5.9		
1994-95	7.3	*Source:* RBI	
1995-96	7.3		

Numbers Tell the Story

The Indian economy has changed beyond recognition in the past 25 years. The 'Hindu rate of growth' has been left behind, and India's GDP growth rate is now among the highest in the world. India has become far more open to the world, with trade as a percentage of GDP rising sharply. This applies not only to merchandise exports but also to trade in services, including 'invisibles' such as IT services. At the same time, inward remittances from India's vast diaspora have soared, making India the largest recipient of remittances in the world. While imports have risen on account of higher growth, the current account gap has been filled by inflows from FIIs and of FDI, thanks to more foreign investors betting on the India story. That, in turn, has led to the RBI buying dollars hand over fist to keep the value of the rupee down to maintain export competitiveness. Competition has increased, helping to keep a lid on inflation, although the recent rise in prices of commodities, including crude oil, has led to a rise in the wholesale price index. The sizzling growth rate has also led to greater demand pressures and infrastructural constraints. It is important to realise that these are problems of optimism, rather than the problems of disillusionment that we had 26 years ago.

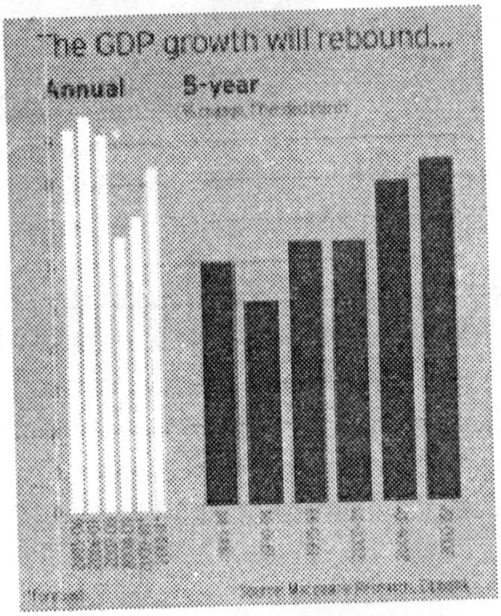

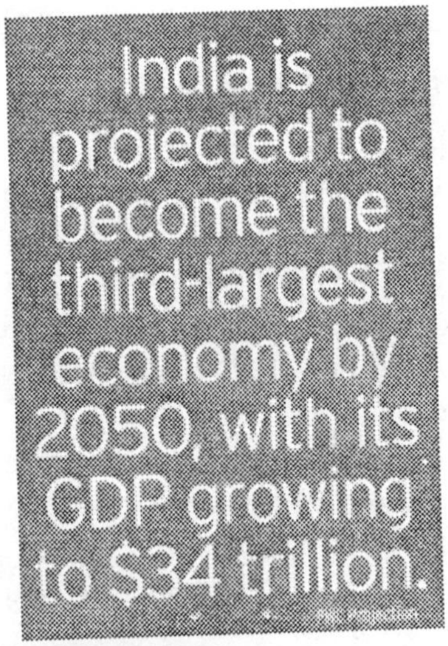

APPENDIX - 001

Kautilya's Game Theory: The Art of Tackling Your Competitor

The famous Hindu text on Polity, the Arthashastra, the kernel of which dates back to (400 B.C.), the state was highly organised and all branches of human activity were hemmed in by many troublesome regulations enforced by a large corps of government officials.

Kautilya 'Chanakya' (400 B.C.)

The Treatise on Material Gain (Arthashastra) of Kautilya reflects, in a striking manner, the social and political forces which were at work in India. Arthashastra may be said to have given quite a new orientation to political theory and practice.

Kautiliya defines Arthashastra as the science which treats of the means of acquiring and maintaining the earth and indeed deals with practical government administration.

Start your Business Now

Starting your own business and running, it is no easy task, especially when you have no previous business experience. But that is how entrepreneurs are born. They start with an 'idea' and a dream to succeed with that idea.

Most of them do not know the path but the confidence that they have takes them through all the ups and downs to reach the final destination where the idea is finally converted into a 'financial success.'

The most critical period in an entrepreneur's life is when he has already experimented with his idea a bit and struggled a lot — but 'money' is yet to fill his pockets.

At this point, he sits down and wonders what went wrong? It's during this period that all near and dear ones would have an opportunity to prove that you were wrong to have taken this path.

Hold on! As Kautiliya says, do not get into a mental trap at this stage:

"Wealth will slip away from the foolish person, who continuously consults the stars; for wealth is the star of wealth; what will the stars do? Capable men will certainly secure wealth at least after a hundred trails" (9.4.26) Starting a new business is no more limited to the rich class.

In today's corporate scenario, there are multiple opportunities for anything that you want to do. Yet, we find people sad and stressed out worrying about the future.

Kautiliya suggests, *"Having found a matter for consideration, he should not allow time to pass."* (1.15.45)

Do not wait for any 'golden' moment to start what you always wanted to do. The best time is not the *mahurat* that the pundit suggests, nor even the dates that come in a calendar. It is right here and now!

After having considered a matter, start work on it immediately. Remember always that the journey of a thousand miles begins with the first step. While starting any project or assignment, a few steps would be helpful.

(1) Self Effort

There is always a problem in starting anything. Maximum energy is required at this point. You need to challenge yourself to get out of your laziness. Do not get caught with the postponement attitude. A work started is a work half done. Just start!

(2) Prepare a Plan

Starting does not mean getting excited. You need to have a direction for how you are going to reach your goal. Take a piece of paper (or open a new file on your computers) and make a note of your points. Give shape to your thoughts. Prepare a blue print of what you want to do. Begin with the end in the mind.

(3) Consult an Expert

As we are not sure of our ideas being practical, take the advice of an expert. Take the help of a person who can guide you in making your dream a reality. It is very important not to go to people who say, "It will not work." Beware of such negative energy in the beginning. You will kill the child even before it is born. Your consultant should himself be a person of positive attitude an should be a success in his own field.

(4) Work out your Plan

All said and done, you have to work out your plan. Do not spend too much time trying to make your plan perfect. Plans are theories that can be successful only if they are given wings of practical application. Once you start, help and the required resources will come. You will learn a lot as you keep putting more and more of your own effort. You can keep improving your plan on the way.

However, it is important to complete what you have started to achieve. It is not important how many new things you have started. What is important is how many of them you have completed. Complete what you have started. And, then, start again after you have completed!

Game theory

Now, let us discuss about one very important stage of conducing business — the 'Game Theory' All management personnel and economists are familiar with this, and use it, very often to analyse situations, and, especially, competition.

Chanakya was a pioneer of the Game Theory in *Arthashastra,* it is called the *Mandala Theory* ('Circle of Kings'). It consists of various multiple permutations and combinations of dealing with the enemy, or the *Shastra.* In a battle, when face-to-face with the *Shatru,* Chalukya says, *"If near him (enemy), he should strike in his weak point."* (7.2.12)

But how does one strategise and make his move against the enemy (competitor) in today's corporate world? Here are some tips:

(1) Study the Competition

Before attacking, one should always know everything there is to know about the person or entity that needs to be countered. Remember, war is 99 per cent preparation and 1 per cent execution. So prepare well before you make moves. Accurate information should be gathered about the competitor, his plans and objectives.

(2) Practise Well

Never ever go rushing into the market (or your own office, for that matter) seeking a direct confrontation with the BIG guys. Gain experience first by practising well in your own region and tasks. The bigger the competitor, the more you need to prepare. In fact, it would pay to seek counsel from an experienced person. His advice can turn things for you.

(3) Know the Rules of the Game

This is the most essential part! The rules of the game are the frame work within which you can conduct your business or day-to-day affairs. It would be highly regarding if you understand them very well. Think about it — it's only after you have become well-acquitted with the rules that you can change them.

Just look at how the Indian hockey team was tackled. They had become invincible at the Olympics for years together. Then the competition studied the rules. They understood that Indians were unbeatable on grass. They changed the rules of the game, and the 'turf' it is played on, literally. Since then, even on modern-day 'Astroturf', it continues to be a struggle for Indians.

All said and done, when the time comes to counter your competitor's moves, do not sit back. Execute. And during execution, do not strategise. The best performers have always defeated their competitors in a single move! It will work for you too.

Conclusion

Kautiliya firmly believed the game. For him, playing the game by rules is the adopted form. He adopted all types of means to excel and achieve the goals. For noble acts mean's does no matter at all.

It may be difficult to answer categorically the question of whether wrong means can be justified for achieving noble ends. Even Lord Krishna couldn't stick to the narrow and straight path. As they say, sometimes, the shortest distance between two points in life may not be a straightline. But how much crookedness is acceptable calls for a sense of perspective; a sense of balance. Leadership has much do with acquiring this balance.

APPENDIX - 002

Milton Friedman on Business & Social Responsibility

When I hear businessmen speak eloquently about the "social responsibilities of business in a free-enterprise system," I am reminded of the wonderful line about the Frenchman who discovered at the age of 70 that he had been speaking prose all his life. The businessmen believe that they are defending free enterprise when they declaim that business is not concerned 'merely' with profit but also with promoting desirable 'social' ends. In fact they are preaching pure and unadulterated socialism. Businessmen who talk this way are unwitting puppets of the intellectual forces that have been undermining the basis of a free society these past decades.

The discussions of the "social responsibilities of business" are notable for their analytical looseness and lack of rigour. What does it mean to say that 'business' has responsibilities? Only people can have responsibilities. A corporation is an artificial person and in this sense may have artificial responsibilities, but 'business' as a whole cannot be said to have responsibilities, even in this vague sense. The first step towards clarity in examining the doctrine of the social responsibility of business is to ask precisely what it implies for whom.

Presumably, the individuals who are to be responsible are businessmen — individual proprietors or corporate executives. Most of the discussion of social responsibility is directed at corporations. Therefore, I shall mostly neglect the individual proprietors and speak of corporate executives.

In a free-enterprise, private-property system, a corporate executive is an employee of the owners of the business. He has direct responsibility to his employers. That responsibility is to conduct the business in accordance with their desires, which generally will be to make as much money as possible while conforming to the basic rules of society. Of course, in some cases his employers may have a different objective. A group of persons might establish a corporation for an eleemosynary purpose — for example, a hospital or a school.

In either case, the key point is that, in his capacity as a corporate executive, the manager is the agent of the individuals and his primary responsibility is to them. Of course, the corporate executive is also a person in his own right. As a person, he may have many other responsibilities that he recognises or assumes voluntarily — to his family, his conscience, his clubs and his country. He may feel impelled by these responsibilities to devote part of his income to causes he regards as worthy. If we wish, we may refer to some of these responsibilities as 'social responsibilities'. But in these respects he is acting as a principal, not an agent; he is spending his own money or time or energy.

What does it mean to say that the corporate executive has a 'social responsibility' in his capacity as businessman? It means that he is to act in some way that is not in the interest of his employers. For example, he is to refrain from increasing the price of the product in order to contribute to the social objective of preventing inflation.

In such a case, the corporate executive would be spending someone else's money for a general social interest. The executive is exercising a distinct 'social responsibility', rather than serving as an agent of the stockholders or the customers or the employees, only if he spends the money in a different way.

But if he does this, he is in effect imposing taxes, on the one hand, and deciding how the tax proceeds shall be spent, on the other. This process raises political questions on two levels: principle and consequences. On the level of political principle, the imposition of taxes and the expenditure of tax proceeds are government functions.

Here the businessman is to be simultaneously legislator, executive and, jurist. He is to decide whom to tax by how much and for what purpose, and how he is to spend the proceeds. The whole justification for permitting the corporate executive to be selected by the stockholders is that the executive is an agent serving the interests of his principal. This justification disappears when the corporate executive imposes taxes and spends the proceeds for 'social' purposes.

He becomes in effect a public employee even though he remains in name an employee of a private enterprise. On grounds of political principle, it is intolerable that such civil servants should be selected as they are now. If they are to be civil servants, then they must be elected through a political process.

On the grounds of consequences, can the corporate executive discharge his alleged 'social responsibilities'? Suppose he could get away with spending the stockholders' or employees' money. How is he to know how to spend it? He is told that he must contribute to fighting inflation. Even if he could answer these questions, how much cost is he justified in imposing on his stockholders, customers and employees for this social purpose?

The situation of the individual proprietor is somewhat different. If he acts to reduce the returns of his enterprise in order to exercise his 'social responsibility', he is spending his own money, which is his right. Of course, in practice, the doctrine of social responsibility is frequently a cloak for actions that are justified on other grounds rather than a reason for those actions.

It would be inconsistent of me to call on corporate executives to refrain from this hypocritical window-dressing because it harms the foundations of a free society. That would be to call on them to exercise a 'social responsibility'! If our institutions, and the attitudes of the public make it in their self-interest to cloak their actions in this way, I cannot summon much indignation to denounce them.

The shortsightedness is exemplified in speeches by businessmen on social responsibility. This may gain them kudos in the short run. But it helps to strengthen the already too prevalent view that the pursuit of profits is wicked and must be controlled by external forces. Once this view is adopted, the external forces that curb the market will not be the social consciences of the pontificating executives; it will be the iron fist of bureaucrats.

The political principle that underlies the market mechanism is unanimity. In an ideal free market resting on private property all co-operation is voluntary. There are no values other than the shared values and responsibilities of individuals. The political principle that underlies the political mechanism is conformity. The individual must serve a more general social interest. Unfortunately, unanimity is not always feasible. There are some respects in which conformity appears unavoidable, so I do not see how one can avoid the use of the political mechanism altogether,

But the doctrine of 'social responsibility' taken seriously would extend the scope of the political mechanism to every human activity. It does not differ in philosophy, from the most explicitly collectivist doctrine. It differs only by professing to believe that collectivist ends can be attained without collectivist means. That is why, in my book *Capitalism and Freedom,* I have called it a "fundamentally subversive doctrine" in a free society, and have said that in such a society, "there is one and only one social responsibility of business — to use its resources and engage in activities designed to increase its profits so long as it stays within the rules of the game, which is to say, engages in open and free competition without deception or fraud."

APPENDIX - 003

Experiences in 'Cooperation'

In 1986, the National Wasteland Development Board, recognising the experience that the National Dairy Development Board (NDDB) had in promoting milk co-operatives, sought its help in setting up village cooperatives to restore the tree cover on degraded lands, termed "wastelands", around villages across the country. It was proposed that Tree Growers Co-operative Societies (TGCS) be set up which would lease parcels of revenue wastelands around the villages, grow trees and bring wastelands into productivity. The members of the cooperative, particularly the poor, would gain in terms of firewood, fodder and small timber,

Amrita Patel

Ideal as this appeared to be, the experience of a few years gave National Tree Growers' Co-operative Federation (NTGCF) a deeper understanding of the local social dynamics and land use realities. It highlighted incompatibility of the structural design of co-operatives with the efforts to both improving the health of degraded lands as well as meeting the basic biomass needs of the rural poor. In fact, the TGCS, with their emphasis on voluntary membership and profit motivation, had the potential to turn what were hitherto common lands into property that became the privilege of an exclusive group mostly comprising the traditionally powerful and articulate sections of the village.

Further, the cooperative had little interest or incentive to allow local use of the land arising from the efforts at regeneration. Once the merchandising mindset took hold, meeting local needs and valuing the ecological services provided by the regenerated lands was taking a backseat.

On another plane, 'wastelands' were rarely lands laid waste, barren or abandoned as unproductive. While these lands appeared unproductive from a timber production forestry perspective, such lands are repositories of local biodiversity, particularly of grasses, shrubs and also trees with their complementary fauna. Degraded they may have been, but these lands have been the source on a diminishing scale of nearly all the firewood, fodder and pasture requirements for the community, especially the poorer households which owned little or no land. And while the state had its rules about ownership of these lands, in many places these were viewed as common lands open to all local residents with fairly well formalised traditional institutions with defined access and user entitlements and responsibilities.

While in many areas revenue wastelands were available in isolated patches limiting scope for expansion, the advent of the watershed development programmes and the joint forest management arrangements threw up opportunities both to work on larger tracts including degraded forest lands as well as with alternative institutional options such as village forest committees. We, therefore, decided to work to restore true forests and grasslands instead of just tree plantations, and meet local needs instead of merchandising tree produce.

In the process we soon recognised the true value of restoring forests — as the indispensable infrastructure necessary to maintain the vitality and viability of agriculture and animal husbandry in the rural economy and as providers of water and habitats of biodiversity and biomass.

By concentrating on 'co-operation' and universal franchise as the founding principles of local self-governance of the natural surroundings, we found ourselves engendering political and economic space for the poor as well as working with many forms of village level institutions and at a scale where ecological services were palpable and appreciated. By working with various categories of land and forms of institutions rather than limiting ourselves to 'revenue wastelands' and 'cooperatives' alone, we could expand the scale of ecological restoration from 5,000 hectares that was possible in the first decade, to an additional 75,000 hectares in the ensuing decade.

In this process of reorientation, we have moved from our earlier narrowly conceived view to the wider vision of recognising the broader dimensions of "co-operating" to achieve a vision of ecological security, not merely in microcosms such as village communities but in much wider national and regional dimensions.

Dr. Amrita Patel is Chairman of NDDB and the Foundation for Ecological Security

National Dairy Plan

The tough target of doubling the country's milk production in the next 10 years can be achieved only if business, and not politics, becomes the driving force of dairy co-operatives. This is what NDDB is trying to infuse in the dairying sector by promoting a new generation of co-operatives called producer companies.

Ever since the Central government passed the Producer Company legislation in 2003 which provides for co-operatives to register under the Companies Act, NDDB has helped set up over 6,900 milk producers' institutions, having 1,20,000 members, in Andhra Pradesh, Gujarat, Haryana, Jammu & Kashmir, Madhya Pradesh, Maharashtra, Rajasthan and Uttar Pradesh. Collectively, they procure on an average about 6,35,500 kg. of milk per day.

"The Producer Company legislation has been crafted to combine the institutional and philosophical strengths of the co-operative with the flexibility, autonomy and discipline of the company law, thus providing a true level playing field to the co-operative form of business enterprise," says Patel. "The co-operative character of the Producer Company is protected by the mandatory provisions of mutual assistance principles of voluntary membership, democratic governance, a cap on dividend, a bar on trading of shares except between members and co-operation among producer companies and other organisations following similar principles," she adds. While the co-operative laws allow non-members to contest election to the board, the Producer Company legislation lets only the members to contest the board election.

Y.K. Alagh, who headed the committee that formulated the Producer Company legislation, says the Producer Company format is a better way organising poor producers, compared to the co-operative format, which is known for its inadequacies. "It offers an opportunity for them to compete and collaborate with other business organisations such as large companies.

As a first step towards bringing in a professional approach to the business of the dairying sector, NDDB has brought in Sangeeta Talwar, the high-profile executive director of Tata Tea, as managing director and chief executive officer of NDDB Dairy Services, a special purpose vehicle formed for the execution of the Rs. 7,300 crore National Dairy Plan (NDP).

With an outlay almost 10 times more than Operation Flood, NDP will be implemented by NDDB as a multistate initiative, in phases with assistance largely from the World Bank. Spread over a span of 26 years, Operation Flood had financial of Rs. 1,750 crore. The first phase of NDP, with an outlay of Rs. 1,600, will be kicked off from April 2011.

Though India's milk production is registering an impressive 4 per cent growth rate, which is double the pace of the world's milk production, the average annual incremental production is 2.5 million tonnes, which has to increase to 5 million tonnes to meet the projected demand of 180 million tonnes by 2020-21. NDP has proposed to increase the country's milk production from the current 108 million tonnes to meet this projected demand, commence once the government of India and the World Bank approve the projects," says Patel.

The efforts needed to achieve the ambitious goals set out under the proposed NOP would require NDDB to offer financial and a range of technical services on a much wider scale and in a far more intensive manner than is being done at present. "To do so, an adequate number of qualified and competent professionals will be required. The nature of skills and competencies required to deliver technical and management services to cooperatives in a market-driven economy is quite different from those required for planning, providing finance, appraisal, information management and policy making the NDDB is presently engaged in," points out Patel.

Sangeeta Talwar: All for private sector participation

It was therefore considered necessary to develop teams of professionals for these two sets of activities through distinct structures. It was under such a backdrop that a separate special purpose vehicle, NDDB Dairy Services was launched.

The NDP has three major components: enhancing milk production through increased productivity of milch cattle by promoting better breed of animals and introducing balancing of feed; strengthening and expanding the infrastructure for procurement, processing, marketing and quality assurance; and human resource development.

To provide a thrust to improve productivity through better genetics, NDDB has entered into collaboration with various public research institutions to implement progeny testing programmes for five breeds. The aim is to produce high genetic merit bulls.

Adding value to feed

With a view to providing a right mix of animal feed, which accounts for about 70 per cent of the cost of milk, NDDB has initiated steps to intensify the dissemination of various technologies that add value to feed and reduce the cost of milk production. This includes ration balancing advisory services at the village level. NDDB has already pilot-tested a comprehensive information system that would lead to a live database to support programmes in animal breeding, nutrition and health.

With a view to get rid of intermediaries in dairy business, NDDB has introduced a centralised computer database with telecommunication facilities with which information on supply of milk by producers can be managed on a real-time basis. The growth of Internet banking and the efforts of banks to roll out business communication to promote inclusive banking have offered new ways of linking producers, making milk payments reach them directly and facilitate producers to transact their business with efficiency and ease. Smart cards, which are photo cards with biometric identification and storage of data, have been successfully pilot-tested in about 150 villages covering close to 4,000 milk producers in Karnataka.

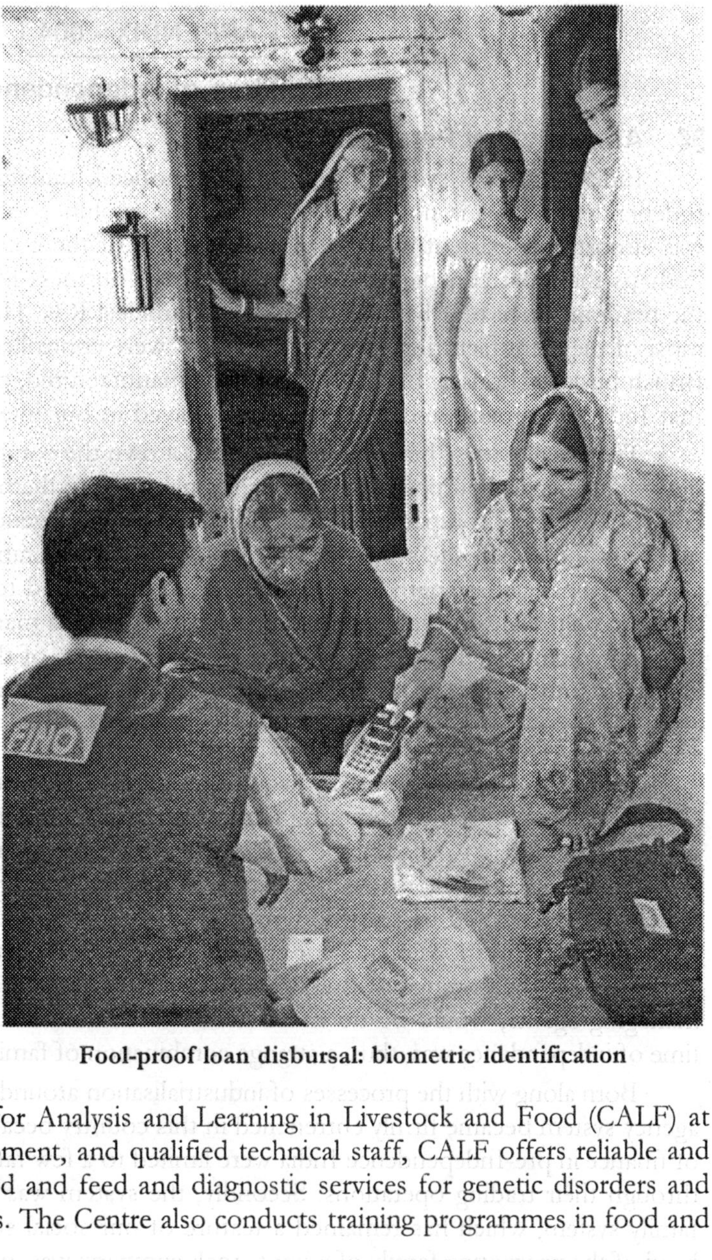

Fool-proof loan disbursal: biometric identification

Recognising the importance and need for reliable and efficient laboratory services for the livestock, dairy and food sectors, NDDB has established a Centre for Analysis and Learning in Livestock and Food (CALF) at Anand. With state-of-the-art equipment, and qualified technical staff, CALF offers reliable and accurate analytical services for food and feed and diagnostic services for genetic disorders and animal health at reasonable charges. The Centre also conducts training programmes in food and feed analysis.

NDDB is also in the process of setting up a dedicated national-level human resources development facility to train thousands of village-based community resource persons and professionals willing to work for and engage with rural producers and their institutions.

APPENDIX - 004

Children of Independence

An Analytical Perspective

India's business system has, almost unnoticed, undergone a virtual transformation since Independence. This is not so much due to the evolution of the country's public sector, which was almost non-existent in 1947, as it is because of the convulsions in the private sector itself. Perhaps the most conspicuous feature of India's business life on the eve of Independence was the predominance of a handful of business families. R.K. Hazari, the economist, estimated that most of the manufacturing companies in 1947 were controlled by just 18 Indian families and two British business houses. Between them, they manufactured, practically, all the industrial products that India then made, and they were all involved in our international trade too.

Technically, these business houses did not own the companies that constituted their empires, but, for all practical purposes, the companies belonged to them. These families were able to exercise control over their companies because of the managing agency system. While the family was the pivot around which the system revolved, the modus operandi was simple. When a family with adequate financial strength and business standing decided to enter a business, it would do two things simultaneously. One, it would declare itself to be a managing agency; usually, a partnership of family members. Two, it would allot to the members of the family, and their relatives, a large enough number of shares such that they could control the nascent concern.

The Family and the Agency System

Although the new company would be an independent corporate entity under the Indian Companies Act, with the promoting family having a controlling stake in it, it was a mere formality for its shareholders to entrust the task — through a formal resolution at their very first meeting — of managing it to the managing agency. Moreover, the terms and conditions under which this would be done would be so wide-ranging that, in effect, it would mean the complete surrender of the rights and responsibilities for critical decisions and strategic actions to the managing agents. Even though the company would have a board of directors, its members, hand-picked by the managing agents, would be no more than a decorative facade. Corporate management at the time of independence was, thus, a strange combination of family control and joint stock companies.

Born along with the processes of industrialisation around the mid-19th Century, the managing agency system became firmly entrenched in this country because of two factors. First, the sources of finance in pre-Independence India were limited to a few families which had accumulated capital through their trading operations. Secondly, the system was eminently consistent with the joint family system, which has remained a feature of our social structure over the decades. Since the head of the promoting family of a joint stock company was, usually, also the head of the managing agency, the system entailed little, or no threat to his authority.

In that sense, the structure of business management was coterminous with the structure of family management in this country. That India did not have an investor class, and stock market operations were yet to gather sufficient momentum only provided reinforcement to the managing agency system of family control. However, the system was open to abuse, and most of the managing agents did misuse their privileges, providing fodder for sharp, and persistent, attacks on this form of management for more than half a century before Independence. But it survived because of the social and economic realities of the Indian situation. Of course, the glamour became increasingly virulent as India's destiny passed into her own hands.

The Family and the Financial Institution

Yet, the (New) Government of India chose to impose only cosmetic restrictions on managing agents and, by implication, on family control over the nation's business when the Indian Companies Act was amended in 1956. For, the government was acutely aware that the ground realities that continued to provide nourishment to family business would take time to change. Instead of submitting to the liberal rhetoric that sought the immediate abolition of the managing agency system, it therefore left the arrangement, more or less, undisturbed for, eventually, 15 more years. If the government had hoped that, during the interregnum, the situation would change to the extent that it would render painless the demise of the system, its thesis was borne out by events. Eventually, the managing agency system did die unwept, unsung, and unnoticed on April 1, 1970, yielding to a new system and provided for a functional chairman managing director and a board of directors as the decision-makers in a company.

Initially, it appeared that the change was merely one of form as the erstwhile managing agents quickly embraced new designations.

INDIA'S TOP 25 BUSINESS FAMILIES

Group-2001 *Top 25 Groups — 2001*	*2001* *Sales*	*2001* *Net Profit*
Reliance Group (Ambani)	59,592.35	4,222.78
Tata Group	30,200.08	1,091.57
Aditya Birla Group	16,905.91	1,306.35
B.K. Birla Group	5,389.87	123.55
Thapar Group	5,231.29	–506.87
Bajaj Group	5,273.74	223.68
Mahindra & Mahindra Group	4,966.03	204.92
Om Prakash Prakash Jindal Group	4,489.61	162.72
Hinduja (Ashok Leyland) Group	4,107.16	195.84
Hero (Mumjals) Group	3898.72	254.33
C.K. Birla Group	3,412.66	–24.44
Essar (Ruia) Group	3,406.53	–261.63
ISPAT (Mittals) Group	3,382.36	–521.25
RPG Enterprises Group	3,336.98	–135.26
Chidambaram M.A. Group	3,295.02	106.09
Videocon Group	3,244.05	134.52
TVS Iyengar Group	3,213.5	132.68
Wipro Group	3,135.54	657.42
Godrej Group	3,125.4	34.66
Lalbhai Group	2939.34	–295.76
Murugappa Chettiar Group	2799.92	94.44
Rucin Group	2,727.92	20.25
Wadia (Bombay Dyeing) Group	2,654.69	43.18
Nirma Group	2,429.22	249.71
Hari Shankar Singhania Group	2,266.86	–19.03

Source: CMIE. Figures in Rs. crore.

Gradually, however, it became clear that the end of the system would have a profound impact on not only the structure of the corporate sector, but also its composition. Infact, the smoothness of the transition to the new system was not due to legal reasons alone; it was also a reflection of a new set of social and economic forces that the business family would have to contend with; Perhaps the most important change was the nation's resolve to accelerate the pace of economic development as reflected by the Five Year Plans. In most cases, the nature of the projects that the private sector was expected to implement to accomplish the Plans' objective was such that no business family could finance them on its own. With the passage of time, the family as a source of Industrial finance ceased to be as indispensable as it had been before Independence. In the meantime, new sources of industrial finance emerged, most of which were under government control, on which the business families had no choice but to depend. And, in most cases, their dependence was so great that, in effect, the financial institutions — and not the business families themselves — ended up acquiring a controlling interest in companies.

Family Controlled Business — Birla Group

C.K. Birla Group

Hindustan Motors
Orient Paper & Industries
Hyderabad Industries
National Engineering Industries

B.K. Birla Group

Century Textiles & Industries
Century Enka
Manjushree Plantations
ECE
Kesoram Industries
Akzo Nobel Chemicals

M.P. Birla Group

Vindhya Telelinks
Birla Ericsson Optical
Universal Cables
Birla Corporation
Indian Smelting & Refining

K.K. Birla Group

Zuari Industries
Chambal Fertilisers & Chemicals
Taxmaco
The Hindustan Times
Upper Ganges Sugar & Industries
Oudh Sugar Mills
New India Sugar Mills
Gobind Sugar Mills
Sutlej Industries
Indian Steamship Company

Aditya Birla Group

Grasim Industries
Indian Rayon
Hindalco
Indo Gulf
Birla Global Finance
HGI Ind. & Essel Mining
Tanfac Industries
Indal
PSI Data Systems
Bihar Caustic
Idea Cellular
Birla Sunlife Group

S.K. Birla Group

Birla VXL
Mysore Cements
Saurashtra Chemicals
XPRO India
Cimmco Birla

Yash Birla Group

Zenith
Birla Yamaha
Dagger Forest Tools
Birla Perucchini
Birla Kennamental
Birla Transasia Carpets
Birla 3M

As family-owned businesses increase in size, their requirements increase too. Business groups, like the Tatas, the R.P. Goenka Group, and the Mahindra Group, for instance, have exhibited five year average sales growth-rates of 19 per cent, 17 per cent, and 21 per cent, respectively. They will, therefore, require a larger number of professional managers, a more robust organisational structure, better-defined policies and practices, more capital, and heightened visibility. In short, they will have to rethink the way they conduct their business.

Family has played a crucial role in the industrialisation of the country. Although, professionals are playing an effective role in running the industries, it is the family gives its trust, confidence and vision to development.

INDIAN DYNASTIES

Some Major Indian Business Families and their Founders

Birlas Sheonarayan Birla	1862
Tatas Jamshetji Nusserwanji Tata	1868
Wadias Nowrosjee Wadia	1879
Burman S.K. Burman	1884
Godrej Ardeshir Burjori Godrej	1897
Murugappas A.M. Murugappa Chettiar	1900
Kirloskars Laxmanrao Kirloskar	1910
TVS T.V. Sundaram Iyengar	1911
Lalbhai Kasturbhai Lalbhai	1931
Modis Rai Bahadur Gujar Mal Modi	1932
Thapar Karam Chand Thapar	1943
Escorts Har Parshad Nanda and Yudhisthir	1944
Bajaj Jamnalal Bajaj	1945
Mahindras Jagdish and Kailash Mahindra	1945
MRF K.M. Mammen Mappillai	1946
Ambanis Dhirubhai Ambani	1969

Note: Many of these groups had trading and other operations dating back to even earlier. (The Wadias have been in ship building for more than 250 years.)

Source: Business India Compilation.

01 The Tata Engineering and Locomotive Company
02 Bajaj Auto
03 MRF
04 Larsen & Toubro
05 Amul
06 Atul
07 Mahindra & Mahindra
08 The Great Eastern Shipping Company

THE TATA ENGINEERING AND LOCOMOTIVE COMPANY WAS ESTABLISHED IN 1945

Horn OK Please TATA: The legend is painted on the back of almost every truck made by the erstwhile Tata Engineering and Locomotive Company (Telco), now rechristened Tata Motors Ltd. (TML). The Tatas began manufacturing trucks towards the end of World War II. Operations were started in an old workshop of the East Indian Railway at Jamshedpur. In 1945, Tata Sons bought the Singhbhum work-shop for Rs. 25 lakh to make steam locomotive boilers and, later, complete locomotives. By 1957 the company had reached its target of producing 100 locos annually. Daimler-Benz AG wanted a partner to start a plant to manufacture commercial vehicles. The Tatas, like Barkiss, were willing. On 15 October 1954, the first vehicle was assembled from a completely knocked down pack of Daimler-Benz aggregates. Twenty-five years later, seven out of every 10 trucks on India's roads bore the jaunty TATA message. Over 500 ancillary suppliers of all kinds of components also came up. In the 1960s, Telco decided to build a second facility in Pune...

Adapted from The History of Indian Business by P.N. Agarwala

The Daimler-Benz collaboration for trucks ended in 1969, but Telco entered into a joint venture with the German company in 1994, for the manufacture of the Mercedes-Benz cars in Pune — a facility that has since become a DaimlerChrysler subsidiary. TML's turnover was Rs. 5,338.87 crore in 2004-05.

Ratan Tata has expanded the group to foray into telecom, bought over VSNL, took Tata Consultancy Services public and made the first Indian car — Indica. Its greatest accomplishment came in 2008, with Tata Nano, a Rs. 1 lakh car, which will change the face of the automotive industry in the world. Also, with a relaxation in government norms, the group has been able to expand overseas and buy foreign assets: Tata Tea acquired Tetley, Tata Steel acquired the Anglo-Dutch giant Corus and Tata Motors got Jaguar and Land Rover; maintaining the strong ethical and social values it inherited from its rich legacy.

THE BAJAJ SCOOTER WAS UBIQUITOUS

Unbeatable, Bajaj may well claim to be. But the two- and three-wheeler manufacturer, which has its roots in the trading firm Bachraj and Company, set up by Congress party treasurer Jamnalal Bajaj in the throes of the Independence movement, has had its share of ups and downs. The fights began with the Firodias' Bajaj Tempo, where Rahul Bajaj began his career in 1964 after his MBA at Harvard. The grass strip separating the Bajaj Auto and Tempo plants in Pune has become a wall, which is a constant reminder of the rift between the two families. By September 1968, the 20-year-old partnership was kaput. The two fought a bitter battle for Bajaj Auto in the boardrooms, the stockmarket and the courts, going all the way up to the Supreme Court. Bajaj had an equally tempestuous relationship with Piaggio of Italy, with which it had its first tie-up to make scooters. A decade after the collaboration ended in 1971, Piaggio went to court in California, accusing Bajaj of pilfering its designs. The case ended with an out-of-court settlement. Piaggio has since come back to India.

The fight with the Firodias resurfaced in 2005, when the latter decided to rename their company Force Motors — a move Bajaj

bitterly opposed on the basis of his shareholding, taking the matter up to the Supreme Court again, before losing his argument. Bajaj Auto had sales of Rs. 6,335.2 crore in 2004-05.

After five decades of ruling the roads with its scooters, Bajaj is now concentrating on motorcycles, in what managing director Rajiv Bajaj describes as a decision that's ratioinal rather than emotional. And going beyond two- and three-wheelers, the company has also tied up with French auto major Renault to make a small car in India.

MRF WAS STARTED IN 1946 IN TIRUVOTTIYUR, MADRAS BY MAMMEN MAPILLAI

With an initial investment of Rs. 10,000, Mammen started the Madras Rubber Factory to produce toy balloons. The venture was a success and the market was soon flooded with cheap Japanese balloons. But it was the potential to expand into the manufacture of tyres, that caught Mammen's eye.

The Indian tyre industry was then dominated by foreign companies like Dunlop, Firestone and Goodyear. This forced the government to step in and encourage Indian companies in the rubber industry to develop a relatively capital- and technology-intensive industry, seeing that it would be crucial for the country's defence.

Mammen mastered the technology of manufacturing tread rubber, the raw material required for re-treading. But competition was cause for concern. "This was our first battleground," he says. "And the lessons we learnt here shaped our later policies, particularly with regard to maintenance of quality and the priceline."

A series of breakthroughs followed: a rubber research centre', manufacturing Nylon passenger tyres commercially, and the development of sturdy tyres for heavy-duty trucks. In the 1950s, MRF became the market leader in India with a 50 per cent share of the tread-rubber market. MRF's presence had in fact, become so overwhelming that it became the major reason for the withdrawal of some large multinationals from the tread rubber business. Today, MRF'S turnover has crossed Rs. 3,000 crore.

LARSEN AND TOUBRO, FOUNDED AS A PARTNERSHIP FIRM, BECAME A LIMITED COMPANY IN 1946

Henning Holck-Larsen and Soren Kristian Toubro were second-class citizens in the India before independence... What promoted these two Danes to give up the security of their jobs and start a business in a country that was battling for its freedom and whose industrial prospect appeared far from promising?

The appeal of India was on several levels for these entrepreneurs. Here was a vast, virgin country, bafflingly innocent of the simplest mechanical wit and ingenuity, wholly open ended, profound, speculative and intensely responsive to technique and humane good sense. The partners knew that they had first to attract and organise the skills needed to satisfy the emerging needs and requirement of India's developmental plans.

They found safety pins were imported. Knives and forks and spoons were Sheffield. Bathtubs and toilet fixtures were Shanks. Sewing thread was DMC... Cigarettes were Navy Cut. There was Lever Brothers behind every soap, bath or washing...

The partners looked around this scene and found there was lots of place for them... So they set up business in India, but rarely ever travelled in the exclusive first-class apartments of the Indian Railways. Equally important they did not lose contracts by making a poor impression. Once on a windswept railway station, the partners got their tickets upgraded for the final lap of the journey. Early the next morning, looking fresh and first-class, they descended from the train to find to their disappointment that the board member himself had not come, but had sent some of his assistants to meet them.

Adapted from Standing Tall, The Story of Larsen and Toubro Limited.

L&T today manufactures equipment for a variety of industries including cement, sugar, paper and steel mills, with a turnover of almost Rs. 13,200 crore this year.

The company was clearly drifting away from its main business, *viz.,* engineering and construction. And not all these activities were entered into by choice. Many were due to compulsion and lack of alternatives available in the Licence Raj. Not surprisingly, the company that helped build India was looked at as directionally dysfunctional by the investment community.

Under the leadership of A.M. Naik, who was appointed as MD in 1999 and CMD in 2003, L&T has regained its focus and become one of India's most valuable companies. Its current market cap is Rs. 94,000 crore.

ON 14 DECEMBER 1946, THE KAIRA DISTRICT CO-OPERATIVE MILK PRODUCERS' UNION WAS REGISTERED

In January 1946, a meeting of milk producers was convened by local Congress leaders at the village of Samarkha in Anand. Poison's Dairy had pushed the milk producers and traders of Kaira too far this time. Polson (originally Pestonji Eduiji Dalal, who gave himself the western sounding name Poison) had obtained from the Bombay government an executive order that gave him, in effect, monopoly over milk procurement rights in the area...

An appeal to Sardar Patel drew from him a reiteration of his opinion that the milk producers should unite in a cooperative society. As his representative, Sardar Patel sent Morarji Desai, the Congress leader beginning to be known as the Sardar's lieutenant.

At a historic meeting under a shady tree in the village of Samarkha on 4 January 1946, Sardar Patel's message was read out. He had a simple proposal: the producers should sell their milk to a cooperative that would own and run a milk processing plant. It was also decided that farmers would refuse to sell milk to any contractor in Kaira...

The milk strike achieved its purpose: after 15 milkless days the (Bombay) government gave in. By October, two cooperative unions were formed. They had fewer than 100 members apiece and they collected scarcely 250 kg of milk.

Amul's Sheer Spread, Size and Depth...

Members: 13 district co-operative milk producers' unions

Producer Members: 2.79 million
Village Societies: 13,328
Total Milk Handling Capacity: 11.22 million litres per day
Total Milk Collection: 3.05 billion litres ('08-09)
Daily Average Milk Collection: 8.4 million litres ('08-09)

1970 Operation Flood Phase I launched.

1977 *Manthan*, a movie made by Shyam Benegal and produced by GCMMF about the cooperative movement in Anand, wins the national award. It is, perhaps, the only "corporate film" to win such a prestigious prize.

1996 Amul revenues top Rs 1,500 crore.

1997 Amul launches ice creams in Mumbai after entering the segment in 1996. Claims #1 spot by 2003.

2002 Amul launches retail parlours to reach out to consumers and avoid "getting squeezed" by retailers. Today, over 5,000 parlours generate Rs 200 crore worth of revenues.

2003 Amul launches pouched milk in Delhi, a stronghold of Mother Dairy, founded by NDDB.

2007 Amul becomes the country's first and only billion-dollar cooperative. Also, the first cooperative to introduce sugar-free, probiotic ice creams.

2008 HUL's market share is below 10% as compared to almost 30% in 1997 in the ice cream segment.

2010 Amul claims #1 spot in the Delhi pouched milk market.

Amul Growing Up with Competition

Dec. 1946 Tribhuvandas Patel, Founder, GCMMF, organises dairy farmers to register in the Kaira District Cooperative Milk Producers Union in revolt against the monopolistic practices of Polson, a Mumbai-based dairy sanctioned by the British to collect milk from Gujarat.

1950

Dr Verghese Kurien joins KDCMPUL as GM.

1952 Under Kurien's leadership, KDCMPUL's milk capacity reaches 20,000 litres per day, up from 200 litres in 1948.

1955 Butter launched, the first brand of Amul. Kurien starts with an advertising budget of Rs 2 lakh to take on competition from MNCs.

1956 Amul starts making condensed milk after Nestle's brass snubs Kurien, contending that condensed milk manufacturing was something it "could not leave to the natives to make".

1962 Amul launches cheese to take on foreign imports in urban markets.

1965 NDDB registered as a society under Kurien's leadership.

1967

The Amul "Butter Girl" is born in response to the Polson butter girl.

ATUL PRODUCTS (NOW ATUL LTD) WAS REGISTERED ON 5TH SEPTEMBER 1947

With the coming of Independence, Kasturbhai Lalbhai, like many Indian businessmen, began to dream of glory. Having conquered the textile industry, he went in search of new businesses. He got the idea of making synthetic dyes and colours, which the textile industry needed in vast quantities. Until then dyes had been imported.

Kasturbhai flew to New York, where he signed an agreement with American Cyanamid to design and provide technical expertise for a new chemical plant. He registered the company on 5 September 1947. It was the beginning of a brand new industry in India. He called it Atul, meaning the "incomparable".

Soon a spanking new town came up around Kasturbhai's plant in the wilds of Gujarat. Kasturbhai employed local illiterate villagers. In March 1952, he invited Jawaharlal Nehru to open it. But Nehru refused. He had recently committed the nation to the socialist goal of central planning, and he was certainly not going to inaugurate a capitalist factory.

A few weeks later, however, Nehru relented, justifying to himself that his "third way", or the Congress planning model, did not totally reject private enterprise — as long as it was under social controls. Besides, Kasturbhai had been persistent and had infected him with his enthusiasm. (That his own sister, Krishna, was married to Kasturbhai's son, Gunottam Hutheesing, might have had something to do with it.)

In 2004-05, Atul had a turnover of Rs. 699.4 crore with profits of Rs. 18 crore.

M&M BECAME MAHINDRA & MAHINDRA LIMITED IN 1948

During his stay in the United States, Kailash Chandra Mahindra met Barney Roos, the inventor of the jeep who suggested that it was the ideal vehicle for India and be would be happy to be associated with the Mahindras in their quest for rapid economic development.

The two brothers, Jagdish Chandra and K.C. Mahindra, Keshub Mahindra's father, together with Ghulam Mohammed, incorporated Mahindra & Mohammed in October 1945. Keshub graduated from Wharton, did his apprenticeship in an engineering company in Pittsburgh, and on his return joined the group in 1947.

The name of the company changed to Mahindra and Mahindra in 1948 when Ghulam Mohammed left on being invited to be Pakistan's first finance minister. (According to M&M vice-chairman and MD Anand Mahindra, the company could not afford to scrap all its stationery, which already said M&M. Thus came the name became Mahindra & Mahindra.) The beginnings were humble, and business in early days consisted of assembling jeeps from completely knocked down parts imported from the US.

The Mahindra group is a $2.59-billion company, and is the largest utility vehicle manufacturer in the country.

THE GREAT EASTERN SHIPPING COMPANY WAS INCORPORATED ON 3RD AUGUST 1948

It has been an eventful 60 years for Great Eastern, India's largest private sector shipping company.

Prodded by an entrepreneurial urge, Maneklal and his second brother, Chunilal had embarked from their hometown of Wadhwan, in Saurashtra, for Africa in the beginning of the last century to try their hand at various businesses. Their efforts had ranged from selling oranges to trading in textiles, but not much had worked out. The crestfallen duo decided to return to India and, as their ship approached Bombay, their youngest brother Jagjiwan was waiting to greet them. The three of them looked at various options and tried their hand at various business ventures.

Jagjiwan started trading in textiles, and was so successful that he started a textile mill and invited his brothers to join him. After some years, Chunilal, who was spiritually inclined, withdrew from business, but his two brothers forged on. They diversified into sugar and, in the early 1920s, started importing the commodity from Java and, a few years later, from Russia as well. Simultaneously, they entered other trades.

A meeting of providence

They were doing well till the Great Depression that began in 1929. The brothers sustained heavy losses in the stock market and the textile mill had to be closed. As they looked frantically for the right business opportunity, they met Hanuman Patel, who happened to be the chief accountant to the Bhiwandiwallas, a Parsi family of considerable wealth and diverse business interests. Ardeshir Hormusji Bhiiwandiwalla, the scion of the family, was looking for a trusted man to help him run the business and Patel offered to introduce the Sheths to him.

The Sheths were evidently so convincing that Bhiwandiwalla promptly offered them a job with a generous salary. But, despite the dire straits they were in, the two brothers politely declined and stressed it was business that they were interested in getting into. In hindsight, they felt these were brave words for someone who had just experienced failure.

The incisive man that Bhiwandiwalla was, he saw promise in Maneklal and Jagjiwan and was willing to back his instincts and give them a chance. He made the Sheths an offer. He would finance a company with the two brothers as partners. For every 16 annas — equivalent to a rupee in those days — the business earned, the Sheths would get one anna for their efforts, while the Bhiwandiwallas would get the balance 15 annas for the capital they had put in. At a time when intellectual capital didn't command the same respect as ready cash, the deal was deemed fair by all concerned.

As to the nature of business, they concurred it would be sugar, as the brothers brought with them valuable experience in that industry. A.H. Bhiwandiwalla & Co, chaired by Ardeshir Hormusji, opened its doors in April 1932. Hard work paid off and in a few years the firm was controlling around 30 per cent of India's sugar trade. They were dubbed the sugar kings of India. World War II brought a period of acute sugar shortages and to fulfil the worldwide demand, the firm chartered ships to import sugar from Indonesia, even setting up an office in Java. Indeed, the Sheths were instrumental in the opening up of two new ports in India — at Porbunder and Okha — to handle sugar imports.

Meanwhile, the next generation of Sheths was growing up. Jagjiwan's eldest son, Jayantilal, looked after the sugar factories, while his second son, Kantilal, a surgeon, took keen interest in the business as well. Maneklal's older son, Sevantilal, managed the family's trading activities. Now that the new generation was ready to play its role, Jagjiwan and Maneklal were ready for new challenges.

From sugar to shipping

Opportunity presented itself in 1948. World War II had ended and the US Maritime Commission decided to auction off some of the Liberty ships that had been used for carrying war material. Daunted by this leap from sugar to shipping, the brothers went to a dose family friend and advisor, H.T. Parekh, the legendary founder of HDFC. He endorsed their decision, but counselled against linking sugar trading with shipping.

Thus, on his advice, Bhiwandiiwalla helped the Sheths form a new company — The Great Eastern Shipping Company Limited — in August 1948. The impeccable business record of the promoters made it easy for them to secure finance from the First National City Bank of New York, in Bombay. Bhiwandiwalla became chairman of the company and, in recognition of his contribution, Great Eastern's logo is a standard that bears the initials AHB. Jagjiwan's youngest son, Vasant, was appointed managing director and he steered the company to greater heights until his untimely death in 1992.

Maneklal and Jagjiwan, the brothers who started it all, and Bhiwandiwalla, who gave shape to their soaring ambitions

Vasant (Sheth) did not easily get unnerved and, with his dynamism, he established more useful contacts. Great Eastern grew and bought more second-hand ships, in the first instance. It was decided that the company should operate in the world market, not only on the Indian coast or on a liner basis. The times were propitious and with Vasant's dynamism and the support of the elders of the family, the company grew in stature.

Vasant soon visited foreign countries, especially Japan. The shares of Great Eastern became the popular counter of the stock exchange and the climate was favourable to raise more capital for the company. Initial generation of cash was also large and the young company and its executives succeeded in taking it far and wide. The company came to be recognised in the international shipping world.

Though initially, Vasant had a very hard task. The very first trip of the ship to Australia, in 1948-49, created labour trouble. Labour being a dominant factor in Australia, the ship could not be moved for almost a year and, in the first year of Great Eastern's existence, the company suffered a loss of Rs. 20 lakh.

The company is a premier shipping and offshore oil fields company with revenues of over Rs. 2,000 crore.

For the Sheths, it has been a saga of spirited enterprise, from trading in sugar to promoting India's largest private sector shipping firm that clocked revenues in excess of Rs. 3,200 crore last year.

The Great Eastern Shipping Company Limited has navigated an eventful course since the time it purchased a single coal-fired cargo vessel from the United States Maritime Commission in 1948. The company's shipping division has 43 vessels, including the 1,58,344 dwt double hull tanker *Jag Lalit,* the pride of its fleet. Its offshore arm has five ships, including three platform supply vessels, with eight more assorted ships on order.

The Mumbai-based company, which has two subsidiaries — Greatship Offshore Service Pte Ltd and Greatship Global Energy Services Pte Ltd — in Singapore, has traded 200 ships over its 60-year lifespan. And, while its ships carried a combined cargo of 1,52,763 tonnes in its first year of operation, its formidable present-day fleet freighted a total 31.09 million tonnes of consignments last year. In contemporary terms, the first year's cargo would have fit comfortably in the hold of just one of its large ships today.

"Great Eastern now has a strong footing and it is a matter of great personal satisfaction for me to know that, even after I bow out, it will continue to prosper, growing from strength to strength," says its 76-year-old Chairrman, Kanaiyalal (Kanu) Sheth. "It has been said that, if you want to go far in business, you've got to stay close to it and I believe in that implicitly," notes Sheth, one of the two sons of Maneklal, who, with his brother Jagjiwan, had established the shipping enterprise six decades ago. "Great Eastern's success has been, in a large measure, due to the fact that we have had our operations under tight control; we've kept our watch on quality, technical innovation, skilled manpower, financial controls ... everything."

Kanu Sheth has been associated with his family company for 57 of its 60 years

GROWTH OVER THE DECADES

(Rs. crore)

	1948-49 *1st year*	*1957-58* *10th year*	*1967-68* *20th year*	*1977-78* *30th year*	*1987-88* *40th year*	*1997-98** *50th year*	*2007-08** *60th year*
Revenues	0.4	3.7	9.8	34.3	116.0	964.1	3,203.5
Operating profit	0.0	1.2	3.9	7.1	50.4	420.6	1,893.2
PBT	0.03	0.7	2.2	–8.8	19.5	191.2	1,403.0
Net profit	0.03	0.6	2.2	–8.8	16.4	166.9	1,356.8
Fixed assets	0.2	4.6	18.8	150.6	223.6	1,448.3	4,832.6
Equity share capital	0.2	0.9	2.4	15.3	55.6	287.6	152.3
Reserves & surplus	0.03	1.9	6.5	19.8	39.2	911.4	4,005.1
EPS (Rs.)	1.5	7.2	9.1	–5.6	2.9	5.8	89.1

Period ending 30th June.

* Period ending 31st March.

APPENDIX - 005

Leadership Communication Choices

Leaders come in different hues and their chosen styles of speaking and writing also differ. Some of the common styles are:

Autocratic: Usually operating from the paradigm "I know best", such leaders are given to issuing peremptory diktats, preferring to order not consult. On the positive side, such leaders are typically clear, decisive and quick in their communication and believe in giving prompt feedback. Flamboyance and personal idiosyncrasy/es often characterize their communication. Think Richard Branson and Lee lacocca.

Participative I democratic: These leaders believe that the team must together "buy" the common dream or corporate goal and hence work hard towards explaining and clarifying issues and motivating their people. Hence they have teams that are largely happy with the group involvement, thought there would be occasional exasperation due to lengthy communication cycles and the subsequent delays in decision-making. Team with such lenders display trust and open-mindedness when it comes to sharing ideas, with lesser fear of criticism. Formal and informal feedback are both high.

How does one balance the large volume of communication with efficiency? Says Manoj Sharma, a senior trainer with a nationalized training college for bankers, "leaders must be careful to avoid over communication. Micro managing must be avoided. At the same time, the team needs to be completely aware of the organisation's plans and accordingly, the expectations that the top management has from them."

Bureaucratic: The "pukka sahibs" of the leadership world, these chieftains are most comfortable with formal communication, using precise language, and invariably indicating impersonal decision making. They prefer to rely on e-mails, letters, and memos, rather than the quick phone call or a casual, verbal instruction. A lot of emphasis is placed on past precedence and appropriateness of form.

Diplomatic: Taking a leaf from Chanakya's book, these leader favour glib, non-threatening talk. Networking figures high on the priority list here. Persuasive communication, using formal communication networks as well as the informal "grapevine" at office, are seen.

While most leaders display the characteristics of predominantly one style of leadership, situation-specific flexibility also exists. Which means, the usually participative leader, when faced with a crisis that requires urgent decisions, may choose the autocratic style of management for a short while.

A brief checklist of tips that good leaders use for effective communication may include the following;

- Good leaders are invariably great listeners, paying attention not only to the words, but also to the hidden nuances of communication.
- Good leaders use the 3 C's of communication, that is, they are consistent, clear and complete, while communicating their plans to the team.

- Timely and objective feedback is critical; its absence could kill a project, the morale of the group and even the year's sales targets.
- The ability to consider and respect the other person's point of view and accordingly tailor make the message, is an invaluable tool in the leader's basket of skills.

The late *Sumantra Ghoshal,* former professor of Strategic Leadership at London business School, had said, "Effective leaders intuitively understand people's feelings and have the ability to shape and leverage those feelings to attain collective goals. They create and manage pride, fear, shame, anxiety, anger and other strong and weak feelings that move people to do things. "Taking this a step further, one may thus surmise that communication, for leaders, is then the conduit for successfully articulating and merging individual dreams into a desirable collective reality.

APPENDIX - 006

A New Wave of Entrepreneurs

Enterprise is the agent of change and development. Enterprise is the creative effort of entrepreneurs. Most importantly, entrepreneurship built and sustained on the true set of value system is ready for the marathon race in the competitive global economy. Entrepreneurial ethics, values, principles, conscience and social responsibility are key matrixes to judge entrepreneurship in the 21st century. In fact, there is a new wave of entrepreneurs.

Over the past five years, though, companies in the small and medium enterprises (SMEs) sector have been outperforming their larger rivals by a wide margin, in particularly every financial measure. The SMEs have emerged tougher and more globally competitive. Several of the enterprises that are medium-sized today are already on their way to becoming tomorrow's blue chips.

SMEs have proved as the entrepreneurial engine. Hence, SMEs have become the darlings of Corporate India.

Since SMEs contribute so much to employment and exports, the spillover effects of supporting them are considerable. Hence, the government does have a role to play. The best policy would be to create an environment of risk-taking and entrepreneurship where seed capital is readily available for start-ups and where SMEs have access to their technology and training needs. The key to wearing away the large, under-employed population from the low productivity agricultural sector lies in the growth of SMEs."

⌘ Entrepreneurial Teams

The numbers and quality of entrepreneurs are increasing at a breathtaking pace. Many more senior executives are willing to leave their jobs and start companies. Similarly a lot of people who are recent graduates are willing to take the risk. However, even now most "mid-level" professionals are unwilling to take professional risk. Further, while many people are keen to start companies, most are still not keen to join a start-up. Thus, the apex of the entrepreneurial pyramid is developing quickly but the base to support it is not developing as fast. This will create many starts-ups that are unable to scale.

⌘ Money

The money available to early-to-mid-stage companies has increased nearly ten-fold in the last year; and promises to further increase this year. This is an encouraging change in a very short period. The increased willingness to invest in less mature companies has many reasons. These include overcrowding in late-stage company investing, arrival of investors who have experience with early-stage investing elsewhere, the "feel good factor" becoming even stronger and giving everyone more confidence, global historical data that early stage investing gives great returns, and the emergence of India as a promising investment destination. Venture firms have attracted operationally experienced professionals who provide "active-capital" where entrepreneurs can benefit from mentorship and support to help bridge some of the gaps.

Box - 1

THE BIGGEST ENTREPRENEURIAL SUCCESS STORY

In 1881, the year Business World began, a group of seven dissatisfied computer programmers wanted to break out on their own. So at a time when entrepreneurship was still a taboo world among the middle class, they quit their regular jobs and set up their own company — in a small flat with a starting capital of $250, which one of its founders borrowed from his wife. The man was N. R. Narayana Murthy, and the company, Infosys. The rest, as they say, is history. Nevertheless, a history worth recounting as we take a trip down the start-up lane. In 1992, the Rs. 46-crore company raised Rs. 13 crore from the public and bet it all on a Rs. 18.76-crore state-of-the-art software development centre in Bangalore. The result? From Rs.14.52 crore in 1993, Infy's revenues shot upto Rs. 260 crore in 1998. Today, it is a $2.7 billion company.

Among the risks are high valuations driven by excess supply of capital — companies are more expensive than comparable-stage companies in other countries, despite less-proven markets. Many investors will lose money, like in the US, where half the venture capitalists lose money. The bet is that this pond is getting bigger and hence more smallish will get an opportunity to grow.

Box - 2

FUELLING ENTREPRENEURSHIP

Infosys was seeded in N.S. Raghavan's Matunga house in Mumbai in 1981. Twenty-five years later, Raghavan continues to fuel the flame of entrepreneurship, mentoring and funding several new companies. His Nadathur Holdings and Investments has funded 17 companies in IT, life sciences and engineering services, including Connexios Life Sciences and Reach Technologies. He also supports IIM Bangalore's Nadathur S. Raghavan Center for Entrepreneurial Learning, with six companies in incubation, including Aparoksha Technologies, a speech processing firm, and Brain League Consulting an IP management company.

N.R. Narayana Murthy and **Sabeer Bhatia** have inspired thousands of start-up artistes who now throng the country and have changed the entrepreneurial landscape forever. Many new entrepreneurs who were inspired by the duo have now made it to the big league. Now, society celebrates entrepreneurs, and even the wealth they create. Gradually, it also began to accept failure as a part of an entrepreneur's risks.

Of course, there are a lot of unreal fantasies and undeserved hype. But the country today is much wiser from a period of intense agony when several dreams were punctured. The dotcom bust at the turn of the century and the hundreds of flame-outs that followed have brought in a sense of reality and reason to entrepreneurial expectations. That was a painful phase. But it was much needed. It tested and refined the spirit of entrepreneurship; it did not kill it.

According to a survey published in September 2006, 74 first-generation entrepreneurs like the ones on the covers have become billionaires in the past five years. Their combined wealth was estimated to be Rs 75,204 crore as on 31 March 2006. This page is a celebration of their enterprise. That is why the entrepreneurial fever is still raging.

START-UP FACTORIES

⌘ WIPRO

In the past 10 years, it has thrown up more than 50 start-ups and 88 CxOs, many of who have set up projects and India operations for international giants like Lucent, Hewlett-Packard and Philips. Even hot Silicon Valley start-ups such as Amber Networks and Armedia (now Broadcom) have head-hunted at Wipro.

⌘ PATNI COMPUTER SERVICES

It seeded one of the best-known entrepreneurial stories of our tunes — Infosys Technologies. All seven founders — N.R. Narayana Murthy, Nandan Nilekani, N.S. Raghavan, S. Gopalakrishnan, K. Dinesh, S.D. Shibulal and Ashok Arora — were working with Patni.

⌘ INDIAN DRUGS AND PHARMACEUTICALS

It went into losses in the early 1990s. But not before it gave birth to several entrepreneurs who went on to start successful pharma and health care companies. K. Anji Reddy, founder of Dr. Reddy's, is one prime example.

⌘ DCM DATA PRODUCTS

Shiv Nadar is the most famous entrepreneur to come out of DCM. His HCL group also spun out entrepreneurs, including Dhadan Bhai of PCL fame and Rajendra Pawar of NUT.

BREAKING NEW GROUND

China is the new land of opportunity for a growing tribe of young Indian entrepreneurs who're launching businesses ranging from *tandoori* restaurants to pharma drugs to construction chemicals.

Abhishek Vaidya, Vaidya 33 (Nelscrop International), Ravi Mehrotra, Sanjeev Goswami (Tandoor chain), and Munu Swamy Gnanavelu (Kitchen Group of Companies) are all part of the famed breed that's now known and respected worldwide for its enterprise. These men have ventured into a hitherto alien territory that many Indians had kept away from, largely due to its closed economy and some unsavoury historical baggage. The trickle has began and promises to turn into a tide simply because of what Vaidya describes as "the scale of opportunity."

By sheer hand work, ingenuity, perseverance and a bit of luck, Indians are learning to crack the Chinese markets. Even though China is often touted as business friendly nation, devoid of red tape, entrepreneurs feel that's true only for big businesses. Small businesses still have to struggle to find their way through myriad Chinese regulations.

The number of Indians in China has increased five-fold over the last six years, and the number of entrepreneurs is set to increase as well. They are spread across China, and can be found from Beijing in the North to Guangzhou in the south, and even in places like XiaoXing, a textile city near Shanghai. With the opportunity only set to multiply, this breed of China aspirants is set to multiply. Munuswamy sums up: "I'm amazed to see young Indians in China. They say 'my future is here, and I am mentally committed to China.' The number of Indians who want to work and do business in China is increasing everyday." To that we say, *"Jia you, Jia you"* (which, loosely translated, reads 'Way to go.")

Likewise, the Indian/Indian-origin entrepreneurs throughout the world are launching and running businesses ranging from hospitality, trade to pharma and IT business and earned the trust of the locals in good measure.

Knowledge entrepreneurship which is not only be outsourcing-driven but also idea and innovation-driven has opened immense opportunities to entrepreneurs in various fields.

Opportunities Elsewhere

With over 44,000 engineering graduates and diploma holders, 2,3 million arts, science and commerce graduates, and 3 lakh post-graduates added every year, and the largest English-speaking worldforce, India is one of the largest talent pools in the world. Besides IT, newer avenues have opened beyond IT-enabled services.

Legal services: Several international firms, publishing companies, legal research firms and multinational companies are now sourcing services — secretarial support, voice-messaging, legal assistance and support by professional lawyers — from India. Companies like General Electric, Oracle, Sun and Cisco have even moved part of their in-house legal departments to India-based units. This segment is expected to touch **$20 billion** by 2015.

Animation and gaming: The sector, currently estimated at **$250-300 million,** is stated to grow by 30 per cent annually in the next 4-5 years.

Engineering, research, and development services: Companies are sourcing these services in sectors such as telecommunications and aerospace, in areas such as telecommunications and aerospace, in areas such as offshore product development. The services sourced from India have almost doubled from $1.7 billion in 2003-04 to **$2.2 billion** in 2004-05.

Financial and accounting services: This includes general accounting and transaction management and makes up approximately 40 per cent of the Indian ITES-BPO industry. It is estimated to touch $25.3 billion by 2009.

Pharmaceutical industry: According to Associated Chambers of Commerce and Industry of India (assocham), the $13 billion Indian pharmaceutical industry is expected to grow to **$25 billion** by 2010.

Customer interactive services: This segment accounts for approximately 46 per cent of the Indian ITES-BPO demand worldwide and is projected to increase between **12-13 per cent** within five years. It concludes IT-enabled customer contact, inbound and outbound voice or non-voice based support, sales and marketing.

Source: NASSCOM Strategic Review, 2006.

Raghunath Medge

Head of Dabbawalla Union. One of two Dabbawallas to attend the Royal Wedding

Tiffin Titan

Raghunath Modge represents Mumbai's spirit. In an age when companies are finding it difficult to discipline employees, he has managed the impossible: creating a team of 5,000 dabbawallas who have maintained an efficiency level of 99 per cent. Thanks to Medge's efforts, the dabbawallas are on the world map today. One never imagined a day when dabbas could be booked on the Internet. Medge must be given credit for sustaining their business despite the growing trend of eating out.

Sigma sensation

Forbes has awarded his Dabbawala system the Six Sigma performance rating.

Power lunches

Surprises students of business schools with his slick Power Point presentations.

Naina Lal Kidwai

CEO of HSBC India, Harward grad, Wearer of elegant sarees.

She was always a quiet leader, formidable yet sexy. I shall never forget the sight of impeccable Naina heading to the disco.

LESSONS FROM EAST ASIA

K. Migara O. De Silva of the World Bank lists some points that Indian SMEs can learn from countries like Taiwan

Size per se was not the only criterion for promoting SMEs in East Asia; 'productivity' was.

Subcontracting as opposed to vertical integration (trying to produce all in-house) was a key aspect of SME growth.

SMEs received little 'protection' from competition. Policies by and large focused on 'promoting' SMEs.

Growth did not take place merely as a result of removing few administrative barriers. A number of other conditions mattered such as the existence of a good investment climate, institutional reforms (legal/linkages/processes etc.), financial base and links with MNCs.

Competition in export markets provided the necessary incentives for SMEs to adopt appropriate technology, marketing strategies, etc.

Enterprise is the agent of change and growth. Leading an enterprise is by mentoring by example innovation and productivity are the core values of an enterprise. Enterprise means fairness. Entrepreneurs never cheat Frankness is one of the core values.

The following statistical data goes to prove the unique contribution of SMEs in acceleration of the Indian economy and economic development.

PERFORMANCE OF SSI SECTOR

Year	*Production (at 1993-94 prices, Rs. cr)*	*Employment (million)*	*Exports ($ billion)*
1989-90	1,89,900	11.96	4.58
1990-91	84,728	15.83	5.39
1991-92	87,355	16.60	5.63
1992-93	92,246	17.48	6.14
1993-94	98,796	18.26	8.07
1994-95	1,08,774	19.14	9.26
1995-96	1,21,175	19.79	10.90
1996-97	1,34,892	20.59	11.06
1997-98	1,46,263	21.32	11.96
1998-99	1,57,525	22.06	11.64
1999-00	1,70,379	22.91	12.51
2000-01	1,84,401	23.87	15.28
2001-02	1,95,613	24.93	14.94
2002-03	2,10,636	26.02	17.77
2003-04	2,28,730	27.14	21.25
2004-05	2,51,511	28.26	24.45
2005-06	2,75,581	29.49	28.15

Notes:
1. Data have been revised sine 1990-91 on the basis of the findings of the third all-India Census of SSI units.
2. Data at constant prices is deflated on the basis of growth rates achieved in SSI sector from 2001-02 to 1990-91.
3. Production at constant prices for the year 2004-05 is estimated on the growth rate of 8.89 per cent achieved during the period April-December 2004.
4. Production at current prices is complied on the basis of average WPI 165.6 of manufactured product for the period April-December 2004.

Source: Ministry of Small Scale Industries, Government of India.

HOW SMEs HAVE GROWN

Smaller Companies have growth more than larger ones

SMEs with turnover of	*Net sales*	*Operating profit*	*Net profit*
Rs. 1 crore-50 crore	175.0	301.6	701.8
Rs. 50 crore-100 crore	125.0	101.0	961.1
Rs. 100 crore-Rs. 200 crore	102.5	115.5	713.7
Rs. 200 crore-Rs. 300 crore	79.6	90.8	365.9
Rs. 300 crore-Rs. 400 crore	86.6	97.9	153.7
Rs. 400 crore-Rs. 500 crore	89.2	89.7	559.0
Rs. 500 crore-Rs. 1,000 crore	63.1	61.1	143.8
> Rs. 1,000 crore	86.4	92.4	169.9
Total	89.1	95.6	206.8

Figures are growth in per cent between 2001 and 2006.

Small Companies' Share of Sales and Profits has gone up

SMEs with turnover of	*2006*			*2001*		
	Net sales	*Operating profit*	*Net profit*	*Net sales*	*Operating profit*	*Net profit*
Rs. 1 crore-50 crore	4.6	4.7	4.3	3.2	2.3	–2.2
Rs. 50 crore-100 crore	3.7	3.0	2.3	3.1	2.9	0.7
Rs. 100 crore-Rs. 200 crore	6.2	5.4	3.6	5.8	4.9	1.4
Rs. 200 crore-Rs. 300 crore	4.2	3.4	2.8	4.4	3.5	1.9
Rs. 300 crore-Rs. 400 crore	3.5	3.8	3.4	3.5	3.7	4.1
Rs. 400 crore-Rs. 500 crore	2.7	3.1	2.5	2.6	3.2	1.2
Rs. 500 crore-Rs. 1,000 crore	7.6	8.1	7.2	8.8	9.8	9.0
> Rs. 1,000 crore	67.6	68.5	74.0	68.6	69.7	84.1

Figures are share of total sales, operating profits and net profits in per cent.

Margin Growth has been better for Smaller Companies

SMEs with turnover of	*2006*		*2001*	
	Operating profit	*Net profit*	*Operating profit*	*Net* profit
Rs. 1 crore-50 crore	18.7	8.3	12.8	–3.8
Rs. 50 crore-100 crore	14.7	5.4	16.4	1.2
Rs. 100 crore-Rs. 200 cror	15.9	5.1	14.9	1.3
Rs. 200 crore-Rs. 300 crore	14.7	6.0	13.8	2.3
Rs. 300 crore-Rs. 400 crore	19.9	8.7	18.8	6.4
Rs. 400 crore-Rs. 500 crore	21.5	8.3	21.4	2.4
Rs. 500 crore-Rs. 1,000 crore	19.6	8.3	19.8	5.6
Rs. 1,000 crore	18.5	9.6	17.9	6.7
Total	18.2	8.8	17.6	5.4

Figures are margins in per cent; Base for all tables: 2,418 non-financial companies.
Source: Capitaline Plus

SSI Outstandings

Bank outstandings to SSIs as a percentage of total outstandings to small, medium and large industries

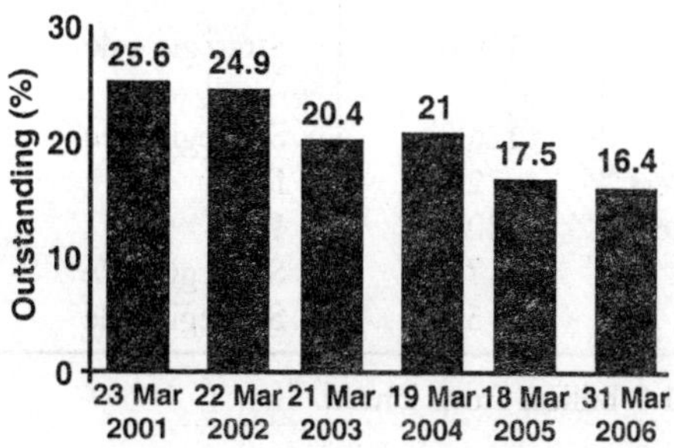

Source: RBI

Outstandings in Scheduled Commercial Banks' Loans to SSI Sector

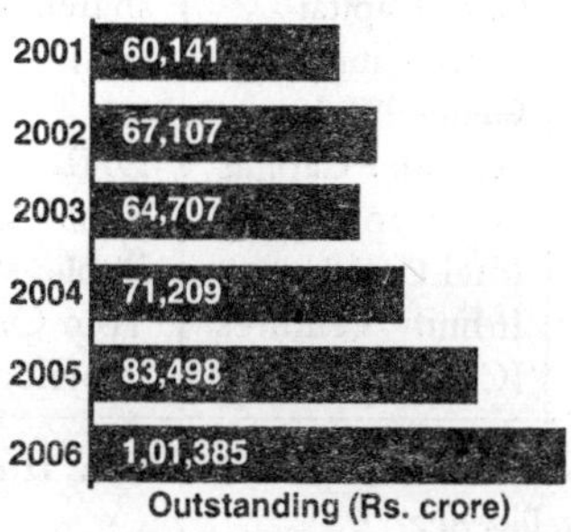

Figures are for end-March Source: RBI

Sick SSI Units Financed by Commercial Banks

Year end-March	*No. of sick units*	*Outstandings (Rs. cr)*
2000	304,235	4,608.43
2001	249,830	4,505.54
2002	1,77,336	4,818.92
2003	167,980	5,706.35
2004	138,811	5,284.54
2005	138,041	5,380.13

Source: RBI

PRIMARY CAPITAL ISSUES: THE 'SMALL' PICTURE

The Bull Market of 2004-05 saw few SMEs going public

Year	*No. of issues below Rs. 50 cr.*	*Amount raised (Rs. cr)**	*Change in amount raised (%)*
1998-99	336	2,966	—
1990-00	455	4,433	49.46
2000-01	491	3,912	–11.75
2001-01	305	3,232	–17.38
2002-03	423	2,475	–23.42
2003-04	574	1,958	–20.89
2004-05	264	2,625	34.07

*Total money raised by SME IPOs of Rs. 50 crore.

Note: The amount raised by the Rs. 10 crore-50 crore bracket is the largest over the years. But there was a drop between 2001 and 2004.

Source: CMIE.

EXIT RECORD

Some of the Key SME Exits in the Past Seven Years

Company	*Seller*	*Buyer ($mn)*	*Deal value*	*Exit type*
Bharti Tele-ventures	Warburg Pincus	Vodafone	847.5*	Strategic sale
Suzlon	Citigroup, ChrysCapital	Public shareholders	340.0	IPO
Daksh eServices	Actis, Citigroup, General Atlantic	IBM	160.0	Strategic sale
Blue Dart	Schroder Capital	DHL	126.0	Strategic sale
Biocon	GW Capital, AIG	Public shareholders	72.0	IPO
Sasken	Intel Capital	Public shareholders	30.2	IPO
Indiagames	Infinity Ventures	Tom Online	17.0	Strategic sale
Indus League	ICICI Venture	Pantaloon	5.3	Strategic sale

* Warburg sold 5.65 stake for $847.5 billion. It earned $1.9 billion from Bharti.

Source: Venure Intelligence.

OFFSHORE ENTERPRISE

Twenty five Global Indian Entrepreneurial Success Stories

Laxmi N. Mittal, Ispat International: With an empire spanning five continents and valued at £900 million, the UK-based steel sultan is the richest Indian abroad.

The Brothers Hinduja, Srichand, Gopichand, Prakash, Ashok: With a $15-billion business, the controversy ridden Hindujas remain one of the most influential business families. They have interests in oil, finance and telecom.

Jasminder Singh, Edwardian Group Hotels: Even as his up market chain of hotels across eight countries suffers the 9-11 effect, its value stays high at £400 million.

Vijay & Bhiku Patel, Waymade Healthcare: In less than three decades, the Patel brothers have transformed a lone store in Basildon, UK into a £298-million pharma retail business.

Lord Swaraj Paul, Caparo Group: The Lord Paul of Marylebone is one of the most respected NRIs in the UK. The turnover of his nine listed companies with interests in steel and engineering exceeds £525 million.

Anil Chandaria, Comcraft: He has interests in steel, chemicals and plastics. His UK-based flagship company Comcraft's turnover alone is £200 million.

Tom Singh, New Look Clothing: Founded in 1969, Singh's clothing retail chain has over 500 stores in UK with a turnover of $650 million.

Sir G.K. Noon, WT Foods: Noon's WT Foods is one of Europe's leading suppliers of ethnic food with sales of £150 million.

Lord Raj Kumar Bagri, Metdist: The first non-Briton to head the prestigious London Metal Exchange, Lord Bagri runs one of the largest non-ferrous metals businesses in the UK. His net worth is close to £80 million.

Gururaj 'Desh' Deshpande, Sycamore Networks: A student of IIT-Madras, Deshpande founded the Massachusetts-based $14.5-billion Sycamore Networks

Reuben Singh, RS Group: The 26-year-old runs an internet company RS International, and is the UK's youngest millionaire with a personal fortune of £35 million.

Sanjiv Sidhu, i2 Technologies: Sidhu and i2 were once Wall Street favourites. But the techmeltdown saw his fortune plummet from a high of $9.6 billion in 1999 to $400 million today.

Naveen Jain, Infospace: Jain quit Microsoft in 1996 to found Infospace. The NASDAQ listed company has more than 700 employees and a turnover of $162 million.

Vivek Wadhwa, Relativity Technologies Inc: Forbes called him a "Leader of Tomorrow" while **Fortune** thinks his $118 million company Relativity, belongs in the list of 25 "coolest" companies in the world.

Vinod Gupta, infoUSA Inc.: The IIT .Kharagpur grad's $300 million infoUSA Inc. sells databases of 12 million businesses and 200 million households across the US.

Sabeer Bhatia: From the heady days of Hotmail to Page 3, it's been one helluva ride for the BITS Pilani alumnus. After his latest venture Arzoo's failure, Bhatia has chosen to play angel.

Lata Krishnan, SMART modular: Kerala-born Krishnan's SMART Modular, a memory modules manufacturer, netted more than $700 million last year and, according to *Fortune,* is one of the 50 fastest growing tech companies.

Ranjan Marwah, Executive Access: He came to Hong Kong on a holiday 28 years ago with $300 rolled in his socks and started a search firm whose annual income today is in excess of $200 million.

Vinod Khosla: His investments in a handful of now-hot telcos like Infinera, Asera and Centrata shows why Khosla, a co-founder of Sun Microsystems, is the greatest VC of all time. His net worth is estimated to be around $550 million.

Rajendra Singh, Telecom Ventures: He grew up in a small Rajasthan village and now runs a company that's into wireless and long-distance telephony. His net worth is close to $ 1.1 billion.

P. Mohammed All, Galfar: Ali landed in the Gulf as a 22-year-old with a diploma in civil engineering. Today his $250 million company has interests in oil drilling and infrastructure.

Amar Gopal Bose: Bose launched his first product in 1968. Today Bose Corporation has a turnover of $600 million and is synonymous with premier audio products.

Nav Sooch, Silicon Labs: Sooch runs a chip design company and with a networth of $186 million he is the highest-ranked Indian American on *Fortune's* list of the richest Americans below 40.

Rakesh Mathur: Mathur made $180 million in a stock deal when Amazon decided to buy his net start-up Junglee Corp. He now runs a data management company.

Kanwal Rekhi: The son of Sikh refugees who landed in the US in 1967, Rekhi became a pioneering VC. He funded Exodus Communications; today, the company is worth $15 billion.

APPENDIX - 007

Jain Religion and Business Leadership

The history of the success stories of Jain businessmen and industrialists, in India has many facets to it. Of course, there is the pre-independence era to consider and then the resurgence of Jain businessmen in the more modern era of recent decades. However, it must be said that Jains for all their cultural values, core beliefs and traditional ethos have adapted very well to changing modern mores and technological-driven times.

But, despite the attendant pressures, compulsions and rigours of modern life, they have not compromised on any of their core beliefs and values. Now the Jains are present in every conceivable business domain, industry and sector in the country. They have carved out niches in various different fields and have established mega empires in certain industries. These industries include manufacturing, services, retail, automotive, SME sector, entertainment, media, foods and hospitality Many young entrepreneurs and even progenies of successful and dynastic businessmen have start-up businesses in the more 'fashionable' IT, ITeS, pharma, biotechnology, life sciences industries too-testifying to the inherent industrious and missionary zeal for trade and commerce of this rich values-based and vibrant community.

The Jains are also well known for their generous donations, their philanthropic activities, their community service programmes, their cultural celebrations. They have always stepped forward to help entire communities and Indian citizens during floods, famines, earthquakes, tsunamis and other calamities. The Jain spirit of 'giving and sharing' is quite universal — given that they have formed successful communities in many other countries of the world like the US, UK, Canada, South Africa, Australia etc.

In the community, it is indeed the businessmen who have shown the way in charting out their own individual and unique niches in business and society. Conscious of their duty towards

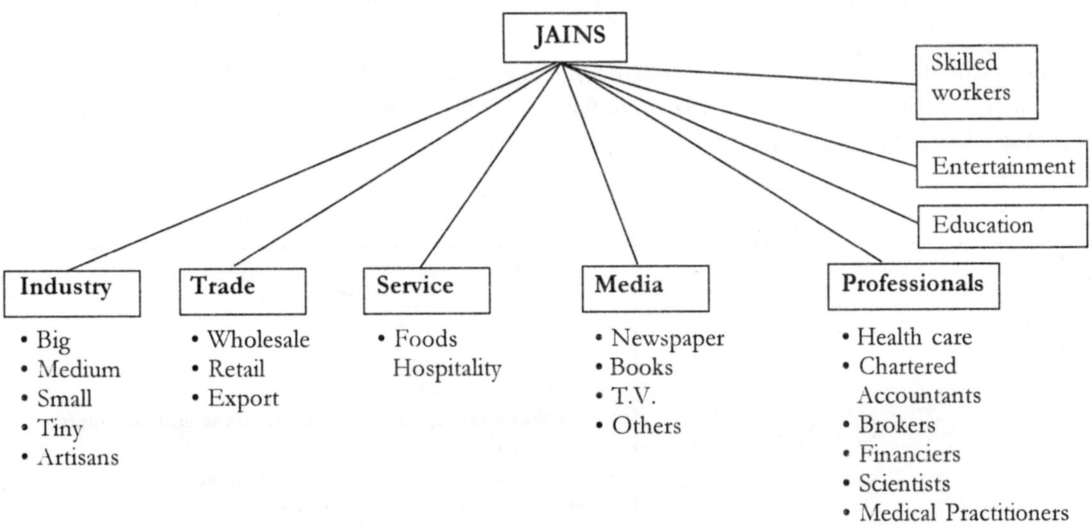

Diversified Interests of the Jain Community

society and their own people, they have been extremely proactive in spreading the message of seva (service), Knowledge and economic empowerment for all.

As the ways to do business evolve at an electric pace, renewed means have emerged to keep up with this sweeping change. One of the oldest and most trusted tools of business is networking, something the most business savvy community of India, the Jains, seem to have mastered over a period of time. They might be small in number, constituting only 1 per cent of the total Indian population, but the Jain community occupy a significant position in the Indian landscape. They have been venerated as a highly literate community, with Jain women being identified as being more educated than their counterparts in other communities, as per the 2001 census.

Primarily belonging to the Vaishya or business caste of the Hindu Varna system, the microsized Jain community has made a distinct name for itself in trade and commerce with significant emphasis on what is called 'ethical business practices.' Immense stress is laid on the right knowledge, cutting edge competence, fellowship spirit and the highest ethical and moral values.

So what keeps this group commercially so vibrant and visible? Well, it's the community's immense endeavour to keep all its members networked with each other. As a community, there's constant stress on staying connected with other Jains everywhere. This helps them keep abreast with the best business practices and with changes in the system. Says Sandeep Bafna of Fort Point, "Business is our main occupation. We are not many in number, but we form associations and conduct conventions in India as well as abroad to share information and establish good networking on business, trade, commerce and industry."

Jain International Trade Organisation (JITO), a global organisation has now come to the fore to bring the Jain communities together and forge a special unity in order to serve the cause of human kind more. It wishes to establish networks to plan, strategise and open avenues to solve issues regarding trade and industry, which in turn helps the growth of the global economy. In spite of the micro size of the Jain population, their leadership in trade and commerce has made its recognition worldwide.

The spirit of collaboration and association is very strong within the community. The JITO fair will help in promoting the Products manufactured by entrepreneurs from the community. In my opinion, this is just the beginning of a system of networking in the Jain community."

Jain Philosophy	*Jain Business Practices*
• Non-violence (Ahimsha) • Moral values • Ethical values • Charity • *Anekantvaad*	• Identifying newer business opportunities • Creating a knowledge base • Networking • Sharing and Caring • Nurturing leaders • Fostering enterprises in industry, trade and commerce • Compliance • Encouraging ethical business practices • Setting up charitable institutions • Good governance Economic empowerment.

One of the primary aims of the meet is to give youngsters an opportunity to meet entrepreneurs from their community. Otherwise, it is not possible for young business aspirants to know Jain business. leaders. These trade meets are a platform for networking within the group.

JITO's Objectives

- Strengthening the Jain community's effectiveness in dealing with threats to socio-economic empowerment, social cohesion, acquiring knowledge, peace and security.
- Building greater capacities among Jains of the globe and work for maximising co-operation amongst the fellow members to counter odds and obstacles.
- Ensuring equitable burden sharing and more effective activities to resolve the existing problems.
- Advancing with a well-crafted strategy to make the community of global Jains more cultured, empowered, skilled, caring, contented and prosperous.

The business-savvy Jain community of India is keeping itself abreast with the latest global business best practices through active intra-community networking.

The community is striving to take business leadership quality to the next generation. Towards this special emphasis is laid on merging Jain business practices and management studies. Their goal is to work on a vision that is strategic and farsighted, a collaborative exercise that was aimed at crystallising various stages of networking with the fellow members of the society for its all-round development.

TOWARDS THE LIGHT

- Average number of shops per 1,000 persons in the U.S.A. and the UK: **4 & 5.**
- Average number of shops per 1,000 persons in India, country with highest shop density worldwide: **11.**
- Chances that shops in India occupy less than 500 sq. ft. in space: **96 in 100.**
- There are over 121 lakh shops in India, competing and catering to the customer needs.
- Over 50 per cent of the workforce in India is self-employed.
- The culture of entrepreneurship is in the genesis of Indian and it to be harnessed.

VISION

"We strive to impart management education to prepare business leaders and entrepreneurs **to stand up to** global competition."

Late Syt. G.D. Birla
A Lofty Visionary

Syt. B.K. Birla
Our Founder & Patron

MISSION

"We are committed to make the institution a hallmark in management education **by achieving** Excellence with Values."

APPENDIX - 008

Theory of Happiness

Introduction

Every one in this world desires happiness and dislikes misery. Hence, happiness is the goal of life and all economic activities. Happiness is as mucha subjective concept as truth or history. It is impossible to define a person's happiness through some predetermined set of quotients. The theory of happiness dwells on the key aspects and their relationship.

Happiness can't be limited to a few pleasant sensations, to some intense pleasure, to an eruption of joy or a fleeting sense of serenity, to a cheery day or a magic moment that sneaks up on us in the labyrinth of our existence. Such diverse facets are not enough in themselves to build an accurate image of the profound and lasting fulfilment that characterises true happiness. By happiness I mean here a deep sense of flourishing that arises from an exceptionally healthy mind. This is not a mere pleasurable feeling a fleeting emotion, or a mood, but an optimal state of being.

Happiness is also a way of interpreting the world, since while it may be difficult to change the world, it is always possible to change the way we look at it. Changing the way we see the world does not imply neive optimism or some artificial euphoria designed to counterbalance adversity. The search for happiness is not about looking at life through rose-coloured glasses or blinding oneself to the pain and imperfections of the world. Nor is happiness a state of exaltation to be perpetuated at all costs; it is the purging of mental toxins, such as hatred and obsession, that literally poison the mind. It is also about learning how to put things in perspective and reduce the gap between appearances and reality. To that end we must acquire a better knowledge of how the mind works and a more accurate insight into the nature of things, for in its deepest sense, suffering is intimately linked to a misapprehension of the nature of reality.

Several studies rate various countries as being the happiest. The University of Liecester rated Denmark as the happiest country. Bhutan even has a Gross Happiness Index which defines prosperity, not just in terms of economic growth but also average level of happiness of the people. A recent University of Warwick study found a correlation between happiness and level of blood pressure of people. On this basis, Sweden tops the list.

Happiness and Economic Growth

"It's good to be just plain happy, it's a little better to know that you're happy; but to understand that you're happy and to know why and how and still be happy, be happy in the being and the knowing, well that is beyond happiness, that is bliss."

The economic growth should aim to make the people happy and contented. It is time we focussed not just on GDP, but on sense of well-being (SWB) and General Well Being (GWB)

People who take the time to chat over the fence to their neighbours, have plenty of sex with the same companion and care about endangered species tend to be happier, according to a report by Britain's "department for happiness". Gardening, praying and going to walks are also all linked to broader smiles.

While the idea of a Whitehall-defined unit of happiness may not fill that many people with joy, its supporters hope that by pinpointing what makes people happy, taxpayers' money could be spent with greater effect on national well-being. "If the aim of policy were to alleviate misery, there may be some justification for targeting women as they tend to exhibit higher levels of depression."

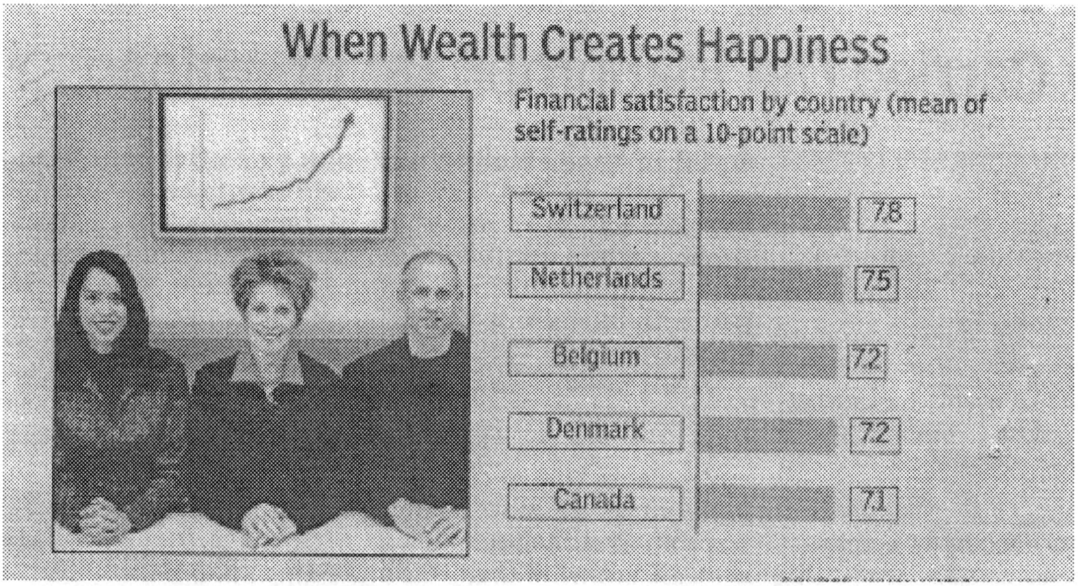

With an annual growth rate of 3.2% per head since 2000, the world economy is heading towards notching its best decade ever. And market capitalism, the engine that runs it, seems to be doing its job well.

But is it? Once upon a time, that job was generally agreed to be to make people better off. Nowadays that is not so clear. A number of economists and politicians think that it ought to be doing something else: making people happy, says **The Economist** in an article titled **Happiness (and how to measure it).**

The view that economics should be about more than money is widely held in continental Europe. In debates with Anglo-American capitalists, wily **bons vivants** have tended to cite the idea of quality of life to excuse slower economic growth. But now David Cameron, the latest leader of Britain's once rather materialistic Conservative Party, has espoused the notion of general well-being (GWB) as an alternative to GDP. In the US, meanwhile, inequality, overwork and other hidden costs of prosperity were much discussed in the mid-term elections; and wellness (as opposed to health) has become a huge industry, catering especially to the prosperous discontent of the baby-boomers.

Much of this draws on the upstart science of happiness, which mixes psychology with economics. Copious survey data has revealed a paradox: affluent countries have not got much happier as they have grown richer.

The science of happiness offers two explanations for the paradox. Capitalism, it notes, is adept at turning luxuries into necessities — bringing to the masses what the elites have always enjoyed. But the flip side is that people come to take for granted things they once coveted from afar.

Economists traditionally assume that people know their own interests, and are best left to mind their own business. How much they work, and what they buy, is their own affair. A properly brought up economist seeks to explain their decisions, not to quarrel with them. But the new happiness gurus are much less willing to defer to people's choices.

Take work, for instance. In 1930 John Manyard Keynes imagined that richer societies would become more leisured ones, liberated from toil to enjoy the finer things in life. Yet most people still work hard to afford things they think will make them happy, only to discover the fruits of their labour sour quickly. They also aspire to a higher place in society's pecking order, but in so doing force others in the rat race to run faster to keep up. So everyone loses. Yet it isn't self-evident that less work would mean more happiness. Indeed, another side of happiness economics busies itself studying the non-monetary rewards from work: most people enjoy parts of their work, and some people love it.

But if growth does not make people happy, stagnation will hardly do the trick. A flourishing economy, on the other hand, creates what biologists call "a tangled bank" of niches. Tytler Cowen, of George Mason University points out that America has more than 3000 halls of fame, honouring everyone from rock stars to pickle-packers. In such a society, everyone can hope to come out on top.

To find the market system wanting because it does not bring joy as well as growth is to place too heavy a burden on it. Capitalism can make you well off. And it also leaves you free to be as unhappy as you choose; To ask any more of it would be asking too much.

Having more doesn't make you happier

Paradoxically, having more does not necessarily make you happier. And pragmatists advice one to value what you have here and now.

Gregg Easterbrook explored the phenomenon in a book called *Progress Paradox*, while experts like British psychologist Michael Eysenck invoked the hedonic treadmill theory, which compared the pursuit of happiness to a person's state of being on a treadmill — grunting and groaning to keep working just to stay in the same place.

Numerous other studies have found that as they keep on pounding the hedonic treadmill, the level of happiness throughout people's life undergoes a U-shaped transformation: with folks becoming increasingly dissatisfied as they approach their 40s and then rebounding back from the trough.

Nor is it very clear why people become grumpy in middle age. One reason could be disenchantment and loss of innocence brought on by the realisation that you may not have everything that you'd wished for through your 'dream-eyed' younger phase of life. Eventually, however people learn to adapt, even to their sense of disquiet. That's when their happiness levels begin to bounce back. Now by choosing the right goals and strategies you could minimise these swings and downturns. The other, tougher option is to obtain satori.

Can money buy you happiness?

Psychologists say that a house can be bought with money but a home remains a far away dream where money matters rules the roost

Children, friends and pets are more likely to make us smile than a big wad of cash, according to a new survey.

The A C Nielsen survey, polled 1471 Australians to find out what made them smile.

The saying that 'money can't buy happiness' was confirmed in the survey which revealed 91 per cent of the Australians rated factors other than money as things that make them smile most. Incidentally, even Indian psychologists maintain similar beliefs.

The survey found that children and babies made 33 per cent of people smile, followed by family and friends (28 per cent), then pets and animals (22 per cent), nature (8 per cent), while money only made 6 per cent of teh smiel factor.

Dr Timothy Sharp from the Happiness Institute said the results indicated people gained more happiness from relationships.

The findings support the theory that happy people have more and better quality relationships than those who don't smile, because it is an important non-verbal sign we give to others as a way of sharing and eliciting positive emotions, say the researchers. Work on relationships and happiness will eventually follow in time.

Economic growth a limited indicator

Finally, we seem to have arrived at a pretty simple and straightforward way to measure, or at any rate, corroborate happiness levels in a society — blook pressure levels. The time has, therefore, come to set aside GDP as the mother of all policy goals. After four centuries of industrialisation, it has become quite clear that material well-being derived from higher and higher production does not always make people feel happier. Rather, they develop a range of stress-related disorders, by virtue of being caught in a treadmill of over-increasing production and consumption. Economic well-being is one thing, and wellness quite another.

Researchers at Warwick University have discovered a strong correlation between a country's happiness and its blood pressure prolbelms. Sweden, Denmark and Britain are on top of the BP-based happiness league, while Germany, Portugal and Finland do worse on the BP front Economists conceded decades ago that GDP does not translate into welfare, and that happiness depends on a range of factors such as availability of public goods to all, status of women, trade-off between work and leisure, levels of political empowerment, state of the environment, a society's political and social history, and above all spiritual and psychological well-being.

Instead of looking at BP as a purely physiological problem, policy-makers should try to link their actions to impact on culture and society — and eventually an individual's BP. With modern ailments such as hypertension and BP on the rise even in developing countries like India, it is time that policy-makers here as well shed some of their single-minded focus on GDP growth. Fortunately, India has the spiritual resources to cope with the afflictions of modernity.

It should not only draw more on these reserves, but also export its yoga, health food, meditative techniques, traditional healing methods and classical music to the West. The entire world must learn how to live more in harmony with nature, the challenge of peaceful coexistence is not just an economic question, but a cultural and spiritual one as well.

Happiness Quotient

Business strategies are increasingly being based on bringing a smile to the customer's face.

It's all about making an emotional connect. Corporates have woken up to the fact that such advertisements are better able to break the clutter.

Marketers are seeking to adjust consumers' happiness thermostat. The concept of happiness is being seriously studied in marketing circles: How to keep your consumer happy, how to get the consumer to love your brand, how to go about enabling happy customers to become brand advocates.

Samsika Marketing's managing director Jagdeep Kapoor highlights four major trends in the marketplace, which aim to keep the smile on the consumer's face.

Loyalty value joy, and confidence

Understanding customers' preferences and preempting the decision making process is another good way to connect emotionally. "Preempting the usual will ensure a good reference."

Last but not the least, corporates should always try to surprise their customer. Joy, faith, hope and confidence would keep the surprise element fresh.

The trend is to connect with the intangibles, not just the tangibles. Though several companies are moving in this direction, others are moving in quite the opposite way. Competing on lower price is passe. "It is not important that 'brand *sasta hai*', it is important that customer hasta hai.'

Some Observations

- Economic growth is measured in terms of money.
- Money does not bring happiness.
- Happiness is a socio-psychological phenomenon.
- Happiness grows with bonding relationship, trust, understanding and love.
- Mushroom economic growth divides society and increases class conflict.
- Economic growth should run parallel to social development
- In the West and in India the number of philanthropreneur is growing.
- Philanthropreneurs seek happiness in giving.
- Cultural enrichment will sustain and enhance happiness.

Entrepreneurial Happiness

Entrepreneurial happiness enhances with growth. It exists in varied parameters like dream realisation, vision translation, implementation of start-up project, production of goods and services and their acceptance. Profit generation, creation of employment and wealth, empowerment of people, trust of employees, stakeholders and customers, loyalty of customers, image building, innovation, blossoming of creativity and self-management.

In fact, the Hindu world-view advocates the pursuit of the four *purushaarthaas* or the four-fold goal of human life: *dharma* (meaning, righteous or harmonious conduct), *artha* (wealth or material gain), kaama (pleasures or desires) and *moksha* (salvation and realisation). And all actions carried out in the course of performance of one's duties are sacrosanct as long as they subserve *saamaanya* Dharma.

For leaders of business, Chanakya had laid it out quite pithily:

Sukhasya Moolam Dharman
Dharmasya Moolam Artham
Arthasya Moolam Rajyam
Rajyasya Moolam Indirya Vijayam

The root of happiness is Dharma. The root of dharma is resources or wealth legitimately generated or earned (Remember, it's not just *laabh,* but *shubh laabh*, meaning, gain or profit mediated by Dharma that every Indian engaged in trade prays for throughout the year). The root of such wealth is kingdom or enterprise. The root of enterprise is self-control. As the last line of this *sutra* connotes that self-management is the key to successful entrepreneurship as with self-control comes emotional equanimity, which is very crucial in the world of business at all times. In today's globalised business environment especially, equipoise is called for in the midst of intense activity. And if you can manage yourself, then managing an enterprise, however huge, will be child's play.

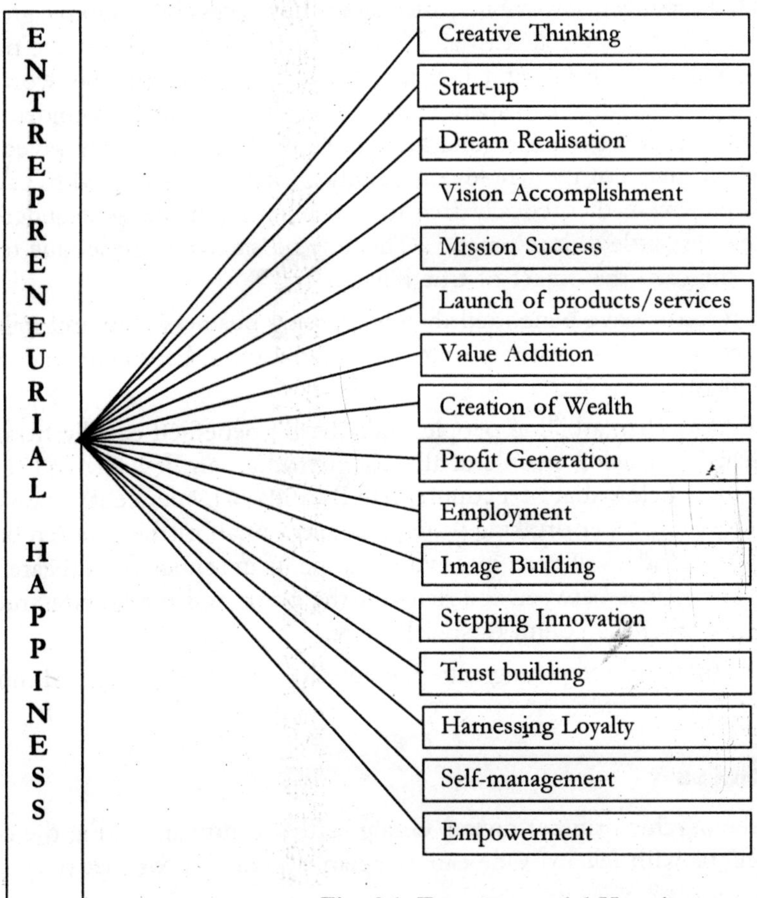

Fig. 8.1: Entrepreneurial Happiness

Arguably, all innovation is a result of a certain amount of dissatisfaction with the *status quo*. Early man was tired of lumbering around with heavy loads, and so invented the wheel to make transporting things easier. Indeed, it may be bad for a nation to have its people content. Contentment stifles innovation and originality. It encourages people to stay in a rut and perpetuate the existing state of affairs. It is only when people want more, and want it enough to work hard for it that the nation as a whole can progress. Happiness works best as the pot of gold at the end of a rainbow that everyone strives towards, but can never achieve.

INDIA'S INCREDIBLE JOURNEY

In the context of India, economic reforms initiated in 1991 have created a new world that simply did not exist earlier. The spirit of enterprise; creativity, innovation blossomed and hard work that Indian businessmen and professionals have come to exemplify. The Indian economy has experienced unprecedented change and growth in the last two decades. There is a new sense of optimism and a willingness to take risk and think big among the leaders of business in India today. After four years of above 8 per cent growth, which in itself is unprecedented in our history, our's economy is poised to repeat this performance for years to come.

To all the successful entrepreneurs who have benefited from the process of economic growth, my advice is to treat their wealth as a societal trust and manage it for the welfare of the nation at large. Lord Keynes, analysing the role of capitalists in 19th century Britain in his work *The Economic Consequence of Peace*, said "If the rich had spent their new wealth on their own enjoyments, the world would long ago have found such a regime intolerable. But like bees they saved and accumulated, not less to the advantage of the whole community... (they) were allowed to call the best part of the cake theirs and were theoretically free to consume it, on the tacit underlying condition that they consumed very little of it in practice. The duty of 'saving' became nine-tenths of virtue and the growth of the cake the object of true religion."

Though the economic reforms have benefitted the enterprising business men and millions of educated Indians, they have left a vast majority untouched. Education, healthcare and water remaining just a dream for them.

But being a country of more than a billion people, India hasn't benefited equally from the reforms. There are more than 380 million people in the country who earn less than $1 a day; adult literacy rate at 61 per cent is below that of a country like Rwanda (64.9 per cent); about 150 million people don't have access to proper drinking water; and almost half of the children below five years of age are underweight. India will need massive investments in schools, healthcare, and sanitation, if it has to keep the divides between the rich and the poor, and the literate and the illiterate, among others, from tearing the country's social fabric.

The mute question is whether the enterprising entrepreneurs and millions of educated Indians are happy in its true sense?

The Secret of Happiness

The happiness lies in the psychic or inner divine. Going to that centre and living the outer human life from there will fill us with felicity. One can make an experiment for that purpose. I shall start with an analogy.

A work exists at several levels of skills, talents, capacities, endowments, accomplishment, from the low crude completion of utility to highly professional execution of a graceful act. At two ends, if these extremes exist, we find ourselves at some middle level. Placed as you are at your middle level, if you acquire the endowment of any higher level. LIFE can take you sooner or later to that levels.

Sutra

A happy life must be to a great extent a quiet life, for it is only in an atmosphere of quiet that true joy can live. Bertrand Russell.

APPENDIX - 009

A Matter of Trust

Introduction — Trust at Workplaces

Trust, That Psychological state that allows people to 'accept vulnerability based on positive expectations of the behaviour of another,' has always been a subject of great interest the world over. The reigning assumption is that trust is built over time.

Deepak Malhotra says 'People do have the ability to take advantage of each other, but you still need to trust. You just can't work without it,'

According to Malhotra's research, people want to trust, especially when they are dependent on each other. In such situations, trust is built very easily and rapidly. This goes against the grain of popular organisational behaviour theories, which say that trust is built gradually. 'My findings are quite the opposite,' he says. 'People don't want to be trusted little by little. They want to be trusted fully and they want to trust others fully. Trust is psychologically satisfying.'

As the word 'trust, is usually used, it represents such a general (and sometimes emotionally charged) concept that very little is communicated about the real meaning of the word in a given context, or how we are to behave if we want to be trusted by others at home and at work. We tend to treat the idea of trust as desired behaviour in any given situation, when it is actually an outcome of a desired set of needs or conditions being met.

Once we begin to view trust as an outcome, it is easier to see that trust flows from a set of specific conditions which, taken together, not only define trust but also provide a process for building and managing trust.

Trust is usually treated as a concept.

When we say that we trust someone or that we don't trust someone, we are really making a bottom line statement of our perception of that person based on mixing together our view of their behaviour and Performance over a collection of dimensions thus creating a single 'package.' To predictably build and manage trust, we have to define trust in terms of these component dimensions. We need to open the package and see what we find inside.

The Concept

We are often quick to make decisions about whom we trust. Studies show that in face-to-face interactions, we often make these decisions in the first few minutes. In telephone interactions, we make these decisions even more quickly — often in seconds. One line of research into how we decide who to trust and whom to not trust, expresses this trust decision as a function of three variables:

$$Trust = f[(credibility) \times (empathy)] / (risk)$$

This means that as a prelude to the creation of a climate of trust and safety and to building the foundations for relationship, we will mentally ask three questions:

— Do I perceive that this person is credible? (Defined as the quality or power of inspiring belief).

— Do I perceive that they understand and are sensitive to my feelings and thoughts without me having to explicitly state them? (Empathy)

— To what extent do I perceive that I am at risk in this situation?

We have found it to be highly constructive to embrace the idea that without empathy, credibility alone is seldom enough to establish trust. The default in the modern world is to drive credibility, often at the expense of empathy.

Empathy includes the ability to share someone else's feelings or experiences by imagining what it would be like to be in their shoes. Defining credibility (according to the dictionary) as the quality, capability, or power to inspire belief is not by itself particularly actionable. Further examination of the package of credibility is in order.

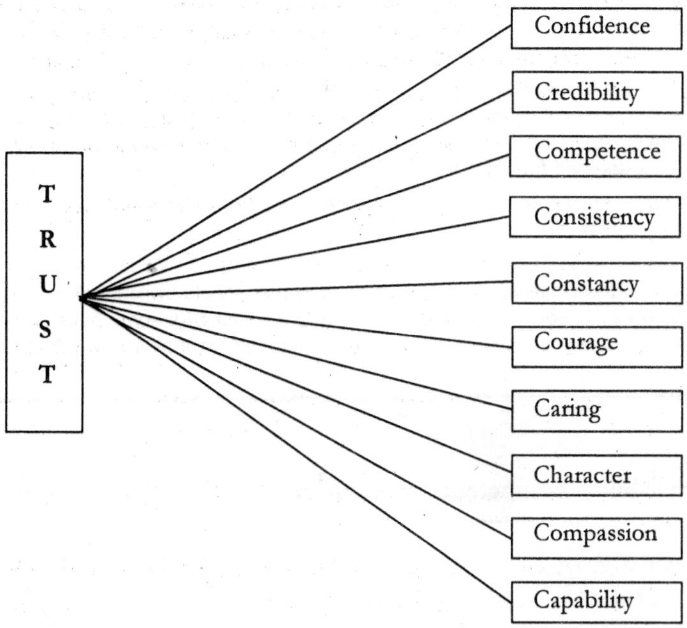

Fig. 1. Characteristics of Trust

Trust also means confidence. Confidence in the enterprise. Peoples integrity and abilities. Trust is core factor in entrepreneurial adventures and start-ups.

Trust is the foundations of faith. Trust is one of the important trait of entrepreneurship. Trust must be constantly managed and managing trust is a core function of entrepreneurial leadership. Trust has a unique relationship between levels of trust in a business system and its performance. The entrepreneur always strive to build trust relationship in people and business system that will go a long way in building a thriving business enterprise. In fact, economic growth, development depends on trust in the entrepreneurial community trust plays a unique role in building and fostering entrepreneurial leadership in the country. Broadly, trust refers to six Cs — competence, consistence, courage, caring, characters and compassion.

Trust has wide applications from individual human interaction to business management. Entrepreneurial trust is being applied in negotiations, partnership, building brands, nurturing value systems, human relation, finance, marketing and varied other fields/stakeholders.

Box - 1

TRUST MAKES STATE-RUN SBI AND LIC TOP THE CHART

Despite all the competition, old warehouses such as the State Bank of India (SBI) and the Life Insurance Corporation (LIC) have scored high on the loyalty factor. The big thing going for these two entities is that they have been around for a long time. They enjoyed a near monopoly status until the mid-1990s and have a strong presence in the market. Go anywhere in India, there will be billboards of SBI and LIC staring at you.

There is another reason why these players enjoy cult status. The new age players in the banking and insurance sectors are yet to make an impact in the great Indian hinterland. They are confined to the metros and large cities. There is a whole universe of customers to whom catchy slogans and sundry brand ambassadors make little sense. Many have no idea what world class service is. For them, SBI and LIC are synonymous with banking and insurance.

A key factor that drives loyalty is trust, which both SBI and LIC enjoy. The fact that both are state-run gives them an edge with customers who have seen several financial scams in the past. The likes of Global Trust Bank folded up. Then there was the Madhavpura Co-operative Bank fiasco. There is also the case of state-run Unit Trust of India going bankrupt but here the Centre stepped in with a lifeline.

The message here is: customers are ready to compromise on convenience for trust; they believe the authorities will step in if SBI or LIC were to hit an air pocket.

Yet another factor that may explain why SBI and LIC still top the mindshare game could be customer lethargy and lack of awareness. Take LIC. There are no compelling reasons why a customer should switch his/her policy from LIC to a new player. For them, a plain-vanilla policy is good enough. Same goes for SBI: some of its branch managers may go out of the way to help a customer without charging extra, something that a new private or foreign bank will never do.

Competence

Trust is closely related with reliability, competence and credibility. This will go long way in building relationships and strengthening the organisation.

In organisational life, the dimension of competence may be the single most critical factor used by managers to evaluate the credibility of a recommendation offered by a direct report before taking action based on that recommendation.

Clearly, technical competence is an important element of being viewed as competent in one's job. And technical competence doesn't always mean 'hands-on' or' bench' competence; it may also include the ability to understand concepts being communicated to us by highly specialised associates, and it certainly may include knowledge of the industry and business and knowledge of the competition and of customer needs. It may mean being able to see the "big picture" and to communicate it to others.

For people in leadership positions in organisations, technical competence must be matched by leadership and managerial competence-the ability to lead others, to influence others, to obtain needed resources, to be "in the know," to manage the 'politics' and get things done in the system, to create a vision and provide direction, to be organised and effective at setting and managing priorities, and so on.

Consistency

The other facets of trust are reliability, consistency, constancy and predicability. The last two elements are subtler than the element of reliability. In these cases, the individual behaviour is driven by some set of stable core values.

For an organisation, constancy may mean that our organisation values are a constant, that, for example, if we claim to be ,customer focused,' when we are faced with difficult decisions and trade-offs, we do indeed make customer driven decisions. Similarly, if we hold ourselves out to be an organisation that values treating our employees with dignity and respect, we will treat them that way even when touch decisions have to be made

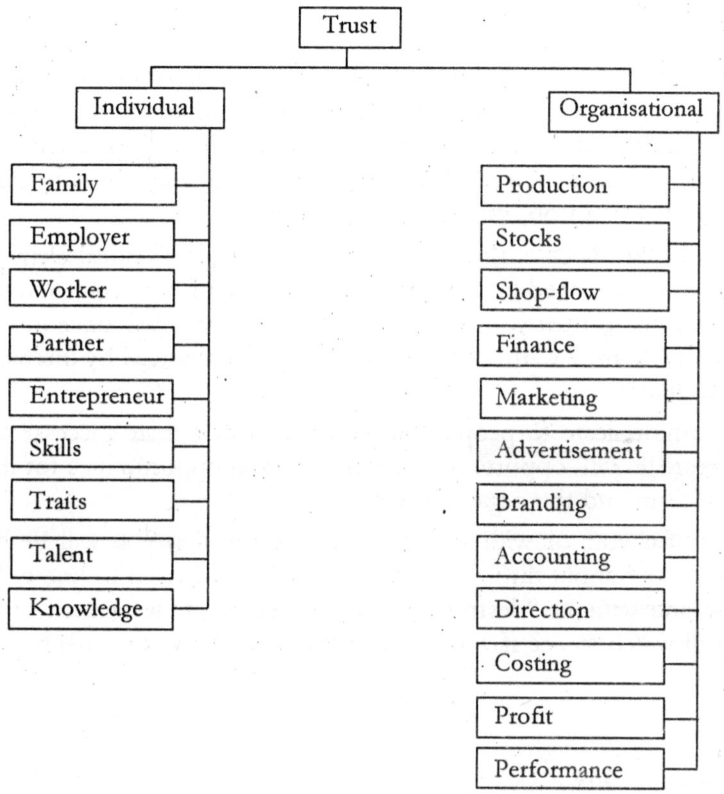

Fig. 2: Type of Trust (Illustrative)

Courage

Courage means taking action even when we don't know for certain the outcome we are likely to produce. Courage also means taking actions that may be unpopular or not politic. Courageous leaders also allow themselves to be challenged by their peers and direct reports, and they "own" their own decisions versus blaming people above them for decisions and actions taken. Leaders with courage ask for feedback about their own performance problems that arise from time-to-time in their work groups; and they don't avoid giving people tough, feedback.

We can also get a sense of how much to trust you by the amount of gossiping you engage in and the amount of blaming you do of other people, teams, and departments. It's hard to trust people who make disparaging and destructive comments about other people and groups, because we don't know if we can trust what you will say about us to others when we are not present. We will perceive this behaviour as a lack of courage.

Perhaps the most direct way we have of observing your courage is to notice whether or not you are willing to say in the meeting (foreground conversation) what you just said in the hallway (background conversation, or what Chris Argyris calls 'the left hand column' in his work on productive dialogue). For you to be credible, you will need to exhibit the courage to have the foreground conversation and the background conversation march.

Caring

For caring to be fully experienced by others, it must flow from empathy. The Merriam-Webster definition of the word is somewhat daunting: Empathy: the quality or action of understanding, being aware of, being sensitive to, and vicariously experiencing the feelings, thoughts, and experience of another without having the feeling, thoughts, and experience completely communicated in an objectively explicit manner.

Being mindful of other people, their situation and needs, is a critical element of managing trust at home and at work. We need to demonstrate awareness of our actual and potential impact on others. In order for me to trust you, I need to believe that you will have my best interests at heart in all of our interactions. I want to know that I will be enhanced by interactions with you-or at least not diminished.

How do you communicate to people that you care about their success? Will you, as my manager, help me create growth opportunities for myself, and opportunities for me to contribute to the growth of the team and the organisation?

Whether I work for you, or with you, I need to know that you will be honest with me about my performance and about difficult situations that arise. I need to know that we will deal with conflict openly and without "destroying" each other or "putting each other down." If I make a mistake, I will watch to see if you can correct me directly and openly and still preserve my dignity.

Character

Too many trust means character

Fortune Magazine noted that when it comes to leadership, "Ninety-five per cent of American managers today say the right thing, five percent do it."

With that quote, the Fortune editors have captured the essence of one of the most basic elements of character-namely, integrity. Do you walk the talk? In other words, do you have an underlying code of values and do you live your values?

Do you, for example, treat people ethically and honestly in all of your personal and business dealings with them? Or, are people constantly finding hidden agendas and ulterior motives that drive your behaviour?

In this way trust also relates to other values of truth, integrity, confidence, arrogance of people working in an organisation and/or entrepreneurial leadership. We also expect people with character to be committed to improving themselves to be constantly striving to be the best they can be. When people with character receive feedback, they take action for further growth and development based on the feedback. Another element of character has to do with the degree to which you serve as a credible role model for how to behave under the day-to-day pressures and crises that occur at work.

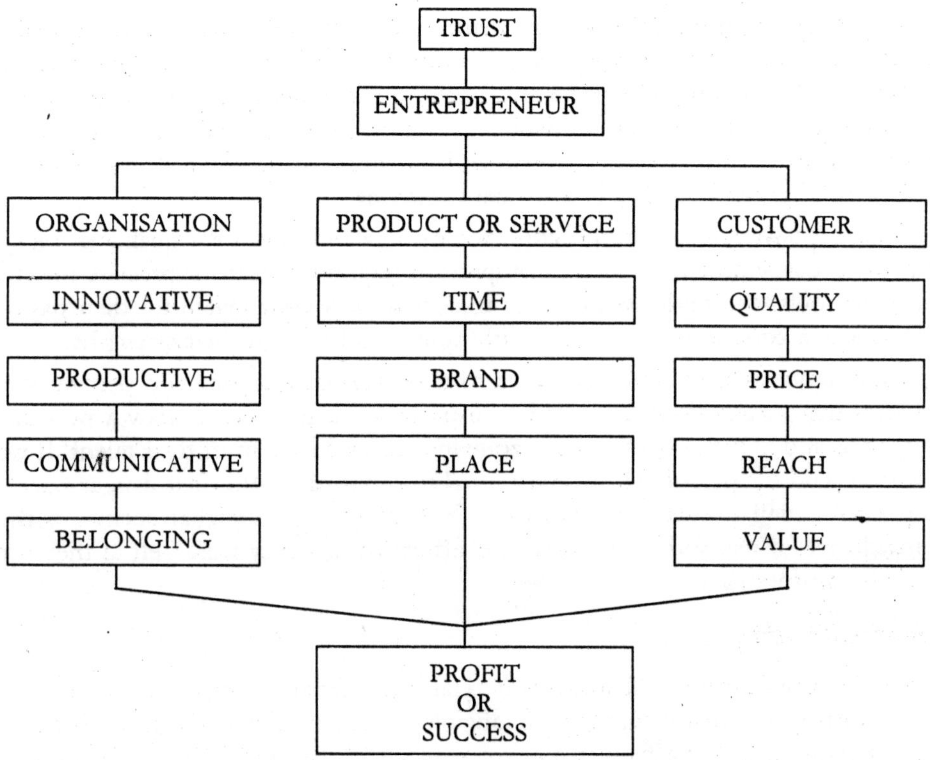

Fig. 3: Entrepreneurial Trust

During organisational changes, for example, your direct reports and peers may observe your responses and take their cues for how to respond from your behaviour and attitude under pressure. How well you manage your own resistance to change, how well you "bounce back" from a temporary setback, how you respond to imposed deadlines, how you respond to mistakes that are made — these are all aspects of your behaviour that people observe to assess your character. If you shout at people and pound the desk, if you get irritable or short-tempered with people when the pressure is on, you won't get high marks for composure plus you will certainly destroy your empathy rating and along with it the presence of trust.

Compassion

Compassion is sometimes offered as a word synonymous with empathy. We propose an important distinction here and offer compassion as a component of empathy.

We believe the work of leadership and management is to turn passion and talent into successful performance. People are likely to be good at, *i.e.,* have talent for, those things they are passionate about and love to do. Talent in this context is defined as any recurring pattern of thinking, feeling or behaving that can be productively applied.

The process of turning talent into performance means drawing out the potential that lives within people and supporting the successful expression of this potential in the external world. Implicit in the meaning of passion is the idea that unrecognised and unexpressed potential becomes a suffering. Certainly this is true for the individual who suffers the failure to achieve their potential. Ultimately this is also true for the organisation and the world at large where the suffering is in the form of the loss of potentially significant contributions.

As we talk about compassion in this context we are talking about the quality of recognising and supporting the development of talent. Compassion requires of us to appreciate the suffering of the majority of souls who find themselves in roles that are a poor match for their passion and talent-that we make a commitment to work with people to build on their strengths.

Compassion requires that we are sensitive to the levels of risk a person perceives in their relationship with the organisation or us. This is especially the case as we draw a person out of their comfort zone and into the performance zone in the development of their talent. If we push too hard, we may send the person we are committed to supporting into their danger zone. If this happens the person will experience a level of fear in reaction to what seems to them an overwhelming degree of risk and they will be less effective than they were before they ventured forth from their comfort zone.

The Speed of Trust

Here's a simple formula that will enable you to take trust from an intangible and unquantfiable variable to an indispensable factor that is both tangible and quantifiable. The formula is based on this critical insight: Trust always affects two outcomes — speed and cost. When trust goes down, speed will also go down and costs will go up. When trust goes up, speed will also go up and costs will go down. It's that simple, that real, that predictable. Consider an example. The Sarbanes-Oxley Act was passed in the US in response to the Enron, World-Com, and other corporate scandals. While it appears that Sarbanes-Oxley may be having a positive effect in improving or at least sustaining trust in the public markets, it is also clear that this has come at a substantial price.

In fact, a recent study pegged the costs of implementing one section alone at $35 billion — exceeding the original SEC estimate by 28 times! Compliance regulations have become a prosthesis for the lack of trust. We come back to the key learning: When trust is low, speed goes down and cost goes up.

So what is trust? Simply put, trust means confidence. When you trust people, you have confidence in them — in their integrity and in their abilities. Relationships of all kinds are built on and sustained by trust. They can also be broken and destroyed by lack of trust. Try to imagine any meaningful relationship without trust.

Trust is invariably a two-way street and it's unlikely that A will trust B if B does not trust A. And though people want it, trust is also fragile and easily shattered. One implication is that contracts and monitoring systems can be damaging in that they impede people's natural desire to trust. If an organisation installs surveillance cameras, thereby demonstrating that it doesn't quite trust its people, employees are not likely to trust its people, employees are not likely to trust their management. But then again, employer surveillance may be necessary for gaining the trust of clients. If sensitive data is at stake. Stakeholders trust organisations for different, opposing reasons. Organisations have to decide which stakeholder's trust is most important.

The real world has always been interested in the dynamics of trust. People trust others based on their integrity, benevolence, technical and managerial competence.

To ask a person if they trust you is a question that may need to be asked in a more focused way. Whether or not people trust you includes how they view your character, caring, and compassion, your courage, competence and consistency.

In other words, when you ask me, "Do you trust me?" You are asking for a great deal more than a simple "yes" or "no"; you are asking me to think about how well you do your job, whether or not you follow through on your promises, whether or not you demonstrate courage and character in my dealings with you, and whether or not I can trust that you will honor my interests in our relationship.

Asking someone if they trust you may involve a complex response. It should also be clear that there is a good deal of overlap across dimensions. For example, a manager who yells at his or her people when he or she is under pressure will probably be seen as lacking courage. At the same time, such behaviour may also be taken as an indication of a low level of caring or empathy.

Returning to our formula, notice if, as risk escalates in business situations and in life, your own tendency is to attempt to further establish your credibility. Many Asian cultures consider this an American obsession. We watch cooperation between intact teams and work groups begin to break down and we watch attempts to fix the situation by driving up the credibility component of trust. This is unlikely to work. When things start to break down, as risk starts to go up, we need to build a spirit of empathy to balance perceived risk and establish the levels of trust required for challenges to be effectively embraced and for opportunities to be successfully pursued.

My answer to the question "Do you trust me?" is really my assessment of your behaviour across the empathetic dimensions of character, caring, and compassion, packaged with the credibility dimensions of courage, competence and consistency. In any given situation the degree of risk that I perceive can dramatically impact my willingness to be trusting. Empathetic behavior will lower my levels of perceived risk, reduce my levels of fear, and raise our levels of trust.

Source: Adapted from Stewart and Joan Energy Studies.

APPENDIX - 010

Herd Instinct Model

The world of retailing is becoming hugely more competitive and more influential, both with consumers and manufacturers. Significantly, today it is the consumer who is taking control. Empowered by a wealth of readily available knowledge and an extraordinary set of choices, consumers often have all the material possessions they need, and now seek a different way of engaging their time with brands. They are seeking products, services and environments that connect with them emotionally; that enhance their lives beyond functionality, and deliver experiences that match their aspirations.

Retail now is about putting ideas and experiences of products, services and environments into context and circulation, in ways that are innovative and convincing to today's savvy consumers. As a result, we at Fitch, create distinct and active experiences that engage consumers emotionally rather than treating them as passive recipients.

Box - 1

EDWARD DE BONO

Born: 1933

Education: Ph.D. and D.Phil. in Medicine from Cambridge University; Doctor of Design from the Royal Melbourne Institute of Technology and LLD from University of Dundee.

Claim to Fame: The originator of lateral thinking, de Bono is also a key proponent of teaching deliberate thinking in schools and has come up with various proprietary tools that can be used to learn to think creatively. He established the World center for New Thinking that promotes 'new thinking' for the future.

Author of: *Six Thinking Hats, The Use of Lateral Thinking, New Think, Six value Medals.*

Key Concepts: Creativity should be producible on demand – formation of new ideas cannot be left to change. According to de Bono, most problems in thinking are at the perceptual level. He developed the Six Thinking Hats technique and the Direct Attention Thinking Tools framework to facilitate lateral thinking.

Companies who use his techniques: Boeing, Nokia, Rolex, Siemens, GM, Nestle, Goldman Sachs.

Recognising the herd instinct has important consequences for marketers. They should focus on the most influential customer; that is the consumer who holds the greatest sway over the majority of his or her peers. Herd Instinct Model is one of the key input strategy of marketing in the global environment by engaging consumers emotionally through the peers.

If Marketers want to wield greater influence over consumer behaviour, they must learn to accept that people do not act autonomously but largely follow what other people do. Over the past 10 years or so clusters of cellophane-wrapped bunches of flowers seem to have appeared with increasing frequency on Britain's roadsides. It is a phenomenon that satirical magazine Private Eye has dubbed the 'cellotaph' syndrome — the setting up of floral shrines to the victims of traffic accidents. But how did these shrines start? And how did they spread and the practice become 'just what we do' when a few years ago it was not? One line of explanation is that each flower is the result of an independent decision based on some cost-benefit trade-off, or is driven by a desire to express an individual's grief. This is what we assume when we conduct marketing research: we ask individual consumers what they do now, why, and what they might do in the future.

We also work on the basis that individuals decide what they do independently of others and can tell us about it. Almost everything of worth in our world — including the power we have over the future of the planet — comes from this herd nature and our ability and passion for social interaction and collaboration. The same is true of the technologies that are reshaping the media environment: SMS and the internet are built on our species' inherent desire and need to interact with others.

Recognising the herd instinct has important consequences for marketers. For a start, it explains why mass behaviour is so hard to change. Most public-policy initiatives struggle to demonstrate any long-lasting change in citizens' behaviour, while most change programmes within companies fail to produce the radical alterations in employee behaviour specified in the objectives.

In theory, marketers should be experts at changing mass-behaviour: after all, we have the experience, analytics and practical tools to understand, describe and reshape it. Putting the consumer at the heart of business is supposedly our raison d'etre. And yet, despite the rightly-praised exceptions — Tesco, Dove, Innocent and iPod — most marketing activity struggles to demonstrate the kind of significant sustainable change in customer behaviour that we imagine is our right. Moreover, this has been the case for as long as most of us can remember; marketing scientist Professor Andrew Ehrenberg once suggested that keeping things the same would represent a reasonable success for most promotional campaigns.

We may have become better at managing things well at the edges in the short term. After all, much of the appeal of the revolution in one-to-one marketing over recent years seems to lie in harvesting marginal opportunities — the 'low-hanging fruit'. But in the main we are no better at creating sustainable changes in mass behaviour than our peers in other disciplines; the changes we do create are minor and feeling.

The next step is to look at marketing as consumer-to-consumer, rather than business-to-consumer. This means recognising that the most important relationship is not between the company or brand and any given consumer, but between the latter and other individuals. What matters in real life is what matters to or between them.

The acceptance of our herd nature is changing the way some media players are evaluating media channel options. While most of the media world is getting excited about moving on from counting audiences and weighting them according to their wallets, to counting them according to how 'engaged' they are with the medium, agencies such as Naked have proposed that the real currency of the media world should be the extent to which an audience passes messages on to others beyond it; the 'propagation' value. For example, in terms of sales or readership a brand may only reach half the number of people through an ad in The Guardian than in The Daily Telegraph, but each Guardian reader might influence several times the number of people their Telegraph-reading counterpart does.

This is significant, and represents the first major shift away from thinking about media as 'channels' down which we tip messages and information; media become important only in so far as they serve and help advertisers access and harness the power of the social networks which lie behind them.

At the same time, the dubious idea of exploiting the most valuable Customers must be ditched. This kind of micro-targeting has no impact on the mechanisms of mass behaviour and risks letting the market move away, suddenly and rapidly. Instead, marketers should focus on the most influential customer; that is the consumer who holds the greatest sway over the majority of his or her peers. Marketers must understand the types and sources of influence that shape customers' behaviour both positively and negatively and think about how their opinions, and more importantly, their actions, can fuel this.

❑ ❑ ❑